O9-BSU-495

POLITICAL ORDER

NOMOS

XXXVIII

NOMOS

Harvard University Press

I	*Authority* 1958, reissued in 1982 by Greenwood Press

The Liberal Arts Press

II	*Community* 1959
III	*Responsibility* 1960

Atherton Press

IV	*Liberty* 1962
V	*The Public Interest* 1962
VI	*Justice* 1963, reissued in 1974
VII	*Rational Decision* 1964
VIII	*Revolution* 1966
IX	*Equality* 1967
X	*Representation* 1968
XI	*Voluntary Associations* 1969
XII	*Political and Legal Obligation* 1970
XIII	*Privacy* 1971

Aldine-Atherton Press

XIV	*Coercion* 1972

Lieber-Atherton Press

XV	*The Limits of Law* 1974
XVI	*Participation in Politics* 1975

New York University Press

XVII	*Human Nature in Politics* 1977
XVIII	*Due Process* 1977
XIX	*Anarchism* 1978
XX	*Constitutionalism* 1979
XXI	*Compromise in Ethics, Law, and Politics* 1979
XXII	*Property* 1980
XXIII	*Human Rights* 1981
XXIV	*Ethics, Economics, and the Law* 1982
XXV	*Liberal Democracy* 1983

XXVI	*Marxism* 1983
XXVII	*Criminal Justice* 1985
XXVIII	*Justification* 1985
XXIX	*Authority Revisited* 1987
XXX	*Religion, Morality, and the Law* 1988
XXXI	*Markets and Justice* 1989
XXXII	*Majorities and Minorities* 1990
XXXIII	*Compensatory Justice* 1991
XXXIV	*Virtue* 1992
XXXV	*Democratic Community* 1993
XXXVI	*The Rule of Law* 1994
XXXVII	*Theory and Practice* 1995
XXXVIII	*Political Order* 1996
XXXIX	*Ethnicity and Group Rights* (in preparation)
XL	*Integrity and Conscience* (in preparation)
XLI	*Global Justice* (in preparation)

NOMOS XXXVIII

Yearbook of the American Society for Political and Legal Philosophy

POLITICAL ORDER

Edited by

Ian Shapiro, *Yale University*

and

Russell Hardin, *New York University*

NEW YORK UNIVERSITY PRESS • *New York and London*

NEW YORK UNIVERSITY PRESS
New York and London

Political Order: NOMOS XXXVIII
edited by Ian Shapiro & Russell Hardin

Library of Congress Cataloging-in-Publication Data
Political order / edited by Ian Shapiro and Russell Hardin.
p. cm. — (Nomos ; 38)
Based on presentations from the meeting of the American Society for Political and Legal Philosophy, held in conjunction with the annual meeting of the American Political Science Association in Washington, D.C., September 1993.
Includes bibliographical references and index.
ISBN 0-8147-8029-6 (alk. paper)
1. Political stability—Congresses. 2. Democracy—Congresses. 3. Nationalism—Congresses. 4. Political culture—Congresses. I. Shapiro, Ian. II. Hardin, Russell, 1940– . III. American Society for Political and Legal Philosophy. Meeting (1993 : Washington, D.C.) IV. American Political Science Association. Meeting (1993 : Washington, D.C.) V. Series.
JC330.2.P64 1996
320'.01'1—dc20 95-50664
CIP

New York University Press books are printed on acid-free paper, and their binding materials are chosen for strength and durability

10 9 8 7 6 5 4 3 2 1

To the memory of J. Roland Pennock
1906–1995

CONTENTS

Preface xiii

Contributors xv

Introduction
IAN SHAPIRO AND RUSSELL HARDIN 1

PART I: ORDER VERSUS DISORDER

1. Political Theory, Order, and Threat
PASQUALE PASQUINO 19

2. State Simplifications: Nature, Space, and People
JAMES C. SCOTT 42

3. Modeling Political Order in Representative Democracies
NORMAN SCHOFIELD 86

4. Institutions and Intercurrence: Theory Building in the Fullness of Time
KAREN ORREN AND STEPHEN SKOWRONEK 111

5. *E Pur Si Muove!* Systematizing and the Intercurrence Hypothesis
WALTER DEAN BURNHAM 147

6. Looking for Disagreement in All the Wrong Places
MORRIS P. FIORINA 156

7. Reply to Burnham and Fiorina
KAREN ORREN AND STEPHEN SKOWRONEK 167

PART II: DEMOCRACY AND NATIONALISM

8. Thinking about Democratic Constitutions: Conclusions from Democratic Experience
ROBERT A. DAHL 175

9. Majority Rule and Minority Interests
NICHOLAS R. MILLER 207

10. Deliberative Equality and Democratic Order
THOMAS CHRISTIANO 251

11. Five Theses on Nationalism
ELIZABETH KISS 288

12. The World House Divided: The Claims of the Human Community in the Age of Nationalism
DEBRA SATZ 333

13. From Post-Liberalism to Pluralism
JOHN GRAY 345

PART III: POLITICAL CULTURE

14. Democratic Autonomy and Religious Freedom: A Critique of *Wisconsin v. Yoder*
RICHARD J. ARNESON AND IAN SHAPIRO 365

15. In Defense of *Yoder:* Parental Authority and the Public Schools
SHELLEY BURTT 412

16. Spheres of Political Order
LAINIE FRIEDMAN ROSS AND DAVID SCHMIDTZ 438

17. Violence against Women: Challenges to the Liberal State and Relational Feminism
JENNIFER NEDELSKY 454

18. Structures of Political Order: The Relational Feminist Alternatives
ROBERT E. GOODIN 498

Index 523

PREFACE

This, the thirty-eighth volume of NOMOS, began life as the 1993 meeting of the American Society for Political and Legal Philosophy, held in conjunction with the annual meeting of the American Political Science Association in Washington, D.C. in September of that year. As the final results here attest, Russell Hardin organized a superb program for that meeting. I was delighted that he agreed to join me as associate editor of the present volume. His inimitable mix of sound judgment and cooperativeness was greatly appreciated throughout.

The contributors, without whom there would be no volume, all merit praise. Writing for NOMOS can be demanding, even irritating at times, and I appreciate the good cheer with which the authors responded to our demands. Kathryn McDermott managed to extract the relevant pieces of paper from the relevant persons at the relevant times, retrieve manuscripts that appeared to have lost themselves on the information superhighway, and keep all the necessary wheels turning in the appropriate directions at the appropriate times. For all this thankless work I offer our collective thanks.

Niko Pfund and Despina Papazoglou Gimbel at NYU Press are also deserving of great gratitude for their flexibility and efficiency in guiding the manuscript into print.

I.S.

CONTRIBUTORS

RICHARD J. ARNESON
Philosophy, University of California, San Diego

WALTER DEAN BURNHAM
Political Science, University of Texas, Austin

SHELLEY BURTT
Political Science, Yale University

THOMAS CHRISTIANO
Philosophy, University of Arizona

ROBERT A. DAHL
Political Science, Yale University

MORRIS P. FIORINA
Government, Harvard University

ROBERT E. GOODIN
Philosophy, Australian National University

JOHN GRAY
Jesus College, Oxford University

RUSSELL HARDIN
Political Science, New York University

ELIZABETH KISS
Politics, Princeton University

NICHOLAS R. MILLER
Political Science, University of Maryland, Baltimore County

JENNIFER NEDELSKY
Law, Political Science, and Women's Studies, University of Toronto

KAREN ORREN
Political Science, University of California, Los Angeles

PASQUALE PASQUINO
CNRS–CREA École Politechnique, Paris

LAINIE FRIEDMAN ROSS
Medical Ethics and Pediatrics, University of Chicago

DEBRA SATZ
Philosophy, Stanford University

DAVID SCHMIDTZ
Philosophy and Economics, University of Arizona

NORMAN SCHOFIELD
The Center in Political Economy, Washington University

JAMES C. SCOTT
Political Science, Yale University

IAN SHAPIRO
Political Science, Yale University

STEPHEN SKOWRONEK
Political Science, Yale University

INTRODUCTION

IAN SHAPIRO AND RUSSELL HARDIN

What constitutes a political order? This question has exercised some of the greatest minds in the Western tradition. Plato, Aristotle, Machiavelli, Hobbes, Locke, Montesquieu, and the American Founders all saw it as central to their reflections about politics. Given the political upheavals of our own time, it is scarcely surprising that political order also preoccupies many students of contemporary politics. The momentous collapse of the Soviet empire is, after all, but the most recent reminder that political institutions are human creations that can be designed more or less well. What is necessary or sufficient for successful design is, today, as intensively debated as it ever has been. Constitutions are being written and rewritten in many parts of the world, a great many possibilities are being explored, and much that matters deeply to millions of people depends on the results.

In the eighteen chapters, all previously unpublished, that make up the present volume, major scholars address some of the most pressing questions about political order. Under what conditions do we get political order rather than political chaos? How is political order sustained once it has been created? Do constitutions matter, and if so how much? Is there one best type of political order, or, if not, what is the range of viable possibilities and how should they be evaluated? Is maintaining political order in a democracy more difficult than in other political systems? If so, what is to be done about it? What are the relations among the prevailing political order and the economic and social orders? What particular problems for political order are posed by the virulent ethnic and nationalist ideologies that seem so prevalent in the contemporary world? What of the demands of religious and ethnic minorities within countries when these threaten the political order? How should we think about tensions between maintaining political order and achieving social justice? What are the implications of recent feminist scholarship for thinking about political order? Our authors address these and related questions in all their richness and complexity. Some offer prescriptions, others seek merely to illuminate. Collectively, they offer a set of discussions that is both accessible and sophisticated, a combination that is, unfortunately, all too rare.

I. Order versus Disorder

How to create and sustain political order is one of the most vexing questions of political theory. Indeed, the author of our first chapter, Pasquale Pasquino, defines political theory as "the attempt to think of ways to avoid disorder inside human communities." Drawing on the arguments of Machiavelli and Hobbes, he argues that the religious wars of the sixteenth and seventeenth century rendered obsolete the classical political theory of the mixed constitution and introduced such concepts as individual rights, sovereignty, and overlapping consensus to reestablish order and civil peace. The state was, for Pasquino, the central player in creating and institutionalizing these ideas, a fact that tends to be lost in anachronistic "negative libertarian" readings of early modern political theorists.

Pasquino wants to help us understand the structure and norms that shape modern political institutions, by conceiving of them as instruments for generating political order out of the particular circumstances of early modern religious conflict in Europe. James C. Scott, by contrast, is more interested in how modern institutions have shaped the larger political, cultural, and even physical environment so as to produce political order. In chapter two, he argues that agents of the state are obliged to observe and assess the life of their society through a series of fictions and simplifications. These fictions and simplifications are shaped by the purposes state agents pursue, and—since they are underwritten by state power—they have substantial resources to transform the terrain of their observation, to make it conform to their expectations and resemble the grid of their observation. Scott examines this process in the fields of scientific forestry, land tenure, urban planning, and patronyms. The combination of such transforming simplifications together with a "high modernist" faith in the capacity of the state to improve human life by utopian feats of social engineering, he argues, lies behind many of the great development disasters of the twentieth century. Utopian transformative schemes, he contends, ignore—at their peril—the kinds of local knowledge that the Greeks conceptualized by reference to the term *mētis*.

Is the political universe fundamentally orderly or chaotic? Norman Schofield offers a lucid account of how four different traditions within the field of analytical political economy have tackled this question over the past twenty-five years. He distinguishes between traditions that focus on individual choice, collective choice, preferences, and beliefs. In each tradition, Schofield explains the conditions under which equilibrium, rather than chaos, might be thought to arise. As an application, he explores the differences in the electoral systems of Britain, the United States, and the proportional representation systems of Europe, and criticizes a class of arguments to the effect that political choice can give rise to economically irrational policies. He concludes with a discussion of the difficulty of maintaining political consensus in these various types of polities, in situations where distributional conflicts are predominant.

Whereas both Pasquino and Scott locate the search for political order in the peculiar transformations of modernity, the rational choice tradition described by Schofield traces it to the analytical properties of different institutional rules. In their spirited exchange with Walter Dean Burnham and Morris P. Fiorina in chapters 4 through 7, Karen Orren and Stephen Skowronek challenge both. Although they are advocates (and, in other scholarship, practitioners)[1] of studying the evolution of political institutions historically, they are highly skeptical of all attempts to periodize history. Models of political processes that operate at what Burnham refers to as the "macrosystemic" level to "order the infinite mass of available data, and provide some clues as to their relative significance" always conceal as much as they reveal in their view. They illustrate this view by criticizing Burnham's work on electoral realignments and Bruce Ackerman's attempt at a grand synthesis of American constitutional history with reference to three "constitutional moments," the Founding, the Civil War, and the New Deal, that partly parallel Burnham's five party systems.

Orren and Skowronek are no less critical of micro-theories about the dynamics of political order than they are of macro-theories, a view they develop in the course of criticizing Fiorina's rational choice-inspired discussions of the Interstate Commerce Commission (ICC). These, they argue, do not square with the relevant data in crucial respects, a result that they think is likely to attend any reinterpretive analytical matrix. Despite their skepticism of macro-synthetic accounts and rational choice micro-theories, and their advocacy of an historical approach, Orren and Skowronek resist all variants of the suggestion that history is just "one damn thing after another." Instead they argue for a study of institutional history that is geared to explaining how institutions might alter basic assumptions about the political organization of time and space, and the relationship between political order and political change. They contend that both the macro-synthesists and the micro-theorists have been so preoccupied with the issues of stability and order that they have failed to grasp ways in which institutions grind against one another, producing disorder. They argue instead for a type of institutional study that "harbors a more radical theoretical program" and "would root political analysis in a distinctly institutional understanding of history itself." Attention to what they describe as the "intercurrent" relations among political institutions over time, they argue, can best illuminate institutional dynamics.

In their respective replies, Burnham and Fiorina concede, as Burnham quotes Oliver Wendell Holmes, that "the ultimate test is empirical." However, they note that to date Orren and Skowronek have utilized the concept of intercurrence principally as a critical device in dissecting the scholarship of others, so that its empirical utility is yet to be tested. Burnham makes the case that, promising as he thinks the concept is, it will not be able to perform the "supressory function" for scholarship that Orren and Skowronek want. "We seem to be dealing now," Burnham writes of the 1994 elections, "as in the past, with a situation in which one regime order comes to an end, and a genuinely new and quite different order is created." He suspects that it is impossible to account for, perhaps even to perceive, political change without the utilization of some synthetic analytical device of the sort that he has proposed, even if his particular scheme turns out to be flawed. Fiorina thinks that Orren and Skowronek exaggerate both his claims and their empirical differences with him. His study of the ICC was intended, he argues, to be an example of the broader issue of legislative delegation, in which a number of models were "applied," but not "tested," to suggest different explanatory possibilities. Urging the use of multiple models, he challenges Orren and Skowronek to demonstrate that their concept of intercurrence contributes to the explanation of political phenomena rather than their mere description. Noting that he agrees with Orren and Skowronek about both the primacy of political institutions and the necessity to apply multiple models to historical data, he rejects the suggestion that there should be "one true religion" for institutional studies. Their reply indicates that Orren and Skowronek agree with this point and other aspects of Burnham's discussion. They remain skeptical, however, of the coherence of Fiorina's claim that models can usefully be "compared to the historical record" without being "tested," and of Burnham's insistence on the utility of such architectonic concepts as realignment, unless they are supplemented by models that pick out and account for the disruptive political dynamics they identify.

II. Democracy and Nationalism

The ideologies of democracy and nationalism must surely rank as two of the most powerful challenges to political order in the modern world. Sometimes in tandem, sometimes at loggerheads, both have the permanent potential to destroy ordered political relations that have persisted for generations, even centuries. Developments in the post-communist world and Southern Africa since 1989 stand as eloquent testimony to this fact. The enduring presence of both democracy and nationalism might not be providentially ordained, as Alexis de Tocqueville wrote of the idea of equality in 1830, but it often appears as though it might as well be.[2] De Tocqueville's warning that people had better learn to live with and manage egalitarian aspirations, lest they be destroyed by them, seems no less applicable to these ideologies. An analogous warning may be thought of as the animating concern behind the chapters in part II.

Perhaps because democratic and nationalist ideologies exercise so powerful a hold over so many millions of people, political theorists have paid a lot of attention to how, if at all, they might be domesticated. It is a subject that has achieved a degree of urgency in recent years, because attempts are underway to write democratic constitutions in many countries where ethnic divisions are profound and nationalist sentiments are strong. In chapters 8 and 9, Robert A. Dahl and Nicholas R. Miller take up ongoing debates about the utility of various constitutional and electoral devices to mitigate democracy's centrifugal tendencies. "What can we learn," asks Dahl, "from the lengthily and diverse experience of democratic countries with constitutional systems, very broadly defined?" In contrast to much conventional wisdom about institutional design, Dahl argues that the evidence suggests that constitutional arrangements are less important than other favorable conditions. This does not mean that constitutional arrangements are irrelevant, but Dahl contends that relevant criteria for optimal constitutional design are numerous, difficult to pin down, and sometimes mutually incompatible. He argues that if we examine constitutions with just one of these criteria in mind—stability—the evidence suggests that, under favorable conditions at least, constitutional arrangements have no discernible effect. Moreover, Dahl contends that each of the available constitutional alternatives is subject to such great variation in its subordinate arrangements that every country's constitutional arrangements are in some respects unique. It appears from Dahl's discussion of the state of the theory and evidence that there is no one best democratic constitutional system, or, if there is, we do not know what it is.

If constitutional arrangements and electoral rules matter only at the margins, some, presumably, are nonetheless better than others. Even if people in the business of writing constitutions are only dealing with three percent of the problem, they are in a position to make choices about the three percent in question. Particularly in the "third wave"[3] of democratizations since 1974, many of which have taken place in the context of profound ethnic and racial division, constitutional designers have be especially attuned to the problem that de Tocqueville and Mill first identified in the nineteenth century: the possibility that majoritarian democratic procedures will operate systematically to disenfranchise some minority, giving it no incentive to participate and a positive incentive to turn to extra-regime politics if it has the power.[4] The same issue arises in established democracies. In Britain, there is a perennial debate over whether some form of proportional representation would more fairly represent the interests of minority parties—currently the Liberal Democrats—than the first-past-the-post system with single member constituencies. In the United States, it has surfaced as a no less controversial debate about "majority-minority districts," as Lani Guinier discovered to her cost when President Clinton was forced to withdraw her nomination to head of the Civil Rights Division of the Justice Department in 1993.

In earlier work, Miller had defended majority rule against critics in the rational choice tradition, pointing out that although it might be unstable in the technical sense of being vulnerable to cycles, this might actually promote social stability because it means that the same minority need not expect to lose in every circumstance.[5] The very unpredictability that makes majority rule irrational, in the sense of being unable to amalgamate individual preferences into a social welfare function, might be democracy's salvation from this point of view of giving present losers incentives not to defect against the democratic political order itself.[6] In chapter 9 of the present volume, Miller further explores the thesis that "winner-take-all" systems render minority interests irrelevant to the outcomes of democratic processes. He argues that although this can happen in certain circumstances, the general claim stands in need of substantial qualification. He distinguishes three kinds of politics—cleavage politics, ideological politics, and distributive politics—and shows that the issue of majority rule versus minority interests plays out quite differently in each context. In cleavage politics, the conventional assumption (that minorities systematically lose) is fully supported if there is one issue only, but given several issues on which the preferences of different groups are cross-cutting, his earlier finding is robust and the conventional argument must be qualified. In the context of ideological politics, majority rule typically produces compromise outcomes, and the interests of even an ideologically distinctive minority can be expected to receive considerable weight. As far as distributive politics are concerned, majority rule turns out to be fundamentally chaotic, and cannot be credited or blamed for any particular outcome.

Christiano's preoccupation with the tensions between democracy and political stability, the subject of chapter 10, is more explicitly normative in character. Arguing that democracy requires equality in the process of deliberation, he notes that in a democratic society it is practically impossible for citizens who accept this principle to agree on what is required for its implementation. Christiano characterizes as the "inherent contestability" of deliberative equality the difficulty that in a democratic society many will think that their views have not been given a fair hearing while others see no difficulty. As a result, those who feel that their views have been given short shrift will reasonably dispute the claim that the prevailing decision-making procedure makes adequate provision for everyone's participation. Even when everyone agrees, and knows that everyone else agrees, on basic principles, some people thus will have reason to contest the claim that their society is fully democratic. In Christiano's view, this state of affairs poses three related challenges to a democratic political order. First, it suggests that the public institutions of a democracy cannot, even in principle, be fully transparent to its members. Second, it implies that there are bound to be endemic disagreements among the citizenry over what constitutes a democratic political order. Finally, if citizens really prize political equality over other political values, political instability may result. Christiano considers various institutional devices that have been designed to overcome these difficulties, arguing that they have not been successful, and concludes with a discussion of how they might be mitigated.

Elizabeth Kiss directs our attention to nationalism's challenge to political order in chapter 11. Her question is: What attitude should we take toward nationalism if we aspire to create the conditions in which human rights claims have an effective voice? Given the intensity of ethnic and national identities in many parts of the world today, she asks, how can we temper our democratic ideals with a sense of what is possible without giving them up? Kiss develops her response to these questions in five theses. First, she contends that although nationalism is not a primordial force, for practical purposes we should consider it a lasting feature of our world. It can, and no doubt will, continue to serve as a source of both solidarity and conflict for the forseeable future. This does not mean, however, that nationalist sentiments are unalterable. Both nationalism's psychological intensity and its moral and political force should be thought of as dynamic and alterable, at least at the margins. Second, Kiss contends that by itself nationalism cannot generate viable principles of political order. Third, although efforts to elevate nationalism to a principle of political order are for this reason politically dangerous as well as morally unsound, in Kiss's view efforts to denationalize politics are no less suspect. It follows, fourth, that the best approach to nationalism must include institutional strategies of ethnic accommodation. However, Kiss concludes that, while necessary, such strategies are insufficient. Her final thesis is that they must be paired with strategies of cultural inclusion that hold out some hope of eroding nationalism's malevolent dimensions, by emphasizing forms of local identification that are compatible with the claims of our common humanity.

Responding in chapter 12, Debra Satz contrasts Kiss's "ethnic nationalism" with less benign nationalisms that center on questions of state power and sovereignty. In Satz's view, such state-centered nationalisms raise more serious difficulties for Kiss's project of reconciling local forms of identification with universalist moral claims. The reason, according to Satz, is that the state is not merely one actor among many; states raise special kinds of agency and collective action problems. In addition to these difficulties, she notes that, merely by controlling immigration, states reinforce inequalities among nations that can be expected to create massive—perhaps insuperable—obstacles to any project whose goal is to reconcile nationalist sentiment with liberal democratic values and practices.

In John Gray's view, it is wrongheaded even to try. On his account, the liberal values that inform the aspiration to harmonize national and democratic aspirations are the product of a misguided universalist agenda. By this he means that the principles of liberal political theory are generally defended as compelling for all reasonable human beings. Such universalist theoretical aspirations, he argues, assume the possibility of "a foundationalist project for liberal practice that cannot be realized." None of the proposed attempts to give liberal practice a universal claim on reason—such as those of Kant, Mill, and perhaps the earlier Rawls—succeeds. In previous work, Gray had argued for the "post-liberal" view that the near-universal authority of liberal civil institutions could be defended on historicist grounds, despite the failures of foundationalist liberalism.[7] In chapter 13, he retreats to the perhaps more pessimistic position that the post-liberal view was mistaken. The earlier error arose, he now thinks, from a conflation of market institutions, which (in all their manifold variety) may command near-universal authority in our circumstances, with liberal civil institutions, which do not.

Gray now offers an alternative view of liberal civil institutions, in which they are understood to express only one possible way of finding a *modus vivendi* among communities and forms of life that are animated by incommensurable and conflicting values. This, for Gray no less than it was for Hobbes, is the fundamental problem of political order. He argues that there is no particular reason to believe that liberal civil institutions offer the only solution, and several good reasons to suspect that they do not. This observation leads Gray to the contention that strong value-pluralism in ethical theory does not, as is often maintained, support liberalism in political theory. Rather, he makes the case that ethical pluralism supports a commitment to political pluralism. This is the view that a diversity of institutions and regimes—some of them liberal and some of them not—is appropriate and legitimate in most historical contexts, including our own. Liberal democratic regimes, on Gray's pluralist view, receive, and deserve, no special privileges.

III. Political Culture

Liberal political theorists have often been faulted for devoting a disproportion of their energies to the structure of, and justification for, particular national institutions, while devoting little—if any—attention to the structure and operation of civil institutions. To some degree the rise of feminism and communitarianism in recent years (dealt with extensively in NOMOS XXXIV: *Virtue* and NOMOS XXXV: *Democratic Community*) have served to remedy this state of affairs, as has the growing attention, in the democratization literature, to the functional importance of certain types of civil practices in sustaining a democratic political order.[8] These literatures have shaped the concerns of the authors in part III. They turn away from Gray's preoccupation with the challenges posed to liberal democracy by the diversity of possible regimes, and focus instead on the challenges posed to it by cultural diversity within regimes.

In chapter 14, Richard J. Arneson and Ian Shapiro confront this issue through the lens of *Wisconsin v. Yoder*, the 1972 decision in which the U.S. Supreme Court exempted the Old Order Amish from a Wisconsin law requiring compulsory education of all children to age sixteen. Arguing that a democratic state has a responsibility to ensure that children are educated to the point where critical reason is developed and can be deployed, Arneson and Shapiro make the case that *Yoder* was wrongly decided. The state's responsibility for children's education has a dual foundation on Arneson and Shapiro's view: in its fiduciary obligation to protect the basic interests of Amish children, and in its accountability to others in a democracy who have an interest in the existence a citizenry that can participate—in an informed and reflective way—in the collective life of the polity. Whatever the religious convictions of the Amish might be (and a democratic state has no reason to challenge the veracity of their convictions), the fiduciary authority of Amish parents over their children's best interests should not extend to the point that it undermines the state's fiduciary responsibility for children's basic interests. Arneson and Shapiro anticipate and respond to various criticisms of their view, including arguments that it inappropriately privileges some conceptions of the good and disprivileges others. They also take up, and reject, arguments that have recently been put forward by Joel Feinberg, Amy Gutmann, John Rawls, and William Galston, all of whom would grant greater deference to the educational practices of groups like the Amish than Arneson and Shapiro think is defensible.

Shelley Burtt takes the contrary view in chapter 15. Elsewhere she has argued that, as far as children are concerned, the American government has underperformed on its traditional responsibility to guarantee physical security while being overly interventionist in areas that liberals have conventionally regarded as beyond its purview: questions of value and spiritual development.[9] She now extends this view to a defense of *Yoder,* arguing that religious parents should have substantial autonomy in shaping the educational experience of their children. In particular, she argues that once certain minimal standards of educational achievement have been met, the state lacks legitimate authority to insist on a public education that parents deem destructive to their children's religious life or sensibilities. Burtt defends this "principle of parental deference" not on Free Exercise grounds, but rather by defending a particular interpretation of what she describes as "parents' and the state's shared responsibility to meet children's developmental needs, broadly conceived."

Lainie Friedman Ross and David Schmidtz shift our attention to a different aspect of civil society: the family rather than the cultural group. In chapter 16, they develop a critique of Rawls's argument that justice applies only to the basic political structure of society, that it is "the complex web of institutions rather than any particular institution" that must answer to the principles of justice. They note that much of human existence occurs not in the larger polis, but rather in smaller spheres of political order such as the family. They explore various ways in which constraints on such smaller spheres might be derived from Rawlsian principles, and conclude that trying to do this might be constrained by the larger Rawlsian project. In short, applying Rawlsian principles to more encompassing spheres of political order can generate checks on family autonomy. However, the converse is also true, suggesting a possibility that Ross and Schmidtz find agreeable: marking off a sphere of legitimate family autonomy could serve as a "check and balance" on the basic structure in which the family is embedded.

In chapter 17, Jennifer Nedelsky takes an altogether less sanguine view of the place of domestic relations in a liberal political order than do either Burtt or Ross and Schmidtz. Like Burtt, Nedelsky thinks the liberal state has failed to "achieve its minimum goal: security from fear and violence." And, like Ross and Schmidtz, she thinks that there are tensions between the requirements of domestic justice and the larger operations of a liberal polity. Unlike these authors, however, Nedelsky does not think the answer lies in drawing the boundaries around family life differently than they presently are drawn. On her account, domestic violence has its roots in the characteristic liberal conception of rights as boundaries. This violence will not be done away with until the liberal conception of rights-as-boundaries is replaced by a relational understanding of rights. Boundary language is incapable of capturing the horror of types of violence like rape, she argues. Rather, the relations between men and women have to be fundamentally transformed, which implies a project for government that transcends traditional liberal understandings of its appropriate role. "Most accounts of liberalism (not merely libertarian ones) would see taking on the kind of transformation I have in mind as dangerously enlarging the appropriate scope of the state with vague, open-ended and inevitably contested objectives," she writes, "thus inviting both intrusion and expanded state power to which no clear limits could be drawn." Nonetheless, she contends that nothing short of such a transformation can be expected to address the problem.

In our concluding chapter, Robert E. Goodin responds to the challenge to liberal conceptions of political order put forward by such relational feminists as Nedelsky. Goodin agrees with

Nedelsky's Shklarian view that political order should be thought about first and foremost as a solution to the problem of evil. He examines various solutions to this problem in the light of feminist critiques like Nedelsky's. The characteristic liberal view, which they criticize, is an hierarchical one. It is based on subcontracting political authority, with rights (understood as protected choices), being one particular form of subcontracted authority. On Goodin's view, relational feminists rightly criticize liberals' characteristic focus on the hierarchical subcontracting of political order involved in ascriptions of liberal rights, but he has misgivings about their proposed alternative: a project of reconstructing the relationships among subjects, using rights to bind people together rather than keep them apart. This leads him to argue for a view that reconciles the two positions. In the day-to-day workings of a liberal society, he notes, informal relations of trust and fair dealing are in the foreground, with the legal panoply of formal rights remaining as background remedies, "should push come to shove." By analogy, he argues, relational feminists are right to advocate the development of interpersonal relations that are sensitive to feminist concerns, but they should recognize the value of having a liberal rights regime present—in the background—in case the relationships they hope to foster should fail to materialize. Goodin's conclusion thus brings us full circle, back to the problem with which Pasquino began: in the modern world at least, without the existence of a rights-protecting regime it may not be possible for political order to be sustained at all.

NOTES

1. See Karen Orren, *Belated Feudalism: Labor, the Law, and Liberal Development in the United States* (New York: Cambridge University Press, 1991), Stephen Skowronek, *Building a New American State: The Expansion of National Administrative Capacities 1877–1929* (New York: Cambridge University Press, 1982), and Stephen Skowronek, *The Politics Presidents Make: Leadership from John Adams to George Bush* (Cambridge: Harvard University Press, 1993).

2. Alexis de Tocqueville, *Democracy in America* (New York: Anchor Books, 1969). See, in particular, the preface to the twelfth edition, written in 1848, xiii–xiv.

3. Samuel P. Huntington, *The Third Wave: Democratization in the Late Twentieth Century* (Norman, Okla.: University of Oklahoma Press, 1991).

4. On constitutions as coordination devices, see Russell Hardin, "Why a Constitution?" in *The Federalist Papers and the New Institutionalism,* ed. Bernard Grofman and Donald Wittman (New York: Agathon, 1989), 100–120, and, on constitutions as devices to ensure commitment, "One for All" in Russell Hardin, *The Logic of Group Conflict* (Princeton: Princeton University Press, 1995).

5. Nicholas R. Miller, "Pluralism and Social Choice," *American Political Science Review* 77, no. 3 (September 1983): 730–45.

6. For elaboration of the relations between the logic of uncertainty and democratic stability, see Giuseppe Di Palma, *To Craft Democracies: An Essay on Democratic Transitions* (Berkeley: University of California Press, 1990), especially chapters 3 and 4, and Adam Przeworski, *Democracy and the Market: Political and Economic Reforms in Europe and Latin America* (New York: Cambridge University Press), especially chapter 1.

7. See John Gray's discussion in *Post-Liberalism: Studies in Political Thought* (London: Routledge, 1993).

8. For recent discussions, see Robert D. Putnam et al., *Making Democracy Work: Civic Traditions in Modern Italy* (Princeton: Princeton University Press, 1993), Ian Shapiro, "Democratic Innovation: South Africa in Comparative Context," *World Politics* 46, no. 1 (October 1993): 121–50, and Edward N. Muller and Mitchell A. Seligson, "Civic Culture and Democracy: The Question of Causal Relationships," *American Political Science Review* 88, no. 3 (September 1994): 635–52.

9. See Shelley Burtt, "Religious Parents, Secular Schools: A Liberal Defense of an Illiberal Education," *Review of Politics* 56, no. 1 (Winter 1994): 51–70.

PART I

ORDER VERSUS DISORDER

1

POLITICAL THEORY, ORDER, AND THREAT

PASQUALE PASQUINO

Political theory is about order inside the city. I suggest that it is more precisely the series of texts on the means of avoiding *disorder* which threatens coexistence within the political community. The aim of this chapter is to show that transformations of political discourse in the West have been a function of changing conceptualizations of *threat* to the existence of political order and hence of the different ways of envisaging the origin and nature of this threat.

I. Liberalism or the Threat of Exorbitant Power of the Central Political Agency

> In a large society, individual liberty has three kinds of enemies to fear. The least dangerous are malevolent citizens: in order to repress them, ordinary authority is sufficient. . . . Individual liberty is far more endangered by [the second enemy: the] undertakings of the *officers encharged to exercise some part of public power.* Simple isolated public officials, entire bodies, the government itself in its entirety, can cease to respect the rights of the citizens.

I would like to thank Alessandro Pizzorno and Bernard Manin. They first helped me some years ago to understand the role of threat in political theory; the second discussed this text with me on many occasions and I am indebted to him for some formulations born in the course of our discussions.

> Long experience proves that *nations are not sufficiently cautioned against this sort of danger.* How disgraceful to see a public official turning against his fellow citizens the weapons or power he has received to defend them and . . . turning the means entrusted to him for their common protection into instruments of oppression!

After this diagnosis, the author proposes his remedy:

> The *separation,* and a good constitution of public powers are the only guarantee that Nations and Citizens might be preserved from this extreme evil. (emphasis mine)

It should be noted that the third enemy of liberty mentioned in this text is the possible foreign enemy, a question which will be set aside throughout this discussion, since the object—it is better to state it right from the beginning—is that of the threat internal to the society or the city.

The quotation which we have just read is taken from an important, but completely disregarded, text by one of major theorists of the liberal state: the *Préliminaire de la constitution française,* by Emmanuel Sieyes, which was published three times in 1789, and since has been largely forgotten in France.[1] By the expression *liberal theory of the state,* I mean a doctrine which, like the one in the text cited, considers that too much power concentrated in the hands of those who govern or by the organs of the state constitutes a danger to the political order, and to the security and liberty of individuals.[2] In his 1921 book on dictatorship, Carl Schmitt wrote that all excessive political power represents the enemy for Montesquieu and his liberal disciples.[3] One can say that "modern constitutionalism," or more precisely the doctrine of the constitutional state based on the fundamental rights and the division/equilibrium of powers, is in fact a response to the kind of internal threat to the city conceptualized in the text of Sieyes.[4] This response is thus to the liberal preoccupation that could be formulated, "how much governing?"

Liberalism, so defined,[5] is so much part of our intellectual horizon that it is easy to forget that it was not always like that. Nonetheless, if one looks at the first systematic theory of the modern state, the *Leviathan* of Thomas Hobbes, one notices the almost total absence of the "liberal preoccupation" with the limitation of state power. In the sense in which I use the word, the liberal preoccupation is *prima facie* outside of Hobbes's concern.[6] He was concerned in fact to answer a logically prior question, not normally broached by liberal thought (which asks "*how much* governing?"): that of knowing *why* a state? Now, at a first level, it seems to me we find in Hobbes the following answer: the state, or rather in his terms the existence and the power of the representative sovereign (be it an individual or an assembly) is necessary, because its absence would allow a condition (which he calls somewhat ambiguously, a *state of nature*) which represents a mortal threat to the political order and the safety, even survival, of each human being. If the natural condition of mankind constitutes in the Hobbesian conception, for reasons which we will have to try to clarify, a source of disorder, danger, and even war of all against all, the sovereign appears, on the contrary, as *creator et defensor pacis,* as source of order and security and hence even as the precondition of the liberty of his subjects,[7] rather than a source of danger and threat.

II. Republicanism and the Threat Coming from the Absence of Regulation of Conflicts between the Parts of the City

> Machiavelli is the first in Christendom that I can find that wrote of a mixed government. (R. Filmer, *The Anarchy of a Limited or Mixed Monarchy*)[8]

The idea of sovereign-Leviathan is also in fact a recent idea. Since the classical antiquity and until the mid-seventeenth century, the dominant political doctrine in the West went under the name of "mixed constitution" or "mixed government."[9] This doctrine proposes a theory of political order which rests on a conception of society and of its internal threat that is very different from the Hobbesian or liberal one. It may seem strange that I have chosen to illustrate the ancient political doctrine with an author who, as much as Hobbes, has been often considered—one thinks for example of Benedetto Croce and Leo Strauss—as the founder of modern political theory: Niccolò Machiavelli. It suffices, however, to read the first chapters of his *Discourses on Livy,* surely the most important of his works and in any case the most systematic of those concerned with political theory, to realize that this choice is not so strange. If one considers in particular Book I of the *Discourses,* one will see immediately that it concerns neither the protective power of the state nor the limitation of this power. A different language is visible, close to that of the ancient and also to a cluster of political categories which I would like to examine more closely in order to discern the conception underlying the classical theory of mixed government.[10]

Before considering this issue, we need to turn briefly to a methodological question. When one reads such a text as Machiavelli's *Discourses* or Hobbes's *Leviathan,* it is necessary to keep in mind that most of the time the author is trying to persuade a specific public to make certain practical choices through arguments that he considers capable of changing the beliefs of his public (for instance, according to certain interpretations of Hobbes, to accept the 1651 government of the Lord Protector Oliver Cromwell or, in the case of Machiavelli, to press the Florentine aristocracy into a compromise with the middle class—to use an anachronistic word—and to oppose the return to Florence of the Medicis' tyrannical government).[11] This rhetorical[12] and contextualist dimension of most political works, absolutely crucial for a correct understanding of the meaning of these texts,[13] should not make us forget that in works produced by people with the intelligence and the intellectual passion of Machiavelli or Hobbes, the contextualist dimension does not exhaust the significance of the text,[14] because it contains an intellectual structure which provides and continues to provide food for thought for a much larger public than that for which it was written: such a public as the readers of this article who are trying to reflect today on political theory just as others did in the past.

In any political community *("republica"),*[15] wrote Machiavelli, there is and there will always be[16] *two different groups* of individuals: the *grandees ("grandi")* and the *people.*[17] These two groups constitutive of every city or political community are characterized by two dispositions, two different *humors:* "the people do not want to be dominated or oppressed by the grandees, and the grandees want to dominate and oppress the people."[18] We find the same idea in the *Discourses* I, 5: "It will be seen that in the former [the grandees] there is a great desire to dominate and in the latter [the people] merely the desire not to be dominated."[19] Now, the existence of these two groups with their opposed humors not only manifests the essential and ultimate structure of the city, being its constitutive, elementary, and irreducible elements, but also represents the source of the disorder that threatens it. In chapter 1 of Book III of *Florentine Histories,* we read: "All the serious though natural enmities which occur between the common people and the nobility are caused by the desire of the latter to command and the former not to obey, these two humors are the origin of all the evils that arise in cities."[20] We see then that Machiavelli identifies, in the dualist and conflictual structure of the city, the threat which calls out for a theory of political order. "*Ordine, ordini*" is key in the Machiavellian vocabulary. By this term, one should understand the constitutional provisions, and constitution has to be taken here in the Greek sense of *politeía,* because it is a matter of both order of the government and that of the city.[21]

As Felix Gilbert has remarked,[22] the first eighteen chapters of the *Discourses* constitute more a general treatise on republics than a commentary on Livy. I would go so far as to say that they contain an answer to the problem posed in chapter 9 of *The Prince* and in Book III, chapter 1, of *Florentine Histories:* i.e., the Machiavellian doctrine of the "mixed constitution." The latter is developed notably in chapters 2–6, Book I of the *Discourses.* These pages of extraordinary richness and power deserve a precise and thorough commentary. I will limit myself here to a few essential points. In chapter 2, Book I, which concerns the different forms of republics in the general sense of political communities, Machiavelli takes up the theory of *anakyklosis* ("the cycle through which all commonwealths pass")[23] presented by Polybius in Book VI of his *Histories.* Machiavelli then arrives at the following conclusion:

> I maintain then, that all the forms of government mentioned above are far from satisfactory, the three good ones [monarchy,

> aristocracy, democracy] because their life is so short, the three bad ones [tyranny, oligarchy, ochlocracy *(licenza)*] because of their inherent malignity. Hence prudent legislators, aware of their defects, refrained from adopting as such any one of these forms, and chose instead one that shared in them all, since they thought such a government would be stronger and more stable, for if in one and the same state there was principality, aristocracy and democracy each would keep watch over the other.[24]

The mixed constitution is thus for Machiavelli the true republic and even the "perfect commonwealth."[25] This chapter has posed a number of problems of interpretation. The first one hardly interests here; it concerns how Machiavelli could have read book 6 of Polybius's *Histories* given that he did not know Greek and at that time no Latin translation of that text existed.[26] A much more important question, to which we will return, consists in trying to understand why the author of the *Discourses* took up the ternary model of the mixed constitution considering that the framework in which he poses the question of political order is of a "sociological" type and dualist like that of Aristotle.

The relation between Machiavelli and Polybius has been the subject of a number of studies;[27] fewer have examined the relation of the political theory of the *Discourses* to Aristotle's *Politics.* Nonetheless, the formal parallel between the analyses of the city proposed by the two authors is perfectly clear, and did not escape the notice of Father Walker.[28] In fact, in a number of passages in the *Politics,* Aristotle contrasts the notables and the rich to the poor or the people (the Greek text speaks of *eúporoi* as opposed to *áporoi* or of *gnorímoi* as opposed to *démos*).[29] It is never been sufficiently pointed out that the entire theory of *politeíai,* which means constitutions or forms of government, and which seems moreover to conclude with the preference for mixed government[30] rests for Aristotle on the "anatomy of the city" which he proposes in Book IV of the *Politics.* Classical political-constitutional theory, from Aristotle until the Hobbesian revolution, is essentially tied to the theory of the "parts of the city" *(mére tès póleos),*[31] which we have seen at the very heart of Machiavelli's political analysis. It would go far past the confines of this chapter to take into account the extraordinary richness and somewhat incoherent structure of such a book as Aristotle's *Politics,* which his author likely never actually wrote out. Nonetheless, I would like to add a remark. Sometimes Aristotle presents his anatomy of the city in a slightly different manner; for example, in the *Politics* IV, 11, 4 [=1295b1–3], one reads: "In all cities there are three parts of the city: those who are very well off, those of very modest means and thirdly those intermediate between them *(mésoi).*" Aristotle distinguishes, moreover, the *politeía* in the narrow sense, meaning the mixed constitution, from the *mése politeía,* which one could possibly translate "middle constitution,"[32] which, in order to produce social equilibrium, stability, and integration of the parts of the city, rests in the middle classes.[33] Besides the basic dualistic model, Machiavelli himself uses this tripartition in a very important text, the *Discursus florentinarum rerum,* which was a constitutional project for the Florentine republic written in 1519–20, when the cardinal Giulio de' Medici came to Florence to put order in its government after the death of his brother Lorenzo il Giovane. Here one reads: "Those who organize a republic ought to provide for the three different sorts of men who exist in all the cities, namely, the most important, those in the middle, and the lowest *[primi, mezzani e ultimi].*"[34] Marcia L. Colish comments thus on this text: "The three councils in his system are designed to accommodate these differences in ambition. He [Machiavelli] also points out that his provisions for veto and appeal enable the three groups to scrutinize each other's actions, thus preventing the abuse of power by all branches of government."[35] Here it is important to notice that the three branches of government are the *immediate* expression of the groups or social parts constitutive of the city; this not being the case at all in the doctrine of the separation of the powers, such as appears for example in Sieyes.

Generally speaking, one should keep in mind that for Aristotle, Polybius,[36] and Machiavelli the constitutional model of the *optima respublica* implies both an ideal of moderation and the project of integrating the social groups which are the basic element of the city, and this by their direct or indirect participation to the public magistracies. In the words of Nippel[37] writing about Aristotle, it is a matter of creating an equilibrium between the different groups of citizens; or, with regard to Florence at the beginning of the sixteenth century, of the integration into the same political community of the urban aristocracy and the artisans.[38] One should note, moreover, that for the Florentine as already for the Stagirite, the mixed government or constitution was contrasted not only to tyranny but also with democracy or popular government. One can see this clearly if one compares the *Discourses* of Machiavelli with the most important political text of Girolamo Savonarola, which was in a sense his spiritual testament, the *Trattato circa el reggimento e governo della città di Firenze,* published in 1498;[39] or if one reads Machiavelli's judgment of the Athenian constitution, also in chapter 2, Book I of the *Discourses:*

> and though . . . Athens returned to liberty because it again adopted a democratic form of government in accordance with Solon's laws, it did not retain its liberty for more than a hundred years. For, in spite of the fact that many constitutions were made whereby to restrain the arrogance of the grandees and the licentiousness of the poor, for which Solon had made no provision, nonetheless Athens had a very short life as compared with that of Sparta because with democracy Solon had not blended princely power and that of the aristocracy.[40]

It would be worth reflecting on the reasons which drove our two authors to the proposition and defense of mixed government. For Aristotle, the constitutive social groups of the city were both (or all three) bearers of positive values, none of which may be renounced in a good and ordered social life without reintroducing disorder. Quite the contrary for Machiavelli: his popular sentiments, at least in the *Discourses,* lead him to accept the idea of the mixed government for the simple reasons of "political realism," the same which had led him to write in *The Prince,* chapter 15: "because I want to write what will be useful to anyone who understands, it seems to me better to concentrate on what really happens rather than on theories or speculations. For many have imagined republics and principalities that have never been seen or known to exist."[41] Thus, this political realism was the reason for his preference for mixed government over popular government, since even if one could kill all the grandees they would reappear *more fungorum,* given, as we have seen, that they are a constitutive part of the city. The anti-aristocratic sentiment is much more subtle in the constitutional project of 1520—one should take into consideration the special character of this text and the occasion which motivated Machiavelli to write it. Here one reads, for instance, "nonetheless some of her [Florence's] citizens have ambitious spirits and think they deserve to outrank the others; these must be satisfied in organizing a republic; the last government, indeed, fell for no other cause than such a group was not satisfied."[42] Here we see his realism reappear! In any case, the popular tendency of Machiavelli led him to write the surprising chapter 5, Book I, of the *Discourses* which concerns the "guardianship of liberty." Guicciardini, closer to the *ottimati,* was moved to criticize this text in his *Considerations on the Discourses of Machiavelli,* where he wrote "I do not understand what it means" *("Io non intendo el titolo della quistione").* One should understand this guardianship of liberty as a type of control on the maintenance of the mixed constitution, assured by popular magistrates.

To conclude these brief remarks on Machiavelli, note that the theory of the mixed constitution represents his response to an analysis of society which sees in the ambition of the grandees the structural source of the disorder menacing the life of the city: not only that ambition[43] but also a form of social conflict in which both parts refuse to compromise and seek to destroy the dualistic structure of the city. Hence, the mixed form of the constitution. The conflict between the parts of the city is for Machiavelli, as he shows in his *Florentine Histories,* the key to understanding politics as much as history. The mixed constitution is not a negation or a mere acceptance of conflict, but its *disciplining* and *institutionalization.* Consequently, the existence of social conflict is not the final word in Machiavelli's political theory. Only conflict coupled with moderation, meaning the willingness to live together with other parts of the city and hence to share the political magistracies, produces political order. In the absence of moderation, social conflicts become the source of anarchy, or undermine the republican regime and become the rationale for the establishment of a principality. This is why in the *Florentine Histories* one finds the thesis that conflict can give rise to two different effects: political order, stability, and grandeur as in the case of Rome, but also civil war as in the history of Florence.[44] In fact, it is only by constitutional management and regulation of social conflicts—a *concordia discors* of which the Roman republic was for Machiavelli a shining example—that one could guarantee the order, liberty, and survival of political community.

III. Sovereign State, Religious Conflicts, and Overlapping Consensus

1517 Annus Mirabilis

Right from the beginning of the modern theory of the state, one finds a systematic and radical critique of mixed constitution by Bodin[45] and Hobbes. This critique has often been reduced to the absolutist character of their thought, which obstructed a proper understanding of the Copernican revolution represented by the texts of these authors. I shall concentrate on several aspects of Hobbes's political theory in order to point out the novelty of his concepts of order, threat, and the anatomy of the city.

In terms of the historical context of Hobbes's political works, one first of all should give consideration to the constitutional conflict that shook England in the 1630s, on the eve of the Great Rebellion, in particular to the conflict between the King and the Parliament with regard to the prerogative, in this case the right claimed by the King of England in 1636, to impose a special tax *(ship money)* on the coastal towns, without asking Parliament's permission.[46] The very interesting debate that followed focused on the question of sovereignty, in the sense of the right or prerogative to give authoritative commands in exceptional circumstances, such as the existence of extraordinary and imminent danger demanding an immediate decision without preliminary debate (in particular according to the King the danger of attack by the Dutch against the English coasts). Hobbes's position in his *Elements of Law* of 1640 is completely favorable to this prerogative, although he was unable to give firm arguments in favor of the exercise by the monarch (rather than by an elected assembly) of this extraordinary and extralegal power. A detailed discussion of the historical context is not possible here, but I will identify certain underlying concepts in the political theory that Hobbes defended throughout the English civil war and within which behind the conflict over the constitution, one detects the rumblings of the religious wars.

Hobbes repeatedly said that the aim of his political reflections was to analyze the "*bellorum et pacis causae*," and hence the origin and *raison d'être* of political order and civil war.[47] It is evident, if one takes account of the entirety of Hobbes's thought, that the real origin of disorder is to be found in false or seditious beliefs and doctrines.[48] The constitutional conflict racking the England of the Stuarts was exacerbated by a conflict which derived from "false" religious beliefs.[49] It is the nature of this *conflict* and the *threat* that it represents, in Hobbes's view, for political order, on which I would like to focus now.

Chapter 25 of the *Elements of Law*[50] is particularly relevant to this question, and one wonders why it has hardly attracted attention from Hobbes's interpreters, even from those recently interested in his writing on religion. At the beginning of this chapter Hobbes, believing that the question of the threat that mixed constitution[51] represents for political order had been settled by his theory of sovereignty,[52] introduces his reader to another type of threat or reason for disorder: "a difficulty, which, if it be not removed, maketh unlawful for any man to procure his own peace and preservation."[53] He continues, "And the difficulty is this: we have amongst us the Word of God for the rule of our actions."[54]

What does he mean by this? Hobbes's thesis is that the Reformation had introduced a threat to the order of the city which calls for a radical reformulation of political theory and in particular the abandonment of the classical doctrine of the mixed constitution and of the political anatomy that constituted its foundation. This threat consisted in the continual possibility of conflict between the word of the sovereign and that of God,[55] since every individual was according to the Reformed doctrine an authoritative and legitimate interpreter of the latter.[56] In other words, to point out the worrying radicality of this "difficulty," political order, civil peace, and even the life of individuals can be brought into question and reduced to nothing by the preoccupation with salvation, that is, with eternal life or death.

We know that Machiavelli had insisted on the danger that Christian religion represented for political order to the extent that it alienated citizens from public life in the city. Now, in 1517, an *annus mirabilis* amongst few others, at exactly the same time as the Florentine secretary was in the process of completing the last great work of the classical political culture, a monk in the north of Germany was posting his incendiary thesis on the doors of the chapel of Wittenberg castle. For more than a century, continental Europe was entirely set alight by wars of religion.[57] The conflict at the heart of Christianity was perceived by Hobbes as a conflict between political and religious loyalties. Hence for him the necessity of showing that obedience to the Leviathan-state could guarantee both life, in the sense of self-preservation, *and* salvation. But let us return to chapter 25 of the *Elements*.

That the order of the city is subject to a *novel threat* which arises with the Reformation is exactly what one may read in Hobbes:

> This difficulty hath *not* been of *very great antiquity* in the world. There was no such dilemma amongst the Jews; for their civil law, and divine law, was one and the same law of Moses: the interpreters whereof were the priests, whose power was subordinate to the power of the king . . . Nor it is a controversy that was ever taken notice of amongst the Grecians, Romans, or other Gentiles. . . . Also those Christians that dwell under the temporal dominion of the bishop of Rome, are free from this question. . . . This difficulty therefore remaineth amongst, and troubleth those Christians only, *to whom it is allowed to take for the sense of the Scripture that which they make thereof, either by their own private interpretation, or by the interpretation of such as are not called thereunto by public authority*.[58]

The former demand all the time liberty of conscience, the latter finding themselves obliged to obey two sovereigns, which is not possible without contradiction and conflict.[59] The modern difficulty of which Hobbes speaks consists thus in the threat to the order of the city which arises from a type of conflict completely different from that which is the object of classical and republican political theory of the mixed government. The conflict between the rich and the poor or the grandees and the people could be mediated; the conflict to which modern political theory had to respond was on the contrary a conflict over truth and salvation. It could not be resolved in the same manner that one might envisage resolving *social* conflict. It is self-evident that neither truth nor eternal life can be shared or compromised upon.

In the face of this type of conflict, political order to Hobbes is founded on an *overlapping consensus*[60] and is based on an anatomy of the city thought as a *society without qualities.* With Hobbes, the "parts of the city," so crucial to classical political views, completely disappear from political discourse. This Hobbesian leveling produces two new subjects: individuals entitled to equal rights and their representative sovereign. This much we know. On the other hand, and this is worth focusing on a bit, Hobbes proposes a model of order for the city which involves neutralizing religious conflicts (meaning in the first place the conflict between religion and politics) by reliance on the existence of a minimal core of shared beliefs, adhesion to which may guarantee earthly peace *and* eternal salvation, because there exists the possibility of building an overlapping consensus amongst all the families of Christianity based on it.

It is also in chapter 25 of the *Elements* that this model of order and pacification is presented; Hobbes introduces the distinction between *fundamental* and *superstruction.*[61]

> And under a Christian sovereign we are to consider, what actions we are forbidden by God Almighty to obey them in, and what not [where from could arise a conflict between religious and political obligation]. The actions we are forbidden to obey them in, are such only as imply a denial of that faith which is necessary to our salvation; for otherwise there can be no pretence of disobedience. For why should a man incur the danger of a *temporal death,* by displeasing of his superior, if it were not for fear of *eternal death* hereafter? It must therefore be inquired, what those propositions and articles they be, the belief whereof our Saviour or his apostles have declared to be such, as without believing them a man cannot be saved; and then all other points that are now controverted, and make distinction of sects, Papists, Lutherans, Arminians, . . . must needs be such, as a man needeth not for the holding thereof deny obedience to his superiors. And for the points of faith necessary to salvation, I shall call them *fundamental,* and every other point a *superstruction.*[62]

The fundamental area of agreement between the different Christian churches, around which it is possible to build an overlapping consensus, is for Hobbes the belief *(unum necessarium)* which says that "Jesus is the Christ."[63] It follows from this reasoning,

> it will easily appear: that under the sovereign power of a Christian commonwealth, there is no danger of damnation from simple obedience to human laws; for in that the sovereign alloweth Christianity, no man is compelled to renounce that faith which is *enough for his salvation;* that is to say, the fundamental points." (my emphasis)[64]

This model of order thus permits the defusing of the conflict between religious sects as well as its source: the conflict between individual conscience and the commandments of political authority.

I would like to suggest in conclusion that there is no contradiction between what has just been presented and what Hobbes claims in the first two parts of the *Leviathan* about conflict and political order.[65] One could argue that the Hobbesian theory of state of nature presents, in a sense, the modern type of the conflict in its most general and abstract form. Here the threat, even that for the survival of individuals, derives from the impossibility of finding agreement on truth and particularly as to what and who constitute a danger.[66] It follows that the threat to political order comes from the impossibility of a common objective recognition of what or who constitutes the threat.[67] The contract or authorizing act which gives the rationale for obedience to the sovereign is conceived by Hobbes in terms of a consensus on the idea of *self-preservation* and abandonment of *jus in omnia.* Here again, one should distinguish between a *fundamental* which one must not renounce *(self-preservation)* and the *superstruction* constituted by the *jus mei regendi meipsum.*[68] In both cases, the order founded on an overlapping consensus is not possible without the pacifying reason of the state.[69]

NOTES

1. To my knowledge, this text has never been translated into English. The quotation is to be found in the 3d ed. (Paris: Baudouin, 1789), 29–30: "La liberté individuelle a, dans une grande société trois sortes d'ennemis à craindre. Les moins dangereux sont les citoyens malévoles. Pour les réprimer, il suffit d'une autorité ordinaire . . . La liberté individuelle a beaucoup plus à redouter des entreprises des Officiers chargés d'exercer quelqu'une des parties du pouvoir public. Des simples mandataires isolés, des corps entiers, le gouvernement luimême en totalité, peuvent cesser de respecter les droits du citoyen. Une longue expérience prouve que les Nations ne sont pas assez précautionnées contre cette sorte de danger. Quel spectacle que celui d'un mandataire qui tourne contre ses concitoyens les armes ou le pouvoir qu'il a reçu pour les défendre, et qui ose changer en instrumens d'oppression les moyens qui lui ont été confiés pour la protection commune. . . . La *séparation,* et une bonne constitution des pouvoirs publics, sont la seule garantie qui puisse préserver les Nations et les Citoyens de ce Malheur extrême."

2. Liberty of citizens is in this conception the foundation and the essence of political order and hence the goal to be realized. That is why one may place liberty and order on the same level.

3. *Die Diktatur,* 2d ed. (München und Leipzig: Duncker und Humblot, 1928), 104: "Jede unverhältnismässige politische 'Über'-Macht ist nach jener Lehre der Feind." It should be added that Schmitt is far from understanding the reasons for Montesquieu's hostility towards despotism; but that is not the point here.

4. For a somewhat more detailed analysis of this text as well as that of Sieyes's liberalism, see P. Pasquino, "The Constitutional Republicanism of Emmanuel Sieyes," in *The Invention of the Modern Republic,* ed. B. Fontana (Cambridge: Cambridge University Press, 1994), 107–17.

5. I should note I do not take this conception to be a reasonably accurate description of contemporary Western states.

6. *Prima facie,* since the power of the Hobbesian sovereign also has a limit: the life (and up to a certain point the well-being) of his subjects may not be touched and even requires a guarantee.

7. On the concept of liberty in Hobbes, cf.: Q. Skinner, "Thomas Hobbes on the Proper Signification of Liberty," *Transactions of the Royal Historical Society,* series V, 40 (1990): 121–51, and P. Pasquino, *Thomas Hobbes: Stato di natura e libertà civile* (Milano: Anabasi, 1994), 35–58.

8. In *Patriarcha and Other Writings,* ed. J. P. Sommerville (Cambridge: Cambridge University Press, 1991), 134. Filmer's claim is false. Before Machiavelli and from Thomas Aquinas on, the majority of medieval political thinkers spoke of mixed government; cf., now, J. M. Blythe, *Ideal Government and the Mixed Constitution in the Middle Ages* (Princeton: Princeton University Press, 1992). It shows nonetheless that Machiavelli's point was correctly understood by the author of *Patriarcha.*

9. The fundamental book on this topic is W. Nippel, *Mischverfassungstheorie und Verfassungsrealität in Antike und früher Neuzeit* (Stuttgart: Klett-Cotta, 1980), supplemented by Chiara Carsana, *La teoria della "costituzione mista" nell'età imperiale romana* (Como: Edizioni New Press, 1990). For the Middle Ages, see Blythe's book, cited in the previous footnote.

10. This language has been called *republicanism,* first in the works of Hans Baron then continued by J. Pocock and Q. Skinner. Unfortunately none of these three authors have given the necessary relevance to the theory of the mixed constitution which is an essential aspect of classical republicanism.

11. One should not forget that Machiavelli did not allow the publication of the *Discourses* (nor that of the *Prince*) during his life. The *Discourses,* as we know, were written for the attention of the members of the anti-Medicean Florentine aristocracy which used to meet at the *Orti Oricellari.* The two major political texts by Machiavelli were published after his death by Father Giovanni Gaddi, probably with the help of the Italian poet Annibal Caro, both persuaded of the extraordinary literary value of the two manuscripts. Cf. S. Bertelli and P. Innocenti, *Bibliografia Machiavelliana* (Verona: Edizioni Valdonega, 1979), XXXIII–XXXVI. *Habent sua fata libelli!*

12. Here with the signification of "aiming to persuade."

13. One can think, to give an impressive and persuasive example, of the book by John Dunn, *The Political Thought of John Locke* (Cambridge: Cambridge University Press, 1969).

14. In the same direction, J. Dunn, *Histoire de la théorie politique* (Paris: Mentha, 1992).

15. This term, as well as *politeía* in Aristotle, has a twofold signification. It means, on one hand, simple political community (as in this case), and on the other hand, the perfect form of this community, i.e., the mixed constitution.

16. Concerning the ahistorical dimension of Machiavelli's political-constitutional theory see the preface to Book I of *Discourses.*

17. We find the same dualistic conception of the anatomy of the city in all Machiavelli's important political works, from *The Prince* to the *Discourses on Livy,* from the *Discursus florentinarum rerum* to the *Florentine Histories.* Q. Skinner in his article "The Idea of Negative Liberty: Philosophical and Historical Perspectives," *Philosophy in History,* ed. R. Rorty, J. B. Schneewind, and Q. Skinner (Cambridge: Cambridge University Press, 1984), especially 204–21, starts from the same point, but reaches conclusions largely different from those of the present article.

18. *The Prince,* chapter 9, ed. Q. Skinner and R. Price (Cambridge: Cambridge University Press, 1988), 34. In the original: "Il popolo desidera non essere comandato né oppresso da' grandi, e li grandi desiderano comandare et opprimere el populo."

19. Ed. B. Crick (Harmondsworth: Penguin Books, 1983), 116: "Si vedrà in quelli desiderio grande di dominare ed in questi solo desiderio di non essere dominati."

20. "Le gravi e naturali inimicizie che sono intra gli uomini popolari e i nobili, causate dal volere questi comandare, e quelli non ubbidire sono cagione di tutti i mali che nascono nelle città; perché da questa diversità di umori tutte le altre cose che perturbano le repubbliche prendono il nutrimento loro."

21. At least in the sense of the attribution of the magistracies to the constitutive parts of the city. It is of some interest to notice that Sieyes in his *Préliminaire,* 34, defines, on the contrary, the constitution as follows: "[it] embrasse à-la-fois: *La formation et l'organisation intérieure des différens pouvoirs publics; leur correspondance nécessaire, et leur indépendance réciproque;* Enfin, *les précautions politiques dont il est nécessaire de les entourer, afin que toujours utiles, ils ne puissent jamais se rendre dangereux*" (the emphasis is by Sieyes; here, we can see again what I have called the liberal preoccupation). On the concept of constitution, see also *Qu'est-ce que le Tiers etat?* ed. J.-D. Bredin (Paris: Flammarion, 1988), chapter 5, 121–46.

22. "The Composition and Structure of Machiavelli's *Discorsi,*" *Journal of History of Ideas* 14 (1953): 136–56.

23. *Discourses,* 109.

24. *Discourses,* 109: "*perché l'uno guarda l'altro, sendo in una medesima città il principato, gli ottimati e il governo popolare.*"

25. *Discourses,* 111.

26. The answer can be found in C. Dionisotti, *Machiavellerie* (Torino: Einaudi, 1980), 139–40.

27. See especially the scholarly, but slightly long-winded, essays by G. Sasso, *Machiavelli e gli antichi ed altri saggi* (Milano-Napoli: Ricciardi,

1987), vol. 1 ("Machiavelli e la teoria dell'*anacyclosis*" and "Machiavelli e Polibio: Costituzione, potenza, conquista").

28. Cf. his commentary to the *Discourses,* volume II (New Haven: Yale University Press, 1950), 273 and *passim.*

29. Cf. M. Venturi Fertriolo, "Aristotele: Democrazia: il nome, la cosa, il concetto," *Quaderni di Storia* 7 (1978): 67–96. The Greek word *dêmos* means the poor people, those who live on the countryside, by opposition to *eudaímones,* (fortunate, wealthy) and *dunatoí* (mighty, powerful); cf. P. Chantraine, *Dictionnaire étymologique de la langue grecque* (Paris: Klincksieck, 1968), vol. 1, 273.

30. Cf., for instance, *Politics* IV, 8 and 9.

31. Cf. P. Accattino, *L'anatomia della città nella Politica di Aristotele* (Torino: Tirrenia Stampatori, 1986), notably chapter 3: "Le componenti della città ed i regimi politici possibili," 71ff. Cf. also E. Schütrumpf, *Die Analyse der Polis durch Aristoteles* (Amsterdam: Verlag B. R. Grüner, 1980).

32. On this point, cf. Nippel, *Mischverfassungstheorie,* 52ff.

33. This idea can be found in the speech of Barnave of August 11, 1791, at the French Constituent Assembly, which is one of the most important texts for understanding the theory of the representative government. The text of this speech can be read in the *Moniteur* 9 (1791): 376.

34. English translation by A. H. Gilbert, in Machiavelli, *The Chief Works and Others* (Durham, N.C.: Duke University Press, 1989), vol. 1, 107; "Coloro che ordinano una repubblica, debbono dare luogo a tre diverse qualità di uomini che sono in tutte le città; cioè, primi, mezzani et ultimi."

35. "Idea of Liberty in Machiavelli," *Journal of History of Ideas* 32 (1971): 343.

36. I refer here to the interpretation of Polybius's mixed constitution propounded by D. Musti, "Polibio," in *Storia delle idee politiche, economiche, e sociali,* volume 1, ed. L. Firpo (Torino: UTET, 1982), 609–43. From his analysis, it appears that Polybius tried to give an account of the Roman republic with its institutional tripartition of consuls, senates, and popular magistracies (tribunes and comitia) using such Greek political categories as that of mixed constitution. This is why the triadic structure superimposed on the dualist model of an Aristotelian type has the consequence of obscuring it. That did not happen in Machiavelli, who also worked with the triadic structure of the Roman constitution and with the sociological dualism of patricians and plebeians. In any case, Musti writes: "The consul represents more

a specific 'organ' than a 'part' *(méros)* of the State, a part to be considered on the same level as the two other *mére,* the senate, and the people. The latter are, on the contrary, the institutional expression of distinguishible social entities: the ruling class, on one hand, and the popular classes, on the other," 619.

37. Nippel, *Mischverfassungstheorie,* 59, n. 28a.

38. Ibid., 163–64.

39. See D. Weinstein, *Savonarola and Florence: Prophecy and Patriotism in the Renaissance* (Princeton: Princeton University Press, 1970), particularly chapter 9, at 288ff.; the author summarizes Savonarola's definition of "civil government" (which he opposes to the *regno*/monarchy and the *governo delli ottimati*/aristocracy) as follows: "others have decided that government should remain in the hands of all the people, who then distribute the magistracies as they see fit" (296); this definition shows more a Thomist than an Aristotelian derivation of the concept. N. Rubinstein in his "Politics and Constitution in Florence at the End of the Fifteenth Century," in *Italian Renaissance Studies,* ed. E. F. Jacob (London: Faber and Faber, 1960), 160, relying on L. Minio-Paluello, claims an equivalence between *governo civile, regimen politicum* (the republican form of government, by opposition to the monarchy) and *πολιτεια*, but he does not seem to understand what Aristotle meant by that word. J.-L. Fournel and J.-C. Zancarini, in their presentation of Savonarola, *Sermons, écrits politiques, et pièces du procès* (Paris: Le Seuil, 1992), which includes the French translation of the *Trattato* (139–83), make the following correct remark: "Savonarola ne discute pas toutes les formes classiques de gouvernement possibles et n'envisage pas un régime "mixte," qui mêlerait savamment les qualités des unes et des autres en éliminant les défauts de chacune d'elles. Il met au contraire en place une rigoureuse alternative logique, suivant laquelle le renoncement au 'gouvernement civil' du Grand Conseil provoquerait nécessairement l'instauration de la tyrannie" (22).

40. *Discourses,* 110 (translation slightly modified): "Benché, dipoi anni quaranta . . . tornasse Atene in libertà, perché la riprese lo stato popolare secondo gli ordini di Solone, non lo tenne più che cent'anni, ancora che per mantenerlo facessi molte constituzioni, per le quali si reprimeva la insolenzia de' grandi e la licenza dell'universale [the people], le quali non furono da Solone considerate: nientedimeno, perché non le mescolò con la potenza del principato e con quella degli ottimati, visse Atene a rispetto di Sparta brevissimo tempo."

41. *The Prince,* ed. Q. Skinner and R. Price, 54.

42. A. H. Gilbert's translation of *The Chief Works,* vol. 1, 107–8:

"nondimeno sono in quella alcuni che sono di animo elevato, e pare loro meritare di precedere gli altri; a' quali è necessario nell'ordinare la repubblica satisfare: né per altra cagione rovinò lo stato passato che per non si essere a tale umore satisfatto."

43. On this concept, see R. Price, "*Ambizione* in Machiavelli's Thought," *History of Political Thought* 3 (1982): 382–445.

44. *Historie fiorentine* III.1: "La quale diversità di effetti conviene sia dai diversi fini che hanno avuto questi due popoli causata. Perché il popolo di Roma godere i supremi onori insieme coi nobili desiderava, quello di Firenze per essere solo nel governo, senza che i nobili ne partecipassero, combatteva." Cf. G. Sasso, *Niccolò Machiavelli,* II, La storiografia (Bologna: Il Mulino, 1993), chapter 2: "Il conflitto sociale," 169–218, particularly 174–75. See also G. Bock, "Civil Discord in Machiavelli's *Istorie Fiorentine,*" in *Machiavelli and Republicanism,* ed. G. Bock, Q. Skinner, and M. Viroli (Cambridge: Cambridge University Press, 1990), 190–91; A. Pizzorno, "Come pensare il conflitto," *Alle radici della politica assoluta* (Milano: Feltrinelli, 1993), 188–90. None of these interpreters points out the intrinsic relation between the problematics of social conflict, mixed constitution, and parts of the city. The crucial role of the mixed constitution in Machiavelli's political thought had, on the contrary, already drawn the attention G. Cadoni, in two important articles: "Libertà, repubblica e governo misto in Machiavelli," *Rivista internazionale di filosofia del diritto,* series III, 39 (1962): 462–84; and "Machiavelli teorico dei conflitti sociali," *Storia e politica* 17 (1978): 197–220.

45. See J. Franklin, "Sovereignty and Mixed Constitution," *The Cambridge History of Political Thought: 1450–1700,* ed. J. H. Burnes (Cambridge: Cambridge University Press, 1991), 298–328.

46. See R. Tuck, *Hobbes* (Oxford: Oxford University Press, 1989), 23–24.

47. *Opera philosophica quae latine scripsit,* volume I, ed. W. Molesworth (London: John Bohn, 1839), 7 *(De corpore).*

48. Cf. *Leviathan,* ed. R. Tuck (Cambridge: Cambridge University Press, 1991), chapter 29, at 223ff; and *De cive,* chapter 12.

49. On Hobbes's critique of fanaticism and religious superstition, see the important book by D. Johnston, *The Rhetoric of Leviathan* (Princeton: Princeton University Press, 1986).

50. I shall quote the edition of this work by J. C. A. Gaskin (Oxford University Press, 1994); chapter 25 corresponds to the chapter 6 of the second part in Toennies's edition. Hobbes comes back to the questions discussed in this chapter in chapter 43 of *Leviathan* (cf. also *De cive,* chapter 18). Nonetheless, the text of the *Elements* is the most clear and telling.

51. Unlike Bodin, who had a classical understanding of the mixed constitution, close to that presented in the previous paragraph (cf. chapter 1 of Book II of the *Republic*), Hobbes picked up this expression from the English constitutional debate of his period and understood it as the idea of any division of power, notably that one between the King and the Parliament.

52. *Elements* II, 25 § 1, at 141: "Having showed that in all commonwealths whatsoever, the necessity of peace and government requireth, that there be existent some power, either in one man, or in one assembly of men, by the name of the power sovereign, to which it is not lawful for any member of the same commonwealth to disobey."

53. We must notice here a relevant shift with regard to classic political tradition: in Hobbes the question is not only that of the order of the city, but also that of peace and self-preservation for everybody. *Elements,* 141.

54. Ibid.

55. *Leviathan,* chapter 43, ed. Tuck, at 402: "The most frequent praetext of Sedition, and Civill Warre, in Christian Common-wealths hath a long time proceeded from a difficulty, not yet sufficiently resolved, of obeying at once, both God, and Man, then when their Commandements are one contrary to the other."

56. Cf. *De cive* 18 § 1: "Causa difficultatis est, quod . . . quæ [scripturæ sacræ] a diversis diverse accipiuntur." *De cive,* ed. Warrender (Oxford: Clarendon Press, 1983), 280. See also what Hobbes says concerning this question in *Behemoth*'s First Dialogue, and the comments of S. A. Lloyd in her very imaginative book, *Ideals as Interests in Hobbes's Leviathan* (Cambridge: Cambridge University Press, 1992), notably 199–201.

57. See the exhaustive book by D. Crouzet, *Les guerriers de Dieu: La violence au temps des troubles de religion (vers 1525–vers 1610)* (Champ Vallon: Seyssel, 1990).

58. *Elements* II, 25 § 2, at 141–42 (emphasis mine).

59. These two situations are concretely different, but from the formal point of view the conflict is of the same type: the will of the sovereign, the civil law, may contradict God's will as interpreted by the individual conscience or by a religious representative who claims his autonomy from the political representative.

60. I take this expression from John Rawls's political vocabulary; at the beginning of his last book, *Political Liberalism* (New York: Columbia University Press, 1993), he refers to the religion wars.

61. The term was used in seventeenth-century English as equivalent of "superstructure"; I cannot prevent myself from thinking that it

would call to the reader's mind the term "superstition." It is anyhow worth noticing that S. Sorbière, in his 1652 translation, rendered the English "superstruction" with the French "superstition"!

62. *Elements* 25 § 5, at 144.

63. On this point, besides *Elements,* 25, see also *De cive* 18 § 6, Annotatio, and *Leviathan,* chapter 43, ed. Tuck, at 407ff. Here we read: "The (Unum Necessarium) Onely Article of Faith, which the Scripture maketh simply Necessary to Salvation, is this, that Jesus is the Christ." See, moreover, A. P. Martinich, *The Two Gods of Leviathan* (Cambridge: Cambridge University Press, 1992), 308–10.

64. *Elements,* 25 § 11, at 152–53.

65. Cf. the excellent account by R. Hardin, "Hobbesian Political Order," *Political Theory* 19 (1991): 156–80.

66. "Alii hostem, alii amicum, eundem putant," we read in chapter 17 of the Latin edition of *Leviathan* (1668); the English says: "he that by one part is held for an enemy, is by another part held for a friend" (ed. Tuck, 119); cf. also *Elements,* 14, § 8: "every man by right of nature is judge himself of the necessity of the means, and of the greatness of the danger." We know, moreover, that Hobbes stressed the absence of "recta ratio in rerum naturae," cf. *Leviathan,* chapter 5, ed. Tuck, 32–33; *Elements,* 29 § 8. Cf. also R. Tuck, *Hobbes,* 65: "people have—in the state of nature—no reason to prefer their own judgement to that of another person." *De cive* 18 § 1: "utrum vero id *quod* imperant, sit contra imperata Dei necne, id nesciunt, sed fluctuante obedientia inter pœnas mortis *temporalis, & spiritualis,* tamquam navigantes inter *Scyllam & Charybdim* incurrunt sæpe in utramque," ed. Warrender, 280–81 (the emphases are in the text).

67. For a less rushed analysis, I refer to my article, "Thomas Hobbes: La condition naturelle de l'humanité," *Revue française de science politique* 44, no. 2 (1994): 294–307.

68. My own right to govern myself in deciding what represents a danger for me.

It is possible to illustrate what I have been arguing as follows:

FIGURE 1

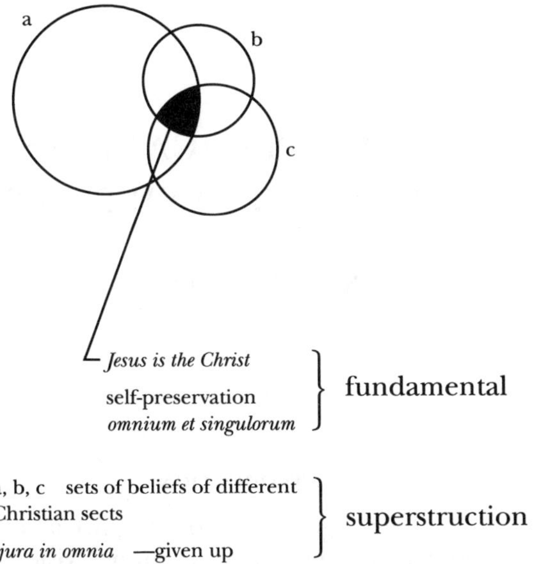

At any rate, one should keep in mind that, in the non-consensual areas, idiosyncratic religious beliefs can survive in the *forum internum.* Conversely, the *jus mei regendi meipsum* can simply be overruled in the commonwealth.

69. According to Hobbes, the sovereign is also the head of the Church in all political societies.

2

STATE SIMPLIFICATIONS: NATURE, SPACE, AND PEOPLE

JAMES C. SCOTT

I. Introduction

Certain forms of knowledge and control require a narrowing of vision. The great advantage of such tunnel vision is that it brings into very sharp focus limited aspects of an otherwise far more complex and unwieldy reality. This very simplification, in turn, makes the phenomenon at the center of the field of vision far more legible and, hence, more susceptible to careful measurement, calculation, and manipulation.

The invention of scientific forestry in late-eighteenth-century Prussia and Saxony serves as a model of this process.[1] While the story of scientific forestry is important in its own right, I plan to use it here as a metaphor for the forms of knowledge and manipulation characteristic of large institutions with sharply defined interests, of which the state is perhaps the outstanding example. Once we have seen how simplification, legibility, and manipulation operate in forest management, we can then explore how a similar optic is applied by the modern state to urban planning, rural settlement, land administration, and agriculture.

II. A Parable of the State and Scientific Forestry

The early modern European state, even prior to the development of scientific forestry, viewed its forests primarily through the fiscal lens of revenue needs. To be sure, other concerns such as timber for masts, shipbuilding, state construction, and sufficient fuelwood for the economic security of its subjects were not absent from official management. These added concerns, too, had heavy implications for state revenue and security.[2] Exaggerating only slightly, one might claim that the crown's interest in forests was resolved through its fiscal lens into a single number: that number being the revenue yield of the timber which might be extracted annually.

The best way to appreciate exactly how heroic is this constriction of vision, is to notice what is left out of its field of vision. Lying behind the number indicating revenue yield are not so much trees as "commercial wood," representing so many thousands of board feet of saleable timber and so many cords of firewood fetching a certain price. Missing, of course, are all those trees, bushes, and plants holding little or no potential for state revenue. Missing as well, are all those aspects of trees—even "revenue-bearing" trees—that may be useful to the population but whose value cannot be converted into fiscal receipts. Here I have in mind the uses of foliage as fodder and thatch, fruits as food for domestic animals and people, twigs and branches as bedding, fencing, hop poles, and kindling, bark and roots for medicine and tanning, sap for resins, and so forth. The actual tree with its vast number of possible uses is replaced by an "abstract" tree representing a volume of lumber or firewood.

From a naturalist's perspective, nearly everything is missing from the state's picture. Gone are the vast majority of flora, the grasses, flowers, lichen, ferns, mosses, shrubs, and vines. Gone, too, are reptiles, birds, amphibians, and innumerable species of insects. Gone is the vast majority of fauna except, perhaps, those of interest to the crown's gamekeepers.

From an anthropologist's perspective, nearly everything touching on human interaction with the forest is also missing from the state's tunnel vision. Except for its attention to poaching, which does impinge on either the state's claim to revenue in wood or its claim to royal game, the state typically ignores the vast and complex, negotiated social uses of the forest for hunting and gathering, pasturage, digging valuable minerals, fishing, charcoal-making, trapping, and food collection as well as its significance for magic, worship, refuge, and so forth.[3]

If the utilitarian state cannot see the real existing forest for the (commercial) trees, if its view of its forests is abstract and partial, it is hardly unique in this respect. A certain level of abstraction is necessary for certain forms of analysis and it is not at all surprising that the abstractions of state officials should reflect the paramount fiscal interests of their employer. The vocabulary used to organize nature typically betrays the overriding interests of its human users. In fact, the term "nature" is, in utilitarian discourse, replaced by the term "natural resources" in which the focus is on those aspects of nature that can be appropriated for human use. A comparable logic extracts from a more generalized natural world those flora or fauna that are of utilitarian value (usually marketable commodities) and, in turn, reclassifies those species which compete with, prey on, or otherwise diminish the yields of the valued species. Thus, *plants* that are valued become *crops;* the species that compete with them are reclassified as *weeds,* and the insects that ingest them are reclassified as *pests.* Thus, *trees* that are valued become *timber* while species that compete with them become "trash" trees or underbrush. The same logic applies to fauna. Those *animals* which are highly valued become *game* or *livestock,* while those animals which compete with or prey upon them become *predators* or "*varmints.*"

The kind of abstracting, utilitarian logic which the state, through its officials, applies to the forest is thus not entirely distinctive. What is distinctive, however, is the narrowness of its field of vision, the degree of elaboration to which it can be subjected, and above all, as we shall see, the unique capacity of the state to impose (in part) its optic on the very reality it is observing.[4]

Scientific forestry was developed from about 1765 to 1800, largely in Prussia and Saxony. Eventually, it would become the basis of forest management techniques in France, England, the United States, and throughout the Third World. Its emergence hardly can be understood outside the larger context of centralized state-making initiatives of the period. In fact, the new forestry science was a sub-discipline of so-called cameral science—an effort to reduce the fiscal management of a kingdom to scientific principles that would allow systematic planning. Traditional domainal forestry had hitherto simply divided the forest into roughly equal plots—the number of plots coinciding with the number of years in the assumed growth cycle.[5] One plot was cut each year on the assumption of equal yields (and value) from plots of equal size. Owing to poor maps, the uneven distribution of the most valuable large trees *(Hochwald)* and very approximate cordwood *(Bruststaerke)* measures, the results were unsatisfactory for fiscal planning.

The first attempt at more precise measurement was made by Johann Gottlieb Beckmann on a carefully surveyed sample plot. Walking abreast, several assistants carried compartmentalized boxes with color-coded nails corresponding to five agreed upon size-categories of trees. Each tree was "tagged" with the appropriate nail until the whole sample plot was covered. Having begun with a specified number of nails, it was a simple matter to subtract those remaining from the initial total and arrive at an inventory of trees by size-class for the entire plot. The sample plot had been carefully chosen for its representativeness, allowing the foresters then to calculate the timber and, given certain price assumptions, the revenue yield of the whole forest. For the forest scientists *(Forstwissenschaftler)* the goal was always to "deliver the greatest possible *constant* volume of wood."[6]

The effort at precision was pushed further as mathematicians worked from the cone/volume principle to specify the volume of saleable wood contained by a standardized tree *(Normalbaum)*. Their calculations were checked empirically against the actual volume of wood in sample trees.[7] The final result of such calculations was the development of elaborate tables with data organized by classes of trees by size and age under specified conditions of normal growth and maturation. References to these tables coupled with field tests allowed the forester to estimate closely the inventory, growth, and yield of a given forest. In the regulated, abstract forest of the *Forstwissenschaftler*, calculation and measurement prevailed and the three watchwords were "minimum diversity," "the balance sheet," and "sustained yield."

The achievement of German forestry science in standardizing techniques to calculate the sustainable yield of commercial timber and, hence, revenue, was impressive enough. What is decisive for our purposes, however, is the next logical step in forest management. That step was to attempt to create, through careful seeding, planting, and cutting, a forest that was easier for state foresters to count, manipulate, measure, and assess. The fact is that forest science and geometry, backed by state power, had the capacity to transform the real, disorderly, chaotic forest so that it more closely resembled the administrative grid of its techniques. To this end, the underbrush was cleared, the number of species was reduced (often to monoculture), planting was done simultaneously and in straight rows for large tracts. These management practices, as Lowood observes,

> produced the monocultural, even-age forests that eventually transformed the *Normalbaum* from abstraction to reality. The German forest became the archetype for imposing on disorderly nature the neatly arranged constructs of science. Practical goals had encouraged mathematical utilitarianism, which seemed, in turn, to promote geometric perfection as the outward sign of the well-managed forest; in turn the rationally ordered arrangements of trees offered new possibilities for controlling nature.[8]

The tendency was toward "regimentation" in the strict sense of the word. The forest trees were drawn up into serried ranks, as it were, to be measured, counted off, felled, and replaced by a new rank-and-file of look-alike conscripts. At the limit, the forest itself would not have to be seen; it could be "read" accurately from the tables and maps in the foresters office.

This utopian dream of scientific forestry was, of course, only the *immanent* logic of its techniques. It was not, and could not, ever be realized in practice. Both nature and "the human factor" intervened. The existing typography of the landscape and the vagaries of fire, storms, blights, climatic changes, insect populations, and disease conspired to thwart foresters and to shape the actual forest. Given the insurmountable difficulties of policing large forests, the adjacent human populations also typically continued to graze animals, poach firewood and kindling, make charcoal, and generally make use of the forest in ways that prevented the foresters' management plan from being fully realized.[9] Though, like all utopian schemes, it fell well short of attaining its goal, the critical fact is that it did partly succeed in stamping the actual forest with the imprint of its designs.

III. Facts-on-Paper, Facts-on-the-Ground

The administrators' forest cannot be the naturalists' forest. Even if the ecological interactions at play in the forest were known, they would constitute a reality so complex and variegated so as to defy easy shorthand description. The intellectual filter necessary to reduce the complexity to manageable dimensions was provided by the state's interest in commercial timber and revenue.

If the natural world, however shaped by human use, is too unwieldy in its "raw" form for administrative manipulation, so too are the actual social patterns of human interaction with nature bureaucratically indigestible in their raw form. A hypothetical, but realistic, case of land tenure arrangements may help demonstrate why this is so. The land tenure practices I describe here are all ones that I have encountered in the literature or in the course of field-work.

Let us imagine a community in which families have usufruct rights to parcels of cropland during the main growing season. Only certain crops, however, may be planted and every seven years the usufruct land is redistributed among families according to family size and the number of able-bodied adults. After the harvest of the main season crop, all cropland reverts to commons where any family may glean, graze their fowl and livestock, and even plant quickly maturing, dry-season crops. Edible wild plants growing on the margins of fields, along water courses, and on bunds, are available to those who gather them. Trees that are known to have been planted are, together with their fruit, the property of the family who planted them, no matter where they are now growing. Fruit fallen from such trees, however, is the property of anyone who gathers it. When a family fells one of its trees or it is felled by wind, the trunk of the tree belongs to the family, branches to the immediate neighbors, and the "tops" (leaves, twigs, fronds) to any poorer village who carries them off. Land is set aside, exceptionally, for use or leasing out by widows with children or dependents of conscripted males. Usufruct rights to land and trees may be "let" to anyone within the village but not to anyone outside the village unless no one in the community wishes to use it.

Let us also imagine that fishing rights are distributed so that anyone may take fish (by net, weir, or hook-and-line) from canals and streams. In flooded usufruct fields, however, while anyone may fish with hook-and-line for small fish, the larger fish—taken usually when the field is drained—belong to the owner of the crop growing in that field.

After a crop failure leading to severe food shortage, many of these arrangements are readjusted. Better-off villagers are expected to assume some responsibility for poorer relatives—by sharing their land, by employing them, or by simply feeding them. Should the shortage persist, the council of lineage heads may inventory food supply and begin daily rationing. In case of an outright famine, the women who have married into the village but have not yet borne children will not be fed and are expected to return to their natal village.

This description could be further elaborated; it is itself a simplification. But it does convey some of the actual complexity of property relations in contexts where customary local arrangements have tended to prevail. Even to describe the usual practices in this fashion, as if they were laws, is a serious distortion. They are better understood as a living, negotiated tissue of practices which are continually being adopted to new ecological and social circumstances—including of course, power relations. Their very plasticity is the source of micro-adjustments which may or may not lead to shifts in prevailing practice.

Imagine, if you will, a written system of positive law that attempted to represent this complex skein of property relations and land tenure. The mind fairly boggles at the clauses, sub-clauses, and sub-sub-clauses that would be required to reduce these practices to a set of regulations which an administrator might understand, let alone enforce. If, in principle, they could nevertheless be codified, the resulting code would necessarily sacrifice much of the plasticity and subtle adaptability of practice. The circumstances that might provoke a new wrinkle in practices are too numerous to foresee, let alone to specify in a regulatory code. That code would, in effect, freeze a living process. Changes in the positive code designed to reflect evolving practice would, at best, represent a jerky and mechanical adaptation.

And what of the *next* village, and the village after that? Our hypothetical code-giver, however devilishly clever and conscientious, would find that the code devised to fit one set of local practices would not travel well. Each village, with its own particular history, its own ecology, its particular cropping patterns, kinship alignments, and economic activity would require a substantially new set of regulations. At the limit, there would be at least as many legal codes as there were communities.

Administratively, of course, such a cacophony of local property regulations would be a nightmare. Notice, especially, that the nightmare in question is not a nightmare experienced by those whose particular customs are being represented but rather by those—i.e., state officials—who aspire to a uniform, homogeneous, national administrative code. Local practice is perfectly legible to those inhabitants who "live" it on a day-to-day basis. Its details may be often contested and far from satisfactory to all of its local practitioners, but there is no doubting its familiarity; local residents have no difficulty in grasping its subtleties and using its flexible provisions for their own purposes. State officials, on the other hand, cannot be expected to decipher and then apply a new set of property hieroglyphs for each jurisdiction. The very concept of the modern state is inconceivable without a vastly simplified and uniform property regime that is legible, and hence manipulable from the center.

Use of the term simple to describe modern property law, whose intricacies provide employment to armies of legal professionals, seems grossly misplaced. It is surely the case that property law has in many respects become an impenetrable thicket for ordinary citizens. The use of the term simple in this context is thus both *relative* and *perspectival.* Modern freehold tenure is tenure that is mediated through the state and therefore readily legible only to those who have sufficient training and grasp of the state statutes to allow them to decipher it. Its relative simplicity is lost on those who cannot break the code, just as the relative clarity of customary tenure to the villagers who live it is lost on the mystified outsider.

The major, but not the only, driving force behind a simple and legible system of property is the need for a reliable format for taxation. Here, there are some instructive parallels between the development of modern, fiscal forestry, and modern forms of taxable property in land. Premodern states were no less concerned with tax receipts than modern states. But, like premodern state forestry, the techniques and reach of the state left much to be desired.

Absolutist France in the seventeenth century is a case in point.[10] Indirect taxes—e.g., excise levies on salt, tobacco, tolls, licenses and the sale of offices and titles—were favored forms of taxation inasmuch as they were easier to administer and required far less in the way of information about landholding and income. The tax-exempt status of the nobility and clergy meant that a good deal of the landed property was not taxed at all, transferring much of the burden to wealthy commoner farmers and the peasantry. Common land, though it was a vitally important subsistence resource for the rural poor, yielded no revenue either. In the eighteenth century, the physiocrats would condemn all common property on two presumptive grounds; that it was inefficiently exploited and that it was fiscally barren.[11]

What must strike any observer of absolutist taxation is how wildly variable and unsystematic it was. Collins found that the major direct land tax, the *taille,* was frequently not paid at all and that no community paid more than one third of what they were assessed.[12] The result was *routine* state reliance on exceptional measures to make good shortfalls in revenue or to pay for new expenses, particularly military campaigns. The crown exacted "forced loans" *(rentes, droits aliénés)* in return for annuities which it might or might not honor; it levied exceptional hearth taxes *(fouages extraordinaires)* and, above all; it billeted troops directly on communities, often ruining them in the process.

The billeting of troops, a common form of fiscal punishment, was to modern forms of systematic taxation as the drawing-and-quartering of would-be regicides (so strikingly described by Michel Foucault at the beginning of *Discipline and Punish*) was to modern forms of systematic criminal incarceration. Not that there was a great deal of choice involved. The state simply lacked both the information and administrative grid that would have allowed it to exact a regular revenue from its subjects more closely tied to their capacity to pay. As with forest revenue, there was no alternative to rough-and-ready calculations with a corresponding fluctuation in yields. Fiscally, the premodern state was, to use Charles Lindblom's felicitous term, "all thumbs and no fingers"; it was incapable of fine-tuning.

Here is where the rough analogy between forest management and taxation breaks down. In the absence of reliable information about sustainable timber yield, the state might either inadvertently overexploit its resources and threaten future supply, or else fail to realize the level of proceeds it might sustain.[13] The trees themselves, however, were not political actors while the taxable subjects of the crown were most certainly political actors. They signalled their dissatisfaction by flight, by various forms of quiet resistance and evasion, and *in extremis,* by open revolt. A reliable format for taxation of subjects thus depended not just on discovering what their economic condition was, but also on trying to judge what exactions they would vigorously resist.

The next step, one to which all modern states aspire, is to measure, codify, and simplify land tenure in much the same way as scientific forestry reconceived the forest. In no way could the state begin to incorporate the luxuriant variety of customary land tenure. The historical solution, at least for the liberal state, has typically been the heroic simplification of individual, freehold, tenure. Land is owned by a legal individual who disposes of wide powers of use, inheritance, or sale and whose ownership is represented by a uniform title deed enforced through the judicial and police institutions of the state. Just as the flora of the forest were reduced to *Normalbaum,* so were the complex tenure arrangements of customary practice reduced to freehold, transferrable, title. In an agrarian setting, the administrative landscape was blanketed with a uniform grid of homogeneous land, each parcel of which has a legal person as owner and, hence, taxpayer. How much easier it becomes to assess such property and its owner on the basis of its acreage, its soil class, the crops it *normally* bears, and its assumed yield, than to untangle the thicket of common property and mixed forms of tenure. The cadastral survey, the "permanent revenue settlement" and the Torrens system of land titling in British colonies were precisely the technique by which a simplified fiscal space could be defined.[14] As in the case of the forest, it provided the means to extract a presumably sustainable fiscal yield. The modern land register and its tax roll was the equivalent, for land tenure, of the scientific foresters' table of timber growth and yield.

The creation of a regional or national market in land and a cadastral survey for tax assessment by officials from outside the community required, above all, a standard measure for land. Customary land measures in most of Europe varied widely by locality and reflected a far greater interest in crop yields and the labor needed to achieve them than in the more abstract qualities of a field, such as how many square meters it enclosed. Thus, in different parts of France, units such as *journal, morgen, hommée,* and *fauchée* indicated how long it would take a man to plow a field. A five journée field could be plowed by a man using standard gear in five days. Depending on the soil, the slope of the land, the kind of plow animals, the plowshare, and so on, a journal would vary greatly from locality to locality as it was a unit of work, *not an abstract unit of area.* In the same fashion, the Irish would refer to "a farm of two cows or a farm of five cows." The amount of land required for a "farm of two cows" might be much greater in a region of poor land in western Ireland than in a rich central county. A centralized cadastral survey, though it might also include a classification of the soil quality and field use (e.g., arable, meadow, pasture, wood lot), had to replace these exotic local measures with a standard, universal measure that was the same throughout the country.

Occasionally, as in Sweden, the customary term might be preserved but its plasticity eliminated forever by fixing it as a uniform areal measure. Customary forms of measurment (not just for land but for weights, textiles, volumes of grain, and so forth) were simply not sufficiently legible either to commodity markets or to central administrators. As one study put it, "The complexity of such early units of measurement, their incompatibility with other measures, and their variation made them unsuitable for cadastral mapping and with capitalism, for which uniform and simple systems are needed."[15] Freehold title and standard land measurement were to the market in real estate what central bank currency was to the marketplace.

If the web of customary land tenure was a mystifying hieroglyph to outsiders and state officials, the new forms of individual, freehold tenure were now mystifying to those whose terrain was being recast. The new forms of tenure, however simplified and uniform they might seem to an administrator, flung villagers willy-nilly into a world of unfamiliar objects and institutions: title deeds, land offices, law, courts, fees, assessments, applications, and cadastral surveys. They faced powerful new specialists in the form of district officials, surveyors, lawyers, and judges whose rules of procedure and decisions were unfamiliar. A central consequence of the new tenure system—one might more accurately say its very purpose—was to map a terrain of taxable real property that was perfectly legible to any clerk or trained state official. At the same time, it radically devalued local knowledge and autonomy. Such forms of specialized knowledge backed by state authority profoundly changed the balance of power between the locality and the state. Where the new tenure system was a colonial imposition—i.e., where the new system was totally unfamiliar, imposed by alien conquerors using a radically different language and institutional context—the transformation conferred unique opportunities for those who first plumbed the mysteries of tenure administration. Thus, the Vietnamese *secrétaires* and *interprètes* who served as intermediaries between the French officials in the Mekong Delta and their Vietnamese subjects, were in a position to make great fortunes. By concentrating on getting the paperwork in order—the title deeds and appropriate fees—they occasionally became, overnight, landlords to whole villages of cultivators who had imagined they were opening common land free for the taking. They might, of course, occasionally use their knowledge to see their compatriots safely through the new legal thicket. Whatever their conduct, their fluency in a language of tenure specifically designed to be legible and transparent to administrators, coupled with the illiteracy of the rural population under them to whom the new tenure was undecipherable, was a momentous shift in power relations.

The actual practices of land tenure—the facts-on-the-ground—did not yield quickly, passively, or entirely to the new tenure regime. Owing to the vagaries of enforcement and the practical interests and values of villagers, a wide variety of unsanctioned and/or illegal tenure practices persisted. Forms of common property survived in popular practice though they might now be legally defined as poaching or trespass. Customary restrictions on sale might continue to be observed for fear of informal local sanctions, although not recognized in law. If the real forest never quite came to resemble the simple homogeneity of the scientific forest's tables, even less did real tenure practices quite come to resemble simple transferrable, freehold property so long as the people on whom it was being imposed had vital interests which led them to resist it. The new scheme, thanks to the power behind it, however, as in the case of scientific forestry, did shape actual tenure practices increasingly in its mold.

IV. "Vos Papiers, Monsieur"

This stock phrase, by which a gendarme addresses a man he wishes to question, illustrates the degree to which even face-to-face encounters in the modern state are mediated by standardized documents. Just as paper currency, as an abstract and uniform unit of value, permits many-tiered exchanges between economic actors who are not known to one another, so do the citizens of the modern state come to be symbolized by paper representations: birth certificates, identity cards, title deeds, tax returns, death certificates, and so forth.

As "representations," these pieces of paper come to take on a life of their own. Consider the following experience, not at all unusual, I believe, from the U.S. Army: A recruit, having recently finished basic training was assigned by his major the task of preparing his regiment's account books for the monthly inspection by the divisional authorities. The books were in complete disorder. Being a clever fellow, the recruit soon realized that the validity of the books mattered less than their conformity to the canons of military accountancy. Accordingly, he made certain that all the figures tallied correctly and that every transaction was represented by the appropriate purchase orders and receipts. Where a paper trail was absent, he manufactured one, whether or not it recorded an actual transaction. The tidy and "paper-perfect" account books were judged the best of all regiments in the division and his commanding officer won much praise for the regiment's financial order. Winning the "divisional colors" every month for the best-kept accounts was important enough to the regiment's commander that he promised the recruit "permanent" leave as long as he repeated his success. Now that he had mastered the creation of "paper-order" in the account books, the recruit vacationed for four weeks each month, returning two days before the inspection of the accounts to reproduce his small miracle.

The first thing to appreciate about the modern state is that most of its officials are, of necessity, usually at least one step—and often several steps—removed from direct contact with citizens. *They observe and assess the life of their society by a series of simplifications and shorthand fictions that are always some distance from the full reality these abstractions are meant to capture.* Thus the foresters' charts and tables, despite their power to distill many individual facts into a larger pattern, do not quite capture (nor are they meant to) the real forest in its full diversity. Thus the cadastral survey, the title deed and tenure contracts are a very rough, and sometimes misleading, representation of actual existing rights to land use and disposal. The functionary of any large organization actually "sees" the human activity of interest to him largely through the simplified approximations of documents and statistics: e.g., tax proceeds, lists of taxpayers, land records, average income, unemployment numbers, mortality rates, trade and productivity figures, or the cases of cholera in a certain district. These stylized facts are, of course, a powerful form of state knowledge making it possible to discover and intervene early in epidemics, understand economic trends that greatly affect public welfare and/or state power, and generally to form policy with many of the crucial facts at hand.[16]

State simplifications, by their very nature, have a particular character. Most obviously, they are observations of those aspects, and only those aspects, of social life that are of official interest. They are also, of course, nearly always written or numerical facts recorded in documents. Third, they are typically *static* facts. Even when they appear dynamic, they are typically the result of multiple static observations through time. Observation of, say, land records or income figures over two or more points in time may reveal a greater inequality in landownership or an increase in income, but it will not reveal how this new state-of-affairs came about or whether it will persist. Finally, most stylized state facts are aggregate facts. Aggregate facts may be impersonal (e.g., the density of transportation networks) or simply a collection of facts about individuals—e.g., employment rates, literacy rates, residence patterns. For most purposes, state officials need to group citizens in a way that permits them to make a collective assessment.

Facts that can be aggregated and presented as averages or distributions must forcibly be *standardized* facts. However unique the actual circumstances of the various individuals who make up the aggregate, it is their sameness, or more precisely, their differences along a standardized scale or continuum that are of interest. The working lives of many people, for example, are exceptionally complex and may change from day-to-day. For the purposes of official statistics, however, "gainfully employed" is a stylized fact; one is or is not gainfully employed. The problems of how to categorize many rather exotic working lives are, in the final analysis, covered over by the categories reflected in the aggregate statistics.[17] Those who gather and interpret such aggregate data understand that there is a certain fictional and arbitrary quality to each of the categories they must employ—that they hide a wealth of problematic variation. Once set, however, these thin categories operate unavoidably *as if* all cases similarly classified are in fact, homogeneous and uniform. All *Normalbäume* in a given size range are the same; all auto-workers (if we are classifying by industry) are the same, all Catholics (if we are classifying by religious faith) are the same.

To this point, I have been making a rather straightforward, even banal, point about the simplification, abstraction, and standardization which are necessary for the observation by state officials of the circumstances of some or all of the population. I want, however, to make a further claim, analogous to that made for scientific forestry, that *the modern state, through its officials, attempts—with varying success—to create a population with precisely those standardized characteristics which will be easiest to monitor, count, assess, and manage.* The utopian (immanent) tendency of the modern state, continually frustrated, is to reduce the chaotic, disorderly, social reality beneath it to something more closely resembling the administrative grid of its observations.

This tendency is perhaps one shared by almost all large hierarchical organizations. As Donald Chisholm, reviewing the literature on administrative coordination concludes, "Central coordinating schemes do work effectively under conditions where the task environment is known and unchanging, where it can be treated as a closed system."[18] The more static, standardized, and uniform a population or social space is, the more legible it is to the techniques of state officials. I am suggesting that state officials endeavor to transform the population, space, and nature under their jurisdiction into the closed system without surprises that they can best observe and control. The reason that they can, to some considerable degree, make their categories stick and impose their simplifications, is because the state, of all institutions, is best equipped to *insist* on treating people according to its schema. If you want to defend your claim to real property you are normally obliged to defend it with a document called a property deed, and in the courts and tribunals created for that purpose. If you wish any standing in law, you must have the documents (e.g., birth certificate, passport, identity card) that officials accept as a claim of citizenship. The categories used by state agents are not merely a means to make their environment legible; they are an authoritative tune to which much of the population must dance.

Some of the most taken-for-granted categories with which we now routinely apprehend social reality had their origin, I believe, in just such state projects of standardization and legibility. Consider something so fundamental as naming practices. Until at least the fourteenth century, the great majority of Europeans did not have permanent patronyms. An individual's name was typically an amalgam of his (if male) given name and his father's given name. Thus, in the English case, William *Robertson's* male son might be called Thomas *Williamson* (son of William) while Thomas's son might be called Harry *Thompson* (Thomas's son). Note that the grandson's name, by itself, no longer bears any evidence of his grandfather's identity, making any tracing of descent through names impossible. The adoption of a *permanent* patronym—a largely state project connected to taxation and inheritance—greatly improved the legibility of kinship and property. The last names were often quite arbitrary; John who owned a mill became, say, John Miller, while John who made cartwheels became John Wheelwright, and their male descendants retained the patronym whatever their subsequent occupations. *Universal* last names, something that was achieved quite late, particularly among the propertyless, was a great step forward in the legibility of the entire population to state officials—most especially tax officials. It is a process still occurring in much of the Third World. One might, in this context, examine still other state-impelled standard specifications which further improved the capacity of state agents to identify an individual. Here the creation of birth and death certificates,[19] *specific* addresses (e.g., not John-on-the-Hill), identity cards, passport numbers, and social security numbers. Such legibility plays an enormous role not only in taxation, but also in conscription, criminal investigations, and so forth.[20] The standardization of individual identities goes hand in hand with the creation of standardized, homogeneous space. Specifying settlements with permanent, official names, creating municipalities, counties, all with sharp, unambiguous boundaries such that all space was named, has also been a vital element of state-formation—allowing state officials to locate—to pinpoint—a specific individual in its grid.

A great part of state-making consists in the comprehensive

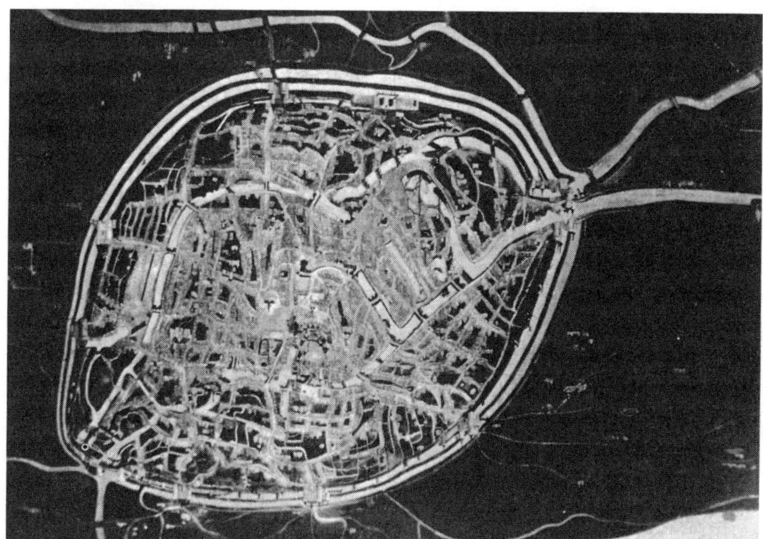

Bruges c. 1500

mapping of a nation's population, its physical space, and its natural resources. Without such mapping—and without the simplifications, standardization, naming, and classification that make it possible—most of the activities of the modern state would be inconceivable.

V. Cities: Legibility from Above and from Below

An aerial view of most medieval cities, or of the oldest quarters *(medina)* of a Middle Eastern city that has not been greatly tampered with, has a particular look to it. It is the look of disorder. More precisely, it conforms to no overall, abstract form. Streets, lanes, and passages intersect at varying angles with a density that resembles the intricate complexity of some organic processes. In the case of a medieval town where defensive needs required walls, and perhaps moats, there might be traces of inner walls superseded by outer walls, much like the growth rings of a tree. A representation of the city of Bruges around 1500 illustrates the pattern. What definition there is to Bruges is provided by the shape of the river and canals which were (until they silted up) the lifeblood of this cloth-trading city and by the marketplace and castle square.

The fact that the city plan, having developed without any overall design, lacks a consistent geometric logic does not mean that it was in the slightest mystifying to its inhabitants. One imagines that many of its cobbled streets were nothing more than the surfacing of footpaths that repeated use had traced. For those who grew up in its various quarters, the town would have been perfectly familiar, perfectly legible. For a stranger or trader arriving for the first time, however, the town was almost certainly confusing, simply because it did lack a repetitive, abstract logic that would allow a newcomer to orient herself. The cityscape of Bruges in 1500 could be said to privilege local knowledge over outside knowledge—including that of external political authorities. Historically, the *relative illegibility* of some urban neighborhoods (or of their rural analogues of hills, marshes, and forests) to outsiders has provided a vital margin of political safety from control by outside elites. A simple way of determining whether this margin exists at all is to ask whether an outsider is likely to need a local guide (a native tracker) in order to find her way successfully. If the answer is yes, then the community or terrain in question enjoys at least a small measure of insulation from outside intrusion. Coupled with patterns of local solidarity, such insulation has proven politically valuable in such disparate contexts as eighteenth- and early-nineteenth-century urban riots over bread prices in Europe, the F.L.N.'s (Front de Libération Nationale) tenacious resistance to the French in the casbah of Algiers,[21] or in the politics of the bazaar that helped bring down the Shah of Iran. Illegibility has been and remains, then, an important resource for political autonomy. It functions, spatially, in much the same way a difficult or unintelligible dialect would function linguistically, to impede communication and understanding.

States and city planners have striven, as one might expect, to overcome this spatial unintelligibility, and to make urban geography transparently legible from without. Their attitude toward what they regarded as the higgledy-piggledy profusion of unplanned cities was not unlike the attitude of foresters to the natural profusion of the unplanned forest. While there is very definitely a political and administrative logic to geometrically regular cityscapes, there is also a strong aesthetic associated with the Enlightenment that looks with approval on straight lines and visible order. The prejudice is nowhere more clearly expressed than by Descartes himself:

> These ancient cities that were once mere *straggling* villages and have become in the course of time great cities are commonly quite *poorly laid out,* compared to those *well-ordered towns that an engineer lays out on a vacant plane* as it suits his fancy. And although, upon considering one-by-one the buildings in the former class of towns, one finds as much art or more than one finds in the latter class of towns, still, upon seeing how the buildings are arranged—*here a large one, there a small one*—and how *they make the streets crooked and uneven,* one will say that *it is chance more than the will of some men using their reason that has arranged them thus.*[22]

Descartes's vision conjures up the urban equivalent of the scientific forest: streets laid out in straight lines intersecting at right angles, buildings of uniform design and size, all built according to a single overarching plan. There are, of course, many cities approximating the Cartesian model. For obvious reasons, most have been planned from the ground up as new, often utopian, cities. Where they have not been built by imperial decrees, they have been designed by the founding fathers of new towns so as to create repetitive and uniform squares for future settlement.[23] A bird's-eye view of central Chicago in 1893 (Philadelphia in the mid-eighteenth century would do equally well) may serve as an example of the grid city.

From an administrator's vantage point, the ground plan of Chicago is nearly utopian. It offers a quick appreciation of the ensemble, since the entirety is made up of straight lines, right angles, and repetitions. Even the rivers seem scarcely to interrupt the city's relentless symmetry. For an outsider—or a policemen—finding an address is a comparatively simple matter; no local guides are required. Local knowledge is not especially privileged vis-a-vis that of outsiders. If, as is the case in upper Manhattan, the cross streets are consecutively numbered and

Chicago 1893

are intersected by longer Avenues, also consecutively numbered, the plan acquires even greater transparency. Delivering mail, collecting taxes, finding a felon or conscript—providing he is at the address given!—planning public transportation, water supply, and trash removal are all made vastly simpler by the logic of the grid.

Two aspects of this geometric order in human settlement bear emphasis. The first is that the order in question is most evident, not at street level, but rather from *above* and *outside.* Like a marcher in a parade, or like a single riveter in a long assembly line, the larger design of the city is not instantly accessible to a pedestrian in the middle of this grid. The symmetry is either grasped from a representation—it is in fact what one would expect if one gave a schoolchild a ruler and a blank piece of paper—or from the vantage point of a helicopter hovering *far* above the ground: in short, a God's-eye view. This spatial fact is perhaps inherent in the process of urban or architectural planning itself, a process that involves scale models and miniaturization upon which patron and planner gaze down exactly as if they were in a helicopter.[24] There is, after all, no other way of visually imagining what a large-scale construction project will look like when it is completed except by a miniaturization of this kind. It follows, I believe, that such plans, which have the scale of toys, are judged for their sculptural properties and visual order, often from a perspective that no (or very few) human observers will ever actually replicate. The grand plan of the ensemble is likely to be far removed from the experience of those "living" in the city at ground level.

A second point about an urban order easily legible from outside is that it has no necessary relationship to the "order" of life as it is experienced by its residents. While certain state services may be more easily provided and distant addresses easier to locate, such apparent advantages may be negated by perceived disadvantages such as the absence of a dense street life, the intrusion of hostile authorities, the loss of the very spatial irregularities that make for gathering places, informal recreation, coziness, and neighborhood feeling. The formal order of a geometrically regular urban space is just that: formal order. Its visual regimentation has a ceremonial or ideological quality, much like the order of a parade or a barracks. The fact that such order "works" for municipal and state authorities in administering the city is no guarantee that it is satisfactory for citizens. Provisionally, then, we must remain agnostic about the relationship between formal spatial order and social experience.

The vast majority of Old World cities are, in fact, some historical amalgam of a Bruges and a Chicago. Although more than one politician, dictator, and city planner has devised plans for the total recasting of an existing city, the cost of such dreams—both financial and political—has generally meant they never left the drawing boards. Piecemeal planning, by contrast, is far more common. The central, older core of many cities remains somewhat like Bruges while the newer outskirts are more likely to exhibit a regularity of several sets of plans. Sometimes, as in the sharp contrast between old Delhi and the imperial capital of New Delhi, the divergence is formalized.

Occasionally, authorities have taken quite draconian steps to *retrofit* an existing city. The redevelopment of Paris by Baron Haussmann under Louis Napoleon was an enormous public works undertaking stretching from 1853–1869. It absorbed unprecedented amounts of credit, it uprooted thousands of peo-

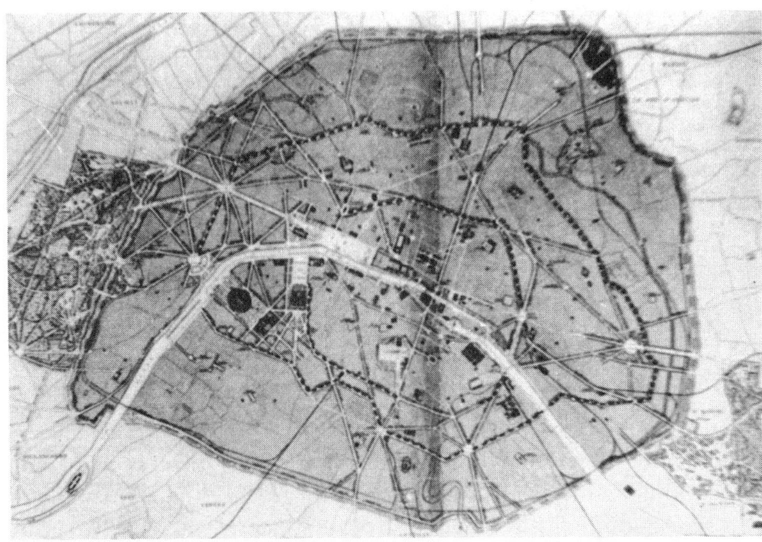

Paris c. 1860

ple, and it could only have been accomplished by a single executive authority not directly accountable to the electorate.

The plan reproduced here shows the new boulevards constructed to Haussmann's measure as well as the prerevolutionary inner boulevards which were widened and straightened. For all its disruption and the legibility it added, the retrofit bears strong traces of its accommodation with an older Paris. The outer boulevards, for example, follow the line of the customs wall of 1787. Haussmann's scheme was far more than a new street plan. The increased legibility of the boulevards was replicated above and below ground in rail lines and terminals, centralized markets (Les Halles), water and gas lines, and a new public drainage system.[25] Even with unprecedented authority and financial resources, however, the existing city and its inhabitants proved a more formidable obstacle to the imposition of planned spatial grid than did the forest or the city begun from zero.

VI. High Modernism and State Power

If we hope to understand the wellsprings of many of the massive, failed experiments in twentieth-century social engineering—unprecedented experiments whose cost in human suffering has been equally unprecedented—then, the mere logic of state simplification and order will not suffice. It is a necessary ingredient but not in itself sufficient.

Aspirations for the "rational" organization of society and nature have nearly always far outstripped the actual capacity for planning and control. Enlightenment advances in scientific observation and experiment, which we saw at work in the case of forestry, certainly raised those aspirations to a new level and fueled hopes of their realization. Until the nineteenth century, however, the reach of state-planned order greatly exceeded its grasp. As an extractive mechanism, the eighteenth-century European state was a great advance on its predecessors. It had become increasingly efficient in pumping revenue, grain, and conscripts from countryside and city. State officials, especially under absolutism, had mapped much more of their kingdoms' population, land tenure, production and trade than before. Yet, there is more than a little irony in the term "absolutism" itself, inasmuch as it was more an assertion and claim than a reality. The authorities lacked the consistent coercive power, the fine-grained administrative grid, or the detailed knowledge that would have permitted them to undertake more intrusive experiments in social engineering. To give their aspirations full reign, they required an even greater confidence or hubris, a state machinery that was apparently equal to the task, and a society they could master.

The template for many of the tragic development failures in the Second and Third World can be located, as many have recognized, in Western historical experience. Outcomes, however, have been generally more tragic in the ex-Second and Third World than in the West. The kinds of failures I have in mind are collectivization in the ex-Soviet Union, communalization and the Great Leap Forward in China, massive population resettlements and frontier cultivation schemes (e.g., Virgin Lands Scheme, Ujamaa Villages), large scale "conquests of nature" such as huge dam and irrigation projects, the diversion of rivers, and so forth.

My argument is a provisional attempt to account for the difference in outcomes by specifying which elements of Western development ideology and practice were shared by the (ex-) Second and Third Worlds and which were not. I hope the rest of this chapter will go some way toward establishing the first part of my case, but I will, for clarity's sake, state the larger argument here.

Many of the most tragic episodes of "state development" in the late nineteenth and early twentieth century originate, I would argue, in a particularly pernicious combination of three elements. The first is the aspiration to the administrative ordering of nature and society, an aspiration we have already seen at work in forestry, but raised to a far more comprehensive and ambitious level. *High modernism* seems an appropriate term for this ideology which I believe was shared, until very recently, by virtually all "developmental elites," whether their names were David Lilienthal, Vladimir I. Lenin, or Julius Nyerere. The second element is the use of the power of the modern state, without restraint, as an instrument of these designs. The third is a weakened or prostrate civil society which lacks the capacity to resist these plans. The ideology provides, as it were, the desire, the modern state, the possibility of acting on that desire, and the incapacitated civil society the levelled terrain on which to build (dys)utopias.

We will return shortly to the premises of high modernism. But here it is perhaps important to note that with the great, and diagnostic, exception of Nazism,[26] the great state-sponsored calamities of the twentieth century have been the work of progressive elites calling themselves socialists or communists. Why? Because, I believe, it is usually only progressives (again, Nazism is the exception) who want to bring about *huge*, often utopian, changes in people's habits, work, living patterns, moral conduct, and world view. They want these changes urgently enough that they are willing to bring them about by the only institutional mechanism powerful enough to enforce them: namely, the state. Thus it is that utopian plans of social engineering are joined to statist and anti-democratic tendencies. The potentially lethal combination is often encouraged by the slowness and recalcitrance of the "human material" who are the objects of the exercise. If, as is often the case, the progressive elites take power on the heels of a revolution and/or after a devastating war, they inherit a relatively prostrate society which they can imagine refashioning root-and-branch. The revolutionaries of 1789 were not the last to believe they were making a fresh start with "year one" of the revolutionary epoch and with the names of the days of the week and month suitably redesigned. The conceit of a "year one" or "year zero" found, say, in the Russian and Cambodian revolutions is a trademark of high modernism's rejection of history and tradition. After a revolution with considerable popular backing the elites are likely to begin with the political capital of enthusiastic support from those who share a part of the same vision of progress or, at the very least, a common hatred for the previous order.

Conservatives are rarely prone to such calamities of hubris because their ambitions are so much more limited. They may care little for civil liberties and may undertake whatever brutalities seem necessary to remain in power. But they do *not* require huge utopian changes which necessitate turning society upside down to create new collectivities, new cities, new family and group loyalties, and new people.

It is not that utopian aspirations per se are dangerous. As at least one political philosopher remarked, a map without utopia on it is not worth having. One can scarcely imagine a social or political vision that does not assert that purposeful human action can improve the conditions of life for one's fellow citizens. Where this utopian impulse goes wrong, I believe is when it depends exclusively on the application of state power for its achievement. Where it goes brutally wrong is when the use of state power is not restrained by an elite commitment to democracy and civil rights or by, above all, a mobilized civil society that can put up stiff resistance and force a compromise.

What is high modernism, then? It is best conceived as a *strong* version of the beliefs in scientific and technical progress associated with the process of industrialization in Western Europe and North America from, say 1830 until the World War I. At its center was a supreme self-confidence about continued linear progress, the development of scientific and technical knowledge, the expansion of production, the rational design of social order, the growing satisfaction of human needs, and, not least, an increasing control over nature (including human nature) commensurate with scientific understanding of natural laws. *High* modernism in this context is a particularly robust, comprehensive version of these convictions that looks to apply the benefits of technical and scientific progress—usually through the state—in all fields of human activity.[27]

It would have been hard *not* to have been a modernist of some stripe at the end of the nineteenth century if you were living in industrializing Europe. How could one fail to be impressed—even awed—by the vast transformations wrought by science and industry? Anyone who was, say, sixty years old in Manchester, England, would have witnessed in that lifetime a revolution in cotton and wool textile manufacture, the growth of the factory system, the application of steam power and astounding new mechanical devices to production, a revolution in metallurgy, transport (especially railroads), and growth of mass-produced cheap commodities. Anyone even slightly attentive to scientific discovery, the advances in chemistry, physics, medicine, math, and engineering would have almost come to expect a continuing stream of new marvels—e.g., the internal combustion engine, electricity. The unprecedented transformations of the nineteenth century marginalized and impoverished many, but even the victims recognized that something revolutionary was afoot. All this sounds rather naive today when we are far more sober about the limits and costs of technological progress, and have a post-modern skepticism of any "totalizing" discourse. Still, it is to forget the degree to which modernist assumptions still implicitly prevail in much of our lives and, above all to overlook the great enthusiasm and revolutionary hubris that was part and parcel of high modernism.

Although high modernism may have originated in later nineteenth-century Europe and North America, it has spread far beyond its *locus classicus* in both space and time. It appeals widely because it promises to deliver the goods (i.e., material progress) and also because, as we will see in detail later, it promises to place great authority in the hands of state officials and experts. It is compatible with wildly divergent political commitments. Thus, such disparate figures as Franklin Roosevelt's New Deal planners (e.g., the founders of the Tennessee Valley Authority), the factory owner Robert Owen, and the planner/architect Le Corbusier shared a high modernist faith with the likes of Lenin, Krushchev, Abdul Nasser, the Shah of Iran, and Julius Nyerere. In each case, their resources, the kind of state power available to them, and the resistance of civil society determined how much of their high modernist vision was, in fact, implemented, but their commitments to rational, state-assisted, progress through planning were remarkably similar.

High modernism as a variant of modernism, in my use of the term, has several distinctive features that bear emphasis. First and foremost, it implies a truly radical break with history and tradition. Insofar as rational thought and scientific laws could provide a single answer to all empirical questions, nothing ought to be taken for granted. All of those human habits and practices from the structure of the family, the patterns of residence, moral values, and forms of production which were inherited, and hence not based on scientific reasoning, would have to be reexamined and redesigned. The past was typically the product of myth, superstition, and religious prejudice. It followed that "scientifically" designed schemes for production and social life would be superior to received tradition. No wonder, as Bauman observes, that modernity "is an age of artificial order and grand societal designs, the era of planners, visionaries and—more generally—*'gardeners'* who treat society as a virgin plot of land to be expertly designed and then cultivated and doctored to keep to the designed form."[28]

The implications of this view are deeply authoritarian. If a planned, scientific social order is simply better than the accidental deposit of historical practice, two conclusions follow. Only those who have the scientific knowledge to discern and create this social order are fit to rule in this new age and those who, through retrograde ignorance, refuse to yield to the scientific plan of the future deserve to be swept aside.

There is no mistaking the utopianism here either. If one thinks of native tongues as the most distinctive and entrenched of customary practices, then the international Esperanto movement that aimed to replace European tongues with a single, scientifically designed, artificial language was surely emblematic of utopian high modernism. The high modernists of linguistics prepared a language they hoped people would want to speak in (because of its obvious superiority) just as the high modernists of urban design prepared a city they hoped people would want to live in.[29]

A second feature of high modernism is that it not only envisions a change in people's material environment, but it envisions improving human nature itself. At the high tide of modernism most people were convinced that social and genetic engineering could produce human material that was healthier, more intelligent, more productive, and aesthetically more pleasing. Here I am not only referring to pseudo-science of phrenology, eugenics, and race science which reached its grisly culmination in Nazi Germany. This was just one possible tangent of a primary belief in human self-determination and perfection: the belief that human nature was a *tabula rasa* on which science could write something new. Milder forms of human engineering were practiced on the industrial working class. In Robert Owen's New Lanark and later at the Cadbury model town, Bourneville, attempts were made to regulate the intimate details of daily life as well as work rhythms. In Bourneville, residents were instructed to close their mouth while sleeping and to brew their tea for precisely three minutes.[30] Social reformers in the United States in the early twentieth century, convinced of their scientific knowledge of domestic order, hygiene, and child-rearing attempted to change the furniture, clothing, eating habits, house-cleaning, and infant-care practices of European working-class families. At one point bottle feeding was preferred over nursing, precisely because a scientific formula, virtually by definition, had to be superior to mother's milk. The growth of public health, sanitation, medical, mental health, and police bureaucracies which supplied the scientific rationale for such micro-interventions in personal life have been analyzed in some detail, thanks in large part to the work of Michel Foucault.[31]

The third, and most obvious, aspect of high modernism is its nearly limitless ambition to transform nature to man's purposes.[32] How completely the utopian possibilities gripped intellectuals of almost every political persuasion is captured in this paean to technical progress in the Communist Manifesto, where Marx writes of "subjection of nature's forces to man, machinery, the application of chemistry to agriculture and industry, steam navigation, railways, electric telegraphs, clearing of whole continents for cultivation, canalization of rivers, whole populations conjured out of the ground."[33] It was, in fact, this promise, made plausible by capitalist development which was for Marx the point of departure for socialism which would, for the first time, place it at the service of the working class. The intellectual air in the mid-nineteenth century was filled with vast engineering projects for the benefit of mankind. In 1869, one such project was completed with enormous consequences for trade between Europe and Asia: the Suez Canal. The pages of *Le Globe,* the organ of utopian socialists of St. Simon's persuasion discussed an endless stream of massive development projects: e.g., the Panama Canal, the development of the U.S., gigantic energy and transportation plans. This belief that it was man's destiny to tame nature in mankind's interest and safety was perhaps the keystone of high modernism, if only because so many of the results of vast engineering projects were already manifest.

Once again the authoritarian and statist implications are clear.[34] The very scale of such projects means that, with few exceptions, such as the early canals, they require large infusions of tax monies or debt. Even if one could imagine, in a capitalist economy, financing them privately, they typically require a vast public authority empowered to seize private property, relocate people against their will, and coordinate the work of many separate state agencies. In statist societies such power is often already built into the political system—whether that system be Louis Napoleon's France or Lenin's Soviet Union. In non-statist societies such tasks have required new public authorities or "super-agencies" having quasi-governmental powers to construct great flood control projects, road and transportation systems, new towns and cities, or, to send men to the moon.

High modernism ought to appeal greatly to those classes and strata who have most to gain from this world view. It is *par excellence* the ideology of the bureaucratic intelligentsia, technicians, planners, and engineers. Only they have the skills and knowledge to conceive, plan, and carry out such great works. The position accorded them is not just one of rule and privilege but rather one of responsibility for the great works of nation-building and social transformation. Under their hand rivers are tamed for irrigation and power, new industrial complexes built and set in motion, populations resettled, new cities created. It is a role tailor-made to raise an elite avant-garde to prominence. Some of the "heroes" of high modernism in the twentieth century, capitalist West include David Lilienthal, Robert Moses, Hyman Rickover, Jean Monnet, and Robert McNamara.

Those who have most to lose from high modernism are, roughly speaking, those whose lives as producers are small scale and autonomous, inasmuch as high modernism favors the large-scale and the hierarchical. Smallholding peasants, independent artisans, petty-traders and shopkeepers would fall into this category as well as, perhaps, independent professions.[35] High modernism of the capitalist or statist variety is likely to threaten their livelihood.

State socialism, as one might expect, has been a very hospitable soil for high modernist thought and practice. A combination of revolutionary victory, the social destruction of a devastating civil war, a Bolshevik worship of modern technology and the machine (above all, the tractor and electricity), and popularly shared utopian expectations conspired to produce an especially robust version of high modernist gigantism. The Bolsheviks ushered in an age of engineers and huge schemes: the White Sea Canal, collectivization, crash industrialization, and so forth. It was a statist, "developmental" utopia. That is, it brought together an older "administrative utopia" tradition preoccupied with the regimentation of the population and of physical space with a renewed intelligentsia desire for "forced march" modernization and industrialization.[36]

An early critic of Bolshevism in power, Jan Waslow Machajski, pointed directly to the privileges it accorded the educated.[37] In his book, *The Mental Worker,* he used Marx, Michels, and Mannheim to label Marxian social democracy as the "self-interested ideology of the radical intelligentsia." He argued that the socialist intelligentsia wanted to abolish capitalism and nationalize production. The workers would become the wage-slaves of the intelligentsia who would, in turn, live like the bourgeoisie.

If, as is often the case, the intelligentsia conceives its mission as one of raising the cultural level of the population, then its role is doubly grandiose. It is not just changing the work-life and material conditions of its people, it is making them a better and more enlightened people. The project of electrification was for Lenin and most Bolsheviks not merely the delivery of a vital service but part of a vision of bringing light, sanitation, hygiene to their dark (narod) subjects sunk in poverty and ignorance. Lest this seem a uniquely Bolshevik conceit, the same sense of cultural mission can be found in the early years of the Tennessee Valley Authority or the Rural Electrification Administration during the New Deal in the United States. Trotsky, for his part, emphasized planned urbanism as an integral part of the Bolshevik cultural mission. He wrote of new cities (see *Literature and Revolution*) built with the compass and the ruler that would replace the chaos of traditional cities. Against those "disurbanists" who would abandon the city, he was adamant.

> [The City] lives and leads. If you give up the city . . . there will remain no Revolution, but a bloody and violent process of retrogression. Peasant Russia, deprived of the leadership of the city, not only will never get to socialism, but will not be able to maintain itself for two months, and will become the manure and peat of world imperialism.[38]

High modernism joined to a cultural project not only makes the technical intelligentsia into a benevolent patron and educator of its people. It provides intellectuals with the large historic responsibility that may contribute to their morale, their solidarity, and the sacrifices they are prepared to make. High modernist, utopian plans serve two other functions. First, they offer a vision of the future that is in sharp contrast to the disorder, misery, and unseemly scramble which elites in all likelihood see in their daily foreground. One might in fact speculate that the more intractable and resistant the real world the planner faces, the greater the need for utopian plans to fill, as it were, the void that would otherwise inspire despair. Second, high modernism raises, by definition, the status of the intelligentsia who become an exemplar of the learning and culture to which their compatriots might aspire. Given its ideological advantages as a discourse, it is hardly surprising that so many Third World elites have marched under the banner of high modernism.

VII. *Mētis:* Particular Knowledge with a Context and a History

When state simplifications take on heroic dimensions, when they are part of a utopian modernist vision and backed by the full weight of state power, they can be, and have often been, deadly. Why? One way of understanding the harm they may inflict is to examine the way in which they make abstractions of nature, of human activity, *and* of the human actors who engage in that activity. The Greek concept of *mētis* provides us with a means of comparing local knowledge to the more general, abstract knowledge deployed by the state and its technical agencies. Before explaining the concept itself, a brief example will illustrate the "vernacular" character of "local" knowledge.

When the first European immigrants to North America were learning how and when to plant new cultivars, such as maize, their Native American advisors instructed them to "plant corn when the red oak leaves were the size of a squirrel's ear." Embedded in this advice is a finely observed sense of the succession of natural events (e.g., the particular plant that flowers, just before a certain species of bird returns, just before the first hatch of a certain insect) which always, or nearly always, happens in that precise sequence. A botanist might observe that the first growth of red oak leaves is keyed to the rising temperature of the ground that, in turn, assures that maize will grow and that the probability of a killing frost is very small. Compare this advice to that typically found in a farmer's almanac which might suggest planting corn after, say, the first full moon in May or after a specified date, say, May 20. This formula requires adjustment by latitude and altitude; it would not work equally well in Connecticut and Vermont, on the coast and inland, or in valleys and on the hills. The date is also probably arrived at on a fail-safe basis, as the worst thing that can happen for those who sell an almanac is to have its advice lead to a crop failure.

As a result of this "commercial" caution, some valuable growing time may be sacrificed in the interest of certainty. The Native American maxim about corn planting is "vernacular" in the sense of relying upon the local ecosystem (red oaks and squirrels) rather than on a nearly universal code (the calendar). Nevertheless, it is applicable wherever red oaks and squirrels jointly occur, it is quite precise in its own terms, and it almost certainly gains a few days of growing time while not appreciably raising the risk of a hard frost.[39]

The Native American advice on when to plant maize represents the accumulated wisdom of local experience as it is embedded in actual practices. These forms of local knowledge I call *mētis,* following the usage of Jean-Pierre Vernant and Marcel Detienne in their discussion of Greek concepts of knowledge in *Cunning Intelligence (Mētis) in Greek Culture and Society.*[40] The failures, both human and technical, of many high modernist experiments in social engineering occur, I believe, not merely because they are bureaucratic and inflexible but because they ignore or violate precisely this sort of knowledge embedded in local practice.

Odysseus is frequently praised for having *mētis* in abundance, although its typical english translation as "cunning" hardly begins to do it justice. *Mētis,* broadly understood, represents the kind of practical skills acquired in responding to a constantly changing natural and human environment.[41] Sailing, boxing, fishing, and (more cooperatively) dancing or team sports are good examples of skills that require constant adjustments and finely tuned reactions to an environment that cannot simply be controlled or engineered. Other spheres of activity that typically have a high component of *mētis* (virtually any activity requires some mētis) are those of professionals who respond to accidents or natural disasters. Successful emergency medical teams, line crews after a storm, Red Adair's team capping oil well-head blowouts and fires, and farming and pastoralism (particularly in precarious environments), all require a high degree of *mētis.* What is distinctive about the situations in which *mētis* is relevant is that (1) they are similar but never precisely identical, (2) they require quick and practiced adaptation that becomes almost "second nature" to the practitioner, (3) they may involve "rules of thumb," but skill typically is acquired through practice (often apprenticeship) and a developed "feel" or "knack" for strategy, (4) they resist simplification to deductive principles which can successfully be conveyed through book-learning, and (5) the environments in which they are practiced are so complex and non-repeatable that formal procedures of rational decision-making are impossible to apply. A shorthand way of assessing the degree of *mētis* implicated in an activity is to ask whether one would prefer as a guide (e.g., mountain climbing guide, airplane pilot, orthopedic surgeon),[42] someone with long and successful experience to someone who had learned the activity as a formal, didactic exercise. *Mētis,* then, is a particular kind of wisdom possessed by someone (or, by a group) who has acquired a practiced "touch" or "eye" for an activity based on practical experience.

It is apparent that *mētis* is nearly the opposite of the formal model of scientific method and Cartesian reasoning from first principles.[43] It is, in turn, at loggerheads with state simplifications which require a uniform administrative grid of categories which can be applied across the board. The two ways of proceeding are, I think, largely incommensurable. A farmer's intimate knowledge (some of it the distilled wisdom of his/her community and ancestors) of such things as the micro-climates, soil, water flows, crop successes and failures, seed varieties, or pests and weeds on a particular farm is irreducibly local. In another setting it would have to be greatly revised. The same would be the case with local forms of land tenure, forest use, grazing, subsistence routines, petty-trade, and so forth. It is just such successful local adaptations embodying the *mētis* of individuals, kinship groups, and communities over which the abstractions of state-sponsored high modernism run roughshod. The results are typically melancholy not just for the human subjects of the experiment, but also for the state itself when its utopian expectations fail.

The simplification and abstraction required in any large-scale administrative exercise is not, in itself, injurious. They are, in fact, a necessary concentration of focus that permits measurement, quantification, and comparisons. One can hardly expect the office of land records to pay meticulous attention to such matters as kinship ties, ecology, or informal exchanges of work and grain. In this respect, the narrow optic of state simplification is not unlike the restricting of focus in scientific experiments on the key variables of direct interest.

Agronomy as a scientific field can be taken as representative. Experiments typically involve a single crop and its response to variations in a specified input (e.g., one kind of fertilizer, pesticide, moisture) with all other factors held constant so the results will be unambiguous. The "response" in which the experimenters are interested is also monochromatic; usually it is the "yield per unit of land" or the net profit per unit of land. The level of simplification and abstraction from ordinary agricultural practice is necessarily heroic. Actual farmers, to take West Africa as an example, may plant several crops similtaneously in the same field (e.g., intercropping, relay cropping) and, of course, they have in mind a host of other outcomes beside yield. To mention only a few other aims that farm households might be interested in: they may want to harvest a crop before the sons go off to work in town; they may want to spread the labor peaks of harvesting so they don't have to hire non-family labor; they may want a crop that will store or transport well; they may want a crop which will provide straw or grazing stubble for their livestock; they may want stable yields; they may want a crop that is tasty, and so on. All these considerations are eminently rational and each household will have its own mix of concerns, ones that may change season to season. No agricultural research station could possibly build all these motives into its experiments or it would be, in the end, reduced to having an experiment design for each household, each season.[44]

The fact that actual farmers neither farm on experimental plots where conditions can be controlled nor have single quantitative objectives that can be unambiguously maximized *does not preclude* a fruitful relationship. Scientific agricultural research does discover important new facts and regularities and farmers are not uninterested in crop yields and net return. So long as farmers are free to modify, adopt, or not adopt the knowledge from agro-economic research, it becomes another source of possible innovation in cultivation practices.

While actual farmers are likely to try, or at least consider, the knowledge provided by scientific agriculture, the reverse is very rarely the case. It is perhaps the ideology of scientific method and the episteme of the controlled experiment that leads to a form intellectual imperialism in which knowledge not gained through the instruments of scientific experiment is not considered knowledge at all. A kind of willful neglect of the agricultural and ecological knowledge embodied in many traditional practices has, until recently, greatly handicapped scientific research in agriculture, particularly in the Third World. As Paul Richards has shown, the actual practices of West African cultivators have quite consistently been more successfully (even by the narrow criterion of yields) adapted to the soils, rainfall, and ecological conditions of a highly diverse landscape than the typical recommendations of Western-style agricultural research stations.[45] The fact that scientific agricultural research operates under the self-imposed handicap of ignoring the wisdom of practice *(mētis)* is not directly injurious to cultivators themselves, although it does sharply limit potential benefits.

When this tunnel vision becomes potentially deadly is when it is deployed by a coercive state determined, usually in the name of progress, to use its techniques to totally transform the life of its subjects.

Space restrictions and, perhaps, the reader's patience as well, preclude a more detailed discussion. Still, a brief example may help clarify what I mean and may suggest the possible value of a more elaborate analysis. The residential pattern of many Tanzanian peoples, most particularly their geographical dispersal, typically reflected a very complex adaptation to grazing and subsistence requirements of a semi-arid environment—the *mētis* of long experience. The ruling party's (TANU and Nyerere's) decision in the 1970s to settle nearly everybody into new *(ujamaa)* villages was taken in relative ignorance of these complexities. Imagining that a concentration of population would make it easier to deliver services (education, health care, water), to inaugurate mechanized cooperative farming under TANU supervision, and to spur the production of cash crops for export, the state bureaucracy pushed ahead. Simple, quantitative goals prevailed: e.g., the number of *ujamaa* villages that officials in each district had "created." The new villages were laid out in legible grids by state surveyors following the standard ("one size fits all") format; houses only a few feet out of alignment with the new grid were occasionally knocked down and rebuilt to bring them into perfect accord with the surveyor's line. The result, as one might have suspected, was economically and socially disastrous for much of Tanzania's rural population inasmuch as it violated any number of sensible practices necessary to pastoralism and agriculture as well as to the diversification of subsistence sources based on long experience. It has taken years to undo the damage it did to viable, productive human communities.

The "sub-species" of high modernism driving Nyerere and TANU bore (not excluding their "socialism" and infatuation with the Chinese communes of the day) a distinct Western intellectual lineage. The logic behind *ujamaa* villages was that large scale farms were inherently superior to small farms, that the more mechanized the enterprise the better (hence the emphasis on tractors), and that concentrated "town" living was inherently superior to rural dispersal. One could find almost exactly the same suppositions behind Lenin's view of Russian agriculture[46] or among the planners of the Tennessee Valley Authority during the New Deal of Franklin Roosevelt.

For all his rhetorical attention to African traditions, when Nyerere wrote that it was high time Tanzanians were made to live in "proper villages," it was a cultural revolution he had in mind. This variant of high modernism serves several manifest and latent purposes. It elevates the knowledge and values of the vanguard elite; it gives them the high goal and responsibility of modernizing their people; it justifies their rule and whatever draconian measures they feel is necessary; and finally, it radically *devalues* the knowledge and practices of the population whose lives they are transforming. Popular resistance can be dismissed as obscurantism and "starting from zero" may be justified. It is only such strong convictions, I believe, that can explain why such policies (e.g., collectivization, *ujamaa* villagization) are pursued long after evidence accummulates of the suffering they are causing, of the coercion required to apply them, and of the actual failures of production which they have brought in their wake.

NOTES

1. Henry E. Lowood, "The Calculating Forester: Quantification, Cameral Science, and the Emergence of Scientific Forestry Management in Germany" in *The Quantifying Spirit in the Eighteenth Century*, ed. Tore Frangsmyr, J. L. Heinbron, and Robin E. Rider (Berkeley: University of California Press, 1991), 315–42. The following account is largely drawn from Lowood's fine analysis.

2. The most striking exception was the royal attention to the supply of "noble game" (e.g., deer, boar, fox) for the hunt and hence to the protection of its habitat. Lest one imagine this to be a quaint premodern affectation, it is worth recalling the enormous social importance of the hunt to such recent "monarchs" as Erich Honneker and Tito.

3. For an evocative and wide-ranging attempt to explore the changing cultural meaning of the forest in the West, see William Pogue Harrison, *Forests: The Shadow of Civilization* (Chicago: University of Chicago Press, 1992).

4. This last is a kind of reverse Heisenberg principle. Instead of altering the phenomenon observed through the act of observation, so that the pre-observation state of the phenomenon is unknowable in principle, the effect of (interested) observation in this case is to alter the phenomenon in question over time so that it, in fact, more closely resembles the stripped down, abstract image the lens had revealed.

5. In the late seventeenth century, Colbert had extensive plans to "rationalize" forest administration both to prevent poaching and to generate a more reliable revenue yield. To this end, Étienne Dralet's *Traité du Régime Forestier* proposal regulated plots (tire-aire) "so that the growth is regular and easy to guard." Despite these initiatives, nothing much came of it in France until 1820 when the new German techniques were imported. Peter Sahlins, "Forest Rites: The War of the 'Demoiselles' in Ariège, France (1829–1831)," unpublished paper presented to the Program in Agrarian Studies, Yale University, January 1992.

6. Lowood, "The Calculating Forester," 338.

7. Various techniques were tried: cutting an actual tree into very tiny bits and then compressing it to find its volume; putting wood in a barrel of known volume and adding measured amounts of water to calculate the volume of the barrel *not* occupied by the wood, and so forth. Lowood, "The Calculating Forester," 328.

8. Lowood, "The Calculating Forester," 341. See also Harrison, *Forests*, 122–23.

9. See, for example, Honoré de Balzac's *Les Paysans* (Paris: Pleiades, 1949); E. P. Thompson's *Whigs and Hunters: The Origin of the Black Act* (New York: Pantheon, 1975); Douglas Hay, "Poaching on Cannock Chase," in *Albion's Fatal Tree,* ed. Douglas Hay et al. (New York: Pantheon, 1975); and Steven Hahn, "Hunting, Fishing, and Foraging: Common Rights and Class Relations in the Postbellum South," *Radical History Review* 26 (1982): 37–64. For a directly opposite German case, see one of Karl Marx's first published articles linking the theft of wood to the business cycle and unemployment in the Rhineland, reported in Peter Linebaugh, "Karl Marx, the Theft of Wood, and Working-Class Composition: A Contribution to the Current Debate," *Crime and Social Justice* (Fall–Winter 1976): 5–16.

10. This brief description is drawn largely from James B. Collins, *Fiscal Limits of Absolutism: Direct Taxation in Early Seventeenth-Century France* (Berkeley: University of California Press, 1988).

11. P. M. Jones, *The Peasantry in the French Revolution* (Cambridge: Cambridge University Press, 1988), 17.

12. Collins, *Fiscal Limits of Absolutism,* 201, 204. It was precisely this capacity to evade taxes that gave the fiscal regime a degree of unintended (from the top at least) flexibility and avoided even more open rebellion in the troubled seventeenth century.

13. This assumes that the crown wants to maximize its long run proceeds. It was and is common, of course, for regimes in political or military crises to mortgage their future by squeezing as much as possible from their forests and/or their subjects.

14. It goes without saying that the homogenization that serves fiscal ends also is crucial for commodities entering the market. A modern market in land is virtually inconceivable where every property bears all the particular traces of the land rights and customary arrangements from which it arises.

15. Roger J. P. Kain and Elizabeth Baigent, *The Cadastral Map in the Service of the State: A History of Property Mapping* (Chicago: University of Chicago Press, 1992), 122. See also Eugen Weber, *Peasants into Frenchmen: The Modernization of Rural France, 1870–1914* (Stanford: Stanford University Press, 1976), chapter 3, "The King's Foot."

16. See Ian Hacking, *The Emergence of Probability: A Philosophical Study of Early Ideas about Probability, Induction, and Statistical Inference* (Cambridge: Cambridge University Press, 1975).

17. There are at least three problems here. The first is the hegemony of the categories. How does one classify someone who works largely for relatives who may sometimes feed him, sometimes let him use some land as his own, and sometimes pay him in crops or cash?

The decisions, sometimes quite arbitrary, about how to classify such cases are obscured by the final result in which only the prevailing categories appear. The second problem, and one to which we shall return, is how the categories—more particularly the state power behind the categories—shape the data. For example, during the recession of the 1970s in the United States there was some concern that the official unemployment rate which had reached 13 percent was greatly exaggerated. A major reason, it was claimed, was that many nominally unemployed were working in the informal economy "off-the-books" and would not report their income or employment for fear of being taxed. One could say then and today that the fiscal system had produced an "off-stage" reality that was designed to stay out of the data bank. The third problem is that those who collect and assemble the information may have very special interests in what the data show. During the Vietnam War the importance of "body-counts" and "pacified villages" as a measure of counter-insurgency success led commanders to produce inflated figures which pleased their superiors—in the short run—but increasingly bore little relation to the facts-on-the-ground.

18. Donald Chisholm, *Coordination without Hierarchy: Informal Structures in Multiorganizational Systems* (Berkeley: University of California Press, 1989), 10.

19. It was not only Nikolay Gogol in *Dead Souls* who was struck by the fact that fiscal death and physical death were not the same. For tax purposes fiscal death in Tsarist Russia was delayed and a family was obliged to pay the full annual head tax on any family member who had been alive during even a minute portion of the fiscal year. It is a staple and bitter irony of many colonial literatures.

20. In the film *Witness,* a modern detective finds himself at a loss when thrust into an Amish community with no telephone numbers and a small number of very common last names. I owe this astute observation to Benedict Anderson.

21. Eventually broken, though at great long-run political cost, by tenacious police work, torture, and networks of local informers.

22. René Descartes, *Discourse on Method,* trans. Donald A. Cress (Indianapolis: Hackett Publishing, 1980), 6. Quoted in Harrison, *Forests,* 111–12, emphasis added.

23. Petersburg is the most striking example of the planned utopian capital, a city Dostoyevsky called "the most abstract and premeditated city in the world." See Marshall Berman, *All That Is Solid Melts into Air: The Experience of Modernity* (New York: Penguin, 1988), chapter 4. The Babylonians, Egyptians, and of course, the Romans built "grid-

settlements." Long before the Enlightenment, right angles were seen as a cultural work of superiority. As Sennett writes, "Hippodamus of Miletus is conventionally thought the first city builder to conceive of these grids as expressions of culture; the grid expressed, he believed, the rationality of civilized life. In their military conquests, the Romans elaborated the contrast between the rude and formless camps of the barbarians and their own military forts, or castra." Richard Sennett, *The Conscience of the Eye: The Design and Social Life of Cities* (New York: Norton, 1990), 47.

24. See the mind-opening book by the geographer Yi-Fu Tuan, *Dominance and Affection* (New Haven: Yale University Press, 1984).

25. As Mark Girouard notes, the plan included public facilities and institutions such as parks (notably, the huge Bois de Boulogne), hospitals, schools, colleges, barracks, prisons, and a new opera house." *Cities and People: A Social and Architectural History* (New Haven: Yale University Press, 1985), 289. Roughly a century later, against greater odds, Robert Moses would undertake a similar retrofit of New York City.

26. I will not pursue the argument here, but Nazism is, I think, best understood as a reactionary form of modernism. Like the progressive left, the Nazi elites had grandiose visions of state-enforced social engineering which included, of course, extermination, expulsion, forced sterilization, selective breeding, and the like, and which aimed at "improving" genetically on nature. The case for Nazism as a virulent form of modernism is made brilliantly and convincingly by Zygmunt Bauman in *Modernity and the Holocaust* (Oxford: Oxford University Press, 1989). See also Jeffrey Herf, *Reactionary Modernism: Technology, Culture, and Politics in Weimar and the Third Reich* (Cambridge: Cambridge University Press, 1984).

27. I have benefitted greatly from David Harvey's discussion of modernism in *The Condition of Post-Modernity: An Enquiry into the Origins of Cultural Change* (Oxford: Blackwell, 1989). See also Marshall Berman's insightful book, *All That Is Solid Melts into Air.*

28. Bauman, *Modernity and the Holocaust,* 113, emphasis added.

29. The problem was that both Esperanto and the completely planned city were alien products to the people who were expected to speak it and live in it, respectively. Their own language and towns were, by contrast, things they and others like them had had some small hand in shaping.

30. Robert Fishman, *Urban Utopias of the Twentieth Century: Ebenezer Howard, Frank Lloyd Wright, and Le Corbusier* (New York: Basic Books, 1977), 93.

31. Michel Foucault, *Discipline and Punish: The Birth of the Prison,* trans. Alan Sheridan (New York: Vintage Books, 1979).

32. Here I want to disassociate myself from the broadside case made against the Enlightenment by Adorno and Horkheimer to the effect that the celebration of purely instrumental reason leads directly to the extermination camps. This is to miss, as many others have pointed out, the contribution of the Enlightenment to the dignity of the individual and the liberal insistence on enshrining individual rights in positive law.

33. Quoted in Harvey, *The Condition of Post-Modernity,* 99.

34. Proudhon's early critique of state-based utopian socialism is prophetic. They would "reconstruct society on an imaginary plan, much like the astronomers from their own calculation would make over the universe." "In promoting a radical, generally egalitarian restructuring of society, the aim of the utopian socialists and the others may be laudable in itself, but their schemes become pernicious when combined with the belief that their goals are to be achieved through the agency of the state or of some other organ whose decisions will be imposed on the whole. The communist project is betrayed by the governmental idea." From *General Ideas of the Revolution,* 90, 106, quoted in George Crowder, *Classical Anarchism: The Political Thought of Godwin, Proudhon, Bakunin, and Kropotkin* (Oxford: Clarendon Press, 1991), 98.

35. The difficulty with independent professions, in this context, is that most professionals can be readily absorbed into large bureaucratic structures, both private and public. Many professionals, perhaps most, actually work as architects, engineers, designers, or physicians within state-like hierarchical institutions. They are thus "amphibians" in a way that the independent peasant or artisan is not.

36. Both strains are analyzed with great insight in Richard Stites, *Revolutionary Dreams: Utopian Vision and Experimental Life in the Russian Revolution* (New York: Oxford University Press, 1989).

37. Ibid., 73.

38. Ibid., 197.

39. The Bavarian peasant formula was that the danger of a killing frost was past when the first grape vine leaves appeared. See Erich Landsteiner, "Bauerlische Meterologie," *Historische Anthropologie: Kultur, Gesellschaft, Alltag* 1, no. 1: 43–62.

40. Originally published in French as *Les ruses d'intelligence: La metis des grecs* (Paris: Flammarion, 1974).

41. I have benefitted here from Steven Marglin's paper, "Farmers, Seedsmen, and Scientists: Systems of Agriculture and Systems of

Knowledge," unpublished. Compare my use of *mētis* with his contrast between *techne* and *episteme.*

42. Notice how "local" and "specific" the expertise of these specialists is: the climbing guide may be best at Zermatt where his experience lies, the airplane pilot best at Boeing 747s, and the orthopedic surgeon best at knees. It is not entirely clear how much of their *mētis* is transferrable if it were a question of the Matterhorn, 727s, and hands, respectively.

43. I overlook, for the moment, the important fact that ethnographies of actual scientific practice have emphasized the role which *mētis*-like aptitudes for improvisation, metaphorical understanding, and experienced "hunches" play in the actual conduct of scientific research.

44. I ignore here the complications that would arise from distinguishing the obvious differences in preference schedules that are likely to characterize each member of a given household.

45. Paul Richards, *Indigenous Agricultural Revolution: Ecology and Food Production in West Africa* (London: Hutchinson, 1985).

46. Lenin's determined emphasis on electrification was perhaps unique—in degree if not in kind. The silence, invisibility, and long-distance transmission of electricity gave it, I think, almost magical properties for early modernists.

3

MODELING POLITICAL ORDER IN REPRESENTATIVE DEMOCRACIES

NORMAN SCHOFIELD

I. Introduction

An extremely powerful notion to use in attempting to understand human society is that of the *market,* conceived in the broadest sense. Each individual is endowed with intellectual, physical, and moral resources and uses these in a rational way to attain personal goals. Implicit in this conception is the ancillary notion of free trade: that each individual has the ability and opportunity to trade with others who are so inclined. In economic versions of the market a price vector may determine the content of permissible trades. Under certain conditions (basically to do with the extent to which individual desires are private) the "equilibrium," x, of the market is *Paretian:* that is there exists no other state y which is preferred by everyone to x.

However, it is implausible that all human desires are private-regarding: we all need companionship, security, love, interaction, and so forth. It is not at all clear that such aspects of our lives, often called public goods, can be attained in some

The ideas presented in this chapter are an attempt to draw substantive conclusions from theoretical work supported by NSF Grant SBR-94-22548. I thank Annette Milford for preparing this manuscript.

reasonable fashion by a market. It is possible, however, that some of these goods can be created in the context of a political market. The fundamental question, then, for political economy is whether the political market can create such public goods as order and security in a Paretian fashion. This concern with equilibrium and Pareto optimality has led to a lively theoretical debate over the last thirty years. Indeed, this debate has spilled back into economic theory, since it is now realized that economic markets can be disordered or chaotic. There has also been a (mostly empirical) debate over the degree to which activity in the political market place can contaminate the equilibrium or Paretian features of the economic market.

I propose in this chapter to present my own views on these debates, to ascertain how they may illuminate the notion of political order. My view is that the theoretical framework that underlies both the economic and political market is that of rational choice theory (RCT), and it is necessary to start with a reasonable understanding of four interconnected facets of RCT.

II. Four Research Programs in Rational Choice Theory

Figure 1 charts four research programs, and distinguishes between preferences and beliefs on the one hand and individual and collective choice on the other.[1] To deal first with the contrast between preference and belief, it is evident that in modeling individual choice, say, it is important to deal not only with the individual's preferences, or desires; it is also necessary to understand how that individual conceives of the world, and its behavior. Just to get at the difference, does a juror who asserts a defendant is innocent do so because of a *preference* for innocence, or because of a belief in innocence? A belief may be changed as new evidence comes to light, but a preference may stay unchanged.

The contrast between individual and collective conceptions is to some extent a matter of degree, but "individual" models focus on the rational decision-making of a single entity examining all possibilities or eventualities. On the collective side, al-

FIGURE 1. *Research Programs in Rational Choice Theory*

	Individual	*Collective*
Preferences	Nash	Arrow
Beliefs	Aumann	Condorcet

though the collectivity is made up of rational individuals, there is in general no attempt to fully model all the possible choices made by each individual. These distinctions may become clearer below. For the moment, it is worth emphasizing that the earliest work in RCT was by the Marquis de Condorcet (1745–1794) who studied both belief and preference (collective) choice.

In my view, collective choice is conceptually akin to field theory in physics—namely gravitation, originating in the work of Newton (1642–1727), and electromagnetism, integrated by Maxwell in 1864. The individual choice theories are twentieth-century inventions and are conceptually close to the quantum theories of the weak and strong nuclear force. There is a further connection concerning computability: full analysis of quantized systems involving three or more entities can be astonishingly complex. In the same way, game theoretic analysis of individual choice involving two agents is often possible, but when there are three or more individuals and no symmetry it is often impossible to fully elaborate the likely behavior. For this reason, it is usually necessary to use collective choice theory as an approximation, because of the intractibility of working at the individual level. In physical science, field theory is a limiting case when there are many interacting bodies. In rational choice theory, the move from the individual level to the collective level is sometimes more a matter of faith than of proof.

There is one other connection between the physical science research programs and the rational choice programs, or more particularly between the program based on gravitation/mechanics and the collective preference program. Although the "Newtonian" inverse square law of gravitation provided the theoretical basis for the development of mechanics, there was deep concern over the computability of the model of the solar system. The problem was this: although the dynamical system involving one planet and one sun could be written down explicitly, it was unclear whether a model involving two planets and a sun was computationally stable. More particularly, small perturbation effects of planet *A* on planet *B* might imply that the orbit solution for *B* was non-convergent. Empirically this could mean that calculations for *B* would, over time, become inaccurate. If the perturbation errors remain small, then the system of planetary equations is called *structurally stable.* Laplace, in his work on celestial mechanics (1799–1825) conjectured that the system was indeed structurally stable. An attempt at a proof by Henri Poincaré (1854–1912) in 1890 suggested that a planetary system could be highly unstable. (In fact, recent analysis using high speed computers suggests that the solar system is basically structurally stable.) However, Poincaré's work laid the foundations for the qualitative study of dynamical systems, and for one of the fundamental theorems of mathematics of the twentieth century. If the underlying space of the dynamical system has no more than two dimensions, then almost all such systems are structurally stable.[2] However, if there are at least three dimensions, then there is a rich class of *chaotic* systems.[3] A chaotic system is one that exhibits an extreme form of dependency on initial conditions or parameters. Although it might be possible to examine a chaotic system in qualitative terms, it is almost impossible to predict exactly how the system will behave. To come back to celestial mechanics, it is known that chaotic planetary systems consisting of three bodies are a theoretical possibility.[4] It is also possible that some small but important components of the solar system (such as asteroids, comets, and minor moons) have chaotic behavior. Smale's result suggests that there are dynamical systems described by completely deterministic equations that are fundamentally chaotic and thus, to all intents and purposes, unpredictable.

One of the main topics for debate in rational choice theory has concerned the possibility for chaos within collective choice mechanisms. Although the debate has cooled off recently, I still view it as of fundamental importance for any formal model of political or economic markets.

The Arrow "Collective Preference" Program

Arrow's Impossibility Theorem is the fundamental result in the theory of collective choice: No aggregation procedure which combines "rational" individual preferences (transitive in both strict preference and indifference) can result in a "rational" social preference ordering respecting both the Pareto criterion (unanimity) and non-dictatorship.[5] Since voting is one of the fundamental collective choice procedures, we can interpret Arrow's result through its implications for (deterministic) voting. In this context, the requirement that the procedure gives a "rational" ranking is obviously unnecessarily strong. All that we really need is that the procedure give a "choice," and this can be guaranteed if the ranking is required to be acyclic (that is, lacking in cycles of the form: x preferred to y, . . . preferred to z preferred to x).

An important situation is where the set of alternatives has a geometric form (given by a particular dimension). In this case, the "choice" or collective equilibrium of the procedure is usually called the *core*. It was shown by Black[6] and Downs[7] that if this "policy space" of alternatives was one-dimensional, then a core could be guaranteed if preferences were "convex." More recently, it has been demonstrated that a non-veto voting process (labeled $\mathfrak{D}$) has a number $v(\mathfrak{D})$ (called the Nakamura[8] number or *stability dimension* of $\mathfrak{D}$), which partially classifies the process in the following way. If the dimension is no greater than $v(\mathfrak{D})$, then a core must always exist.[9] However, if the dimension is $(v(\mathfrak{D})+1)$ then a core need not occur. Instead, voting cycles are possible. However, these cycles must belong to the Pareto set, and in general, the phenomenon of cycling will be constrained. Disorder, even if it occurs, can still be compatible with a reasonable ordering of collective choice. However, this insight, which was first due to Tullock,[10] is invalid in higher dimensions. In particular, for each process, $\mathfrak{D}$, there is a second classifying integer, $w(\mathfrak{D})$, with the following property. If the dimension is at least $w(\mathfrak{D})$ then a core *almost never* exists. Thus cycles are *generic,* in the sense that, for almost all preference configurations, cycles must occur. Even more seriously, if the dimension is at least $(w(\mathfrak{D})+1)$, the "chaos dimension," then it is *generically* the case that these cycles fill the space. In other words, from any one point in the "policy space" it is possible to construct a political agenda which will lead to any other point.[11]

These results are essentially based on a particular condition due to Fan[12] applied to a correspondence F that describes the voting process, $\mathcal{D}$. That is, for any point x, let $F(x)$ be the set of points that beat x under the rules $\mathcal{D}$ of the procedure. The Fan condition is that at every x, $F(x)$ lies in a "half space." If the dimension is less than $v(\mathcal{D})$, then the "Fan" condition must be satisfied, no "cycles" can occur and a core must exist. We can infer that chaos is impossible. On the other hand, if the dimension exceeds $w(\mathcal{D})$ then, generically, there is an open dense set S in W such that the Fan condition *fails* at every point x in S. This implies the S-reachability condition: that every point x of S is reachable from any point in S. Notice that this does not quite imply the existence of chaos. However, it does imply that there exists a selection f (a function) from F such that the process $\{x, f(x), \ldots, f^k(x), \ldots\}$ is chaotic.[13]

The two differing situations, with and without equilibrium, can be characterized in a geometric way which is intuitively satisfying. In the equilibrium case, below the stability dimension, there is at every point a *social welfare gradient* which determines the permissible or socially feasible moves. "Rational" moves or transitions made by the society will then lead into the equilibrium. This gradient represents in some abstract sense the local *consensus* that the society can attain. It is precisely at the instability dimension $w(\mathcal{D})$ that there can occur points where no consensus (or social welfare gradient) is possible, while at the chaos dimension consensus is almost always impossible. (These results concern deterministic voting, where it is assumed that any individual is always in a position to rank alternatives. "Probabilistic" voting has different features and is discussed below.)

These abstract voting theorems have engendered considerable controversy on the viability of democratic institutions[14] and on the extent to which such institutions are in fact stable.[15] A recent literature has focused on the evident fact that real political institutions have a great deal more structure than is assumed in these theorems.[16] Indeed, it is obvious that with restrictions on coalition power and the existence of multiple veto groups there can exist equilibrium. The question remains however: if it is no more than certain specified rules that keeps the equilibrium-inducing institutional structure in place, then what happens when the rules are broken? At the time of writing, it is evident that the enormously complex and rule-bound institutional structure of the Soviet Union and most of Eastern Europe is being transformed. In both the political and economic realm there is strong evidence that chaos in the technical sense is occurring. While new institutional structures will doubtless appear, I for one would not hazard a guess as to their form.

The "chaos" voting theorems[17] should perhaps be viewed as a possibility result: that is for any type of non-dictatorial or democratic voting system it is possible, given high enough dimensionality, for complete "disorder" to occur. "Neo-institutionalism" on the contrary emphasizes the fact that political choice is constrained by particular decision-making structures, by transaction costs, by lack of information, by norms and conventions, and so forth.[18] Recent work on modeling "representative" or parliamentary political systems generally concludes that an "equilibrium" can be plausibly maintained when the representatives make choices in a well-structured context, where they have consistent beliefs about the motivations of the electorate, of other representatives, and of the rules of interaction and of political discourse.

The chaos voting theorems are only directly relevant for models of committee choice in situations where the policy dimension is sufficiently high. Below the instability dimension, the models do suggest that majority rule committees (choosing in a two-dimensional space) will make choices that are Paretian, and generally centrally located. Indeed, if there are many voters (as in an electorate), then the collective choice can be expected to belong to a very small area in the Pareto set.[19] To go beyond these models, to make inferences about representative democracy on the basis of collective choice procedures is unwarranted without a fully developed model of the decision calculus of political agents, namely candidates, parties, representatives, and so forth. Most of this work lies within the Nash program and will be discussed below.

The Nash and Aumann "Individual" Programs

As we noted earlier, the existence of the competitive equilibrium in an economic market is of fundamental importance. In this model, each individual acts out of rational self-interest to maximize utility on a budget set or production set, taking prices as exogenously given.[20] Moreover, under certain private regarding conditions, there will exist a price vector such that all markets clear. Now, in some sense such a model does not fully detail rational behavior. If individuals have reason to believe that their choice will affect prices, then they should build such reasoning into their choice. There are formal results[21] that imply that manipulation of various kinds is a possibility for a "rich" class of economies.

However, manipulation necessarily involves forming beliefs about the way the world and people behave. So before pursuing the notion of manipulation further, it is useful to discuss results in the Aumann program of individual belief aggregation.

To give a simple case, consider a committee of experts, each of whom has some private information, and thus a set of prior probabilities about the state of the world. If the experts have commonly understood models of the world, and their deliberation results in a "statistic" that encapsulates their information, then each can update their prior probability to form *a posteriori* probability distributions. Eventually their posterior probabilities will converge.[22] However, this convergence depends on certain "common knowledge" assumptions that may not be valid in more general situations.

In a more complex situation such as the market, individuals not only have private information, but quite distinct preferences. Thus, to model an individual's rational calculation, we may have to model that individual's beliefs about other agents' beliefs, and model their beliefs about others, and so forth. As Arrow has noted,[23] an understanding of markets may require a solution to this underlying "common knowledge" problem. One recent technical result by Nyarko[24] suggests that general models of markets, involving both beliefs and preferences, tend to bifurcate into two classes. For certain "equilibrium" markets, the underlying fundamentals of the game imply that reiteration results in a contraction to beliefs and behavior which are mutually consistent. For other markets, given *any* possible behavioral trajectory, there is some system of initial "hierarchical" beliefs which can trigger the trajectory.

Thus, while there may well exist a "Nash" equilibrium in a relatively simple market game, a more structured game form, where individual rational behavior is modeled more fully, can be chaotic.[25] The transition from equilibrium to chaos can also be seen in public goods or "prisoners dilemma" (PD) situations. The standard view of the one-shot prisoner's dilemma is that each individual should rationally defect. Consequently, the Pareto preferred cooperative outcome will not occur. The "irrationality" of this Hobbesian non-cooperative outcome is usually viewed as a basis for the necessity of government for public goods provision.[26] Many authors have argued that cooperation can be maintained if the PD is reiterated in time.[27] The seminal work by Kreps, Milgrom, Roberts, and Wilson,[28] however, indicated that, as the iterated game nears its end, then complicated behavior can be sustained by quite reasonable beliefs about others' behavior. Since rational behavior by each individual in the PD is thus based on common knowledge foundations, it is in principle possible for "anything to happen." This is the basis for the so-called folk theorem[29]. To relate this back to the ideas of chaos, Richards has shown that "empirical chaos" can occur in two-person prisoner's dilemmas.[30] Other instances of chaos at the theoretical level include models of bandwagon effects, fashions, and fads.[31] and the bifurcation into equilibrium or chaos shown in *n*-person collective action games by Huberman and Glance.[32]

The point of this observation is not just to assert that chaos is possible, but to emphasize that any theoretical model which attempts to demonstrate that some phenomenon is likely in a particular collective context is probably wrong.

This caveat should be kept in mind when considering the various models that have been proposed to describe political competition. Deterministic models of two-candidate or two-party competition have had to deal with the chaos results mentioned earlier. The various models vary somewhat with regard to the assumptions made about the motivations of the candidates, but in general they assume that the fundamental motivation is to win. Since there can in general be no certainty of winning (and indeed no equilibrium), it has been proposed that the candidates converge toward a set known as the uncovered set.[33] The logic of this is that the candidates use mixed strategies, randomizing among a set of possible policy objectives. However, it is difficult to regard this as a serious model of candidate behavior. Perhaps a more plausible situation to model is one where candidates owe obligations to particular interest groups, and so have "induced policy preferences." Rational candidates might then choose policy points near the center of the electoral distribution. I have tentatively proposed an equilibrium notion called the "heart,"[34] which is defined, and continuous, in the voter preferences, and can be thought of as an "attractor" for candidates. However, "policy-driven" models of this kind do not generally exhibit the degree of candidate convergence found in one-dimensional Downsian "policy-blind" models of political competition.

Coherent models with more than two parties are even more difficult to construct. The earlier literature assumed parties attempted to maximize the number of seats or votes they won in the election.[35] Such an assumption is open to criticism and it is more plausible to assume that parties are committed to certain policy positions, but perhaps modify these positions before the election both with regard to electoral returns and the constraints these declared objectives will have on negotiation over government. It is evident that such models have to address the degree of credible commitment that the parties have towards their declared policies. For example, in Britain the Labour Party has clearly attempted, over the last four years, to move towards the "political center," yet under Kinnock and Smith the electorate found the various declarations less than credible. Perhaps with Blair as the new leader of the party, it will be possible for Labour to take over the middle ground. It is obvious that the electoral response involves beliefs as well as preferences. However, details of the electoral system can be very important in turning beliefs into votes and seats. A later section will return to this theme.

The Condorcet "Collective Belief" Program

Condorcet's idea was that politics can be thought of as the aggregation of the beliefs of the many concerning the truth.[36] The simplest situation is one where each individual k, has some probability, π_k of making the "correct" choice in binary decision. It is usually assumed that each $\pi_k > 0.5$ and that the voter choices are independent. In this case, the probability p that a majority chooses the correct option exceeds 0.5 and indeed if the size of the society approaches infinity, then p approaches 1.[37]

We can use this model to approximate political competition between two candidates. Suppose now there is an underlying policy space within which the candidates compete for votes. Suppose further that the two candidates pick positions, x,y, and for convenience call the candidates x,y. For each voter, k, let (x_k, y_k) be the "distances" x_k and y_k from voter k's position. Let π_k be the probability that k votes for x. Suppose that the probability π_k has the property that $\pi_k = 1/2$ if $x_k = y_k$, while π_k approaches 1 if y_k approaches ∞. For each (x,y) let $\pi(x,y)$ be the average of π_k. In general if the π_k's are independent, and if $\pi(x,y) > 1/2$ then the probability $p(x,y)$ that x wins will exceed $\pi(x,y)$. Moreover, if the size of the society approaches infinity, then $p(x,y)$ approaches 1. In this model of collective belief aggregation no mention has been made about "preferences". We have only modeled the nature of beliefs in terms of some underlying parameter space. The model has the feature under further "concavity" assumptions on the π_k's that if the candidates desire to win then they will choose identical positions ($x = y$). Moreover these positions are, in some sense, optimal in that they minimize the average distance $\Sigma\, x_k$ between the "winning" position and the voters. That is to say, the equilibrium position, x, is at the "barycenter" of the voter positions.[38] Many probabilistic voting models have similar features.[39] My view is that these "probabilistic" models should be regarded as belief aggregation procedures rather than preference aggregation mechanisms. As we have noted above with regard to preference aggregation, if voters choose "deterministically" which candidate they prefer, then chaos can occur. It is still a lively debate in rational choice theory whether the equilibrium results of belief aggregation models or the political chaos of deterministic, preference aggregation are more appropriate for interpreting political competition. My view is that political aggregation involves both preference and belief and that we are not yet in a position to fully model political behavior. However, we can perhaps draw some broad inferences depending on the general structure of the political institutions. The reader will have noticed that the previous discussion has been void of any mention of real political institutions. What I propose to do now is sketch out the differences between American and British political institutions on the one hand, and the European political systems based on proportional representation. I shall attempt to use the RCT theories outlined above to draw inferences about the general features of these institutions.

III. Political Institutions

The United States

Any elementary description of the United States distinguishes between the legislature, executive, and judiciary. The fact that these three institutions are so distinct is the unique, characteristic feature of the United States. To formally describe the relationship between the institutions is overwhelmingly complex, but I shall, nonetheless, present my own views on this. I assume that both the House and Senate are characterized by weak parties; that representatives and senators reflect heterogeneous, local preferences. Analyses of voting behavior in both houses[40] indicates that there is an underlying two-dimensionality in voting behavior in the Congress. I infer that there is a strong geographical structure to this heterogeneity. Intuitively, I would say one dimension is an East-West cleavage, and we can think of it as old industry–new industry. A second dimension can be thought of as north-south, possibly pro- and anti-government intervention. The formal results by Schofield and Tovey mentioned earlier,[41] given this heterogeneity, imply that the "heart" for both houses is small and centrally located. Small changes in election results may cause this "heart" to move, but only "continuously." Log-rolling or vote exchanges in both houses are likely to lead to legislation in this heart. Compromise between the houses results in outcomes in the intersection of House and Senate hearts.

I conjecture that the same underlying "policy" space describes the system of electoral preferences in the population at large. However, presidential candidates for the two parties are generally committed, through the operation of a system of primaries, to distinct policy positions. Because there is a significant degree of uncertainty in the outcomes of presidential elections, a probabilistic policy-driven model of two-candidate competition is plausible. As I emphasized, such a model does not display convergence. Instead, each candidate chooses a declaration that optimizes with regard to the policy commitment necessary to obtain endorsement, and with respect to the candiates' information or belief over the probability of election. There is no reason to believe the equilibrium position of the winner belongs to the House-Senate heart. After the election, it is plausible that the president then has to face the incompatibility between his underlying commitment on certain issues, his electoral promises as well as the difference between these and reasonable compromises (in the heart) with the House and Senate.

My view of the role of the judiciary requires that we introduce the notion of social or political risk. It is plausible that well-structured political institutions should be designed to deal with risk in different ways. I infer that, in general, a president is risk-preferring, that the House and Senate are risk-neutral (because of their heterogeneity) while the judiciary is risk-averse. To elaborate on this inference would require a book by itself. Perhaps it is sufficient to say that these underlying risk postures are sustained by beliefs and negotation both within and between these three institutions.

Britain

Unlike the United States, Britain has a parliamentary system with a number of strong parties. The electoral system is first-past-the-post (FPP), which implies there is a relatively low correlation between the proportions of votes cast for each of the parties and the proportion of seats they receive.[42] Small, but geographically concentrated parties, such as the Scottish or Welsh Nationalists, tend to do quite well, proportionally.

The two current center parties, liberals and social democrats, even though they recently coalesced, gained very few seats given their electoral vote (less than 5% compared to 20%). There is a strong north-south feature to electoral politics, with the Conservative strength concentrated in the south and Labour strength in the north. Given what appears to be a fundamental uni-dimensionality, there is little evidence of "Downsian" convergence to a voter median. To compare with the Downsian model, suppose that there were only two parties and a single dimension in Britain. Clearly policy commitment by either party would make it vulnerable to defeat by the other, and a strong centralizing tendency could be expected. This tendency with Blair and Major as the respective leaders (recently called Blajorism) is still quite weak. Assuming that the parties do indeed attempt to maximize the expected number of seats they obtain, subject to their ideological constraints, then we are led to infer that there is both a high degree of uncertainty imparted by the electoral system and more than one dimension to the political conflict. (It is possible that disagreements over European integration comprise a second independent dimension from the usual economic dimension.) It may be the case that a Condorcet model of probabilistic voting is the appropriate one to use. Even so, the subtlety of the electoral system means that no simple assertion regarding the optimality of the winning party position can be made. Note also the difficulty with the Duverger hypothesis that only two parties can survive in a FPP system. Although the center parties are relatively impotent in parliamentary terms, they still obtain significant electoral support.

European Multiparty Systems

With an electoral system based on proportional representation (PR), political fragmentation (defined in terms of the pattern of parliamentary seat ratios) can be very high (as in Finland or Italy). Classical arguments against PR relate the electoral system to fragmentation and so to unstable government. The oddity of this argument is that parliamentary coalitions in a number of European countries are very often based on a center party, generally called a Christian Democrat party.[43] However, this "centrality" may be a phenomenon of the past. In Italy, the dominance of the centrist Christian Democrat Party (DCI) was destroyed in 1992. The results of the May 1994 election in the Netherlands have led to the loss of power of the Christian Democratic Appeal (CDA) and a new "purple" coalition involving Labor, Liberals, and Democrats '66.

In contrast to the centrist systems of Belgium, Italy (until 1992), and the Netherlands (until 1994), strong left-wing parties in the Scandinavian countries have often resulted in minority socialist governments, alternating with right-wing or bourgeois coalition governments. Empirical analyses of party declarations and government policy-making[44] suggest that the policy space in these countries involves at least two dimensions—one economic and one concerning social welfare. The models of coalition government that have been proposed give theoretical reasons why centrist policies associated with a social consensus should result. It is entirely possible that these inferences are dependent on a particular historical context that is fading. For example, the reunification of Germany has lead to the formation of new parties (Republicans) and the weakening of the centrist Free Democrats. The existence of social consensus in the new Germany may be a thing of the past.

However, it is plausible that the overall centrist consensus in the European polities (other than Britain) lies near an electoral European "heart." This may suggest a reason why the current British government finds this European consensus so difficult: as I have suggested, the electoral system in Britain does not appear to induce centrist government policies.

Japan

Japan has a rather unusual political system, presumably rooted in the nature of the electoral system. In the past, multi-seat districts gave rise to intense competition between factions within the Liberal Democratic Party (LDP).[45] LDP factions jockeyed for power and contributions but still maintained the pretense of a unified party. This "stability" has recently collapsed, as small LDP factions allied themselves with the non-LDP parties. Recently, of course, the anti-LDP coalition broke down as the Socialists in turn changed their allegiance. If, in fact, the Japanese polity is fundamentally zero-sum rather than policy-oriented, then full-scale chaos could occur.

IV. The Economic Irrationality of the Polity

In this section, I review the general argument that political intervention in the economic market gives rise to economic irrationalities. To give the argument in its most blunt and abstract form, suppose that x_1 is the economic equilibrium outcome which we can assume to be Pareto optimal with regard to private goods distribution. It is well known that the private goods economy is unable to deal with public goods provision, so assume first that the public goods allocation y_1 is zero. A government is formed and levies some tax, say, to create an "optimal" level of public good, y_2 (we return to the method of public good provision in a moment). By definition taxation effects the private good economy, so the outcome is now (x_2,y_2). We can assume that (x_2,y_2) is unanimously preferred to $(x_1,0)$. Once government is in place, it gives entry to interest groups who "manipulate" the economy to secure rents, and so forth. The manipulated outcome (x_3,y_3) is preferred to (x_2,y_2) only by these interest groups. The alleged irrationality results because economic productivity is higher at (x_2,y_2) than at (x_3,y_3). By definition this means that the GNP (gross national product), say, is higher at (x_2,y_2), so there is a system of transfers within the economy from the economically efficient state (x_2,y_2) to a state (x_4,y_4) that is preferred by almost everyone to (x_3,y_3). Figure 2 gives the logic of this argument.

Note that it is assumed that once the move to the economically inefficient outcome (x_3,y_3) has been made, it is politically impossible to move to (x_4,y_4). The reason for this is that the interest group prefers (x_3,y_3) to (x_4,y_4) and exercises a veto, so that the move from (x_3,y_3) is politically infeasible.

FIGURE 2

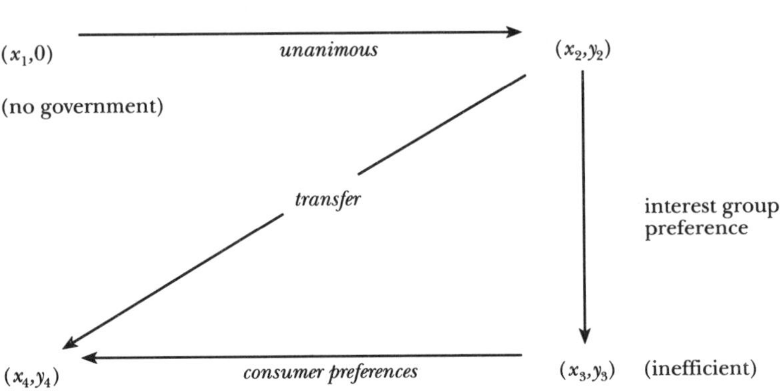

The Rise and Decline of Britain

Olson's arguments in *The Rise and Decline of Nations* can be interpreted in terms of this diagram.[46] The interaction of interest groups is essentially a prisoner's dilemma: a group, such as a trade union, will defend its interests by pushing for higher wage rates, restricting the implementation of new technology to maintain employment for its members, or protecting against foreign imports. While such a strategy is rational for the group, it is socially irrational, as it reduces social output in the long run. Once one group manipulates in this way, others follow suit, and total output declines further. Olson further suggests that the periods of long political stability facilitate interest group activity of this kind, while countries (such as Germany) that have had severe social crises, such as defeat in war, have weaker interest groups and are less susceptible to this dilemma of democracy. It should be remembered that Olson was writing at the end of the 1970s with the aim perhaps of explaining the relative decline of Britain and the United States. While the framework lacked a specific model of interest group behavior, it did appear consistent with the events under the Heath and Callaghan governments in Britain. Beer provided a related model of the "new group politics" in Britain.[47] With the decline of party identification, small groups in the economy became unconstrained in pressing their claims in the political arena for subsidies, excess pay rewards, and other benefits. Although Beer does not emphasize this point, it is possible that the FPP system in Britain had the effect of magnifying the power of such interest groups. However, it is also fairly obvious that the trade union groups that Olson had in mind in Britain have been more or less emasculated in the last fifteen years. Clearly, neither Olson nor Beer had a formal model of political activity in mind, and their arguments tend to some extent to be contradicted by the models involving political equilibrium discussed earlier.

Public Goods in the United States

A somewhat related literature has developed over the last few decades on the provision and distribution of public goods. In the classical public finance literature, the public good is financed by a tax-rate which is chosen by majority rule. Since the choice of a tax schedule is a uni-dimensional problem, standard Downsian arguments[48] would suggest the existence of a median tax equilibrium for the political economy. It is evident, however, that evaluation of a given tax rate is dependent on the subsequent choice of what public goods are to be created. Moreover, any public project is likely to have geographically local effects on employment and factor prices. Thus, any public good decision, and more generally any major government spending decision, has some distributional consequences. In a sense, Thurow is correct to refer to the "zero-sum society."[49] Various authors have argued that political mechanisms, designed to deal with public goods conflicts, will lead to overprovision of the goods. Thus, political representatives propose pork barrel projects that benefit their own constituencies, knowing that most of the cost will be faced by other voters. Weingast, for example, has argued that "universalistic" coalitions including nearly all legislators are likely and that these will continuously overprovide public goods.[50] Since the tax costs of this overprovision will be high, one might expect increasing budget deficits (I return to this point in a moment). Although certain aspects of this argument may be justified, some difficulties should be mentioned. I assume that the pattern of preferences of U.S. representatives is quite heterogeneous, but that the policy problem is not completely distributional. In this case, theory suggests that vote trading in Congress will result in a small domain of possible legislation. By definition this means the coalition is not universalistic. However, it is true that evaluation of policy outcomes may not involve a complete economic pricing. Thus, political outcomes may lead to budget deficits, but not necessarily as high as implied by the universalistic model. However, it is also true that past compromises in the "congressional heart" have resulted in mandated transfers that are difficult to change. On the other hand, transformations in government expenditures that do not affect large numbers of people are politically feasible (the recent reductions in military expenditure resulting from the end of the cold war are good examples).

Now consider the ability of interest groups to manipulate the U.S. economy. In the political choice of economic strategy, it would appear appropriate to use the results of Condorcet belief aggregation. Because of the heterogeneity of the representatives, it is reasonable to infer that the consequence of voting on issues that are fundamentally uncertain will result in "centrist" policies. For example, there is, in the United States, great variety in popular opinions over the virtues of free trade and the appropriate way to deal with crime. The content of the trade and crime bills do not suggest that they were captured by special interests. Beliefs about the appropriate pattern for health care in the United States are even more complex. However, it is possible that a Condorcet compromise will eventually be found.

The argument just outlined is that heterogeneous beliefs in Congress generate a "Condorcet" belief equilibrium that need not be identified with any particular party. This equilibrium will change over time as new information becomes available to voters and representatives. It is fairly apparent that the United States has responded quite vigorously to the structural transformation that is affecting the world economy. In general, low productivity jobs are being eliminated; the automobile industry which was regarded as incompetent a decade ago has responded vigorously to foreign competition; protection against imports is fairly weak. All of this is quite contrary to the Olson thesis concerning the ability of interest groups to protect themselves. This does not mean there is consensus, in the generally accepted meaning of the word, but there does appear to be a belief equilibrium. Perhaps unfortunately, one aspect of this "equilibrium" is that the tax base of many U.S. cities has been depleted, and poverty and crime are endemic.

Social Compromise in PR Polities

Many authors have used the term consociationalism to describe a situation where bargaining and compromise dominate in the political arena.[51] In particular, coalition governments in PR polities are based on negotiation between a number of relatively small parties. To relate these ideas to the inferences on multiparty PR systems in Europe, it is plausible that social consensus is attained through the presence of a relatively large "centrist" party which is able, in general, to maintain itself in government by bargaining with smaller allied parties. Crouch's work, on evaluating the success that the European countries had in moderating inflation and unemployment in the 1970s, suggests that high political fragmentation in countries such as Belgium, Denmark, and Finland made consensus difficult to attain.[52] So we can infer there is a conflict between centralism and fragmentation. What I wish to suggest is that the nature of the social consensus in the European polities is based on preference aggregation, and focused in general on a dominant center party. Usually this consensus involves agreement in the polity over the nature of the social contract: that is the level of government expenditure, minimum wage legislation, health and unemployment benefits, access to education, and so forth. One aspect of the social contract that is relevant is, of course, the level of trade protection implied by the Common Agricultural Policy. The quite pronounced differences between the general understanding of the social contract in the PR parties of the European Union and the nature of the belief equilibrium in the United States suggests one way of interpreting the disagreements over agriculture that attended the recent GATT negotiations. Since the European Center parties are committed to the social consensus, it has proved very difficult for them to adapt to recent structural changes in the international economy. Economic protection and the relatively high social cost of labor has lead to exceptionally high levels of unemployment. Recent unemployment figures are 23.5% (Spain), 13.1% (Belgium), 11.6% (France), 10.1% (Denmark), 12.4% (Italy), 8.3% (Britain), 8.3% (Germany), and 7.2% (Netherlands).[53] Meanwhile the U.S. rate is 5.6%. Of course these countries are at different stages of the business cycle. However, it does seem to be the case that one of the consequences of the technological transformation that faces us all is a rapid rise in white-collar unemployment. If this is a permanent feature, then the European centrist social consensus will be difficult to maintain. This may be the reason why small extreme parties have been able to gain support recently in France and Germany.

V. Conclusion

In the last two sections, I have written as though equilibrium necessarily exists in the various polities that were discussed. The instability results from the Arrow program suggest, on the contrary, that chaos is a real possibility, but only when the underlying dimension of the policy space becomes sufficiently high. In other words, in times of economic downturn the political game may more closely approximate a zero-sum situation. In the context of the U.S. Congress, this would imply that the heart explodes out to the full Pareto set. In European multiparty polities, the center party would no longer be able to control, indirectly, the path of policy-making. Instead, one would expect constantly changing coalition government. In Britain, the implicit electoral coalitions underlying the majority party would become unstable. It is possible that political representatives in developed democracies take care to prevent, if they can, the occurrence of such zero-sum chaos. Of course, the international economic tribulations and the oil crises of the late 1960s and 1970s did induce some degree of chaos. The 1980s and early 1990s on the contrary, were a period of economic and political recovery from this instability. It is possible that attempts to mitigate the effects of the current economic transformation could make the eventual disorder more extreme than it might otherwise be.

NOTES

1. The programs are named after the following seminal works. K. J. Arrow, *Social Choice and Individual Values* (New York: Wiley, 1951); R. J. Aumann, "Agreeing to Disagree," *Annals of Statistics* 4 (1976): 1236–39; M. J. A. N., marquis de Condorcet, *Essai sur l'application de l'analyse à la probabilité des décisions rendues à la pluralité des voix* (Paris: Imprímerie Royale, 1785); J. F. Nash, "Non-Cooperative Games," *Annals of Mathematics* 54 (1951): 289–95.

2. M. Peixoto, "Structural Stability on Two-Dimensional Manifolds," *Topology* 1 (1962): 101–20.

3. S. Smale, "Structurally Stable Systems Are Not Dense," *American Journal of Mathematics* 88 (1966): 491–96.

4. D. Saari, "On Oscillatory Motion in the Problem of Three Bodies," *Celestial Mechanics* 1 (1970): 343–46; D. Saari, "The N-Body Problem of Celestial Mechanics," *Celestial Mechanics* 14 (1976): 11–19.

5. Arrow, *Social Choice and Individual Values.*

6. D. Black, *The Theory of Committees and Elections* (Cambridge: Cambridge University Press, 1958).

7. A. Downs, *Economic Theory of Democracy* (New York: Harper and Row, 1957).

8. K. Nakamura, "The Vetoers in a Simple Game with Ordinal Preference," *International Journal of Game Theory* 8 (1979): 55–61.

9. N. Schofield, *Social Choice and Democracy* (Heidelberg: Springer, 1985).

10. G. Tullock, "The General Irrelevance of the General Impossibility Theorem," *Quarterly Journal of Economics* 81 (1967): 256–70.

11. N. Schofield, *Social Choice and Democracy;* R. D. McKelvey and N. Schofield, "Structural Instability of the Core," *Journal of Mathematical Economics* 15 (1986): 179–88.

12. K. Fan, "A Generalization of Tychonoff's Fixed Point Theorem," *Mathematische Annalen* 142 (1961): 305–10.

13. D. Saari, "Price Dynamics, Social Choice, Voting Methods, Probability, and Chaos," in *Lecture Notes in Economics and Mathematical Systems* 244, ed. C. D. Aliprantis, O. Burkenshaw and N. J. Rothman (Heidelberg: Springer, 1985).

14. W. Riker, *Liberalism against Populism: A Confrontation between the Theory of Democracy and the Theory of Social Choice* (San Francisco: Freeman Press, 1982); W. Riker, *The Art of Political Manipulation* (New Haven: Yale University Press, 1986).

15. G. Tullock, "Why So Much Stability?" *Public Choice* 37 (1981): 189–205.

16. K. A. Shepsle, "Institutional Arrangements and Equilibrium in Multidimensional Voting Models," *American Journal of Political Science* 23 (1979): 27–60; K. A. Shepsle and B. R. Weingast, "Structure Induced Equilibrium and Legislative Choice," *Public Choice* 36 (1981): 221–337.

17. McKelvey and Schofield, "Structural Instability of the Core."

18. See D. North, *Institutions, Electoral Change, and Economic Performance* (Cambridge: Cambridge University Press, 1990), for an extensive discussion.

19. N. Schofield and C. Tovey, "Probability and Convergence for Supra-Majority Rule with Euclidean Preferences," *Mathematical Computer Modeling* 16 (1992): 41–58.

20. K. J. Arrow and G. Debreu, "Existence of an Equilibrium for a Competitive Economy," *Econometrica* 22 (1954): 265–90.

21. Some of these are discussed elsewhere: N. Schofield, "Chaos or Equilibrium in a Political Economy," in *Chaos and Society,* ed. A. Albert (Amsterdam: IOS Press, 1995).

22. R. D. McKelvey and T. Page, "Common Knowledge, Consensus, and Aggregate Information," *Econometrica* 54 (1986): 109–27.

23. Arrow, "Rationality of Self and Others in an Economic System," *Journal of Business* 59 (1986): 5385–99.

24. Y. Nyarko, "Convergence in Economic Models with Bayesian Hierarchies of Beliefs," typescript, New York University, 1993.

25. W. Brock, B. Le Baron, and D. Hseih, *Nonlinear Dynamics, Chaos, and Instability* (Cambridge: MIT Press, 1991).

26. M. Taylor, *Anarchy and Cooperation* (London: Wiley, 1976).

27. M. Taylor, *Community, Anarchy, and Liberty* (Cambridge: Cambridge University Press, 1982); R. Hardin, *Collective Action* (Baltimore: Johns Hopkins University Press, 1982); R. Axelrod, *The Evolution of Cooperation* (New York: Basic Books, 1984).

28. D. M. Kreps, P. Milgrom, J. Roberts, and R. Wilson, "Rational Cooperation in the Finitely Repeated Prisoner's Dilemma," *Journal of Economic Theory* 27 (1982): 245–52.

29. D. Fudenberg and E. Maskin, "The Folk Theorem in Repeated Games with Discounting or Incomplete Information," *Econometrica* 54 (1986): 533–54.

30. D. Richards, "Is Strategic Decision-Making Chaotic?" *Behavioral Science* 35 (1990): 219–32.

31. S. Bikhchandani, D. Hirschleifer, and I. Welsh, "A Theory of Fads, Fashions, and Cultural Change as Information Cascades," *Journal of Political Economy* 100 (1992): 992–1026.

32. B. A. Huberman and N. S. Glance, "Beliefs and Cooperation," typescript, Xerox Research Center, Palo Alto, Calif., 1994.

33. R. D. McKelvey, "Covering, Dominance, and Institution-Free Properties of Social Choice," *American Journal of Political Science* 30 (1986): 283–314.

34. N. Schofield, "Party Competition in a Spatial Model of Coalition Formation," in *Political Economy: Institutions, Competition, and Representation,* ed. W. Barnett et al. (Cambridge: Cambridge University Press, 1993).

35. K. A. Shepsle ably summarizes this literature in *Models of Multiparty Electoral Competition* (Chur, Switzerland: Harwood, 1991).

36. Condorcet, *Essai*

37. K. Ladha, "Condorcet's Jury Theorem, Free Speech, and Correlated Votes," *American Journal of Political Science* 36 (1992): 617–34.

38. K. Ladha and N. Schofield, "Comparison of Two-Party Competitive Models Based on Maximization of Expected Value and Win Probability," in preparation, Center in Political Economy, Washington University,

39. J. Enelow and M. Hinich, *The Spatial Theory of Voting* (Cambridge: Cambridge University Press, 1984); P. Coughlin, *Probabilistic Voting* (Cambridge: Cambridge University Press, 1994).

40. K. Poole and H. Rosenthal, "Patterns of Congressional Voting," *American Journal of Political Science* 35 (1991): 228–78.

41. Schofield and Tovey, "Probability and Convergence."

42. N. Schofield, "Multiparty Electoral Politics," forthcoming in *Perspectives on Public Choice,* ed. D. Mueller (Cambridge: Cambridge University Press); R. Taagepera and M. S. Shugart, *Seats and Votes* (New Haven: Yale University Press, 1989).

43. See M. Laver and N. Schofield, *Multiparty Government* (Oxford: Oxford University Press, 1990); N. Schofield, "Multiparty Electoral Politics."

44. I. Budge, D. Robertson, and D. Hearl, eds., *Ideology, Strategy, and Party Change* (Cambridge: Cambridge University Press, 1987); M. Laver and I. Budge, eds., *Party Policy and Government Coalitions* (New York: St. Martin's Press, 1992).

45. N. Schofield and J. Wada, "Bargaining in the Liberal Democratic Party of Japan," forthcoming in *Social Choice and Political Economy,* ed. N. Schofield (Dordrecht: Kluwer-Nijhoff).

46. M. Olson, "Stagflation and the Political Economy of the Decline in Productivity," *American Economic Review: Papers and Proceedings* 72 (1982): 143–48; M. Olson, "The Political Economy of Comparative

Growth Rates," in *The Political Economy of Growth,* ed. D. C. Mueller (New Haven: Yale University Press, 1982); M. Olson, *The Rise and Decline of Nations* (New Haven: Yale University Press, 1982).

47. S. Beer, *Britain against Itself* (London: Faber and Faber, 1982).

48. A. Denzau and R. Parks, "Existence of Voting-Market Equilibria," *Journal of Economic Theory* 30 (1983): 243–65.

49. L. C. Thurow, *The Zero-Sum Society* (New York: Basic Books, 1980).

50. B. R. Weingast, "A Rational Choice Perspective on Congressional Norms," *American Journal of Political Science* 23 (1979): 345–63.

51. G. Lehmbruch, "Consociational Democracy, Class Conflict, and the New Corporatism," in *Trends towards Corporatist Intermediation,* ed. P. C. Schmitter and G. Lehmbruch (London and Beverly Hills: Sage, 1980); A. Lijphart, *The Politics of Consociational Democracies* (Berkeley: University of California Press, 1976).

52. C. Crouch, "The Conditions for Trade Union Wage Restraint," in *The Politics of Inflation and Economic Stagnation: Theoretical Approaches and International Case Studies,* ed. L. N. Lindberg and C. S. Maier (Washington: Brookings Institution, 1985).

53. *The Economist,* July 15, 1995. Volume 336, number 7923.

4

INSTITUTIONS AND INTERCURRENCE: THEORY BUILDING IN THE FULLNESS OF TIME

KAREN ORREN AND STEPHEN SKOWRONEK

Theorizing about political institutions has taken as its central task the explanation of order and regularity over time. The rationale for this seems so straightforward as to appear almost definitional. Institutions persist through time, organizing politics into something more than a seamless flow of activities and events. Carrying forward objectives instilled in them at their time of origin, they infuse their environments with durable norms and predictable rules of action.

There is no denying that without institutions stability and continuity would be in short supply. The task of uncovering the historical patterns that institutions establish is a vital one. Our contention, however, is that political scientists have cast their theories too narrowly upon these premises, missing the great paradox inherent in the ordering capacities of institutions. The very tendency of institutions to persist means that at any moment in time several different sets of rules and norms are likely to be operating simultaneously.[1] To the extent that the idea of order presumes institutions synchronized with one another, entailing their creation all at once, something unlikely to be accomplished by even the most radical revolution. These insights take on special significance in the case of political institutions, because political institutions are inherently other-directed; that is, they seek to control individuals or other institutions outside their own sphere.[2] As a consequence, different institutional rules and norms will abut and grate as a normal state of affairs.

The durability of institutional purposes, the nonsimultaneity of institutional origins, and the other-directedness of political action all serve to complicate our identification of institutions with order and to problematize the temporal dimension of politics generally. These attributes of political institutions suggest a picture in which the boundaries that have traditionally separated the study of political order from the study of political change are dissolved and the passage of time is filled with contentious interactions among different ordering arrangements. Such a perspective directs the analyst to the disjointed character of political development and to the tensions among relatively independent institutional orderings as these become formative of political action at any given moment. As the traditional study of order and regularity gives way, this "new institutionalism" illuminates sustained and ingrained asymmetries in the organization of civic power, a political landscape riddled with incongruities and subject to continuous friction among its various components.

In place of the concept of a "political system"—an integrated whole in which institutions work together, more or less well, to meet demands from their environment—we posit a political universe organized and activated by intercurrence—engagements throughout the polity of the different norms embedded in institutions, the terms of control contested, more or less intensely, in the ongoing push and pull among them. By adopting the term "intercurrence" for political analysis, we do not mean to suggest a pathological condition. Discordant standards, each with its own institutional foundation, will be acted upon at the same time as a matter of course, their meaning and future development shaped by their impingements and oppositions. As political actors, inside and outside of institutions, manipulate, elaborate, and oppose the norms and procedures at hand to achieve their ends, they amplify the dissonances inherent in the institutional organization of political space. In this way, the intercurrence of different ordering arrangements becomes the medium of change through time.

At the risk of trivializing what we see as a pervasive and often subtle determinant of politics, we might reference some of the more glaring incongruities that have shaped American political development: the enforcement of ancient, common-law rules under the new, market-oriented constitutions of the post-Revolutionary era; the constitutional incorporation of slavery within a regime of personal liberties; the development of mass-based parties alongside a pre-democratic Constitution premised on their absence; the emergence of an integrated national economy within a federalized system of economic regulation; the expansion of national administrative controls through a Congress organized to protect localities. Among the prominent abrasions at work today are patriarchal prerogatives in the family against a profusion of legal rights in other spheres and the claims of national sovereignty against the realities of international business. All of these call attention to the multiple orders that comprise the institutional firmament and activate the polity.

The particular multiplicities mentioned no doubt would be admitted and each attributed to historical circumstance. Coming to terms with the analytic implications of their describing a normal state of affairs, however, requires more than the ritual acknowledgment of the historical character of institutions. What remains to be confronted is the institutional character of history. To this point, the theoretical program of explaining order and regularity has been sustained by holding historical sensibilities in abeyance and tying political analysis to extra-institutional assumptions about the wholeness of systems and the homeostatic character of change. To the extent that they associate institutional politics with "normal politics" and "politics in equilibrium," these efforts have preempted a forthright assessment of the distinctive way in which institutions organize time and space.

To illustrate the problems we see inherent in theories of politics that rely on extra-institutional assumptions, we will examine two strategies current in political science for dealing with questions of order and change in the American context. They are first, the periodizing of whole system dynamics, and second, the modeling of regularities within particular institutional settings. These are not exclusive strategies; we recognize that some researchers have attempted to combine their insights.[3] But integrating the different conceptions of institutional politics already extant is no substitute for further theoretical advance. Proceeding by way of critique, we take up in parts I and II work in which leading exponents of each approach have wrestled with the problem of history in institutional analysis and have articulated a case for the concepts used to deal with it. We point to ways in which a presumption of intercurrence would reconceptualize the particular problems they engage, and we suggest more broadly how theories built on this premise might, in many instances, constructively supersede those that presume temporal order and institutional regularity. The old saw that institutions must be understood in their historical context will yield here to the more fundamental truth that in any complex society each institution will, to some extent, have its own history.[4] We conclude in part III by describing what we call "the fullness of time" and distinguishing "historical institutionalism" as the program best suited to analyzing it through the elaboration of theories of intercurrence.

I. Ordered Systems: The Pitfalls of Periodization

The most explicit method of addressing questions of political order over time has been to periodize. Here the division of history into discrete eras or blocks of years becomes the premise for analyzing the subdivisions according to principles said to order them. In the words of historian Martin Sklar, periodization establishes "the ground of coherence and objective inquiry" in history.[5] For reasons that will become apparent, we do not follow Sklar in the assertion that periodization is "no different" in its proper application from theory in the physical sciences. We agree with him, however, that it is a valuable method of empirical inquiry in the social sciences and will continue to do a major share of the constructive theoretical work in political science. By relating order *to* time, periodization schemes lay a foundation for theorizing about the role of temporality in political life. The critical question lies in how we go about employing this method and the claims we draw from it.

The utility of periodization for the study of institutions has been diminished unnecessarily, we believe, by a failure to distinguish between two distinct analytic moves, each involving a separate ordering principle. The first move entails separating history into discernable periods ordered sequentially according to a principle of division seen to motivate an institution or set of institutions over time. The principle of division may imply cycles (party alignments, presidential regimes, constitutional moments), or it may imply linear progression (state-building, liberal development, the consolidation of capitalism), or both. This principle might be self-consciously elaborated or all but implicit. Indeed, one might argue that this periodization move is made whenever social scientists speak of something as being "pre" or "post" (as in "pre-Revolutionary" or "post-New Deal"), or "early" or "modern" (as in "early Republic" or "modern presidency").

The second move entails describing politics within divisions or periods according to a principle of synthesis seen to distinguish one period from another. The principle of synthesis may be closely tied within the scheme to the principle of division—"liberalism," or the "modern presidency"—where features attributable to the institutions in question also demarcate the period; or this move might be substantively independent, as are the different historical motifs of various "party systems." Insofar as principles of synthesis identify themes or conditions that constrain institutions and actions in the period in question, they are unexceptionable if not indispensable, and in any case are consistent with the basic rationale of dividing up time in the first place. However, typically they take on wider proportions, with the objective of demonstrating the coherence and cohesiveness of the political system as a whole. That is to say, we use periodization schemes as if they are paradigms in a natural science, testing their value by how much more of the data known about a period they can explain or synthesize than can alternative schemes. This procedure has the effect of encapsulating time within periods, as institutions come to be treated as bulwarks supporting the premise of this synthetic temporal order, and the analysis of the politics of the period is placed on some extra-institutional ground of thematic unity.

To illustrate, consider the periodization of party realignments, arguably the leading conceptual picture of American political development.[6] A foremost architect of this paradigm, Walter Dean Burnham, has written that these realignments "involve constitutional readjustments in the broadest sense of the term," influencing both the "grand institutional structures of American government" and "the roles played by institutional elites."[7] When taken to task by the historian Richard L. McCormick for overstating the explanatory range of the "system of 1896" and thereby ignoring very different determinants of politics in the Progressive era,[8] Burnham responded forcefully. The purpose of a periodization scheme, he claimed, is to exploit its synthetic possibilities:

> Any periodization scheme is or implies a schedule of priorities. It is or implies a set of generalizations which order the infinite mass of available data, and provide some clues as to their relative significance. Ultimately, the periodization scheme permits the telling of a causal story about collective human affairs which could not be told without it. But there are many possible stories one might tell. The key issues about any given causal story are, first, whether it is inherently credible at all, and second, assuming that it has some credibility, whether it is to be preferred to another story with legitimate truth claims of its own.
>
> There really are two alternatives here, assuming that a causal story which purports to prioritize, explain, and therefore, suggest useful research programs is already before the court of professional opinion. The first of these is to propose an alternative story as an ordering, integrating device superior to the one currently under review. The second is to assert with full radicalness, that everything flows, everything is change, or in short, that history is one damned thing after another.[9]

The choice Burnham presents—between maximum possible analytic unity and one damned thing after another—is, as we shall see, not unique to advocates of periodization. As appealing as the prospect of analytic unity may be, and however daunting the prospect of capitulating to the view that everything flows and everything is change, we contend that neither of these alternatives allows for what a distinctly institutional view of history has to offer. In particular, neither points to the operation of several relatively stable configurations of rules and meanings in constant communication with the environment around them but nonetheless distinguishable from that environment and from one another. Both selections in Burnham's choice—synthesis and seamless flow—are at odds, in other words, with intercurrence, with a conception in which political institutions hold the formative or fundamental position in politics.

Analysis anchored in a more distinctly institutional conception of history would move social science away from the notion of synthesis toward a paradigm that engages several periodization schemes at once, each exposing a different institutional element in play in the politics of the moment. Used in this way, periodization schemes are not contestants for the prize of most powerful ordering device, but emerge rather as different components of an analysis that exposes the push and pull among diverse institutional orderings. Notice that neither the party alignment scheme nor similar ordering devices are discarded here; they remain essential parts of such an analysis. But the overall view of politics is no longer that of an integrated order punctuated periodically by radical change. Rather, it is one of multiple and disjointed orderings that overlay one another, with the interplay among them breaking down the period-bound distinction between order and change.

This alternative picture is already evident in much of the recent political-historical work in which institutions figure prominently. Besides our own efforts[10] Tulis has traced the origins of modern presidential politics to an overlay of Wilsonian plebiscitary politics upon older norms of constitutionalism.[11] Balogh has disaggregated the "organizational synthesis" of progressive politics to expose the disjointed and incomplete implementation of principles of bureaucratic organization over the course of the twentieth century.[12] Polsky has described the travails of the juvenile court system in the persistent collision between rules of the old judicial establishment and rules of the new institutions of social work.[13] Finegold and Skocpol have reinterpreted the New Deal political reconstruction,[14] rooting the different outcomes of reform in industrial affairs, labor affairs, and agricultural affairs in the divergent prior histories of policy in each sphere.[15]

But if an alternative to ordered systems can be found in a variety of specific historical and institutional settings, the advantage of this general approach to institutional analysis must ultimately be determined, as Burnham says, by its ability to tell a causal story that better explains what is observed. To elaborate the case for intercurrence, we will set up a small test on Burnham's own ground, the electoral realignment of 1896. Let us accept for purposes of discussion his thesis that by providing fewer competitive electoral districts, by dividing the parties sharply along sectional lines, and by virtually guaranteeing the northern Republican party control of the entire federal apparatus this alignment contributed mightily to the corporate consolidation of American capitalism. Let us also agree, as a platform for our divergent perspectives, that in 1911 the Supreme Court removed the single most important obstacle to this consolidation when it ruled in the *Standard Oil* case that the Sherman Anti-Trust Act, passed by Congress in 1890, prior to the realignment, forbade all but only unreasonable restraints of trade.

The question, analytically speaking, is how to regard the Court's actions. From the perspective of period synthesis, the decision of 1911 was as predictable as it was monumental, for it at once completed the logic of the system of 1896 and created institutional support for the new ordering principle. Burnham credits this interpretation himself. He cites approvingly the work of Martin Sklar, mentioned earlier, whose study of the corporate reconstruction of American capitalism highlights the importance of the Court's 1911 decision. Having long contended that the critical realignment synthesis offered parsimonious, credible, and useful periodization of subjects with which scholars (especially historians) must deal, Burnham points to Sklar's "comparatively grounded, state-centered analysis of American politics" as a contribution to this synthetic project.[16]

Is this persuasive? From a multiple-orders perspective, there is a good deal more action here than the judiciary's consolidation of a prior political decision. Rather than elaborate the synthetic idea, the historical institutionalist would underscore the "anomalous" situation from 1896 until 1911, during which time the Supreme Court actively imposed a reading of the Sherman Act that was hostile to the principles of the new party system. Sklar recounts that in 1897, in its first major interpretation of the Act, the Court ruled that *all* restraints of trade were illegal, and it persisted in that line of argument until a new majority formed in 1911 to overturn it. "The corporate reorganization of the economy," he observes, "went forward within the framework of an incongruent legal order," and "this legal incongruity directly translated itself into a political conflict that became central to national politics."[17]

Of course, the mere fact that the Supreme Court continued for fifteen years to interpret the major statute on the central issue of the period as designated by the party system in a manner contrary to that same system's purported logic is not itself fatal to a synthetic view. Burnham might well allow for a long and complicated institutional adjustment to the new ordering principle established by the system of 1896. Still, it does not appear on the record that in imposing its own view of the Sherman Act the Court was an uncertain laggard, awkwardly trying to regain its bearings in a new political environment. The Court, on the contrary, played a decidedly unsynthetic role as an aggressive and formative institutional player, its majority developing new doctrines to justify its position.

Nor did time simply "pass," neutral in its effects, until the Court came around. Indeed, the issue is fully joined when we observe the destabilizing effect of the Court's interim behavior on the party system itself. Following the Court's 1897 ruling, as Sklar details, both Republican presidents and Republican majorities in Congress scrambled to produce the needed clarification of the Sherman Act. Their failure in the face of judicial independence to agree on a solution, moreover, put such pressure on the new governing coalition that by 1911, when the Court finally fell into (would-be) line, Republicans in the other branches were a spent force as a governing instrument. Already in 1910, the issue of corporate consolidation had fractured the coalition seen analytically to have ushered it in, giving way to resurgent Democrats and insurgent Progressives who were avowed enemies of corporate consolidation.

The attempt by a Democratic president and Congress to refortify the 1890 Sherman Act against the Court's 1911 decision with the 1914 Clayton Anti-Trust Act did not halt the reconstruction of American capitalism. But neither did it merely extend the reform path already paved.[18] Just as surely as the Court ultimately conformed to the logic of the party system of 1896, it had by then transformed that system and redirected its course. Reform was not conducted or contained by a single period logic but contested by different ordering principles and at least two logics, each situated in a different institutional sphere. Actions taken in one sphere impinged and folded in upon the other, altering both in the process.

Were there no accounting for the specifics of this push and pull, such an interpretation might well throw the analysis of politics back into the seamless flow of "one damn thing after another." There are, however, some obvious institutional factors at work that make the outcome predictable, and in regarding them, we stand to gain a clearer picture of the seams and fissures that institutions introduce into the relationship between order and change. In this instance, each factor refers back to the Court's distinctive institutional characteristics, independent of the 1896 election: an ideological disposition in favor of precapitalist business by judges trained in an earlier era; an adherence by a rule-bound judiciary to the rule that clear legislative declarations overrode common law standards; and the relative imperviousness of life-time appointees to electoral realignments.

One or all of these might be at work here; our point is that each resists the notion of a synchronized order that coheres until it is replaced by another. In this case, as elsewhere, we have been too prone to resolve "anomalies" discovered in trying to synthesize politics around one ordering principle by ignoring institutional patterns tied to different ordering principles. Instead of filling in Burnham's story line, intercurrence tells a different story. The "anomalies" refer to distinctly institutional features of politics, features essential to any explanation of how one gets from one point in the period to another. To understand the sequence of events, it is necessary to disassemble the period; to examine the patterns and tempos of separate institutions, including the social conflict swirling around them; and to analyze the interactions of these separate spheres over time.

In fairness, explaining movement between realignments is not Burnham's aim. He merely projects how what we have called a principle of division, party realignment, might be joined to a principle of synthesis, the "corporate reconstruction of American capitalism." Therefore it is instructive to consider another effort at periodizing order and change that he regards as in substantial "consilience" with his own, the work of constitutional scholar Bruce Ackerman.[19] As his principle of division, Ackerman employs a distinction between "constitutional politics" and "normal politics" that yields three "constitutional moments" (1789, 1866, 1933), moments of popular transformation of government that partly parallel Burnham's five party systems, and three intervals or periods of "normal politics," in which institutions carry out the will of the people as expressed in their last clear act of constitutional redirection. Where Ackerman would seem to add most to Burnham's scheme, then, is in his analysis of synthetic politics within periods, his "closing the ring"—to use Burnham's own assessment—"between the Supreme Court and the rest of the political order."[20]

For Ackerman, whose empirical focus is the Supreme Court, synthesis refers to more than a system-wide theme or project but rather to the actual process of interpretation through which members of the Court superimpose and reconcile through adjudication the various principles laid down by "we, the people" at critical constitutional moments. Thus, for instance, in one of several high-wire acts of synthesis he attributes to the Court, Ackerman reads *Lochner v. N.Y.* as the Court's reconciling equal protection under the Fourteenth Amendment (period 2) with the Founders' solicitude for private property (period 1). Likewise, *Brown v. Board of Education* demonstrates period 2's aim of racial equality, now reinterpreted according to New Deal–style activist government called for by "we, the people" in period 3.

Ackerman's analysis breaks new ground by building into the Court's interpretive processes the multiple orders and temporal overlaps that in our view infuse institutional—that is to say, political—life, and in particular the judiciary's engagement both with other government institutions and the electorate. More notably still, Ackerman's principles of synthesis, separately applied to the many complex domains of the Court's jurisdiction, reflect backward and forward on one another in different historical contexts, motivated by identifiable institutional actors. But while he incorporates subtle historical crosscurrents into his analysis of how the Court goes about synthesizing the politics of different periods, his basic commitment to demonstrating synthesis within periods dictates a radically truncated explanation of the historical process itself. When he lays out the "path of the law" that leads from one point in the Court's historical jurisprudence to another, the intricate edifice of institutionalism he has constructed gives way, and the argument is placed on the steeper planes of a priori categories.

Ackerman takes his rendering of constitutional history—of "constitutional" moments and the principles of synthesis in-between—as his starting point and contends that the Court has in fact arrived at decisions consistent with his scheme. What he forgoes is any concrete explanation of how the rules and procedures of the Court, either separately or together with the institutions around it, produced the results observed. Consider in this regard his description of how period 2's commitment to equal protection is transformed from its particularized racial interpretation in the *Slaughterhouse Cases* to its generalized protection of contract and property in *Lochner:*

> Think of the American Republic as a railroad train, with judges of the middle republic sitting in the caboose, looking backward. What they see are the mountains and valleys of dualistic constitutional experience, most notably the peaks of constitutional meaning elaborated during the Founding and Reconstruction. As the train moves forward in history, it is harder for the judges to see the traces of volcanic ash that marked each mountain's political emergence onto the legal landscape. At the same time, a different perspective becomes more available: As the second mountain moves into the background, it becomes easier to see that there is now a mountain range out there that can be described in a comprehensive way.

This changing perspective is intended to explain the shift from particularistic to comprehensive synthesis. Old judges die, and new ones are sent to the caboose by the engineers who happen then to be in the locomotive. The new judges' views of the landscape are shaped by their own previous experiences in life and in the law, as well as by new vistas constantly opened up of the mountains as the train proceeds, rearlong, into the future.[21]

No doubt this metaphor conveys important truths about how Court doctrine changes over time. But as an account of "normal politics"—and there is nothing more systematic offered than this—it leaves much to be explained, and on reflection, it offers less hope than Burnham thought for "closing the ring" on the analysis of order within periods. It might be recalled, for example, that at the very time that the Court observed the synthetic rule of free contract in *Lochner,* it was insisting upon a rigid reading of the Sherman Act that radically restrained business' contractual freedom. In fact, the majority opinion in both *Lochner* and in *Trans-Missouri Freight Association,* the 1897 decision denying that the common-law rule of reason mitigated legislative strictures of anti-trust, were written by the same Justice, Rufus Peckham. Again, the point is not that there are no arguments available to reconcile these positions: the Court may have exhibited deference to national statutes at the same time it resisted state statutes; it could have adhered to common law in matters of master-servant and bowed to legislation in matters of commerce; perhaps Peckham, one of Grover Cleveland's three appointees on the Court, saw both decisions as supporting a constitutional preference for laissez faire of an older individualist variety. The point is, even if one were to stay with Ackerman's picture of cabooses, an actual explanation would require more than one institutional track, perhaps another landscape, and likely also a switching station or two.

It is not incidental that Ackerman's purposes include refuting the idea that the Supreme Court has acted as an independently creative institution—a "counter-majoritarian" force—in American politics. Thus his interpretation of *Brown.* To the extent that periodization schemes provide a basis for subordinating distinctive institutional logics to system-wide principles of order based on external directives, they are likely to convey just such a message. On the other hand, if periodization is used to illuminate the manner in which different institutions proceed, according to their own rules, in their own cycles and at their own rates, it will become apparent how the intersections and collisions among institutions form the substance of any individual political episode. Based on the assumption of multiple, disjointed institutions, any given periodization becomes an entry point into many others, and the key to political analysis becomes conjuncture not synthesis, timing not order.

II. Simplicity Itself: The Science of Modeling Through

Among the different branches of rational choice theory flourishing in the social sciences, the positive theory of institutions (PTI) may be distinguished for its attention to the organization of political space. In this respect, PTI would seem to offer a remedy for many of the shortcomings we have identified in simple periodization schemes. Instead of fitting the operations of the various parts of the political system to some historically delimited principle said to underlie the whole, PTI examines the parts, seeking to uncover their separately structured logics of action. Applied broadly to different political institutions operating simultaneously, such an approach might be expected to reveal the systemic incongruities, frictions and inefficiencies that characterize politics in time.

But while PTI may generate a picture of the political universe not unlike the one we propose, it is not at all clear that it can follow through. The difficulty is in fitting this picture to an appropriate corresponding conception of change or development without at the same time rendering the theory itself a fairly empty shell. Like all rational choice theories, PTI is an equilibrium theory, committed to the familiar conception of change as episodic and homeostatic—a momentary transition between stable states—precisely the conception called into question by the discovery of ingrained asymmetries in the institutional organization of political space as a whole. The problem is notable because rational choice theorists came to the study of institutions out of a felt need to shore up their theory against what it was telling them about the inherently elusive character of equilibria in politics.[22] We suspect that PTI's program will not serve to bolster its major theoretical premise but to direct attention to empirical investigations that further undermine it. Be that as it may, the integrity of the theory seems to rest at present on alternative extraneous conceits: either that particular institutional regularities can be abstracted from the larger institutional universe and modeled in isolation, or that some single institution (usually the Congress) is the prime mover of the system, to which the operations of the whole are geared.[23]

Analytic power purchased in this way comes as a cost to empirical plausibility even higher than that extracted by the ordering of periodization schemes. Both approaches sustain a program of explaining regularity, and both do so by moving away from a distinctly institutional conception of history; but they move in opposite directions. Unlike simple periodization schemes, PTI does not aim to encapsulate time in comprehensive period syntheses; rather, it effectively removes time from particular historical contexts. Time passes in the sequential play of a game, which may be replayed in dispersed historical episodes. Instead of trying to explain as much as possible within a period—spatially, as it were, across diverse institutions—with reference to a central ordering principle, these theorists seek to "specify the 'objective function' of agents in a way that is separable from the context of decision."[24] In its most ambitious and arresting applications, then, rational choice modeling offers explanations for relatively timeless and spaceless regularities, for "stylized facts," and shows these tied to abstract logics of institutional structure.

Launching a theory of institutional politics on such an ahistorical platform runs certain inevitable risks. On the one side, explanations of particular episodes of interest will be hard pressed not to import their organization of time and space from outside the model, relying on conventional historical accounts. In that case, theory verges on rhetoric, adding little more than ingenious argumentation for the proposition that political actors are rational and behave strategically. On the other side, the promise of generalization, of taming the facticity of institutional politics by a set of universalizing analytic tools, risks the same result in reverse. Conceiving temporal and spatial relationships in terms of isolated institutions, with the object of translating diverse historical materials into the details of a generalizable game form, threatens to remove theory so far from the historical episodes in question that it becomes difficult to determine what if anything of an empirical nature has been explained.[25]

But is it possible to steer a middle course? How broad is that middle range in which rational choice theory might illuminate the institutional organization of time and space? Let us consider these questions with reference to three widely cited articles by Morris Fiorina on the legislative choice of regulatory forms.[26] These articles use rational choice models to explore the inception and persistence of an important pattern in policy making and political development: Congress's propensity, since 1887, to establish administrative agencies rather than lay down clear legislative standards of regulation to be enforced by the courts. Putting positive theory at its most elegant up against institutional history at its most formative, they offer a self-conscious review of the challenge posed by a theory that conflates rather than discriminates among historical contexts. Cautioning us to "proceed against a backdrop of historical awareness," to recognize structural changes in the Congress over time, Fiorina suggests that useful theory will take in just the right amount of history: a model "which ignores the details of the legislative process may be inherently incapable of enlightening us about legislative outcomes, and a model which incorporates too much detail may provide a good accounting of the Occupational Safety and Health Act of 1970 but not of the Federal Communications Act of 1934, or the Interstate Commerce Act of 1887."[27]

The tensions between history and theory, between the welter of detail and the world of generalization, are resolved through the construction of simple causal models, connecting individual calculations in rule-bound settings to patterned policy effects. Thus, in expounding upon how different concentrations of congressional winners and losers will effect a given legislator's choice of regulatory form, Fiorina affirms that "reasonably simple models can produce relatively general statements about various patterns, trends and other regularities in the politics of regulation."[28] Similarly, in arguing that support and opposition to given regulatory forms under conditions of uncertainty will be affected by how advantageously a legislator is situated to influence commission behavior in the future, Fiorina avers as to how such a "simple and obvious abstract proposition suggests an array of empirical relationships when interpreted in light of various features of the American political system."[29] Much as Burnham warned us against analytic capitulation to the seamless flow of events, Fiorina lays down a stern challenge to political scientists who "continue to argue that it all depends on some critical incident or personality": "they will have to shoulder the blame" when others "continue to ask what political science has to say about regulatory policy."[30]

Like Burnham's, Fiorina's challenge may be best answered against the historical record, for therein, we believe, lies the test of its merits as a framework for understanding institutional politics. Focusing on the case of the Interstate Commerce Commission (ICC), we propose to do this in somewhat greater depth than with periodization schemes. Unlike the latter, which serve mainly to organize and reinterpret political history, rational choice accounts reconstrue history at its presumed sources in strategic action. This places a heavy burden on getting the story right, lest the empirical gain from modeling be not just negligible but negative. It is important, however, to stress that the questions in our evaluation are not quibbles about whether a given detail is included or emphasized over some other. We are concerned here with fundamentals, with rational choice taken on its own terms: we ask whether a regularity of historical outcomes—an empirical question itself—may be understood plausibly in terms of a regularity of behavior—another empirical question—seen to be its cause; and whether historical material may be approached as a repository of examples to prove models that presume, a priori, not only the specific content of both causes and outcomes, but also the dynamic that relates the two.

Fiorina models two regularities: an outcome or developmental result—the proliferation of commission forms of regulation, understood as one regulatory design picked by Congress over a competing design of direct statutory prohibitions and penalties enforceable directly through the courts; and a behavior seen to produce it—the tendency on the part of reelection-seeking Congressmen to select the commission form (or not) under the institutional conditions specified. To explain their connection, he recommends a variation on another model in which Congressmen from single member districts attempt to make policy choices in order to maximize the probability of their reelection. This is the "shift the responsibility" (SR) model: if a member of Congress expects the net effects from regulation to be negative on her district, she will prefer delegation to an administrative agency over laws to be enforced by courts, since the former choice lowers the costs of regulation that constituents will attribute to legislative action. Again, the virtue of simplicity: the SR model "provides a simple explanation for such seemingly perverse phenomena as overwhelming support for patently inefficient government activities," including regulation by administrative commission.[31]

Let us begin with the core assumption of reelection-seeking Congressmen. Minding Fiorina's caution concerning the "backdrop of historical awareness" evokes the following: because of the relative prominence of party organization and the intense level of party competition within districts during the period of the passage of the Interstate Commerce Act (ICA), there was a high rate of turnover of seats in the House, i.e., in that chamber whose members were the only single-member district election seekers in the situation. Another, constitutional feature of the time was that Congress went on with its business for a full year until members chosen in the previous election were seated. This meant that some portion of the membership during the interim session would have been defeated and serving as lame ducks. These are straightforward historical conditions, well within the institutional bounds set by the SR model; yet going no farther than this, theory and history will be seen to have diverged so far that the former can be sustained only by discarding the latter altogether as "too much detail."

Consider this divergence with direct reference to the Interstate Commerce Act, rightfully identified by Fiorina as a watershed event in need of explanation. When the final House bill on the Commerce Act was voted upon, for example, in the summer before the 1886 fall elections, 104 or 32 percent of the House members were not candidates for reelection. And, in early 1887, when a total of 318 members of the House voted upon acceptance of the conference bill that instituted the ICC, there were 100 or 31.4 percent who were retirees and another 28 or 8.8 percent who were lame ducks. In other words, when the ICA was adopted, a full 40 percent voting were not members rationally choosing anything based on calculations of their possible upcoming reelection to the House. Furthermore, an analysis of House votes on the same conference bill shows that the choice made by members who were not reelected, and who therefore lacked the incentives postulated by the model, differed in no significant way from the choice of members who were.[32]

Nor does the SR model's assumptions concerning the regularity of the commission form and its selection in the ICA fare better against the record of events. What is striking about the legislative history of the ICA is that in 1886, on the last vote of the House on its railroad bill, the commission form was rejected by a majority of House members, who are, again, the only actors elected by the single-member districts contemplated in the model. Instead, the form of legislative standards and court enforcement was chosen by the House majority, just as it had been repeatedly endorsed by the House from the time of its first presentation in the Reagan bill in 1878. By contrast, the only occasion on which the commission form was ever supported by the House majority was in the vote on the conference bill in 1887, when the choice was between commission regulation and no regulation at all, and when the compromise also contained an express prohibition against pooling, a paramount goal of the forces behind the Reagan bill. True, the SR model does not predict the commission form will always be chosen by single-member district representatives; it only specifies the conditions under which it will be the choice. However, in the case that set the historical pattern at issue in the model there is no connection demonstrable between the regularity to be explained, delegation to commission, and the regularity claimed to explain it, blame shifting by single-member district representatives.

An awareness of this absence of fit between theory and history may have been what prompted Fiorina in a subsequent article to concentrate on the institution of the Senate, which in 1886 selected the Cullom bill, providing for railroad regulation by commission, over court-enforced legislative standards, with this choice incorporated into the final version of the ICA.[33] Here Fiorina develops the idea of uncertainty and suggests how legislators resolve elements of indecision about which regulatory form to choose, given various positions of support and opposition relative to the preferences of the chamber as a whole. In an effort to identify factors that "might bear a systematic relationship to distance from the legislative median and to optimism and pessimism about agency enforcement," he hypothesizes that institutional structures, such as committees and the like, will be an important determinant. For the Senate, he concentrates on the future role of senators in advising and consenting to commission appointees: those legislators who expect to be in the majority party will be more inclined, other things being equal, to support commission forms of regulation. With specific regard to the passage of the ICA he remarks: "One wonders whether Reagan's forces in the House would have opposed commission enforcement so intensely had they been the majority that would advise and consent to commission appointments."[34]

Again, a test of this hypothesis against the empirical rather than "stylized" facts of the case deepens doubts that the Senate's action may be plausibly analyzed as one instance in a regular pattern described. When the Cullom bill was voted by the Senate in 1886, it received overwhelming support from both parties, including Democrats, who were the minority. (Republicans supported the bill 26–0, Democrats 20–4; with 26 senators, split between the parties, not voting.) Now, conceivably, Democratic senators might be looking to the upcoming elections and holding out hopes of soon becoming members of the majority party, a possible calculation in the spirit of Fiorina's hypothesis. Therefore, the vote on the conference bill, after the election, with Democrats knowing for certain that they will be in the minority, is even more interesting. This time, the Republicans voted to reject (recommit) the final compromise establishing the ICC by a vote of 20–16, while Democrats voted to accept it (i.e., by a vote against recommittal) by a majority of 21–5.

To be sure, the conference did not present a pure test of the choice of commission form, for it also contained the outright prohibition against pooling that was anathema to some Republicans in the Senate. What the voting pattern, in both the House and the Senate, suggests is that pooling, rather than support or opposition to the commission form, may have been the deciding issue, and that the commission form rode into history on the back of Congress's stronger preference for a court-enforceable standard. This, of course, would be a very different history from the one modeled, but, notably, it is one that does not stray from data entirely within the congressional arena where Fiorina would confine it. Furthermore, this different history supports two claims in our brief for "intercurrence." One is that institutional consequences are often unintended, in the sense that they result from institutional motives, principles, and causes not plausibly deduced without specific historical investigation. Second is that this mix of institutional motives becomes part of the design of new institutions, which carry forward these rival conceptions in their own functioning. In the case of the ICA, the contradiction between commission form and legislative standards enforced by courts characterized the ICC's controversial career from then on.

At this point, our assessment touches even more basic issues: what reason is there to suppose that the prominence of commission forms in American regulatory history, or even the tendency of Congress to adopt commission forms, can be usefully explained by hypotheses that pertain solely to Congress's rules and behavior—without reference to the presidency, the courts, the regulatory commissioners, the groups regulated, the party system, not only as these appear in the perceptions of maximizing congressmen but as these institutions acted independently, overruling and upending the plans of congressional majorities? Taking into account only the role of the Supreme Court, for instance, there arises the prior question of which institution, Congress or the Court, should be considered the prime mover in the story of the ICA. In 1886, the Court voided all state regulation of interstate commerce; by 1898, it had gutted most of the duties assigned to the Interstate Commerce Commission; and it was the Court in 1910, not the Congress, that established the precedent of judicial deference to Commission decisions.

Or, at another level, what constitutes the episode of choosing? The actions the Congress actually took in creating the ICC suggest an institutional calculus very different from that which Fiorina's models outline. Congress specifically did not, for example, make a choice between regulation and court enforced standards in 1887. Section 9 of the original ICA provided that any party aggrieved under the Act might appeal either to the ICC or to any district or circuit court in the United States. Furthermore, when it became clear that commissioners as well as railroads had a different understanding of the strictures of the ICA, Congress moved to impose and strengthen both standards and penalties. In 1903, for example, Congress passed the Elkins Act against rebating, providing criminal penalties in addition to the qualified and non-criminal prohibitions in the original ICA, all independently enforceable in court. In 1910, the Mann-Elkins Act similarly re-outlawed pooling; and as a result of the Supreme Court's acquiescence in the railroads' ignoring the long-and-short haul clause against the orders of the Commission, Congress in Mann-Elkins also struck out the vague language that had vitiated its force.

Searching for alternative explanations for the ICA in keeping with our inter-institutional approach, we would propose that if Congress was in important respects a different institution in this period than it later became, then the same may well have been true of the other institutions implicated in Fiorina's model. Thus, perhaps the increasingly independent mood of the late-century judiciary toward economic regulation made it reasonable for congressmen to calculate that laying down standards to be enforced in court was an even more thoroughgoing shift of responsibility than delegation to a commission. Here the historicity of the rational calculus presses in with such force that the comparative statics of the choice simply dissolve, and the theory of equilibrium readjustment becomes a hollow metaphor for understanding the politics in play. Instead, we see an extended struggle over railroad regulation, organized by a host of intercurrent tensions among institutions and the political actors arrayed within them. The initial delegation of power to the commission becomes but the opening salvo in what would prove to be decades of institutional pushing and hauling. Far from a contained episode in a relatively timeless game, the creation of the ICC appears as a politically transformative event forcing all the relevant actors to rethink their interests and strategies in a prolonged series of institutional confrontations.

Stepping back from these observations, we might speculate how PTI advocates would answer when confronted with this empirical state of affairs. One response might be to concede, as Fiorina now seems to have done, that the ICA was not a good case for testing.[35] Given that the case in question remains a watershed instance, we would argue that this concession is reason enough to replace timeless models with a new kind of study that addresses particularity as well as fit. A second response could be to object to the manner in which we have tested the hypotheses, and to assert that party position, electoral ambitions, perceived costs and benefits to the district, and so forth must be more subtly transposed upon one another to yield the retrospectively predicted choices of legislators. This move in itself, however, would compel recognition that the processes of legislative choice are not definable in simple models of single institutions but are multi-layered and intercurrent arrangements of causal factors, involving aspects, for example of the two-party system, not deducible from congressional behavior or rules.

A third response might be to say that all of the relevant variables can, eventually, be factored into the rules of the models employed. Fiorina suggests as much himself. In discussing possible extensions of his uncertainty model to account for the question of the breadth (rather than the form) of delegation he offers the following paragraph to explain what seems to have been a shift in recent years in congressmembers' preferences regarding regulation:

> In plain English, a perception of increasing bias in the administrative process coupled with increasingly broad but asymmetric delegations would lead to a decline in support for administration relative to courts. Speculating a bit, as the myth of the disinter-

ested expert died and evidence of agency capture accumulated, congressional support for the traditional administrative process should have weakened. That judicial deference to administration has weakened is well known. Briefly, from the 1940s to the 1960s courts deferred to agencies, checking for adherence to the Administrative Procedures Act (APA) and other pertinent statutes but generally accepting agency decisions so long as they were based on some evidence (not "arbitrary and capricious"). But as some courts came to accept interest-group interpretations of American politics in general, and of regulation in particular, judicial deference to agency expertise began to decline. Analogous developments occurred in Congress. Much of the legislation establishing the "new social regulation" was filled with detailed procedural requirements going far beyond the APA. Congressional majorities encouraged an accessible rulemaking process, sometimes going so far as to subsidize intervenors. And these same majorities provided every opportunity for disgruntled interests to shift the conflict from the administrative arena to the judicial. Though such developments admit various interpretations, they are consistent with legislators trying to counter increasingly evident biases in administrative processes.[36]

Finally prompted to describe how we get from one "episode" to another, Fiorina has sketched a picture of institutional politics much like the one we are advancing as an alternative to PTI. This supplement is apparently offered at the expense of simplicity, not regularity, since Fiorina would encompass it within "p" in his model, that is, congressmember's estimates of the probability of given levels of enforcement by agencies versus courts. We are tempted here to rest our case, and say that if all these relationships can be packed into "p," fine, much of the important analytical work has been accomplished. We are constrained, however, to notice that what remains of the original search for regularity is largely psychology, the rational behavior of legislators when they make choices as against—it is no longer clear what: irrationality? a world in which legislators have no choices? Nor does the baggage now loaded onto this psychological vessel contain a patterned understanding—an order—of any kind. Rather, it exhibits the complex, multi-level, time-bound pushing and hauling among institutions (not to mention the conventional narrative of them), from which rational choice analysis was supposed all along to emancipate our studies.

Given the obstacles to delivering on PTI's promise of simplicity in analyzing institutions in diverse time periods, it comes as no surprise that "thinner" versions of the theory have begun to proliferate that place more weight on historical context. Since we would distinguish this retreat to more complicated, and more familiar, ground from an analytic program that proceeds upon an institutional understanding of history itself, we will (more briefly) consider a recent reconciliation of theory and history attempted by John Ferejohn. In an article entitled "Rationality and Interpretation: Parliamentary Elections in Early Stuart England" Ferejohn confronts head on what he says is sometimes thought, that if rational choice is right, interpretive explanations—by which he means the world as it existed in the minds of actual participants in historical events—must be wrong, and vice versa.[37]

Ferejohn concludes that both approaches are "incomplete." Rational choice analysis (here called "Neo-Whig" for its insistence on the similarities between today's elections and those in the seventeenth century) explains electoral phenomena in the earlier period as the realization of an implicit game form. In this game potential aspirants for office agree to collude (to not contest seats); in this last respect seventeenth-century elections are seen as different from modern ones, but still analogous. On the other hand, such a "rationally reconstructed Whig account," according to Ferejohn,

> lacks any way of selecting which of the many possible equilibria will be played. Indeed, it contains no internal reason to believe that collusive equilibria could be reached or sustained. It does not say who will stand and who will not; it makes no unique prediction as to the level of competition; it is as consistent with high levels of competition as with lower ones.[38]

For these reasons, there is virtue in combining the two accounts:

> There is something in the meanings shared by members of that time and place, in their identities and self-understandings, that make some equilibrium outcomes not just plausible but more

> natural, and even more inevitable than others. Interpretivists are right to suggest the self-understandings of members of a hierarchical and unified society as the likely source of this selection. But if appeals to tradition and to the internal norms of an ordered society are essential components of explanation, they do not exclude that part of the explanation that results from principles of rationality. . . . However they construct their worlds, agents' actions must make sense to themselves in some way not merely appropriate but as representing the best actions they could choose.[39]

On its face, Ferejohn's analysis would seem to be advantageously open-ended; applied to behavior separated by several centuries rather than decades, it makes no attempt to retrospectively "predict" specific outcomes. Readers are directed to the thoughtful treatment of the various possible game forms and equilibria, how mechanisms in place might enforce collusive agreements, and how different types of constituencies or election rotations might produce different sorts of equilibria. They will also encounter a satisfying example of what a detailed interpretivist reading, based on the cultural or intersubjective understandings of the time, can fill in: why families claimed seats in Parliament, why others deferred to their claims, why, when contests occurred, they took the form that they did. However, as the two quotations above show, having abandoned the rigors of regular predetermined effects, Ferejohn places the historical study of institutions squarely where Fiorina, in his description of congressmember's changed perceptions quoted earlier, left it: with a psychological mode—rationality—the applications of which are now defined by "thick" historical descriptions already extant plus, arguably, a new conceptual vocabulary to use in cross-historical comparisons. But with game forms and equilibria determined by historically idiosyncratic perceptions, what, besides models, is left to compare?

Our point is not to deny that intersubjective understandings in any period (including those of social scientists) are an important part of politics; it is rather to say that in juxtaposing rational choice analysis to interpretivist history, even in an effort to reconcile them, Ferejohn has set up another false dichotomy. Interpretivism is not the only alternative to rational choice;

conceptually, it is not much of an alternative at all. Rational choice *and* interpretivist models present institutions as order; in the former, institutions are ordered by equilibria of varying stability, observed post hoc by the social scientist interpreter; in the latter, institutions are ordered by culture, presumed stable enough to be written backwards onto the motives of only loosely specified participants. Both may pack a lot of information into these essentially static perspectives; neither breaks new ground in conceptualizing the relationship between order and change in time.

III. Intercurrence: A Theoretical Foundation for Historical Institutionalism

Current theories of institutional politics have sought in various ways to hold history at bay. As a result, the study of institutions comes to us isolated on a stark conceptual field. The study of order is defended against capitulation to the seamless flow of history; the search for regularities weighs in against undue attention to the idiosyncrasies of personalities and events; deductive modeling offers a hedge against rampant interpretivism. As should be amply clear by now, however, these alternatives do little to illuminate what is most distinctive about the institutional organization of time and space. So long as the analytic choices are conceived in this way, the terrain available for theory building will remain quite narrow.

History is not a problem to be eluded by institutional theory; it is the central theoretical puzzle posed by the subject matter of political institutions. Hard pressed to avoid it, we need better ways to confront it. The approach we have sketched out for this purpose begins with a recognition of the ordering propensities of institutions, but opens onto an analysis of the multiple, incongruous orders that are formative of politics at any given moment; it proceeds on an acknowledgment of historical patterns but leads to an analysis of timing and conjuncture in the explanation of political change; it contends with the limits of interpretivism but advances to theories of intercurrence.

The concept of intercurrence presumes neither order nor disarray, though it can accommodate degrees of either in particular historical settings. It does so by replacing the expectation of an ordered space bounded in synchronized time with the expectation of a politicized push and pull arrayed around multiple institutional arrangements with diverse historical origins. With this image of the political universe in view, attention is directed to the ways in which different ordering principles converge, collide, and fold onto one another. Theories of politics formulated on the presumption of intercurrence will, like all theories, stand or fall on their capacity to tell an empirically refutable story which is, on the known evidence, more convincing than others. But their particular attributes, when extended along the standard dimensions of space and time, indicate a distinctive research program that may appropriately be labeled "historical institutionalism."

The Institutional Construction of Space

In the alternatives reviewed above, institutions are set in an environment in which are located the major forces of their motivation and change. In the work of Burnham and Ackerman, party systems and constitutional regimes, respectively, are demarcated and organized by public opinion, cues mediated but not determined by the institutional processes they set in motion. In PTI, rationality appears against "a backdrop of historical awareness": in Fiorina's episodes, this amounts to shifting party practices and public demands for regulation that exist outside the institution of the Congress itself; in Ferejohn's "rationally reconstructed Whig account," the critical variable is "the self-understanding of members of a hierarchical and unified society."

This separation is a convention, an exaggeration accepted for purposes of analysis, but its implications are not insignificant. The effect is to overstate the independence of action on either one or the other side of the environmental-institutional divide. The alternative offered by the concept of intercurrence removes this analytic barrier, without at the same time collapsing the analytic field into some hopelessly tangled morass. It does so, first of all, by specifying as a fundamental property of political institutions their regular outreach and continuous engagement with others, who in so far as they are acting politically, also act in institutional settings. Analysis can then move either inside out or outside in; institutional rules and norms will appear as the vehicles either way. Whether institutional rules are applied or resisted, juxtaposed or transformed, they shape and direct the actions of both institutional incumbents and those who seek their control.

Institutional engagements may be exhibited in formal designs, as in the routine checks and balances of the U.S. Constitution; in anticipated tensions, as when one court overrules another; or in confrontations between state and society, the latter organized into parties, interest lobbies, or movements. Even the least organized aspects of politics—public opinion or constituency pressures—will be seen to be oriented around, directed at, and conveyed through an institutionally constructed political space. Any line attempted between institutional politics and such forms of individual expression would blur precisely where the latter become most salient politically; that is, where they are registered, gathered, and transmitted, through channels that claim greater or less legitimacy, and that delimit possibilities for accommodation and resistance on both sides. Nor are the fluidity and spontaneity associated with such interventions diminished by this formulation. To the extent that a range of different institutional rules and norms claim legitimacy within a polity, intercurrence will specify a political universe that is inherently open, dynamic, and contested, where existing norms and collective projects, of varying degrees of permanence, are buffeted against one another as a normal condition.

That said, the element of structure—the primary characteristic of all institutional analysis—remains, with the explanation of political action continually referred back to rules and norms that persist within concrete institutional forms. The multiple-orders thesis merely decouples the idea of structure from the presumption of historical fit, allowing the analyst to consider rule-governed behavior without abstracting political dynamics to the level of comparative statics. To the extent that existing theories have identified regularities with clear institutional referents, for example the cycles of party realignment, the premise of intercurrence would employ them, requiring only that other patterns—other orders imposed by other institutions—be juxtaposed. Thus reformulated, we would see how each episode is reshaped and distinguished by its encounter with other relatively independent institutional formations.

Although political institutions are intent on ordering politics within a large and open sphere, institutional politics is not in this view inherently conservative, resistant to "forces of change," or antithetical to creativity. On the contrary, once it is appreciated that political settings do not typically present a single set of institutional constraints, the potential for creativity by actors of all sorts becomes evident. Multiplicity thus conceived will be distinguishable also from pluralism, a theory which in its classic formulations present different groups of actors with conflicting interests competing with each other around one agreed upon set of rules. Both David Truman's "rules of the game"[40] and Robert A. Dahl's "eight conditions of polyarchy"[41] run directly against the presumption of intercurrence, that the foundations of conflict and competition lie in the asymmetry of different sets of rules and their complex temporal structure.

It should be underscored that the political universe is no less patterned for different regularities ingrained in separate but intersecting locales. No encompassing environmental sea motivated by mysterious tides of consilience will be needed to situate institutions or the boundaries of the political space they construct. Theories of intercurrence will make it less plausible to assert distinctions between, on one side, periods of order and normality, and, on the other, periods of transformation and crisis. They will undermine the presumption that change is usefully understood as a movement from one equilibrium state to another; but they do not discard the insight that institutional rules and purposes shape the behavior of their incumbents. In theories of intercurrence, the institutional structure of politics remains; only its spatial and temporal organization is altered.

The Institutional Construction of Time

The persistence of institutions implies that the objectives they pursue at any given moment will reflect the resolution of earlier encounters, and that new purposes and procedures will accumulate over time. Analysis in this frame is therefore drawn back to the circumstances in which the different rules in play originated, and individual institutions themselves will be described as a layering of divergent experiences and imperatives. Principles of political organization, for example, hierarchy, individualism, or majority rule, would be expected to play a greater or lesser role within different institutions, forming overlapping streams of what Ferejohn refers to as the "meanings shared" by participants in a given political culture. Likewise, ideas, such as "corporatism," "equal protection," and "property rights," would always be represented institutionally as hybrids, mixed with other ideas carried over from earlier.

The construction of time that follows from this view of the historical character of institutions is, we believe, the distinctive contribution institutional study has to offer the social sciences. Consider, first, the prevalent understanding in which time "passes," independently and continuously. The work we have criticized makes an advance on this view by suggesting that time is channeled, bent, or slowed by institutions: insofar as individual actions or events are concerned, their occurrence within institutions changes their position from mere happenstance—one damn thing after another—to an observable pattern that orders them and relates them to other comparable and contrasting actions or events. However, time still "marches on," even as institutions "lag behind," "catch up," or "overreach" developments elsewhere.

This conception of time as flowing through and around institutions supports the artificial separation of institutions and their environment. In breaking down the distinction between institutions and environment, the concept of intercurrence reverses this temporal field. In place of the conventional picture of time as one wide stream surrounding institutional action and deflected by it, intercurrence shows time filled up, sculpted, so to speak, by the different historical trajectories that institutions bring into play. What is revealed is no longer the problematic character of institutions in history, but the institutional character of history itself. No longer do institutions float "in" time; time is a construct of the intercurrence of institutions. In place of an undifferentiated environment, something selectively organized or imported opportunistically for analytic purposes, as in Ferejohn's study, or explored for signs of consilience, as Burnham recommends, time is "told" at every moment by its institutional content.

The sense of time we have in mind may perhaps be conveyed graphically, by a table of the sort commonly found in atlases of world history. Each downward column separately marks off one damn thing after another: national dynasties and revolutions, important military battles, technical advances, landmarks of religion and the arts, scientific discoveries. Although chronological dates are listed along the sides of the page as well, they are external to the sequences presented. The significance of any particular date will be established by reading across the table, to the various events that comprise any particular historical conjuncture and also perhaps to those adjacent, in the near-past and near-future. There can be no blank spots or float in this rendering, for time is filled by the intercurrence of events and demarcations that comprise it.

This fullness of time, and theories built upon its assumptions, should account for phenomena in political analysis often discussed but without adequate or articulated theoretical foundation. One of these, for example, is the notion of unintended consequences. A better understanding of the manner in which institutions and practices are connected to one another promises to explain effects that are as regular as they are unanticipated. Another is the problem of causality, and multi-causality. By itself, multi-causality exists as an unformed concept, often suggesting no explanation at all; in any case, it reiterates the pattern of inside and outside forces characteristic of so much political institutional analysis. In the perspective of intercurrence, the entire issue of causality in politics will require a reexamination. An inquiry that has interconnectedness and separation, continuity and discontinuity as its focal point should, as have similar reflections in the disciplines of history and historical sociology, permit a more satisfying treatment of the relations between agents and structures, intentionality and events.[42]

These are not new questions, to be sure; but their exploration in political science has been stunted by the stubborn conceit of order. Historical institutionalism may claim as its distinctive province the creation of historical-institutional grids that bend, shape, and construct time, and the development upon them of theories of politics that highlight the collisions and combinations, the changes and cycles, of institutions in their various internal and external relations. Political action *in* time will then be understood as purposeful human behavior within, motivated by, conforming and in opposition to, impacting and with repercussions upon, this impinging political world.

NOTES

1. James G. March and Johan P. Olsen, "The New Institutionalism: Organizational Factors in Political Life," *American Political Science Review* 78 (1984): 734–49; Douglass C. North, *Institutions, Institutional Change, and Economic Performance* (New York: Cambridge University Press, 1990); William H. Sewell, "A Theory of Structure: Duality, Agency, and Transformation," *American Journal of Sociology* 98 (1992): 1–29; Margaret R. Somers, "Rights, Relationality, and Membership: Rethinking the Making and Meaning of Citizenship," *Law and Social Inquiry* 19 (1994): 63–112.

2. Karen Orren and Stephen Skowronek, "Beyond the Iconography of Order: Notes for a 'New Institutionalism'," in *The Dynamics of American Politics: Approaches and Interpretations,* edited by Lawrence C. Dodd and Calvin Jillson (Boulder, Colo.: Westview Press, 1994), 311–30.

3. Terry Moe, "Interests, Institutions, and Positive Theory: The Politics of the NLRB," *Studies in American Political Development* 2 (1987): 236–302.

4. Maurice Mandelbaum, *Purpose and Necessity in Social Theory* (Baltimore: Johns Hopkins University Press, 1987), 156.

5. Martin Sklar, "Periodization and Historiography: Studying American Political Development in the Progressive Era, 1890–1916," *Studies in American Political Development* 5 (1991): 181–83.

6. A. G. Bogue, "The New Political History of the 1970s," in *The Past before Us: Contemporary Historical Writing in the United States,* edited by Michael Kamen (Ithaca: Cornell University Press, 1980).

7. Walter Dean Burnham, *Critical Elections and the Mainsprings of American Politics* (New York: Norton, 1970), 9–10.

8. Richard L. McCormick, "Walter Dean Burnham and 'The System of 1896'," *Social Science History* 10 (1986): 245–63.

9. Walter Dean Burnham, "Periodization Schemes and 'Party Systems': The System of 1896 as a Case in Point," *Social Science History* 10 (1986): 265.

10. Karen Orren, *Belated Feudalism: Labor, the Law, and Liberal Development in the United States* (New York: Cambridge University Press, 1991); Karen Orren, "The Work of Government: Recovering the Discourse of Office in *Marbury v. Madison*," *Studies in American Political Development* 8 (1994): 60–80; Stephen Skowronek, *Building a New American State: The Expansion of State Administrative Capacities, 1877–1920* (New York: Cambridge University Press, 1982); Stephen Skowronek, *The Politics Presidents Make: Political Leadership from John Adams to George Bush* (Cambridge: Harvard University Press, 1993).

11. Jeffrey Tulis, *The Rhetorical Presidency* (Princeton: Princeton University Press, 1987).

12. Brian Balogh, "Reorganizing the Organizational Synthesis: Federal-Professional Relations in Modern America," *Studies in American Political Development* 5 (1991): 119–72.

13. Andrew Polsky, *The Rise of the Therapeutic State* (Princeton: Princeton University Press, 1991).

14. Kenneth Finegold and Theda Skocpol, *State, Party, and Policy: Industry and Agriculture in America's New Deal* (Madison: University of Wisconsin Press, 1995).

15. In a kindred spirit, though more grounded in ideas than in institutions, see Smith on the "multiple traditions" of liberalism with respect to race. Rogers Smith, "Beyond Tocqueville, Myrdal, and Hartz: The Multiple Traditions in America," *American Political Science Review* 87 (1993): 549–66.

16. Walter Dean Burnham, "Pattern Recognition and 'Doing Political History': Art, Science, or Bootless Enterprise," in *The Dynamics of American Politics*, edited by Lawrence C. Dodd and Calvin Jillson (Boulder, Colo.: Westview Press, 1994), 68–69.

17. Martin Sklar, *The Corporate Reconstruction of American Capitalism, 1890–1916* (New York: Cambridge University Press, 1988), 170.

18. Scott James, *The Politics of Coalition-Building, the Democracy, and the Construction of Regulatory Institutions, 1884–1936* (Ph.D. dissertation, University of California, Los Angeles, 1993); Gerald Berk, "Neither Markets nor Administration: Brandeis and the Anti-Trust Reforms of 1914," *Studies in American Political Development* 8 (1994): 24–59.

19. Bruce Ackerman, *We the People: Foundations* (Cambridge: Harvard University Press, 1991).

20. Burnham, "Pattern Recognition and 'Doing Political History'," 64–65.

21. Ackerman, 98–99.

22. William Riker, "Implications from the Disequilibrium of Majority Rule for the Study of Institutions," *American Political Science Review* 74 (1980): 432–46; Kenneth Shepsle, "Studying Institutions: Some Lessons from the Rational Choice Approach," *Journal of Theoretical Politics* 1 (1989): 131–47.

23. A literature on point is recent efforts to use rational choice modeling to study judicial interpretation of statutes, said to reflect the "strategic setting." See John A. Ferejohn and Barry R. Weingast, "A Positive Theory of Statutory Interpretation," *International Review of Law and Economics* 12 (1992): 263–79. Courts and Congress are both modeled; however, the behavior of judges is determined by their calculations of what they expect Congressmembers will do in response to their decisions. Moreover, there is no theory analogous to Congressmembers' desire for re-election of why judges would "maximize" in the predicted way. In the article cited, it is presumed that decision makers want their handiwork to endure (266). It is not theorized why judges might choose one or another means, i.e., jurisprudential rules or interpretation, to that end. For a sympathetic critique along similar lines, see Frank H. Easterbrook, "Some Tasks in Understanding Law through the Lens of Public Choice," *International Review of Law and Economics* 12 (1992): 184–88.

24. John Ferejohn, "Rationality and Interpretation: Parliamentary Elections in Early Stuart England," in *The Economic Approach to Politics: A Critical Reassessment of the Theory of Rational Action* edited by Kristen Monroe (New York: HarperCollins, 1991).

25. Donald P. Green and Ian Shapiro, *Pathologies of Rational Choice Theory: A Critique of Applications in Political Science* (New Haven: Yale University Press, 1994).

26. Morris Fiorina, "The Legislative Choice of Regulatory Forms: Legal Process or Administrative Process," *Public Choice* 39 (1982): 33–66; "Group Concentration and the Delegation of Legislative Authority," in *Regulatory Policy and the Social Sciences* edited by Roger Noll (Berkeley: University of California Press, 1985); "Legislator Uncertainty, Legislative Control, and the Delegation of Power," *Journal of Law, Economics, and Organization* 2 (1986): 33–51.

27. Fiorina, "The Legislative Choice of Regulatory Forms," 34.

28. Fiorina, "Group Concentration and the Delegation of Legislative Authority," 196.

29. Fiorina, "Legislator Uncertainty, Legislative Control, and the Delegation of Power," 48.

30. Fiorina, "Group Concentration and the Delegation of Legislative Authority," 197.

31. Fiorina, "The Legislative Choice of Regulatory Forms," 42. The probability of a Congressmember's reelection is assumed to be a monotonically increasing function of the net benefits flowing to the district from any given regulatory policy.

32. James, *The Politics of Coalition-Building.*

33. Fiorina notes this discrepancy as a "historical footnote" in "The Legislative Choice of Regulatory Forms," 50.

34. Fiorina, "Legislator Uncertainty, Legislative Control, and the Delegation of Power," 45, 47.

35. Morris Fiorina, "New Institutionalism, 'Old' Institutionalism, and the 'New' Historical Institutionalism," remarks presented at the plenary session, Annual Meeting of the Social Science History Association, 1993. Forthcoming in *Social Science History.*

36. Fiorina, "Legislatory Uncertainty, Legislative Control, and the Delegation of Power," 49.

37. Ferejohn, "Rationality and Interpretation."

38. Ferejohn, 298.

39. Ferejohn, 298–99.

40. David Truman, *The Governmental Process* (New York: Knopf, 1951).

41. Robert A. Dahl, *A Preface to Democratic Theory* (Chicago: University of Chicago Press, 1956).

42. See Mandelbaum, *Purpose and Necessity in Social Theory;* Paul Ricoeur, *Time and Narrative,* vol. 1 (Chicago: University of Chicago Press, 1984); Sewell, "A Theory of Structure: Duality, Agency, and Transformation."

5

E PUR SI MUOVE! SYSTEMATIZING AND THE INTERCURRENCE HYPOTHESIS

WALTER DEAN BURNHAM

As is their wont, Karen Orren and Stephen Skowronek have given us a forceful challenge in their chapter, "Institutions and Intercurrence." Art is long, life short, and elaborate controversies often tedious; therefore my response will be brief. For a moment, the thought crossed my mind that I could confine it to a four-digit number: 1994. For "realignment theory" has never been in better shape for decades than it is just now: the behavior of the voting citizenry in this election has seen to that. Still, some further discussion seems warranted. Brevity will necessarily result in failing to give anything like complete justice to a paper having the intelligence, richness, and awareness of nuance that we have come to expect from Orren and Skowronek. It will serve, however, to concentrate on what I perceive to be the heart of the matter, so far as their attentions to my own work are concerned.

We begin by noting what should be obvious. The authors have a great deal to say that is of real importance about the constitutionally embedded intercurrence of governmental institutions that are condemned to compete as well as cooperate with each other. This intercurrence is a prime reality of political action in the United States, and it is eminently reasonable to center analysis upon it and its implications for an institutionally centered account of what happens, and has happened, in American politics. If there were nothing more involved, there would be no reason to do more than acclaim the result. But the authors think it necessary to devote close to one-third of their text to my own and Bruce Ackerman's understandings of this political world. This of course means that quite a lot more is involved.

Perhaps part of their attention may grow from pique at an earlier argument of mine that history was either one damned thing after another or that it had some ascertainable macrosystemic pattern. This would leave no middle ground, i.e., no room for "what a distinctly institutional view of history has to offer."[1] The possibility may surely be conceded that my dichotomy was a false one. I would in principle have no difficulty accepting this institutional view as being perfectly legitimate for dealing with issues at an appropriate level of analysis. By much the same token, for example, the pluralism that so long dominated authorative explanations of American politics in action seems to me to continue to have a distinct, if also distinctly limited, explanatory role to play even today. Its universalistic claims have fallen pretty much into the discard, because over the past generation it has become obvious that the pluralist model is simply not equipped to account for important aspects of political reality.

This concession still implies, however, that there is some sort of hierarchical progression from "Brownian movements" to middle-range phenomena (and their attendant theories) to macrosystemic phenomena (and their theories). The basic critical purpose of "Institutions and Intercurrence" is to make room for the authors' model by demolishing the efforts of others—myself and Ackerman, for instance—to construct models at this macrosystemic level. There is a certain kind of imperialism involved in such an endeavor. We should immediately add, however, that such moves to dominate subsequent scholarly agendas are extremely commonplace in academe. They are part of a normal competitive battle among models and modelers: realignment theory, after all, implies an imperialism of its own. Every model is a proposed schedule of priorities. It is a vehicle through which to see the world as it hasn't been seen before, and to guide research into sorting out what is relatively more and less important, and why, in the subinfinite flow of data with which scholarship has to deal. Ultimately, any model is as good as its ordering power, its capacity to help me or others to explain what is sought to be explained. As Justice Holmes used to say, the ultimate test of truth is acceptance in the marketplace of ideas. My own judgment is that intercurrence, at least so far as developed in the pages of this chapter, clearly comes to grips with important realities of American politics that have not been addressed head-on before; yet there are realities at least as important that are not so addressed, with the authors appearing to deny their reality.

We may make this discussion a bit more concrete by asking one set of a host of possible questions. Was there such a thing as the System of 1896 or not? If there was, how does this fact and the many arguments related to ,it (systemwide punctuational-change transformations, succeeding regime orders, and so on) impact on and are shaped by the intercurrence processes of the Orren-Skowronek account? If there wasn't, then how do we account for a wide variety of fact situations that we know existed in the period 1894–1932 (or–1937), and at no other time in our history?

People who have made the bet that some such system and other systems in political time have existed are left essentially without any intellectual purchase on the problem by the kind of "institutional view" proposed here. They might well be concerned with the extent to which such a perspective seems somehow introspective, free-floating, acontextual and even, perhaps, in some sense ahistorical. One thinks of a non-official institution—the party system and its major components—that is only sporadically present in Skowronek's otherwise superb, pathbreaking study, *The Politics Presidents Make,*[2] and which is certainly not at center stage in the pages of this chapter.

Such considerations seem particularly relevant at the moment. I submit that the combined policy-constitutional "revolution" which congressional Republicans of 1995 are trying to accomplish—not to mention the abrupt elevation of the House of Representatives in the general institutional scheme of things in Washington—cannot he accounted for in terms of the intercurrence construct developed by the authors. To do so requires work at a different and—dare I say it?—a higher, system-centered level of analysis. But, as I read their essay, Orren and Skowronek are basically saying—despite some elegant qualifiers here and there—that there *is* no attainable level of integration higher than the largely disintegrated activity of institutions-in-motion on which their interest centers. If that is indeed what they are saying, one can leave many of the counterarguments to the events of 1994, 1995, and the very immediate future: they alone will carry most of the weight of refutation. *Res ipsa loquitur,* as the jurists say.

By way of suggesting what a detailed rejoinder might look like if there were the space or the will to produce one, let us now look at two issues the authors raise as part of their demolition project. The first deals with their discussion of pre-1911 antitrust jurisprudence as an "anomaly," and the second with some reflections on Bruce Ackerman's celebrated *We The People: Foundations.*[3] As to the first issue, it is of course quite true that only with the 1911 *Standard Oil* case did the Supreme Court finally substitute the "rule of reason" doctrine for its previous view that *all* restraints on trade were illegal. Equally clearly, the former clearly fits the "logic" of the System of 1896 far better than the latter—and fifteen years is certainly a long time to wait for the Justices to come around. But I don't believe that this antitrust "anomaly" will bear the load the authors place on it. For they are quite right to say that I would argue for a "long and complicated institutional adjustment to the new ordering principle established by the system of 1896."[4] I have never thought it necessary (or intellectually in the slightest degree plausible) that either instantaneous or complete integration across all domains should arise out of systemic transformations. One deals instead, as it were, with statistical probabilities and central tendencies, not absolute conformity. It is thus not necessary to have so heroic a standard as suggested by the authors in order to sustain the system-level case for the real-world existence of a phenomenon we conceptualize under the rubric, the System of 1896.

One can even provide another counterexample, this one going in just the opposite chronological direction. Let us take a "flagship" decision of the 1895 Court, *Pollock v. Farmers' Loan & Trust Co.*[5] Reversing a "century of error" going back to *Hylton v. U.S.*,[6] the Court struck down congressional power to levy a federal income tax, a power freely deployed during the Civil War. This decision would have seemed to be fully consonant with the "ordering principle" of the System of 1896; yet this system's dominant Republican majority could not live with it, even in the intermediate run. On July 12, 1909, the Sixteenth Amendment, designed specifically to overrule the *Pollock* decision, received the necessary two-thirds support of both houses of Congress, and was sent to the states for ratification. At this time, following the solid and to-be-expected Republican victory in the 1908 election, there were 59 Republicans and 33 Democrats in the Senate, and 219 Republicans and 172 Democrats in the House. The amendment was declared ratified on February 25, 1913. During the time of ratification, Republicans controlled both houses of at least twenty-four of the state legislatures.

Now the full pro-corporate rigor of the 1896-system narrative would clearly have been better served had *Pollock* remained good law until the New Deal, or the Supreme Court's famous "switch in time" in 1937. But so what? With or without *Standard Oil* or the Sixteenth Amendment lying in our path, I think we would find near-unanimous agreement among scholars of American constitutional history that a periodization of the years 1895–1936 is not only plausible but, for many purposes, is analytically mandatory to make sense of what was going on. In this period the Court constructed a dense and generally coherent (or convergent) network of constitutional doctrines aimed at imposing very considerable limits on the power of both federal and state governments to regulate the economy. Obviously such doctrines had a prehistory (e.g., in the pre–1895 dissents of Justice Stephen Field), but they did not achieve hegemonic position until the "revolution" of 1895 and its sequelae that issued forth over the next decade. They were to have no history worth mentioning after April 1, 1937.

The Supreme Court as an institution acquired in crucial and easily specifiable domains of public policy an ascendancy never achieved before or after the 1895–1936 period. The literature is so vast and generally convergent on this basic point that it seems a tedious exercise in supererogation to provide extensive citations here. Let me simply note that a most knowledgeable contemporary, Robert H. Jackson—just before his own elevation to the Supreme Court—published a credible if partisan view of this whole era in Supreme Court history in a work whose title precisely captures the point: *The Struggle for Judicial Supremacy*.[7] In the presence of this huge mass of evidence, we hardly need to belabor our own point further. The eager search for and discovery of specific jural "anomalies" here and there cannot seriously disturb two propositions. First, there was a System of 1896 with clear doctrinal as well as other boundaries. Second, one of the most defining characteristics of this system was the specific institutional position of the Court within it, a position not to be detected either before or after it.

As for the authors' discussion of Ackerman, I gladly leave him to defend himself, should he so wish. But, as one not entirely without training and background in American constitutional history, let me dwell on a very few points. There is no doubt that Ackerman has his own agendas. These importantly include an account that is aimed at rescuing the Supreme Court's meta-political role in a democracy from the countermajoritarian difficulty. All this and more will form matters of controversy among law-school faculties and political scientists which we may leave for them to sort out. Let me simply give here as my opinion that his crucial identification of "constitutional moments" and their place in the greater historical scheme of things makes empirical sense. By the same token, from the perspective of reshaping constitutional order in quite major if not ultimately revolutionary ways, his three-republics periodization of American constitutional history is also persuasive.

As Ackerman stresses, at such constituent moments the formative role of the Supreme Court as an institution is altogether overshadowed by the energized mobilization of many other actors. These actors centrally include the electorate. The dynamics involved here are clearly those of critical realignment, even though Ackerman's particular tools of analysis pick up only some, rather than all, events that fall into that category. Ackerman also stresses the *proactive* role of the electorate at such "moments," so strikingly different from its usual semi-passive, reactive stance. Nor is this merely the conceit of a scholar whose basic professional interests and analytic tools lie in the domain of legal and political theory. Precisely the same account of this phenomenon is given, not only by contemporaries who live through such rare transforming moments in our political history, but also by those who have given much of their professional lives to their empirical study.[8] Here we are at quite a distance from an institution-centered account with intercurrence at its center. Yet one wonders how it can be denied that these and other "abnormal" states of affairs are centrally involved in recasting some of the most important dimensions of political action. Such dimensions, we speculate, would surely include the terms of trade within which the interaction of governmental institutions unfolds.

Nor, after all, need we necessarily rely upon such indirect if frequently compelling evidence. My provisional working hypothesis is that 1994 inaugurated a realignment sequence. If so, we can ourselves gain a direct, existential, personal insight into what such events may have been like in the past. Moreover, those who have taken power in the wake of the 1994 election have made it crystal-clear that their objective is to produce yet another in our series of "constitutional moments." This would lead, presumably, to a Fourth American Republic whose basic contours can already be delineated with some accuracy. Even if they do not realize their maximum program, there is considerable chance that some such transition will in fact be realized, in however messy and semi-integrated a way. That considerable chance exists because the "basement," the foundation both geopolitical and socioeconomic on which all political superstructures rest has been so modified in recent years as to make such a development plausible, likely even.

Now what does the institutional view of American political evolution presented in "Institutions and Intercurrence" have to say to all this? We can hope that Orren and Skowronek will inform us in due course. As matters now stand, if one wants to construct an explanation of what was going on, say, in the 1890s, the 1930s, and the 1990s, the model presented in this chapter will not, without more, be particularly helpful. Institutional intercurrence is a significant idea well worth developing and exploiting. But it can perform no such supersessory function for scholarship as the authors claim for it. We seem to be dealing now, as in the past, with a situation in which one regime order comes to an end, and a genuinely new and quite different order is created, one which is also genuinely an *order*. One suspects that only a model that can produce some sort of ordering for the study of political change at a given level of action will suffice for those trying to solve puzzles at that level. Nor need such a model be in any way identical with that I have proposed. The only requirement is that it provide a credible and verifiable set of ordering propositions to explain things that have to be explained. As Justice Holmes also used to say, the ultimate test is empirical.

NOTES

1. Karen Orren and Stephen Skowronek, this volume, 117.
2. Stephen Skowronek, *The Politics Presidents Make: Leadership from John Adams to George Bush* (Cambridge: Harvard University Press, 1993).
3. Bruce Ackerman, *We the People: Foundations* (Cambridge: Harvard University Press, 1991).
4. Orren and Skowronek, 119.
5. 158 U.S. 601 (1895).
6. 3 Dall. 171 (1796).
7. Robert H. Jackson, *The Struggle for Judicial Supremacy* (New York: Knopf, 1941).
8. See in particular Paul Kleppner, *Continuity and Change in Electoral Politics, 1893–1928* (Westport, Conn.: Greenwood Press, 1987), and especially his discussion of this issue in "Appendix: Realignment Theory Since Key," 239–49. Very worth reading as background to the Reconstruction-era "constitutional moment" in Ackerman's scheme is Eric L. McKitrick, *Andrew Johnson and Reconstruction* (Chicago: University of Chicago Press, 1960). A major theme of this work is that by the summer of 1866 at the latest, a very large part of the Northern electorate had given unmistakable signs that they would not stand for anything remotely resembling President Johnson's proposed solution of the Southern Question. It would seem that adoption of the Fourteenth Amendment had become a minimally acceptable baseline for such

voters. McKitrick's narrative correctly stresses the outcome of the 1866 congressional election as central to and the *sine qua non* of everything that happened to politics and policy concerning Reconstruction thereafter. The vital importance of this election was thoroughly understood by all the actors involved, as McKitrick documents. He also more than once discerns the element of proactivity among voters that both Kleppner and Ackerman also stress: "Meanwhile, the Republican campaign in that state, as an Ohio historian remarks, was 'quite spirited', reaching unusual heights of enthusiasm, energy, and vitality: there was a sense in which 'the people' had taken it over" (446).

6

LOOKING FOR DISAGREEMENT IN ALL THE WRONG PLACES

MORRIS P. FIORINA

Scholars can be arrayed along many dimensions, one of which ranges from conflict to cooperation. On one end of this continuum are scholars who believe in sharpening lines of difference and disagreement—even in inventing them when necessary. On the other end are scholars who search for commonalities and complimentarities. Orren and Skowronek (hereafter OS) clearly fall into the former camp; increasingly, I find myself in the latter.

In this note I will first correct the more important misreadings of my work that form the basis of OS's critique. Then I turn to their multisyllabic exhortations in an attempt to determine what really is at issue.

Delegation and the ICC: Getting the Story Right

OS stress the importance of getting the story right when doing historical analysis. I wish they had followed a similar admonition when reading my work. As I explained to them in a long letter several years ago, I did not try to explain the establishment of the Interstate Commerce Act with a "shift the responsibility"

(SR) model. Hence, much of their unhappiness with my specific work (as opposed to the general PTI approach) is a figment of their willful misunderstanding.

By way of explanation it might be useful to practice a little intercurrence and put the articles in question into their temporal and institutional context. In 1980, I was commissioned to write an article explaining why Congress prefers to regulate via centralized bureaucratic "command and control" rather than via decentralized "incentives-based" schemes such as emissions taxes, markets in licences, and so forth. As soon as I began to think about the question I began to doubt that it was the one I wanted to answer. In the first place, if one adopted a broad definition of regulation, the underlying claim was questionable. The Internal Revenue Code, for example, could be viewed as a gigantic incentives-based economic regulatory scheme, many of whose details reflect precise statutory enactments. In the second place, the original question conflated two questions. The regulatory instruments or techniques Congress chooses (incentives versus command and control) and the agent it charges with enforcing regulation (administrators versus judges) are distinct questions, each worthy of examination.

The second question struck me as prior to the first. After all, Congress began to regulate long before the fertile minds of modern economists had thought of emissions taxes and the like. But some contemporary economists—the intended audience—did not share my priorities. I turned to the ICC in an attempt to persuade those who viewed regulatory *bureaucracy* as "natural," in need of no explanation.

The ICC was a useful case for three reasons. First, it was established well before Pigou's thinking laid the groundwork for modern incentives-based regulatory schemes; "command and control" was the only option on the table. Second, this first major federal regulatory intervention was not just another step along a well-trod policy path. The states had tried both statutory and administrative forms of regulation, and the congressional battle over these alternatives significantly delayed the legislation. Thus, the ICC was a genuine collective choice, not simply an extension of familiar choices from the past. Third, the era was one of a strong Congress and relatively weak Presidency. What better time to focus on *legislative* calculations underlying delegation to administrators?

For all these reasons I regularly used the example of the ICC to *motivate* my general interest—the delegation of legislative authority.[1] But my broader explanatory concern was legislative delegation, not the history of the ICC. In the first article OS cite,[2] *five* separate models are offered as possible explanations of delegation, one of which is the SR model they criticize.[3] The only reference to the ICC in the section discussing the SR model is a single sentence that notes how different distributions of benefits and costs across states and congressional districts could have led majorities to vote differently, even if the same model were operative in both House and Senate.[4] That observation also applies, of course, to the other models, and, indeed, to any model that includes constituency benefits and costs.

In the article that develops the SR model at length, the ICC is again used to motivate attention to the question of delegation[5], but in the specific development of the model,[6] the ICC disappears, save for a single sentence[7] noting that one could not infer who benefitted from ICC regulation in 1887 based on who benefitted in the 1950s. Various "economic" theories of regulatory origin (eg. Stigler, 1971) commit just that fallacy, and I referred to the ICC rather than another commission simply because as the oldest regulatory bureaucracy, the fallacy was clearest there.

A third article[8] does apply a specific model to the ICC, but not the SR model. Rather, I modify and extend another of the five models presented in the first article, a decision-making under uncertainty model that conceptualizes legislators as choosing between enforcement lotteries. Neither judges nor administrators can be expected to be perfectly faithful agents of legislative majorities. What expectations would explain taking a gamble on one as opposed to the other?

OS give this third article a strange spin—that it reflects my decision to concentrate on the Senate because I could not explain the House. They have lost me here. The uncertainty model explicitly addresses the question of why the Senate and

House *differed* in their preferences for judicial as opposed to commission enforcement. OS observe that

> pooling, rather than support or opposition to the commission form, may have been the deciding issue, and that the commission form rode into history on the back of Congress's stronger preferences for a court enforceable standard.[9]

This suggestion overlooks the important difference between Senate and House preferences, but it is not inconsistent with my argument in this third and final article that

> The House majority grudgingly accepted the commission only upon winning an explicit prohibition against pooling and a stronger long- and short-haul provision.[10]

In sum, OS are locked in mortal combat with straw men. They go to great lengths to criticize a model that is not used to explain the establishment of a railroad regulatory commission. Then they give short shrift to and misinterpret a model that I do offer as part of the explanation. *And in the end they arrive at an interpretation similar to mine.* Are they so disturbed at the prospect of any agreement between us that they feel it necessary to trump up a specious account of what I have written?

Before moving on to broader questions, there is one other OS criticism that deserves rebuttal. OS reject the models I explore because these models are constituency benefit models. "Gotcha!" say OS. One-third of the House did not stand for reelection in 1886 and fully forty percent of the members in the lame-duck session were lame ducks. That the voting patterns of the lame ducks and the holdovers did not differ is damning evidence against constituency benefit models inasmuch as the lame ducks "lacked the incentives postulated by the model."

Please. As one who spent more hours than I care to remember compiling data on the shape of House careers,[11] I am well aware of the contours of House careers in the 1880s. True, career representatives were relatively rare in the mid-1880s, but career *politicians* were not. Not only was there more in-out-in movement than today, but more importantly, service in the House was often just part of a longer political career. There is no reason to believe that members abandoned all fealty to local constituencies, and to local parties who controlled patterns of advancement, just because they did not expect to return to the House for the next Congress. That the voting patterns of the lame ducks did not differ from the holdovers may only indicate that there were about the same proportions of professional politicians in both. Despite their emphasis on history, OS seem to have overlooked these historical specifics.

In general, while reelection-seeking representatives might plausibly be assumed to maximize net benefits to their constituencies, even those not seeking reelection may have the same goal, whether because they plan to return to Congress at some future time, plan to seek another office whose constituency overlaps with their congressional constituency, or even because they consider doing good for their constituencies to be their proper "role" as a representative. The maximization of constituency benefits is as consistent with the selfless advocacy of constituency interests as with single-minded seeking of reelection. OS argue that because reelection-seeking representatives would maximize net benefits to their constituencies, non-reelection seeking representatives would not. This is an elementary logical fallacy.

PTI Models and the ICC

In the research program summarized in the 1982, 1985, and 1986 articles, I was exploring a phenomenon that I did not view as bound by time or by a specific legislative institution. That phenomenon was delegation, the willingness of any legislators at any time to cede power to others. The ICC was a vehicle by which I sought to persuade an audience accustomed to thinking of delegation as "natural" that it was in fact a significant question.[12] Ultimately I decided that the ICC was not *primarily* a reflection of calculations about legislative delegation, although contrary to OS comment, I did not decide that the ICC was "a bad case" for testing.[13] Rather, my continuing research, including preliminary roll-call analyses, indicated that the railroad regulation issue was bound up in the larger electoral struggle of the time, when control of the House and the Presidency were in question in each election. Maintaining a majority coalition in the House required a delicate balancing act: pooling would be banned for the benefit of long-haulers, but short-haulers had to be protected from the natural consequences.[14] In such a situation log-rolling and/or coalition formation models would be more illuminating. Delegation mattered in that substantive commitments made in the Democratic House would be less credible if enforced by a commission controlled by a Republican Senate than if enforced by independent courts. That the House conceded on procedure (accepting the Commission), while the Senate conceded on substance (accepting pooling and a stronger long- and short-haul provision) presumably reflected different constituencies, different bets about the future, and different institutional prerogatives, as well as other things that I did not care to study.

This brings me to a larger confusion about the use of formal models. These models are not "tested" against historical data; rather, they are "applied." The models are logical constructions, their propositions are logically true. The question is whether they are useful, which is to say, whether they enable the scholar to better understand the empirical world. A model is compared to the historical record, and if it "fits," if its propositions are reflected in the empirical record, then it is a candidate for being an element of the explanation of that record. Even where a model does not fit, the very lack of fit can point us to the features of an empirical situation that are not incorporated in the model. Most of the assumptions of models, especially the motivational assumptions, can not be directly tested. If the models fit, even in a time or place where we might not expect them to, my reaction is not to dismiss such fits as coincidence, but to search for equivalents of or substitutes for critical assumptions that explain the degree of observed fit.

What Do Orren and Skowronek Want?

OS are obviously exercised about something. What is it that they see as the surest path to knowledge? What are they exhorting the rest of us to do? Their prose is difficult to interpret, but as best as I can translate, "intercurrence" has two important components. First, it means the use of multiple, differing models; second, in these models political institutions should play a preeminent role. Thus, "political institutions hold the formative or fundamental position in politics." And, "the overall view of politics is no longer that of an integrated order . . . Rather, it is one of multiple and disjoint orderings that overlay on one another."[15]

Such sentiments seem reasonable enough, insofar as I understand them. As for the primacy of institutions, I think that more properly should be a conclusion than an assumption, but I resonate with OS's apparent belief that institutions have at least as much to do with shaping culture, interpretations, and other subjectivities as vice versa. And as for multiple models, if only OS read less selectively. I wrote in 1985:

> To be sure, there are a variety of political reasons to delegate, only one of which—shifting responsibility—has been examined here. Elsewhere (Fiorina, 1982) I have surveyed some of these, each of which deserves a great deal more investigation. Moreover, others could undoubtedly produce numerous other political considerations after giving the question some thought.[16]

And I am only talking about delegation—a specific kind of legislative action—here! The explanation of any important political institution, significant event, or dramatic change will normally require the application of multiple models incorporating multiple causal influences. People in the PTI camp are just as likely to believe this as historical institutionalists are.

Things can not be so simple, however; surely OS must be trying to say something beyond the assertions that institutions are important and politics are complicated. Perhaps the controversy lies in how we approach that complexity. Those of us in the PTI tradition approach it by breaking it down into component parts, attempting to work out the various principles, logics, and problems that generate institutions and that institutions generate. We are well aware that we have isolated only a piece of the complexity and that our model may address only some aspect or aspects of that piece. (I'm sure the same is true for those like Ackerman and Burnham who come from other traditions, but it would not be rational to use my limited space to defend them.)

OS appear to believe that such a parsing of the problem into component parts is inherently impossible, which I interpret to be a claim that the interactions among components are sufficiently strong and complex that partial analyses of components are impossible. Thus, OS reject the notion that separate analysts working on separate pieces of the problem can ever produce the knowledge that will allow others to put the whole together. They seem to demand that each analyst embrace the whole institution-in-time at once and apply all possible relevant logics or models. If this is their argument, then I have a simple suggestion: put up or shut up.

OS are making an empirical claim; namely, that they can provide superior explanatory accounts via their strategy of intercurrence. Maybe they can; show us. Few scholars are persuaded by discussions that trumpet that "my approach is great, but yours is worthless." If OS wish to persuade the skeptics, they should do it by demonstrating that they have a better way of explaining patterns, outcomes, or changes, and I emphasize the notion of "explaining," as opposed to providing a thicker description. Show us that the strategy of intercurrence does not lead to a slide down Burnham's slippery slope of putting "one damned thing after another." Show us that analysts following such a strategy can do solid social scientific work and not just tell stories couched in difficult prose.[17]

Stability and Change

Finally, I point out that OS are focused on the subject of political change. Obviously change is important, but it is not the only important focus of institutional studies, or political studies generally.[18] The 1994 congressional elections marked a great change in American electoral politics, but they do not alter the fact that the Democrats controlled the House of Representatives for forty years. Stability can be as interesting and as important as change, a proposition OS implicitly appear to deny.

Thus, OS quote me at length on the subject of change in

patterns of regulation, describing the passage as "telling," and noting with apparent satisfaction that "Finally prompted to describe how we get from one 'episode' to another, Fiorina has sketched a picture of institutional politics much like the one we are advancing as an alternative to PTI."[19] It is of little concern to me whether my "sketch" resembles OS's notion of intercurrence, for the article was not about getting from one episode to another, and I wasn't "prompted" to do any such thing. The article developed a model of delegation. At the end of the article, I speculated about how events and developments outside the model could lead to changes in the parameters within the model and thereby lead to different predictions. While I thought that such speculation was worthwhile, the article mainly addressed legislative decision at a particular time. Do OS believe that only *changes* in decisions are important?

Both stability and change are important, of course. Contemporary PTI models mostly address stability. They take fundamental preferences and beliefs as givens.[20] Here is where I find historical institutional studies valuable. If such studies can explain the genesis of preferences and beliefs, and how they change, then in combination with PTI models they will be important elements of explanations of political change. I say "in combination with" rather than "by themselves" because PTI models demonstrate that changes in beliefs and preferences do not inevitably generate changes in outcomes, and conversely, changes in outcomes do not necessarily indicate changes in preferences.[21] A full account of change will require attention to both beliefs and preferences, and institutions.

Thus, I return to an emphasis on complimentarities. Different approaches have strengths and weaknesses, and that of OS is no different in this regard. Practicing scholars will continue to pick and choose among approaches and develop new ones. OS are wasting their time if they think that by preaching intercurrence as the one true religion they can whip heterogeneous subfields of political science and history into line behind their particular vision of institutional studies. But as long as they seem determined to try, positive research will be more persuasive than tortured critiques.

NOTES

1. I also used the case to cast doubt on some existing theories of regulation, such as the Kolko-Stigler "cartel by design" theory. Gabriel Kolko, *Railroads and Regulation* (New York: Norton, 1965); George Stigler, "The Theory of Economic Regulation," *Bell Journal of Economics and Management Science* 2 (1971): 3–21.

2. Morris Fiorina, "Legislative Choice of Regulatory Forms: Legal Process or Administrative Process," *Public Choice* 39 (1982): 33–66.

3. Although restated in rational choice terms, the principle underlying that model is common in the mainstream "institutional" American politics literature. See, for example, Peter Woll, *American Bureaucracy*, 2d ed. (New York: Norton, 1977), 113.

4. Fiorina, "Legislative Choice of Regulatory Forms," 49.

5. Morris Fiorina, "Group Concentration and the Delegation of Legislative Authority," in *Regulatory Policy and the Social Sciences*, edited by Roger Noll (Berkeley: University of California Press, 1985), 183–88.

6. Ibid., 188–195.

7. Ibid., 193.

8. Morris Fiorina, "Legislator Uncertainty, Legislative Control, and the Delegation of Power," *Journal of Law, Economics, and Organization* 2 (1986): 33–51.

9. Orren and Skowronek, this volume, 131.

10. Fiorina, "Legislator Uncertainty, Legislative Control, and the Delegation of Power," 38; in a further recognition of the importance of the pooling issue, I noted that one of the three Senate conferees refused to sign the conference report (34).

11. Morris Fiorina, David Rohde, and Peter Wissel, "Historical Change in House Turnover," in *Congress in Change*, edited by Norman Ornstein, (New York: Praeger, 1975), 24–57.

12. Theodore Lowi, *The End of Liberalism* (New York: Norton, 1979).

13. Morris Fiorina, "Rational Choice and the New (?) Institutionalism," forthcoming in *Polity*.

14. Thus, Poole and Rosenthal find that the votes on the ICA fall neatly along the major ideological dimension underlying congressional alignments of the time. Keith Poole and Howard Rosenthal, "The Enduring 19th Century Battle for Economic Regulation: The Interstate Commerce Act Revisited," *Journal of Law and Economics* 36 (1993): 837–59.

15. Orren and Skowronek, 117.

16. Fiorina, "Group Concentration and the Delegation of Legislative Authority," 196.

17. OS might reply that they already have provided such demonstrations, but I am not sure from their article who is in and who is out of their camp. For example, I think that Skocpol's *States and Social Revolutions* is a model of historical institutional research, but they do not cite it in their list of officially approved works. Is she not intercurrent enough?

18. Obviously, I will not agree to define institutional study as the study of institutional change.

19. Orren and Skowronek, 134.

20. Although some models allow fundamental preferences to be learned, and beliefs to be updated.

21. As an example of the former, in a median voter model voters on both sides of the median can switch positions all they want, but if the position of the median voter does not change, the outcome stays the same. As an example of the latter, if the status quo in a voting model changes for some reason, the outcome may change even if all preferences remain constant. An example would be the Wabash decision voiding all state regulation of interstate railroads.

7

REPLY TO BURNHAM AND FIORINA

KAREN ORREN AND STEPHEN SKOWRONEK

We speak first to the remarks of Burnham, who has responded to our efforts with his usual graciousness. The farthest thing from our mind was to "demolish" party realignment as an organizing construct. On the contrary, the idea of intercurrence depends on the clear identification of patterns through time, and we will go so far as to say that at present realignment theory is the best-articulated and most productive pattern we have. Nor do we insist on one particular anomaly such as anti-trust to prove our point. Our argument is that there will be several patterns at work in any specific historical incident, that these may present themselves as if they were anomalies, and that developing concepts that relate these patterns to each other will both resolve anomalies and add dimension to our empirical accounts.

Burnham references various turning points, including the New Deal with its definitive "switch in time," as support for his own position. Our perspective does not preclude attention to turning points; in fact everyone in this discussion would consider the New Deal, for example, an important one. Each of us understands the New Deal differently, however. For Orren, it registers the overcoming through collective action of common-law ordering, this time of master and servant, and the furtherance of the historical shift to legislative sovereignty. To Skowronek, it signals the impact of a secular trend toward the thickening of social and political organization on a recurrent pattern of institutional renewal. These perspectives are by no means incompatible with the fact of party realignment; but they do not track from 1896 and are not contemplated by that scheme. The essential disagreement, then, is on the *principle* of relying on any single construct to explain what happened.

Having said this, we heartily agree that much more will be required in the way of future theoretical development to sustain a notion like intercurrence. He is quite right when he points out that it is impossible to study everything, especially at once. Our interest is in clarifying that institutions neither sit there, in time, promoting order, nor move together synchronically, through time, as available conceptions of change, including party realignment, would seem to indicate. The agenda projected is to devise methods to uncover the distinctly institutional aspects of the organization of politics, rooted as we see them in nonsimultaneous origins and multiple orderings.

Fiorina's remarks leave us as mystified as he says ours do him; likewise the letter he mentions having sent us about a different version of this paper. In the first place, it is flatly untrue that we fail to take proper account of his 1986 article that applies an uncertainty model to ICC. Nor do we treat that article as if it applied the SR model, as he suggests; nor do we limit our observations to such "straw men" as pooling, about which he says we agree. His article hypothesizes that U.S. Senators in the majority party will, unlike House members, prefer commission to court enforcement because of the Senate's role in the appointment of ICC commissioners. His rejoinder above reiterates: Republican Senators were willing to trade away pooling for agency delegation because of their "bets about the future, and different institutional prerogatives." We tested this. It didn't work. Republicans had controlled the Senate in every Congress except one (1879–1881) since the Civil War and they would continue as the majority until 1893. But their majority status did not cause them to support to the Commerce Act, with its commission form, in greater numbers than Democrats; on the crucial conference bill vote, the contrary was true.[1]

Similarly, we tested the SR model. For all his disclaimers, Fiorina has given us no convincing reason why this should be prohibited. The model's stated basis for House members to prefer one form of regulation over the other is their desire for reelection. Therefore, we looked to see whether or not there was any difference in voting between House members seeking reelection and those already defeated or retiring. We found there wasn't. Fiorina chooses to see this as a game of "Gotcha!" Please. If he now wants to complicate the SR model with the career patterns of late-nineteenth-century politicians, we would need to know why politicians in constituency-diverse states (who *might* be) eyeing state-wide offices, gubernatorial, presidential appointments, or whatever, would be expected to follow the SR logic of the House and not some other more closely attuned to these different prospects. More directly, our argument is that the SR model is undermined at its logical foundations by the changing patterns of officeholding over time, exactly the sort of historical "noise" we have in mind when we speak of intercurrence.

Through all the smoke and flapping of arms it is apparent that the source of the heat is not that we were negligent in testing only one or even two of Fiorina's "five" models—the one he agrees he "applied" to the ICC and the other he says the ICC merely "motivated." The real issue is that we had the temerity to test these models at all. Models, Fiorina informs us, are to be "compared to the historical record," not "tested." If one doesn't "fit" the historical record or, according to a method yet to be designated, explains only a small part of some variance or other, move on to another. Maybe the SR model might fit the FTC, for instance, or the uncertainty model might. But if the creation of every regulatory agency is to have its own model or set of models, then what of the promise that "reasonably simple models can produce relatively general statements about . . . regularities in the politics of regulation"? This is the point addressed in our paper and the reason we took up these articles in the first place. We argued that the promise of broad historical application is unlikely to be fulfilled by a procedure that isolates institutional rules and freezes them in timeless models. Fiorina's rejoinder marks a retreat.

We seekers—no, "inventors"—of disagreement are constrained to answer when a self-proclaimed champion of complementarities purrs, "put up or shut up." Both of us have written about the ICC's origins; some of our thoughts about intercurrence came from this work. Orren depicted an ICC premised on an interplay between the voluntary rules governing commerce in the late nineteenth century and the coercive rules governing labor. Skowronek related the stillbirth of administrative regulation in 1887 to the dominance of courts and parties in late-century governance. Both of us extended our analysis to other agencies. Whether these accounts are sufficiently simple to satisfy Professor Fiorina is neither here nor there. But someone so ready to hear "my approach is great but yours is worthless" behind straightforward critiques might think to practice what he trumpets. Incidently, to the extent that Fiorina's models are logically but not empirically true, who here is "just tell[ing] stories?"

We wrote the essay against precisely the ritual invocation of "commonalities" that is at odds with intellectual (and professional) reality. We chose strong and influential scholarship to discuss, scholarship located at various points on the methodological spectrum, and that when viewed together illustrates the conceptual lacunae in question. We represent no subfield or group of scholars.[2] Fiorina claims we are interested in change and not stability. Our purpose was to break through the dichotomy that divides the analysis of stability from the analysis of change. We aimed by our critique to show how this dichotomy hampers our understanding of both political institutions and political life.

NOTES

1. Nor did Senate Republicans vote in significantly higher numbers for the commission form than their fellow party members in the House. We tested for this in response to Fiorina's stress on the differ-

ence between the two houses in his rejoinder. In the first vote in the 49th Congress (1885–86), which was in effect to substitute a commission-form bill for the the Reagan bill, 92 House Republicans voted in favor, and 6 voted against. On a second vote to substitute the House Reagan bill for the Senate commission bill, 85 House Republicans favored the commission and 13 voted against. Admittedly, these figures are not comparable with the second Senate vote we cite because the House bills did not incorporate the anti-pooling provision. Therefore we tested for a Senate-House difference in the 48th Congress, when there was no anti-pooling provision attached to any commission bill. Here House Republicans supported the commission bill when it was matched up against the Reagan bill by a margin of 73–7; in the Senate, the number was 28–3.

We are aware that this is not a perfect test of Fiorina's argument. (The question of how members of the Democratic majority in the House might have acted were they, like Senators, overseeing commission appointments must remain where Fiorina left it, in the realm of speculation.) However, if the cross-party Senate comparisons reported in our paper on the point of majority status are somehow off the mark, surely intra-party comparisons across the houses must have some bearing on his hypothesis that institutional position and not party or ideology is important in the choice of regulatory enforcement (1986, 47). This is not to say there is no rationale that might be constructed to explain these figures, but we suspect not one able to satisfy Fiorina's standard of simplicity *and* travel across time.

2. Still less, if possible, did we seek to indicate who is in or out of any "camp," as Fiorina insinuates in his altogether curious footnote 17. This volume, 166.

PART II

DEMOCRACY AND NATIONALISM

8

THINKING ABOUT DEMOCRATIC CONSTITUTIONS: CONCLUSIONS FROM DEMOCRATIC EXPERIENCE

ROBERT A. DAHL

When the Framers of the American Constitution undertook the task of designing a framework for a broadly based representative republic they had no strictly comparable body of historical experience on which to draw. Sheer necessity compelled them to reason from cases that were, at best, only weakly comparable.

By contrast, during the intervening two centuries representative democracy and constitutional government have developed, and sometimes perished, in so many countries that conscientious members of a constitutional convention today might suffer more from an excess of relevant information than from a deficit. A score of countries exist today that have steadily maintained democratic institutions for nearly a half-century or longer. During that same period an even larger number have managed to retain constitutional democracy after gaining it for the first time or restoring it after a breakdown. Breakdowns, too, provide a highly relevant body of experience: in this century, democracy has been displaced by a nondemocratic regime on more than fifty occasions.

Taken together, this large body of historical experience is a rich lode of information from which to mine judgments about democratic constitutions—a challenging program for a science of politics conducted in the spirit of Aristotle's study of the constitutions of Greece or James Madison's pre-Convention study of the history of confederacies and their vices.[1] The range of relevant experiences such a program would have to examine is so vast that it may well never be completed. Nonetheless, parts of it could yield information about the tendencies and likely consequences of alternative constitutional arrangements that would enable those engaged in creating new constitutions or modifying existing ones with some reasonable judgments. Drawing on the experiences of a wide array of countries, a number of scholars recently have made substantial contributions to our understanding of several of the major constitutional alternatives suitable for a democratic country.

In what follows, I am going to draw freely on this recent work in order to formulate some propositions about democratic constitutions that, I believe, are supported by democratic experiences over the past century. So far as possible, I cast these propositions in a form that will facilitate their confirmation or rejection after further experience and analysis is available.

Assumptions

To avoid misunderstanding, however, I need to clarify several of my assumptions. The unit with which I am concerned is a country. As to countries, we need to distinguish between (1) the basic political institutions that define a country as a "democracy"; (2) the conditions that favor the existence of these institutions; and (3) a country's constitutional arrangements.

1. A country is classified as politically "democratic" if certain basic political institutions exist in that country. Because the political order formed by this set of political institutions, taken as a whole, is historically unique, and clearly different in important ways from earlier democracies and republics, it is sometimes helpful to distinguish modern democracy in the nation state by referring to it as a polyarchy or a polyarchal democracy.[2] Therefore I do not discuss constitutions that might have been

suitable for comparatively small city-states in earlier centuries, or for subordinate units of government or very small associations today.

The effective presence of the basic political institutions of a polyarchal democracy also serves to distinguish democratic countries from countries with nondemocratic regimes.[3] I count as "stable" or "older" democracies[4] those countries in which the key institutions of polyarchal democracy have existed continuously for several generations, specifically from 1950 until the present. As I have already mentioned, these number about twenty.[5] "Newer" democracies, then, are countries in which the institutions have not existed continuously since 1950 but did exist in the early 1990s. Among the newer democracies, I should point out, are several (such as Uruguay) which were also democratic in 1950, but where democracy later broke down and was subsequently restored.[6]

2. From a comparison of the experience of the stable democracies with that of countries where the institutions of polyarchy have broken down, are relatively new, or are in varying degrees defective or absent, we can draw some reasonable inferences as to the conditions that favor the development and maintenance of the political institutions of polyarchal democracy. In a moment I shall list some of the most important of these favorable conditions.

3. Finally, then, we need to distinguish a country's constitution both from the basic political institutions of polyarchal democracy and from the conditions that favor their existence. By "constitution," however, I mean the term in a broad sense to include rather enduring political structures, particularly party systems and electoral arrangements, that in conventional usage might not be counted as part of a "constitutional" system. I do so because these interact in crucial ways with the arrangements specified in a country's "constitution" in the conventional sense.

In discussing constitutional alternatives it is also helpful to draw a rough and ready distinction between *major* alternatives and *subordinate* arrangements. For example, among the major constitutional alternatives are Proportional Representation (hereafter PR) versus plurality elections. Given a PR system, a subordinate arrangement would be a requirement that in order to gain representation in the legislature a minimum threshold of votes must be cast for a party's candidates, such as 5 percent.

Keeping these definitions and assumptions in mind, let me now offer some conclusions that I believe are warranted by democratic experience.

I. For developing and maintaining democratic political institutions, constitutional arrangements are less important than the existence of certain favorable conditions.

Among the most important of these conditions are:

The means of violent coercion, mainly the military and police, are effectively under the control of elected and constitutional leaders, or else highly dispersed or otherwise neutralized.

The country possesses a modern dynamic pluralist market-oriented society. That is, by historical and comparative standards the country has high rates of economic growth, high levels of education, an extensive array of relatively autonomous associations and organizations, and so on.

The country is culturally homogeneous; or, if it is heterogeneous, it is not segmented into strong and distinctive subcultures; or, if it is so segmented, its leaders have succeeded in creating a consociational arrangement for managing subcultural conflicts.

Its citizens participate in a political culture that encourages behavior and beliefs, particularly among political activists, that support the institutions of polyarchal democracy.

The country is not subject to intervention by a foreign power hostile to the existence in that country of one or more of the political institutions of polyarchy.

If a country lacks these favorable conditions, or if the obverse (unfavorable) conditions are present, it will almost certainly be governed by a nondemocratic regime. In countries with mixed conditions, some favorable, some unfavorable, if polyarchal democracy exists at all it is likely to be unstable. In some countries with unfavorable conditions, the regime may oscillate between polyarchy and a nondemocratic regime.[7]

II. Creating favorable conditions is difficult, uncertain, and slow, whereas constitutional arrangements are more open to deliberate choice.

We often (indeed to some extent always) confront fundamental conditions that have powerful and lasting effect on outcomes but over which we can exercise little if any deliberate control, such as the effects of climate and rainfall on agricultural production. However, more or less fixed conditions may nonetheless leave us with alternatives. Sometimes our choices may be so constrained as to be trivial; but they are not always so limited. For example, given climate and rainfall we might consider whether it would be best to raise cattle, wheat, or fruit trees. So too with constitutional arrangements. To a far greater extent than the conditions mentioned above, constitutions are subject to deliberate choice.

III. To judge whether differences in constitutional arrangements matter, we need criteria. Reasonable criteria for judging the relative desirability of different democratic constitutions are, however, numerous.

Without intending to imply that the following list is either complete or very precise, let me suggest some reasonable criteria for appraising the achievemens of a democratic constitution:

1. *Contributing to the stability of basic democratic political institutions.* A primary requirement of a good democratic constitution is, of course, to provide a democratic framework of government and to help to preserve the necessary guarantees these institutions require. Although this is the criterion on which I focus later, clearly it is only one of a number of reasonable criteria.

2. *Protecting majority and minority rights and duties.* Here, I single out for extra emphasis the basic rights and duties that provide guarantees for both majorities and minorities. It goes without saying that what constitutes a proper balance is inordinately complex and highly debatable.

3. *Maintaining neutrality.* Having insured fundamental rights and duties, constitutional arrangements should insure that the process of making laws is designed neither to favor nor penalize the views or the legitimate interests of any citizen or group of citizens.

4. *Preserving accountability.* Citizens should be able to hold political leaders accountable for their decisions, actions, and conduct within a "reasonable" interval of time.

5. *Providing fair representation.* What constitutes "fair repre-

sentation" in a democracy is, as everyone knows, the subject of endless controversy. Not to put too fine a point on it, let me say that if by fair representation we mean that groups of citizens with common interests bearing on laws and policies ought to be represented in the legislature in proportion to their numbers, then the most obvious and direct way to achieve it is by some system of PR. But of course fair representation in this sense may clash with other desirable ends, of which two immediately follow.

6. *Aiding the integration of interests: Gaining an informed consensus on laws and policies.*[8] The very electoral arrangements that provide fair representation could also prevent citizens and leaders from engaging in a search for a broader, more informed consensus and thus weaken the capacity of the government for discovering and acting on the more inclusive common interests—the common good, if you will—of its citizens. A good democratic constitution would help to create opportunities and incentives for political leaders to engage in negotiations, accomodation, and coalition building that would facilitate the integration of diverse interests.

7. *Providing effective government.* By effectiveness I mean that a government acts to deal with what citizens understand to be the major issues and problems they confront, and for which they believe government action is appropriate. Effective government is particularly important in times of great emergency brought on by war, the threat of war, acute international tension, severe economic hardship, and similar crises. But it is also relevant in more ordinary times, when major issues head the agendas of citizens and leaders. To be sure, in the short run a nondemocratic government might sometimes meet this criterion better than a democratic government; though whether it would do so in the long run seems more doubtful. In any case, we are concerned here with governments functioning within democratic limits. Within those limits, it seems reasonable to want a constitutional system that has procedures for avoiding protracted deadlock, delay, or evasion in confronting major issues and undertaking actions intended to deal with them.

8. *Facilitating competent decisions.* We would not praise a gov-

ernmental system, however, that facilitated decisive and resolute action but was incapable of drawing on the best knowledge available for solving the urgent problems on the country's agenda. Decisiveness is no substitute for brains.

9. Operating with transparency and comprehensibility. By this pair of criteria, I mean that the operation of the government is sufficiently open to public view and simple enough in its essentials that citizens can readily understand how and what it is doing. Thus, it must not be so complexly constructed that citizens cannot understand what is going on, and, because they do not understand their government, cannot readily hold its leaders accountable, particularly at elections.

10. Being adaptive and resilient. A constitutional system should not be so rigidly constructed or so immutably fixed in writing and tradition that it cannot be adapted to novel situations.

11. Contributing to legitimacy. Meeting the previous ten criteria would surely go a long way toward providing a constitution with sufficient legitimacy and allegiance among citizens and political elites to insure its survival. Yet in a specific country certain constitutional arrangements might be more compatible than others with widespread traditional norms of legitimacy. For example, maintaining a monarch as head of state and yet adapting the monarchy to the requirements of polyarchy has—paradoxical though it may seem to many republicans—conferred additional legitimacy on democratic constitutions in the Scandinavian countries, the Netherlands, Belgium, Japan, Spain, and (at least until recently) Britain. Elsewhere, any attempt to blend a monarch as head of state would clash with widespread republican beliefs. Thus Alexander Hamilton's proposal at the Constitutional Convention for an executive with life tenure—an "elective monarchy"—was rejected almost without debate. As Elbridge Gerry remarked, "There were not 1/1000 part of our fellow citizens who are not against every approach to monarchy."[9]

Although stating these criteria so briefly does an injustice to the complex task of constitution-making, perhaps these phrases catch the essence of some reasonable though not exhaustive criteria for a good democratic constitution.

IV. Because these criteria are numerous and conflicting, it is impossible to judge any democratic constitution as superior to others in all important respects.

Even if we were to set out the criteria more precisely and in greater detail, any list that provides more than a few criteria for guiding decisions inevitably creates space, as judges and policymakers well know, for varying judgments; with eleven criteria, the space is very generous indeed. Moreover, the criteria sometimes conflict with one another. Consider fair representation. Perfectly fair representation might seem to require an extreme form of PR. Yet extreme PR can make both the process of integrating interests and achieving effective government more difficult, whereas plurality elections, it can be argued, would do more to facilitate integration of interests, the ready and clear-cut formation of majority coalitions, and thus government decisiveness. Further conflicts among reasonable criteria for a good constitution would show up if we were to examine some of the other fundamental constitutional alternatives listed earlier—federalism versus unitary government, judicial review versus legislative supremacy, and so on.

Finally, there appear to be no meta-principles that would somehow allow us to arrive at uncontestable solutions to the conflicts.

If it is true that criteria for a good constitution are numerous, that they conflict with one another, and that there are no meta-principles we can employ to judge that one solution is invariably better than all the known alternatives, then how can we reasonably justify a judgment that one constitution is better than the alternatives?

So much for theoretical argument, one might say. Can we not draw on experience with the various alternatives to support practical judgments about their relative desirability? Why not bypass the problem of conflicting criteria by testing the performance of democratic countries against a single criterion at a time? To consider all of the major alternatives in the light of each of the relevant criteria is, however, a task of staggering proportions. Is it possible to draw on recent work to reach some reasonable judgments of narrower applicability?

But what *are* the major constitutional alternatives that might be appraised according to that criterion and the others?

V. Among the older democracies, constitutional arrangements have varied widely.

The stable democracies have definitely *not* adopted just one basic type of constitution. On the contrary, they have persistently maintained several different types. Some of the ways in which the constitutional arrangements of the older democracies vary are:[10]

1. Whether a constitution is written or unwritten. Among the older democracies (and assuredly among the newer ones), an unwritten constitution is a result of highly unusual historical circumstances, as it was in the three exceptional cases of Britain, Israel,[11] and New Zealand.

2. Whether the constitution includes an explicit bill of rights. Again, although its absence is the exception an explicit constitutional bill of rights is not universal among the older democracies.

3. Whether the rights specified in a constitution are exclusively political rights or include social and economic rights as well. Although the American Constitution and those that survive from the nineteenth century in the older democratic countries generally have little to say explicitly about social and economic rights,[12] those adopted since World War II typically do include them.

4. Whether the government is to be federal or unitary. Among the twenty-two older democratic countries, only six are strictly federal. In all six countries, federalism is the result of special historical circumstances.[13]

5. Whether the legislature is to be composed of more than one chamber. Although bicameralism predominates, Israel has never had a second chamber and since 1950 the five Nordic countries and New Zealand have all abolished their upper houses.

6. Whether a judicial body—a supreme or constitutional court—can declare unconstitutional laws properly enacted by the national legislature.

Judicial review has been a standard feature in democratic countries with *federal systems,* where it is seen as necessary if the national constitution is to prevail over laws enacted by the states, provinces, or cantons. But the more relevant issue is whether a court can declare a law enacted by the *national* parliament unconstitutional. Switzerland, in fact, limits the power of judicial review *only* to cantonal legislation. As we just saw, however, most democratic countries are not federal, and among the unitary systems only about half have some form of judicial review. Moreover, even among countries where judicial review does exist, the extent to which courts attempt to exercise this power varies from the extreme case, the United States, to countries where the judiciary is highly deferential to the decisions of the parliament.[14]

7. Whether members of the higher courts, in particular the supreme or constitutional court, are appointed for life tenure or for limited terms. In contrast to the United States, some democratic countries that have explicitly provided for judicial review in constitutions written after World War II (with American experience in full view) have rejected life tenure and instead have chosen to provide for limited, though lengthy, terms, as in Germany, Italy, and Japan.

8. Whether national referenda are possible, or in the case of constitutional amendments, even obligatory. Switzerland provides the limiting case: there, referenda on national issues are permissible, obligatory for constitutional amendments, and frequent. At the other extreme, the U.S. Constitution makes no provision at all for referenda. In more than half the old democracies, however, a referendum has been held at least once.[15]

9. Whether the constitution prescribes a presidential or a parliamentary system.

10. Whether members of the national legislature are chosen by PR or a plurality (first-past-the-post) system. As I suggested earlier, although this choice need not be specified in the "constitution" *sensu strictu,* it is highly relevant because of the way electoral systems interact with other parts of the constitution, and in particular with a presidential versus a parliamentary form.

Although the list of alternatives could be extended even further, it is surely enough to show that constitutional arrangements among the older democracies vary widely.

But do constitutional differences like these really matter? In what ways? According to what criteria? In what follows, I draw on a large amount of recent work that helps us to arrive at some judgments about the consequences of several of the constitutional alternatives for meeting the first and perhaps the most important criterion listed above: maintaining the basic democratic political institutions.

VI. The experience of the stable democracies shows that in countries where the conditions are highly favorable, constitutional variations have no effect on the stability of basic democratic institutions.

Because each of the constitutional alternatives listed earlier has existed in at least one stable democracy, it appears that polyarchal democracy is compatible with many different constitutional arrangements—given the favorable conditions that have prevailed in those countries.[16] Obviously there are limits: the British constitution of the eighteenth century had to change in important ways to accomodate the political institutions of twentieth-century polyarchy. But within broad limits, democratic countries have a wide choice of constitutions.

A particularly conspicuous example of variations in democratic constitutions is provided by alternatives 9 and 10 above.

VII. One important variation in constitutional arrangements is the choice between parliamentary or presidential government and between PR or plurality elections. Each of the major combinations has been chosen by one or more of the stable democracies.

VIII. Among the stable democracies, however, the combination of parliamentary government with PR is far and away the most frequent; the alternative of parliamentary government with plurality elections is limited to several English-speaking countries; while a presidential system with PR, or with plurality elections, each exists in only one stable democracy.

As Arend Lijphart has pointed out, "Two fundamental choices that confront architects of new democratic constitutions are those between plurality elections and proportional representation (PR) and between parliamentary and presidential forms of government."[17] Taken together, these two "fundamental choices" provide four basic options, each of which in turn permits an almost limitless variety of more specific choices: (1) parliamentary government with a PR electoral system; (2) parliamentary government with plurality elections; (3) presidential government with plurality elections; and (4) presidential government with PR elections.

To these four more or less "pure" combinations we need to add (5) the option of a hybrid system that combines elements of presidential and parliamentary government, such as the quasi-presidential system of the French Fifth Republic or the unique plural executive of Switzerland. Further, in a hybrid system elections might be conducted under either a PR or a plurality electoral system. Finally, the electoral system could combine elements of both PR and plurality, as in Germany.

Consider the choices made among the four "pure" combinations and the fifth mixed bag, leaving to one side for the moment significant variations among countries within each of the categories.

1. Parliamentary government with a PR electoral system. Parliamentary government is the overwhelming choice of the older democracies, and among democracies generally it predominates over presidential government. It is worth remarking that whether a country is federal or unitary has no particular bearing on its choosing between a parliamentary and a presidential system. Of the federal systems among the older democracies, four are parliamentary (Australia, Austria, Canada, and Germany) while only the United States is presidential, and Switzerland is a unique hybrid. Thus we can discount federalism as a factor that determines the choice between presidentialism or parliamentarism.

Likewise, among the older democracies, PR is clearly the predominant electoral system. Until 1993, only six of the older democratic countries exclusively employed a plurality system in national elections.[18] With France as a partial exception,[19] five were English-speaking countries in which the traditional English system was adopted with little or no consideration of PR as an alternative. Otherwise, all the older democracies employed PR exclusively or as a significant modification of plurality elections.[20]

It is fairly obvious, then, that the favored combination among the older democracies is a parliamentary system in which members are elected by some system of Proportional Representation. This is predominantly so in Europe, where the newer democracies have also followed the standard European path.[21] Consequently I refer to this combination as the *continental European option*. It is important to keep in mind that the constitutional systems included in this category are in fact of great variety, a point I return to below.

2. *Parliamentary government with plurality elections.* Because of its origins and its prevalence in the English-speaking democracies (other than the United States), we might call this the *British option*. Only four of the older democracies have adopted this solution; not surprisingly, they were the UK, Canada, Australia, and New Zealand.

3. *Presidential government with plurality elections.* Because the United States stands alone among the older democracies in employing this combination, we may call it the *U.S. option*. A half-dozen newer democracies have also chosen this solution.

4. *Presidential government with PR elections.* In their strong preference for presidential government, Latin American countries have followed the same constitutional path as the United States. But in their choice of electoral systems, they have entirely followed European practice. By so doing, they have created a combination distinctly different from that of both the European democracies and the United States. In the fifteen Latin American countries where democratic institutions were more or less in place in the early 1990s, the basic constitutional pattern was a combination of presidential government and PR.[22] It is appropriate therefore to call this the *Latin American option*.

It is striking that with a single exception *none* of the older democracies has selected this option. The exception is Costa Rica, which (unlike every other country in Latin America) has been steadily democratic since about 1950. Although as we have seen the older democracies are strongly predisposed to PR, we have also observed that they have overwhelmingly rejected presidential government.

5. Finally, three democratic countries, all of them older democracies, have created systems that combine aspects of both presidentialism and parliamentarism in various ways: the French Fifth Republic,[23] Finland, and with its unique plural executive consisting of members by elected by parliament for fixed terms, Switzerland.

IX. Each of the major constitutional alternatives is subject to such great variation in its subordinate arrangements that every country's constitutional arrangements are unique.

For example, the last category, "mixed" systems, is hardly more than a catch-all for systems that do not fit the other categories. Yet even the more homogeneous categories prove on inspection to contain great diversity. The differences among European parliamentary systems are in some respects as interesting and as important as their similarities. For example, they may require that parliamentary elections be held *only* at regular four year intervals, as in Norway; that cabinet members *cannot* hold seats in parliament, as in Norway and the Netherlands; that the government can be dismissed only by a "constructive vote of nonconfidence" that elects a replacement, as in Germany, and so on.

Likewise, although I have deliberately ignored variations among countries with some form of PR, the fact is that systems of proportional representation are capable of almost infinite variation. To evaluate PR as if it were a single type, as is the common practice in American discussions, is fatuous. In addition, we need to keep in mind not only that PR itself comes in innumerable flavors, but also that PR and plurality systems can be judiciously combined in different ways.[24] The German option under which half the members of the Bundestag are chosen in single-member districts and half by PR (from national party lists) is widely admired and justifiably so, since it provides a balance between the competing claims of representativeness, favored by PR, and government effectiveness. In several countries where either a PR or plurality system has been a basic element in the constitutional system since democratic institutions were introduced, discontent has been sufficiently great to bring about demands for a version of the German option. Thus, on the heels of a referendum in 1993 in which voters decisively rejected the existing PR system for electing members to the Senate, Italy adopted a new system of plurality elections modified by PR. In that same year but moving in the opposite direction, following a referendum that registered great discontent with the existing plurality system, New Zealand made the first historic break in the ranks of the English-speaking democracies by adopting the German option.

X. In countries where the conditions for democracy are not highly favorable, the greater incentives and opportunities for accommodation provided by a parliamentary system are likely to contribute more than presidential systems to the stability of the basic democratic institutions.[25]

As we have seen, in countries where the conditions are highly favorable for the development and maintenance of democratic institutions, differences in constitutional arrangements appear to have had no perceptible effect on stability (though they may have other important consequences). But in many countries the conditions are not altogether favorable. This is particularly true in countries highly divided by ideological, ethnic, racial, or religious cleavages. Under these conditions, if democratic institutions are to survive—if, for example, a military coup is to be avoided—political leaders will need both strong incentives and significant opportunities for striving to overcome these differences by accommodation, compromise, and building coalitions that cut across the cleavages.[26] To be sure, if conditions highly adverse to democracy are deeply rooted and persistent, then even skillful leadership may be unable to find solutions that will overcome the differences; or, fearing loss of influence, their own incentives and opportunities for compromises and inclusive coalitions will weaken; or, they will be replaced by leaders who seek to profit from confrontation. In the face of highly adverse conditions, constitutional arrangements can go only so far, and may be swept away by nondemocratic forces.

Nonetheless, constitutional arrangements might sometimes make a crucial difference. In particular, parliamentary systems appear to provide more opportunities and incentives for accommodation than do presidential systems:

1. In parliamentary systems, the executive is chosen by the legislature and the legislature by the voters. In presidential systems, the president and the legislature are separately chosen by the voters. In parliamentary systems, then, the executive has no special claim to democratic legitimacy independent of the legislature's claim. In presidential systems, on the other hand, president and legislature can each claim democratic legitimacy from their election by "the people." Typically they do.[27]

2. In parliamentary systems, there is a single electorate. In presidential systems, there are two electorates, and they are not identical. The president is likely to be more responsive to his own electorate, and legislators to theirs.

3. In parliamentary systems, the tenure of the executive is dependent on the continuing support of a majority of legislators, or at least on the unwillingness or inability of a majority to support an alternative to it. In presidential systems, the tenure of the executive is largely independent of the legislature.

4. In presidential systems, the office of the chief executive is occupied by a single person. In parliamentary systems, the cabinet tends to be more collegial.[28]

Certain consequences follow from these different arrangements. Because a president and the legislature look to different constituencies, their policies are likely to conflict. In case of conflict, each can legitimately claim to represent the people. Yet because of their mutual independence, conflicts between president and legislature cannot be easily resolved. They may, indeed, result in deadlock. In a parliamentary system, conflicts between cabinet and parliament are much less likely to arise, and if they arise and persist, the executive can be replaced. In general, then, a parliamentary system provides the cabinet and leaders of the majority coalition in parliament not only with with stronger incentives for resolving conflicts but also with strategic opportunities for doing so. In presidential systems the incentives are weaker—indeed, may work to sharpen the conflict—and opportunities for resolving it are much more limited.

In a country with relatively favorable conditions, such as the United States, that also has a political culture in which the values and practices of compromise and conciliation are deeply embedded, a presidential system may work well enough to avoid outright breakdown.[29] But in countries where the conditions are less favorable, a presidential system is likely to be riskier than a parliamentary system.[30]

Evidence of the relative frequency of breakdowns in countries with parliamentary and presidential systems provides some support for this judgment. From 1973 to 1989, democratic institutions were introduced in fifty-three countries outside the OECD group of advanced industrial democracies. In almost half (twenty-five countries), a presidential system was installed; in the rest (twenty-eight), a parliamentary system was chosen. Democratic breakdowns were frequent: democratic institutions survived continuously for ten years or more in only twenty-two countries. Of these democratic survivors, however, seventeen, or 61 percent, had pure parliamentary systems; only five, or 20 percent, had presidential systems. To put it another way, during the last several decades the rate of breakdown in presidential systems was more than twice as high as in parliamentary systems. Moreover, during this same period military coups were much more common in presidential than in parliamentary systems.[31] Whether democratic experience over the entire twentieth century shows a significantly greater frequency of coups and breakdowns among presidential systems is, however, unclear.[32]

XI. In countries with sharply divided societies, consociational arrangements may help to provide stability.

It is hardly surprising that democracy often breaks down in countries where people are sharply divided by differences in language, religion, race, ethnicity, region, ideology, or combinations of these. What *is* surprising is that a few countries have managed to maintain democratic institutions by developing arrangements that help to overcome the political consequences of such strong cleavages. Consociational arrangements have made a crucial contribution to stability in several older democracies in countries with distinctive subcultures. Arend Lijphart has argued that consociational arrangements might also serve to overcome subcultural cleavages in some newer or emergent democracies as well.[33]

XII. Because of differences in the incentives and opportunities for accommodation they create, electoral systems also make an independent contribution to democratic stability.

In the English-speaking democracies, the winner-take-all character of plurality systems provides little in the way either of incentives or opportunities for accommodation or building coalitions across partisan divisions.[34] As we have seen, among the stable democracies as a whole, PR systems are by a large measure the most numerous. And some scholars contend that in countries where democratic institutions are relatively weak, PR may provide stronger incentives for accommodation and coalition building than plurality systems. As its advocates point out, contrary to conventional views in the English-speaking democracies, PR systems can easily be designed to avoid the extreme multiplication of parties that make the formation and stability of governing coalitions difficult or impossible.[35]

Although there is not space here to discuss the differences among PR systems and their likely consequences, it is important to keep in mind that the list system of PR that most European countries have adopted is not the only alternative to the British and American first-past-the-post system. Donald L. Horowitz has argued that of the three major alternatives—list system PR, the single transferable vote, and the alternative vote—the latter would do the most to strengthen leaders' incentives and opportunities for building political coalitions *across* cleavages.[36] However that may be, in thinking about constitutional arrangements his central point is highly important: Electoral systems should be appraised by, among other things, the opportunities and incentives they provide political leaders for building coalitions that cut across the major cleavages, particularly in countries with highly divided societies.

XIII. Of all the major alternatives, presidentialism with PR—the Latin American option—may be the most unstable.

Many attempts have been made to combine presidentialism with PR, and many have broken down. As we have seen, among the stable democracies only Costa Rica retains this combination. Although the number of significant parties depends in part on the specifics of the PR system, when a multi-party system is combined with presidentialism deadlock between the executive and legislature is more likely than under "either parliamentary systems or two party presidentialism," and it is also more difficult to build interparty coalitions.[37] Again, the explanation is to be found in the shortage of incentives and opportunities for either president or party leaders in the legislature to construct solid coalitions that bridge the political gap between the two branches.

On present evidence, then, a newly democratized country seeking an appropriate constitution would be ill-advised to choose the Latin American option.

XIV. To summarize: Judged by the criterion of stability—helping to maintain the basic democratic institutions—in countries where the conditions are not highly favorable, the best option appears to be parliamentary government with a PR system carefully designed to limit the number of parties. Neither plurality electoral systems nor presidential government provide comparable incentives and opportunities for accommodation and coalition building. The worst of the major alternatives is the combination of presidentialism and PR.

So far, we have examined only two sets of major constitutional alternatives, judging them against only one criterion: stability. Obviously, to undertake a similar appraisal of the other alternatives, judged against some of the other criteria, would be a staggering undertaking. Let me conclude, however, by briefly examining the consequences for stability of one other set of alternatives: judicial review versus parliamentary supremacy.

XV. Among the stable democracies, evidently judicial review is not necessary for maintaining the basic political institutions of polyarchal democracy. However, it might contribute to stability in countries where conditions are less favorable.

Judicial review appears to be a growing feature of democratic constitutions. Many of the constitutions adopted in democratic countries since World War II have adopted some form of judicial review by a constitutional court: for example, Japan, Germay, Austria (re-establishing in 1945 the 1920 constitution),

Greece with the restoration of democracy in 1975, Portugal in 1976 after the fall of the Salazar regime, Spain in 1978 after the fall of Franco.[38]

An American unfamiliar with democratic experience elsewhere might argue that to protect and preserve the constitutional framework of government, the basic democratic institutions and the essential rights and duties they require, particularly the rights of minorities, a democratic constitution must necessarily provide for judicial review of laws enacted by the national legislation. Many Americans—and not a few constitutional lawyers—would, I suspect, find it hard to believe that democracy could function without a supreme court endowed with the power of judicial review. Yet because, as we have already seen, some democratic countries manage without judicial review—among the old democracies, the United Kingdom, New Zealand, Belgium, Finland, Luxembourg, Netherlands, and Switzerland (with respect to national legislation)—it is simply impossible to demonstrate that judicial review is a necessary requirement for the stability of democratic institutions.

Nevertheless, our advocate might argue that in countries that do provide for judicial review, fundamental rights are *better* protected than in democratic countries without it. In particular, one might contend that thanks to the vigorous exercise of judicial review, fundamental rights have been more firmly protected in the United States than in democratic countries where the judiciary has entirely lacked this authority or has exercised it within very narrow limits. So far as I know, however, no systematic studies exist that would support this hypothesis.

Casual evidence, on the other hand, lends it scant support. As to political rights, in perhaps none of the older democracies—with or without judicial review—have unpopular political groups suffered so much discrimination, notably, of course, communists. In fact, in exercising judicial review the Supreme Court has sometimes been a major factor in *depriving* persons of the most fundamental of human and political rights: e.g., slaves (Dred Scott in 1857) and newly freed slaves (the Civil Rights cases of 1883). As to what now would be widely regarded as social and economic rights, the U.S. Supreme Court has sometimes exercised its authority to strike them down—notoriously in the case of child labor—long after they had successfully been enacted into law in some other democratic countries.[39]

One might argue further, of course, that although judicial review may not be necessary in all democratic countries, the special conditions of the United States do make it imperative there, and perhaps in some other democratic countries as well.[40] In a moment, I want to say a word about the importance of designing a constitution to meet a country's special conditions. Meanwhile, we can accept as at least plausible that in countries where democratic institutions and the rule of law are less firmly established, judicial review might add some protection. At the same time, however, precisely because of those conditions it would be risky for a court to exercise its power in a contest with the legislature or executive, or both, on a highly controversial issue.[41]

XVI. The preceding judgments, like all general judgments about constitutional arrangements, should always be tempered by the need to adapt constitutional arrangements to the special conditions of a country.

A country's special conditions—historical, cultural, ethnic and racial, territorial, economic, social, ideological, and others—may often require special arrangements. The Swiss constitutional system, with its consociational arrangements, plural executive at the national level, strong decentralization of authority to relatively small and homogeneous cantons, and frequent use of national referenda to reach a settlement on issues over which the Swiss people are divided, is unique. As best one can judge, among the Swiss it works well. Yet in almost any other country it would probably work badly. No other country seems to have found a plural executive workable. Uruguay's 1919 constitution prescribed a modified plural executive that ended in dictatorship in 1933. Its 1952 constitution, adopted by referendum, established a "true plural executive," which, however, was abolished by referendum in 1967.[42]

As in Switzerland, the constitutional systems of the United States, Canada, Australia, and Germany are federal. In each of these countries, historical conditions provided a strong early justification for federalism. It is virtually irrelevant to ask whether a unitary constitution would have served these countries better. For example, given the political conditions of the United States in 1787 a unitary system was simply not possible. Once well established, federalism became so deeply embedded in American political life, culture, practices, and beliefs that to abolish it was downright unthinkable. Would a unitary constitution have served the United States and the other federal countries better than federalism? Conversely, would all democratic countries be better off under a federal system?

Democratic countries vary so greatly in their conditions that no single constitutional order can be suitable for all. Despite the widespread belief among U.S. citizens that their constitutional system is the best in the world, the record decisively demonstrates that the U.S. system is simply not for export. The "Westminster model" of two-party parliamentary government in a unitary system with plurality elections in single-member districts, which English and American political scientists often upheld as a model, has been successfully adopted in a number of very small Caribbean countries (Belize, for example). But as we have seen, it has been rejected by continental Europeans. Even the home of the Westminster model has not for some years had a two-party system. What is more, two of Britain's offspring—Canada and Australia—chose federalism and three-party systems, while New Zealand, for generations the unflawed embodiment of the Westminster model, has opted for PR and, as a likely consequence, a multi-party system.

XVII. There is no one best democratic constitutional system.

From the argument presented here, a reader might conclude that on the whole the continental European option is—in my view, at least—the best democratic constitutional system. However, let me restate several reasons for rejecting that conclusion. First, that option, we must remember, is defined by two very general alternatives—presidential versus parliamentary government and PR versus plurality elections—each of which, as I have repeatedly emphasized, covers an enormous range of actual and possible variations. Constitution-makers cannot just buy a single standard model off the floor and let it go at that. Here, as elsewhere, God, and the devil too, is in the details.

Second, mixed or "impure" systems may in some circumstances be better than a "pure" option: for example, the German combination of PR and plurality elections, which has recently replaced pure PR in Italy and pure plurality elections in New Zealand; or the French Fifth Republic mix of presidential and parliamentary government; or—given Switzerland's special conditions—the unique Swiss system.

Third, the continental European option, like the others, is defined by only two extremely simplified constitutional alternatives. I listed eight others that require choices just as fundamental: judicial review, federalism, and so on. Thus, to choose the continental European option would at most be no more than a beginning to the difficult task of creating a democratic constitution.

It is true, surely, that if a constitutional convention were to assemble today for the purpose of constructing a constitution for an existing or evolving democratic country, its members would have vastly more experience on which draw than has ever before been available. As a result, they could be far more fully informed by relevant knowledge than could any previous constitution-makers, even so recently as a few generations ago. If, and as, the Aristotelian-Madisonian program is carried further, to arrive at wise constitutional judgments should be less difficult than it was in 1787. Yet the task is inherently so complex that it will never be easy.

NOTES

1. Cf. William Lee Miller, *The Business of May Next, James Madison and the Founding* (Charlottesville: University of Virginia Press, 1992), 15–16.

2. With this understanding, in what follows I use such terms as democracy, modern democracy, polyarchy, democratic countries, and

the like, as interchangeable. The seven basic political institutions that, taken together, distinguish polyarchal democracy are that elected officials are constitutionally vested with control over government decisions about policy; elections are free and fair; suffrage is inclusive; the right to run for office is widely extended; freedom of expression is effectively protected; alternative sources of information are accessible; and citizens and groups have an effective right to associational autonomy. Further elaboration of, and the rationale for, this definition is set forth in Robert A. Dahl, *Democracy and Its Critics* (New Haven: Yale University Press, 1989), chapter 15, 213–24. See also Robert A. Dahl, "Procedural Democracy," in *Philosophy, Politics, and Society,* ed. Peter Laslett and James Fishkin (New Haven: Yale University Press, 1979).

3. The institutional criteria above were converted by Michael Coppedge and Wolfgang H. Reinicke to a scale for measuring polyarchy, which they then applied to 170 countries that were independent in 1985. See their "Measuring Polyarchy," in *On Measuring Democracy: Its Consequences and Concomitants,* ed. Alex Inkeles (New Brunswick, N.J.: Transaction Publishers, 1991), 47–68. The classification below of democratic countries as "stable" (or "older") and "newer" draws on their work, slightly modified by later information.

4. Note that stable democracy in this sense is not equivalent to what is often referred to as "governmental stability," i.e., the relative rate of turnover of cabinets or "administrations." It is one thing for a democratic "government" (in the European sense) to fall; it is quite another for a democratic regime to fall. In the first case, democracy persists; indeed, the fall of the "government" may be a sign of democratic vigor. In the second case, democracy is replaced by a nondemocratic regime. Among the stable democracies, some have had much higher rates of cabinet turnover—instability of "governments"—than others. Even cabinet turnover, however, can be misleading if, as in Italy until 1993, the "new" government consisted for the most part of the same persons who made up the old government.

5. Arend Lijphart has cited twenty-one countries as continuously democratic "since about World War II," *Democracies, Patterns of Majoritarian, and Consensus Government in Twenty-One Countries* (New Haven: Yale University Press, 1984), Table 3.1, at 38. These countries are also substantially the same as Samuel P. Huntington's survivors from the first (1828–1926) and second (1943–1962) waves of democratization. *The Third Wave: Democratization in the Late Twentieth Century* (Norman, Okla.: University of Oklahoma Press, 1991), 15. To Lijphart's list Costa Rica should be added because it has been steadily democratic since about 1950. The present constitution was adopted in 1949 and the first

elections under it were held in 1953. By virtue of the constitutional shift from the Fourth to the Fifth Republic in France, Lijphart's twenty-one countries actually furnish twenty-two constitutional systems, or, with the addition of Costa Rica, twenty-three. Michael Coppedge and Wolfgang H. Reinicke ranked all these countries (with the exception of Israel) in the highest of eleven scale types in measuring the degree of polyarchy in 170 countries in the mid-1980s. "Measuring Polyarchy," 60. Because of some limits on freedom of expression, Israel was placed in the next scale type. In his annual Comparative Survey of Freedom, Raymond D. Gastil also rated Israel somewhat lower than older democracies. See "The Comparative Survey of Freedom: Experiences and Suggestions," in *On Measuring Democracy: Its Consequences and Concomitants,* ed. Alex Inkeles (New Brunswick, N.J.: Transaction Publishers, 1991), 21–46. In the discussion that follows, however, Israel is included among the older democracies.

6. In 1993, the political institutions of polyarchal democracy existed in at least twenty countries at levels comparable to those of the older democracies. In another ten countries, the institutions were largely intact but in some respects impaired.

7. For reasons of space and relevance, this summary of the favorable conditions is a radically shortened and simplified version of the discussion in chapters 18 and 19 of my *Democracy and Its Critics,* chapters 18 and 19, 224–64. See also Seymour Martin Lipset, "The Social Requisites of Democracy Revisited" (Presidential Address, American Sociological Association, 1993). A detailed comparison of eighteen European countries during the interwar period, comparing eight countries in which it survived with ten in which it failed, yields a rather similar set of favorable conditions. See Dirk Berg-Schlosser and Gisèle de Meur, "Conditions of Authoritarianism, Fascism, and Democracy in Inter-War Europe: Systematic Matching and Contrasting of Cases for 'Small-N' Analysis" (unpublished manuscript, 1993) and "Conditions of Democracy in Inter-War Europe—Reduction of Complexity for a Small-N Analysis" (unpublished manuscript, 1992).

8. In political science jargon, this is often called interest aggregation, a term that seems misleading in its implication that simple additivity will do the trick.

9. According to Madison's notes, in a lengthy speech on June 18, 1787, Hamilton remarked, "As to the Executive, it seemed to be admitted that no good one could be established on republican principles. . . . The English model was the only good one on this subject. . . . Let one branch of the Legislature hold their places for life or at least during good behavior. Let the Executive also be for life." See Max Farrand,

ed., *The Records of the Federal Convention,* vol. I (New Haven: Yale University Press, 1966), 289. Gerry's comment on June 26 is at 425.

10. For a brief discussion of the principal alternatives adopted by the older democracies, see Lijphart, *Democracies,* on which I have drawn freely.

11. Through a series of enactments by the parliament sitting as a constitutional body, Israel has been converting its constitutional arrangements into a written constitution.

12. Some social and economic rights have been added to the American Constitution directly, as with the Thirteenth Amendment abolishing slavery, or via congressional and judicial interpretation of the Fifth and Fourteenth Amendments.

13. These are Australia, Austria, Canada, Germany, Switzerland, and the United States. Lijphart, Tables 10.1 and 10.2, at 174, 178. Because of its regional decentralization, Belgium might reasonably be added to the list. As with other constitutional arrangements, the categories "federal" and "unitary" include significant variations.

14. As in the Scandinavian countries. In France, the constitution of the Fifth Republic modified the practice of the Third and Fourth Republics according to which the judiciary was expected to defer completely to parliamentary decisions. Although, once promulgated, "a parliamentary enactment *(loi)* was (and allegedly, still is) absolutely unchallengeable in any court, including the Conseil Constitutionel," during the short period between parliamentary approval and promulgation, the Constitutional Court can be asked to pass on its constitutionality. Originally interpreted in very strict fashion, the Constitutional Court has somewhat expanded its claims. Mauro Cappelletti, *Judicial Review in the Contemporary World* (Indianapolis: Bobbs-Merrill, 1971), 153–60.

15. See Lijphart, *Democracies,* Table 12.1, at 262.

16. That the conditions were and are relatively favorable is, of course, an empirical assertion. Here I adopt it by assumption. The evidence is, however, quite extensive. See, for example, *Democracy and Its Critics,* chapter 18, "Why Polyarchy Developed in Some Countries and Not Others," 244–65, and Seymour Martin Lipset, "The Social Requisites of Democracy Revisited" (Presidential Address, American Sociological Association, 1993).

17. Arend Lijphart, "Constitutional Choices for New Democracies," *Journal of Democracy* 2 (Winter 1991): 72–85, at 72.

18. In late 1993, one of these, New Zealand, abandoned that system in favor of the German solution, where half the seats are awarded

by PR and half are chosen by plurality elections in single-member districts.

19. The French system might be regarded as a majority system (not a plurality system) because of the requirement of a run-off if no candidate receives a majority of votes.

20. In 1993, Italy shifted from an exclusively PR system to a modified plurality system in which only 25 percent of the seats were awarded by PR and the rest by voters in single-member districts. Also in 1993, a reform-minded government in Japan proposed to replace multi-member districts with single-member districts.

21. Of nineteen old and new democratic countries in Europe in 1993, fourteen combined parliamentary government with some form of PR. As noted in note 20 above, in 1993 Italy greatly reduced the proportion of parliamentary seats chosen by PR. Because of the weakness of the presidents in Austria, Iceland, and Ireland, "these systems are unambiguously parliamentary." Arend Lijphart, "Presidentialism and Majoritarian Democracy: Theoretical Observations" in *The Failure of Presidential Democracy,* ed. Juan J. Linz and Arturo Valenzuela (Baltimore: The Johns Hopkins University Press, 1994), 91–105, at 95.

22. For details, see Dieter Nohlen, "Sistemas Electorales y Gobernabilidad," in *Elecciones y Sistemas de Partidos en America Latina,* ed. Dieter Nohlen (San Jose, Costa Rica: Instituto Interamericano de Derechos Humanos, 1993), 391–424. See also Dieter Nohlen, ed., *Enciclopedia electoral Latinoamericana y del Caribe* (San Jose, Costa Rica: Instituto Interamericano de Derechos Humanos, 1993). In counting fifteen Latin American countries, I exclude the island countries of the Caribbean together with Guyana and Belize on the mainland. In 1990, twelve independent countries in the Caribbean region, including Guyana and Belize, were members of the British Commonwealth. Prior to independence all had been British colonies, most of them for two centuries or more. Of these, only Jamaica and Trinidad/Tobago had populations greater than one million; of the rest, none except Guyana exceeded approximately a quarter of a million in population. Without exception, all twelve had adopted the British (Westminster) constitutional model. See Bernd Hillebrands, "El Desarollo de la Democracia Westminster en los Micro-Estados del Commonwealth-Caribe," in *Elecciones y Sistemas de Partidos en America Latina,* ed. Dieter Nohlen (San Jose, Costa Rica: Instituto Interamericano de Derechos Humanos, 1993), 355–90.

23. Following Maurice Duverger, "A New Political System Model: Semi-Presidential Government," *European Journal of Political Research* 8,

no. 2 (1980): 165–87, Lijphart contends that "the Fifth Republic is, instead of semipresidential, usually presidential and only occasionally parliamentary." See "Presidential and Majoritarian Democracy," 95.

24. Moreover, as Steven J. Brams reminds us an alternative to both plurality elections and PR is *approval voting*, which he argues is markedly superior to both. See Steven J. Brams and Peter C. Fishburn, *Approval Voting* (Boston: Birkhauser, 1983) and "Approval Voting and the Good Society," *The Newsletter of PEGS* 3, no. 1 (Winter 1993): 10.

25. In what follows, I owe a heavy debt to the work edited by Juan Linz and Arturo Valenzuela cited in footnote 21, and particularly to Linz's opening chapter, "Presidential or Parliamentary Democracy: Does It Make a Difference?" 3–87. In addition to his essay and the chapter by Stepan and Skach cited above, I have drawn on Arend Lijphart, "Presidentialism and Majoritarian Democracy: Theoretical Observations," 91–105, and Giovanni Sartori, "Neither Presidentialism nor Parliamentarism," 106–18. Earlier versions of Linz's argument, both published and unpublished, have fueled a considerable controversy. See Linz's "The Perils of Presidentialism," *Journal of Democracy* 1 (Winter 1990): 51–70, and the criticism by Donald L. Horowitz, "Comparing Democratic Systems," *Journal of Democracy* 1 (Fall 1990): 73–79. Arend Lijphart, ed., *Parliamentary versus Presidential Government* (Oxford: Oxford University Press, 1992) contains selections from thirty-four essays by different authors dealing with aspects of this question. See also Scott Mainwaring, "Presidentialism, Multipartism, and Democracy: The Difficult Combination," in *Flying Blind: Emerging Democracies in East Central Europe,* ed. György Szoboszlai (Budapest: Hungarian Political Science Association, 1992), 59–85; and Arturo Valenzuela, "The Crisis of Presidentialism," *Journal of Democracy* 4 (October 1993): 3–16.

26. This point is strongly emphasized by Donald L. Horowitz, *A Democratic South Africa? Constitutional Engineering in a Divided Society* (Berkeley: University of California Press, 1991).

27. For the development of this claim by American presidents from Andrew Jackson on, see Robert A. Dahl, "The Pseudodemocratization of the American Presidency," *The Tanner Lectures on Human Values* X (1989), ed. Grethe B. Peterson (Cambridge: Cambridge University Press, 1988), 33–72.

28. This feature is emphasized by Lijphart in "Presidentialism and Majoritarian Democracy," 91–105. He argues that "the prime minister's position in the cabinet can vary from preeminence to virtual

equality with the other ministers, but there is always a relatively high degree of collegiality in decision making," 93.

29. It would be a mistake, however, to attribute the American Civil War to the defects of presidentialism. By expressing a willingness to accept slavery in the Southern states, Lincoln's determined efforts in 1861 to negotiate a compromise went far beyond the moral and political limits that he came to insist on by 1863. The American Civil War demonstrates that conflicts in interests, values, and ways of life are sometimes so profound that no constitutional system can overcome them.

30. I should point out that Giovanni Sartori is somewhat skeptical of the predominant thrust of the contributors to the Linz volume, cited above. "My stance is . . . that semipresidentialism can improve presidentialism and, similarly, that semiparliamentary systems (if I may so call the *Kanzler* or premiership formulas) are better than plain parliamentary ones." See "Neither Presidentialism nor Parliamentarism," in *The Failure of Presidential Democracy,* ed. Juan J. Linz and Arturo Valenzuela (Baltimore: The Johns Hopkins University Press, 1994), 110.

31. Alfred Stepan and Cindy Skach, "Presidentialism and Parliamentarism in Comparative Perspective," in *The Failure of Presidential Democracy,* ed. Juan J. Linz and Arturo Valenzuela (Baltimore: The Johns Hopkins University Press, 1994), 119–36, Table 4.3, at 124, and Table 4.4, at 125.

32. Mathew Soberg Shugart and John M. Carey, *Presidents and Assemblies: Constitutional Design and Electoral Dynamics* (Cambridge: Cambridge University Press, 1992), count thirty-nine cases of democratic breakdowns in the twentieth century. Of these twenty-one were parliamentary systems, twelve were presidential, and six were mixed systems. (See Table 3.1, at 40.) From this evidence they conclude that there is "no justification for the claim of Linz and others that presidentialism is inherently more prone to crises that lead to breakdown" (42). However, since they do not show relative *frequencies,* it is hard to know what to make of their finding. Moreover, probably because of differences in criteria (39) their list of twentieth-century breakdowns is substantially different from that of Frank Bealey, "Stability and Crisis: Fears about Threats to Democracy," *European Journal of Political Research* 15 (1987): 687–715. Bealey lists fifty-three breakdowns (excluding nine cases of foreign occupation during World War II). His list contains twenty-three cases not on Shugart and Carey's list, and theirs contains sixteen not on his. The combined total from both lists would thus be

sixty-nine. Clearly this large number of breakdowns invites further analysis.

33. See Arend Lijphart, *Democracy in Plural Societies* (New Haven: Yale University Press, 1977) and *Power-Sharing in South Africa* (Berkeley: University of California Institute of International Studies, 1985). In facilitating the creation of consociational arrangements and their dissolution when they are no longer necessary, parliamentary government with a PR electoral system may have an advantage over the winner-take-all presidential system. See Lijphart, "Presidentialism and Majoritarian Democracy," 97. During Holland's consociational period from 1917–1967, the parties continued to be represented in parliament according to their popular votes and the cabinets were made up of shifting coalitions. By contrast, when Colombian party leaders sought to ward off the danger of a repetition of the earlier costly civil war, they inaugurated a system from 1958–1974 that required alternation between liberals and conservatives in the presidency and parity in seats in the Congress. In effect, voters were disfranchised in the interests of stability.

34. So many other factors help to account for the breakdown of the British model among African countries that it can hardly be assigned major responsibility. However, among the twelve Caribbean countries that adopted the British model after gaining independence from Britain, breakdowns occurred in two countries that suffered from an extreme polarization that political leaders not only failed to overcome but probably exacerbated. In Guyana, the polarization took place along ethnic lines, in Grenada on ideological lines. See Hillebrands, cited above in footnote 22.

35. Arend Lijphart argues that it is possible to avoid "extreme PR, which poses few barriers to small parties" by "applying PR in small districts instead of large districts or nationwide ballotting, and requiring parties to receive a minimum percentage of the vote in order to gain representation, such as the 5 percent threshold in Germany. The Dutch, Israel, and Italian systems exemplify extreme PR and the German and Swedish systems, moderate PR." "Constitutional Choices for New Democracies," *Journal of Democracy* 2 (Winter 1991): 72–84, at 73. Moreover, despite the well-known tendency of PR to generate a multiparty system, two-party systems have effectively existed in several countries with a high degree of political homogeneity where the two largest parties ordinarily have won, despite PR, an overwhelming share of the vote. Examples are Costa Rica, Ireland, Uruguay, and Venezuela. For Uruguay and Venezuela, see Bernhard Thibaut, "La Estruct-

ura y Dinámica de la Competencia Partidista y el Problema de la Estabilidad de las Democracias Presidenciales en Costa Rica y Venezuela," in *Elecciones y Sistemas de Partidos en America Latina,* ed. Dieter Nohlen (San Jose, Costa Rica: Instituto Interamericano de Derechos Humanos, 1993), 269–314. For the two-party system of Uruguay, see Julio Barreiro, "El Sistema de Partidos Políticos en Uruguay," Working Paper 65, Institut de Ciències Polítiques i Socials (Barcelona, 1993).

36. Horowitz, *A Democratic South Africa?* chapter 5, 163–203. See also his "The Challenge of Divided Societies," *Journal of Democracy* 4 (October 1993): 18–38.

37. Scott Mainwaring, "Presidentialism, Multipartism, and Democracy: The Difficult Combination," in *Flying Blind: Emerging Democracies in East Central Europe* ed., György Szoboszlai, (Budapest: Hungarian Political Science Association, 1992), 58–85. See also his "Presidentialism in Latin America," *Latin American Research Review* 25, vol. I (1990): 157–79.

38. Mauro Cappelletti, *The Judicial Process in Comparative Perspective* (Oxford: Clarendon Press, 1989), 187–88. Perhaps the most interesting case is France, where "separation of powers" had long been interpreted to mean that judges could not rule on the constitutionality of parliamentary legislation. Under the Fifth Republic, however, a limited form of judicial review has developed. Ibid., 153–60.

39. Congressional legislation outlawing child labor was passed in 1916 and declared unconstitutional by the Supreme Court in 1918 by a vote of 5–4. The majority opinion was delivered by Justice Day, who had been appointed fifteen years earlier. In 1922, the Court ruled unconstitutional a second congressional law passed in 1919. As a further indication of widespread support, Congress was able to pass a constitutional amendment in 1924, but the amendment failed to gain the support of three-fourths of the states. Legislation passed in 1938 was finally accepted as constitutional by the Court in 1941.

40. It is worth noting that for courts with the authority to exercise judicial review of legislation, life tenure for judges is not demonstrably the best solution. Although tenure for life helps to insure judicial independence, the combination of judicial review with lifetime tenure, as in the United States, increases the possibility that members of the judiciary appointed in an earlier period will resist changes widely supported by legislative and popular majorities. Indeed, that possibility is presumably the purpose of life tenure. However, an unintended consequence is to make appointments to the Supreme Court matters of intense political and ideological controversy. As we saw earlier,

other democratic countries that have created constitutional courts have provided the justices with lengthy but not life terms.

41. As the experience of the Russian Constitutional Court in 1993 illustrates.

42. Harry Kantor, "Efforts Made by Various Latin American Countries to Limit the Power of the President," in Lijphart, *Parliamentary versus Presidential Government,* 101–9.

9

MAJORITY RULE AND MINORITY INTERESTS

NICHOLAS R. MILLER

I. Introduction

The nomination in the Spring of 1993 of Lani Guinier to be Assistant Attorney General for Civil Rights, and the concomitant attention focused on her law review articles,[1] might have generated a useful public discussion on the relationship between majority rule and minority interests. But the discussion that got under way was hardly constructive or enlightening and, in any case, it was aborted along with the nomination. This essay attempts, in what is surely a very limited and incomplete way, to advance such a discussion.

In the introductory chapter to her book, *The Tyranny of the Majority,* Guinier discusses examples of collective choice in which majority rule implies that "the numerically more powerful majority choice simply subsumes minority preferences." In such cases, "the majority that rules gains all the power and the minority that loses gets none." Thus, in some circumstances—in particular, in a "racially divided society"—"majority rule may

This chapter was presented as a paper to the Yale Workshop in Political Theory, January 1995, and to the 1995 Annual Meeting of the Public Choice Society, Long Beach, March 1995. I am grateful to Brian Barry, James Buchanan, Lani Guinier, Jack Nagel, Hannu Nurmi, Jason Saving, and Ian Shapiro for comments and suggestions.

be perceived as majority tyranny," operating in a "winner-take-all" fashion that cleanly (but unnecessarily) partitions society into political "winners" and "losers."[2] Members of the minority, though equally enfranchised in formal terms, gain nothing with respect to collective choice from their enfranchisement.

The view that there is a fundamental incompatibility between majority rule and minority interests (a view which in fact Guinier does not unconditionally endorse) is commonly advanced and has, at first blush, a compelling plausibility. *Of course,* minority interests must suffer under majority rule. The only question seems to be whether one's reaction is: "so much the worse for minority interests" or "so much the worse for majority rule."

I hope to show that this surface plausibility is less compelling on closer analysis. This chapter attempts to clarify, and in so doing substantially qualify (though not totally negate), the common argument that majority rule invariably operates on a "winner-take-all" basis that renders minority interests irrelevant.

I undertake this task in a distinctive fashion, by employing the particular style of analysis associated with formal political theory and social choice theory.[3] Works within this tradition have significantly clarified the logical nature of majority-rule decision making, but they have rarely addressed the issue of majority rule versus minority interests,[4] even though this issue has an ancient pedigree in political theory and is a standard debating point in practical political arguments. I hope to show that the logic of formal political theory in fact provides helpful insights into this long-standing issue. More specifically, I distinguish among three types of politics—here labelled "cleavage politics," "ideological politics," and "distributive politics"—and show that the issue of majority rule versus minority interests plays out quite differently in each context. In the context of cleavage politics, the common argument is fully supported if there is just one issue; but, given several issues on which preferences are crosscutting, the argument must be qualified. In the context of ideological politics, majority rule typically produces compromise outcomes, and the interests of even an ideologically distinctive minority typically receive considerable weight. In the context of distributive politics, majority rule is chaotic and cannot be blamed or credited for any particular outcome.

Adopting the social choice framework has implications for the scope of this study that should be explicitly noted.

First, in considering majority rule within the framework of social choice theory, we are solely concerned with "majority rule" as a formal "decision rule"—that is, as a procedure or institution for collective choice; we are not concerned with the social locus of political power or electoral enfranchisement, as we would be in speaking of the "movement towards majority rule" in Europe a century ago or in South Africa much more recently. And whereas "majority rule" may have had distinctively "radical" or "progressive" implications for government policy in the past (or in present South Africa), it may have "conservative" ones in mostly affluent industrial or post-industrial societies (especially those with racial or similar minorities). Insofar as the following analysis suggests why present racial or similar minorities may not fare too badly under majority rule, it also suggests why economic minorities (e.g., the rich) also have not fared badly.

Second, it needs to be emphasized that the concept here counterposed to "majority rule" is "minority interests"—not, as is more commonly the case, "minority rights."[5] The issue of "majority rule versus minority rights" is an important and difficult (though probably mislabelled) one in political practice and constitutional law, but the issue need not in principle raise a problem within the context of social choice theory. Social choice theory often assumes (as we do here) that a collectivity has made a prior "constitutional agreement" concerning the domain of activities that are subject to collective decision—the scope of powers "delegated" (so to speak) to the collectivity—and concerning the decision rule (majority rule or otherwise) to be employed in making these decisions.[6] In the complementary domain of activities "reserved" (so to speak) for individual choice, the rights of individuals hold sway.[7] Thus majority rule operates in one domain, the rights of individuals—regardless (and this is why the issue may be mislabelled) of whether they belong to particular majorities or minorities—in another. The minority interests we are concerned with here are not those interests that are secured (at least in principle) as individual rights but precisely those interests unquestionably at play within the domain of collective control and choice.

Finally, our concern is with the implications for minority interests of majority rule operating at the level of the overall political institutions of society. To bring the issue of majority rule versus minority interests most directly into focus, we assume that "simple majoritarian power relations" exist within society. This means that any coalition in society comprising a majority of the whole can bring about whatever political outcomes (within the domain of collective control and choice) it wants.[8] We are not, therefore, particularly concerned with the issue of "majoritarian" versus "proportional" electoral systems (which, of course, is Guinier's principal concern), since legislatures and parliaments, however elected, typically use majority rule to enact their decisions. It is worth emphasizing that, insofar as there is a conflict between majority rule and minority interests, a proportional electoral system by itself does little to mitigate the conflict. Indeed, given legislative majority rule, it follows that a society that uses proportional representation to elect its parliament is if anything even more reliably majoritarian in its overall power relations that one that uses a "majoritarian" electoral system.[9]

II. The Social Choice Framework

In this section, I sketch out a social choice framework that unavoidably entails a vastly oversimplified representation of any political system. But it allows us to think clearly about the relationship between majority rule and minority interests.

We suppose that a political system has three ingredients: (1) a set of "issues" concerning activities within the domain of collective control that accordingly must be resolved by collective choice; (2) a set of "citizens" endowed with "preferences" (or "interests") with respect to these issues; and (3) a political "decision rule" that determines how citizen preferences ultimately count in resolving these issues. In these terms, we also distinguish among three types of politics.

1. *Issues*

Formally, an issue is a set of two or more mutually exclusive *alternatives* (possible policies, programs, budgets, etc.), exactly one of which must be collectively chosen by the polity.

Some issues are *discrete,* with a finite, and typically small, number of distinct alternatives. The simplest kind of issue is *dichotomous*—that is, one with just two alternatives ("pro" and "con," "*X*" and "not *X*," "NAFTA" and "not NAFTA," or whatever). A more complex kind of issue is *polychotomous*—that is, one with multiple distinct alternatives ("NAFTA," "not NAFTA," and "NAFTA with specified amendments," or whatever).

Other issues are *continuous,* with an infinite number of alternatives. Social choice theorists customarily think of such an infinite set as an *alternative space* of one or several dimensions. Suppose, for example, that an issue that must be resolved is the funding level of some collective activity or the provision of some *public good.* The "space" of possible funding or provision levels is infinite—a continuum running from zero upwards. An alternative space might also represent an *ideological* spectrum running along a continuum from left to right. Some continuous issues are multidimensional. *Allocative* issues provide an example. For example, if a fixed supply of some *private* good (benefit) or bad (cost) must be divided three ways, every point on the surface of an equilateral triangle represents a possible alternative.

2. *Preferences*

We now consider the *citizens* who may participate in the political system and who have *preferences* on issues. We suppose that these preferences are (to use a technical term) *separable* by issues. This means that preferences on one issue are not conditioned on the resolution of other issues.[10]

Preferences over discrete issues are described by orderings of the alternatives from most to least preferred. (For simplicity, we suppose that no one is indifferent between discrete alternatives.)

With respect to continuous one-dimensional issues, we make a more powerful (but plausible and standard) assumption. We suppose, first, that each citizen has a most preferred alternative or *ideal point* on the issue continuum and, second, that, in comparing two points on the same side of his ideal point, each citizen prefers the one closer to his ideal to the one more distant from it. Such preferences are called *single-peaked,* for reasons that are evident if one imagines drawing a "utility curve" (or "function") to describe preferences over the issue continuum.[11]

We need also to specify preferences in a more comprehensive way. Several issues may (at least implicitly) be considered jointly, so we must suppose each citizen has preferences over *political outcomes,* i.e., combinations of alternatives, one for each issue under consideration. If the issues are discrete, these outcomes are likewise discrete (though relatively numerous) and preferences over them can be described by an ordering. Separability restricts what orderings can occur, however. Suppose that two dichotomous issues, X_1 (with alternatives x_1 and $\bar{x}_1$) and X_2 (with alternatives x_2 and $\bar{x}_2$), are under simultaneous consideration. There are four possible outcomes: (x_1,x_2), $(x_1,\bar{x}_2)$, $(\bar{x}_1,x_2)$, and $(\bar{x}_1,\bar{x}_2)$. Given separability, any citizen who has a first preference of outcome (x_1,x_2) must have a last preference of the "opposite" outcome $(\bar{x}_1,\bar{x}_2)$, and so forth. But, at the same time, two citizens with the same first (and last) preferences may have orderings that differ with respect to their *intermediate* (second and third) *preferences.* Put substantively, two citizens with the same first preferences may differently answer the question: "If you could get your way on just one of the two issues, which one would it be—that is, with respect to which issue is your preference more 'intense'?"

A multidimensional space results if a continuous issue has two or more dimensions or if several continuous issues are considered together. Given such a multidimensional space, we often suppose that citizen preferences over it have this property: preferences over the alternatives lying on any straight line through the space are single-peaked preferences in the multidimensional, as well as one-dimensional, context.[12]

Allocative issues—for example how to divide up benefits

(or costs) among members of society—are also continuous and multidimensional, with essentially as many dimensions as there are individuals (or groups or geographical entities) in society. But preferences over allocative issues surely are not single-peaked; plausibly, they are *individualistic,* i.e., given two alternatives, each citizen prefers the alternative that provides him with more benefits or imposes lower costs on him.

3. The Decision Rule

The "issues" discussed above belong to the domain of collective control and choice. The political system needs some *decision rule* by which citizen preferences over issues are aggregated into collective choices. Here we suppose that the applicable decision rule is *majority rule*—that is, in choosing between any two alternatives or outcomes, collective choice is determined by the preferences of the greater number of citizens. As a result, the political system is *majoritarian,* so that any majority of citizens is empowered to bring about any political outcome within the domain of collective choice.

The operation of majority rule is most transparent in resolving a single dichotomous issue considered in isolation, and indeed informal discussions of the relationship between majority rule and minority interests often do not look beyond this simplest case. In section III, we will see how majority rule extends (with some complexities) to polychotomous or multiple issues.

4. Three Kinds of Politics

Within the social choice framework outlined above, we can define three different contexts of collective choice that are relevant for our discussion, and we can link each reasonably clearly with different kinds of practical politics in terms of which we label them.

Cleavage (or Group) Politics. In this context, issues arise that are "naturally" discrete and in fact (we will here assume) dichotomous. Accordingly, each such issue partitions (or "cleaves") the population of citizens into two clusters, each of which is internally homogenous, but between which there is total conflict, with respect to preferences on the issue. As a matter of sociological description (not necessarily entailed by our social choice framework), the issue may engage and the preference partition reflect some underlying "social cleavage" or stigmatic criterion that divides the population into different ethnic, linguistic, religious, territorial, occupational, etc., groups. It is in the context of cleavage politics that the issue of majority rule versus minority interests—indeed of "*the* majority" versus "*the* minority"—can arise most starkly. In this context, collective choice appears unavoidably to be a matter of winner-take-all.

Ideological (or Public Goods) Politics. In this context, issues arise that are "naturally" continuous and over which preferences are single-peaked. Examples include the level of provision of public goods or of government activity or the trade-off between two or more such goods or activities (e.g., "guns versus butter") within a fixed budget. Or perhaps various issues fit into one or a few ideological dimensions. In any event, in this context, collective choice is not so clearly a matter of winner-take-all.[13]

Distributive (or Private Goods) Politics. In this context, issues arise that pertain to the allocation of a fixed supply of divisible and essentially private goods. The archetypical distributive issue is often described as that of dividing $1—though, in the age of big government, dividing $1 trillion might be a better description. The allocation of "pork-barrel" projects, together with the sharing out of their costs, provides a more realistic description of distributive politics. Since the benefits in question can be parcelled out in any fashion, distributive politics need not be winner-take-all.

III. Properties of Majority Rule

Research within the social choice tradition has significantly clarified the properties of majority rule and the logical nature of majority-rule decision making. Here I provide a very brief overview of some of that research.

1. May's Theorem

Given a single dichotomous issue, majority rule strikes most people as fair and reasonable in the abstract. Many years ago, Kenneth May formalized our intuition, by identifying four conditions that we may want a decision rule to meet when applied to a dichotomous issue and demonstrating that majority rule, and only majority rule, meets these conditions.[14] May's conditions are these: *decisiveness*—however citizen preferences are distributed, there is always a clear result (even if it is a tie); *anonymity* (of citizens)—we do not need to know who has which preferences to determine the collective choice (we just count preferences); *neutrality* (between alternatives)—we do not need to know how alternatives are labelled (e.g., "status quo" versus "change in the status quo") to determine the collective choice; and *positive responsiveness*—if alternative x at least ties y and then someone changes his preference ordering so it is more favorable to x, then x is certainly the collective choice. *Unanimity rule* (as used by juries) violates decisiveness; *weighted majority rule* violates anonymity; *supra-majority rule* (such as two-thirds majority rule) violates either neutrality (if—as in practice—failure of the alternative entailing change in the status quo to receive the requisite supra-majority support results in choosing the status quo) or positive responsiveness (if failure of either alternative to receive the requisite supra-majority support results in a "tie"). May demonstrated that majority rule meets all four conditions and is the only decision rule that can do so.

2. The Rae-Taylor-Straffin Theorem

Suppose citizens are negotiating a "constitutional agreement" and are choosing what decision rule they would like the political system being formed to use in resolving a series of dichotomous issues that will arise in the future. Each citizen aims to maximize the proportion of times that the collective choice agrees with his own preference (i.e., each aims to maximize what we may call his *political satisfaction* over the long run). No citizen knows how his preferences will be related to those of other citizens. From behind this "veil of ignorance," each supposes that his probability of supporting an alternative on any issue is proportional to the overall support for that alternative. It then follows that majority rule maximizes the prospective satisfaction of every citizen.[15]

3. Multiple Alternatives and Condorcet Winners

Both May's Theorem and the Rae-Taylor-Straffin Theorem deal with collective choice on a single dichotomous issue, in which context the meaning of majority rule is straightforward. Some citizens prefer one alternative, others prefer the other, and—at least if the number of citizens is odd and they are never indifferent between alternatives—one or other alternative is the *majority winner* on the issue, i.e., is the first preference of a majority of citizens.

But if an issue has multiple alternatives, or if several dichotomous issues are considered together (generating multiple outcomes), it is likely that first preferences will be sufficiently dispersed among the multiple alternatives or outcomes that no majority winner exists. What then does majority rule imply for collective choice?

One possibility is that the *plurality winner* becomes the collective choice. The plurality winner—one weakening of the notion of majority winner—is the alternative that is the first preference of the greatest number of citizens, even if that number fails to constitute a majority. Apart from the possibility of ties, a plurality winner always exists, regardless of the number of alternatives and the nature of citizen preferences over them. But social choice theory shows that in other respects the plurality winner is an unreliable basis for collective choice from among multiple alternatives, as it changes erratically in response to small changes in the nature of alternatives, in the number of alternatives, or in citizen first preferences. Moreover, few practical political institutions and processes base collective choice on the plurality winner. Most notably this is true of parliamentary voting in a legislative setting.

Given three or more alternatives, it seems desirable—and, in a legislative setting, generally true—that collective choice meet the following conditions: (1) it should take account of citizens' full preference orderings (not just their first preferences); and (2) it should proceed on the basis of pairwise choices, with respect to each of which majority rule can be straightforwardly implemented. (If the second condition is realized, the first also is, since many pairwise choices will necessarily involve alternatives not the first preference of many citizens.)

Two centuries ago, the Marquis de Condorcet proposed that collective choice should comply with both conditions, by being based on what contemporary social choice theory calls the "majority preference relation."[16] Consider any two alternatives x and y. Some citizens prefer x to y; others prefer y to x. (We continue to rule out indifference.) Suppose the number of citizens preferring x to y exceeds the number preferring y to x. Then we say x beats y under majority rule. If we consider all possible pairs of alternatives in this way, we discover the *majority preference relation* over the entire set of alternatives. Condorcet's candidate for collective choice under majority rule is customarily dubbed the *Condorcet winner.* A Condorcet winner is an alternative that beats every other alternative under majority rule and, in that sense, stands at the top of the majority preference relation. Clearly, for any given set of alternatives and preferences, there can be no more than one Condorcet winner.[17]

Several points follow. First, a majority winner x is preferred *by the same majority* (i.e., the majority of citizens all of whom share x as their first preference) to every other alternative (though this "permanent majority" may be augmented by different sets of additional citizens in different pairwise comparisons). Therefore, a majority winner is necessarily a Condorcet winner. But the converse is not true. In general, a Condorcet winner may *beat different alternatives through different* (or "shifting") *majorities,* rather than through a single "permanent majority." Indeed (if there are at least four alternatives), these majorities may have no citizen in common. Another way to put this point is that a Condorcet winner may fail to be the first preference of *any* citizen (so it is clear the Condorcet winner may be distinct from the plurality winner). The Condorcet winner is therefore another weakening of the notion of the majority winner—one that has more theoretical appeal than the plurality winner.

Nevertheless, the extension of majority rule to multiple alternatives is not entirely straightforward, due to a characteristic of the majority preference relation that Condorcet was fully aware of. This is its possibly *cyclic* nature: x may beat y, y may beat z, and yet z may beat x. This possibility is most readily illustrated by the following three citizen preference orderings over the three alternatives x, y, and z.

1	*2*	*3*
x	y	z
y	z	x
z	x	y

Note that each alternative is beaten by one other alternative, so a Condorcet winner fails to exist. This phenomenon has been called the "Condorcet effect," the "Arrow problem," the "paradox of voting," and (perhaps most illuminatingly) "cyclical majorities." It evidently was first discovered by Condorcet, and it was then alternately forgotten and rediscovered until the work of Duncan Black and Kenneth J. Arrow some forty years ago firmly placed it in the minds of social choice theorists.[18]

Notice that cyclical majority preference requires that different majority preference relationships be effected through different majorities. Thus in the example above, x beats y through the majority of 1 and 3, y beats z through the majority of 1 and 2, and z beats x through the majority of 2 and 3. If any citizen is a "permanent winner"—that is, belongs to all majorities through which majority preference relationships are effected—majority preference must be identical to that citizen's preference ordering and is therefore non-cyclical, and the most preferred alternative of the "permanent winner" is the Condorcet winner.[19]

4. The Median Voter Theorem

Consider a continuous issue X over which the preferences of all n citizens are single-peaked. Each citizen has an ideal point somewhere along the continuum, and these ideal points can be ordered from (let us say) "left" to "right," and we can accordingly label them $x^1, x^2, \ldots, x^n$. If the number n of citizens is odd, a unique ideal point x^m (where $m=(n+1)/2$) occupies the median position in this ordering. A social choice result of fundamental importance, originally due to Duncan Black and commonly known as the *median voter theorem,* is that x^m is the Condorcet winner on issue X.[20] To verify this, consider any point to the left of x^m; x^m is preferred by the median citizen and all citizens to the his right, by definition a majority of citizens, so x^m beats every alternative to its left. By similar argument, x^m beats every alternative to its right. Thus x^m beats every other alternative and is the Condorcet winner.

5. *Multiple Dimensions and "Chaotic" Majority Rule*

In a multidimensional issue space with single-peaked preferences, a unique median ideal point exists only if ideal points are distributed in a distinctly fortuitous fashion; consequently, there is almost never a Condorcet winner.[21] Moreover, in the almost certain event that there is no Condorcet winner, a global majority preference cycle encompasses the entire issue space.[22] Because of these results, majority rule on a multidimensional issue space has been characterized as "chaotic." However, further results indicate that, even in the multidimensional case, majority rule has a strong centralizing tendency, so that collective choice based on majority rule typically leads to selection of a relatively centrist (in the sense of median) alternative (e.g., one belonging to the "uncovered set"), even though we cannot say exactly which one.[23]

However, this centralizing tendency does not apply to allocative issues. In this context, majority rule appears to be genuinely "chaotic."[24] Collective choice appears to be governed not by preferences and the decision rule but by fortuitous coalition formation or by specific (and arbitrary) features of institutional context.[25]

6. *Majority Rule and Political Process*

Having summarized results on the theoretical properties of majority rule, it may be worthwhile to ask to what extent the political process in (more or less) majoritarian political systems is governed by these results, and particularly by the median voter theorem applied in the context of ideological politics.

In a legislature with weak or non-existent party discipline (e.g., the United States), we might expect that any proposal would be successfully amended until the ideal point of the median legislator was (approximately) reached. (Some majority of legislators always has the incentive to introduce and support such amendments.) Furthermore, the ideal point of the median legislator ought to be quite similar to that of the median citizen. (Details of the electoral system—in particular, the extent to which it is majoritarian or proportional—would influence the spread of legislator ideal points but would have little influence on the location of their center.)

In a legislature with two strongly disciplined parties (e.g., the United Kingdom), in the preceding electoral campaign (or in anticipation of the subsequent one), each party—whether influenced by the desire for simple electoral victory or by the desire to maximize its policy goals (or, more plausibly, by a mixture of these goals)—would offer an (approximately) median platform or establish a similarly centrist record in office.[26]

In a legislature with multiple disciplined parties (presumably elected by some variant of proportional representation), the median party has an overwhelming bargaining advantage in getting into a coalition government and in imposing its preferred position on that government, and in turn (given the proportional electoral system) the median party ought to represent the median citizen accurately.

Of course, participants in the political process often make mistakes and fail to exploit available opportunities, so collective choices may be made and endure even though some majority exists that prefers another outcome but "can't get its act together." But such "failures" in the political process can hardly be blamed on the institution of majority rule, the consequences of which we are evaluating.

IV. Cleavage Politics

In this section, we examine the consequences of majority rule for minority interests in the context of cleavage politics. We examine in turn collective choice on a single dichotomous issue considered in isolation, two dichotomous issues considered independently, two dichotomous issues considered jointly, and finally a series of such issues.

1. Single-Issue Cleavage Politics

Let us designate the one issue X with alternatives x and $\bar{x}$. Issue X partitions the set of citizens into two complementary subsets according the their preferences on the issue: a larger subset who prefer the majority winner x and a smaller subset who prefer the minority alternative $\bar{x}$. Let p (between 1/2 and 1) designate the proportion of all voters who prefer the majority alternative. We call p the *level of popularity* of x. To the extent that p approaches 1, issue X is *consensual;* to the extent that p approaches 1/2, it is *divisive.*

It is in the context of a single dichotomous issue that the problem of majority rule versus minority interests arises most starkly. The majority wins totally and the minority loses totally. Moreover, this partitioning of society into winners and losers depends in no way on the size of the minority; a large minority does no better than a tiny minority. Likewise, collective choice is unaffected by the "distance" (if we can speak of such a thing in the context of cleavage politics) between the majority and minority alternatives. Minority preferences are indeed "subsumed" by the "numerically more powerful majority choice"; it makes no difference for collective choice whether members of the minority are enfranchised or not.

Insofar as this situation may be deemed socially unfortunate, we should note that it comes about essentially because of the nature of the issue and preferences regarding it, not because of the nature of the decision rule used to resolve the issue. If there are truly only two ways to resolve the issue (i.e., if the issue is truly dichotomous), to choose the only other way that is available would almost surely be regarded as an even more socially unfortunate resolution. And if other more appealing resolutions of the issue are available, we are beyond the scope of a single dichotomous issue.[27]

2. *Two-Issue Cleavage Politics*

Suppose we have two dichotomous issues X_1 and X_2. We use the same notation introduced above with the respective subscripts.

The two issues partition the set of citizens into four subsets or clusters according to their first preferences regarding issues X_1 and X_2, as follows. The *majority cluster* is composed of citizens who prefer the majority alternatives on both issues; their first preference is the outcome (x_1,x_2), their last preference is $(\bar{x}_1,\bar{x}_2)$, and their intermediate preferences—with respect to $(x_1,\bar{x}_2)$ and $(\bar{x}_1,x_2)$—may vary. The *minority cluster* is composed of citizens who prefer the minority alternatives on both issues; their first preference is $(\bar{x}_1,\bar{x}_2)$, their last preference is (x_1,x_2), and their intermediate preferences—with respect to $(x_1,\bar{x}_2)$ and $(\bar{x}_1,x_2)$—may vary. The two *mixed clusters* are composed of citizens who prefer the majority alternative on one issue and the minority alternative on the other. One such cluster has the first preference of $(x_1,\bar{x}_2)$ and the last preference of $(\bar{x}_1,x_2)$; the other cluster has the reverse first and last preferences. The intermediate preferences of both mixed clusters—with respect to (x_1,x_2) and $(\bar{x}_1,\bar{x}_2)$—may vary (both between and within clusters).

The relative size of these clusters depends on three parameters: the *level of popularity* of each majority alternative and the *degree of association* or *reinforcement* between preferences on the two issues. Levels of popularity are indicated by the fractions p_1 and p_2. The degree of association or reinforcement between preferences on the two issues is indicated by the (positive or negative) parameter r, which represents, as a fraction of all citizens, the amount by which the size of each of the majority and minority clusters exceeds (or falls below) the "baseline" fraction that would result if preferences on the two issues were statistically independent. (The mixed clusters necessarily deviate by the same magnitude in the opposite direction.) Using these symbols, the relative frequency distribution of citizens over the four clusters is shown in figure 1.

Examination of the expressions in the cells of figure 1 confirms (as should be intuitively evident) that: (1) the majority cluster is never empty and always exceeds the minority cluster

FIGURE 1

Preferred Position on X_1 ⇓ \ on X_2	x_2	$\bar{x}_2$	Popularity
x_1	*Majority Cluster* $p_1p_2 + r$	*Mixed Cluster* $p_1(1 - p_2) - r$	p_1
$\bar{x}_1$	*Mixed Cluster* $(1 - p_1)p_2 - r$	*Minority Cluster* $(1-p_1)(1-p_2) + r$	$(1 - p_1)$
Popularity	p_2	$(1 - p_2)$	1.00

in size; and (2) the combination of the majority cluster and *either* mixed cluster must itself be a majority.

If preferences on the two issues are perfectly *crosscutting*, r equals zero, so the fraction of citizens in each cluster is just the "baseline" fraction. To the extent that issue preferences are *positively reinforcing*, r is positive, so the fraction of citizens in the majority and minority cluster is greater, and in each mixed cluster is less, than the "baseline" fraction. When preferences are as positively reinforcing as possible (given the popularity levels), at least one mixed cluster is empty. To the extent that issue preferences are *negatively reinforcing*, r is negative, so the fraction of citizens in each mixed cluster is greater, and in the the majority and minority cluster is less, than the "baseline" fraction. When preferences are as negatively reinforcing as possible (given the popularity levels), the minority cluster is empty.

The size of the majority cluster increases with the level of popularity of each majority alternative and the degree of positive reinforcement of preferences on the two issues. If the majority cluster is itself of majority size, we may speak of a *universal majority*. We also dub each member of the majority and minority clusters a *universal winner* and *loser,* respectively. (These terms are more natural when we move to multiple issues).

Let us use the following simple (inter-personally comparable) scale of political satisfaction (in the manner of the Rae-Taylor-Straffin analysis): a citizen's *level of political satisfaction* is equal to the fraction of issues on which his preferred alternative is collectively chosen. If we suppose for the moment that each majority alternative is collectively chosen, *average* satisfaction over two (or more) issues is simply their average popularity level and is independent of how reinforcing or crosscutting preferences are. Given our concern with minority interests, however, we must focus on how *unequally* satisfaction is distributed, and this does depend on how reinforcing or crosscutting preferences are. Specifically, *if we suppose that the majority alternative on each issue is collectively chosen,* the status of minority interests depends largely on the degree of positive reinforcement in preferences. If preferences are highly reinforcing in the positive direction (and especially if the issues are highly divisive), there are relatively many universal losers. If preferences are crosscutting (and especially if the issues are quite consensual), there are relatively few universal losers. And if preferences are sufficiently reinforcing in a negative direction, universal losers disappear entirely.

3. *Coalitions of Minorities*

Outcome (x_1,x_2) is the outcome composed of the two majority winners on the two issues considered separately. But if the issues are considered jointly, we must examine majority preference over all pairs of outcomes. Outcome (x_1,x_2) certainly beats both $(x_1,\bar{x}_2)$ and $(\bar{x}_1,x_2)$ under majority rule. Both pairwise comparisons involve outcomes that differ with respect to only one issue, and with respect to that issue (x_1,x_2) gives (by definition) the more popular alternative. But it does not follow that (x_1,x_2) beats $(\bar{x}_1,\bar{x}_2)$ under majority rule.

Thus we should not jump too readily to the conclusion that the collective choice will be the pair of majority winners, for *if the two issues are considered jointly* an effective "coalition of minorities" may exist. In terms of the majority preference relation over political outcomes, an effective *coalition of minorities* is a majority that prefers outcome $(\bar{x}_1,\bar{x}_2)$ to outcome (x_1,x_2), with the result that (x_1,x_2) is *not* the Condorcet winner among the four outcomes.[28]

Let us count up citizens who may have the required preferences to belong to a coalition of minorities. Certainly members of the minority cluster have the required preference for $(\bar{x}_1,\bar{x}_2)$ over (x_1,x_2). Equally certainly, members of the majority cluster have the opposite preference and cannot be part of such a coalition. Members of the mixed clusters may or may not have the requisite preference, depending on their *intermediate preferences* or, in more substantive terms, depending on which issues they care about more intensely. Therefore, whether there is an effective coalition of minorities depends on the size of the respective clusters and the intermediate preferences (or distribution of intensities) in the mixed clusters.

With respect to intermediate preferences, let the *fraction with majority intensity* be the fraction of citizens in the mixed clusters who prefer (x_1,x_2) to $(\bar{x}_1,\bar{x}_2)$—that is, who prefer getting their way only on the issue on which they prefer the majority alternative to getting their way only on the issue on which they prefer the minority alternative. Let the *fraction with minority intensity* be the fraction of citizens in the mixed clusters who prefer $(\bar{x}_1,\bar{x}_2)$ to (x_1,x_2)—that is, who prefer getting their way only on the issue on which they prefer the minority position to getting their way only on the issue on which they prefer the majority position.[29]

Holding the distribution of intermediate preferences in the mixed clusters constant, the possibility of an effective coalition of majorities decreases with the size of the majority cluster, which in turn increases with the level of popularity of majority alternatives and with the degree of positive reinforcement. However, increasing the popularity of majority alternatives increases average satisfaction with the outcome (x_1,x_2) and, in that sense, makes the possibility a coalition of minorities less important. In this respect, therefore the degree of positive reinforcement is probably most important.[30]

The condition for an effective coalition of minorities is that the minority cluster plus the fraction of the mixed clusters with minority intensity must be greater than the majority cluster plus the fraction of the mixed clusters with majority intensity. From this, we can readily identify two *necessary* conditions for an effective coalition of minorities. First, a coalition of minorities is effective only if the majority cluster is of less than majority size. Turning the proposition around, one condition that precludes an effective coalition of minorities is the existence of a universal majority, which can occur if one or both issues are quite consensual or preferences are quite positively reinforcing. Otherwise, the effectiveness of a coalition of minorities depends on the intermediate preferences of voters in the mixed cluster. An effective coalition of minorities can exist only if the fraction with minority intensity is greater than the fraction with majority intensity.[31] (In this sense, an "impartial" distribution of intensities means that coalitions of minorities can never be effective.) The required advantage of the fraction with minority intensity over the fraction with minority intensity depends in turn on the size of the majority cluster relative to the minority.

Finally, we observe that if one issue is of overwhelming *salience,* so that *all citizens care about it more intensely than about the other issue,* it follows that all members of mixed clusters with majority intensity belong to the *same* mixed cluster, that this mixed cluster together with the majority cluster is a majority, and that therefore there can be no effective coalition of minorities.

In the absence of an effective coalition of minorities, (x_1,x_2) is the Condorcet winner among the four outcomes generated by considering the two issues jointly. But if there is an effective coalition of minorities, i.e., if $(\bar{x}_1,\bar{x}_2)$ beats (x_1,x_2) under majority rule, it does not follow that $(\bar{x}_1,\bar{x}_2)$ is the Condorcet winner. Indeed, it is clear that both $(x_1,\bar{x}_2)$ and $(\bar{x}_1,x_2)$ beat $(\bar{x}_2,\bar{x}_2)$, for both pairwise comparisons involve outcomes that differ with respect to only one issue, and with respect to that issue $(\bar{x}_1,\bar{x}_2)$ gives (by definition) the less popular alternative. Therefore, *an effective coalition of minorities implies that majority preference is cyclical and that there is no Condorcet winner at all.*[32] Collective choice with an effective coalition of minorities is therefore unpredictable and depends on factors independent of the institution of majority rule. Given two-issue cleavage politics, we cannot say, even if the conditions for an effective coalition of minorities holds, that the two minorities will be substantially satisfied. But we can say that either minority or their intersection *may* be fully satisfied; nothing in the institution of majority rule implies that they must be dissatisfied.

4. Multiple-Issue Cleavage Politics

Suppose we have a series of dichotomous issues X_1 through X_k. The general nature of the previous analysis may be extended to this general case. As before, there is a single majority cluster (whose members prefer the majority alternative on every issue) and a single minority cluster (whose members prefer the minority alternative on every issue). But once the number of issues exceeds two, the majority cluster may be empty (and, once the number of issues exceeds three, may be empty even when the minority cluster is not). In addition, there are now many mixed clusters, which run from being *imbalanced in the minority direction* (made up of citizens who favor minority alternative on most issues) through being *balanced* (made up of citizens who favor majority alternatives on about half the issues) to being *imbalanced in the majority direction* (made up of citizens who favor majority alternatives on most issues). Unless preferences are systematically and positively reinforcing in a high degree, almost all citizens belong to mixed clusters.

Increasing the number of issues has no systematic impact on the average level of satisfaction, which (if majority alternatives are consistently chosen) is simply the average level of popularity of those alternatives. But, to the extent that preferences are crosscutting, increasing the number of issues does have a systematic effect on the distribution of satisfaction (even if majority alternatives are consistently chosen). The more issues there are, and the more preferences on these issues are crosscutting, the more citizens bunch up in mixed clusters and particularly mixed clusters that are balanced or (to the extent that majority alternatives are popular) somewhat imbalanced in the majority direction, so the more equally political satisfaction with outcomes is distributed. If some pairs of issues are negatively reinforcing, universal (or even near-universal) winners and losers disappear, further reducing inequality in satisfaction. One the other hand, systematically and positively reinforcing preferences tend to polarize citizens into universal winners and losers.[33]

At the same time, if preferences are crosscutting, the more issues there are, the more likely it is that at least one coalition of minorities will be effective and consequently that majority alternatives may *not* be consistently chosen. In the manner described in the previous subsection, we can check whether there is an effective coalition of minorities with respect to any pair of issues. And even if there is no effective coalition of minorities on any *pair* of issues, there may be an effective coalition of minorities with regard to some *larger set* of issues. As we consider the effectiveness of coalitions of minorities with respect to an expanding set of issues, two competing considerations arise. On the one hand (unless preferences are positively reinforcing in high degree), the size of the *potential* coalition increases, as more and more citizens find themselves in the minority on at least one issue. On the other hand, finding the right distribution of intermediate preferences (intensities) to support an *actual* coalition of minorities becomes more complex. Citizens in many mixed clusters prefer majority alternatives on most issues, and it is unlikely that they will care enough about the smaller number of other issues to prefer to get their way on those at the cost of not getting their way on the greater number of issues on which they prefer the majority alternative. On the other hand, citizens in other mixed clusters prefer minority alternatives on most issues, and it is likely that they will care enough about these issues to prefer to get their way on them at the cost of not getting their way on the small number of issues on which they prefer the majority alternative. Finally, citizens in balanced mixed clusters face tradeoffs similar to citizens in the two mixed clusters in the two-issue case. To the extent that issues tend to be consensual, the first class of mixed clusters will be the largest, making an effective coalition of minorities with respect to the expanded set of issues rather unlikely. On the other hand, as the set of issues expands, it evidently becomes more likely that a coalition of minorities will be effective with respect to *some* subset of issues.

The upshot is that citizens with minority interests on a particular issue *X* are unlikely to be in a minority with respect to all or even most issues, if there are a number of issues and preferences are at least somewhat crosscutting. Moreover, under the same circumstances, there is a reasonable probability that the minority in question will find itself part of an effective coalition of minorities with respect to *X* (and one or more other issues), in which case the minority alternative on issue *X* itself may well end up being collectively chosen under majority rule.

V. Ideological Politics

While cleavage politics partitions citizens into discrete clusters on the basis of their first preferences, ideological politics spreads citizens over a continuum with respect to their first preferences (or ideal points). One point on the continuum must be collectively chosen and becomes binding on the whole collectivity.

It is possible and useful in this context to introduce another crude measure of citizen satisfaction. We may suppose (very justifiably) that a citizen is totally satisfied if the collective choice is identical to his ideal point and is increasingly dissatisfied as the distance between the collective choice and his ideal point increases. (This is no more than the single-peakedness assumption stated in terms of satisfaction.) For simplicity (but with somewhat less justification), we shall further suppose that *dissatisfaction* for each citizen is a simple linear function of this distance. Moreover we shall continue to suppose that dissatisfaction is interpersonally comparable, so that we can speak of the minimum, maximum, average, etc., level of dissatisfaction with collective choices (by equating each with the minimum, maximum, average, etc., distance from each ideal point to the collective choice).

We should also observe that the notion of "winning" versus "losing" is greatly softened in the ideological context. It is true that, if the political process converges on the Condorcet winner through a series of parliamentary style votes (as suggested in section III.6 with respect to a political process with weak parties), winners and losers are generated on each pairwise vote.

But the tally of such wins and losses will have little to do with how satisfied or dissatisfied citizens are with the ultimate collective choice. For example, if the initial proposal is far to the right and is then progressively amended toward the median, extreme leftwing citizens will consistently "win" and rightwing citizens will consistently "lose" in the sequence of votes, but the final (centrist) choice will be (more or less) equally unsatisfactory to both.

1. Ideological Politics with a Single Preference Distribution

In the context of ideological politics, with ideal points spread over a continuum, the notion of a "majority group" versus a "minority group" is rather murky. This is especially true if the distribution of ideal points is given by a single, more or less bell-shaped, frequency curve. In this subsection, we suppose that this is the case, although we do not suppose that the frequency curve is necessarily normal or even symmetric in shape. In this case, an ideological minority consists of citizens whose ideal points put them at one extreme of the distribution. But there are necessarily two extremes and two ideological minorities, one at each end of the distribution. Clearly if any change in collective choice gives greater satisfaction to members of one ideological minority, it must at the same time—and in approximately the same magnitude—give less satisfaction to members of the other ideological minority. Apparently the conflict here is not so much majority interests versus minority interests but (one set of) minority interests versus (another set of) minority interests.

Given ideological politics on a single dimension, collective choice of the median ideal point (i.e., the Condorcet winner) has this desirable property: it *minimizes the average dissatisfaction of citizens*—any other collective choice results in greater total (and average) dissatisfaction.[34] But of course, to the extent that preferences are dispersed, levels of satisfaction will likewise be dispersed about this (optimal) average. And if our concern is to minimize the damage done to minority interests, we might want to proceed in a Rawlsian manner by minimizing the maximum level of dissatisfaction in society.[35] How does majority rule fare

FIGURE 2

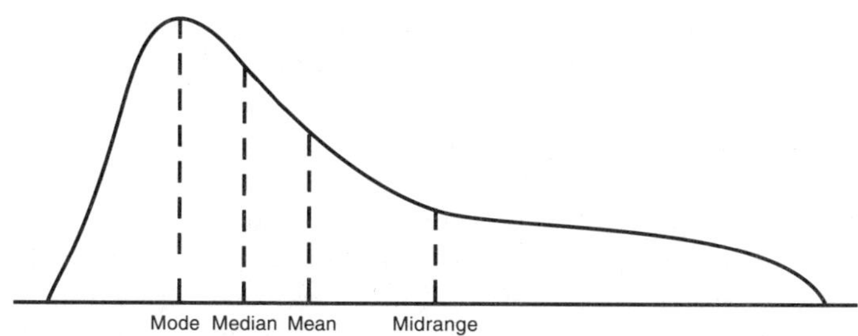

in this respect? This "minimax" criterion dictates that the collective choice should be the *mid-range,* i.e., the point exactly halfway between the ideal points of the most leftwing and the most rightwing citizens. Whatever the collective choice, it is clear that one or other of these two extreme citizens must be the most dissatisfied. The midrange makes them equally dissatisfied and any change in collective choice must increase the dissatisfaction of one or the other. It follows that majority rule conforms with this "minimax" criterion if the distribution of preferences is symmetric (so that the mirror image of the distribution is indistinguishable from the original distribution), in which case the median and midrange coincide.

Figure 2 shows a (bell-shaped but) asymmetric distribution of ideal points over an ideological continuum, and it shows the resulting discrepancy between the median and midrange. A compromise collective choice is the *mean,* which has the property that the average algebraic deviation from it is minimum and in fact equals zero; put more substantively, if the collective choice is the mean, the total "leftwing" dissatisfaction is just equal to the total "rightwing" dissatisfaction.[36]

Collective choice could conceivably be made by dividing the continuum up into small intervals of equal length, asking citizens to vote for one interval, with collective choice being the *plurality winner.* Provided that everyone votes "sincerely," this would produce the *mode* as the collective choice. Collective choice as the mode has the property of maximizing the proportion of citizens who are (essentially) fully satisfied. It can treat one or other ideological extreme very badly, however, as the distribution in figure 2 illustrates.

Finally, we may note that if the ideal points of voters at either ideological extreme (say the right in figure 2) were to shift outwards and become even more extreme, collective choice as the mean or midrange would move somewhat in the same direction. In some respects, and in terms of being solicitous of minority interests in particular, this might be regarded as a desirable trait in collective choice. But, in another respect, it could be a severe drawback, for by responding to extreme preferences in this way, it would give citizens with moderately extreme preferences an incentive to *express* far more extreme preferences, in the hope that the resulting collective choice would be close to their true (and more moderate) preferences. Since citizens on both extremes could play this game, there would be a widespread tendency to feign extreme preferences.[37] In any event, collective choice as the median is resistant to (real or feigned) changes in extreme preferences. This gives majority rule in the context of ideological politics a quality of "strategyproofness."

Moving from one to two or more ideological dimensions has two effects. First, there are no longer just two ideological minorities; rather ideological minorities populate the entire "boundary" of the distribution. But such minorities come in "antipodal" pairs with directly opposed interests, with respect to which similar considerations arise as in in the one-dimensional case. Second, it is very unlikely a Condorcet winner exists, but the literature cited in section III.5 suggests majority rule is still likely to produce outcomes near the center of the distribution.

2. *Ideological Politics with a Distinctive Minority*

As we have seen, if ideological politics involves a single (bell-shaped) distribution of ideal points for the whole society, the issue of majority rule versus minority interests somewhat disappears from view. However, we can recover much of the dualistic conflict between majority and minority interests by assuming that a minority group of citizens exists that is (in some degree) *ideologically distinct* from the larger majority group, in that (1) each group has its own (bell-shaped) preference distribution

FIGURE 3

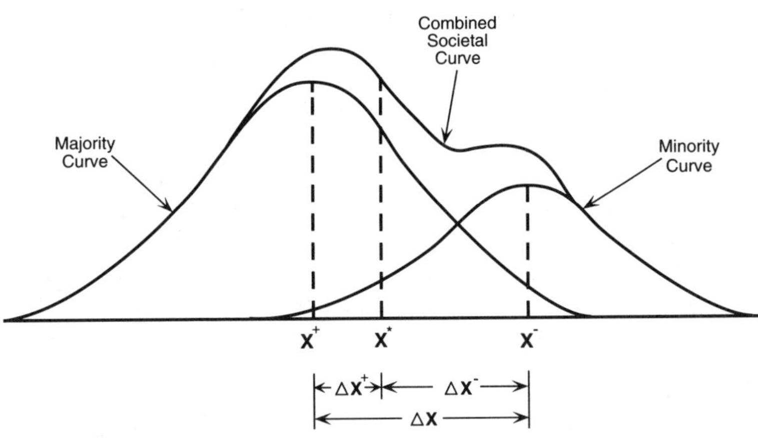

and (2) the two distributions are differently centered. The preference distribution of the whole society therefore is combination of the two distributions, and this combined societal distribution is typically *bimodal* and *asymmetric,* as illustrated in figures 3 and 4.

For purposes of specific illustrations and calculations, it is

FIGURE 4

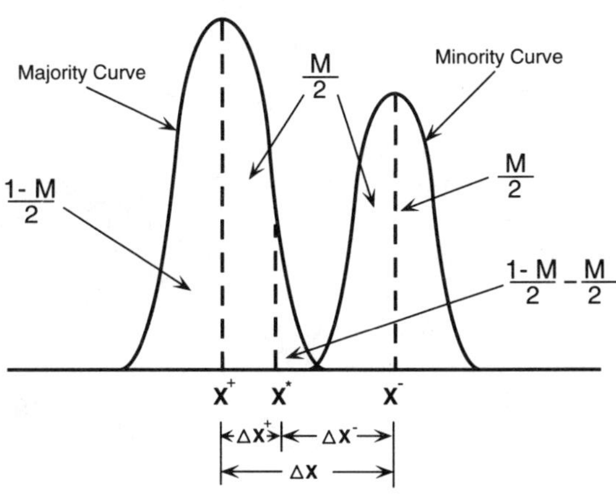

convenient to assume that the majority and minority groups have symmetrically—and indeed normally—distributed ideal points. However, the general thrust of the conclusions reported here holds for any bell-shaped curves.

The collective choice situation that results from ideological politics with a distinctive minority is described by a number of parameters, which we now consider.

The first is *relative size of the minority group*. Let the size of the minority group relative to the total society be given by the fraction M, where M lies strictly between zero and ½. Geometrically, M is the area under the minority curve as a proportion of the area under the societal curve. In figure 3, M is about 0.25; in figure 4, M is about 0.4.

The next parameters are the *centers* (means) of the majority and minority distributions, which we designate x^+ and x^- respectively. Given that both distributions are symmetric, these means are also medians. Thus, by the median voter theorem, x^+ is the (hypothetical) *majority collective choice*—that is, x^+ is what the collective choice would be if the majority group were choosing (by majority rule) unilaterally (e.g., if the minority were disenfranchised). Likewise, x^-, is the (hypothetical) *minority collective choice*—that is, x^- is what the collective choice would be if the minority group were choosing (by majority rule) unilaterally (e.g., if the majority were disenfranchised).

The two means may be collapsed into a single parameter—the magnitude of *ideological polarization* between the majority and minority groups, given by the length of the interval along the ideological continuum from x^+ to x^-, which we designate Δx.

The third and fourth parameters pertain to the level of *ideological cohesion* of the majority and minority groups, respectively. A perfectly cohesive group is monolithic or homogenous in its preferences; a less cohesive group is dispersed or heterogenous in its preferences. Let D^+ and D^- designate the dispersion of the majority and minority distributions, respectively—specifically, the standard deviations of their ideal points; D^+ and D^- measure (inversely) the cohesiveness of the two groups.

We are concerned here with majority and minority groups that are ideologically distinct. This means that each group has its own preference distribution differently centered on the ideological continuum, so that there is some degree of ideological polarization between them. *Ideological distinctiveness* is a matter of degree, however, and it depends on the cohesiveness of the two groups as well as their polarization. For example, if we compare figures 3 and 4, polarization is greater in figure 3 but the majority and minority are more distinctive in figure 4 because both groups are more cohesive. Ideological distinctiveness determines the amount of "overlap" between the two frequency curves. Thus the minority depicted in figure 4 is essentially *totally distinctive,* in that there is virtually no overlap between the two curves.

The notion of ideological distinctiveness implies that, for fixed levels of cohesion for the majority and minority groups, there is a *critical threshold* of polarization just sufficient (virtually) to eliminate overlap between the two frequency curves, so that the minority becomes totally distinctive. The polarization depicted in figure 4 is just about at this critical threshold; if it were diminished at all, the frequency curves would begin to overlap substantially.[38]

Finally, we label as x^* the societal collective choice—that is, x^* is what the collective choice actually is given that the whole society is choosing by majority rule. By the median voter theorem, x^* is the median of the combined societal distribution, and it is apparent that x^* lies somewhere in the interval between x^+ and x^-. Therefore the interval Δx can be subdivided into the two subintervals from x^+ to x^* and from x^* to x^-, as shown in figures 3 and 4, which we label Δx^+ and Δx^- respectively.

The first subinterval Δx^+ may be characterized as the *minority impact* on collective choice, as it represents the impact that the presence of the enfranchised minority has on collective choice under majority rule. To say that "the numerically more powerful majority choice simply subsumes minority preference" is to claim, in this context, that Δx^+ is (essentially) zero.

The second subinterval Δx^- may be characterized as *collective minority dissatisfaction,* as it represents the gap between the collective choice the minority would make if it constituted its own polity and the collective choice that binds it when it is part of the larger polity.[39]

The focus of our analytical concern in the remainder of this subsection is the location of the societal collective choice x^* between x^+ and x^- (and thus the magnitude of minority impact Δx^+) as a function of the parameters we have just discussed.

It may be worth observing that collective minority dissatisfaction is in large measure a function of the magnitude of the polarization between the majority and minority groups and, in particular, that (given majority rule) minority dissatisfaction can be reduced to zero only if polarization is reduced to zero. But if polarization is reduced to zero, the minority impact on collective choice is necessarily reduced to zero also. That is, the only kind of minority that can have an impact on collective choice under majority rule is a distinctive one that is also bound to be at least somewhat dissatisfied with that collective choice (even after having its impact on it).

The next point is that there is almost always a minority impact, and that the magnitude of this impact almost always depends on the size of the minority. That is, minority interests are almost never entirely "subsumed" in ideological politics. In this respect, ideological politics, even with a distinctive minority, differs from single-issue cleavage politics.

Let the cohesion of the majority and minority groups be fixed and let polarization reach the critical threshold. The magnitude of minority impact is the distance between the majority and societal medians. Since the minority is (essentially) totally distinct, (essentially) the entire minority frequency lies on the x^- side of x^* (as is true in figure 4 but not figure 3). Thus the interval from x^+ to x^* is essentially the interval required to make the area under the majority frequency curve that lies between x^+ and x^* equal to half the total area under the minority curve.[40]

If we measure minority impact in terms of the *area* under the majority curve that lies between x^+ and x^*, it follows that this impact, as a function of minority size M, is $M/2(1\text{-}M)$. Thus a small minority, with for example $M = 0.1$, has a very small area impact (i.e., 0.056). But as minority size increases, area impact increases faster, until a minority of maximum size (i.e., M just short of 0.5) has a maximum area impact (likewise just short of 0.5).

Our real concern, however, is minority impact measured in terms of the *displacement of collective choice* along the ideological continuum toward the minority distribution, i.e., the interval Δx^+. Since the height of the (normal) majority frequency curve is declining in this range—and declines especially rapidly from about $0.5D^+$ to about $1.5D^+$ away from x^+, increases in minority size M (and in area impact $M/2(1-M)$) produce increasingly large increases in the displacement of x^* along the continuum. Minority impact Δx, where Δx is expressed in terms of D^+, increases roughly linearly from 0 to about $1D^+$ as M increases from 0 to 0.4 and increases rapidly to about $2D^+$ as M increases to 0.49.

Suppose ideological polarization increases while group cohesion is constant, so that polarization goes beyond the critical threshold. *For fixed minority size, minority impact does not further increase as polarization increases beyond the critical threshold.* However, the relationship between minority size and minority impact remains as before, so *larger minorities have greater impact than small ones no matter the degree of ideological polarization.* In the first respect, ideological politics with a distinctive minority resembles—but, in the latter respect, contrasts with—single-issue cleavage politics.

Finally, suppose that polarization is reduced while the cohesion of both groups remains the same, so that polarization falls below the critical threshold, and the two frequency curves overlap substantially. The minority curve now straddles x^* (and perhaps x^+ as well, as in figure 3). Since a portion of the minority lies in the majority side of the societal median x^*, the area under the majority curve between x^+ and x^* is now less than $M/2$. Moreover, area impact is now less responsive to variation in minority size. As polarization vanishes (and the majority and minority become ideologically indistinguishable), minority impact likewise vanishes (and necessarily becomes unresponsive to minority size), though collective minority dissatisfaction disappears.

To this point, we have assumed that majority (and minority) cohesion are fixed, and we have described minority impact in terms of D^+-units. For example, we have seen that, with polarization at or beyond the critical threshold, $M=0.4$ produces a minority impact of about $1D^+$. But the actual magnitude of this impact, i.e., the amount of displacement along the ideological continuum, obviously depends in turn on the magnitude of D^+. That is, *minority impact depends,* not only on minority size, but also *on the cohesion of the majority group.* Other things constant, *minority impact on collective choice decreases as majority cohesion increases.* Further, *minority impact becomes less responsive to variation in minority size as majority cohesion increases.* Both effects reach their logical maximum when the majority become fully cohesive (i.e., $D^+ = 0$); in this circumstance, no minority of any size (and regardless of the level of minority cohesion or polarization between majority and minority) can have any impact on collective choice. In this special case, we are in effect back to the realm of single-issue cleavage politics.[41]

So long as ideological polarization is at or beyond the critical threshold, *minority cohesion has no effect on collective choice.* However, below the critical threshold of polarization, both minority impact on collective choice and the responsiveness of that impact to minority size increase (though only modestly) with minority cohesiveness. In fact, if polarization is low and the minority is so much more cohesive than the majority that the majority distribution "straddles" the minority distribution in the manner of figure 5, societal collective choice x^* can lie closer to x^- than to x^+.

FIGURE 5

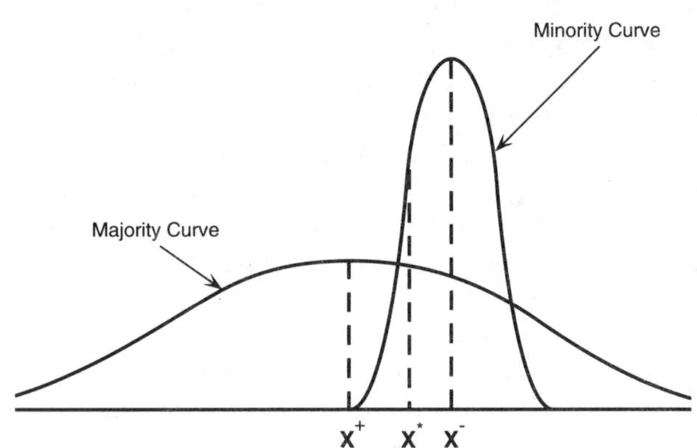

We have seen that group cohesion—and especially majority cohesion—is an important determinant of minority impact on collective choice. This raises the question of a *collusive majority*—that is, a majority in which a high degree of (apparent) cohesion is artificially enforced. More particularly, members of the majority group might agree on a common alternative (perhaps x^+) and then act as if they all shared this alternative as their ideal point; then, just as if the majority were in fact fully cohesive, "majority choice simply subsumes minority preferences."[42]

Such collusion, however, is intrinsically difficult to enforce. Whatever instruments of enforcement may be available are beyond the scope of our social choice framework, and the institution of majority rule itself tends to undermine such collusion. Whatever the parameters of the situation may be, the majority frequency curve straddles x^*—that is, some members of the majority are highly satisfied with x^*. More importantly, a significant minority of them prefer x^* to x^+ and—since x^* is the Condorcet winner—this minority of the majority group together with the minority group itself constitute a societal majority. Therefore, there is no reason within the abstract logic of the situation why these critical members of the majority group would join a collusive agreement on x^+ (or, for that matter, any alternative on the x^+ side of x^*).[43]

VI. Distributive Politics

Under majority rule, citizens (and the votes they cast) are *formally interchangeable* (or "fungible"); May's Anonymity Condition expresses this formal property. Essentially, this means that any one citizen (and vote) is as good as any other in building or sustaining a majority coalition. In this formal sense, majority rule entails "equality of political opportunity."

But, given any actual occasion for collective choice, citizens (and their votes) are attached to preferences (or interests), and the preferences to which they are attached are typically *not* interchangeable—some preferences are compatible with one another, others are not.[44] In this substantive sense, one citizen (and one vote) may not be as good as another in building or sustaining a majority coalition *in support of a particular policy*.

This is most strongly the case in single-issue cleavage politics, or multiple-issue cleavage politics with positively reinforcing preferences or with one issue of overwhelming salience. It is somewhat less strongly the case with multiple-issue cleavage politics with cross cutting preferences and dispersed intensities or in ideological politics, especially if preferences are reasonably dispersed.

In the realm of distributive politics, however, citizens (and the votes they cast) in fact are fully interchangeable. While citizens (and votes) are attached to (individualistic) preferences, such preferences are all identical from the point of view of third parties looking around for coalition partners to support some allocative alternative. Put otherwise, given any present majority controlling collective allocation, anyone outside that majority (presumably receiving nothing at the moment) can advantageously make an offer to displace any member of the present majority that will be appealing to other members of that majority. Thus we may expect to see a constant shifting (or generic instability) of majorities and allocative outcomes. This expectation is confirmed by formal results in social choice on the structure of majority rule over the space of allocative alternatives. First, there is no Condorcet winner. Second, a global majority preference cycle encompasses virtually all allocative alternatives (even inefficient ones that waste a portion of the good being allocated). Third, even such refined "solutions" as the "uncovered set" that give (even in the face of global cycles) considerable coherence to majority rule on multidimensional alternative with single-peaked preferences spaces effectively break down in the allocative context with individualistic preferences by expanding to include essentially all efficient alternatives.[45] In sum, in the context of distributive politics, majority rule is chaotic and cannot be blamed or credited for any particular outcome.

A consequence of the interchangeability of preferences in distributive politics is that, within our social choice framework, we have no way to identify or define a minority or minority interests. In cleavage and ideological politics, minorities and minority interests may be defined in terms of preference distributions, and exactly for this reason members of such minorities may not make desirable coalition partners. But in the context of distributive politics, all citizens have, in a relevant sense, identical preferences, so the only way minority status may be defined is in terms of some exogenously fixed stigmatic criteria (such as race, language, religion, and so forth).

Given the chaotic nature of majority rule in the context of distributive politics, majority rule itself cannot really be blamed if outcomes systematically discriminate against stigmatic minorities by excluding them from collectively chosen allocations. But it is also true that the chaotic nature of majority rule may give room for such seemingly arbitrary factors to exert an influence that they would not (directly) exert in the realm of cleavage or ideological politics, where collective choice under majority rule is more clearly determined by preferences.[46]

Three sorts of "solutions" have been proposed for the problem of allocation by majority rule. Consider the archetypical divide-the-dollar game with three players. Many years ago, John von Neumann and Oskar Morgenstern proposed that certain "standards of behavior" would emerge to constrain collective choice to a particular "solution" (subset of allocative alternatives) that would exhibit two types of stability. First, such a solution would exhibit *internal stability* in the sense that no alternative in the solution would be beaten by any other alternative in the solution. Second, such a solutions would exhibit *external stability* in the sense that any alternative outside the solution that beats an alternative inside the solution would in turn be beaten by another alternative in the solution.[47] They then showed that the three-player allocation game possesses two types of solutions. The first is the *main simple solution,* which consists of the three allocations that give each member of each two-player majority half of the spoils and gives the remaining player nothing. The second is an infinite family of *discriminatory solutions,* each containing an infinite number of alternatives all of which have this property: two players collude, by conceding some small amount of spoils to the third player and implicitly agreeing to deal no further with him, and then bargaining over the remainder.[48]

A third type of solution has been proposed in the more empirically oriented work on legislative choice (with the U.S. Congress especially in mind). This is the *universalistic solution* that consists of the single alternative the gives each player an equal share of the spoils. The universalistic solution is internally stable in a trivial way. But it is externally stable only in a long-run sense and with additional assumptions (e.g., about attitudes toward risk). And its realization may depend on characteristics of the organization of a legislature that compromise its majoritarian character.[49]

The main simple and universalistic solutions treat all players symmetrically, but—as its name suggests—the discriminatory solution does not. Indeed both the nature and name of this solution suggest (but only suggest) how stigmatic characteristics might influence collective choice of allocative outcomes under chaotic majority rule. But it bears repeating that nothing in the logical character of majority rule implies that an exogenously defined minority must do poorly in distributive politics.

VII. Conclusion

On the basis of formal analysis, we have seen that the argument that majority rule renders minority interests irrelevant—that "the numerically more powerful majority choice simply subsumes minority preferences"—must be importantly qualified. The argument in effect assumes that politics is invariably cleavage politics with a single issue or with highly reinforcing preferences. In other political contexts—cleavage politics with cross-cutting preferences, ideological politics (even with a distinctive minority), and distributive politics—minority preferences significantly influence collective choice. Real-world politics of course is a complex mixture of cleavage, ideological, and distributive politics; such complexity probably gives minority interests additional influence, but taking account of such complexity is largely beyond the present power of formal political theory. Real-world political outcomes clearly are also influenced by factors other than preferences and decision rules. Whether and how such additional factors affect the fortune of minority interests must await further analysis; clearly they are likely to affect different minorities (sociologically defined) in different ways.

NOTES

1. "The Triumph of Tokenism: The Voting Rights Act and the Theory of Black Electoral Success," *Michigan Law Review,* 89 (1991): 1077–154; "No Two Seats: The Elusive Quest for Political Equality," *Virginia Law Review,* 77 (1991): 1413–514; "The Representation of Minority Interests: The Question of Single-Member Districts," *Cardozo Law Review,* 14 (1993): 1135–74; "Groups, Representation, and Race-Conscious Districting: A Case of the Emperor's Clothes," *Texas Law Review,* 71 (1993): 1593–642.

2. *The Tyranny of the Majority* (New York: The Free Press, 1994). This book contains the law review articles, together with an introductory chapter and some other material.

3. "Classic" works in this genre most notably and relevantly include: Kenneth A. Arrow, *Social Choice and Individual Values,* 2nd ed. (New York: Wiley, 1963); Duncan Black, *The Theory of Committees and Elections* (Cambridge: Cambridge University Press, 1958); Anthony Downs, *An Economic Theory of Democracy* (New York: Harper & Row, 1957); and James M. Buchanan and Gordon Tullock, *The Calculus of Consent* (Ann Arbor: University of Michigan Press, 1962). A survey (together with a somewhat idiosyncratic thesis) is provided by William H. Riker, *Liberalism Against Populism: A Confrontation between the Theory of Democracy and the Theory of Social Choice* (San Francisco: Freeman, 1982).

4. A partial exception is my own "Pluralism and Social Choice," *American Political Science Review,* 77 (1983): 734–47, which this essay in some ways extends. Another partial exception is Brian Barry, "Is Democracy Special?" in *Philosophy, Politics, and Society,* 5th series, edited by Peter Laslett and James Fishkin (New Haven: Yale University Press, 1979). I should say that both of my essays owe much to Barry's work.

5. For example, Henry Steele Commager, *Majority Rule and Minority Rights* (New York: Oxford University Press, 1943).

6. See, in particular, Buchanan and Tullock, *The Calculus of Consent.*

7. Some social choice theorists have formulated the problem of collective decisions and individual rights in another way that *has* raised all sorts of theoretical complexities. This formulation is due to Amartya K. Sen, "The Impossibility of a Paretian Liberal," *Journal of Political Economy,* 78 (1970): 152–57, and it has generated an enormous literature.

8. See Nicholas R. Miller, "Power in Game Forms," in *Power, Vot-*

ing, and Voting Power, edited by Manfred J. Holler (Vienna: Physica-Verlag, 1982); and Miller, "Pluralism and Social Choice."

9. Under a typical "majoritarian" (Anglo-American style) electoral system based on single-member districts, some majority coalitions are impotent because of their particular geographical configurations. Proportional representation assures that any majority coalition in the electorate, whatever its geographical configuration, can secure majority representation in the legislature and thus (given legislative majority rule) can control legislative outcomes.

10. Of course, preferences on many distinct issues (as the term is ordinarily used) are not separable. (For example, how much money you want to spend on Project *X* likely depends on how much is spent on Project *Y* and also on what the Tax Rate *Z* is.) Our assumption can be justified on two grounds. First, the distinction between majorities and minorities, defined in terms of their preferences on issues, becomes murky if preferences are not separable, so informal discussions of political majorities and minorities tend implicitly to make the same assumption of separability. Second, we can simply define a set of alternatives as constituting a distinct issue only if preferences on it are in fact separable.

11. Such preferences were first formally described and named by Duncan Black, "On the Rational of Group Decision-Making," *Journal of Political Economy,* 56 (1948): 23–34; also see *The Theory of Committees and Elections,* 6–8. With respect to alternative funding levels, the implication of single peakedness is that a citizen who most prefers a low level also prefers a moderate to a high level, and a citizen who most prefers a high level also prefers a moderate to a low level. It should be emphasized that single peakedness is neither a logical necessity nor always plausible. For example, a citizen who most prefers a high funding level for a program may also believe that, in the event such funding is not provided, little or no funding would be preferable to an intermediate amount that would not accomplish its purpose.

12. In the terminology of formal political theory, such multidimensional preferences are "strictly quasi-concave"—a term that seems worthwhile to avoid in the text of this essay.

13. Insofar as the label "ideological politics" may suggest a politics in which participants are rigid and uncompromising, the label is misleading. The reader should bear in mind that it is the structure of collective choice (i.e., selecting a point along a continuum), not the behavior of the participants, that is being characterized.

14. "A Set of Independent Necessary and Sufficient Conditions for Simple Majority Decision," *Econometrica,* 20 (1952): 680–84.

15. This problem was first formally posed by Douglas W. Rae, "Decision-Rules and Individual Values in Constitutional Choice," *American Political Science Review,* 63 (1969): 40–56. Rae assumed that each citizen expects to have a 0.5 probability of supporting a given alternative on any issue, and his argument proceeded in a way that was persuasive but not logically conclusive. Shortly thereafter Michael Taylor, "Proof of a Theorem on Majority Rule," *Behavioral Science,* 14 (1969): 228–31, provided a general proof for all probabilities. Philip D. Straffin, Jr., "Majority Rule and General Decision Rules," *Theory and Decision,* 8 (1977): 351–60, subsequently provided a proof that was both more concise and covered a more comprehensive domain of possible decision rules.

16. *Essai sur l'application de l'analyse à la probabilité des decisions rendues à la pluralité des voix* (Paris, 1795). See Black, *The Theory of Committees and Elections,* 159–80.

17. If we allow for citizen indifference and/or an even number of citizens, so that "majority preference ties" may result, there may be several alternatives not beaten by any other.

18. Black, "On the Rational of Group Decision-Making"; Kenneth A. Arrow, *Social Choice and Individual Values,* 1st ed. (New York: Wiley, 1951); Black, *The Theory of Committees and Elections.*

19. A "permanent loser" also ensures non-cyclical majority preference, and his least preferred alternative is the Condorcet winner.

20. Black, "The Rationale of Group Decision-Making," and *The Theory of Committees and Elections,* 16. If the number of citizens is even, ideal points $x^{n/2}$ and $x^{(n/2)+1}$ jointly define the median; all alternatives in the interval connecting these points tie each other, every alternative in the interval at least ties every other alternative, and every alternative outside the interval is beaten by some alternative in it. Regardless of whether n is even or odd, single-peakedness precludes cyclical majority preference.

21. Charles R. Plott, "A Notion of Equilibrium and Its Possibility under Majority Rule," *American Economic Review,* 57 (1967): 787–806.

22. Richard D. McKelvey, "Intransitivities in Multidimensional Voting Models and Some Implications for Agenda Control," *Journal of Economic Theory,* 12 (1976): 472–82; and "General Conditions for Global Intransitivities in Formal Voting Models," *Econometrica,* 47 (1979): 1085–112.

23. Nicholas R. Miller, "A New Solution Set for Tournaments and Majority Voting," *American Journal of Political Science,* 24 (1980): 68–96; Richard D. McKelvey, "Covering, Dominance, and Institution Free Properties of Social Choice, *American Journal of Political Science,* 30

(1986): 283–314; Gary W. Cox, "The Uncovered Set and the Core," *American Journal of Political Science,* 31 (1987): 408–22; Scott L. Feld, Bernard Grofman, and Nicholas R. Miller, "Centripetal Forces in Spatial Voting Games: On the Size of the Yolk," *Public Choice,* 59 (1988): 37–50; Craig A. Tovey, "The Instability of Instability," Naval Postgraduate School Working Paper, Monterey, California, May 1991, and "The Almost Surely Shrinking Yolk," Political Economy Working Paper No. 161, School of Business and Center in Political Economy, Washington University, January 1992.

24. Benjamin Ward, "Majority Rule and Allocation," *Journal of Conflict Resolution,* 5 (1961): 379–89; Nicholas R. Miller, "The Complete Structure of Majority Rule on Distributive Politics," paper presented to the Annual Meeting of the Public Choice Society, San Antonio, Texas, March 1982; David L. Epstein, "Uncovering Some Subtleties of the Uncovered Set," paper presented to the American Political Science Association, Washington, D.C., September 1991.

25. On the latter point, see for example David P. Baron and John A. Ferejohn, "The Power to Propose," in *Models of Strategic Choice in Politics,* edited by Peter C. Ordeshook (Ann Arbor: University of Michigan Press, 1989).

26. Here we invoke the well-known result concerning "Downsian" party competition (Downs, *An Economic Theory of Democracy,* chapter 8), embellished in many subsequent works. For the extension to policy-motivated parties, see Randall L. Calvert, "Robustness of the Multidimensional Voting Model: Candidate Motivations, Uncertainty, and Convergence," *American Journal of Political Science,* 29 (1985): 69–95. The same results, applied at the level of single-member districts, help justify the conclusion in the weak-party case that the median legislator closely resembles the median citizen.

27. Consider an example that Guinier uses (*Tyranny of the Majority,* 2). Responding to a problem posed in a children's magazine (what game would a group of six children play when four vote to play tag and two vote to play hide-and-seek?), her four-year son proposed this "untraditional" but appealing solution: they would take turns (perhaps playing tag about two-thirds and hide-and-seek about one-third of the time). But what has happened here is that an issue originally posed as dichotomous has been converted into a continuous one (i.e., what proportion of the time should each game be played?). And, if preferences on this issue are reasonably spread out over the resulting continuum, majority rule will produce (on the basis of the median voter theorem) a "taking turns" solution. (It seems doubtful, however, that a "taking turns" solution is practicable for many substantial and divisive

issues of public policy. We really can't make abortion legal on Mondays, Wednesdays, and Fridays, and illegal on Tuesdays and Thursdays.) However, if the four children are tag-playing fanatics, *all* of whom want to play tag *all* the time every day, majority rule will *not* lead to the compromise of "taking turns," even if such a compromise is available. (We will reach this conclusion more formally in section V.2.)

We might note that even a fanatical tag-playing majority might choose to compromise with the minority because (we may suppose) the whole group of children share a common desire to play *something* together, and the disgruntled minority of two might (or might threaten to) secede from the group if they were not accommodated in some degree. The bargaining power of minorities to withdraw cooperation or even secede is indeed a check on the power of majorities, but it obviously is not a check that derives from the nature of majority rule itself.

28. Stated otherwise, distinct "intense minorities" can "trade votes" or "logroll" to bring about an outcome that includes the minority alternative on the issue each cares about the most. The term "coalition of minorities" is due (I believe) to Anthony Downs (*An Economic Theory of Democracy,* 55–62). Robert Dahl's discussion of "minorities rule" in *A Preface to Democratic Theory* (Chicago: University of Chicago Press, 1956), 128–29, focuses on the same phenomenon.

29. The fraction in each category need not be the same in the two mixed clusters; all that matters in determining the effectiveness of a coalition of minorities is the overall fraction.

30. In "Pluralism and Social Choice," I argued that crosscutting preferences made effective coalitions of minorities more likely and reinforcing preferences made them less likely. An analysis by Tse-min Lin ("The Paradox of Voting and the Equilibrium Cycle," paper presented to the 1991 Annual Meeting of the American Political Science Association, Washington, D.C., August 29–September 1, 1991) shows that this proposition needs to be refined. The original distinction in sociological literature between "reinforcing" and "crosscutting" patterns of cleavage (to which "Pluralism and Social Choice" referred) concerned cleavages (for example, religion, language, region, and so forth) that had no common polarity such as "low" and "high." In this context, one could talk only about pairs of cleavages being either (in some degree) reinforcing or crosscutting—no distinction between positive and negative reinforcement was appropriate. However, when we extend the notion of crosscutting versus reinforcement to preferences on dichotomous issues, in conjunction with a focus on the operation of majority rule that leads us to label issue alternatives as "majority"

versus "minority," a common polarity is introduced, so it becomes possible and natural to distinguish between positive versus negative reinforcement, as I have done explicitly in this essay. While it was not explicit, the discussion of "reinforcing preferences" in "Pluralism and Social Choice" referred to *positively* reinforcing preferences only—for example, "reinforcing divisions of a population into majority and minority groups" (740). It is clear that the possibility of an effective coalition of minorities increases (i.e., the required fraction with minority intensity decreases) monotonically as the degree of positive reinforcement decreases towards crosscuttingness (popularity remaining constant). But the required fraction with minority intensity is not at its minimum when preferences are perfectly crosscutting. It continues to decrease (though only slightly) as preferences become negatively reinforcing, and the minimum is achieved at maximum negative reinforcement.

31. Downs, *An Economic Theory of Democracy,* 64–69, refers to the ineffectiveness of a coalition of minorities as *rule of the passionate majority.* The terminology may be slightly misleading. First, no interpersonal comparisons of preference intensity are relevant—the question is how *individual citizens* make issue tradeoffs within their own preference orderings. Secondly, how citizens within either the majority or minority clusters make such tradeoffs is also irrelevant—the question is only how citizens within the mixed clusters make such tradeoffs. Finally, it is not necessary for all citizens in the mixed cluster to prefer to get their way on the issue on which they prefer the majority alternative in order to produce "rule of a passionate majority"; it is always sufficient that at least one-half of such voters have such preferences (we may refer to this condition as a "generalized passionate majority"), but even this is almost never necessary. How great this proportion must be depends on the size of the several clusters.

32. An early result in formal political theory, provided independently and more or less simultaneously by many different researchers, was this demonstration that an effective coalition of minorities entails cyclical social preference. For a general review, see Nicholas R. Miller, "Logrolling, Vote Trading, and the Paradox of Voting: A Game-Theoretical Overview," *Public Choice,* 30 (1977), 51–75.

33. Note that preferences cannot be systematically and negatively reinforcing, since if issues 1 and 2 are negatively reinforcing and issues 2 and 3 are negatively reinforcing, issues 1 and 3 are positively reinforcing.

34. This follows because the median has the property that the average absolute deviation from the median is less than the average

absolute deviation from any other point. See Herbert Weisberg, *Central Tendency and Variability* (Newbury Park, CA: Sage Publications, 1992), 25–26. Start at the median ideal point x^m and move any distance D toward the left. You are *increasing* the dissatisfaction of the median citizen and every citizen to the his right by the same amount D for each of these $(n+1)/2$ citizens. *At best* you are *reducing* dissatisfaction of the left-of-center citizens by the same amount D for each of these $(n-1)/2$ citizens. (If you move beyond the ideal point of any left-of-center citizen, you reduce his dissatisfaction by less than D or even increase it.) So the overall effect of the move is to increase total dissatisfaction by at least D and average dissatisfaction by at least D/n. Obviously the same argument holds for any movement to the right.

35. John Rawls, *A Theory of Justice* (Cambridge: Harvard University Press, 1971).

36. Weisberg, *Central Tendency and Variability*, pp. 28–29. We might alternatively suppose that dissatisfaction increases, not linearly with distance from one's ideal point, but with the square of that distance. (Such "quadratic loss functions" are sometimes used in formal political theory.) It then follows that collective choice as the mean, rather than median, minimizes average dissatisfaction.

37. A "split-the-difference" arbitration rule (i.e., the midrange rule) is widely recognized to encourage such behavior in bilateral choice.

38. Given that the majority and minority distributions are normal with standard deviations of D^+ and D^- respectively, we may deem the critical threshold of polarization to be about 2.5 $(D^+ + D^-)$. (In a normal distribution, fewer than 1 percent of the points lie more than 2.5 standard deviations in either direction from the mean.)

39. We are characterizing both intervals from the minority point of view. From the majority point of view, Δx^- may be characterized as the "majority impact" and Δx^+ as "collective majority dissatisfaction." Note that we refer to Δx^- (or Δx^+) as *collective* minority (or majority) dissatisfaction, since some individual citizens (though necessarily a minority) within the minority (or majority) group may actually prefer x^* to x^- (or x^+). (If the minority group is highly distinctive, however, this minority within the minority must be vanishingly small; the corresponding minority within the majority would usually be relatively substantial. See figure 4.)

40. Then the total area under the curves on the x^+ side of x^* is equal to $(1-M)/2 + M/2$, and the area on the x^- side is $[(1-M)/2 - M/2] + M$, and elementary manipulation shows that these magnitudes are equal. If polarization falls much below the critical threshold, a significant portion of the minority distribution lies on the x^+ side x^*, so

the area under the majority curve between x^+ and x^* can be less than $M/2$.

41. The case of the fanatical tag-playing majority discussed in footnote 27 is an example of a fully cohesive majority that precludes minority impact.

42. The term "white primary" comes to mind; see V. O. Key, Jr., *Southern Politics* (New York: Alfred A. Knopf, 1949), chapter 29.

43. As the previous footnote suggests, one can think of reasons that might well arise in real social situations to promote such collusion. It follows from the previous discussion that there is no incentive for minority collusion if polarization is at or beyond the critical threshold. There is an incentive for minority collusion if polarization falls below the critical threshold, but in that case minority collusion presents the same dilemma as majority collusion invariably does.

44. See Charles R. Beitz, "Equal Opportunity in Political Representation," in *Equal Opportunity,* edited by Norman E. Bowie (Boulder, Colo.: Westview Press, 1988).

45. See footnote 24.

46. Such stigmatic criteria may account for the cleavages in cleavage politics or for a distinctive minority in ideological politics, of course.

47. *The Theory of Games and Economic Behavior* (Princeton: Princeton University Press, 1944).

48. Note that such collusion is far more likely to succeed than that discussed in the previous section, because this is not collusion that attempts to displace a Condorcet winner.

49. Barry R. Weingast, "A Rational Choice Perspective on Congressional Norms," *American Journal of Political Science,* 23 (1979): 245–62; Morris P. Fiorina, "Universalism, Reciprocity, and Distributive Policy Making in Majority Rule Institutions," in *Research in Public Policy Analysis and Management,* edited by J. P. Crecine (Greenwich: JAI Press, 1981); Gary J. Miller and Joe A. Oppenheimer, "Universalism in Experimental Committees," *American Political Science Review,* 76 (1982): 561–74; Barry Weingast and William Marshall, "The Industrial Organization of Congress," *Journal of Political Economy,* 96 (1987): 132–63.

10

DELIBERATIVE EQUALITY AND DEMOCRATIC ORDER

THOMAS CHRISTIANO

Deliberation has acquired a privileged status in recent work in democratic theory. Many have claimed that democracy without deliberation is an unstable system wherein the desires of citizens clash without regard to the common good and even without concern for the reasonableness of the desires themselves. Some, inspired by the ideas of Jürgen Habermas and John Rawls, have argued that the process of social discussion among equals is itself intrinsically valuable and ought to be thought of as the preeminent value underlying democratic institutions.[1] Others, such as this author, give deliberation a more instrumental role in enhancing citizens' understanding of their and others' interests and in encouraging individuals to abandon the pursuit of naked self-interest. Moreover, equality in this process of discussion is itself essential to democratic equality and thus is required by the principles of justice underlying democracy.

Contemporary theorists are certainly right to point to the importance of open discussion among equals in a democratic society. But placing deliberation among equals at the heart of democratic values entails important theoretical and perhaps practical costs. Though a principle of equality in the process of deliberation can be defined, the principle is such that in a pluralistic democratic society it is practically impossible for citizens who adhere to the principle to agree generally on what is required for its implementation. Many individuals in a democratic society will reasonably think that their views have not been given a fair hearing, while others see no difficulty. This I call the inherent contestability of deliberative equality. As a result, many citizens can reasonably dispute the claim that the collective decision-making process makes adequate provision for everyone's participation. They often will have reason to contest the claim that the society is fully democratic. And they will have reason to deny that the decision-making procedure is fully legitimate even when everyone agrees and knows that everyone else agrees on the basic principles. The trouble is that people will quite reasonably disagree as to whether the ideal of equality in public discussion is satisfied and though there may be a truth of the matter, they are not going to know it. Thus arises a constant contest among citizens over how to structure the very institutions of political equality themselves. This contest is of the very same nature as those disagreements about how to organize the society which lead citizens to demand political equality in collective decision making in the first place.

This ongoing contest constitutes a challenge to political order in a number of ways. First, it implies that the public political institutions of a democratic society in principle cannot be fully transparent to its members. Second, it suggests that there will be serious disagreements about what that order is. Third, it may indeed lead to political instability inasmuch as all citizens prize the ideals of political equality. And it can lead to this kind of instability even when everyone agrees on the same ideals. These difficulties are inherent in the very ideals of democracy themselves.

In what follows, I will show how this problem arises. First, I will defend and define a conception of democratic equality, then will demonstrate the importance of deliberation among equals to democratic politics in this view. I will develop a conception of the ideal of deliberation among equals as an ideal of qualitative equality. It raises the problem of the contestability of deliberative equality. I subsequently will discuss a number of institutional devices designed to overcome the problem of contestability and show how they fail. I will conclude with some remarks about the implications of this problem and how it may be mitigated.

Democratic Equality

Democratic decision making is an intrinsically valuable process that lends legitimacy to its outcomes; its core ideal is political equality. The rationale for these claims basically is that democracy is a just way of resolving certain kinds of conflicts of interests. Citizens have many interests which are deeply interdependent with those of other citizens. These interests involve aspects of social life such that one person's well-being cannot be affected for better or worse without involving the interests of most if not all other citizens. These are collective features of social life. Some examples are such collective goods as pollution control and defense against outside aggressors. Others are the structure of property rights in the society and contract and tort law. There are also such cultural goods as the display of public monuments and the structure of public education. Communitarians have rightly insisted that individuals have important interests in these features of society: these features define the environment which frames people's relations with each other, structures the possible courses of life they can lead, and forms their characters. These features can also be the source of either alienation or a sense of belonging for individuals inasmuch as they understand, recognize, and adhere to the cultural and moral norms embodied in the social arrangements that shape their lives. But communitarians have ignored the profound conflicts of interests and disagreements over these collective properties of society. Modern societies are characterized by deep differences in conceptions of norms of justice, cultural traditions, and conceptions of the good of human beings. These differences lead to conflict over the level of provision of public goods and the structure of property, as well as the social and psychological conditions of a flourishing life. Some of these conflicting interests can be handled in the context of smaller voluntary associations and private life, but many of the interests are too interdependent and must be adjudicated on a society-wide level.[2]

The interests of each must be given equal consideration because these conflicts must be resolved in a just manner. Only democracy can embody this equal consideration in these contexts. Contrary to my claim, many would argue that the interests of each are given equal consideration when a regime of equal well-being is established. Thus, a just society ought to be arranged as to promote equality of well-being. The process of democratic decision making must be evaluated in terms of whether its outcomes approach as closely as possible to equality of welfare. Democracy, on this account, is not intrinsically valuable and cannot by itself confer legitimacy on its outcomes. In my view, this interpretation of equal consideration of interests cannot be sustained; the only full embodiment of this principle of justice is equality in the resources individuals command for having an influence over the collective decision-making process. Equality of welfare is not an ideal for political institutions because the demands made on our ability to know when such equality is in place or approximated cannot even in principle be met. First, our conceptions of our interests are necessarily incomplete. We have some knowledge of what is in our interests, but only a bit. Second, our conceptions of our interests are constantly changing. We learn about our interests as we live and across generations but this process is never completed. Thus, the unit to be compared in a principle of equality of welfare is necessarily inaccessible. Third, the relative importance and means of measuring the satisfaction of one person's interests with others' is a subject of constant disagreement in society. The measures and standards are deeply contested. So even if we had full conception of our interests, we would not be able to agree on any standard by which to compare them. These three facts of ignorance about interests combine to suggest that if equality of welfare were the ultimate standard of justice, social justice itself would be in principle beyond human ability to assess. Social justice is not a mysterious principle, but one to be assessed in public. In a just society the equal public status of individuals is made evident through the functioning of its institutions. A proper interpretation of equal consideration of interests must satisfy this basic test and the ideal of equality of welfare cannot do so. On the other hand, a principle which assigns to individuals equal means for discovering and pursuing their interests does signal to each and every citizen in a public way that their interests are being given equal weight in the collective decision-making process. And citizens can be assured of their equal status by a principle which assigns to citizens equal means for resolving contests over the collective properties of society and resolving disagreement over how interests and goods are to be compared.[3] Thus, in the context of collective decision making, equality of resources is the only reasonable embodiment of equal consideration of interests.

Equality in Cognitive Conditions

On this view, democratic decision making involves two important components. It involves an adversarial and a deliberative element. The adversarial aspect consists in the distribution of votes and voting power in collective decision making as well as resources for coalition building and bargaining. This aspect is a necessary part of democracy insofar as decisions must be made in an egalitarian way despite as yet unresolved disagreement and conflict of interests. The equal distribution of voting power and coalition building resources is a publicly ascertainable method of advancing the interests of each and every citizen. But it is only a part of democratic equality.

In the light of the problem of ignorance about interests, individuals need time and other resources to develop their understanding of their interests as well as just ways of putting together their interests with those of others. The equal consideration of interests requires that these resources be distributed equally. Egalitarian institutions are charged with the task of disseminating understanding widely so that individuals have the means to comprehend and advance their interests and convictions. Those who do not know what policies will advance their interests or their conception of what is best are not likely to have much real power. Compare a person at the wheel of a working automobile who does not know how to drive it, with someone who has a car who does know. The first person is powerless because of her inability to use the resources at her command due to ignorance while the second, who has the same resources, does have control. This is similar to the comparison between those who vote on the basis of some real understanding of politics and those who have little. There is a considerable differential in power because while the ignorant might sometimes be able to block the knowledgeable from getting what they prefer, they rarely get what is in their interest except by accident.

Such ignorance also undermines a person's ability to control his life in the case where he has very confused or distorted conceptions of his interests. Compare the person with a car, who knows how it works, but has only confused ideas of where he wants to go, to the person who has an idea of where she wants to go. The first person is at a considerable disadvantage in power compared to the second. He will drive around aimlessly without achieving any end while the second person will be able to achieve some end that she desires. This is a real difference in power.

In addition, a person whose conception of his interests is more or less arbitrarily arrived at is at a disadvantage in relation to a person who has thought about her aims and has some basis for pursuing her ends. He may not always do worse but in general he is more likely not to pursue aims suitably related to his real interests. This is because a person who has not consciously examined his interests is likely to have an unstable conception, especially when he is confronted with many alternatives. Plato's discussion of justification and its worth expresses this well:

> true opinions, as long as they remain, are a fine thing and all they do is good, but they are not willing to remain long, and they escape from a man's mind, so that they are not worth much until one ties them down by giving them an account of the reason why.[4]

The person who has a poorly reasoned or unreflective conception of his aims is a person who is unlikely to achieve much of worth to himself. Such a person will be easily subject to confusion, arbitrary changes in opinion as well as manipulation by others. Thus, inasmuch as it is important to advance the interests of any person, it is also important for him to have some reasoned grasp of his interests.

Democratic Deliberation

Democratic institutions and in particular institutions of discussion and deliberation have a large impact on whether individuals have the opportunities to reflect on and come to a better understanding of their interests. They can provide resources for learning and reflection. Egalitarian institutions of discussion and deliberation provide individuals with equal resources for reflecting on their interests. Hence, democratic institutions ought to be structured in such a way as to provide wide and roughly equal access to information relevant to democratic decision making. Discussion and deliberation thus contribute importantly to egalitarian democratic institutions and the principle of equality provides a rationale for distributing the resources for deliberation equally. Contrary to the objections of critics, these claims are derived entirely from a principle of equal consideration of interests when there is considerable ignorance about the interests that are to be advanced.[5] Institutions of deliberation and discussion advance political equality.

We must devote time, resources, and energy to acquire knowledge. It might appear that what is necessary for access to understanding politics and the interests and moral aims it can serve, is that each person have the resources for developing his or her own understanding of politics and interests. Each person can be set up with his or her own computer, telephone, and money to acquire information. But this would be an unfortunate solution since it is not very efficient to have everyone seeking out information on his or her own. In politics, the time and resources needed for developing any real understanding of what is going on and where one's interests really lie as well as what might be just or unjust are very great because of the complexity of the issues. We need only observe the resources that go into think tanks, political parties, interest groups, universities, and policy studies centers for the purpose of achieving some understanding. The processes of developing an understanding of politics require organization, specialization and expertise, all of which is beyond the ability of any single citizen to cultivate. As a consequence, organization is necessary to a desirable process of democratic deliberation. We also must think of interest groups and political parties as the main institutions that perform this role in the democratic process. At the same time these institutions make a large contribution to the understanding of those who are not specialists. Thus they are institutions of democratic discussion.

Equality in the Deliberative Agenda

We have seen the importance of deliberation among equals to political equality and the significance of institutions for this process. Some remarks about the nature of equality in deliberation are in order. Let us distinguish between two kinds of equality. One might be called numerical equality and the other, qualitative equality. In numerical equality persons are treated as equals when resources are distributed equally to persons. Hence, when we give individuals the vote we assign equal votes to each person. In qualitative equality, persons are treated as equals when resources are divided equally among certain qualities of persons. For example, if we value two distinct group projects equally, we might distribute monies to them equally regardless of how many persons are involved in each. Each project is treated equally, though those in the larger group would get fewer resources per person.

The equality we should aim at in the deliberative process is closer to qualitative equality. There are a number of reasons for this. First, a deliberative process aims at achieving the truth in the subject being discussed. Citizens desire primarily to advance a view because they think it is *true,* not because it is *their* view. This is in contrast to voting and bargaining wherein each pursues his or her own separate interests or aims. Social discussion and deliberation presuppose a kind of common aim: one does not lose by having one's opinion refuted; indeed, this is a gain since one learns something new.

By way of illustration, in a seminar with ten persons who disagree on two views wherein seven support *A* and three support *B*, what is of prime importance to each is the assessment of the truth or falsehood of the views. That more people favor *A* than *B* does not enter into determining how much time ought to be devoted to each view. Suppose John and Jane support *A* and Joel supports *B*. For John it matters that *A* is taken into account and the same goes for Jane. But this "mattering" does not add up. The fact that two people wish that *A* be taken into account does not entail that *A* ought to be taken into account twice in discussion. For each, it matters only that *A* be taken into account. Thus, equal time should be given to opinions *A* and *B*.

A second reason for giving equal time to *A* and *B* is the fact that ideas have a certain "jointness of supply."[6] The ideas do not have to be divided up in order for everyone to benefit from them. And the same is true for discussion. John's view is given as much hearing as Joel's, and Jane's view is also given as much hearing when *A* is given the same amount of time for a hearing as *B*. This jointness of supply is relevant to the discussion of opposing points of view in a democracy where different positions may reflect different interests. Citizens' interests are, to an extent, unintentionally reflected in the points of view they advance, especially when it comes to the organization of society. In discussion, individuals have various reasons to want their views expressed: one is that the very preparation for expressing one's views to others stimulates one to more serious reflection on what one is about to say. Thus the chance to express oneself in public gives one an invaluable motive for thinking and learning. Another is that such expression enables those who have the opinion to hear how others respond to it. If I have no opportunity to raise questions or say what I think to others about some issue, then I will not be able to benefit from hearing what they have to say about it. I will not be able to learn from those others on matters which are of importance to me and in particular which relate to my interests. Thus I have a great interest in having my views expressed.

This value of expression is not based in the intrinsic importance of expressing oneself. It is based on the fact that one learns a lot by receiving a response to one's views. This also implies that it is not essential that I do the expressing. What is important is that the view be properly aired by someone and that it be answered by others. Hence, if ten people have the same view, given jointness, they will all learn from the responses to one single expression of the view. Indeed, if more time is given to their view than to others' because they are fewer in number, the interests in learning of the ten will be better served than those of the lesser number. Thus, a principle which assigns more time for the discussion of a single view than to others merely on the basis of the greater number of believers behind that view treats the interests of the greater number with more than equal consideration. Therefore, the principle of equal consideration of interests requires a principle of qualitative equality in determining how resources are allocated to the expression and discussion of views. Thus we have two arguments for qualitative equality as an egalitarian principle for regulating the agenda for deliberation.

The logic of this argument is clear when we attend to the conclusion about the importance of organization in the process of developing knowledge about the various interests in society. The best way to develop understanding about interests is not to have each person try to figure things out for himself or herself. This ignores the importance of specialization in the process of learning. It is clear that resources among persons ought to be pooled in order to support specialization and expertise in developing the understanding of their interests as well as points of view. Thus, speaking in an idealized way, for each set of interests or points of view, there ought to be pooling of resources devoted to the greater understanding of these interests or points of view. But if we distribute resources to persons equally, then those who share interests with greater numbers of persons will have more resources devoted to understanding their interests and points of view because the resources would be pooled so as to have a much better funded organization to understand those interests. If more resources are devoted to views or interests that are shared by more persons, then the means for understanding one's interests will vary from person to person depending on how many other persons have those interests. But this seems to constitute an important form of unequal consideration of interests among individuals. Some have more resources devoted to understanding their interests than others.

What we need is a qualitative principle for distributing the cognitive conditions. Resources for developing understanding should be distributed equally to each kind of *view,* not to each *person.* Only on such a principle, is each person's access to the cognitive conditions equalized. Since organizations are formed for the purpose of articulating conceptions of the interests and moral aims individuals have in the society, they must have roughly equal resources for developing their point of view. Only in this way does each citizen have the same resources devoted to the cultivation of his or her understanding. This is a necessary condition for giving equal consideration to each interest.

This principle of qualitative equality introduces special problems. It suggests that in order to know whether a system of associations devoted to deliberation is egalitarian or not we have to have some knowledge about the set of relevant interests and points of view in the society that ought to be cultivated. Only if we know what the relevant interests and points of view are can we know whether the principle of qualitative equality is satisfied. There are a number of difficulties here, however. First, there are many different kinds of interests and points of view which vary along a number of dimensions. Second, many interests are simply ignored because of a previous history of oppression and lack of collective action. Third, there are controversies about the importance of interests as well as the significance of the differences between interests or points of view. In short, there are many questions about which interests should be counted and what the relative importance of these interests are. In the next section, I shall lay out some of the main dimensions of contestability of this deliberative agenda. I then will lay out a more sophisticated version of the principle of qualitative equality. We will see that the contestability of the agenda is inherent in the democratic process when we survey the various different ways in which one might try to overcome the problem and how they fail.

Dimensions of Contestability of the Deliberative Agenda

There is considerable disagreement about what interests people have and with whom they share those interests. There also are differences about justice. Therefore, the deliberative agenda is likely to be quite complex. As we have seen, an important function of interest groups is to help individuals more clearly understand their interests. They enhance social discussion on interests and justice. Equality requires that there be a wide variety of social groups that reflect the different interests and sectors of the society as well as the different points of view. Thus any system of interest groups and political parties which sustains an egalitarian process of social discussion will be quite complex along a number of dimensions.

One main dimension on which associations might differ is the *importance* to the members or the society of the issues with which they are concerned. Some associations are concerned with issues that are of manifestly less significance than others to anyone in the society. For any interest group, some or even many may not think that the concerns they express are particularly important. Some may not identify with the other members of the supposed group. For example, many African-American persons may not think of their ethnic heritage as an important distinguishing feature of their lives. They may see the difference between white and black as not very salient. They do not identify themselves as African-American. Thus the groups that claim to "represent" them are not very important to them. Another example is the scope of the concerns of an association. Some are concerned with only a few issues in politics. For instance, anti-abortion groups are often concerned with only that issue. Environmental groups are concerned with wider issues but they are not usually concerned with the whole gamut of political issues. Business and labor groups are also quite diverse. They can, as does the AFL-CIO, concern themselves with the whole range of political issues in society.[7] Here, the question is, ought points of view on matters of greatly different importance be treated equally? Obviously, they should not but it is not clear how we can properly accommodate this fact since the matter of importance will be a subject of controversy.

A second dimension is the extent to which interest groups are *significantly different* from others. Two groups may be concerned with issues that are very similar and may have views that are very close. Surely, in this case it would be unfair to treat these groups as on a par with some other association which represents a very different view on the issue at hand. As with the matter of importance, there may be a lot of controversy about whether the views or interests of two groups are relevantly different in a particular case. In many cases, some groups will see their interests as being quite different from each other while many outside those groups may not see much difference between their concerns.

A third difficulty is that groups in the society encounter different *obstacles* to organization. First, there are collective action problems which are more and less difficult to solve for different groups. Second, there are problems concerning the quantity of resources that sectors of society have with which to organize groups. These latter two problems bring it about that some parts of society are merely latent in their ability to form associations. Inasmuch as the associations perform a crucial deliberative function, certain interests for which there is no organizational support may go unrecognized by many including those who share them.[8] Thus some interests are simply not acknowledged even by those who have them. But what these interests are, as well as the nature of the group that has them, are likely to be topics of considerable contention within the society.

A fourth kind of variation is in the *credibility* of groups. Some interest groups simply do not advance credible claims on the society. For example, many would agree that those who insist that the theory of creation ought to be treated on a par with evolutionary biology in the school curriculum, or that it should be given precedence, do not advance credible claims. Ought these groups really to be treated on a par with others? Ought the principle of qualitative equality require that these groups have as many resources as other more credible associations?

Clearly this would be illegitimate. Yet, there is likely to be some serious disagreements about which groups are credible.

A fifth important kind of variation is among groups that hold to tyrannical conceptions of the aims of society. Such groups refuse to treat some other groups in the society as equals. Their positions are based on a denial of equal consideration of interests to certain citizens. An example of this is the Nazi party in the United States. They simply refuse to grant equal status to many of their fellow citizens. Surely such groups are not entitled to be treated on a par with those whose views are compatible at least with some rough interpretation of equal status among citizens. Consistency suggests that views which imply that some people's interests ought not to be treated equally need not benefit from a scheme of equality. Only non-tyrannical views ought to be treated as equals in an egalitarian deliberative agenda.

Some may think that a sixth dimension ought also to be taken into account. Associations might be distinguished by whether they advance *special interests or the common good.* Religious, ethnic, and socioeconomic associations promote the concerns of sectors of the society on the assumption that they have distinctive interests and points of view. The parts of the society they "represent" are independent of the existence of the associations and they claim to represent the interests of those who are not members of the group but who are in the relevant sector of the society. By contrast, environmental, consumer, and other general reform associations do not claim to represent the interests or points of view of any particular sector of the society. They are groups of people who are united on the basis of shared opinions about the common good. They cannot claim to represent the points of view of anyone outside the group, and they do not represent anyone's interests; they have opinions about the common good. That some groups take positions on the common good and others on the good of a particular sector of society would appear to make a difference to the appropriate allocation of resources to groups in the process of discussion. The difference between public special interest groups, some would say, ought not to be ignored in our conception of what equality in the process of social discussion consists in.

This distinction, however, is problematic in a number of ways. Many so called "special interest groups" advance points of view on the common good of the entire polity. For example, unions as well as trade associations make claims to speak for the public interest and these claims ought not to be dismissed merely as bad faith. Though they tend to be biased towards their own interests, they do offer legitimate contributions to debates about how the society ought to be structured. Furthermore, socioeconomic, ethnic, and religious groups usually offer judgments about what fairness demands in accommodating their interests. Thus they advance claims about the society as a whole. Furthermore, public interest groups, to some extent, are not free of bias towards particular interests either. Environmental groups, for example, tend to reflect the interests of upper-middle-class Americans and downplay the interests of working-class persons. This is not a cynical observation on the concealed motives of these individuals, but rather a remark on the necessary cognitive bias involved in any assertion of important social goals.

Another element of this distinction is that some groups advance *judgments* about the common good while others advance the *interests* of a sector of the society. But this is not cut and dry since "special interest" associations do not uncontroversially represent the interests or views of sectors of the population except those of the members. In some cases, alternative associations have different views about the interests and views of the same sector of the society. Indeed, the very idea that the associations represent groups is problematic. What associations of ascriptive groups do in their deliberative function is express judgments about the interests and points of view of their constituencies and the importance of such interests as well as fair ways of accommodating those interests in the society. The claim to represent the people whose interests they describe is not much better than the claim of public interest groups to represent the interests of the citizenry as a whole. Each of these kinds of groups offer controversial judgments about interests and fairness. Thus those groups ought not to be thought of as simply advancing the interests of particular citizens but as advancing judgments about those interests which are to be subject to the scrutiny of all citizens. These two observations seem to me to diminish the importance of the distinction between public interest and special interest groups for a specification of the deliberative agenda. The proposed sixth dimension of complexity safely can be ignored in our attempt to define a viable principle of qualitative equality.

Clearly, however, the five dimensions of complexity must have an influence on how an egalitarian deliberative agenda is to be structured. The distribution of resources to these different groups is the primary determinant of the agenda of public discussion and so far we have seen that qualitative equality is a reasonable principle for distributing resources. But it is clear that this principle must be modified. If a set of issues with which some association is concerned is relatively unimportant, then it is hard to see why we should be worried if it receives less support than organizations which treat more important issues. Such an organization ought not to have as prominent a place on the agenda for discussion. Furthermore, if two organizations are concerned to advance nearly indistinguishable points of view on various issues, we should not be disturbed if one or both do not occupy as important a position in the deliberative agenda as a group that advocates a distinctive set of ideas. Giving all three groups equal attention would violate the principle of qualitative equality. And groups with ideas that lack credibility ought not to have the same status on the agenda as the more credible. Finally, only associations advocating non-tyrannical points of view ought to be guaranteed an equal place on the deliberative agenda.

Thus the principle of qualitative equality must be quite complex. It states that non-tyrannical and credible groups must be given an equal hearing with other views on issues of the same importance as long as the views are sufficiently distinct; it also requires that no important sectors of the society are excluded from the process of discussion. Tyrannical groups may not be banned but they may not make a claim to equality; such a claim would seem inconsistent.[9] The same conclusion should hold for groups whose claims are not credible. Furthermore, issues of less importance ought to be given less of a hearing. Let us call this modified idea the principle of plural qualitative equality.

The Deliberative Agenda Problem

The principle of plural qualitative equality is a reasonable principle for evaluating an egalitarian deliberative agenda but we should expect considerable controversy regarding the importance, distinctness, credibility, latency, and sometimes even the tyranny of the various different views. The very setting of an egalitarian deliberative agenda itself is likely to be the subject of considerable dispute on all the dimensions. Moreover, this disagreement is of a similar sort as the kind of disagreement and conflict that motivates the demand for democratic equality in the first place. It is disagreement about the relative importance and nature of the interests that individuals have. Therefore, the very disagreement and conflict that calls for a democratic solution also seems to put the characterization of democratic equality into question in any particular case.

The problem to be solved for the democrat is how to establish an egalitarian deliberative agenda in accordance with plural qualitative equality in a manner that takes account of the considerable disagreement on what the proper structure of such an agenda should be. Democrats require that the citizens themselves make the decisions in these circumstances of disagreement. The deliberative agenda must be chosen by the citizens. It ought not to be determined entirely a priori nor ought it be determined by some third party. Both of these methods would be inconsistent with the basic principles that underlie democratic equality: that each must have a say in collectively binding decisions when there is considerable disagreement among them. This is the deliberative agenda problem.

There are two main methods that can be used to make a choice of deliberative agenda: a market method and a collective decision method. The basic market method is to give each citizen an independent choice on the issue. That is, each citizen has the power to bring about what he or she prefers more or less on his or her own. The collective decision method requires that citizens make a choice together. A citizen does not get what he or she wants on his own but can only secure a prefered outcome with the help of most other citizens. All the citizens participate in making one decision.

In the next section, we will consider two general ways to solve the problem of the deliberative agenda. First, we will explore the familiar idea that institutions of deliberation ought to be a marketplace of ideas. Second, we will explore an egalitarian modification of the marketplace of ideas that has been proposed recently. Both of these views propose a market method for choosing the deliberative agenda. We will see how they fall afoul of some important requirements of democratic equality. Third, we will review democratic collective decision making methods for solving the deliberative agenda problem. They too encounter difficulties of practical as well as theoretical significance.

The Marketplace of Ideas

The marketplace of ideas is often used as a way to describe possible institutions of discussion and deliberation. The idea, however, is ambiguous and involves a number of thoughts that ought to be separated. There is a metaphorical ideal and a more literal conception of the marketplace of ideas. On the one hand, the ideal is often used as a kind of metaphor for a set of institutions where ideas are exchanged freely and where each person has the right to make up his or her own mind about which are the best ideas. Thus a seminar might be a marketplace of ideas if all are permitted to say what they think is right and to advance reasons for what they think and each is permitted to make up his or her own mind. Buying, selling, competition, cost, and benefit are all metaphors for the process of agreeing, persuading, and disagreement. In the marketplace, all of these activities can be engaged in freely. The efficiency of markets is a metaphor for the optimistic idea that the good ideas will ultimately drive out the bad in free discussion. This metaphor provides an attractive ideal of social discussion inasmuch as it is egalitarian and open and suggests that the cause of truth will be served. But it fails to provide institutional guidance since it does not include a description of the social costs in time and resources of discussion or the distribution of those costs. Thus it cannot help solve our problem.

On the other hand, the idea of a marketplace of ideas is used in a more literal sense when it is thought of as a method for allocating resources to particular points of view. The idea behind this literal marketplace of ideas is that there ought to be a market in the production and consumption of ideas just as there is in the production and consumption of any other good. Accordingly, the process of discussion should be funded in much the same way that any other economic activity is sponsored. It should be paid for by those who benefit from it. And the beneficiaries should pay only on condition that it is worth their while. The consumers of the information ought to pay for it. This arrangement parallels that wherein consumers pay for the food they consume, or consumers of stereo equipment pay for the equipment. This very same logic is applied to the supply of information. A consumer will buy a book on some subject he or she is interested in only if it is worth the price. The price reflects the cost of production to a great degree so in effect the consumer supports the production of the information. If the consumer does not desire the information sufficiently to pay the price for it, then it appears that it would be more worthwhile to produce something else: either some different information or something altogether different for which people are willing to pay. Thus, though producers must decide what to produce, their decisions will be based on what consumers wish to consume at the prices that must be paid for the objects. The consumer is ultimately sovereign in the marketplace according to this kind of approach.

The theorists of the marketplace of ideas in a literal sense argue that the institutions of deliberation and discussion we are presently contemplating ought to be organized along the same lines as any other market institution. Thus, organizations for elaborating and articulating the interests and points of view of citizens ought to be paid for by those who will consume the information. Only if it is worthwhile to them to pay for the information will it be useful information to produce. The very same efficiency that results from markets in general will also result here.

They argue that the cause of truth will be served since citizens have an interest in hearing what is true and in telling the true from the false. As a consequence, citizens will cease to support those organizations that have proved to be unreliable in producing good information and will transfer their resources to organizations which are more reliable in this respect. The producers of the information have an incentive to improve their products. They do not want to be destroyed in the competition. Since citizens are diverse there will be a great diversity in the kinds of ideas that are expressed. As a consequence, citizens will have a lot to choose from and in the long run the good ideas will drive out the bad.

The market can also determine how much resources to devote to the development and articulation of each kind of knowledge about the different interests and points of view in the society. If citizens find certain kinds of information unimportant, then they will be willing to expend less resources on them. More resources will go to elaborate more important ideas. Citizens will not be willing to support sources that produce roughly the same information. This would just be getting the same information twice. As a consequence, we seem to have a solution to the problems of estimating the credibility, relative importance and qualitative distinctness of different interests and points of view. Citizen consumers decide whether information is credible, how important it is and whether it is sufficiently distinct from the information they already have to be worth their while to purchase. All of these discriminations are adequately handled in a marketplace of ideas of the sort we have described. The problem of the deliberative agenda seems to be solved here.[10]

There are two serious objections to this view, however. The first objection is that the uneven distribution of resources in the society undermines equality in rational social deliberation to the extent that it enables some to support the kinds of organizations necessary to developing and communicating their interests to others, while it disables others from developing and communicating their views. The ability and willingness to pay for anything is partially a function of wealth. As a consequence, we see the wealthy contributing much more resources to organizations devoted to the development of the understanding of their interests and points of view.[11] Naturally, the same holds for large economic organizations such as corporations. Therefore, there will be a bias in a system of organizations structured by the marketplace of ideas towards the interests and points of view of the wealthy. The marketplace of ideas will prove to be deeply inegalitarian.

These observations imply that the marketplace of ideas may fail to ensure the kind of diversity of opinion for advancing the basic epistemic aims of social discussion and deliberation. Such a marketplace may limit what Mill has called "the clash of ideas" and the testing of ideas because of its limitations on sources of ideas outside the wealthier parts of society. Inasmuch as the testing of ideas by competition with other ideas is an essential condition for enhancing the understandings of everyone in society, the uneven distribution of resources is an obstacle to the basic aim of rational social deliberation since it makes it very hard for large sectors of the society to elaborate and articulate their views at all. Inasmuch as the epistemic aim of rational social deliberation as well as equality in the process of discussion can be achieved only when active support is given to a diversity of groups to organize and articulate their views, it appears that the marketplace of ideas cannot be endorsed as the best institutional arrangement for rational social deliberation.

The second objection has to do with the fact that political information is a collective good. Recall that the main purpose of improving one's understanding of political and social matters is to be able to have an impact on the outcome of collective decision making. But for the great majority of citizens, there is little incentive to develop this understanding because they will make little difference to the ultimate outcome. Citizens desire that a lot of information about their interests be available to voters and that voters use that information wisely; but each citizen is far less concerned with himself or herself having that information. Thus, while each would like everyone else to be well informed, they have no reason to inform themselves. At least self-interested citizens are not likely to become informed or pay the price to become informed because they can either rely on others to do the same or they will figure that if others are not very well informed, they will not make much difference to the outcome so they have little reason to become informed. Thus self-interested citizens are rationally ignorant.[12] This would suggest that most citizens radically undersupport the system of secondary associations. They will not pay the price for it because either enough others are paying the price or not enough others are paying the price, in which case it makes little difference whether a particular individual does or not. In general, the principle of consumer sovereignty operates rather poorly in this kind of context.

Given this problem of low information among a large proportion of the electorate, it is not clear how citizens can be in a position to evaluate ideas in the way that is required by the theory of the marketplace of ideas. On a self-interested conception of motivation, while it is true that citizens desire that flawed ideas be rooted out and that the good ideas replace them, they do not have the incentive to invest in the time and resources necessary to make such evaluations on their own. Thus there is little reason to expect that good ideas will drive out the bad, and there is little reason to think that citizens will have the incentive to develop nuanced conceptions of their interests and points of view with regard to the collective properties of society. Thus, at least on the self-interest assumption, the theory of the marketplace of ideas seems to fail to bring about the desirable outcomes that are promised by the theorists.

Furthermore, serious inequalities come about in this context. Individuals receive a large share of their information about politics as a by-product of their other activities when they do not actively seek it.[13] Those who are in professional, large business, and governmental occupational positions in the society tend to receive much more political information than others as a by-product of their work than those who are, say, construction workers, wait persons, or unemployed. Their jobs bring them into contact with government policy quite often. They also tend to be better educated and thus more able to process the information they receive. As a consequence of these two factors, they tend to be much more politically sophisticated and active.[14] Thus interest groups and parties as well as the government are likely to be more responsive to their interests and points of view than those of the less well-to-do. Also, certain groups whose interests are affected in a highly concentrated way by the government will have some incentive to sponsor the generation of knowledge about their interests and points of view and communicate it to the government. They will tend to be overrepresented in the system of interest groups. For example, firms that employ many workers have interests in becoming narrowly informed about occupational regulation; those that experience competition from foreign firms wish to know about laws regulating imports, and potential beneficiaries of public subsidies have interests in knowing about government policy in these areas. But only some are in a position to have these incentives. Finally, since most citizens are not willing to pay for their political information but often receive it from other sources, these groups which have a special interest in government policy have an incentive to subsidize the production and communication of whatever information the citizenry at large receives. That information will tend to be biased in favor of the interests of the groups that do the subsidizing.[15] As a consequence, it appears that the process of social discussion in a large democracy will tend to be deeply inegalitarian if the marketplace of ideas is the main institutional method for organizing it.

We have proceeded as if citizens act on the basis of self-interest alone. While such an assumption is false,[16] it provides illumination into the case where motives of fairness also play a role. For even if we suspend the strong self-interest assumption, we can see that important inequities result from the fact that the cultivation of understanding is a collective good. First of all, even if citizens are willing to cooperate in supporting organizations that develop and communicate knowledge of their own interests and points of view, they still face what is called an assurance problem. They do not wish to contribute resources to an organization if not enough others contribute to such an organization. Such a contribution would be a waste of those resources. But if they cannot tell whether others will contribute to such organization, they will be wiser to allocate their resources in other things. Thus I may be willing to do what I think is my fair share in supporting some cause that I think is important, but if I do not think enough others will do the same, then I will prefer to invest my efforts and resources elsewhere.

This poses a special problem for most people in the society. Since they do not know what organizations will receive sufficient support from others, they cannot tell whether the organizations they favor will receive such support. In short, they experience a massive coordination problem. Coordination problems themselves are difficult and costly to solve. Their solution requires that one become informed about what others are doing and that one informs the others of what one intends to do. Ordinary citizens may well be willing to support collective organizations as long as enough others do but they do not know what the others will support. They will reasonably tend to be cautious in their support for organization. As a consequence, even individuals who are not fully self-interested will tend to undersupport such organizations. Thus the principle of consumer sovereignty fails to operate properly for the vast number of people in society.

These obstacles will be smaller for the well-to-do. First, because of their greater wealth and the diminishing marginal value of each extra bit of wealth, they will be more willing to contribute resources to organizations; they will be a bit less cautious. Second, given their better education and the much greater amount of political information they receive as a by-product of their occupations, they will have more knowledge about the interests they share with others and its relation with politics. Third, some of these will be associated with firms and corporations which receive highly concentrated benefits from the government. These firms have clear cut incentives to cultivate knowledge and understanding of political matters. They will also have greater incentives to subsidize the information that the rest of society receives and in some cases to enlist other parts of the society in tasks which advance primarily their interests and points of view.

Indeed, often the coordination problems that the rest of society must attempt to solve is in part resolved by those who are well-to-do and who have special interests in doing so. We see many examples in modern American politics. When a large firm desires some change in government policy, it lays out enormous funds to find all other people in the society who might also think they can benefit from this change in policy. Then it pays for the organization of those people in the forms of letter writing campaigns, telephone banks, and campaigns for raising money for the cause. It is the large firm that is willing and able to support the costs of coordination and it is its interests and points of view that primarily are expressed. For example, the auto industry managed to defeat provisions of a clean air bill in 1990 by hiring a lobbying firm which "scoured six states for potential grassroots voices, coaching them on the 'facts' of the issue, paying for the phone calls and plane fares to Washington and hiring the hall for a joint press conference." This firm "has a 'boiler room' with three hundred phone lines and a sophisticated computer system, resembling the phone banks employed in election campaigns. Articulate young people sit in the little booths every day, dialing around America on a variety of public issues, searching for 'white hat' citizens who can be persuaded to endorse the political objectives of Mobil Oil, Dow Chemical, Citicorp, Ohio Bell, Miller Brewing, U.S. Tobacco, the Chemical Manufacturers Association, the Pharmaceutical Manufacturers Association, and dozens of other clients."[17] Thus much of the organization that ordinary well-meaning citizens are involved in will be coordinated by and for the interests of large private economic interests.

Therefore, in a society where the institutions of deliberation are structured by a marketplace of ideas, we will see that the wealthy and powerful private economic institutions will dominate the process of discussion which will reflect their interests and points of view primarily.[18] Such a society simply cannot live up to the egalitarian ideals of democracy. It undermines the diversity of voices necessary for a fully informed process of discussion and it undermines equality of citizenship in the process. Ironically, the very ideals embodied in the metaphorical marketplace of ideas are betrayed in its actuality. In what follows, we will review a modified conception of such a marketplace of ideas which attempts to generate its positive results while removing the egalitarian and epistemic objections.

Public Support for Political Parties and Secondary Institutions

The above considerations suggest that some public support is necessary to promote the epistemic aims of rational social deliberation in a democracy as well as the demand for equality in the process. This social support could be in the form of support for political parties and secondary associations which represent broad sectors of the society. Two considerations support this special public support for political parties and interest groups.

First, the public support can guarantee that a number of different voices from different parts of the society have the opportunity to develop and articulate their points of view and interests as well as the ability to communicate them to other parts of the society. It does this by supporting efforts at organization of groups that might not otherwise be able to organize. It can help solve the problems of resource inequality as well as coordination. Thus each group may make a contribution to the epistemic aims of social discussion. Second, public support can guarantee greater equality in the process of deliberation and discussion by supporting and giving public recognition to the diversity of interests and points of view in the society in such a way as to encourage members to make a contribution to the process of social deliberation. It does this by means of redressing the resource inequality in society and by underwriting the cost of coordination among ordinary citizens.[19]

There are different ways in which public support can be provided and we shall consider two: a publicly sponsored voucher system for paying for the costs of secondary associations and a direct subsidy for secondary associations decided upon by the democratic legislature. The first attempts to preserve the idea of the marketplace of ideas while the second uses a collective decision procedure to make this choice.

An Egalitarian Marketplace of Ideas?

Some have argued recently that the state ought to distribute vouchers to all citizens which may be used only for the purpose of supporting secondary associations. Citizens would then distribute their vouchers to the associations of their choice, which would in turn cash them in for resources with which to develop the association.[20] Citizens would receive many vouchers, so they would be able to allocate them in a nuanced way to associations of their choice, giving more to those they see as more important and less to others.

The voucher scheme partially solves the problem of resource asymmetry by giving equal resources to all citizens with which to support organizations. This would enable to flourish such organizations that are concerned with articulating the interests and points of view of the less well-to-do. Thus it would increase the presence of many different voices and interests in the process of discussion and contribute to equality of citizenship as well as the clash of ideas so important to the democratic process. It would mitigate the problem of collective action by discouraging the use of these resources for purposes other than political organization. Citizens would have the choice of either throwing away the vouchers or using them to support the associations they prefer. Presumably they would generally choose to use the vouchers. Therefore, some of the inequalities that arise as a result of the problem of collective action would be lessened. The problem of coordination remains to some extent, since vouchers spent on organizations which receive too little support from others would be wasted, but it is mitigated by the fact that there is no opportunity cost to the political use of the voucher. Since citizens would have nothing to lose in trying to support organizations of their choice, they would not exhibit the same kind of caution as they would with their own money. At the same time, the virtues of the marketplace remain. The support each organization receives would be nuanced in the sense that it would reflect the importance citizens associate with the interests and points of view advanced by the organization. It would also reflect citizens' judgments as to the distinctness of the different organizations. And citizens would not support organizations that they do not regard as credible. This system has some of the virtues of the marketplace but has less of its vices.

Nevertheless, there is a general problem of coordination here. The marginal return from a citizen's expenditure of his or her voucher would depend on what all other citizens are doing as well. If many citizens contribute to a certain group, the marginal return from my extra contribution would be very small while if just enough other citizens contribute to a certain group, the marginal return from my expenditure would be greater and if very few other citizens contribute to the organization, my expenditure may have no marginal return at all if it is not enough to sustain the organization. There is no real price mechanism here since I would not get some definite commodity in return for a definite expenditure. As a consequence, there is at least some incentive to manipulate the system by first determining how many others are going to support an organization and whether it is worth my while to lend my support. Even if an organization is the first on my list for support, I may have reason not to contribute anything as long as enough others do so. I would then throw my support to other groups. Hence the principle of consumer sovereignty would not be fully satisfied.

Second, the distribution of vouchers does not eliminate inequality by any means. The use of private funds to support organization would still be available to citizens and these would be subject to the same logic as in the unmodified marketplace of ideas. This alternative source of funding would bring about inequalities on its own but it would also skew the distribution of vouchers. This is because organizations would have to campaign for the receipt of vouchers from citizens. And this campaigning would inevitably be dominated to a great extent by those with greater funds. Thus those with large private funds as well as those with funds from previous distributions of vouchers would be favored over the less well to do and those who have not entered into the system.

In order to rectify this problem, the process of campaigning itself would have to be publicly funded and private funds would have to be excluded both from the campaigns as well as from the funding of the organizations. But in order to ensure that this was done in an egalitarian way, some non-market process would be necessary in order to decide on the allocation of resources for the campaigns for raising money. Thus it appears that the voucher scheme must fall short of the ideal of equality it attempts to achieve or it must rely on a prior non-market method of ensuring equality in the process of social discussion.

Third, there is another problem with the marketplace of ideas that affects this scheme which I have not yet discussed. If we suppose that individuals would not strategically place their vouchers for organizations so that they always allocate more resources to those organizations that think are the most important, then the system of associations would satisfy the principle of numerical equality appropriate for voting systems and systems for distributing the means for exerting pressure on collective decision making, but it would not satisfy the principle of qualitative equality which is appropriate for institutions of deliberation. The voucher system would ensure that those interests and points of view favored by a larger group of people receive more resources with which to cultivate and develop the understanding of those interests. Thus the interests and points of view of certain citizens would receive more attention than those of others merely on the grounds that more people have those interests and points of view. But this means that some people's interests would be treated more than equally by such a system. It violates qualitative equality and only this kind of equality can ensure that everyone's interests are treated equally.

A Democratic Solution

Recall that the kinds of disagreements about the credibility, importance, and distinctness of interests and points of view are similar to the very problems which led us to accept a principle of democratic equality in the first place. Democratic equality embodies equal consideration of interests when there are severe and inevitable epistemic limitations on our abilities to assess and compare the interests individuals have in collective properties of the society and when we require a coordinated method for deciding on these properties. Now we find that the equality in the process of discovery is itself problematic because it is so difficult to publicly ensure that plural qualitative equality is satisfied due to disagreements about how to compare interests. Furthermore, the marketplace of ideas is unable to provide a coordinated method for establishing equality in the process of social discussion. Thus to establish an egalitarian deliberative agenda seems to require a coordinated and egalitarian collective decision-making process.

The natural solution to this problem is that the ultimate decisions over how to structure the deliberative agenda should be made democratically. The democratically elected legislature would decide by majority rule on the proper distribution of resources to the various secondary associations. They would decide to fund organizations on the basis of a principle of plural qualitative equality taking into account differences in importance, credibility, and qualitative distinctness as well as an assessment of which interests and points of view are merely latent in the society. Furthermore, their decisions could have a remedial function in that they would merely have to subsidize those groups that needed help. Private funding would not have to be excluded, but would merely be supplemented. Thus the problems of inequality and coordination could be solved by this method. As Joshua Cohen and Joel Rogers claim, "Groups so authorized inherit the legitimacy of the authorization."[21] Indeed, this might be a solution to the question of how the system of secondary associations might be thought to be egalitarian.

The Problem of Circularity

This solution, however, suggests that the particular system of secondary associations is both a condition of genuine equality in democratic decision making and the outcome of democratic decision making in a democratic society. This seems to imply a rather serious practical and theoretical problem.

The idea that an egalitarian system of secondary associations is a condition of democratic equality is fairly clear by now. Only if citizens have the wherewithal to develop their understanding of their interests and their points of view on the society, can they genuinely be thought to have some ability to have some say in the direction of their society. Only if citizens have organizations in which they can learn about, and deliberate with, each other, can they be said to have a say in their society. Furthermore, only if citizens' interests and points of view are somehow equally explored in organizations can they be said to have an equal say in their society.

This raises the problem of circularity. The system of secondary associations is thought to have a significant impact on democratic decision making. That is why it is thought that it ought to be subject to some kinds of egalitarian restrictions. In particular, it would seem that in the long run, the system of secondary associations will have a significant impact on the composition of the legislature. A society with very strong business associations and weak associations from other parts of the society will have a legislature dominated mostly by business interests.[22] Such a legislature has a strong bias for retaining the current system of associations. This may be true even in the event that the system of associations straightforwardly overrepresents certain interests and points of view. Inasmuch as the individual legislators owe their positions to the persuasive powers of the associations in place they may be inclined to maintain the arrangement and the democratic solution gives them some ability to do this. If the system of secondary associations is under democratic control, then it will in part determine the composition of the legislature while the legislature determines the system of associations. Such a system of associations could well get "locked in" or become "sclerotic" thus undermining the democratic aspirations of the society. This is not an unusual problem in political societies which give substantial support to secondary associations.[23] It is a serious practical problem for the ideal of democratic equality. It suggests a permanent tendency away from democratic equality inherent in the very institutions of democracy.

In addition to this problem, a democratic legislature will have a difficult time in making the very complex decisions that are necessary to set up or reasonably alter a system of associations satisfying the principle of qualitative equality. The number of such associations seems to be unlimited and the nuances between them are very fine. Perhaps we ask too much of such a system if we ask it to make such fine-grained decisions.

There is a serious theoretical problem here as well. It is hard to see how the system of associations can acquire its legitimacy from being chosen by a majority in the democratic legislature at the same time as being the very condition under which the democratic legislature is legitimized. The very disagreement about the deliberative agenda will imply disagreements about whether the society is fully democratic or not. Those who do not think that the system of associations is egalitarian, and that the deliberative agenda it supports is democratic, will regard the legislature that is elected, partly as a function of such a system, as non-democratic at least to some extent. They will argue that the legislature was elected under circumstances where not everyone has had the chance to become informed.

They will conclude that the interests of everyone are not given equal weight. This suggests that in a democratic society where everyone agrees on the basic principles, there will inevitably be disagreement about whether that society is genuinely democratic. There will be permanent ambiguity and uncertainty about whether the society is fully treating the interest of all of its citizens with equal consideration.

It should not be thought that a unanimity rule would improve this situation. First, a unanimity rule would work against groups of increasing prominence that do not yet have representation in the legislature. This is a problem such a rule would share with majority rule. Second, unanimity rule invariably works to the benefit of certain groups. The rule seems to be inconsistent with equality. A unanimity rule requires that there be a default rule for those occasions when consensus cannot be reached. One default rule might be that the system will remain the same unless there is consensus on change. With this default rule a single party or a small group of parties could hold the system hostage if they wished to retain the status quo. Such a rule gives disproportionate power to those who prefer the status quo. Another possible default rule might be that support for the system of associations will simply end if no agreement can be reached. But such a rule would favor those who could easily do without the public support for the system of associations: those wealthy groups who would tend to do better under the unmodified marketplace of ideas. They might be able to hold the system hostage so as to receive greater allocations of resources from the state. These problems are the familiar difficulties of unanimity rule: it is inegalitarian when some specially benefit from the status quo.

It appears, then, that our search for solutions has not yielded much relief from the problem of how to set up an egalitarian deliberative agenda.[24] The various market mechanisms, modified and unmodified, fail to deliver the qualitative equality necessary for fully democratic discussion. The various collective decision making methods fail to resolve the problem of inevitable disagreement and the consequent sense of illegitimacy that many citizens are likely to have. Let us explore the implications of this conclusion.

We know that in a democracy, citizens are likely never to agree on whether one of the essential elements of equality is satisfied. They cannot reach consensus on whether the deliberative agenda is egalitarian. Since equality in the deliberative agenda is a necessary component of political equality, citizens will disagree on whether the society is fully democratic. And since democratic equality is the embodiment of equal consideration of interests, it is likely that many citizens will have reason to think that their interests are not being taken equally into account. There is a threat that some citizens will think that they are being treated as inferiors. This can lead to instability in the society if everyone is committed to democracy since some will reasonably believe that the society does not fulfill this commitment with regard to their interests. The equal public status of citizens will always be obscured to some degree.

Concluding Remarks

Let us conclude with some remarks that moderate the significance of this problem. First, as long as the electoral and legislative systems are set up along egalitarian lines and individuals are confident that their fellow citizens are doing their best in trying to accommodate the interests of all in the deliberative agenda, then even those who believe their interests are not being given equal attention must acknowledge that it will be hard to do better in terms of equality without making others even worse off. This problem is one that lies at the heart of democratic equality and thus it can be eliminated only by doing away with some or all of the institutions of democracy. Those who contemplate such actions cannot often have the realization of equality as their aim. They would only be sacrificing the interests of others so as to achieve a lesser gain for themselves. Second, those who do not think that their interests are being given equal consideration in the process of social discussion can most likely be assured that their situation is not permanent. Given the shifting distribution of opinions in the society, the chances are that in the future they will either find themselves in a more powerful position to affect the agenda or that more citizens in the society will see that their views are legitimate and important (if their own views do not undergo change). Thus, over time the significance of these inequalities will be mitigated for many groups.

These remarks notwithstanding, there is an essential ambiguity at the heart of democracy which poses a threat to its viability even under ideal circumstances. Citizens can reasonably disagree about whether they are being treated as equals and some can reasonably protest that they are being treated as inferiors. This would be despite general agreement on the principles of democratic equality itself. Any democratic theory which takes deliberation among equals seriously must address this problem.[25]

NOTES

1. See Jürgen Habermas, *Legitimation Crisis,* trans. Thomas McCarthy (Boston: Beacon Press, 1973), part III, and John Rawls, *Political Liberalism* (New York: Columbia University Press, 1993). For recent views, see Joshua Cohen, "Deliberation and Democratic Legitimacy," in *The Good Society: Normative Analysis of the State,* ed. Alan Hamlin and Philip Pettit (Cambridge: Basil Blackwell, 1990), 17–34, as well as Cass Sunstein, "Democracy and Shifting Preferences," in *The Idea of Democracy,* ed. David Copp, Jean Hampton, and John Roemer (Cambridge: Cambridge University Press, 1993), 196–230.

2. This argument is developed in greater detail in my "Social Choice and Democracy," in *The Idea of Democracy.*

3. These arguments for resourcism are developed in greater detail in my "Democratic Equality and the Problem of Persistent Minorities," *Philosophical Papers* 23 (1994): 169–90. There I argue for a moderate resourcism which does not require equality of resources in all distributive contexts but only in those where the epistemic problem above is acute.

4. Plato, *Meno,* in *Five Dialogues,* trans. G. M. A. Grube (Indianapolis, Ind.: Hackett Publishing, 1981), 86.

5. Charles Beitz makes this charge against egalitarian views in his *Political Equality: An Essay on Democratic Theory* (Princeton: Princeton University Press, 1989), 12, and James Fishkin writes as if the aspects of deliberation and political equality should be separated in his *Democracy and Deliberation* (New Haven: Yale University Press, 1991).

6. See Paul Samuelson, "The Pure Theory of Public Expenditure," in *Rational Man in Irrational Society?* ed. Brian Barry and Russell Hardin (Beverly Hills, Calif.: Sage Publications, 1982), for the original characterization of this notion.

7. See David Greenstone, *Labor in American Politics* (New York: Vintage, 1970) for an account of the comprehensive nature of union participation in politics in the United States after World War II.

8. See Mancur Olson, *The Logic of Collective Action* (Cambridge, Mass.: Harvard University Press, 1960) for the seminal discussion of the extensive implications of these difficulties.

9. The fact that it is reasonable to permit tyrannical groups to say what they think but not to have a share in the resources which are devoted to the promotion of democratic discussion seems to me to undermine those who argue that principles of free speech are defensible on grounds of promoting democratic deliberation alone. It also seems to undermine the idea of those who think that a requirement of fair access to the means of communication is inherent in the right to free speech. The American Nazi party has a right to think and say what it believes, but it is not clear that it has a right to be provided with a share of resources that give it access to social discussion. For examples of the democratic discussion argument for free speech see Alexander Meiklejohn, *Political Freedom* (New York: Oxford University Press, 1965), part I, and Cass Sunstein, *Democracy and the Problem of Free Speech* (New York: Basic Books, 1993). These theorists generally defend a fair access provision as part of free speech. For a non-democracy-based argument that includes the fair access condition in the ideal of freedom of expression, see Joshua Cohen, "Freedom of Expression," *Philosophy and Public Affairs* (Summer 1993): 216.

10. See David Kelley and Roger Donway, "Liberalism and Free Speech," in *Democracy and the Mass Media,* ed. Judith Lichtenberg (New York: Cambridge University Press, 1991) for a defense of the literal marketplace of ideas.

11. See Sunstein, *Democracy and the Problem of Free Speech* for an elaboration of this kind of argument.

12. See Anthony Downs, *An Economic Theory of Democracy* (New York: Harper and Row, 1957), 246.

13. See Downs, 221, as well as Samuel Popkin, *The Reasoning Voter: Communication and Persuasion in Presidential Campaigns* (Chicago: University of Chicago, 1991), 22–28.

14. See H. Russell Neuman, *The Paradox of Mass Democracy* (Cambridge, Mass.: MIT Press, 1990) for evidence that these are the most important factors behind political sophistication.

15. See Downs, 235, and Charles Lindblom, *Politics and Markets* (New York: Basic Books, 1977). See Robert Entman, *Democracy without Citizens* (New York: Oxford University Press, 1990) for a very good critique of the marketplace of ideas metaphor along these lines as it applies to discussions of the mass media.

16. See the essays in *Beyond Self-Interest,* ed. Jane Mansbridge (Chicago: University of Chicago Press, 1989) for an elaboration of arguments against the self-interest view.

17. See William Greider, *Who Will Tell the People? The Betrayal of American Democracy* (New York: Simon and Schuster, 1992), 39–40, for this and many other examples of this kind of corporate-led coordination.

18. See Charles Lindblom, *Politics and Markets* (New York: Basic Books, 1977) for arguments to the same conclusion.

19. See Danilo Zolo, *Democracy and Complexity: A Realist Approach* (State College: Pennsylvania State University Press, 1992) for skepticism about public support for parties and secondary associations.

20. See Phillipe S. Schmitter, "The Irony of Modern Democracy," *Politics and Society* (December 1992): 511–12. See also James Fishkin, *Democracy and Deliberation* (New Haven: Yale University Press, 1991) and *The Dialogue of Justice* (New Haven: Yale University Press, 1992) for a tentative endorsement of this kind of institutional arrangement.

21. Joshua Cohen and Joel Rogers, "Secondary Associations and Democratic Governance," *Politics and Society* (December 1992): 451. Cohen and Rogers focus on the role of alternative governance. The authors defend a quasi-public status for secondary associations and argue that when they acquire such power, they ought to have equal power so that when they bargain with each other, they will conform to democratic norms.

22. See Charles Lindblom, *Politics and Markets* (New York: Basic Books, 1977) for an extensive argument to this effect in the United States. See also Thomas Ferguson and Joel Rogers, *Right Turn: The Decline of the Democrats and the Future of American Politics* (New York: Hill and Wang, 1986).

23. See Schmitter, "The Irony of Modern Democracy," 509.

24. Perhaps some combination of the institutional devices we canvassed would do the trick but if such a combination were tried, it would have to be evaluated in terms of its results and thus the disagreements that plague the collective decision solutions to the problem would also be a problem here.

25. I would like to thank Helen Ingram, Deborah Mathieu, John Schwartz, David Snow and Bob Varaty as well as Russell Hardin and Ian Shapiro for their helpful comments on this paper. It was written with the support of a fellowship from the Udall Center for Public Policy Studies at the University of Arizona.

11

FIVE THESES ON NATIONALISM

ELIZABETH KISS

Introduction: Ethnic Nationalism and Political Order

> It is a waste of breath to press the claims of common human identity on men and women prepared to die in defence of their claims of difference. There will be no end to the dying, and no time for the claim of our common species being, until each people is safe within its borders, with a sovereignty which makes them master of their needs. Only when difference has its home, when the need for belonging in all its murderous intensity has been assuaged, can our common identity begin to find its voice.
>
> —Michael Ignatieff, *The Needs of Strangers*

Around the world, appeals to ethnic difference are drowning out claims of common human identity and destabilizing political institutions and borders. Some of the conflicts are new, others just newly visible: but all of them have left scholars, policy-makers and concerned citizens scrambling to understand and respond.[1] This chapter considers the following question: what attitude should we take to nationalism if we aspire to create conditions in which the claims of common human identity have an effective voice? In particular, what role (if any) could nationalism play in the construction of a more humane global political order?

My question is complex, even inelegant. It straddles description and prescription, trying to strike a balance between political analysis and ideal theory. My aim is neither to sketch an ideally just political order nor to assess actual prospects for ethnic toleration. Both of these are valuable enterprises in themselves. But I hope in this essay to offer something rather more foolhardy: to consider what we should do given the current state of the world and the role of ethnic and national identity within it. This approach requires tempering ideals with a sense of what's possible, while remaining committed to devising solutions—combining, as Gramsci put it, pessimism of intellect with optimism of will. Even at its best—which is to say, much better than I can do here—such an approach would probably leave idealists and realists equally dissatisfied. Nevertheless, such hybrid approaches are necessary if we want to bring the insights of normative political theory to bear on the dilemmas of political practice.

I began with Ignatieff's words because he was unusually prescient when he stressed, in 1984, the continuing salience of peoples' claims of difference.[2] The global triumph of a liberal democratic political order which many proclaimed in the closing days of the cold war[3] has now yielded to a picture considerably more complex, ambiguous, and uncertain in its prospects. One of the chief factors complicating the picture is nationalism, particularly what I shall call *ethnic* nationalism. The cruelty, corruption, and inefficiency of Soviet communism has destroyed, at least for the time being, socialism's appeal as an ideal for transforming political order. But another array of ideals has become more powerful in the wake of the Soviet empire's demise. These ideals, which center around ethnicity, religion, and culture, have become the focus of struggles—such as those over borders, the criteria for citizenship, the nature and limits of legal jurisdiction, and the relationship between church and state—which will fundamentally shape the future of our global political order.[4] The most common form of this politics of identity is ethnic nationalism,[5] which has emerged as the pre-eminent politics of difference in the world today, demonstrating that repeated predictions of nationalism's imminent demise under the onslaught of modernization, the homogenizing force of the world market, and the rise of liberal individualism[6] were wrong or, at the very least, dramatically premature. For instance, ethnic nationalism played a significant role in the collapse of the Soviet empire; it was often impossible to disentangle democratic and nationalist aspirations when Lithuanians, Ukrainians, or Poles demanded the right to "govern themselves." More generally, ethnic nationalist conflicts are destabilizing and reconstructing political order throughout what has aptly been termed "the new world (dis)order,"[7] not only in Central and Eastern Europe (the region which forms this essay's primary point of reference), but also in the successor states to the colonial empires of Africa and Asia and in the Western liberal democracies themselves.

By *ethnic nationalism* I mean a politics of identification with and allegiance to a nation, a collectivity defined by what its members regard as a shared descent, history, and culture. I stress the subjective character of this shared identity—it is there because people regard it as being there—since, as scholars of nationalism have long stressed, there are no empirical or objective criteria for defining nations.[8] Nations and ethnic groups typically do possess some shared empirical features such as language, religion, political history, or geographical or racial origin, but none of these, nor any combination of them, constitutes a sufficient condition for a nation. Ethnic nationalists pursue a politics aimed at protecting, preserving, and empowering their nation and its members. I use the term *ethnic* nationalism to highlight the focus on shared identity, culture, and origins and to distinguish the political phenomenon I am investigating here from allegiance to a *state*. While allegiances to a nation and to a state can obviously overlap, they are separable in theory and practice. One can have strong allegiance to a state without identifying with a nation that has a shared culture and history. And one can be an ethnic nationalist while at the same time being the loyal citizen of a multi-ethnic state (indeed, one might base one's loyalty to a multi-ethnic state precisely on its ability to protect, preserve, and empower one's nation). As this last example indicates, I think the specific political aims of ethnic nationalisms can vary. Ethnic nationalists seek resources, power, and respect for their nation, but different ethnic nationalist movements focus on different political means to attaining these goods. For instance, some may stress territorial demands; others, legal jurisdiction over the nation's members; still others, control over cultural, educational, and religious institutions. Ethnic nationalist movements can also have different political ends: some seek to acquire political representation within a larger polity, some try to attain formal territorial or legal autonomy within a polity, some struggle to acquire their own independent state, and others strive to conquer their neighbors and form an empire. Ethnic nationalism, on my view, does not have to take the form of a demand for a nation-state, although this demand is obviously a classic instance of nationalism.

To be sure, ethnic nationalism is a *political* phenomenon, not simply a matter of experiencing oneself as, say, Hungarian or Polish. In practice, however, the lower threshold separating non-political expressions of cultural identity from political expressions of ethnic nationalism can be difficult to specify. Consider an example drawn from ethnic immigrant life in the United States. There is a large community of Armenian Americans in and around Watertown, Massachusetts. They have churches and language schools, publish Armenian newspapers, and hold religious and cultural festivals. They organize demonstrations to commemorate the Armenian genocide by Turks in 1915–17. Armenian businesses help one another, and both Armenian and non-Armenian city and state politicians make a point of demonstrating their support for the Armenian community. Community leaders have lobbied the U.S. government and such international organizations as the United Nations and the Conference on Security and Cooperation in Europe to condemn Turkey for its unwillingness to take responsibility for the Armenian massacres and to deny the Turkish application for entrance into the European Union. More recently, community leaders have organized the collection of money and supplies to support the Armenian effort to gain control of the Armenian enclave in Azerbaijan, Nagorno-Karabakh, and lobbied Congress to support Armenia. Some young people from the community may even have gone to Armenia to fight or in other ways to directly support the war effort. At what point do these activities become examples of ethnic nationalist politics? The line between organized ethnic life within civil society and ethnic nationalist politics is difficult to draw. Most of the activities I listed clearly fit within organized cultural life. But some do aim to have a significant impact on local, national, or even international political order and are best understood as instances of ethnic nationalist politics.

There are also considerable differences among ethnic nationalist self-definitions, and these differences have important moral and political implications. For instance, ethnic nationalist movements characterized by a *cultural* or *linguistic* self-definition tend to be less exclusionary and more tolerant than those which define themselves in terms of *biological* descent, since people can acquire a culture or language but cannot change their biological origins. But these are no more than rough generalizations, since there are historical examples of exclusionary (or coercively assimilationist) cultural nationalisms[9] as well as of more inclusive or tolerant movements based on shared descent.[10]

While the political importance of ethnic nationalism has been recognized for some time by political scientists studying developing countries,[11] it was generally ignored by the mainstream of contemporary Anglo-American political theory until quite recently.[12] Contemporary liberalism offers detailed prescriptions for the domestic legal and institutional frameworks of political order, but it has generally been silent on a number of other issues of political order that are especially germane to ethnic nationalism.[13] So, for instance, in the flowering of liberal theory inspired by John Rawls's *A Theory of Justice,* most theorists took for granted a polity's membership and territorial boundaries and paid little or no attention to cultural influences on political order.[14] Even communitarian critics of liberalism who explicitly stressed the cultural context of political life tended not to interrogate how communal identities arise and take on political significance, and treated cultural communities as homogeneous entities rather than as sites of both internal and external struggle.[15] Only more recently have the challenges posed by cultural difference to political order received sustained attention,[16] as an increasing number of political and legal scholars have noted that ethnic nationalist issues abound in our own backyard.[17]

In the last few years, ethnic nationalist politics has vividly demonstrated not only its capacity to disrupt and remake political order, but also the great moral dangers it can pose. The greatest of these is correctly identified by Ignatieff in the passage I cited at the outset: ethnic nationalism can construct a moral framework which excludes "the claims of common human identity." It can make men and women regard human beings outside of their group as outside the moral community. We are daily reminded of how "the claims of common human identity" have lost all power to constrain the forceful and murderous "claims of difference" being played out on the streets of Sarajevo. People's behavior in ethnic nationalist wars in former Yugoslavia, Azerbaijan, Georgia, Ossetia, in riots by Hindu nationalists in India, and in thousands of individual incidents of violence directed against immigrants in Western Europe—to cite only a few examples—demonstrate how those motivated by ethnic nationalism can come to believe that only members of their own group should have any moral claim, or be entitled to a political voice.

To be sure, our species has always been inventive in formulating reasons why some of its members can and should be ignored, exploited, tormented, expelled, or killed. Hierarchies of gender, class, and caste, and distinctions between religious or ideological believers and heretics or infidels, or between "normal" citizens and "subversives," have served and continue to serve to categorize some as sub-human and to legitimate their abuse. In *laissez-faire* economies unregulated greed leads to brutally exploitative practices which cost vulnerable people their well-being and even their lives. Many of this century's most murderous excesses were not motivated by nationalism, as the records of Stalin, Mao, and Pol Pot show. Thus, while ethnic nationalist politics can be dangerous to the claims of common humanity, it is important to recognize that it is far from unique in this respect. Moreover, in actual political situations one basis for exclusion or resentment frequently maps onto another. So, for instance, ethnic hatreds are sometimes simultaneously class hatreds. An ethnic group may be resented for being, or being perceived as, an elite, as in the hatred directed against Russian administrators and professionals in some of the former Soviet

Republics or against Jews in a number of East-Central European countries. Or an ethnic group may be despised because its members are or are perceived to be lower class, which is no doubt a factor in hatred toward immigrants and guest workers such as Mexicans in the United States, Turks in Germany, and North Africans in France.[18] The mass rapes in Bosnia demonstrate the central role which an oppressive gender politics focussed on women's bodies as objects of protection and violation can occupy within ethnic nationalism's psychological economy of power and self-esteem. Commentators on the Balkan war have also stressed that one rationale for the violence is not so much ethnicity or religion but rather hatred of the city, which helps to explain the relentless destructive force directed against Vukovar, Dubrovnik, and Sarajevo by soldiers drawn overwhelmingly from the countryside.[19] This rural-urban split can also be observed elsewhere, in less murderous forms, in Eastern Europe, such as in the "anti-cosmopolitan" rhetoric of some Hungarian, Polish, and Slovakian nationalist politicians.[20]

What sets nationalism apart to some extent from other rationales of exclusion is precisely its close historical links with democracy. For while all rationales of exclusion serve to unify the "us" that is contrasted with "them," nationalism's inclusiveness tends to invoke democratic ideals both in principle (the nation is vertically integrated, with membership equally shared)[21] and in practice (historically, nationalist struggles have often been democratic struggles against autocratic regimes or multinational empires).[22] It is these strong but ambiguous links with democracy which make nationalism a quintessentially modern political phenomenon and render the task of evaluating it from the perspective of humanity's claims more complex.

As Ignatieff suggests, then, the moral challenge posed by a world of politicized ethnic and national differences is to find powerful ways to voice the claims of humanity, and effective political means to protect these claims. He was also correct in his contention (suggested by the cited passage, and stated more explicitly elsewhere in his book) that the claims of humanity had to be vindicated—or, to use a lawyer's term, "operationalized"—in the political arrangements, institutions, and practices that govern people's daily lives. That is, Ignatieff conceived the task of reconciling commonality and difference as primarily one of domestic political order, of creating workable institutional practices through which people could effectively protect themselves and other members of their group. While he applauded the work of the global human rights movement, for instance, Ignatieff suggested that despite the good intentions and admirable successes of human rights and humanitarian organizations, people whose domestic political arrangements had abandoned them were in most cases subject, like Shakespeare's Lear, to the merciless imperatives of the heath,[23] and the plight of Bosnian victims of "ethnic cleansing" in the face of Western indecision and indifference, or indeed of millions of the world's refugees, bears out his skepticism.[24] Finally, Ignatieff was also right to conceive the task we face as involving, as he put it, finding "a home" for difference, a task which I will describe as requiring the creation of institutional strategies of accommodation as well as cultural strategies of inclusion.

On the other hand, Ignatieff's sketch of a political order which could accomodate both the claims of difference and the claims of humanity was naïve and unhelpful. And his rhetoric suggests that he misconstrued the nature and origins of our differences. I shall argue that "difference"—in this case ethnic nationalist difference—should not serve as a general organizing principle of political order, and that Ignatieff's vision of a world in which "each people is safe within its borders," where each is the sovereign "master" of its needs, is a chimera. This vision ignores the dispersed and mottled nature of ethnic populations, the overlapping territorial claims they make, the population movements that inevitably accompany a globalized economy, and the practical problems these demographic, cultural, and social realities create for the project of constructing a world of homogeneous nation-states. More deeply, it misconstrues the nature of national differences themselves by treating them as a pre-political given. What differences there are, and what they mean morally and politically in people's lives, depends on human action and invention. Ethnic or national differences cannot be explained by appealing to an essential human need for belonging (or a hatred of the "other") which must be assuaged, for the nature, object, and intensity of such needs and their mode of political expression varies with circumstances. While human beings may always identify with particular groups, the rise and politicization of particular ethnic or national allegiances is a much more complex matter than a direct response to a basic human need. Finally, Ignatieff also overestimates the extent to which sovereignty as it is traditionally construed is a viable or even a desirable aspiration for many ethnic national groups.

I will develop my arguments about the relationship between ethnic nationalism and political order in the form of five theses. *First,* we should conceive nationalism as a lasting feature of our world but not a fixed or primordial one. It can and no doubt will continue to serve as a source of solidarity and conflict. But both the strength and the moral and political characteristics of nationalism are dynamic and alterable. *Second,* we should acknowledge that nationalism does not offer a viable principle of political order. *Third,* efforts to elevate nationalism to a principle of political order are morally dangerous, while efforts to denationalize politics are at least morally suspect. *Fourth,* the best approach we can take to nationalism will involve the creation of institutional strategies of ethnic accommodation. *Fifth,* these institutional strategies would be inadequate in and of themselves and must be paired with cultural strategies of inclusion.

Before elaborating these theses, however, I need to explain what I mean by the moral claims of humanity.

Humanity's Claims

My inquiry in this essay is guided by a moral aspiration to foster political and cultural conditions in which the claims of our common humanity have power and meaning, in which humanity is conceived to some significant degree as a single moral community. The core of the ideal I have in mind is the conviction that all human beings have the same basic moral status and should be treated accordingly. This conviction cannot be deduced from the biological fact that we are members of the same species nor logically derived from other facts about human nature. It is an "imagined"[25] or constructed moral community, rather than something ordained by nature, although an appeal to nature (the natural characteristics and fate all human beings share) does play an important role in the process of its construction. Of course, people may commit themselves to humanity as a moral community for many reasons, including comprehensive political or religious ideals. But at a basic level I conceive a commitment to humanity's claims as being rooted in empathetic solidarity arising from a recognition of the aspirations, vulnerabilities, and potentialities we all have in common as individual human beings. However, while denial of our human commonalities is irrational—while it is irrational for someone to believe, for instance, that Jews, blacks, indigenous peoples, or "subversives" are fundamentally different from and inferior to themselves—reason does not dictate that we ascribe value to our commonalities and thereby to every individual's life and well-being. Doing so ultimately involves an act of commitment, a leap of faith.[26]

The most powerful, precise, and widely understood language we have available today for articulating the claims of common humanity is the language of human rights. Starting from background beliefs about the forces and practices which most acutely threaten people's dignity and well-being, the language of human rights elaborates a series of normative relations—permissions as well as constraints—that need to be maintained in order to protect people's status as members of a human moral community. In discussing humanity's claims I shall employ the language of human rights as well as the helpful analysis of rights as networks of liberties, claims, immunities, and powers first developed by Wesley Hohfeld.[27] Promoting the power of humanity's claims, then, may be redescribed, in our day, as striving to create a political order in which the liberties, immunities, claims, and powers central to the human rights ideal are institutionalized and protected, and in which people can appeal to the moral vision of a human community in shaping and challenging the institutions and practices of their society.[28]

But what are these liberties, immunities, claims, and powers? The *content* of human rights can be construed in more minimal as well as more maximal ways. Human rights can be understood minimally as a set of injunctions not to deprive human beings of the possibility of having a basic quality of life. These would include immunities from torture, arbitrary arrest, imprisonment, and killing; they would also include claims not to be deprived of or left without the basic material means of life. Somewhat more robust but still minimal would be the notion of rights to equal protection of the law[29] and equal citizenship, rights designed to protect people from victimization and to provide them with standardized means to seek redress and to publicly voice their demands. Much more robust would be a conception of humanity's claims as encompassing entitlements to the resources and opportunities necessary to flourish or to develop one's capacities more fully.

But who is responsible for respecting and enforcing these rights? Both the addressees of human rights and the scope of their obligations may once again be conceived in more or less robust ways. Construed maximally, respect for human rights would require massive redistributions of resources across familial, communal, and political boundaries; it would make any exclusionary boundary such as any restriction on immigration morally indefensible. The enormous cross-boundary inequalities in our world are, indeed, difficult to defend. But, in line with my attempt to strike a balance between pragmatism and utopianism in this essay, I shall construe human rights more minimally and accept that some exclusion of outsiders and protection of unequal resource distributions is justifiable on the part of polities. This does not mean that I believe more maximal conceptions of human rights are invalid; the choice to adopt a relatively minimalist conception is dictated by my sense that it is more relevant to the concerns of this essay, not by a conviction that minimalist approaches are always better or more justified.

Rather than simply a fixed list of basic norms, however, I would suggest that we think of human rights as an open-ended terrain of contestation. Some norms within that terrain are fixed (like the prohibition on torture) while others (like what equal protection of the law requires) are undergoing constant debate and revision. Above all, the question of which social and legal practices will best protect and promote human rights is an open one and requires attention to particular distributions of power and particular threats to human well-being. The idea I have in mind is that of an ongoing dialogue or struggle (for the process metaphorically resembles conversation as well as war) over the practices required to create societies in which human beings enjoy an equal moral status.

For the purposes of this essay, it is more important to identify features of a political order which are likely to lead to systematic denials or violations of human rights. Clearly, any political order which legitimates torture, *de jure* or *de facto* enslavement, arbitrary imprisonment, or the creation of concentration camps, denies humanity's claims. Any political order in which some suffer starvation or destitution and do not have their basic needs met despite the availability of resources also violates basic or minimal human rights. As this last example shows, a commitment to human rights raises central structural issues about political order. Any political order which systematically excludes some within it from full legal protection, or from participation in public life—which, in other words, grants some people a permanent second class status—is likewise suspect. So, for instance, while the distinction between resident alien and citizen is defensible, so long as there are fair procedures for people to move from one status to another if they wish, two-tier systems in which it is impossible or very difficult for some people to become full citizens are not. Hence the German system (prior, at least, to its recent modification) in which permanent residents who were not ethnic Germans were guaranteed basic immunity rights but denied such rights as those of freedom of assembly, movement, association, and occupation, was deeply problematic from the perspective of humanity's claims because it legally marginalized a sector of society, denying a whole group of residents the domestic institutional means available to others to articulate their needs and demands.[30] Institutionalized patterns of exclusion and marginalization create the conditions in which human rights are likely to be violated or ignored. To be sure, such patterns of exclusion need not be legally codified: gross inequalities of power can have much the same effect even when there is formal equality of legal status.

I would suggest, then, that the obligations on governments entailed by humanity's claims should be construed as obligations to refrain from such practices as those I just listed, that is, obligations not to violate basic liberties or immunities, not to ignore or deny basic powers or claims, and not to create or tolerate institutionalized patterns of exclusion. More difficult is the question of the extent to which governments and the international community as a whole are obliged to come to the aid of human beings outside their own borders or jurisdiction whose human rights are being denied. It is hard to specify a minimum here. But a commitment to intervene to stop the most egregious violations of human rights and some form of globally coordinated refugee policy comprise a minimal conception of species obligations. At the moment, even these very minimal obligations are frequently beyond the capacities of the international community, as demonstrated by its lack of effective action in the last few decades in the face of campaigns of genocide in Kampuchea and Burundi and more recently in response to "ethnic cleansing" in Bosnia. Current efforts to tighten refugee and asylum policies in many countries, including our own, demonstrates how vulnerable such commitments are to domestic pressures. Beyond these minimal obligations there is also a moral and practical imperative, for those committed to human rights, to do what they can to support the creation of conditions in which these rights can be effectively voiced and respected.

One final point about humanity's claims: aspiring to make human rights norms effective around the world does not entail a commitment to cultural homogeneity or to a bland or biased form of universalism. One of the characteristic dangers of ethnic nationalism is that it promotes a rigid politics of difference in which only certain differences count and their meaning is coercively imposed on people. People have to support certain policies in order to be "true" Croats, Serbs, Romanians, or Hungarians; those who do not fit the rigid ethnic definitions (for instance, Jewish citizens of Serbia, Croatia, and so forth, or children of ethnically mixed marriages) are excluded regardless of their personal feelings, treated with suspicion even when they do choose one identity or another, and denied full acceptance when they try to embrace some kind of "hyphenated" identity. By promoting the power of humanity's claims we create a terrain on which new claims of difference can be made. On this terrain those who assert and seek recognition and respect for the ways in which they are different can do so by appealing to the shared human aspirations and vulnerabilities that underlie the differences. And this, in turn, encourages people divided by differences to recognize that they want many of the same things. People may still construe some of their shared aspirations as zero-sum games, and some differences may be experienced as arising from aspirations utterly alien from our own. Nevertheless, encouraging a recognition that shared aspirations underlie claims of difference is likely to make compromise and give-and-take more psychologically palatable and politically possible.

How then, can we promote the power of humanity's claims in a world of potentially exclusionary ethnic nationalist differences? I begin addressing this question by examining the nature of those differences themselves.

Thesis #1:

We should conceive nationalism as a lasting feature of our world but not as a fixed, primordial, or pre-political phenomenon. Nationalism can and no doubt will continue to serve as a source of solidarity and conflict for the foreseeable future. But both the strength and the moral and political characteristics of nationalism are dynamic and alterable.

I defined ethnic nationalism as a politics centered on allegiance to a collectivity whose members regard themselves as having a shared culture, origin, and history. But what are these collectivities, how do they come into being, and how do they become the objects of moral and political identification and allegiance? Most importantly, what forces affect the nature of that moral and political identification and allegiance—its openness and tolerance, the reasonableness of its claims? What are the implications of the answers to these questions for how we should approach the relationship between ethnic nationalism and political order?

Nations are not fixed primordial entities but dynamic historical and political constructs. That nations are social constructs does not mean they are "fake"; social constructs shape reality. Nor does an emphasis on the constructed nature of nations entail that they are easily alterable.[31] Indeed, many modern nations have ancient roots and there are important continuities between modern ethnic nationalism and premodern forms of ethnic mobilization.[32] Nationalist movements derive much of their power from their ability to translate ancient myths into a modern idiom, to graft mythic understandings of existence onto such quintessentially modern issues as employment, education, and trade. History makes a difference; a society's possibilities are constrained by the cultural heritage, the repertoire of stories and meanings, available to its members. But it is important not to exaggerate these constraints. Nationalists movements arise in particular and contingent contexts; their trajectory is not determined in the mists of time but shaped by particular conditions and decisions.[33]

Only in recent times have millions of people around the world conceived themselves as members of nations. In this respect, as scholars of nationalism have repeatedly stressed, nationalism is a modern phenomenon that is "above all not what it seems to itself."[34] Nations are "invented" or "imagined" communities which are then typically primordialized, with their history projected into the dim past. To be sure, as I've already noted, nations are not invented out of thin air; they draw on earlier historical or cultural repertoires, just as national languages are constructed out of older dialects. But neither the boundaries of nations nor the characteristics considered crucial to their identity are preordained; they are the object of intentional choices and often of controversy and change. The construction of nations involves processes not only of external differentiation but also of internal suppression or erosion of difference. Nations are created not only by distinguishing "us" from "them" but also by suppressing, eroding, or forgetting internal differences in order to construct "us."[35]

Eastern Europe provides many examples of the ironies of national construction. In some cases national construction is so recent that it can be traced to the actions of particular individuals[36] and yet the identities thus constructed have been deeply primordialized. The term "Slovene," for instance, was invented in 1809 by a philologist named Jernej Kopitar.[37] While the concepts of the Hungarian and Polish "nations" are older by several centuries, they referred, until the eighteenth century, only to members of the feudal aristocracy, whether or not they spoke a Hungarian or Polish dialect or were of Hungarian or Polish ethnic descent.[38] Serfs and peasants, who comprised the vast majority of the population in Eastern Europe, had local and religious, not national, allegiances and identities. In the Balkans, for instance, the very idea of nationality was alien to people's lived experience until the end of the eighteenth century.[39] Croatian and Serbian nationalist movements arose in the nineteenth century, but they had serious competition from movements which sought to establish a single national identity embracing Croats, Serbs, and other South Slav ethnic groups, the "Illyrian" movement of the 1830s and 1840s and "Yugoslavism" in the late nineteenth and early twentieth century. Both of these movements attracted strong, even fanatical, followers.[40] Serbs, Croats, and Bosnian Muslims are of common ethnic genealogy and their separate national identities were by no means preordained.[41] Hence the ethnic nationalist differences for which people kill and are killed in Bosnia are not primordial identities but constructs, and the political and moral meanings they have taken on in people's lives during the current conflict are relatively recent. In addition, the religious identifications which have increasingly dominated the Bosnian conflict were of little significance in most people's lives before war broke out.[42] The sense of shifting identities was vividly evoked by the personal testimony of a young woman who told a reporter "I have no Serbian identity at all. I am forced to be a Serb by events over which I have no control . . . I am a Yugoslav."[43] The high percentage of intermarriage prior to the conflict among the various ethnic and religious groups,[44] especially in the cities, demonstrates that she was not alone.

If nations are constructs, why are they constructed? An examination of the emergences and re-emergences of nationalism as a moral and political force reveals complex processes driven by many different motives. It is not, as Ignatieff implies, simply a matter of a primordial desire for belonging which wells up and is addressed by nationalism, but rather a convergence of diverse aspirations and interests. These processes no doubt *do* involve basic psychological needs, aspirations, and fears and cannot be understood apart from them—needs and aspirations, for instance, for belonging, recognition, self-respect, power or security, or fears of those different from ourselves. But there is no necessary link between these needs or fears and ethnic national identities; many kinds of groups or associations can give people a sense of belonging or, conversely, become the focus of fears of the "other."[45] Nor is there a necessary link between these needs or fears and their political salience. For instance, suspicion of those who speak a different language may perhaps be an ineradicable element of human life, but this does not explain why such suspicion sometimes comes to occupy center stage in the construction of political order and social life.

Some generalizations can, of course, be made about processes of ethnic and national construction. The first is that these processes are relational and reactive and are shaped by concrete practical exigencies.[46] By this I mean that national identities are drawn and redrawn in reaction to particular historical contexts, and their political salience is shaped by reaction to groups perceived as threats, competitors, or ideals to emulate. Such processes of reaction also played an important role in the nineteenth-century constructions of Eastern European nationalism, with, for instance, the anti-Habsburg Hungarian nationalist movement of 1848 serving as a catalyst for Romanian, Croatian, and Slovakian nationalist movements which feared Hungarian political control and sought to resist coercive Magyarization. The reactive nature of ethnic nationalism is particularly evident in the case of national identities that "nest" within each other and acquire and lose political force as circumstances change. So, for instance, Austrians have historically defined themselves variously as part of, and as distinct from, a German nation; the once powerful idea of Arab nationalism is now being overtaken by contending loyalties to different Arab states as well as by allegiances to Islam which transcend Arabism;[47] during the Tito era many Serbs and Croats conceived themselves as sharing a Yugoslav identity, with the number of Yugoslav citizens who identified themselves as of "Yugoslav" ethnicity on the census growing twenty-fold between 1961 and 1981,[48] and many immigrants from Mexico, Puerto Rico, Cuba, Panama, have united in a "Latino" identity and political movement within the United States today.[49]

A second generalization about ethnic nationalism, and another sense in which the processes of nationalist construction are reactive, is that nationalism frequently arises in opposition to imperialist or authoritarian political orders—or, more broadly, in reaction to political orders that come to be viewed as threateningly unrepresentative of the interests, or demeaning to the dignity, of a group.[50] Nineteenth-century Eastern European ethnic nationalists sought to resist Austro-Hungarian, Ottoman, or Russian imperialism, just as the current wave of nationalism is a reaction to the crumbling Soviet empire. Political mobilization around the nation is thus prompted by frustration over blocked mobility, lack of representation, and lack of public sources of self-respect.[51] These frustrations, in turn, are experienced in different ways by the different social groups who typically play a key role in nationalist revivals, such as intellectuals and politicians.[52] Among nineteenth-century East European nationalists, for instance, we find philologists and other intellectuals who dreamed of creating flowering cultures to rival the national cultures they admired, as well as political and economic modernizers who sought to transform feudal economies. Moreover, as John Comaroff has argued, quite different forces may be at work at different times when ethnic nationalisms are created, sustained, or revived.[53] Thus, both the nineteenth-century and post-communist variants of Eastern European ethnic nationalism have been anti-imperialistic, but there are also crucial differences; post-communist nationalism is not simply the awakening of a "sleeping beauty"[54] frozen during decades of communist rule. In an interesting analysis of post-communist ethnic nationalism, Claus Offe has recently analyzed the complex and at times somewhat paradoxical ways in which communism has shaped post-communist nationalism.[55] On the one hand, nationalism has been a reaction against the aggressive internationalism of the Soviet period, which at any rate sometimes took the form of thinly masked Russian nationalism. At the same time it has also been, paradoxically, a *product* of Soviet and Yugoslav nationalities policies which fostered national identity by organizing political administration along national lines (this is most striking in the case of so-called "titular nationalities" in former Soviet republics which had never created nationalist movements before their Soviet period). In addition, by seeking to destroy or completely co-opt the institutions of civil society, communism eroded other sources of allegiance, such as churches, clubs, and civic and professional associations. Another group which has played a key role in the construction of post-communist nationalism has been former communist politicians like Slobodan Milosevic who desired a source of legitimacy which could keep them in power, distance them from communism's past, and at the same time provide them with an explanation for why they were willing to be communist leaders in the first place. Embracing nationalism enabled them to define themselves in a tradition of anti-Stalinist national communist leaders in the mold of Tito or Nagy.[56]

Why does ethnic nationalism sometimes become such a powerful mobilizing force? Once again, the answer is complex and varies according to different contexts and circumstances. Nationalist appeals are likely to be persuasive in conditions in which many members of society are frustrated with a legacy of repressive foreign rule. Part of the appeal of nationalist political visions, Offe suggests, may be that they offer people a source of pride and self-respect by invoking internal values and heroic memories of a golden past.[57] Above all, the logic of nationalist pride and self-protection becomes a powerful mobilizing force amidst a pervasive atmosphere of fear and insecurity.[58]

What conclusions can we draw from this first thesis about how to approach the relationship between ethnic nationalism and political order? The socially constructed nature of ethnic nationalism does not mean that nationalist allegiances are "false" or "fake"; they are no more "false" than other social identities. Moreover, ethnic nationalist allegiances can survive demystification. Knowing, for instance, that "Slovene" was invented in 1809 need not weaken a Slovenian's national allegiance in any way.

Some false beliefs typical of ethnic nationalism do have predictably pernicious effects. The (always false) conviction that one's nation has been an unblemished victim of history or that it has performed a pure and compassionate civilizing mission vis à vis its neighbors, are likely to lead to moral insensitivity or worse. Nationalists may also regard their nation as "racially pure" when there is no basis for this claim in fact, and then endow these false biological ideas with feelings of superiority; extremist nationalists in Slovakia, Hungary, and Romania have all made factually absurd and morally dangerous claims about their nation's racial or biological purity. False beliefs about racial purity or historical innocence can clearly legitimate the construction of an exclusionary moral order that violates human rights. But not all false beliefs and not all convictions of superiority have morally pernicious effects. I may, for instance, falsely believe that the Pilgrim Fathers were paragons of tolerance and, taking pride in this tradition, embrace tolerance myself. Or I may think that my family, nation, or region is lovelier, more civilized or intelligent, and possesses a richer poetic or musical tradition or a better cuisine than its neighbors, without denying others' claims as human beings. Nor, finally, is it always the case that naturalized or primordialized differences are more divisive than those that are acknowledged to be constructs—ideological allegiances are perceived as constructs but can certainly be dangerously exclusionary. Hence, while many nationalist beliefs are false, and while some of these false beliefs are morally dangerous, nationalist allegiances and beliefs as such cannot be labeled either false or pernicious.

It is important to try to understand nationalist politics and allegiances as in some sense *rational* responses to particular circumstances[59] rather than as *sui generis* and irrational emotional drives. By this I do not mean that we should invariably consider nationalist attitudes and allegiances to be strategic masks for other, more basic needs and desires.[60] But even the most heartfelt, powerful, and irrational nationalist attitudes are better understood not as inescapable aspects of a particular nation's world view ("these Balkan peoples are simply like that") but as specific forms of symbolic politics and self-understanding which have a historical beginning and, given the right efforts and circumstances, could have a historical end. This is true, for instance, of the emotionally powerful anti-semitism, redolent of *ressentiment,* which plays such an important role in East-Central European nationalist rhetoric even, as in Poland, in the absence of a numerically significant Jewish minority.[61]

Contrary, then, to Ignatieff's suggestion that the identity of peoples is fixed, what "differences" there are among human beings and how they matter morally and politically depends on circumstances and on intentional and unintentional human action. An inquiry into political order cannot take ethnic or national differences as given. The genesis of national and ethnic differences and the morality and politics they embrace are themselves political developments. We should seek, then, to understand ethnic nationalisms as human constructs which are subject to change and which can be influenced by political developments as much as they themselves influence political order. Otherwise, we end up mystifying nationalism no less than nationalists themselves do. As Katherine Verdery has argued, we have to lodge agency "back in human beings, constrained by social structures," and avoid a tendency to "treat nationalism itself as a social actor."[62] Ethnic nationalist symbols and political programs are the result of human action and social struggle. As such, they are subject to change. The challenge is to understand how people can affect the moral and political dynamics of nationalism.

Recognizing the constructed nature of nations implies that they are not eternally fixed features of human life. Human beings have not always identified themselves as members of nations. The ethnic national allegiances which are experienced as primordial identities and which shape political order so profoundly today will almost certainly fade and possibly disappear over time. What we might call "denationalization," in other words, is historically possible,[63] though we should not forget that nations may be replaced by other constructed identities that would also be naturalized, and that could also justify dangerous forms of moral and political exclusion.

Denationalization can mean several quite different things. Its strongest meaning would entail the withering away of national identities as such. People would no longer think of themselves as members of ethnic national groups, just as most people today don't think of themselves as members of clans, tribes, or castes, or of "Christendom." The withering away of nations may coincide with the rise of other ascriptive identities (for instance, many homosexuals now identify themselves as members of an ascriptive group).[64] But this strong understanding of denationalization would require that ethnic national allegiances cease to be central to people's self-understanding.

Immigration and the increasing globalization of culture has certainly produced increasing numbers of people with apparently non-national or multiple national identities—people of "hyphenated identities," as Audre Lorde called them. Nevertheless, despite the importance of these trends, we must recognize that ethnic nationalist identities are very important for a large portion of the world's population and that this will not change any time soon. Moreover, such identities can resurface in apparently non-ethnic settings. For instance, while the United States is frequently described as having a civic self-description rather than an ethnic nationalist one, hostility toward Asians or blacks, Spanish speakers, and Muslims demonstrates that racial, linguistic, and religious identifications do, in fact, play an important role in many people's sense of American identity.

We should, then, assume that nationalism will continue to serve as a source of solidarity and conflict for the foreseeable future, but that its strength and moral and political characteristics are dynamic and alterable.

Thesis #2:

Nationalism does not offer a viable principle of political order. It does not provide us with workable answers to basic questions about institutional design, membership criteria, or territorial boundaries.

While ethnic nationalism is likely to continue to be a focus of political allegiance and mobilization in many regions of the world for the foreseeable future, it does not offer a viable framework for determining the basic principles of political order. Ethnic nationalism clearly does not offer answers to the problems of basic institutional design. While, as I've argued above, it has strong links with democracy, ethnic nationalism is not a competitor with the democratic or liberal traditions in the construction of prescriptions for institutional design. Ignatieff and others[65] have suggested that ethnic national differences can provide a general organizing principle for other basic questions of political order, answering the questions of membership and boundaries largely ignored by contemporary liberal democratic political theory. But this vision of the role which ethnic nationalism can play in constructing political order is naïve in several respects. First, and most straightforwardly, "peoples" are scattered in mottled population patterns that make it difficult to decide where borders should lie. As John Stuart Mill observed a century ago, in East-Central Europe, national groups are geographically "so mixed up as to be incapable of local separation," posing an insuperable practical obstacle to the principle "that the boundaries of governments should coincide . . . with those of nationalities."[66] Nor is it only mottled demographics which makes the question of borders contentious, as is shown by the insistence among champions of Greater Serbia that Kosovo, despite its overwhelming Albanian majority, belongs to them by virtue of its prominent place in Serbian history. Nearly every East-Central European nation has, within its historical and cultural repertoire, a memory of a "Greater" homeland, along with tragic stories of how the borders were truncated to their present location.[67] The homes envisioned by different peoples expand and overlap in ways that wreak havoc with Ignatieff's vision of each people safe within "its" borders. In 1990, the fewer than two hundred countries in the world had over eight hundred nationalist movements; and the territorial claims of these movements were such that most often "the vindication of one nationalist destiny would displace another."[68]

It might be said that, *pace* Mill, it is not impossible to use national membership to devise a solution to the problem of mottled demographics—one can move people, either peacefully or through coercion, in order to create ethnically homogeneous states, as the thugs of "ethnic cleansing" and the Geneva negotiators are both, in their different ways, attempting to do in Bosnia. Policies of population transfer are indeed possible, and may in some unstable and dangerous circumstances represent the least evil option. But they have terrible human costs, and in many circumstances will leave people resentful and longing to return to their previous homes. For instance, Stalin's forced resettlements of the Ingush and other ethnic groups have wreaked havoc, half a century later, as these populations try to return to their original homes in the Caucasus.

The model of a homogeneous nation-state, then, is not a realistic one for most of the world's people. Very few states even come close to approximating the ideal type, where the boundaries of the ethno-cultural nation and the political state are congruent and seamless. Nearly all of the world's countries, including those traditionally considered "nation-states," are in fact multicultural.[69] As Tzvetan Todorov has noted, multiculturalism is "neither a panacea nor a threat, but simply the reality of all existing states."[70] What the fact of multiculturalism suggests is that congruence of state and nation is not a viable general principle of territorial order nor an unproblematic principle of political membership. Even leaving aside the continuous influxes of immigrants and refugees, all or nearly all polities have significant minorities, and have to confront their presence in determining the criteria for citizenship. The pressures and opportunities of our increasingly global economy will lead many more people to move to new homes as well. The model Ignatieff proposes is therefore practically inadequate, for it does not address the issue of those who are different within the "home" of difference.

Despite its prominence in innumerable international documents, the national right to self-determination is thus a hopelessly unrealistic guide to creating workable borders and policies of citizenship.[71] Nor, finally, is national sovereignty on the traditional model the guarantee of security which Ignatieff implies that it is. For one thing, sovereignty may hinder, rather than help, a people meet its needs: communist Albania, for instance, was certainly sovereign in its unsplendid isolation and economic and social misery, and Slovakia is likely to do worse after its political divorce from the Czech Republic. More generally, given the multitude of peoples around the world, any feasible attempt to guarantee them "self-determination" will require a willingness to think of "sovereignty" in more flexible terms.[72] A world in which each ethnic national group is safe within its borders and master of its needs is a chimera. Contemporary realities require us to devise approaches to political order which take ethnic nationalist political allegiances into account within an inescapably multi-ethnic world.

Thesis #3:

A commitment to human rights should lead us to regard efforts to elevate nationalism to a principle of political order as morally dangerous and efforts to denationalize politics as morally suspect.

Attempts to elevate ethnic nationalism to a principle of political order are not only impractical; they are also profoundly morally dangerous from a human rights perspective. A commitment to human rights requires us to support the principle of equal citizenship and therefore, given the demographic and political realities I alluded to in my discussion of thesis #2, to oppose conditions in which ethnic national identity becomes the sole criterion of citizenship. The exclusionary potential of such a citizenship policy, and the likelihood that it will produce populations of marginalized and vulnerable people, is simply too great.[73] The only morally acceptable exceptions to this rule arise in circumstances in which defining citizenship in ethnic terms is motivated by concern for human rights—for instance, when members of a particular group are subject to genocide or oppression and granting them citizenship on the basis of group membership elsewhere will facilitate their rescue. But even under these circumstances there are likely to be ethnic minorities present in the polity, making it imperative, from the perspective of human rights, that ethnic membership not be allowed to become either the *sole* criterion of citizenship, or the basis of a higher citizenship status.

A commitment to human rights also requires us to oppose the view that nationalism offers a conclusory criterion for just borders. While the human rights ideal offers no guidance on where borders ought to be drawn, it does require us to oppose approaches to political order that are likely to justify institutionalized patterns of exclusion and marginalization. And, once again, while there are instances in which the drawing or redrawing of borders on ethnic nationalist grounds is morally justified,[74] elevating nationalism to a general principle of just territorial order ignores the pervasive reality and importance of minority issues and is therefore morally unacceptable.

Does a commitment to human rights require us to strive to denationalize politics? It depends on what this "denationalization" means. Ethnic nationalist allegiances and forms of political mobilization are not intrinsically inimical to human rights and may even in some contexts be demanded by human rights commitments.[75] A commitment to humanity as a moral community does not rule out particular commitments to groups or spheres of solidarity smaller than the species, and an ethnic group or nation can be one of these groups. I may take pride in, identify with, and feel special obligations toward my nation or ethnic group without denying humanity's claims. To be sure, as with all particularistic commitments, my commitments to my nation may (indeed almost inevitably will) be in some *practical* tension with my commitments to humanity, for I will favor members of my group and in the process ignore some more urgent needs among outsiders. A recognition of humanity's claims pulls us, as I have already noted, toward questioning the legitimacy of all boundaries. But this universalizing impulse has to be balanced with a recognition that particularistic commitments, such as those to families, cultures, and nations, are constitutive of the legacy of cultural creation that gives human life meaning and interest. So long, then, as I respect humanity's claims, the tension between human commonality and national particularity, while real, does not constitute a moral incompatibility. Moreover, given the reality of group oppression, political mobilization by and on behalf of a particular group is often required to achieve respect for human rights within a society. In some circumstances, then, a commitment to human rights, far from requiring us to oppose all nationalist politics, may demand that we support political mobilization by and on behalf of an ethnic group.

The reality of group conflict and disadvantage also suggests that those committed to human rights should approach efforts to denationalize politics with some scepticism. It would be desirable if ethnic solidarities were no longer politicized but were, as Francis Fukuyama has recently advocated, pushed "into the realm of private life and culture."[76] Fukuyama's vision of a privatized nationalism is an attractive one.[77] But it is unrealistic to demand that ethnic national identities cease to be a focus of strong solidarity and political mobilization in the foreseeable future. The private flourishing of ethnic national cultures depends on public resources and spaces which require political mobilization to create. People need access to schools, cultural institutions, houses of worship, and avenues of social mobility in order to be able to sustain their cultures. As long as ethnicity remains a predictor of marginalization in many societies, ethnic nationalist political mobilization is likely to arise. While a proponent of human rights might prefer political efforts to combat marginalization that do not focus on ethnicity, this does not make ethnic mobilization illegitimate. Human rights advocates must also be cautious in the face of explicit efforts to purge political life of ethnic overtones, since such efforts may exacerbate the marginalization of one ethnic group and may even be intentionally designed to achieve this end. Bulgaria's legal ban on political parties formed along "ethnic, racial, or religious lines," for instance, had the predictable effect of outlawing the Movement for Rights and Freedoms, the major political organization representing the interests of Bulgaria's Turkish minority.[78] Attempts to forcefully denationalize political life may disguise the exclusionary nationalist aspirations of a majority. They may also backfire because such efforts, by polarizing political debate between "bad" nationalism and "good" civic democracy or liberalism, are likely to strengthen the position of extremist rather than moderate ethnic nationalists. The legacy of aggressive internationalism and the nationalist manipulations of the communist era in Eastern Europe, for instance, makes efforts to condemn ethnic nationalism as such counterproductive. Thus, in any region of the world with a recent history of ethnic animosity, denationalization as an explicit political project is morally suspect.

Thesis #4:

Efforts to reconcile nationalism with humanity's claims require the invention of a wide range of institutional strategies of accommodation.

I have argued that while ethnic nationalism will be a political force for the foreseeable future, it should not be construed as an organizing principle of political order. Moreover, in approaching the relationship between ethnic nationalism and political order we have to try to keep in mind how nationalist identities and aims are political constructions and susceptible to revision and challenge. What then, is to be done in trying to promote human rights in a world of ethnic nationalisms? I believe the task is best conceived as involving two interrelated processes by which we try to influence political order. The first is institutional strategies of accommodation, the second, cultural processes of inclusion. Each of these processes in turn should be understood as an attempt, in particular circumstances, to balance the goals of respecting cultural differences and of promoting a sense of common human identity. I offer a sketch of these processes as my two final theses about nationalism.

It is tempting to say, as John Stuart Mill did, that liberal democracy represents a political order in which national differences can flourish within a framework which respects humanity's claims. I agree with Mill to a considerable extent: liberal democratic institutions do represent a very large part of the solution. But liberal democracy is incomplete as a solution to my inquiry for several interrelated reasons. It tends to have difficulty confronting and overcoming the problems of permanently marginalized or disempowered minorities or deep inequalities, precisely the conditions in which ethnic nationalist movements are likely to arise. Its prescriptions for political order—the rule of law, protection of individual rights, and democratic elections to representative legislatures—generally have little to say about some of the struggles most central to nationalist politics, including struggles over cultural recognition and protection; the relative distribution of patronage opportunities, resources, and bureaucratic positions among different groups; and above all the overwhelming problem of fear and insecurity as disincentives to supporting liberal regimes. It has become a central (if contested) theme of American constitutional jurisprudence that policies blind to difference may not alleviate, and indeed may exacerbate, the plight of marginalized groups. The same argument may be made about prescribing liberal democracy as a complete solution to the relationship between ethnic nationalism and political order. Institutional arrangements sensitive to ethnic national differences will have to be designed in order to ensure that the aspirations and interests that fuel nationalist politics are not thwarted in ways that lead people to reject liberal democratic institutions and human rights.

In thinking about the problem of institutional design, we have to recognize that there are no universally applicable solutions, that different arrangements have a better chance of working in different contexts, and that every institutional proposal has its drawbacks and dangers. The most we can do in a general sense is to sketch some goals and offer a kind of institutional toolkit, a range of techniques which may help to accommodate ethnic nationalist aspirations and human rights.

Some generally applicable goals are: reducing group-based fear and insecurity, avoiding conditions in which an ethnic group is permanently marginalized, creating institutional frameworks appropriate to the circumstances in which power is balanced among groups and there are regular avenues for the articulation of interests and the voicing of grievances, ensuring that there are paths of upward mobility available to members of all ethnic groups, defusing tendencies for all social conflict to occur along ethnic lines, and ensuring that state officials do not systematically demean a group.

Another general aim is to try to be sensitive, in deciding which processes to support, to the issues that pose the greatest danger of instability, violence, and extremism in particular contexts. In some places accommodating competing religious demands will be the most urgent priority and the issue that poses the greatest risks; in others, it will be accommodating territorial demands. The institutional arrangements we should support need to be selected with these dangers in mind rather than being simply guided by more abstract moral reasoning. For instance, the integrity of existing borders has little or no moral weight as a general principle of political order, since every existing state border is the result of past conquest and violence and is to a considerable degree morally arbitrary. Nevertheless, in a context like East-Central Europe, where raising the issue of borders could lead to a frenzy of territorial claims and counterclaims and encourage ethnic minorities to be regarded with suspicion and hatred as potentially treacherous secessionists and irredentists, proclaiming a ground rule of territorial integrity may be morally justified—so long as this proclamation is coupled with demands for minority rights throughout the region.

Some of the particular domestic institutional arrangements that might support these aims are:[79] forms of federalism, power-sharing schemes like consociationalism, autonomy regimes that provide ethnic groups with control over local government or over certain areas of public life such as educational and cultural institutions, constitutional protection of minority rights which ensures access to the public goods that enable groups to sustain their cultural life, creation of parliamentary seats to ensure representation for geographically scattered minorities, electoral engineering to promote coalitions across ethnic lines, and mandated proportional representation in police forces, the army, and local civil administration.

None of these is a panacea. All of them require certain contingent circumstances to have any hope of success.[80] Almost without exception they pose the danger of exacerbating conflict and resentment among groups. There are also clearly ways in which these processes will be in unavoidable tension with one another and with other important goals of justice and human rights. Autonomy regimes may, for instance, involve culturally segregated schools, whereas integrated education would be better for inclusiveness. And providing institutional opportunities for group self-determination always leaves open the possibility that the group will oppress its own members.[81] These dangers have to be weighed carefully in assessing particular institutional arrangements before and after they are put in place.

There are also some institutional innovations and processes which regional, international, and non-state actors can undertake to promote processes of accomodating ethnic nationalism and human rights. The "round tables" which achieved a remarkably orderly transition to multi-party democracy in a number of Central European countries offer an innovative model for dealing with ethnic nationalist conflicts and minority issues, and such arrangements are, in fact, being tried at both the domestic and international level in a number of places, including Hungary and Romania.[82] Broader regional treaties to promote uniform standards for minority rights, perhaps in exchange for territorial agreements, could be modelled on the Helsinki Accords. An effort on the part of the international community, particularly the United Nations, to come to grips with the unhelpful vagueness of the "national right to self-determination" and to replace it with more realistic international legal norms concerning the range of recognized forms that "self-determination" might take[83] could be of considerable use, as would serious efforts to revitalize the continually stalled U.N. working group effort to codify minority rights. As many observers have noted, the hasty international recognition of Croatia in the absence of concerted international pressure to ensure respect for the rights of its Serbian minority played a critical part in the exacerbation of ethnic nationalist conflict in former Yugoslavia. More generally, the international community can play a role by placing conditions on aid such as constitutional protection for minorities and other crucial human rights guarantees such as rights to a free and independent press.

As important as these political techniques of accommodation are, we must recognize that institutional engineering will never be sufficient as an approach to ensure a successful accommodation of ethnic nationalism and human rights. For one thing, people have to be willing to go along with institutional changes in the first place. More generally, efforts to challenge extremist, xenophobic forms of nationalism will require confronting the cultural attitudes and fears from which they derive their strength. I turn, in my last thesis on nationalism, to the most difficult challenge of all: that of inventing and promoting cultural processes of inclusion, through which, in Ignatieff's words, difference can find "a home" within a strengthened ideal of a shared human community.

Thesis #5:

Reconciling nationalism with humanity's claims also requires us to create and promote a variety of cultural strategies of inclusion.

Preventing ethnic nationalism from destroying the ideal of human rights requires influencing the trajectory of ethnic nationalist self-definitions and world views so that respect for human rights does not seem to ethnic nationalists themselves to be incompatible with their aims. The terrible potential for extremist nationalism to destroy a sense of shared human identity is obvious: we need only think of the short time it took in Bosnia for some people who had lived all of their lives in a multi-ethnic community, who even, in many cases, came from ethnically mixed families, to come to view the mere presence in their community of those from another group as intolerable. How can this process be prevented, and who can play a role in preventing it?

Insight on these matters will lie, ultimately, in the details of particular cultural contexts and particular histories. Once again, however, I will try to offer a few general goals as well as a few specific suggestions.

Among the general goals of a process of cultural inclusion aimed at reconciling ethnic nationalism and human rights would be preventing nationalism and human rights, or nationalism and liberalism, from being viewed as polar opposites within the political discourse of a society. This means promoting the ideal of the liberal, tolerant nationalist as one who better represents the interests of his or her nation than extremists do. Another goal is to support those elements of a nation's historical self-definition that are more inclusive and tolerant. A third goal is to confront the specific patterns of *ressentiment,* fear, demonization, and exclusion that characterize a particular nationalist tradition's intolerant strands.

These processes of cultural invention require courageous commitment on the part of many people, among them educators, journalists, cultural and religious figures, and politicians. Intellectuals will have to take on the task of being "political therapists"[84] to their society. Historians will have to debunk dangerous myths of national purity, superiority, and innocence. And politicians will have to show moral leadership in opposing demagoguery and extremism. There are many examples of these kinds of actions from East-Central Europe in recent years. For instance, Adam Michnik has argued eloquently that Poles need to be ashamed of Polish fascists in order to have the right to be proud of Polish achievements[85] and Hungarian President Arpád Göncz responded to a sudden upsurge in skinhead attacks against African students by publicly apologizing in the name of the Hungarian nation and by becoming the honorary president of the human rights group the students had formed. Such symbolic gestures will not halt violent and intolerant actions, but they can be of immense value in shaping a society's response.

There are ways in which the international community can help such processes of cultural invention, although intervention in this sphere is always a delicate matter. Some of the suggestions I listed in my discussion of thesis #4 can offer concrete institutional and normative resources to those seeking to promote tolerant forms of nationalist politics in the same way that the human rights norms of the Helsinki Accords offered a standard to which Eastern Europen dissidents could appeal in criticizing their societies. Foreign governments and outside commentators can avoid supporting the view (which has gained too much currency in attitudes toward Eastern Europe) that all politicians can be categorized as either "good" liberals or "bad" nationalists. Governmental and non-governmental agencies can strive to offer support to those who are trying, as the Serbian winner of a human rights award noted recently, to argue that "true patriotism" involves a commitment to tolerance.[86] And they can try to counteract developments (like that of the increasing government monopoly over the media in both Serbia and Croatia) that prevent such voices from being heard.[87]

More generally, of course, we can try to work for an inclusive civic culture in our own societies, and to support the exchange of resources among civic organizations in different societies working toward these ideals. One of the striking characteristics of contemporary political order is the possibilities it offers for rapid cross-cultural learning, a phenomenon which can obviously work for good or ill. Just as skinhead groups in Eastern Europe have received funding and support from the United States, so civic organizations dedicated to pluralism and tolerance can establish contacts with and offer help to their counterparts in other countries.

Conclusion

The approach I have sketched here to the relationship between ethnic nationalism and political order lacks the virtue of theoretical simplicity. It situates itself in an uneasy equilibrium between two approaches that are much more straightforward and elegant: on the one hand, a particularist view that stresses the intrinsic value of cultural difference as something which requires political protection; and on the other, an uncompromising commitment to universal and uniform political principles with no regard for cultural difference. I am uneasy with both of these views, though for different reasons. My uneasiness with particularism is deeper, since such a view ignores the complexity and moral ambiguity of all cultural communities and evades the problem of culturally sanctioned injustice and oppression. Moreover, the principle of "protecting difference" is unworkably vague; political protection for one kind of cultural difference, such as that often demanded by ethnic nationalist groups, privileges that difference and in the process suppresses or obscures others. Thus particularism does not, in my view, constitute a coherent or acceptable substantive moral position. A self-critical, open-ended universalism is worth striving for in part precisely because it creates a framework within which claims for the protection of difference can be made. My uneasiness with universalist positions that rule out political protection of difference is of a different order. Such positions are politically unrealistic. They fail to acknowledge that an insistence on neutral policies can be counterproductive because it does not address people's insecurities and fears or because it fails to address the systematic disempowerment of some groups relative to others.

Political recognition and protection of cultural difference may be the best way to prevent great harm to people and to create the conditions in which they can live in dignity.[88]

Aristotle argued in the *Nicomachean Ethics* that we should not strive to attain more precision in an area of inquiry than is appropriate to the subject matter itself.[89] No doubt a great deal more clarity is possible in discussing ethnic nationalism and political order than I have offered here. But an overarching concern for theoretical precision is not, I think, an appropriate attitude for political and legal philosophers to take when approaching issues of such cultural complexity and political sensitivity as ethnic nationalism. I doubt if precise "solutions" to the challenge of reconciling ethnic nationalism with human rights, or universalizable statements of necessary and sufficient conditions for achieving this goal, are devisable. What theoretical essays like this one have to contribute is something less precise but no less important—arguments about what is morally at stake and about how various and often competing moral aspirations might be weighed and balanced. I have argued that in practice this process should involve strategies of political accommodation of difference. But there is also an urgent need to underline the importance of fostering universalist ideals. Growing rhetorical support for human rights around the world should not blind us to the fragility of the human rights ideal and the ways in which previous attempts to promote a vision of a shared human moral community have foundered and faded under the pressure of exlusionary ideals, greed, violence, and hypocrisy. Since the end of the cold war, the future of our political order has been revealed to be less constrained and more open-ended than it appeared to be for several generations. But these more open horizons also reveal heavier responsibilities. The trajectory that ethnic nationalism will take in the coming years—the ways in which people will challenge and shape it—will help to determine whether future observers will look at the late twentieth century as the promising if difficult adolescence, or the decline and death,[90] of the contemporary ideal of human rights and of a common human moral community.

NOTES

Versions of this chapter were presented to the American Society for Political and Legal Philosophy, at the University of Wisconsin-Madison, and to the Program in Ethics and Public Affairs at Princeton University. I am grateful for the stimulating questions and comments I received from many people on these occasions, and especially from Allen Buchanan, Jeff Holzgrefe, Alan Houston, Debra Satz, Craig Scott, Ian Shapiro, Michael Walzer, and Bernard Yack. I would also like to thank the Harvard Program in Ethics and the Professions for its generous fellowship support.

1. A recent survey in the *New York Times* identified forty-eight major ethnic conflicts worldwide. David Binder and Barbara Crossette, "As Ethnic Wars Multiply, U.S. Strives for a Policy," *New York Times,* February 7, 1993, A1, A14.

2. See Michael Ignatieff, *The Needs of Strangers* (New York: Penguin, 1984), 131.

3. The best known exponent of this view is Francis Fukuyama, "The End of History?" *National Interest* 16 (Summer 1989): 3–18.

4. See, for instance, Samuel P. Huntington, "The Clash of Civilizations?" *Foreign Affairs* 72 (Summer 1993): 22–49; Stanley Tambiah, "Nation State, Democracy, and Ethno-Nationalist Conflict," in *Balancing Power in Multi-Ethnic Societies,* ed. V. Tishkov, (Moscow: Nauka, forthcoming).

5. Religious fundamentalism, for instance, is an important form of identity politics quite distinct from ethnic nationalism, although particular religious fundamentalist movements may also be nationalistic.

6. The view that nationalism was a premodern phenomenon has been widely shared by social scientists of both liberal and socialist persuasion. Even a prominent contemporary scholar of nationalism, E. J. Hobsbawm, concluded a recent book by predicting that it was "most unlikely" that historians of the future would regard nationalism as a central feature of late-twentieth-century politics. E. J. Hobsbawm, *Nations and Nationalism since 1780* (New York: Cambridge University Press, 1990), 181–83.

7. I borrow the term "the new world disorder" from John Comaroff, "Ethnicity, Nationalism, and the Politics of Difference in an Age of Revolution," in *The Politics of Difference: Ethnic Premises in a World of Power,* ed. E. Wilmsen and P. McAllister, (University of Chicago Press, 1996).

8. Max Weber, *Economy and Society,* vol. 11 (Berkeley: University of California Press, 1978), 922.

9. For some striking examples of French cultural nationalists whose politics were by no means tolerant of difference, see Tzvetan Todorov, *On Human Diversity,* trans. Catherine Porter (Cambridge: Harvard University Press, 1993), esp. ch. 3.

10. For instance, political mobilization by indigenous peoples is often based on a genealogical definition of membership, but, at least in some instances, full membership is open to those who marry in (although there are also examples of gender discrimination in the criteria for membership).

11. See, for instance, Walker Connor, "Nation-Building or Nation-Destroying," *World Politics* 24 (1972): 319–55; Walker Connor, "The Politics of Ethnonationalism," *Journal of International Affairs* 27 (1973): 1–21; Nathan Glazer and Daniel P. Moynihan, eds., *Ethnicity: Theory and Experience* (Cambridge: Harvard University Press, 1975); Crawford Young, *The Politics of Cultural Pluralism* (Madison: University of Wisconsin Press, 1976) and "The Dialectics of Cultural Pluralism: Concept and Reality," in *Balancing Power in Multi-Ethnic Societies,* ed. V. Tishkov (Moscow: Nauka, forthcoming); Donald Horowitz, *Ethnic Groups in Conflict* (Berkeley: University of California Press, 1985); Myron Weiner, *Sons of the Soil: Migration and Ethnic Conflict in India* (Princeton: Princeton University Press, 1978). Even in this literature, however, authors frequently described their work as going against the widely shared assumption that national, ethnic, and religious differences would fade with modernization.

12. This tendency for Anglo-American political theory to ignore questions of borders when discussing political order may well reflect the fact that shifting borders are not a part of theorists' own experience. This attitude was best illustrated for me by a childhood friend who once asked me if the Carpathian Mountains were in Hungary. When I replied that they had once been in Hungary but this was no longer the case, he looked utterly bewildered. "What do you mean," he whispered, "they moved?"

13. This point is also stressed by Allen Buchanan, *Secession: The Morality of Political Divorce* (Boulder, Colo.: Westview Press, 1992), ch. 1.

14. One prominent exception is Michael Walzer, who made questions of territoriality and membership central to his discussion of political order and justice in *Spheres of Justice* (Oxford: Blackwell, 1983), esp. ch. 3. See also Michael Walzer, "The New Tribalism," *Dissent* (Spring 1992): 164–71; "Reply" to James B. Rule's "Tribalism and the State,"

Dissent (Fall 1992): 523–24; and "Exclusion, Injustice, and the Democratic State," *Dissent* (Winter 1993): 55–64.

15. For instance, Michael Sandel, *Liberalism and the Limits of Justice* (New York: Cambridge University Press, 1982). Charles Taylor's recent essay "The Politics of Recognition" explicitly confronts issues of multiculturalism but still tends to treat the definition of "culture" and the value of "cultural survival" somewhat uncritically. Charles Taylor, "The Politics of Recognition" in *Multiculturalism and the Politics of Recognition,* ed. Amy Gutmann (Princeton: Princeton University Press, 1992).

16. Of these theorists, Michael Walzer has written most explicitly about ethnic nationalism. See Walzer, "The New Tribalism." See also Allen Buchanan, *Secession: The Morality of Political Divorce* (Boulder, Colo.: Westview Press, 1991) and "The Morality of Inclusion," *Social Philosophy and Policy* 10 (1993): 233–57; Will Kymlicka, *Liberalism, Community, and Culture* (Oxford: Clarendon, 1989) and *Multicultural Citizenship* (New York: Oxford University Press, 1995); Martha Minow, *Making All the Difference* (Ithaca: Cornell University Press, 1990); Yael Tamir, *Liberal Nationalism* (Princeton: Princeton University Press, 1993); Iris Young, *Justice and the Politics of Difference* (Princeton: Princeton University Press, 1990). John Rawls has also reconceived his approach to political liberalism as a solution to political order in culturally and morally plural societies. See John Rawls, "Justice as Fairness: Political not Metaphysical," *Philosophy and Public Affairs* 14 (1985): 223–51; John Rawls, *Political Liberalism* (New York: Columbia University Press, 1993).

17. Recent developments in North America have heightened awareness of ethnic nationalist issues. Canadian scholars have responded to Quebecois separatism and Native American political mobilization, while in the United States, disputes over immigration, language policy, and electoral engineering to support minority representation raise questions typical of ethnic nationalist conflicts in plural societies. The legal order of the United States is also more complex than most citizens realize. For instance, Perry Dane describes a multiple choice question on a poster at Yale Law School which asked how many sovereign governments there were in the United States. The possible answers were one, fifty-one, fifty-three (adding Puerto Rico and Guam) and a number in the high three digit range. To the astonishment of most observers, the correct answer was the last, given the number of Indian tribes who are recognized in U.S. and international law as sovereign entities. Perry Dane, "The Maps of Sovereignty: A Meditation," *Cardozo Law Review* 12 (1991): 959–60.

18. For a detailed discussion of the relationships between ethnic and class conflict see Horowitz, *Ethnic Groups in Conflict,* 22–36 and Tambiah, "Nation State, Democracy, and Ethno-Nationalist Conflict," 12–13.

19. Bogdan Denitch, "Tragedy in Former Yugoslavia," *Dissent* (Winter 1993): 29.

20. "Cosmopolitan" is also a code word for "Jewish" in Eastern Europe. But critics of cosmopolitanism evince a general suspicion of urban life and urban elites which goes beyond, while encompassing, anti-semitism.

21. The internally integrated nature of nationalism is stressed by Paul Brass, *Ethnicity and Nationalism* (Newbury Park, Calif.: Sage Press, 1991), 20. See also Liah Greenfeld, *Nationalism: Five Roads to Modernity* (Cambridge: Harvard University Press, 1992), 10. Of course, this is a general nationalist ideal rather than an actual description of nationalist politics.

22. Nationalist politics need not, of course, be democratic. As Liah Greenfeld points out, collectivist or organicist conceptions of the nation lead to the idea of a nation having a collective will which only a few are qualified to interpret, an idea which legitimates authoritarian political arrangements. Greenfeld, *Nationalism,* 11.

23. Ignatieff, *The Needs of Strangers,* ch. 1.

24. However, as I shall argue in theses 4 and 5, I think the international community's involvement is essential to efforts to create such domestic political practices.

25. The phrase "imagined community" has been made famous by Benedict Anderson's use of it in the title of his book on nationalism. Benedict Anderson, *Imagined Communities* (New York: Verso, 1991).

26. This point is also stressed by Ghia Nodia, "Nationalism and Democracy," *Journal of Democracy* 3 (1992): 1–22. A chilling example of a failure to make this commitment was the matter-of-fact response of a man who had lived on the outskirts of a Nazi concentration camp who was interviewed by Claude Lanzmann in his documentary about the Holocaust, *Shoah.* Asked how he felt about the people he saw daily on their way to the gas chambers, the man replied, "When you cut your finger, it doesn't hurt me."

27. Wesley Newcomb Hohfeld, *Fundamental Legal Conceptions,* ed. W. W. Cook (New Haven: Yale University Press, 1923).

28. Of course, saying this much already evades innumerable difficult moral and philosophical issues. What should we do, for instance, about borderline cases, human beings who have not yet developed, or

have irrevocably lost, the capabilities from which our sense of solidarity arises—the unborn or those in a permanent vegetative state? How do we construe the membership in a common human moral community of those whose capacities are severely impaired? Or of those who fail to respect the humanity of others? And what about the species boundary itself, which, like all moral boundaries, represents exclusion as well as inclusion? Why shouldn't we follow Bentham in believing that all sentient beings have the same basic moral claims on us? I leave aside these questions, while acknowledging their moral importance, because they are not central to the purposes of this essay. For while debates over the moral status of fetuses, comatose people, and animals are crucial, they are not germane to the tension between "us" and "them" constructed by ethnic nationalism.

29. Henry Steiner argues that equal protection is perhaps "the preeminent human rights norm." Steiner, "Ideals and Counter-Ideals in the Struggle over Autonomy Regimes for Minorities," *Notre Dame Law Review* 66 (1991): 1548.

30. Douglas Klusmeyer, "Aliens, Immigrants, and Citizens: The Politics of Inclusion in the Federal Republic of Germany," *Daedalus* 122:3 (Summer 1993): 81–114.

31. I'm grateful to Ian Shapiro and Michael Walzer for pressing me to clarify this point.

32. This point has been developed most fully by Anthony Smith in *The Ethnic Origins of Nations* (Oxford: Basil Blackwell, 1986).

33. I would therefore take issue with Liah Greenfeld's path-dependent treatment of European nationalisms. Greenfeld, *Nationalism.*

34. Ernest Gellner, *Nations and Nationalism* (Oxford: Basil Blackwell, 1983), 56.

35. For instance, the history of nation-building is replete with processes of coercive linguistic homogenization. A striking illustration is provided by the title of a report commissioned by the French National Convention in Year II of the Republic: "On the Necessity and the Means of Annihilating the *Patois* and Universalizing the Use of the French Language." Nathaniel Berman, "Nationalism Legal and Linguistic," *New York University Journal of International Law and Politics* 24 (1992): 1523.

36. For a detailed account of the so-called "awakeners" of Eastern European nationalism, see Emil Niederhauser, *The Rise of Nationality in Eastern Europe* (Budapest: Corvina, 1982).

37. Niederhauser, *The Rise of Nationality in Eastern Europe,* 129, 220–21.

38. George Barany, "Hungary: From Aristocratic to Proletarian

Nationalism," in *Nationalism in Eastern Europe,* ed. Peter Sugar and Ivo Lederer (Seattle: University of Washington Press, 1969); Niederhauser, *The Rise of Nationality in Eastern Europe,* 195.

39. Ivo Lederer, "Nationalism and the Yugoslavs," in *Nationalism in Eastern Europe,* ed. Peter Sugar and Ivo Lederer (Seattle: University of Washington Press, 1969), 399, 401.

40. Lederer, "Nationalism and the Yugoslavs," 414–28.

41. It is one of the ironies of the current war that the Serb militias operating in Bosnia have managed to create a more powerful Bosnian Muslim nationalism than has ever existed before.

42. As a joke making the rounds in Bosnia puts it, the difference between Serbs, Croats, and Bosnian Muslims was that Serbs didn't go to Orthodox church, the Croats didn't go to Catholic mass, and the Bosnians didn't kneel and pray to Mecca. P. J. O'Rourke, "Gang Bang," *Rolling Stone,* January 7, 1993, 41.

43. Robert Sam Anson, "Letter from Yugoslavia," *Esquire,* October 1992, 116.

44. Bogdan Denitch reports that there were two-and-a-half million mixed marriages in Yugoslavia before the war. Denitch, "Tragedy in Former Yugoslavia." The total population of Yugoslavia, according to the 1991 census, was 10,406,742.

45. Robert Lane offers an interesting analysis of the psychological needs addressed by nationalism, but points out that these needs do not necessarily attach to nations. For instance, Lane draws an analogy between nationalists who compensate for personal feelings of failure through exaggerated pride in the achievements of their nation and alumni of elite universities who compensate for their feelings of inadequacy by glorying in the prestige of their *alma mater.* Robert Lane, "The Persistence of Nationalism: Roots in Attachment and Cognition" (unpublished manuscript), 12.

46. This point is stressed by Ivo Lederer in "Nationalism and the Yugoslavs," 405. For a good discussion of the relational quality of ethnogenesis, see John Comaroff, "Ethnicity, Nationalism, and the Politics of Difference in an Age of Revolution," 9ff.

47. Martin Kramer, "Arab Nationalism: Mistaken Identity," *Daedalus* 122 (1993): 171–206.

48. On the 1961 census, 21,638 persons identified themselves as of "Yugoslav" ethnicity; in 1981 this had grown to 473,184. By 1991, it had dropped somewhat to 343,593. My thanks to Matthew Liao for his assistance in finding these census figures.

49. Miren Uriarte, "A Challenge to the Racial Order: Boston's Latino Community," *Boston Review,* September/October 1992, 9–11.

50. John A. Hall, "Nationalisms: Classified and Explained," *Daedalus* 122 (1993): 11.

51. Hall, "Nationalisms," and Gellner, *Nations and Nationalism.*

52. Hall, "Nationalisms," 15 (citing Wlodek Wesolowski).

53. Comaroff, "Ethnicity, Nationalism, and the Politics of Difference in an Age of Revolution."

54. I borrow the phrase from John A. Hall, "Nationalisms," 4.

55. Claus Offe, "The Rationality of Ethnic Politics," *Budapest Review of Books* 3 (1993): 6–13.

56. Offe suggests a number of other sources of post-communist nationalism, including a reaction to the mistreatment of ethnic minorities in neighbouring countries whose plight as second class citizens and scapegoats during the period of communist economic decline had aroused political opposition and concern. Offe, "The Rationality of Ethnic Politics."

57. By contrast, Offe argues, Eastern European liberals appealed only to an uncertain future and to a desire to emulate Western Europe, far less psychologically potent and satisfying ways of mobilizing people. Offe, "The Rationality of Ethnic Politics."

58. István Bibó, "The Distress of East European Small States," in *Democracy, Revolution, Self-Determination: Selected Writings* (Atlantic Research and Publications/Columbia University Press), 42. See also Michael Walzer, "The New Tribalism."

59. Offe, "The Rationality of Ethnic Politics."

60. In some cases this does appear to be the case—few analysts believe, for instance, that Slobodan Milosevic embraced Serbian nationalism out of inner conviction and heartfelt belief.

61. Adam Michnik, "The Two Faces of Europe," *The New Republic,* November 12, 1990, 23.

62. Katherine Verdery, "Whither 'Nation' and 'Nationalism'?" *Daedalus* 122 (1993): 39.

63. I think Michael Walzer, for instance, rather overstates the permanence of particular ethnic national—or what he calls "tribal"—identities in Walzer, "The New Tribalism," 171.

64. As Verdery notes, the title "Queer Nation" is especially apt for this self-understanding of homosexuality. Verdery, "Whither 'Nation' and 'Nationalism'?" 44.

65. This suggestion is advanced, for example, in more detail and with greater sophistication by Bernard Yack, "Nationalism and Liberal Individualism: Odd or Unhappy Couple?" Presented to the 1992 Convention of the American Political Science Association, Washington, D.C.

66. John Stuart Mill, "Considerations on Representative Government," in *Utilitarianism, On Liberty, and Representative Government,* ed. H. B. Acton (London: J. M. Dent, 1972), 394.

67. This fact has been stressed recently by a number of East-Central European commentators cautioning against raising the issue of border changes in the international community. See, for instance, Zoltán Fábián, "Politikai Rasszizmus és nacionalizmus," *Magyar Narancs,* July 1, 1993, and Oszkár Füzes, "Szomszédunk, Magyarország," *Népszabadság,* July 3, 1993: 12.

68. Richard Falk, "Evasions of Sovereignty," in *Contending Sovereignties: Redefining Political Community,* ed. R. B. J. Walker and Saul Mendlovitz (Boulder, Colo.: Lynne Rienner, 1990), 66.

69. The exceptions usually cited are Iceland, Norway, and Portugal. Uri Ra'anan, "Nation and State: Order out of Chaos," in *State and Nation in Multi-Ethnic Societies,* ed. U. Ra'anan, M. Mesner, K. Armes and K. Martin (Manchester: Manchester University Press, 1991), 4.

70. Todorov, *On Human Diversity,* 252.

71. Buchanan, *Secession,* 50.

72. Buchanan, *Secession,* 21; Craig Scott, "Dialogical Sovereignty" (unpublished manuscript).

73. Julie Mostov offers a powerful critique of ethnic criteria for citizenship in "Democracy and the Politics of National Identity," *Studies in East European Thought* 46 (1994): 9–31. A crucial factor in the slide of Yugoslavia toward war was the unwillingness of Croatia to convincingly guarantee its Serbian minority full citizenship rights.

74. The most comprehensive discussion of this issue is Buchanan, *Secession.*

75. For a recent defense of nationalism as being compatible with respect for others, see Yael Tamir, *Liberal Nationalism* (Princeton: Princeton University Press, 1993).

76. Francis Fukuyama, "Comments on Nationalism and Democracy," *Journal of Democracy* 3 (1992): 24.

77. See also Walzer, "The New Tribalism," 170.

78. The proposal to outlaw the Movement for Rights and Freedoms was narrowly defeated on judicial review. See Emil Konstantinov, "Turkish Party in Bulgaria Allowed to Continue," *East European Constitutional Review* 1 (Summer 1992): 11–12; Jon Elster, "On Majoritarianism and Rights," *East European Constitutional Review* 1 (Fall 1992): 19–24.

79. The most comprehensive discussion of such arrangements is Horowitz, *Ethnic Groups in Conflict.*

80. Donald Horowitz has argued that the consociational arrange-

ments championed most famously by Arend Lijphart have a tendency to exacerbate ethnic conflict by focussing all political competition along ethnic lines. Horowitz, *A Democratic South Africa? Constitutional Engineering in a Divided Society* (Berkeley: University of California Press, 1991). But Ian Shapiro has argued that the vote-pooling techniques strongly supported by Horowitz which ask voters to list second and third choices in an effort to encourage cross-national coalitions and campaigning will only work if voters pool their votes across, rather than within, ethnic lines. In fact, this form of electoral engineering is probably only really useful in situations in which ethnic groups are territorially demarcated, and the pooling has to occur across regions. Ian Shapiro, "Democratic Innovation: South Africa in Comparative Context," *World Politics* 46 (October 1993): 146–47.

81. Steiner, "Ideals and Counter-Ideals in the Struggle over Autonomy Regimes for Minorities."

82. See, for instance, David Binder, "Romanians and Hungarians Building a Bit of Trust," *New York Times,* July 20, 1993, and Alan Riding, "9 East Europe Nations to Join Round Table Talks," *New York Times,* May 28, 1994: A17.

83. For a very interesting discussion of these issues, see Scott, "Dialogical Sovereignty." See also Buchanan, esp. 21–22.

84. I borrow the phrase from Sándor Szilágyi's analysis of the sociologist István Bibó, whose essays (written from the 1940s to the 1960s) on such sensitive subjects as nationalism and anti-semitism offer an inspiring example of lucid social criticism combined with a courageous commitment to the fate of his country and its citizens. Sándor Szilágyi, "István Bibó, Central Europe's Political Therapist," in István Bibó, *Democracy, Revolution, Self-Determination* (Highland Lakes, N.J.: Atlantic Research and Publications and Columbia University Press, 1991), 527–46.

85. "More Humility, Fewer Illusions: A Talk between Adam Michnik and Jürgen Habermas," *New York Review of Books,* March 24, 1994, 28.

86. Vesna Pesic, speech accepting the Democracy Award of the National Endowment for Democracy, *Journal of Democracy* 14 (July 1993): 136–37.

87. Cf. the excellent suggestion made by Misha Glenny that the United States should support independent radio and television broadcasts and newspapers that contradict the massive disinformation campaign being waged in the Serbian press. Glenny, "Milosevic's Secret Weapon," *New York Times,* August 4, 1993, p. A32.

88. Will Kymlicka and Joseph Carens offer persuasive arguments

for this position using the example of Canadian native groups and of Fijians, respectively. Kymlicka, *Liberalism, Community, and Culture,* and Carens, "Democracy and Respect for Difference: The Case of Fiji," *University of Michigan Journal of Law Reform* 25: 3–5 (Spring and Summer 1992): 547–631.

89. Aristotle, *Nicomachaean Ethics,* bk. I, ch. 3, 12–14.

90. I borrow the metaphor from Henry Steiner, who pleaded for a recognition that we live in the "youth" of human rights in his review of Louis Henkin's *The Age of Rights.* Steiner, "The Youth of Rights," *Harvard Law Review* 104 (February 1991): 917–35.

12

THE WORLD HOUSE DIVIDED: THE CLAIMS OF THE HUMAN COMMUNITY IN THE AGE OF NATIONALISM

DEBRA SATZ

> Some years ago a famous novelist died. Among his papers was found a list of suggested plots for future stories, the most prominent underscored being this one: "A widely separated family inherits a house in which they have to live together." This is the great new problem of mankind. We have inherited a large house, a great "world house" in which we have to live together—black and white, Easterner and Westerner, Gentile and Jew, Catholic and Protestant, Moslem and Hindu—a family unduly separated in ideas, culture and interest, who, because we can never again live apart, must somehow learn to live with each other in peace.
>
> —Martin Luther King, Jr., "Where Do We Go from Here"

We live in a heterogeneous, diverse world. We differ from one another in virtue of our personal characteristics (e.g., sex, race, mental and physical abilities, vulnerabilities) and our social and cultural circumstances (e.g., country of birth, degree of national freedom and inequality). These differences are facts.

Facts require both explanation and interpretation to establish their moral significance. For example, if a particular cultural difference were the product of oppression and ignorance, rather than a natural consequence of the free exercise of rea-

My thanks to John Ferejohn, Andrew Levine, and Elisabeth Wood for discussion of the issues involved in this chapter.

son, we might not seek its accommodation. Instead, the waning of some cultural diversity might be a predictable, and not altogether lamentable, consequence of the struggle against injustice. Even if we mourned cultural diversity's passing, we might still think that a more homogeneous human community is an acceptable price to pay for ending oppression. Likewise, if the growth of a global economy really meant the end of starvation and famine, the threat it poses to the survival of local cultures justifiably might be considered of lesser importance. Facts alone can not comprise an answer to the question: what political and moral significance should we accord to our differences? How we answer that question will significantly shape our judgments about contemporary politics.

The affirmation of cultural and ethnic "difference" has become a primary focus for contemporary social movements. This is particularly true of movements centered around national identity. Elizabeth Kiss's chapter, "Five Theses on Nationalism" invites us to consider the political and moral status of *nationalist* differences from the standpoint of preserving and encouraging the ideal of humanity as a single moral community. This is an urgent and important question which, until recently, has been largely ignored by traditional political theory. Political theorists have tended to abstract from questions of membership and cultural diversity,[1] assuming a world with fixed borders. But we live in a culturally plural, multi-ethnic world populated with subordinated groups—poor people, women, and non-Europeans—who were not consistently part of liberal political theory's original emancipatory project. What values should we want our society to embody regarding relations between different groups, both in the national and international context?

Kiss offers an insightful and eloquent response to this question in which she attempts to reconcile the values of ethnic nationalism with those of our common humanity. By "ethnic nationalism" she means "a politics centered on identification with and allegiance to a collectivity whose members regard themselves as having a shared culture and history, focused around a common ethnic, racial, or geographic origin, language, or religion."[2] She argues that ethnic nationalism can be compatible with the moral claims of humanity, as codified in the language of human rights. There is, for her, no intrinsic incompatibility between human rights and ethnic nationalism. In her reconciliation project, Kiss uses a "minimal conception" of human rights as "a set of injunctions not to deprive human beings of the possibility of having a basic quality of life. These would include immunities from torture, arbitrary arrest, imprisonment, and killing; they [would] also include claims not to be deprived of the basic means of life."[3]

Concern and respect for these minimal human rights does not, according to Kiss, require denationalization. But it does require that we oppose attempts to elevate ethnic nationalism to a "principle of political order," in which ethnic groups determine questions of membership and boundaries. She persuasively argues that humanity's claims cannot be "operationalized" on the basis of a political order founded on the priority of ethnic nationalism.

The primary reason is that populations are "mottled." We are not only ourselves frequently people with multiple affiliations (e.g., African-American, Jewish-Hungarian, Gay-Latino), but we live amongst others with their own, different hyphenated self-descriptions. We can't establish our own ethnic group in our own national homes because our homes are already inhabited by others. The vast majority of the world's states are multi-national or culturally plural states. We must necessarily live amongst each other in multi-ethnic homes.

But living amongst is not living with. While I agree with much in Kiss's chapter, and find her five theses uncontroversial as stated, I will argue that nationalism is a more serious threat to the realization of humanity's claims than she allows. In particular, I will argue that (1) her definition of "ethnic nationalism" bypasses most of the troubling theoretical and political issues raised by a nationalist group's allegiance to a particular political state; (2) that the existence of sovereign national states creates difficulties for the institutionalization of human rights; and (3) that if we interpret human rights in a more expansive way than Kiss does (as I think we should),[4] the reconciliation project becomes more difficult to accomplish. The existence of sovereign nations and national borders blunts our ability to think about, as well as to redress, the subordination and inequalities which take place between nations. World inequality seriously threatens our ability to meet the claims of our common humanity.

Two Conceptions of Nationalism

Kiss begins her chapter by defining nationalism as a form of political identity in which individuals organize and promote the interests of their own group. In agitating for and promoting their own group's interests, a nationalist group can have a strong impact on political order: it can, for example, demand proportional representation in its country's sovereign bodies, recognition of its own schools and religion, and support for its culture's unique ways of living. But it does not necessarily seek to express its nationalism through allegiance and control of the official state apparatus.

What Kiss refers to as "ethnic nationalism" must therefore be sharply distinguished from what I will call *official or state-centered nationalism.* Ethnic nationalism is a phenomenon which bypasses the historical ties between nationalist movements and states. In doing so, it denudes nationalism of much of its appeal and also its danger. The emphasis on shared forms of culture and identity, even when understood as a political phenomenon, tends to evacuate questions of sovereignty and statehood from nationalism's center. This may be analytically justified, since strong "nationalist" sentiments can sometimes exist without finding expression in movements for state sovereignty,[5] but this conception of nationalism elides an important distinction between ethnicity and nationalism. Much of the power and promise of nationalism has rested on its claim to deliver sovereignty and self-legislation to the members of a cultural or ethnic community who are excluded from the dominant institutions of their country[6] or subordinated to the control of other nations.

I think that state-centered nationalism—which "nationalizes" cultural and ethnic identity—raises quite distinct problems from "ethnic nationalism." While Kiss's chapter opposes attempts to elevate ethnic nationalism to a political principle for settling questions of borders and membership, she fails to identify several specific problems which state-centered nationalism raises. State-centered nationalism poses particular problems because states are not simply one actor among others: they empower a sovereignty to act in the name of vast numbers of people. This is not generally the case with ethnicity: there is no Jewish organization which, for example, is empowered to act in my name simply because I am a Jew.

In classical liberal theory, the empowerment of a sovereign state was justified on the assumption that rational individuals would not voluntarily cooperate to provide themselves with basic public goods, in particular, the goods of social order and defense. States secure these goods through laws, and through a monopoly of the means of legitimate violence.[7]

Consider two problems which arise as the result of state-centered nationalism: First, how does the collectivity, the "nation," actually get its agent, the state, to carry out its will? There is a significant gap between the desires of the "principal" and their enactment by the "agent": the fact that everyone or most people want the state to do something does not make it so. There must be mechanisms by which the desires of the nation are translated into the actions of the state. But any such mechanisms will need to surmount at least three obstacles: (1) the state is a particular organization, which has its own distinct interests, including individuals with interests in the perpetuation of their own positions of power; (2) the state is vulnerable to the unequal power exercised by individuals in society: it can be captured by a well-organized minority; and (3) the "nation" is not itself a unified agent but a collection of diverse groups with conflicting interests who may not be able to converge on a set of political demands and thus may not be able to enforce state compliance with their (divided) will. These problems are exacerbated in ethnically and culturally divided societies.[8]

Second, even if sovereign national states managed to secure public goods for their members, in part through centralization and stabilization of their organization, coordination and collective action problems emerge on a world scale. States that are strong enough to solve their domestic collective action problems may threaten their neighbors. Sovereign states may thereby threaten global order. How then do we get sovereign states to cooperate in the global achievement of mutual security and defense?[9] Who bears the costs—in money and sometimes human life—of enforcing human rights laws? The United Nations and the World Court have been relatively unsuccessful at getting the most powerful nation-states to comply with their sanctions.[10] More seriously, nations have been left relatively free to interpret the meaning of human rights for their own purposes.

One solution to the problem of achieving international cooperation would be to create a world government, an international sovereign body. The construction of such a body, of course, raises extraordinarily complex issues about representation, organizational structure, and feasibility. It is also difficult to imagine the stability of such a body given the divergences in value which characterize the world's populations. Furthermore, the principal-agent problems I mentioned above may be exacerbated when the agent and the principal reside in distant and diverse circumstances. These are practical problems. But many theorists have rejected a form of world sovereignty on moral as opposed to pragmatic grounds.[11] The national state, they claim, is the most appropriate arena for the exercise of sovereignty: a people has a moral right to choose its own form of government, however defective that government from a moral point of view. Critics of the idea of a world government also worry that such a government would override the historical continuity of certain nations by enabling the whole world to choose their laws and institutions. Such a process would undermine the legitimacy of governments, which rests on the consent of the governed and not the views of outsiders.

While I am sympathetic to pragmatic defenses of national sovereignty, I believe that the moral justification of national sovereignty is flawed. In the first place, the fit between "a people " and the nation state is imperfect and often non-existent. Within almost any nation there are already diverse communities and cultures, which coexist (sometimes unhappily and in the presence of great injustice) with a unified government. There is no one-to-one correspondence, no way of identifying a nation with some unified and underlying ethnic or cultural community. There is no single people within most nations, and there are often oppressed minority groups. From the perspective of cultural and ethnic pluralism, structures which institutionalize identity on a supra-nationalist level may be preferable to nations. Supra-nationalist entities such as empires have been more conducive to securing certain human rights for minority groups than nations. For example, the status of minorities in both the Austro-Hungarian and Ottoman empires was, although far from ideal, superior to that of those same minority groups within the individual nation states which arose out of the breakup of those empires.

In the second place, consent is a complex idea. Even in relatively homogenous cultures we cannot assume that popular compliance with existing national arrangements signifies consent. Compliance can reflect many things, including fear, strategic judgment, or lack of knowledge about feasible alternatives. Given the diversity of reasons which can underlie "consent," we cannot assume citizens are deeply committed to their particular nation's form of government because they do not rebel. It is here, again, that facts require interpretation and causal knowledge. Moreover, this knowledge may not always be available to the members of a given nation. Sometimes, outsiders may be in a better position to gather information about the practices in a given country; sometimes outsiders are in a better position to redress a serious injustice.

A world government need not totally supersede national governments which rest on more local agreements, any more than a form of national government totally supersedes forms of state, local, and neighborhood organization. Any practical and desirable form of world government will share sovereignty with other institutions, including nations, and more local forms of association. Sovereignty is not an unbreakable atom; it can be, and generally is, pulled apart. Indeed, contemporary Europe is already moving toward trans-national forms of sovereignty.

Nationalism and Inequality

The existence of severe international inequality also places obstacles before the project of reconciling nationalism with our common humanity. The problem is exacerbated by the fact that the redistribution from rich countries which would be needed to ensure a decent standard of living for poor countries is massive. It is unlikely that individuals in rich countries would agree to the hardships that such redistribution would entail.

But what does nationalism have to do with world inequality? Nationalism, like other forms of community, encourages solidarity among its members. Solidarity requires identification. The existence of solidarity is arguably tied to the equitable treatment of individuals who are understood to be members of the same group. For example, the success of social democracy in Sweden has largely been attributed to its largely homogenous work force and culture. Conversely, racism and ethnic division has undoubtably played a role in the weakness of redistributive institutions in the United States.[12]

Of course, the evidence is far from conclusive as to whether or not local solidarity discourages more global forms of solidarity. Sweden, Norway, and Finland not only have significant national redistribution, but they also give greater amounts of aid to non-governmental agencies in the Third World than do their more culturally and ethnically diverse counterparts. Nevertheless, I believe that nationalism encourages directing distribution to the members of one's own group. The nonmembers of the national community are viewed as "strangers," they have no entitlements to share in the good fortunes of the nation. The idea that a person's entitlements do not reach beyond national boundaries raises a serious problem in light of the fact that the world's neediest people are most frequently strangers to the people who are in a position to do anything about it. But to take that fact seriously means thinking of many redistributive principles on supra-national lines.

Surely individuals can be members of diverse communities—they clearly are. Individuals can be parents, workers, women, and citizens simultaneously. Nonetheless, the roles people occupy and the values which support these roles have complex interrelationships. The value of caring for one's own children, for example, can stand in some tension with the value of treating individuals as equals. While parents can (and are expected to) love their children above all others, nepotism on the job is discouraged or outlawed. Complex mechanisms and forms of organization are needed to deal with such tensions. But in the case of international inequalities, we have few world-wide mechanisms of redistribution. Income transfers tend to take place largely within national borders which serve as a convenient obstacle to exclude those unlucky enough to be born somewhere else. National exclusion is especially troubling if one takes seriously the moral arbitariness of one's place of birth and the greater need experienced by people outside the few islands of wealth.

While egalitarians have focused their attention largely on domestic inequality, such inequality pales by comparison with that between North and South. Even if within each respective nation all citizens' incomes were equal, 75 percent of the present inequality in the world would continue to exist. In other words, 75 percent of inequality *is between nations, not within them.*[13] Without cross-national mechanisms of redistribution, mechanisms which surely compromise national sovereignty and nationalist ideologies, the project of reconciling humanity's claims with ethnic nationalism leaves one of the greatest stains on our common humanity largely untouched.

So Many Particulars

Kiss's chapter opens up the categories we need to address one of the most pressing problems in contemporary politics: that of the relationship between group membership, political order, and our common humanity. She insightfully argues that ethnic nationalism can not offer us a useful or compelling paradigm for constructing political order. Nevertheless, she holds out the hope that nationalist politics can be accommodated by a perspective which places priority on our common humanity, as expressed in the language of human rights. What differences we accommodate—and how—is a political and moral question. I share her view that despite our differences, members of the human species form a single, albeit "imagined" community.[14] But I do not find in her reconciliation project a clear way to get a handle on some of the troubling issues which arise when we take both nation-states and the inequality between them seriously. What justifies ethnic nationalism's exclusion of the needs and entitlements of others?

We live in a "world house" where only a fraction of the inhabitants have a decent standard of living and that standard can be maintained only by strict controls on immigration across national borders. Until the inequities between the fortunes of individuals, rooted in arbitrary facts such as place of birth and ethnicity are addressed, the work of reconciling ethnic nationalism with the common human status of all individuals remains undone.

NOTES

My thanks to John Ferejohn, Andrew Levine, and Elisabeth Wood for discussion of the issues involved in this chapter.

1. An important exception is Michael Walzer, *Spheres of Justice* (New York, Basic Books, 1983).

2. Elizabeth Kiss, "Five Theses on Nationalism," 290.

3. Kiss, "Five Theses," 297.

4. Indeed, it would seem that she does as well, for she writes that "the enormous cross-boundary inequalities in our world are difficult to defend" (298). Nevertheless, from the point of view of her reconciliation project, she excludes such questions on pragmatic grounds. Perhaps this narrowing of focus is inevitable, given the state of the contemporary world. Still, it must be underscored that a "reconciliation" which bypasses the crushing poverty of most nations, and which assumes strict controls on immigration, lies under a shadow. I take this up below.

5. Kiss cites the example of the Armenian community in Massachusetts.

6. State-centered nationalism takes many forms: sometimes the members of the "nation" have been defined biologically; sometimes culturally or linguistically; and in rare cases, through the allegiance of its members to shared principles. Nations have thus drawn their boundaries very differently as to who is and is not a stranger. For discussion, see Ernst Gellner, *Nations and Nationalism* (Oxford: Basil Blackwell, 1983); Liah Greenfield, *Nationalism: Five Roads to Modernity* (Cambridge: Harvard University Press, 1992).

7. Cf. Max Weber, *Economy and Society,* vol. 1, ed. G. Ross and C. Wittich (New York: Bedminster Press, 1968).

8. The current human ravages underway in Rwanda underscore the idea that liberalism has never adequately theorized the relationship between individuals, nationalism, and the nation state. Liberal theory has assumed, following Hobbes, that individuals are characterized by conflicting desires and so need to be constrained in their collective interest by a third party, i.e., by a political state. But consider the case of contemporary Rwanda, an example which turns liberal theory on its head.

Scholars and journalists report that there are no ascribed characteristics which mark Hutu from Tutsi (except for a variation in height), that these groups share a common language and ethnicity, and that for generations intermarriage was so common that "most people did not care who was Hutu and who was Tutsi." See Raymond Bonner, "Rwandan Villagers Fear Leaders, Not Neighbors," *New York Times,* Sunday, August 28, 1994, 3. (Note that the tribes originally occupied different areas and directed themselves to different types of labor.) The salient distinction between the two groups was economic, with the Tutsi controlling most of the country's wealth and excluding the Hutu tribe from power. In 1959, the Hutu rebelled and by 1962 had seized control of the state. Rather than protecting individuals with diverse desires and interests from each other, the Rwandan government (along with the earlier maneuvering of the colonial powers) found it useful to construct differences—preaching racial hatred—in the interest of securing its own power. The differences between Hutu and Tutsi have been *constructed by the state for its own ends.* The Rwandan state, in other words, has not constrained ethnic or group conflict but in fact given it moral and political significance.

9. For one type of answer as to how conditional cooperation between sovereign states is possible, see Kenneth Oye, ed., *Cooperation under Anarchy* (Princeton: Princeton University Press, 1986).

10. Cf. the failure of the World Court to effectively sanction the United States for the mining of Nicaragua's harbors.

11. Cf. Michael Walzer, "The Moral Standing of States: A Response to Four Critics," in *International Ethics,* ed. C. Beitz, M. Cohen, T. Scanlon, and A. J. Simmons (Princeton: Princeton University Press, 1985).

12. Cf. T. Sneeding, M. O'Higgins, and L. Rainwater, *Poverty, Inequality, and Income Distribution in Comparative Perspective* (Washington, D.C.: The Urban Institute, 1990). The authors report that the percentage of persons who are poor after taxation and transfer payments is

4.8 in Norway, 5.0 in Sweden, 6.0 in West Germany, 8.8 in the United Kingdom, 12.1 in Canada, and 16.9 in the United States.

13. Albert Berry et al., "Global Inequality and Its Trends since 1950," in *Economic Inequality and Poverty—International Perspectives,* ed. Lars Osberg (New York: Sharpe 1991), 60–91.

14. The human community is "imagined" because no logical argument can demonstrate our common humanity with others. It is a "leap of faith," a moral construct.

13.

FROM POST-LIBERALISM TO PLURALISM

JOHN GRAY

The liberal project was the project of specifying universal limits to the authority of government and, by implication, to the scope of political life. The task of liberal theory was to specify the principles, and sometimes the institutions, in which this universal limitation on political power was expressed and embodied. To be sure, as a species of the Enlightenment project, the liberal project was often associated with, and dependent on, an historical philosophy of progress, which affirmed that different political regimes were appropriate and legitimate in different historical circumstances. Nonetheless, the goal of liberal theory remained that of specifying principles for the limitation of political power which were universally authoritative in that they applied to the best regime for the entirety of humankind—if only in an unspecified future phase in the historical development of the species. It was acknowledged in liberal theory that the best regime might be unattainable in some historical milieux, and in such circumstances the task liberal thought set itself was that of providing a non-ideal theory of second-best arrangements, which approximated but did not try to meet the requirements specified for the ideally best regime. Again, liberal thinkers recognised that the institutional structure of the best regime might, and indeed would, legitimately vary in different historical contexts. Even where the best regime was attainable, its forms would properly vary, depending on their circumstances and antecedents. With these caveats, however, the goal of liberal theory was and—insofar as the liberal project still lingers on—remains, the articulation of principles for the limitation of governmental and political power that have universal authority.

This liberal project animates all recognisable liberal theorists, including the later Rawls, but it is most self-conscious and systematic in the greatest of them, John Stuart Mill. In Mill's work there is exemplified the paradigmatic liberal programme of stating "one very simple principle" (as he terms it in *On Liberty*) as governing the relations of state and society with the individual; this principle is defended by reference to a conception of man as a progressive being; and Mill makes entirely explicit his conviction that the principle he states is authoritatively applicable in all circumstances in which the species has emerged from barbarism.[1] Again, no doubt the principle will have novel applications, as circumstances, such as changes in technology, for example, throw up new contexts in which it must be applied. How Mill's principle of liberty, or harm principle, applies to the use of electronic bugging devices or long-distance cameras, or to new forms of video or computer-generated pornography, are obviously not questions that Mill could have answered, since such devices were unknown and unthought-of in Mill's time. If Mill's principle is to have the action-guiding force Mill demanded of it, however, it must have definite application in these new contexts. And, again, the applications of the principle will be universally authoritative, provided only that the society in which it is implemented is one that has emerged from barbarism. This liberal project, found prototypically in the work of John Stuart Mill, recurs in nearly all subsequent liberal thinkers. It informs Rawls's conception of the basic liberties, Feinberg's elucidation, restatement, and emendations of the Millian principle,[2] Dworkin's account of equality and rights, and many others.

The liberal project is open to the criticism, which I have developed in earlier work,[3] that the principles it issues in are subject to disabling indeterminacies, arising not merely from the open-texture of their central concepts, but more seriously from incommensurabilities among, and within, the values they invoke. These disabilities in the principles to which the liberal project has given rise are so serious, I have argued, to warrant its abandonment—the relinquishment of the universalist aspiration of liberal theory and the adoption instead of an historicist perspective on liberal institutions and practices. On this post-liberal view, the indeterminacies and incommensurabilities which afflict the principles articulated in liberal political philosophy are resolved, locally and provisionally, in a variety of recurrent political and juridical settlements achieved in the diversity of liberal regimes that are to be found in the real world of history. They are resolved in practice, typically in political practice, in settlements that vary from place to place and time to time. There is no overarching or synoptic normative theory from which these settlements can be derived—no delusive Archimedean point of privileged leverage whereby they can be generated. They arise, and are dissolved, in the contingencies and vicissitudes of practice. In this post-liberal perspective, the conflict of goods, their uncombinability and sometimes their incommensurability, is taken to be the central datum of political morality, and to support a form of theorising in which the ephemeral but real settlements achieved in political practice are preferred to the delusive harmonies of liberal philosophy.

In the work of Isaiah Berlin and of Joseph Raz, the competitive moral pluralism marked by these deep conflicts among goods is invoked to support a novel, and non-standard form of liberalism—what I have termed an agonistic liberalism.[4] What is most distinctive of this species of liberal theory is not its affirmation of the reality of rationally incommensurable values—which is a feature of standard or conventional liberalism of the Rawlsian variety—but its recognition that these incommensurabilities enter into liberal principles themselves and undermine the possibility of a comprehensive system of such principles. On this agonistic view, as on mine, conflicts within liberal political morality—conflicts among important liberties, say—cannot as a rule be decided by appeal to any theory or principle; they are decidable only in practice. Since it is characteristic of political practice, as distinct from that of law, that it issue in settlements that are open to renegotiation, embody compromises of interests and ideals, and carry no presumption of unique rational authority, agonistic liberalism is a genuinely *political* liberalism in a way that Rawlsian liberalism, in which political life is evacuated of virtually all substance, manifestly is not. This much is clear about the species of liberal theory we find, in markedly differing forms, in the work of Berlin and Raz. What is less clear is whether Berlin or Raz would follow me in the historicist move of theorising liberal institutions and practices as particular forms of life having no universal authority whatever.

For my present purposes, I will not at this stage in my argument pursue this last question, except to note my view[5] that from the truth of a plurality of incommensurable values the priority of one of them—liberty, autonomy, or choice-making, say—cannot follow. Value-pluralism cannot entail, or ground, liberalism in any general, still less universal way. The historical fact of a diversity of conceptions of the good, or of world-views, in a particular society may be a good reason for the adoption of liberal institutions in that society; but, if value-pluralism is true, the range of forms of genuine human flourishing is considerably larger than can be accommodated within liberal forms of life. As a matter of logic alone, it is safe to say that value-pluralism cannot mandate liberalism, where that is taken to be a theory or set of principles claiming universal authority. I will, towards the end of this chapter, consider how a fully pluralist position differs from the agonistic liberal standpoint I have attributed to Berlin and Raz. My present purpose is not, however, to argue that value-pluralism cannot entail liberalism, but instead to take this result as a starting point of a further inquiry—an inquiry into what forms of political order follow from acceptance of a strong form of value-pluralism.

In earlier work, defending a position I have termed post-liberal, I argued that the institutions characteristic of liberal civil society are most congenial to the truth of value-pluralism, at any rate in the historical circumstances in which we find ourselves.[6] This was, in effect, a quasi-Hegelian defence of what I called "the living kernel of liberalism," the historic inheritance of liberal civil society. Having interpreted liberalism as a system of ideas characterised by four values or theses—individualism, egalitarianism, universalism, and meliorism—I argued that, whereas these values or theses could not be shown to be rationally compelling, they re-emerge as features of the constitutive practices and institutions of liberal civil society. I specified the four defining features of *liberalism* as follows:

> First, there is the idea of *moral or normative individualism*—the idea that, since nothing has ultimate value except states of mind or feeling, or aspects of the lives of human individuals, therefore the claims of individuals will always defeat those of collectivities, institutions, or forms of life. . . . A second element in the liberal syndrome is *universalism*—the idea that there are weighty duties and/or rights that are owed to all human beings, regardless of their cultural inheritances or historical circumstances, just in virtue of their standing as human beings. . . . This second idea leads, naturally enough, to the third element in the liberal syndrome, namely *meliorism.* By this is meant the view that, even if human institutions are imperfectible, they are nonetheless open to indefinite improvement by the judicious use of critical reason. . . . The fourth and final element of the liberal syndrome issues intelligibly from the first three—liberal *egalitarianism.* By this is meant the denial of any natural moral or political hierarchy among human beings, such as was theorised by Aristotle in respect of slavery and by Filmer of absolute monarchy. For any liberal, in other words, the human species is a single-status moral community, and monarchy, hierarchy, and subordination are practices that stand in need of an ethical defence.[7]

Later in the same study, I argued,

> The four constitutive elements of liberalism as a doctrine . . . re-emerge as characteristics of civil society. The legal structure of a civil society is bound to be *individualist* since none of us is (in the jargon of recent communitarian theory) a radically situated self whose identity is constituted by membership of a single community. . . . Here individualism is affirmed, not as any set of universal normative claims about the species, but instead as a necessary feature of any modern civil society. . . . Similarly with *egalitarianism.* Though a civil society presupposes neither political nor economic equality, it does require equality before the law. For it is a necessary feature of a civil society that, just as no-one in it is above the law, so no-one is denied the protection of the law. . . . What of *meliorism?* . . . Within the history of any particular civil society . . . it makes sense to talk of improvement or decline and

> to frame projects of reform. . . . Discourse as to amelioration or decline will in general be governed by standards that are imminent in the specific histories and traditions of the diverse civil societies. . . . The *universalist* element of liberalism survives, not by civil societies converging on any single model, but in virtue of the universality, or near universality, of civil society itself as a condition of prosperity and peace for any modern civilisation.[8]

By *civil society* I had specified regimes having three features: I contrasted it with the *weltanschauung*-states of ancient and modern times, maintaining that

> In a civil society . . . diverse, incompatible and perhaps incommensurable conceptions of the good and the world can coexist in a peaceful *modus vivendi*. . . . A second feature of civil society is that, in it, both government and its subjects are constrained by *a rule of law*. . . . In any civil society, most social and political activities will take place in autonomous institutions that are protected by the rule of law but independent of government. . . . A third feature of civil society is the institution of private or several property. The importance of several property for civil society is that it acts as an enabling device whereby rival and possibly incommensurable conceptions of the good may be implemented and realized without recourse to any collective decision-procedure. . . . The central institution of civil society—the institution of private property—has its rationale as an *enabling device* whereby persons with radically discrepant goals and values can pursue them without recourse to a collective decision-procedure that would, of necessity, be highly conflictual.[9]

In this argument that the defining features of liberalism as a doctrine re-emerge as constitutive features of modern civil societies, I was concerned to stress the diversity of forms in which modern civil societies may be found. Civil societies need not be liberal democracies—neither Whig England nor, in our own times, Hong Kong or Singapore are such, though they clearly fit the model of civil societies I have sketched—and they need not possess democratic institutions of any other sort. Civil societies need not be, and in their East Asian examples are not, associated with the moral culture of individualism which informs them in their European, and more particularly their American varieties. Nor need the economic system of a modern civil society be that of market capitalism; in parts of the post-communist world, especially Russia, market institutions are emerging that differ in fundamental respects from those of Western capitalism. Nevertheless, I concluded that "On the view presented here, civil societies, in all their legitimate varieties, are the living kernel of what was 'liberalism.' "[10] This was the core of the post-liberal view argued for in my earlier work—that, whereas the foundationalist, universalist, or doctrinal claims of liberalism cannot be defended, the central elements of liberal political morality re-emerge as constitutive institutions or practices in modern civil societies. In other words, whereas any form of fundamentalist liberalism was rejected according to which liberal forms of life possess universal rational and moral authority, the post-liberal view affirmed the near-universality, in the late modern world, of varieties of civil society in whose institutions the elements of liberal political morality were preserved.

This post-liberal view seems to me now to be mistaken. It is mistaken in arguing that strong value-pluralism is, in contemporary historical circumstances, a good reason for the universal, or near-universal adoption of a Western-style civil society, in any of its varieties. In political milieux which harbour a diversity of cultural traditions and identities, such as we find in most parts of the world today, the institutional forms best suited to a *modus vivendi* may well not be the individualist institutions of liberal civil society but rather those of political and legal pluralism, in which the fundamental units are not individuals but communities. In polities that are plural or divided, the legal recognition of different communities, and of their distinct jurisdictions, may well be mandated on the Hobbesian ground that it promotes peace. It may be justified on another, independent ground—that it enables practitioners of distinctive cultural traditions to have these mirrored in the legal orders to which they are subject, without necessitating the secessionist struggles that are unavoidable if a single polity or human settlement which encompasses many peoples also has only a single legal order to which all are subject. Such legal pluralism is justifiable, in other words, not only on the Hobbesian rationale of promoting the peace, but also on the Herderian ground that it allows even peoples who are commingled in the same territories or human settlements to recognise their cultural identities in the legal orders to which they are subject. Such legal pluralism is, in fact, the institutional embodiment of the human need for strong forms of common life in circumstances of substantial cultural diversity. The pluralist standpoint which is here defended aims to answer the question: How may peace and common life be achieved, in historical milieux of great cultural diversity, such as our own?

This pluralist view has in common with the post-liberal position, for which I have hitherto argued, that it takes as a point of departure that the recent liberal ideal of the neutral state is indefensible. It is indefensible, partly because—as Raz has shown[11]—the ideal of neutrality with respect to rival conceptions of the good is itself incoherent. It is indefensible for another reason. The pluralism of values which is invoked, in Rawls and other recent liberal writers, to support the liberal ideal of neutrality, is the attenuated species of pluralism arising from diverse individual life-plans informed by personal conceptions of the good that may be rationally incommensurable. The variety of value-pluralism that is most salient in the context of the world today is not of this of this diluted and individualistic variety, but arises from the plurality of whole ways of life, with their associated moralities and often exclusionary allegiances. The liberal ideal of neutrality is a wholly inadequate response to this form of value-pluralism—the most important and challenging in current circumstances—because the conceptions of the good in which it is expressed resist legal privatisation—that relegation to the private sphere of voluntary association which would be their fate in the neutral state envisaged in recent liberal theory. The liberal ideal of neutrality is, in fact, a demand for the legal disestablishment of cultural traditions, which is to say, a denial of legal recognition to distinctive ways of life. To respond with liberal neutrality to rival demands for legal recognition from different ways of life is a classic example of liberal legalism. Legal pluralism seeks to meet this demand by the creation of a diversity of jurisdictions for the various communities, which—unlike the chimera of a neutral liberal state—is an achievable objective with numerous historical antecedents.

Though it has in common with it a rejection of the liberal legalist utopia of a neutral state, the pluralist view here advocated differs from the post-liberal position in that it does not presuppose, or entail, endorsement of the central institutions of Western civil society. A pluralist regime could exhibit the virtue of toleration with regard to different religions and world-views, according them full legal recognition, and yet be a *weltanschauung*-state. The Moorish kingdoms of medieval Spain and the contemporary Malaysian state are each of them Islamic polities, yet they practice toleration and indeed pluralism in religious matters. The United Kingdom retains an established Anglican church, yet few societies are as latitudinarian as contemporary Britain. Both the Roman and the Ottoman empires were exemplars of legal and religious pluralism, with the Ottoman *millet* system institutionalising legal recognition of the different religious communities, but in each there was an established faith or state cult. Of course, pluralist political orders will resemble civil societies far more than totalitarian states or fundamentalist regimes, in that, though they may be *weltanschauung*-states, they will not be animated by an overriding project of propagating a religion or ideology: any such objective will be subordinated to, or at the very least constrained by, concern for peace and common life among and within the various ways of life the pluralist order contains.

In earlier work, my conception of civil society was developed, in part, contrastively, by reference to regimes—totalitarian and fundamentalist regimes, for example—in which the distinction between the state and society has been obliterated. This contrastive understanding of civil society remains valid, but it is far from exhaustive of the varieties of regime we find in the world. Both civil society and totalitarianism are Western categories which capture Western-derived regimes;[12] and fundamentalism is best understood, in many contexts, as a reactive phenomenon, responsive to Westernisation. As the occidental ideologies continue to wane, and non-occidental cultures assert themselves in political terms, we may reasonably expect, as in earlier periods of history, to see a far wider range of regimes than can be captured in the Western category of civil society and its contraries. The forms in which the institution of property develops, and in which law develops—to take two further constitutive practices of Western civil society—may be expected to be various, and to be different in some important respects from their exemplars in Western civil societies. It is this diversity that the pluralist view aims to theorise.

The pluralist view takes deep cultural diversity to be a common historical occurrence and an ineradicable feature of many, indeed most contemporary societies. This brings out a decisive point of difference between the pluralist view of political order and that maintained by traditionalist or reactionary critics of liberalism. Such conservative critics of liberalism see political order as serving the Old Right project of restoring, or instituting, an "integral" or "organic" culture, and their policy with regard to cultural minorities is one that forces on them alternatives of assimilation or exclusion from the political order. It is unclear if such a contemporary theorist of the Old Right as Roger Scruton would accept this characterisation of his standpoint, but that it has points of affinity with Maurrasian integralist nationalism, say, seems undeniable.[13] The pluralist rejects this Old Right project for the same reason he rejects the Enlightenment project.[14] Both seek to roll back the reality of cultural diversity for the sake of an imaginary condition of cultural unity—whether that be found in a lost past or in a supposed future condition of the species in which cultural difference has bee marginalised in a universal civilisation. Both perspectives are alien to that of the pluralist, which takes the reality of cultural difference as a datum of political order.

A pluralist political order may nevertheless deviate from the central institutions of a liberal civil society at crucial points. It need not, and often will not possess an individualist legal order in which persons are the primary rights-bearers. The principal bearers of rights (and duties) in a pluralist political order will be communities, or ways of life, not individuals. Of course, many pluralist political orders will possess mixed legal systems, and legitimately so: the legal system of contemporary India, for example, is partly the individualist, secular one inherited from the British, partly Islamic, and partly Hindu, with the differences focussing, not unnaturally, on the law of marriage and the family, and conflicts of jurisdiction are not uncommon.

That there should be such mixed systems, which stop short of full legal pluralism, is unavoidable and in many contexts desirable on pluralist grounds. Equally—anticipating a familiar liberal objection—there will sometimes be a good question as to how ways of life are to be individuated so as to make their legal recognition workable. This will plainly be an issue where intermarriage is common between members of different cultural groups, and where plural inheritances are otherwise common. It will also be a question where, in a society divided on religious lines, one or more of the religions permits or encourages conversion, as with Islam in contemporary India (where there is significant conversion from the Hindu caste of untouchables). In most, if not all pluralist political orders, there has been legal provision for migration from community to community, and for those with plural inheritances. There remains still a fundamental difference between liberal civil societies in which individuals are the primary rights-bearers and pluralist orders which vest most rights and duties in communities.

It is important to note that, from the standpoint of pluralist theory, whether a pluralist political order is appropriate is itself a matter of time, place, and circumstance. It is far from being a consequence of pluralist theory that pluralist political orders are everywhere legitimate, necessary, or desirable. In societies with strong individualist traditions and very high levels of interpenetration of cultural traditions, such as the United States, a liberal civil society, whatever its social costs and however reformed, is the only real historical option, no matter what radical communitarians may wish. Equally, liberal civil institutions are clearly appropriate in a society, such as contemporary France, which is multi-ethnic but (unlike the United States) successfully monocultural, or (like contemporary Australia, but again unlike the United States) which is successfully multicultural. In the countries of the European Union, as presently constituted, the institutions of a liberal civil society accord both with long-standing cultural traditions and with contemporary needs. The central proposition of pluralist political theory, which is that different legal and political institutions are desirable and legitimate in different cultural and historical milieux, itself entails that liberal regimes should sometimes be legitimate.

The unit and constitution of a pluralist political order will also properly vary with time, place, and circumstance, according to the pluralist view. In contexts in which a viable national political culture exists and has allowed at least a partial transcendence of ethnic allegiances, the appropriate unit may be the sovereign nation-state, with many functions devolved to regional and local levels. Where commonalities of cultural tradition and economic development are present, supranational associations of such sovereign states may come into being—though we may be sure that such projects as that of a federal superstate in Europe will remain utopian owing to the lack, in any future that is foreseeable or even imaginable, of a transnational European political culture. Where ethnic allegiances prove stronger than a shallow or deformed national culture, and where the non-territorial jurisdictions of legal pluralism are not acceptable to peoples whose mutual relations are ruled by suspicion or enmity, as in former Yugoslavia, there may be no realistic alternative to the construction of ethnically based sovereign states. In this last case, the worst from both a liberal and a pluralist perspective, political practice is likely to give way to war as it becomes increasingly clear that the terms of a political settlement will themselves be substantially determined by the military balance of forces. In some contexts, such as that of the Russian Federation, it is at least arguable that the human costs—in terms of the brutalities of war and the atrocities of "ethnic cleansing"—of setting up sovereign nation-states in territories of long commingled human populations which have never known nationhood may be so vast and terrible as to mandate a neo-imperial regime in which a Hobbesian peace is kept among the rivalrous peoples. The vital point here is that pluralist theory is open as to the form of state organisation—sovereign nation-state, confederal or federal union, or empire—best able in any given historical context to embody the pluralist regime of a peaceful *modus vivendi* among different cultural traditions, ways of life, and peoples.

The pluralist view is permissive and open, also, about the internal constitution of an acceptable regime. It need not contain democratic institutions, nor the institutions of a Western-style civil society. As I understand it, the project currently underway in China is that of developing market institutions, having many features that distinguish them from Western exemplars, *without* the apparatus of democracy or a Western-style civil society. The project may fail; but, if it does, it will be as a result of historically familiar problems of state disintegration in China, not because all polities are fated to converge on Western norms of democracy or civil society. Contrary to the ideologues of the New Right, nothing in the project of constructing or developing market institutions commits anyone to the adoption of the institutions of democracy or civil society.[15] Whether democratic institutions are mandated is, on the pluralist view, a matter of time, place, and circumstance, not of universally authoritative principle. The pluralist standard of assessment of any regime is whether it enables its subjects to coexist in a Hobbesian peace while renewing their distinctive forms of common life. By this standard, the current regime in China might well be criticised for its policies in Tibet; but such a criticism would invoke the intrinsic value of the communities and cultural forms now being destroyed in Tibet, not universalist conceptions of human rights or democracy. The practical and political implications of such a criticism, though they might be radical, would still be very different from those, commonplace in Western countries, which attack the current Chinese regime because it refuses—rightly, in my view—to accept Western norms and practices as authoritative in China.[16] On the pluralist view, there is no democratic project that has authority for all peoples and all circumstances. Like other political institutions, democracy is a convenient device, whose usefulness turns on its contribution to peace and the renewal of valuable forms of common life.

The pluralist view defended here involves the abandonment, not only of any democratic project, but also of the liberal project, even as that is found in such agonistic liberal theorists as Berlin and Raz. The liberal project of stating, and enforcing, universal limits on governmental power, especially when it is coercive, amounts to the prescription that a single form of political order be everywhere installed regardless of the cultural traditions and ways of life of its subjects. That political orders should be vessels for the transmission of ways of life across the generations, and that the forms of government may legitimately vary according to the cultures of the peoples they serve, are propositions rejected by all liberals, new and old. Yet they are implied by strong value-pluralism—especially by its deepest, in which the most radical form of value-conflict is not the competitive moral pluralism which arises when individual life-plans or conceptions of the good express incommensurable values, but rather that which occurs in conflicts between whole ways of life, each with their characteristic, and often exclusionary excellences, virtues, and goods. The pluralist position I have sketched here is, in part, merely an elaboration of one of the implications of this value-pluralist insight—namely, the implication that, if there are ways of life embodying genuine forms of human flourishing that require as their matrices non-liberal social and political structures, then a pluralist moral theory which recognises such forms of human flourishing must be complemented by a pluralist political theory, which recognises as legitimate forms of political order that are not, and will never become, liberal. Standard or conventional liberal thought, as it is found prototypically in the work of Rawls, resists this result, because in it value-pluralism is trivialised and banalised. In its conventional liberal uses, the pluralism of values refers to incommensurabilities arising among and within individual plans of life and personal conceptions of the good, but not to those which arise in the relations of whole ways of life, and liberal principles themselves are supposedly insulated from incommensurabilities arising within and among personal conceptions of the good. If, on the other hand, value-pluralism is not so banalised and trivialised, if it is seen as applying to whole ways of life and as infecting (and disabling) the so-called principles that are articulated in liberal political philosophy, then liberalism itself is undermined. In short, to follow through on the implications of strong value-pluralism inexorably entails relinquishing the liberal project.

Even non-standard or agonistic liberalism is not immune to the subversive force of value-pluralism. There is a tension in the agonistic liberalisms of Berlin and Raz, insofar as they aim to give reasons for according a universal or general priority over other political goods to their differing conceptions of freedom. Berlin's claim that collective well-being, equality, and liberty, for example, are irreducible and incommensurable values is not easily reconciled with the claim he sometimes also makes that freedom—in his preferred conception of negative liberty—is to be accorded a general, though never absolute priority over other ultimate values. In Raz, the priority accorded to autonomy within his perfectionist liberalism is thoroughly problematic. In Raz's account, autonomy derives its value from its status as an ingredient in human flourishing in certain definite social and cultural milieux—those, such as our own (according to Raz), that are characterised by high levels of social and occupational mobility, in which skills of choice-making are functionally indispensable. This is a functional explanation of the value of autonomy, which is nearly indistinguishable from a merely instrumental account;[17] and it is difficult to see how such a radically contextualised, and historicised, view of autonomy, in which autonomy is elevated to the central position in liberal political morality, can be squared with the universalist claims that go with traditional liberalism, or with the strong claims Raz makes for the role of a liberal state in promoting autonomy.[18] If the autonomous life is not in itself better than other forms of life—as Raz has himself rightly stressed[19]—and it makes a vital contribution to a distinct mode of human flourishing only in certain definite social milieux, then it seems reasonable to promote it only insofar as the benefits in terms of human well-being Raz claims for it are clear. Here the empirical record looks a good deal more equivocal than Raz allows. It is in particular far from clear that Asian immigrants, whose cultural traditions do not valorize autonomy, do worse—from the standpoint of individual well-being—than representative members of liberal societies which do so valorize it. Indeed the opposite case could be made, from the available evidences, with equal, or greater conviction: that such cultural groups are doing as well, or better, than most in the liberal societies in which they have formed enclaves. There seems to be a tension, perhaps ineradicable in Raz's liberalism, between the radically historicised and contextualised account of autonomy he advances and the central and dominating role he wishes autonomy to have in political morality.

The upshot of the dominant role autonomy plays in Raz's liberalism—explicitly in his major work, if less unequivocally in later writings[20]—is that a liberal society must be a monocultural society, at least with respect to the mores required by autonomy. Here, I think Raz has grasped a point of fundamental importance, perceived by Mill but not by Rawls—that a liberal state cannot be neutral with regard to illiberal forms of life coming within its jurisdiction. Or, to put the matter still more shortly, Raz is entirely correct in seeing liberalism itself as a whole way of life, and not merely a set of political principles or institutions. The trouble is that, if value-pluralism is true at the level of whole ways of life, then the liberal form of life can have no special or universal claim on reason. This is a difficulty that besets Berlin's liberalism also, even though it resists elevating autonomy to a central or dominating place in liberal morality, since it accords a parallel role to negative liberty. In both cases the liberal project, which is pursued *sotto voce* in their writings, is undermined by the value-pluralism which they also espouse.

The pluralist view here defended cannot but be anathema to fundamentalist or doctrinal liberals. It must be so, in that it repudiates the universalist pretensions of liberal theory, together with the Enlightenment philosophy of history—of the desirability of ultimate cultural convergence on a universal civilisation—on which liberal universalism reposes. It must be so, again, in that the forms a pluralist *modus vivendi* may legitimately assume are not dictated by pluralist theory, but are settled—if at all—in political practice. Agonistic liberal theory, as I understand it, seeks to show that the liberal form of life has a superior claim on reason arising from its supposed tolerance of value-pluralism. This was the view I myself held, and termed post-liberal.

The present discussion has aimed to take our inquiry one step further—from an agonistic liberal, or post-liberal position, in which liberal institutions and practices are commended for their hospitality to forms of moral diversity marked in value-pluralism, to a pluralist view, in which liberal forms of life enjoy no special privileges of any kind.

NOTES

1. J. S. Mill, *On Liberty,* in John Stuart Mill, *On Liberty and Other Essays,* edited by John Gray (Oxford: Oxford University Press, 1991), 13–14.

2. I have offered a critical assessment of Feinberg's restatement of Millian liberalism in my book, *Post-Liberalism: Studies in Political Thought* (London: Routledge, 1993), chapter 16.

3. See my paper, "Agonistic liberalism," *Social Philosophy and Policy* 12(1995): 111–135. and "What Is Dead and What Is Living in Liberalism" in my book, *Post-Liberalism: Studies in Political Thought,* chapter 20. An earlier version of some of these arguments is developed in "After Liberalism," in my book, *Liberalisms: Essays in Political Philosophy* (London: Routledge, 1989), chapter 12.

4. See my paper, "Agonistic liberalism," above. I have discussed Berlin's version of agonistic liberalism more comprehensively in my book, *Berlin* (London: HarperCollins, Fontana Modern Master, 1995).

5. I develop an extended argument for this view in the last chapter of my book, *Berlin.*

6. I argue this in my paper, "What Is Dead and What Is Living in Liberalism."

7. *Post-Liberalism: Studies in Political Thought,* 286–87.

8. Ibid., 319–20.

9. Ibid., 314–15.

10. Ibid., 318.

11. J. Raz, *The Morality of Freedom* (Oxford: Clarendon Press, 1986).

12. I discuss the contrastive relations between civil society and totalitarianism in my essay, "Totalitarianism, reform, and civil society," collected in my book, *Post-Liberalism: Studies in Political Thought,* 156–95.

13. For a good statement of his criticism of liberalism, see Roger Scruton, "In Defence of the Nation-State," in *Ideas and Politics in Modern Britain,* edited by J. C. D. Clark (London: Macmillan, 1990).

14. I have criticised the Old Right project of cultural fundamentalism in my monograph, *The Undoing of Conservatism* (London: Social Market Foundation, 1994), reprinted in my book, *Enlightenment's Wake: Politics and Culture at the Close of the Modern Age* (London and New York: Routledge, 1995).

15. I develop an extended critique of the political thought of the New Right in my book, *Beyond the New Right: Markets, Government and the Common Environment* (London and New York: Routledge, 1993).

16. I have discussed the situation in China, a little more systemati-

cally and comprehensively, in my monograph, *The Post-Communist Societies in Transition: A Social Market Perspective* (London: Social Market Foundation, 1994), reprinted in my book, *Enlightenment's Wake: Politics and Culture at the Close of the Modern Age* (London and New York: Routledge, 1995).

17. On this, see B. Parekh, "Superior People: The Narrowness of Liberalism from Mill to Rawls," *Times Literary Supplement,* February 25, 1994.

18. See J. Raz, *The Morality of Freedom* (Oxford: The Clarendon Press, 1986).

19. In his reply to his critics. See Joseph Raz, "Facing Up: A Reply," *University of Southern California Law Review* 62 nos. 3 and 4, (March–May 1989): 1227 ff.

20. I refer in particular to Raz's article, "Multiculturalism," published in *Dissent* (Spring 1994), in which the strongly assimilationist position he had adopted in respect of illiberal cultural enclaves within a broader liberal society is tempered and qualified.

PART III
POLITICAL CULTURE

14

DEMOCRATIC AUTONOMY AND RELIGIOUS FREEDOM: A CRITIQUE OF *WISCONSIN V. YODER*

RICHARD J. ARNESON AND
IAN SHAPIRO

Democratic politics is constitutionally at odds with paternalism and political hierarchy. For centuries democratic theorists have studied how to structure public institutions so as to diminish inegalitarian power relations, and how to equalize voting power among diverse citizenries in the selection of public officials. Relatively little attention has been paid, however, to what democracy requires of the institutions that make up civil society. This is most notably true of religious and familial institutions which are often—and perhaps in some respects inescapably—hierarchical and inegalitarian in character. This lack of democratic theoretical attention to the structure of civil institutions derives from several sources, prominent among them the preva-

For helpful comments, we wish to thank Amy Gutmann, Steven Macedo, Joseph Raz, Stephen Schiffrin, and participants in Yale's Political Theory Workshop. A version of this chapter was presented at the September, 1992 American Political Science Association meeting, and we wish to thank members of the audience and co-symposiasts Michael Perry and Jeremy Waldron for helpful criticism.

lence of the liberal view that civil institutions form the private sphere that is, or at any rate ought to be, "beyond politics."

In recent years the feminist and communitarian critiques of liberalism have rendered its public versus private dichotomy problematical, if not obsolete. The way is now open for normative reflection by political theorists on the structure of civil institutions.[1] In this essay we take up a small piece of the newly uncovered terrain: we explore the limits of parents' authority in the education of children who have been committed to their charge. Our use of this formulation, rather than parents' authority over "their children," prefigures one of the central claims that we seek to defend and employ: that the relationship between parents and their children is best thought of as one of trusteeship; children are in no sense the property of their parents. Although most people will find the claim thus stated unexceptionable, and few would go so far as to describe their children as their property, it will emerge from our discussion that many of the convictions to which people find themselves drawn in thinking about the authority of parents over children reflect the archaic idea that the child is the chattel of the parent (which once went hand-in-hand with the patriarchal idea that the wife is the chattel of the husband).

It is beyond the scope of our discussion to develop and defend a general theory of parent-child relations. We restrict ourselves, rather, to the specific issue of what the theory of constitutional democracy requires when parents and public officials find themselves in conflict over the compulsory education of children for whom they have overlapping responsibilities. This was the issue presented in *Wisconsin v. Yoder,* decided in 1972 by the United States Supreme Court in favor of Old Order Amish parents, who wanted to remove Amish children from the Wisconsin schools after eighth grade (at age fourteen) in violation of a statutory requirement of compulsory education to age sixteen.[2] The court's decision was something of an outlier in American constitutional jurisprudence: the result was unexpected, and, although it has never been overruled, it has not become a precedent for a general expansion of the domain of parental authority at the expense of the public law of child-rearing. Courts (including the Supreme Court) have tended to limit *Yoder* to its idiosyncratic facts, seeming to avoid opportunities to entrench it or to expand its reach.

Yet the *Yoder* case is a useful vehicle for reasoning about the implications of democratic theory for adult-child relations because of the stark and specific manner in which parental and public authority over children clashed, and because the conflict involved religious freedom as well as the education of children. Whatever our differing moral intuitions about compulsory education taken on its own, few would seriously deny that a substantial degree of religious autonomy of citizens from the state is an important value in a modern democracy. As a consequence, parents' claims that state authority in the education of children should be limited are likely to be especially weighty when their free exercise of religion is implicated in, and supplies the basis for, their arguments. If one is going to argue on democratic grounds, as we do here (in sections III–IV), that the parents' claims should not displace a democratic state's requirement of compulsory education to an age when critical reason is developed and can be fully deployed, then the religious arguments of the kind put forward by the Amish parents are perhaps the most difficult to answer. Answering them is the burden we take on here in arguing that *Yoder* was wrongly decided. In discharging it we hope to render plausible and attractive a fiduciary model of adult-child relations in a democracy that may prove useful in other contexts. Following a discussion of the context of the *Yoder* litigation, what was at issue, and why the result might initially seem attractive from the standpoint of democratic constitutional theory we turn, in section II, to an examination of democratic citizenship and the logic of its requirement of compulsory education to an age where critical reason is developed and can be fully deployed. In section III, drawing on Locke's discussion in the *Two Treatises,* we sketch and defend a fiduciary model of parent-child relations. In parts IV through V we make the case that this model requires a rejection of the Amish parents' free exercise claims and the acceptance by them of a responsibility to develop the critical reason of their charges, even if this threatens the existence of the Amish community from whence they come. In a final section, we draw out some of the implications of analysis of the *Yoder* problem for a democratic theory of civil institutions.

I. *Wisconsin v. Yoder*: The Dispute and Its Implications

Context of the Yoder *Litigation*

The Amish in North America live in self-contained and relatively self-sufficient communities, mainly in Pennsylvania, the Midwest, and Ontario. Their ancestors were the Anabaptists of sixteenth-century Europe whose founder, Joseph Ammann, split from the mainstream of the Swiss Anabaptist church in the 1690s. They do not seek to proselytize, and they have no desire to bring an Amish state into existence. Indeed, since they conceive of themselves as a voluntary community which members are always free to leave (and from which they can be expelled and "shunned"), they are dependent on the existence of a non-Amish outside world. They reject the modern world in all its essentials, preferring a simple agricultural or semi-agricultural life geared to a subsistence existence. Their *Ordnung,* or blueprint for expected behavior, governs all public, private, and ceremonial life. It prescribes the distinctive but unostentatious Amish dress and diet. It specifies their religious rituals, patriarchal family structure, and austere work habits, and among other things it proscribes the use of mechanized farming equipment, ownership of cars, conveniences in the home, participation in worldly public organizations, filing lawsuits, military service, divorce, all jewelry, air transportation, and high school education.[3]

Over a fifth of the children leave the community before adulthood, and very few non-Amish adults ever join. Yet, unlike the Amish communities of Europe that have long been extinct, the North American communities have thrived and expanded, growing from about 3,700 living in 22 church districts in 1890 to over 85,000, living in 526 districts, in 1979. This rapid expansion of between 30 and 48 percent per decade is accounted for by their high birth rate; the average Amish family has seven children.[4]

The Amish people's conception of their community as voluntary extends to their treatment of children. Like other sects of Anabaptist origin, they reject the doctrine of infant baptism.[5] In the Amish view, sin enters the world with a knowledge of good and evil which is unavailable to a young infant; not having sinned, children do not need baptism for the removal of sin. Thus, although Amish children are governed by the *Ordnung,* they do not become members of the church until they choose to be baptized—usually in late adolescence. The vow of baptism "embodies the spiritual meaning of becoming an Amish person, an acceptance of absolute values, and a conscious belief in religious and ethical ends entirely for their own sake, quite independent of any external rewards." It includes total submission to the authority of the Amish church, an implied promise to abide by all Amish rules, and it cannot be reversed. Whereas those who leave the community without taking the vow are not "shunned," those who take it and fail to live up to it are excommunicated from the church, and members of the community will have nothing more to do with them.[6]

Although the Amish believe that the vow of baptism must be taken voluntarily by a mature person, they go to great lengths in designing their system of education and acculturation to ensure that Amish children will take the vow and join the church. Herein lies the source of the half-century of conflict between the Amish and secular educational authorities that culminated in the *Yoder* decision. The Amish educational system is designed to prepare children for life in the Amish community, not the outside world. To this end, the Amish try to shield children from the secular world, and they actively discourage critical questioning of Amish values and beliefs. They are particularly opposed to high school education, which they see as threatening to their entire way of life. By age fourteen, the Amish child knows everything necessary to live successfully in the Amish community; as a result the Amish oppose further schooling, preferring on-the-job vocational training that will ease children into the community.

Amish acculturation practices have led even so sympathetic a commentator as Donald Kraybill to observe that in many respects Amish youth do not enjoy a genuine choice as to whether or not to enter the community. He goes so far as to suggest that by allowing adolescents a few flings with worldliness before they have to confront the baptismal choice, the Amish create an appearance of choice where for many there is no such thing in fact. By the time of the choice, Amish adolescents have been so "thoroughly immersed in a total ethnic world with its own language, symbols, and world view," that to leave would involve a traumatic severing of all their significant friendships. For the great majority who join the church, "the illusion of choice" serves an important function in adult life. "Thinking they had a choice as youth, adults are more likely to comply with the demands of the *Ordnung*."[7]

Since the 1930s, conflicts between the Amish and secular authorities have surfaced whenever compulsory education requirements have seemed to Amish leaders to jeopardize their acculturation program. In 1937 in East Lampner, Pennsylvania, legislation was passed lengthening the school year and increasing the age of compulsory schooling to age fifteen—a prelude to the issues that would fuel the confrontation in *Wisconsin v Yoder*. This produced a flurry of opposition from the Amish, who insisted that the proposed changes would "lead our children away from the faith." The following year, writing to the Pennsylvania Attorney General, Amishman Stephen Stolzfus demanded to know "Why can't the Board of Public Instruction show us leniency and exempt our children when they have a fair education for farm and domestic work? If we educate them for businessmen, doctors and lawyers they will make no farmers."[8] So strongly do the otherwise placid Amish feel on this issue that some have been prepared to go to prison rather than accede to the law's requirements. Other tactics that have been used to keep children out of public high schools include having them repeat eighth grade, or holding them back from first grade so that by the time they reach high school the compulsory age requirement is moot.[9]

The 1937–38 conflict abated after the Amish received a partial exemption from the statutes in question, enabling most children to avoid compulsory high school education. The Amish also began creating, and staffing, their own schools in response to the controversy. Although these schools do not meet the criteria for state certification, state officials have tended to be skittish about withholding it. Perhaps taking the path of least resistance they have adopted a stance of "benign neglect" toward the Amish schools.[10] The unavoidable collision that came about in Wisconsin was the result of the state's decision to enforce legislation requiring compulsory education to age sixteen at a time when the public high school system was being regionalized and consolidated. Attending the public high schools would thus have made mingling in the non-Amish world and confronting secular ideas unavoidable for the Amish teenagers; as a result the Amish leadership opposed the compulsory school requirement. This resulted in the *Yoder* litigation, which found its way to the U.S. Supreme Court in its 1971–72 term.

Logic of the Yoder *Decision*

The opinion of the Court in *Yoder* held that the interests served by Wisconsin's compulsory education law—preparing citizens for effective and self-reliant adult life and social participation—were sufficiently served by the proposed course of action of the Old Order Amish parents. The Amish wished to withdraw their children from the public schools and train them informally in the community (though not in private community schools) for rural life in accordance with Amish religious precepts. These include eschewal of participation in the wider political and legal order, rejection of modern technology and consumer society, and affirmation of a traditional and ascetic way of life that revolves around primitive but effective farming. The Court stressed that it was not dealing "with a way of life and mode of education by a group claiming to have recently discovered some 'progressive' or more enlightened process for rearing children for modern life." In his opinion for the Court, Chief Justice Burger attributed great importance to the fact that the Amish parents were sincere, that they were acting on the basis of a long-established and deep religious conviction, "shared by an organized group and intimately related to daily living."[11]

The Amish parents had contended that the compulsory education statute threatened not only the free exercise of Amish religion, but the very existence of the Amish community. The basis of this claim was their experience that it was after eighth grade that Amish children in the public schools were most likely to develop the desire to leave the Amish community, and act on it. The Court regarded this contention as decisive, "that enforcement of the State's requirement of compulsory formal education after the eighth grade would gravely endanger if not destroy the free exercise of respondents' [the parents'] religious beliefs." The Amish parents indicated that they would not seek to remove their children from the public schools prior to the eighth grade, and some of the justices made it clear that they would find differently were that issue presented. But they accepted as legitimate the Amish conception of education as "preparation . . . for life in the separated agrarian community that is the keystone of the Amish faith," concluding that compulsory education of Amish children beyond the eighth grade was unnecessary, and that as a result the Amish parents were henceforth immune from criminal prosecution for violating the relevant parts of the state of Wisconsin's compulsory education law.[12]

Considerations from Democratic Theory

At first sight the *Yoder* decision might seem attractive from a civil society–centered democratic perspective; the decision was expressly crafted to preserve a viable community that is part of America's pluralistic political heritage. A commonplace of democratic theory since de Tocqueville at least has been that in the modern world a well-functioning democratic political order requires a rich array of civil institutions that operate with relative autonomy from the state, and to some extent in competition with it as a source of values in the culture. True, the Amish community is scarcely itself a paradigm of democracy, but democratic theorists of the relations between civil society and the state have often placed greater weight on the functional importance for democracy of a rich diversity of overlapping civil institutions than on the internal character of those institutions.

De Tocqueville went so far as to suggest that in a democracy, where political equality is the norm, hierarchical civil institutions might offer certain advantages for the authoritative allocation of values. Among contemporary theorists, Michael Walzer insists that although a democratic civil society "is one controlled by its members," this condition does not require that institutions of civil society themselves be internally democratic. According to Walzer, that civil society associations have the capacity to act as shields limiting the domination of state power is intrinsically beneficial to democracy.[13]

This pluralist functional case for the importance of diverse civil institutions in a democracy has a venerable twentieth-century history in American political science, beginning with attempts by the so-called group theorists of American politics in the early twentieth century, of whom Arthur Bentley is perhaps the best known.[14] "For every group an interest, for every interest a group" was their theoretical slogan. They were followed, in the 1950s and 1960s, by the pluralist theorists, who sought to confirm the old group theorists' claim on the basis of a series of empirical studies of American cities that were alleged to show that decision-making power was widely dispersed.[15] But it was in Louis Hartz's *The Liberal Tradition in America,* published in 1955, that the implications of pluralism were first explored systematically. Initially, Hartz wanted to explain why there has never been a powerful socialist tradition in American politics. His answer to this question turned on the claim that in contrast to European societies, which had exhibited a *single-cleavage* between the propertied classes and the rest, America lacked the effects of a feudal past. Hartz portrayed America as a *multiple-cleavaged* society, where there is no basic or enduring division of the socio-economic landscape.[16]

Leaving to one side the much-debated question of how accurately Hartz portrayed the distinctive features of American politics, his distinction between single- and multiple-cleavaged societies has become one of the conceptual building blocks of pluralist democratic theory. The more a society approaches the multiple-cleavaged model, the less likely destabilizing revolutionary change becomes, according to the theory. If I am opposed to you on one issue, but also know that I may be allied with you against another coalition of forces on some future issue, I have an incentive to moderate my opposition to you and search for common ground. No minority ever reaches that proverbial state of affairs where its members have "nothing to lose but their chains." Generalizing this, pluralist theorists have argued that building and sustaining a social landscape made up of cross-cutting cleavages reinforces pluralist-democratic stability.[17]

The pluralist functional standpoint might be thought to support broad tolerance of Amish practices, on the ground that flourishing civil society associations promote the stability of democratic institutions. Indeed, there is special reason to let alone the withdrawing Amish, who do not aim to lasso state institutions in order to achieve their goals. They have interests in common with other groups who favor a heavily decentralized educational system (though they differ with them on other issues); there is no danger of their pushing the nation further in the direction of a single-cleavaged society. But even if a rich diversity of civil associations promotes democratic stability, this hardly generates reasons for tolerating any particular questionable practice of an association. At issue here, after all, is not the mere existence of the Amish (to which we make no objection), but their child-rearing practices. It will become plain later that democratic theory reasonably requires more of civil institutions than that they not be run in such a way as to be threatening to the survival of democracy in the pluralist functional sense.

The functional arguments aside, the *Yoder* decision can seem intrinsically attractive to democrats; it respects the autonomy of a small self-governing group which is a source of meaning and value for its members. Culturally and economically the Amish are self-sufficient, and their mode of social organization has been revealed to be viable by centuries of testing. As Kraybill says, "Without consultants or strategic planners, the Amish, in simple and down-to-earth ways, have devised a social system that not only merits the attention of tourists and scholars but also raises profound questions about the underpinnings of happiness, freedom, and meaning. Moreover. . . . despite the best efforts of the most learned planners and strategists, our modern world is strewn with fragmentation, and despair."[18]

Given the many defects of the world we live in, the Amish might reasonably be thought to exemplify the kind of face-to-face community that participatory democrats in the Rousseauian tradition (at least) would prize as something to be fostered and nurtured, rather than obliterated before the steamroller of abstract democratic principles. It is scarcely surprising, therefore, that many democratically minded communitarians took heart at the decision and have defended it vigorously.[19] Our claim is that these various reasons for supporting the outcome in *Yoder* are not persuasive; now let us begin making that case.

II. Democratic Citizenship

In support of its compulsory-education requirements, the state of Wisconsin advanced two arguments. One is that "some degree of education is necessary to prepare citizens to participate effectively and intelligently in our open political system."[20] The second argument asserts that education is needed to prepare individuals for independent adult existence in modern society. In this section, we consider the first argument.

The Supreme Court majority opinion by Chief Justice Burger accepted that the state has a compelling interest in bringing it about that children are educated in a way that prepares them for the responsibilities of democratic citizenship. Burger held that this interest could be met without keeping Amish children in school past age fourteen. However, the conception of democratic citizenship that figures in the Court's reasoning is sketchy and impoverished. A more adequate understanding of the prerogatives of democratic citizenship compels the conclusion that compulsory high school attendance is a reasonable state requirement for the purpose of preparing youth for the role of citizen.

Burger's argument on this point consists of several independent assertions. He states that the fact that the Amish community has survived for more than two hundred years with little change in its way of life shows that Amish socialization practices must be instilling solid citizen virtues in their youth. Quoting from a letter of Thomas Jefferson, Burger observes that this founding father, who championed education as a shield against tyranny, apparently thought that an education providing basic literacy was adequate for this purpose. In this same vein, Burger adds that an eighth grade education fully satisfies the educational requirements of six states, and some other states have flexible requirements that partially excuse older children past eighth grade from school attendance requirements so that they may take paid employment. Burger asserts approvingly that the Amish community members "are productive and very law-abiding members of society; they reject public welfare in any of its usual modern forms."[21] Finally, Burger offers the conjecture that part of the initial motivation for compulsory-education laws was to prevent unhealthy child labor.[22] Given that the wholesome farm labor imposed on their children by Amish parents is not the sort of unhealthy labor that progressive legislation was designed to prevent, granting the Amish an exemption to the compulsory-education law would not subvert this aspect of the state's legitimate concern, according to Burger.

This discussion is noteworthy for its lack of any specification of the responsibilities of democratic citizenship. Burger's implicit theory of citizenship would seem to be that a good citizen is law-abiding, stays out of trouble, and stays off the welfare rolls. In contrast, we suppose that a good citizen has the capacity to vote in an informed way in elections that determine the membership of legislative assemblies, hence the content of the laws, as well as the identity of public officials and judges who execute and apply the laws. To be able to participate competently in democratic decision-making, voters should have an adequate knowledge of contemporary science in its bearing on public policy issues, an understanding of modern world history and particularly the history of democratic institutions and the culture of their own society, and critical thinking skills that include the ability to represent the situation of others in imagination, to intuit their experience, and sympathetically to analyze and assess their attitudes, principles, and policy arguments.[23] Citizens should have the capacities to keep themselves briefed on current events that are relevant to governmental decisions to be made. In a diverse democracy composed of disparate creeds, faiths, races, worldviews, and concerns, arriving at fair and reasonable decisions about public policy is a task of delicate and complex judgment.[24]

Without entering into an extended consideration of what sort of education best prepares children for the responsibilities of democratic citizenship so conceived, we submit that education beyond basic literacy is needed to increase to an adequate level the likelihood that an individual will have the skills needed for democratic deliberation and the disposition to exercise these skills on appropriate occasions. To this end, a high school education is not a panacea, but it does provide some skills and knowledge needed to be a competent democratic deliberator. One might add that the experience of attending a typical contemporary high school—be it public or parochial—introduces the youth to people from different backgrounds, of different creeds, beliefs, ethnicity, and social class than her own. The experience of informal negotiating with one's classmates and adjustment to differences among them is itself a helpful preparation for the responsibilities of democratic citizenship.

Citizens in a democracy have rights to vote and to influence the opinions of others through practices of free expression and the democratic process. These rights give each citizen a small amount of political power over other citizens; their collective actions produce effects that others have to endure.[25] With power comes the responsibility to use it in ways that do not wrongfully harm those who are affected by one's exercises of it. In a democracy, the responsibilities of guardians of children include the duty to educate youth so that they become competent to exercise the powers of citizenship in ways that do not wrongfully threaten to impose harm on others. If parents and guardians fail to discharge this duty, the state has the obligation to intervene in order to ensure that the obligation is met.

The objection might be raised that the discussion of citizenship and education to this point has set an unrealistically idealistic norm both for citizenship and for the education that is to prepare individuals for citizenship. Actual majority-rule decision procedures are far from functioning as an ideal deliberative democracy. At best, ignorant voters beset by venal and ambitious politicians and by agents of the special interests who stand to profit from manipulation of the law-making process cast ballots that are honestly counted and that determine who rules. High schools in the United States today too often provide unsafe and hostile environments that reinforce the tribal anxieties and prejudices of school-age youth and impede their intellectual development. The Amish refusal to involve their children in this process cannot be plausibly presented as a failure of citizenship responsibilities.

No doubt democratic institutions and educational practices could benefit from improvement. What aspect of contemporary society could not? But the failure of citizens generally to fulfill the responsibilities of citizenship and to provide adequate education preparing youth for future citizenship does not justify a decision by society to cease upholding and enforcing these norms. Similarly, the unfortunate fact that some parents physically abuse their children would not excuse the state's renouncing its attempts to enforce norms against child abuse. The correct inference from the observation that there is a gap between the obligatory norms we profess and the degree to which we fulfill these norms is that we should narrow the gap by doing more to fulfill the norms.

Suppose it is said that if the Amish, a withdrawing sect, do not exercise voting rights, they are not obligated to educate their children into voting competence, since it is reasonably anticipated that the children will also abjure the exercise of voting rights. After all, no American citizen is under any legal obligation to vote. So far as the law is concerned, voting is optional. If the Amish do not take up this option, they have no further obligation with respect to it, and they surely need not train their children for responsibilities they will never face.

Although we would not go so far as to argue that people necessarily have an obligation to vote in a democracy, there surely is a defeasible obligation to vote in any tolerably functioning democracy. Voting by many is necessary if the system is to function properly and there is no obvious fair way to select a subset of voters to whom the obligation to vote does not apply. No doubt there are circumstances in which refraining from voting is permissible and even obligatory. For example, it may well be the case, for all that we say in this essay, that the Amish practice of withdrawal from society is justified. But informed judgment about these matters can only be made by people who understand how democratic systems work, and what the issues at stake in democratic elections are. One needs to be educated for competent citizenship in order to determine whether it is permissible or obligatory to abstain from exercising this or that function of citizenship.

But even if there is no obligation to vote, we still contend that guardians of children have an obligation to develop in their charges the capacities necessary for informed voting. All citizens will have the inalienable right to participate, so all future citizens should be educated so that they can exercise this right competently should they choose to do so. The Amish did not propose to waive their children's future rights of citizenship; nor should any proposal to this effect be seriously entertained, much less ratified.

Even if it is granted that the state has a strong legitimate interest in compelling high school attendance in order to foster intelligent and conscientious citizenship, a judgment call is required when this interest conflicts with rights to the free exercise of religion. In our judgment, even if the state's paternalistic concern for the welfare of Amish children were to be entirely set aside, the imperative of educating future citizens into habits of intelligent and well-informed tolerance suffices by itself to justify compulsory school attendance laws like the one challenged by the Amish in this case. The duty to educate for democratic citizenship trumps any religious exercise claims that might oppose it. But to vindicate this claim, we must clarify the nature of the parental rights and free exercise claims at stake in the *Yoder* case.

III. Parental Rights over Children

In the *Yoder* case, the Court held that the Wisconsin compulsory school attendance law placed a substantial burden on the free exercise by the Old Order Amish of their religion. Having stipulated that the law burdens free exercise, the Court took the view that an exemption from the law must be granted to the Amish (or the law must be struck down), unless the state could show a compelling interest that would have to go unmet if such an exemption were granted. The free exercise interests in question were the interests of the Amish parents in practicing their religion in their traditional way. But the state's expressed interest concerned the education of Amish children. On the face of it, there was a gap between the rights claimed by the parents, having to do with their practice of religion, and the claims of the state, having to do with *the children's* education. How do the Amish parents' rights of religious freedom extend to encompass rights to set limits to the education of the Amish children?

The obvious answer is that rights of religious freedom are understood to include the right to raise one's children in one's own faith. But it is not obvious what the source of these extended parental rights is, nor what their proper limits should be.

One useful canonical text on parental rights and obligations is John Locke's *Two Treatises of Government.* Locke there writes, referring to the natural equality of persons, "Children, I confess are not born in this full state of Equality, though they are born to it. Their Parents have a sort of Rule and Jurisdiction over them when they come into the World, and for some time after, but 'tis but a temporary one. . . . The Power, then, that Parents have over their Children, arises from that Duty which is incumbent on them, to take care of their Off-spring, during the imperfect state of Childhood."[26]

On Locke's view, biological parents have fiduciary obligations to care for their children. Since children are incapable of controlling their own conduct by their reason in a steady way that adequately caters to their prudential long-term interests and the interests of others affected by their conduct, parental obligations include the duty to govern their children. These obligations are oriented to the interests of children and of humanity at large, and the concomitant rights that devolve on parents so that they may fulfill their obligations are rights to act for the good of their children (subject to moral constraints), not rights to use their children as they might wish for the parents' own benefit. On this view, children are not in any respect the property of their parents.

My obligation to raise my children for their present and

future welfare in practice is tantamount to an obligation to raise my children for their present and future welfare as conceived by me. Similarly, my obligation to train my children to respect the rights of others and to give priority to justice and fair play translates into an obligation to train my children into proper morality as I conceive it.[27] In this way, the same paternalistic duty falling on each parent leads each to a different child-rearing policy. Following your lights, you teach your child sound business practices and the lore of your tribe, and following my lights, I teach my child the religion I profess.

Locke may perhaps make too much of biological parenthood, but the rest of the story he tells remains credible. Society assigns major responsibility to particular persons to be primary guardians of particular children; in our society, biological parenthood is one way, perhaps a generally acceptable way, to assign these particular bundles of rights and responsibilities that are conventionally identified with parenthood. Having made an initial assignment, society does better to leave well enough alone for the most part, trusting parents whose competence and motivation have not been impugned by gross and readily verifiable tests to carry out their parental obligations as they see fit.

Society intervenes in the discharge of parental obligations in two main ways. Parents found to be unfit are separated from their children by state authority. In areas such as health, hygiene, and education, the state may set standards to be met, generally leaving wide discretion to parents as to what means to choose to meet these standards.

A complication in this picture is that being a parent looms large in the life plans of many adults who are parents. Since the discharge of parental obligations allows wide scope for parental discretion, choosing and pursuing a child-rearing regimen is for many parents an important mode of self-expression and personal creativity. Since the discharge of parental obligations is sometimes fun, and over the long run deeply satisfying, for many, and for everyone strongly endorsed by powerfully entrenched cultural norms, being able to see oneself as a good parent is often a source of deep satisfaction. Even those who find parenting continuously and aggravatingly frustrating try hard to discover in their experience, or in some dimly imagined transformation of it, what they believe to be the normal pattern of harmony and mutual satisfaction. Moreover, the wide discretionary authority enjoyed by parents allows them to satisfy their own desires and whims in their child-rearing, sometimes in the course of fulfilling their obligations to their children, sometimes in the course of masquerading at fulfilling these obligations. If I fancy putting my child in the Little League, or in the church choir, I generally may do so. Finally, and pertinently to the Amish litigation, parents may find their own fulfillment bound up with having the freedom to raise their children in ways they deem obligatory. As the Amish parents noted, they believe that their own prospects of salvation are tied to their raising their own children properly, which means assuring their salvation, which in turn means raising them so that they in due course become loyal and conforming members of traditional Amish society.

For all of these reasons, parents may feel that their own personal freedom and their rights to pursue their own happiness in their own way require that society grant them wide discretionary authority to raise their children as they see fit. So the interests and freedom of Amish parents, as well as the interests and liberties of Amish children, are at stake in *Wisconsin v. Yoder.*

IV. Free Exercise of Religion Rights

The education of children (as opposed to adult education) by its nature involves an authoritative overriding of the judgment of the recipients of the schooling: educators seek to impart beliefs, values, attitudes, and capacities to those in their care. Indeed part of the mission of the educator of children is to shape their aspirations and desires. We have no quarrel with the conventional understanding that parents have the right to play a major role in shaping the education of their children. Nor do we quarrel with the common opinion that the religious freedom rights of parents include the right to introduce their children to their own religion and to raise their children as practicing adherents of the parents' sect. But in this section, we argue that parents' rights to the free exercise of religion give out at the point where their preferred manner of exercise comes into conflict with the basic interests, including the basic educational interests, of their children. Since parents and guardians do not stand in anything like an ownership relation to their immature charges, the assertion of "parents' rights" to withdraw their children from school in the circumstances of *Yoder* would have to be shown to be compatible with their overriding fiduciary obligations to their children.

What if the free exercise interests of Amish parents and the interests of Amish children are in tension with one another? If there were a conflict between the free exercise interests of the parents and some other legitimate interests of the children which parents had an obligation to preserve (such as an interest in receiving an adequate supply of food), then, on the fiduciary model sketched above, the parents would have an obligation to limit their own free exercise rights. If your own interests prevent you from carrying out your obligations as a trustee, you must give up your fiduciary authority to someone else who is duly authorized to take it on, or to a probate court.

It might be argued that this reasoning simplifies things misleadingly, because part of what is at issue is the free exercise rights of the children. In a dissenting opinion, Justice Douglas objects that the opinions of the fourteen-year-old Amish children were not solicited by the trial court, the implication being that these opinions are relevant to the proper outcome. Here we should distinguish two questions: do children themselves have free exercise rights that courts should respect in such cases as *Yoder,* and should courts take children's views into account when adjucating such cases as *Yoder?* The two are very different. In custody disputes, for example, courts will generally appoint a social worker to interview the children as to their preferences and make a recommendation, and in some states the court is required to appoint an attorney to represent their interests in litigation over custody. Sometimes the judge will interview the children in chambers to elicit their preferences as well. But none of these devices is based on the idea that the minor children are free to choose a custodial parent.[28] Their preferences are one factor that is taken into account along with a variety of other factors, and depending on their age their preferences are given more or less weight. In practice, this is a rough-and-ready calculation, no doubt infected with the judge's own values to some degree, but conceptually it is quite different from the notion that the preferences of less than fully competent adult persons should be dispositive because they are their preferences. After all, if they were fully competent adults they would not need fiduciaries in the first place. Because free religious exercise (as opposed to mindless cultish behavior) can only be entered into by an act of autonomous will, someone (like a child) who by definition is in need of fiduciary supervision in religious matters, cannot engage in free religious exercise. Thus, although Justice Douglas may have been right that the children should have been interviewed, he would have been wrong to have held that their preferences in the matter should have been dispositive. The question has to be, taking everything into account, did the parents abuse their fiduciary authority by removing the children from school?

Conventional opinion in the United States and other countries holds that it is part of a parent's authority qua parent that he or she speaks for the child in religious matters. But why? Because we regard the child as too immature to speak for herself. That is reasonable from the standpoint of the fiduciary model, so long as it is subject to the proviso that the parent cannot pretend to speak for the child while really regarding the child as a mere empty vessel for the parents' own religious convictions. As a fiduciary, the parent is bound to preserve the child's own future religious freedom. Few people would deny this outright. After all, most religious people distinguish between religions and cults and they would see it as part of their responsibility not to let their children become prey to cults. But what is the distinction if it does not turn on preserving some freedom of will, some freedom to reject? This is a fine line, of course. Often religious people think their children should have free choice so long as they make "the right" choice in the end; this appears to be the Amish view of the matter, as we have seen. In reality, such people do not believe in free religious choice.

The parents in *Yoder* did not invoke a fiduciary obligation to their children in support of their actions. Instead, they appealed to a mixture of the right of the Amish community to reproduce itself and the parents' own free exercise rights. We consider each of these in turn.

The first appeal rests on an exceedingly powerful claim for group rights, for which it is difficult to see a coherent justification. Groups and classes are groups and classes of individuals, and talk of the "right" of the Amish community to reproduce itself glosses over the reality that the different members of the group may have conflicting rights and interests. If it is in the interest of Amish children to receive an adequate education, and their receiving it will threaten the existence of the group (assuming for now that this is true), then a conflict of this kind is evidently present. Our claim is that in such an eventuality there is no defensible reason to sacrifice the interests of the children in their education to their parents' desire to reproduce the Amish community in the name of group rights.

Our argument for resisting the notion that there is a right of the Amish community qua community that has to be weighed against other relevant interests should not be misinterpreted. In particular, it does not amount to an affirmative claim that the Amish community has no right to exist, that it should be stamped out by the state. Any such claim would run headlong into freedom of association arguments which constitutional democrats would be bound to endorse. But it is far from saying that adults have the right to associate as an Amish community to saying that adults have a right to violate the rights of children to an adequate education, or to violate the legitimate interests of third parties in the education of children, *in order that they may* associate freely as an Amish community. If rights-violations of either sort really are necessary conditions, then the claims of the Amish adults must give way. This is not because the Amish ought to be stamped out, but because there is no reason that children and third parties should have to endure rights violations so that the Amish may freely associate.[29]

This brings us to the parents' own free exercise rights. In *Wisconsin v. Yoder,* the Court held that the Wisconsin compulsory schooling law, though not discriminatory on its face, in its application to the Amish parents qualified as a burden on the free exercise of their religion. That is, the law significantly hindered a practice that was central to their religious way of life. So far, we agree. In such a circumstance, according to the Court's interpretation of the Free Exercise Clause, the Constitution requires a decision in favor of the Amish that relieves this burden by exempting them from the law. This is so unless the state could show that granting such relief would thwart a compelling state interest, an interest "of the highest order," an interest "of sufficient magnitude" to override the free exercise interest.[30] Balancing the interests at stake, the Court ruled that the fundamental interest in free exercise should trump the state's interest in universal education. We see no convincing basis for the Court's weighing of the interests at stake.[31]

In section III, we argued that the Court understated the importance of the state's interest in ensuring that each child is adequately educated for the responsibilities of democratic citizenship. In section V, we contend that the Court's opinion underestimates the moral imperative of education for autonomy. Here we make the case that the Amish parents' interest in free exercise should give way when that interest comes in conflict with their fiduciary obligations to provide education for their children.

Even if everything at stake in this case except free exercise of religion rights were ignored, the Amish parents' free exercise interest in withdrawing their children from school would be countered by each Amish child's nonwaivable interest in religious freedom (the freedom as an adult to choose one's own faith), which is served by education for autonomy. If the parents' free exercise rights genuinely do clash with the children's rights as defined by the relevant legitimate statute, then the parents must either accept their own loss of religious freedom or, in the limiting case, decline to be parents. If their religion told them to sacrifice their children on an altar we would think nothing of terminating their parental rights (even knowing that God might, after all, be on their side). When Christian Scientists go to court to try to get permission to withhold vital medical care from their children on religious grounds they appropriately lose, and that does not trouble our intuitions either (again God might be on their side, in fact). *Yoder* presents the same kind of issue.

This understanding of parents' fiduciary obligations implies a strong role for the state as the ultimate arbiter of at least some children's interests. But just how strong should that role be? An extreme version of the argument would require us to insist that no one has a right to be a parent. Rights of parenthood are positive rights conferred by the state. They are defined by a bundle of benefits (such as access to certain types of companionship, public esteem, tax breaks) and responsibilities (to nurture their charges, see that they are protected, able to develop into normal adults, and so forth), and can always be rescinded by the state. Although it is true that every state reserves the right to terminate parental rights under some conditions, most democrats would reasonably find this view unacceptably strong; it supplies too little in the way of participation by the relevant parties, and too few limitations on state power.

A weaker and more plausible claim for state authority would be that although no one has an unconditional right to be a parent, people are generally presumed to have that right absent a showing to the contrary. One might start from the premise that the officials in a state (democratic or not) do not know all the answers to what the best ways to raise children are, that there are inherent economies of smallness to such knowledge. This is a plausible, and for many, an attractive thought. Certainly a democratic theory of education should not commit its adherents to any single developmental or psychological theory of education.

On this view, we would say that the state can rule certain things out as clearly abusive of children or subversive of the state's interests in the production of a citizenry able to participate in its operations, but beyond that it must defer to parents. This would issue in a "basic interests" rather than a "best interests" standard for evaluating parents' fulfillment of their fiduciary obligations. On this view, whether or not the Amish parents lose depends simply on whether or not compulsory education up to age sixteen is a basic interest. The parents were explicit in saying that they wanted their children to leave school at age fourteen both because by that age the children already had the relevant skills to survive in the Amish community, and because experience had taught that it was at this age that children were most likely to develop and act on the desire to leave the community. The parents in *Yoder* thus did not begin to make the case that compulsory education to age sixteen is not a basic interest. Indeed, we argue in section VI that the parents' candid admission of motives supplies prima facie evidence that a basic interest of their children was being violated in removing them from school at age fourteen.

It is perhaps worth noting explicitly that a Supreme Court decision that required the Amish to educate their children to age sixteen would not require the Amish to submit their children to secular public high schools. The Amish would be as free as any other citizens to comply with state educational requirements by sending their children to private schools, or to establish their own schools, rather than use the public schools.[32]

V. Autonomy: The Child's Right to an Open Future

Several commentators on *Wisconsin v. Yoder* and related issues in family law have found the key to the puzzle to be a strong value of individual autonomy which finds appropriate expression in "the child's right to an open future." On this view, the aim of education is to prepare children for lives of rational autonomy once they become adults. A "rationally autonomous" life is one that is self-chosen in a reasonable way. Education for rational autonomy thus encompasses two requirements: (1) Upon onset of adulthood individuals should be enabled to choose from the widest possible variety of ways of life and conceptions of the good and (2) Individuals should be trained into habits and skills of critical reflection, so that they attain to the greatest feasible extent the capacity to choose rationally among these alternative ways of life. We shall refer to these two aspects of education for autonomy as (1) the maximization of options and (2) the development of critical reason.

The conflict between the child's right to autonomy so conceived and the claims of the Old Order Amish parents is clear and direct, for the Amish straightforwardly believe that they should educate their children so that they embrace the traditional Amish way and that skills of critical reasoning would alienate their children from wholehearted identification with the right way to live and would therefore be corrupting.

Many commentators on children's rights are attracted to the ideal of individual autonomy. Amy Gutmann writes, "One can concede that any practical standard of education will eliminate some options that might otherwise be open to children when they mature, but so long as we must choose among paternalistic standards we are required to choose those that are most neutral among competing conceptions of the good, standards that expand rather than contract a child's future ability to exercise meaningful choice."[33] Criticizing the reasoning of Chief Justice Burger's opinion of the court in *Wisconsin v. Yoder,* Joel Feinberg comments, "An impartial decision would assume only that education should equip the child with the knowledge and skills that will help him choose whichever sort of life best fits his native endowment and matured disposition. It should send him out into the adult world with as many open opportunities as possible, thus maximizing his chances for self-fulfillment."[34] Discussing the proper basis for child custody decisions in divorce litigation, Jon Elster describes what he asserts to be a "superior way" of conceiving the child's best interests: "Instead of being guided by the substantive preferences and choices that are imputed to the child, one could be led by the more formal goal of protecting the child's opportunity and ability to make choices. On this view, a child should be allowed, as far as possible, to reach maturity with a maximum of potentialities and the autonomy needed to choose which of them to develop. Once that point is reached, what he chooses to make of his life is up to him, but one should not knowingly preempt the choice."[35]

It might seem obvious that if one accepts that children have the right to autonomy as characterized by Gutmann, Feinberg, and Elster, then one should also accept the further claim that the state ought to uphold that right against parents who would deny it, so the state of Wisconsin should have prevailed against the Amish parents—hence *Yoder* was wrongly decided. This conflict between the *Yoder* decision and the child's right to autonomy has not seemed obvious to the commentators who have asserted the child's claim to autonomy. Feinberg views the issue as a balancing problem, with the child's interest in continued education on one side of the balance and the Amish parents' free exercise interest on the other side. In this particular case, only two years of education were at issue, because school attendance under Wisconsin law was compulsory only to age sixteen, and the Amish parents accepted the state law insofar as it prescribed school attendance through the eighth grade (age fourteen). The specific balancing problem presented to the Court was delicate, according to Feinberg, and resolving it in favor of the Amish parents' right of free exercise might have been correct, and certainly was not clearly mistaken.

Gutmann agrees with Feinberg that the amount of education at stake in *Yoder* was too small to force the conclusion that the child's right to education should trump the parent's right to free exercise. She also raises two further considerations that might support the decision actually reached by the Court. She suggests that the worse the education the state provides, assessed according to the standard of how well the state prepares students for successfully negotiating a wide range of valuable ways of life that are feasible in modern society, the weaker the paternalistic rationale for state imposition of an educational regime on recalcitrant parents. Gutmann also flirts with the suggestion that children have a right to autonomy in the strong sense of a right "to be so educated as to be capable of choosing unprejudicially among all conceivable conceptions of the good."[36] She then observes that this right would not warrant state enforcement of education "beyond the basics" because we are substantially ignorant of how education might be set so that it does not instill some prejudices even as it removes others. She writes, "Every educational system now in existence closes children's minds to some potentially desirable conceptions of the good life and the good society."[37] Yes, but this hardly means that all educational systems are on a par with respect to the cultivation of autonomy. If the strong sense of autonomy is so exalted that all feasible educational regimes would equally fail to achieve it, that shows not that autonomy is an irrelevant standard for judging educational regimes but that Gutmann's strong conception of autonomy is not the relevant conception.

In the course of growing up, children acquire values and preferences—a conception of the good. These values and preferences of course do not spring spontaneously from the child's mind, but are the outcome of interaction between the child's innate dispositions and socializing environmental forces. Being social, children have a disposition to adopt the standards that are salient among significant persons in their lives such as playmates, close relatives, teachers, and other adult figures vested with authority. Even if it were somehow possible for an educational regime to abstain from inculcating values in the child, this would not be sensible, for the vacuum left by abstaining educators would be filled by other causal influences. One way or another the child is going to be influenced by the social environment. So the idea of arriving at adulthood without having prejudged some matters of value is a chimera. At any rate, the phenomenon of choice of values by an individual that we associate with attainment of autonomy always presupposes a context in which some standards and values are held at least provisionally fixed and guide choice. So being prejudiced or having one's mind made up on some valuation issues is necessary for autonomy not an obstacle that precludes it.

But then having been inculcated with Amish values as a child is not per se a hindrance to achievement of autonomy any more than having been inculcated with capitalist consumerist values or any other values. So we had better drop the supposed ideal of unprejudiced choice among all possible ways of life and conceptions of the good.

It is worth pointing out that the maximization of options aspect of the ideal is vulnerable also to powerful objections. The idea at issue here is that education should be arranged so that the child is allowed to reach maturity with a maximum of potentialities. In some simple choice problems, this norm might seem to yield advice that is both determinate and plausible. Denial of high school education so that a child can be socialized into an ultra-traditionalist religious farming community seems to open one option while foreclosing many others. The norm of maximizing options supports provision of high school education to every child who is capable of it.

But what exactly is meant by talk of "maximizing options"? To begin with, it is far from clear how to individuate and count options or opportunities. One suspects that from different evaluative standpoints, options would reasonably be individuated in different ways, and that there is no neutral counting of options. From the Amish standpoint, one might say there are two relevant options, turning away from the world toward the Amish community and turning toward the world away from the community. To grant the one option is to foreclose the other. The varieties of worldly options will not appear saliently different from the Amish standpoint, and anyway there are no doubt many various alternative ways of life within the Amish community, suboptions within the unworldly option. Perhaps the neutral-sounding judgment that the Amish rejection of secondary education fails to maximize children's options is just a neutral-sounding way of registering the judgment that the Amish way of life is not worthwhile by comparison to the way of life that secondary education prepares the child for.

Assume for the sake of the argument that the difficulty raised in the last paragraph has somehow been overcome and that the Supreme Court has available to it a neutral standard for counting options which discloses that denial of secondary education reduces the total number of life options available to the child. It still is far from clear that "maximization of options" is unproblematically a good that the state ought to require all parents to provide for their children. Consider that there are many attractive ways of life, such as ballet performance and competitive athletics, that require dedicated singleminded concentration and commitment on the part of any individual who aspires to one of these forms of achievement. This commitment must be made at an early age and sustained through adolescence and young adulthood. Moreover, the tremendous concentration of energy and time required to have a chance at success at a field of highly competitive performance inevitably forecloses many other valuable life options. This is not a choice that can be reserved for the adult. Either a commitment is made before the child is fully in a position to appreciate the nature of this decision problem or the child loses any realistic possibility of success at any career goal that requires early commitment. In order to open this door even by a crack one must simultaneously close many other doors.

No doubt the decision by parents as to whether to permit or

encourage their child to make an early commitment to such a career as ballet is delicate and open to abuse. The point we wish to make in this connection is modest. Even if one countenances the idea that it is possible to count children's opportunities and options so that the idea of educating a child so as to maximize the number of options available at the onset of adulthood is coherent, "maximizing options" is at most one desideratum among many and could not plausibly be regarded as the sole or dominant standard for child-rearing policy. Sometimes the value of a single option is sufficiently high that providing it even at the cost of foreclosing other less-valued options is on balance desirable for the child.

But if concentration on athletic training oriented to Olympic competition can be good for a child even if it effectively rules out college attendance for one who is academically marginal but athletically gifted, then one cannot object to Amish withdrawal of children from school in order to provide a secure Amish way of life for the child simply on the ground that this policy fails to maximize the number of opportunities available to the child at maturity. The maximization-of-options aspect of the ideal of autonomy does not have much force in an argument against the Supreme Court's analyses in the *Yoder* decision. Like the unprejudiced choice notion, the maximization-of-options aspect of autonomy cannot be sustained.

What marks education for autonomy is development of skills and habits of critical thinking. The autonomous person is not the person who bears allegiance only to spontaneously self-chosen values that are untainted by environmental influence. The autonomous person is rather one who is capable of standing back from her values and engaging in critical reflection about them and altering her values to align them with the results of that critical reflection. The difficulty with the Amish program of socialization is not that it instills prejudgments, for any educational program does that, but rather that it fails to train children in skills of critical thinking and to encourage children to place a positive value on engagement in critical thinking about one's fundamental values. The Amish acculturation program is expressly designed to limit critical thinking, to get children to accept things on faith without submitting them to reasoned reflection. As Kraybill makes clear, Amish education is "an effort to manage consciousness, to set and control the agenda of ideas. Abstract and rational modes of thought are simply not entertained in the Amish school. The uniform world view propogated by Amish education funnels ideas in prescribed channels that undergird the ethnic social system."[38] The Amish reject critical reflection partly out of fear of its effects, and partly because they are philosophically opposed to it. According to the Amish sages, the wisdom of the world "makes you restless, wanting to leap and jump and not knowing where you will land."[39]

But is failure to educate for autonomous critical thinking really objectionable? Interestingly, some political philosophers recently have advocated a reduced liberalism stripped of what they regard as sectarian commitments and thereby capable of becoming the object of a broad consensus that includes traditionalist religious advocates. William Galston writes that the "civic standpoint," which he endorses, "does not warrant the conclusion that the state must (or may) structure public education to foster in children skeptical reflection on ways of life inherited from parents or local communities."[40] In a similar spirit, in recent writings John Rawls asserts that the doctrine of autonomy of Immanuel Kant and the doctrine of individuality of John Stuart Mill are accepted by few citizens of modern diverse democracies. According to Rawls, a political conception of liberalism suitable for a modern democratic society must eschew commitment to intractably controversial philosophical views such as those of either Kant or Mill. Otherwise liberalism becomes just another sectarian doctrine, a religious view no more suited than Marxism or Methodism or Buddhism for the role of consensus moral foundation for fundamental democratic practices. Rawls in fact alludes to *Wisconsin v. Yoder* when he draws the line between a commitment to rational autonomy and fair play in the public sphere that is essential to democratic citizenship and a commitment to substantive conceptions of the good and partisan ties in private life that is said to be perfectly compatible with democratic citizenship.[41]

The Galston-Rawls position is buttressed by noting that freedom of speech as commonly understood is the right of a willing speaker to engage any willing audience on matters of public concern. No law in a democratic society commands participation in free speech practices. The laws structuring freedom of expression impose on citizens only the duty to forbear from wrongful interference with the free speech activities of other citizens. Democratic tolerance including a proper respect for freedom of expression is then (on this view) fully compatible with a firm confidence in the correctness or acceptability of one's own present values and a total absence of inclination to subject one's own fundamental values to critical scrutiny. The "civic standpoint" that Galston extolls includes support for the basic institutions of democracy and their underlying rationale. If the underlying rationale of the law of freedom of expression were a commitment to the ideal of rational autonomy, it would seem more appropriate that the law should compel, not merely permit, participation in some free speech activities that would help to stimulate appropriate critical reflection. The ideal of rational autonomy is a species of perfectionism, an ideal of character that might support paternalistic restriction of the liberties of adults who would fail even to try to conform their characters to the ideal in the absence of such restriction. That the law of freedom of expression is permissive rather than compulsive suggests that its underlying rationale is civic tolerance not rational autonomy.

The Galston-Rawls position seeks to detach practices of democratic toleration from the development of critical reason aspect of the ideal of autonomy. Though their arguments differ somewhat, they share a concern that the appeal to a philosophical ideal of autonomy to defend freedom of expression and to determine the limits of religious liberties is sectarian. Many, perhaps most citizens of modern democracies are committed to substantive conceptions of the good and particular ways of life and would not value the freedom to subject their fundamental ends to skeptical scrutiny. Hence, one cannot resolve the conflict between Amish parents and Wisconsin public officials by stipulating that both parties to the dispute accept an ideal of rational autonomous choice of ends and subjection of current ends to critical scrutiny that in effect simply presupposes that the public officials are correct and the Amish have no case. This ideal of autonomy is contested in contemporary society. To argue as though this ideal were uncontroversial is to evade, not settle, the dispute.

In response: Three lines of argument converge in support of the proposition that society through the agency of the state should ensure that children develop the deliberative capacities that are required for autonomy. These arguments are labelled the parallel with autonomous citizenship, the pressure of freedom of expression, and the instrumental case for autonomy.

The Parallel with Autonomous Citizenship

Members of a democratic society are obligated to fulfill the responsibilities of democratic citizenship, which centrally involve the assessment of public policy proposals. In order to assess policy proposals as a citizen one must be able to exercise critical reason by imagining what can be said for and against candidate policies from the different points of view that are represented in the electorate.

The claims that (1) one ought to exercise critical reason in evaluating policies and candidates and (2) one is entitled to eschew critical reason altogether in forming and affirming a view of one's own individual good are in conflict. A plausible surmise is that any view that justifies the claim that future citizens should be trained for the autonomous exercise of critical reason in the democratic deliberations that ought to determine the content of public policy will also justify the claim that citizens should be trained for the autonomous exercise of critical reason in their personal choices of fundamental ends. And any view that denies that citizens should be autonomous in their personal choices of fundamental ends will also deny that citizens should autonomously make up their own minds on issues of collective political choice. Hence, the advocate of the Galston-Rawls position will have to deny that citizens are obligated to develop and exercise their critical reason in making up their minds on public policy issues, and this implication may be difficult to swallow.

The Pressure of Freedom of Expression

A second argument supporting state-mandated provision for autonomy is that in a democratic society that honors freedom of expression, state policy towards the education of children ought to be consistent with the underlying principles that support freedom of expression. Any such policy must be designed to foster autonomy.

"Freedom of expression" refers to the right of a willing speaker to address a willing audience on matters of public concern.

In a 1940 First Amendment case, *Cantwell v. Connecticut,* the Supreme Court states a rationale for broad legal protection for freedom of expression:

> In the realm of religious faith, and in that of political belief, sharp differences arise. In both fields the tenets of one man may seem the rankest error to his neighbor. To persuade others to his own point of view, the pleader, we know, at times, resorts to exaggeration, to vilification of men who have been, or are, prominent in church or state, and even to false statement. But the people of this nation have ordained in the light of history, that, in spite of the probability of excesses and abuses, these liberties are, in the long view, essential to enlightened opinion and right conduct on the part of the citizens of a democracy.
>
> The essential characteristic of these liberties is that, under their shield many types of life, character, opinion, and belief can develop unmolested and unobstructed. Nowhere is this shield more necessary than in our own country for a people composed of many races and of many creeds.[42]

From one angle the Court's position looks puzzling. If speakers are likely to give offense, and upset the cherished views of their audiences, perhaps proselytization across sects and argument across communal groups should be restricted or forbidden in a diverse society "composed of many races and of many creeds" so that each group can follow its own preferred way unmolested by distressing speech. Yet the Court describes free speech as a shield that protects disparate ways of life. What the Court evidently has in mind is that when free speech is protected, individuals will have access to a broad array of views supporting many ways of life, and that individuals who take advantage of the opportunities that free speech provides will make better informed and better considered choices of a way of life for themselves than they otherwise would. The Court asserts a democratic faith that under a regime of free expression on the average and in the long run individuals will make better choices as a result of intelligently sifting through the welter of considerations generated for them by free dialogue—better choices than would be made under a regime that censors speech to protect group and sect sensitivities. Free speech under the conditions of modern democracy produces "enlightened opinion," in the Court's hopeful words. This is a broad and vague empirical claim of a sort for which it is difficult to provide anything that would count as compelling evidence, hence we have characterized the Court's view as resting on a democratic faith. But notice that if one denied this claim one would be hard-pressed to defend legal guarantees of freedom of expression. If one held that under a regime of free expression on the average and in the long run the quality of individuals' choices of ways of life and conceptions of the good deteriorates compared to what that quality would be under a regime of repression, one is well on the way to endorsement of repression. One might blanketly assert that individuals have basic rights to free speech even if free speech leads them to ruin, but such a fundamentalist assertion of right would be quixotic.

If adult society is conceived as a regime of free expression, in which debate is open, robust, and uninhibited, then children in order to profit from that open debate must be trained for it. Guidelines for educational policy are implicit in the rationale for freedom of expression. Education in a democratic society might well be designed to achieve other goals as well, but a society that privileges freedom of expression should establish a system of education that coheres with it.

The Instrumental Case for Autonomy

The relationship between an individual's achieving autonomy and attaining a good life is complex. For one thing, an individual making an autonomous choice might decide to sacrifice her own good for the sake of fulfilling moral obligations or furthering nonobligatory ideals. Leave these cases aside. Though important, they do not pertain to the issues that are central for this essay.

Autonomy might be viewed as a deontological requirement which the individual must pursue. But once we distinguish deciding for oneself as it bears on the interests of other people and as it bears on one's own success in leading a good life, and recall that in this section we are considering only the latter, then it is hard to see how there could be a *moral* requirement to pursue one's own interests in a certain way, namely, autonomously.

The achievement of autonomy might be deemed worthy either instrumentally or for its own sake, quite apart from further consequences of such achievement. Conceived in this latter way, autonomy would have to be judged a sectarian goal, not suitable as a consensual basis for public policy. On what basis would autonomy be imposed on those who would reasonably regard it as not intrinsically worthwhile from the standpoint of their not unreasonable fundamental values?

The instrumental view of autonomy is difficult to disown. The idea is simply that what we now regard as good might not be good in fact, and that to improve the quality of our beliefs we must think for ourselves.[43] Being autonomous helps one discover reasonable values and a reasonable way to live, and discovering such values helps one to attain them. Anyone who accepts that her current beliefs that underlie her fundamental personal values might be mistaken or confused must acknowledge that critical examination of the reasoning supporting her values might reveal confusion of thought, and that further acquisition of factual knowledge might remove false beliefs but for which she would not maintain her commitment to her current values. But people do not merely wish to live a valuable and worthy life according to their current beliefs about what constitutes such a life. They want to lead a life that truly is valuable and worthy. Insofar as critical reflection on one's present values is a useful means to acquiring values that could withstand informed critical reflection and that would be a reliable guide to a valuable and worthy life, one's basic goal of living a good life generates the subsidiary goal of developing and exercising critical reflection. This, as we have seen, is the core defensible aspect of the ideal of autonomy.

The instrumental view of autonomy does not make a fetish of it. Engaging in critical reflection about one's values can improve the quality of the values one eventually affirms, but for most of us continued engagement in reflection quickly becomes subject to diminishing returns. Since time spent at critical reflection is time that could have been spent seeking to fulfill one's current values, the overarching goal of leading a good life does not dictate endless dithering at reflection instead of energetic pursuit if one's aims. In principle, the prudent agent will allocate her time between reflection to improve her values and action to achieve them so as to maximize the extent to which she is successful in leading a life that is good according to standards which she affirms and which could withstand further well-informed rational critical scrutiny. Notice that for any given individual the correct allocation of time between reflection on aims and pursuit of them depends crucially on her native talents that contribute to critical reflection skills. At the limit, a person whose thinking is always unavoidably thoroughly confused would do better to avoid critical reflection altogether and simply accept her given current aims on faith, since she is incapable of improving them by the use of her own critical powers.

In general, the practical alternative to subjecting one's fundamental aims to critical scrutiny is to accept uncritically whatever aims socialization during one's childhood has instilled. The utility of this strategy of trusting local authority as it happens to have impinged on one's life depends among other things on the quality of the local authorities that have acted as socializing agents—but this is not a matter on which one can have a trustworthy opinion prior to broad comparative investigation of one's local ideology rated against other ideologies and other worldviews.

The foregoing discussion of autonomy regarded as instrumental to a good life provides a way to model the decision problem for a guardian choosing an appropriate paternalistic policy for the upbringing of Amish youth. The model suggested here does not invoke controversial premises about the nature of the good life or about the role of the ideal of autonomy within a vision of the good life that are biased against religious traditionalists such as the Amish.

The problem of a guardian choosing an education for a youth entrusted to her care is to maximize the expected value of the life the child will lead, subject to moral constraints reflecting the legitimate interests of others whose lives will be affected. The decision is complicated by uncertainty about the future circumstances in which the child will lead his life and uncertainty about the value to the child of the options to which education can provide access. The Amish parent must choose between a program of withdrawal from worldly concerns that prepares the child only for life in the Amish community and a program of secular education that prepares the child for different ways of life in modern society. So as not to take advantage of the perhaps unwarranted polemical claim that secular education prepares the child for many valuable ways of life, whereas Amish withdrawal prepares the child at most for a single way of life, let us suppose that the child's future can be represented as a choice between just two options, a "religious traditionalist" and a "secular worldly" way of life. No assumption is made about the relative value of the two options, but it is assumed that individuals differ in their traits so that for some individuals, the secular way of life is better, and for some, the traditionalist way is better. The differences among persons that render one way of life or another superior for them cannot be identified in advance of maturity by guardians or by the individuals themselves. To some unknown extent the withdrawing educational program renders the recipient fit for traditionalist life and unfit for worldly life, whereas a secular education to some unknown degree renders the recipient fit for worldly life and unfit for traditionalist life. The choice of an educational program also can affect the child's capability and desire to engage in well-informed critical deliberation issuing in a choice of values and a way of life. At maturity the individual will choose a way of life autonomously or nonautonomously, where choosing one way or the other does not affect the value of the option that is chosen. But it is assumed that choosing after well-informed critical deliberation, or autonomously, increases the probability that an individual will choose the way of life, secular or traditionalist, that is better for her. On these assumptions the better course for a guardian is to choose a secular autonomy-promoting educational program for the child.

The assumptions presented in the previous paragraph are more favorable to the Amish case than any alternative set that could be adopted by public officials monitoring guardians without violating the Establishment clause of the First Amendment. No controversial assumption is made to the effect that Amish education closes off more opportunities for the child than would secular education. No assumption is made as to the comparative value of Amish and non-Amish ways of life. No autonomy-favoring assumption is made that choosing by means of well-informed critical reflection per se enhances the value of whatever way of life is chosen. In this model, autonomous choice is not itself an element of the good life, it is merely a device for discovering the good life. Still, this instrumental value of autonomy suffices to show the superiority of an education that promotes it to one that does not when educational choice must be made *ex ante,* before the individual's type is known. But this assumption that educational decisions affecting a child must be made in substantial ignorance of the child's endowment of traits and dispositions surely is realistic.

This way of framing the issue might be thought to load the discussion against the Amish parent, who surely believes that he knows the comparative value of an Amish versus a non-Amish existence and believes that the former is superior for his children, regardless of their particular idiosyncratic traits. But how could he attain knowledge of these matters without having undertaken a comprehensive comparative study of Amish and non-Amish ways of life of a sort that requires wide empirical knowledge and critical reasoning skills that only secular education claims to provide? Even if he had undertaken such a comparative inquiry, its results could not be extrapolated directly to determine what life is best for his child, because the child's traits and evaluative dispositions might be significantly different in ways that would alter the outcome of the comparisons, and anyway the comparative inquiry would have to be updated with current information and a current scrutiny of pertinent evaluative arguments on offer, in order to yield a decisive answer that could sensibly guide his child's choice.

Of course, in modern diverse societies the law gives parents wide latitude to attempt to pass along their own values to their children in the absence of any presumptive ground for thinking that parents know that their own values are adequate, much less superior to the values affirmed by other members of society. But there are limits to the permissible indoctrination of children by parents. One such limit that is widely accepted is that parents must cooperate with other legitimate authorities in society to develop in their children critical reasoning skills that will enable their children to stand back from the values they have been taught and to subject these values to informed critical scrutiny.

No doubt this limit is contested. But to deny the moral appropriateness of requiring all guardians to promote in their charges the disposition to critical reasoning and the skills needed to practice it, it would seem that one must deny that an individual of normal potential competence is likely to benefit from such exercise of critical reasoning skills. One must hold that the epistemic strategy of uncritical acceptance of the values that the individual was taught is a superior strategy for maximizing the goodness of the life the individual will have. This across the board denial of the efficacy of critical reasoning in human life is a possible position to maintain, but holding that view is incompatible with any plausible rationale for democratic civil liberties including broad freedom of expression. There is no conceptual room for a "civic standpoint" that affirms wide freedom of expression for adult citizens but denies that the development in children of the capacities to engage profitably in free expression practices has any value.

VI. Conclusion: *Yoder* and Democratic Theory Revisited

We have argued that in a democratic society all of us have a "compelling" interest in bringing it about that each member of society is raised with the capacities needed to fulfill the responsibilities of democratic citizenship. These capacities notably include skills and habits of critical thinking that enable one to participate effectively in democratic deliberation. In a democratic society in which there is no established religion or privileged faith, and in which many doctrines and faiths compete for allegiance, it is in each person's interest to have critical thinking skills that facilitate wise choice. In a slogan: democracy and autonomy go together.

These considerations set limits to toleration. Other things being equal, it is desirable to let associations and families carry on their own way of life in their own way, but other things are decidedly not equal in a case such as *Yoder,* in which the perceived religious interests of parents conflict with their basic fiduciary responsibilities as parents. Some parents have scruples of conscience that prevent them from taking care of the basic health care, nutritional, and educational needs of their children, but in these cases conscience must yield to basic needs.[44]

But *is* education at the high school level a basic need? The opinions of the Supreme Court justices in *Yoder* seemed to reflect the view that at the margin, whether to attend or skip two years of high school was not of much importance. In contrast, the Amish defendants themselves seemed to have a lively appreciation of the fact that early adolescence is a crucial period for defining one's identity and one's relation to the values taught as authoritative in one's childhood. If the development of children's minds from ages twelve to fourteen is not consequential, what is the fuss about? Beyond this polemical point, our account has stressed that attaining the autonomy proper to a democratic citizen involves a mastery of sophisticated skills beyond what students could be expected to learn in grade school. So high school is pivotal, and half of high school is significant.

In section I, we mentioned two sets of considerations from democratic theory that might be thought to support the outcome in *Yoder.* First, sustaining a rich civil society fabric of associations may be functional to democracy in a variety of ways. In fact, there are at least two kinds of functional claim in the democratic theory literature that turn out to be pertinent to evaluating what was at issue in *Yoder.* As far as the literature on single- versus multiple-cleavaged societies is concerned, it is clear that the Amish present no threat to the existence of a democratic political order. A (somewhat tendentious) case might be made that they are functional to democracy; certainly they are not dysfunctional in the sense of posing a threat to democratic stability. If that were the decisive test, the Amish should win.

A second functional argument is the Walzer/de Tocqueville claim that internally undemocratic civil institutions are healthy in a democracy. In the allocation of authorative values they act as a counterweight against the potential tyranny of the democratic state, and thus help preserve its democratic character in the long run. Ever since this claim was first put forward by de Tocqueville its democratic credentials have been suspect, not least because the mechanisms by which an internally undemocratic civil society will produce democratic agents and institutions have not been spelled out by its proponents. In most formulations, it seems at bottom to be a liberal rather than a democratic argument, since the institutions of civil society are regarded as important primarily as shields between individuals and the state. In a world in which conventional liberal distinctions between public and private have been called into question, this argument becomes yet more vulnerable still. If politics permeates civil society, a democratic theory of politics which is designed to leave civil society untouched scarcely deserves the name.

We have not argued that the Amish constitute a threat to a democratic political order. We not against tolerating them, only against tolerating their educational practices. Our argument has been that in a democracy, where citizens are affected by the collective actions of the majority, it is necessary that citizens develop the capacities needed to understand and evaluate the policies by which their lives might be affected, and through which they might affect the lives of others. Children in a democracy thus have a right to education to an age when critical reason is developed and can be deployed, and third parties have a right to expect parents and other educators to try to provide children with such an education.

We do not go so far as to argue that citizens in a democracy are obligated to participate in political life. We do insist, however, that even if, when they become adults, those who accept the Amish way of life choose to withdraw from participation in the political order, they need critical reasoning capacities if such a choice is to be authentic. It is because the Amish acculturation program is explicitly designed to prevent the development of critical reason that the Amish should have lost in *Yoder*. In order to respect a person's choice of an Amish way of life, one must have some reasonable confidence in an individual's choice-making competence. This competence, we have argued, is developed in education for autonomy.

The other democratic argument in support of *Yoder* that we mentioned at the outset is communitarian in spirit. The Amish association provides the good of close community ties and a shared sense of worthwhile life for its members by withdrawing from a modern life that breaks down small-scale stable community and all that goes with it.[45] So democratic communitarianism gives one reason to tilt in favor of such groups as the Amish and to applaud the decision in *Yoder* that accorded "greater respect to the claims of our encumbered selves" than the contrary decision would have done.[46]

Talking about "our" encumbered selves in the context of *Yoder* glosses over the distinct perspectives of Amish parents and Amish children. No doubt the child's self will become variously encumbered by the time adulthood is reached, but the issue is, encumbered by what? We have argued that it is good for each of us to become encumbered by the ability and disposition to step back from those of our current values that have been rendered problematic in some way and to think critically about them. In the absence of an argument that shows that it is possible consistently to reject this view without rejecting democratic values wholesale, the exhortation to respect encumbered selves is little more than unreasoned sentimentalism.

NOTES

1. See Michael Walzer, *Spheres of Justice: A Defense of Pluralism and Equality* (New York: Basic Books, 1983); Michael Sandel, *Liberalism and the Limits of Justice* (Cambridge: Cambridge University Press, 1984);

and Susan Okin, *Justice, Gender, and the Family* (New York: Basic Books, 1989).

2. *Wisconsin v. Yoder* 406 U.S. 205 (1972).

3. John A. Hostetler, *Amish Society,* 3d ed. (Baltimore: Johns Hopkins University Press, 1980), 25–92; Donald B. Kraybill, *The Riddle of Amish Culture* (Baltimore: Johns Hopkins University Press, 1989), 94–99.

4. Hostetler, *Amish Society,* 98–108.

5. The term *Anabaptist* originated as a nickname meaning "rebaptizer," practiced by nonconformist Calvinists who believed that nothing in the scriptures supports the practice of infant baptism. Hostetler, *Amish Society,* 26–27.

6. Hostetler, *Amish Society,* 79, 83.

7. Kraybill, *The Riddle of Amish Culture,* 140.

8. Quoted in Kraybill, *The Riddle of Amish Culture,* 123.

9. Kraybill, *The Riddle of Amish Culture,* 127.

10. Kraybill, *The Riddle of Amish Culture,* 137.

11. 406 U.S. 214, 216.

12. Ibid., 216.

13. Tocqueville makes this claim most explicitly while discussing the relative merits of Catholicism over Protestantism in democratic systems. See Alexis de Tocqueville, *Democracy in America* (New York: Anchor, 1969), 449, 450–51. Michael Walzer, "The Idea of Civil Society," *Dissent* (Spring 1991): 302–3. More generally, see Walzer, *Spheres of Justice.*

14. A. F. Bentley, *The Process of Government* (Chicago: University of Chicago Press, 1908); D. B. Truman, *The Governmental Process* (New York: Knopf, 1951).

15. Robert Dahl's study of New Haven, Connecticut, entitled *Who Governs?* (New Haven: Yale University Press, 1961), was the classic of this genre.

16. Louis Hartz, *The Liberal Tradition in America* (New York: Harcourt Brace, 1955). See also Robert Dahl, *A Preface to Democratic Theory* (Chicago: University of Chicago Press, 1956).

17. For a good account of the history of the functional argument and an elaboration of its logic, see Nicholas R. Miller, "Pluralism and Social Choice," *American Political Science Review,* vol. 77, no. 3 (1983).

18. Kraybill, *The Riddle of Amish Culture,* 259.

19. See, for example, Michael Sandel, "Freedom of Conscience or Freedom of Choice?" in *Articles of Faith, Articles of Peace,* ed. James Hunter and Os. Guiness (Washington, D.C.: Brookings, 1990), 90–91.

20. 406 U.S. 205, 221.

21. Ibid., at 222.

22. According to Kraybill, the original motivation was in fact to diminish unemployment in the aftermath of the depression by removing adolescents from the labor market. *The Riddle of Amish Culture,* 122.

23. On the educational attainments that are necessary for intelligent and responsible exercise of the franchise, see John Stuart Mill, *Considerations on Representative Government,* in *Collected Works,* vol. 19, ed. J. M. Robson (Toronto: University of Toronto Press, 1977), 470–71.

24. On the nature of deliberative democracy, see Joshua Cohen, "Deliberation and Democratic Legitimacy," in *The Good Polity,* ed. Alan Hamlin and Philip Pettit (Oxford: Basil Blackwell, 1989); Jon Elster, "The Market and the Forum," in *Foundations of Social Choice Theory,* ed. Jon Elster and Aanund Hylland, (Cambridge: Cambridge University Press, 1986), 103–32; also Jürgen Habermas, *Communication and the Evolution of Society,* trans. Thomas McCarthy (Boston: Beacon Hill, 1979).

25. Interestingly, in this connection the Supreme Court did not encounter any difficulty in 1990 in setting aside a Minnesota Supreme Court decision that exempted an Amish group from complying with a highway safety law. At issue was their refusal to obey a state law requiring reflecting triangles on the rear of slow-moving vehicles on the grounds that compliance would mean they trusted man rather than God. Following its own precedent in *Employment Division v. Smith,* 494 U.S. 872 (1989) (which held that religious groups could not be exempted from criminal laws against drugs on the grounds that these laws violated their religious beliefs), the court denied the Amish request for an exemption. *Minnesota v. Hershberger* 495 U.S. 901 (1990).

26. John Locke, *Second Treatise of Government,* ed. Peter Laslett (Cambridge: Cambridge University Press, 1960), 346, section 55, and (after the ellipses) 348, section 58.

27. Within limits, that is. Since I know that among the set of moral beliefs I now hold to be true, some are doubtless misguided, I have an obligation to teach my child methods of reasoning and inquiry that give her a fair chance of adopting a better morality than my own. The same applies to my conception of what is prudent, which I am entitled to pass on to my child, but with a similar qualification hedging against the likelihood that my conception of prudence is in some respects in error.

28. It is perhaps worth noting that even in the much discussed Gregory Kingsley case in September 1992, where a Florida court terminated a twelve year old's parents' parental rights at his request, this was

not a case of a child "divorcing" his parents as reported in the press. See the *New York Times,* September 26, 1992, 1, 5. The court found that the boy's biological mother had so completely neglected him for so long that her maternal rights should be terminated in favor of the foster parents with whom he had been living for a year. It was novel that the child was the named plaintiff in the suit, a tactical move on the foster father's part (a lawyer), who wanted to avoid having the child taken out of his home while the litigation was pending. But it was not a case of child-parent "divorce" in that the court would not have allowed the boy become parentless on his own motion, or, indeed, to choose new parents other than the foster parents.

29. Given the high rate at which the Amish population is growing (between 30 and 48 percent per decade since 1890 at least, and well in excess of the population at large), these claims about the threat of extinction seem exaggerated. Figures taken from Hostetler, *Amish Society,* 99.

30. At least, that was the constitutional requirement as viewed by the justices who agreed with the verdict in *Yoder.* Since *Employment Division, Department of Human Resources of the State of Oregon v. Smith,* 485 U.S. 660 (1988) and 110 U.S. 1595 (1990), the free exercise constitutional requirement in relation to actions of government that are neither discriminatory on their face nor manifest an intent to discriminate has changed. For analysis and criticism of the Supreme Court's retrenchment on free exercise, see Michael McConnell, "Free Exercise Revisionism and the *Smith* Decision," *University of Chicago Law Review,* vol. 57, no. 4 (Fall 1990): 1109–53.

31. One point should be mentioned here, although its elaboration would take us too far afield. In deciding whether an exemption from state law could be carved out to satisfy a religious interest without unduly frustrating a substantial and legitimate state aim, the extent to which the exemption that is proposed would thwart a countervailing state interest depends in part on how broad the exemption must be. In this connection, note that Justice Burger attempted to narrow the class of claims that could take shelter under the First Amendment Religion Clauses by what looks to be a tautology: "to have the protection of the Religion Clauses, the claims must be rooted in religious belief." But this seeming tautology is actually false. If one objected to compulsory schooling in a case that was just like the case of the Amish, except that the choice against compulsory schooling for one's children was "philosophical and personal rather than religious," it would be utter favoritism toward religion, impermissible under a reasonable construal of the Religion Clauses, to allow the Amish claim for exemption be-

cause it is religious and to disallow the otherwise comparable secular claim just because it is secular in its grounding. See on this point the partially dissenting opinion in *Wisconsin v. Yoder* by Justice Brennan. To specify when a claimed exemption for secular reasons is "otherwise comparable" to an exemption claimed for religious reasons is of course an intricate and difficult undertaking.

32. In other words, a decision against the Amish in *Yoder* could consistently be reconciled with *Pierce v. Society of Sisters,* 268 U.S. 510 (1925).

33. Amy Gutmann, "Children, Paternalism, and Education," *Philosophy and Public Affairs* vol. 9, no. 4 (Summer 1980), 350.

34. Joel Feinberg, "The Child's Right to an Open Future," in *Whose Child? Children's Rights, Parental Authority, and State Power,* ed. William Aiken and Hugh LaFollette (Totowa, N.J.: Littlefield, Adams, 1980), 134–35.

35. Jon Elster, "Solomonic Judgments: Against the Best Interests of the Child," in his *Solomonic Judgments: Studies in the Limitations of Rationality* (Cambridge: Cambridge University Press, 1989), 137.

36. Gutmann, "Children, Paternalism, and Education," 351. In fairness it should be noted that Gutmann alters this way of conceiving autonomy in her book *Democratic Education* (Princeton: Princeton University Press, 1987). See 33–47, where she criticizes theorists such as Bruce Ackerman who espouse the idea that children should be educated in a way that is so far as possible neutral among all conceptions of the good life.

37. Gutmann, "Children, Paternalism, and Education," 352.

38. Kraybill, *The Riddle of Amish Culture,* 131.

39. Quoted in Kraybill, *The Riddle of Amish Culture,* 131.

40. William A. Galston, *Liberal Purposes: Goods, Virtues, and Diversity in the Liberal State* (Cambridge: Cambridge University Press, 1991), 253.

41. We assume that Rawls has *Yoder* in mind when he writes, "Justice as fairness honors, as far as it can, the claims of those who wish to withdraw from the modern world in accordance with the injunctions of their religion, provided only that they acknowledge the principles of the political conception of justice and appreciate its political ideals of person and society." He proceeds to a brief discussion of the education of children from this standpoint. See John Rawls, "The Priority of Right and Ideas of the Good," *Philosophy and Public Affairs,* vol. 17, no. 4 (Fall 1988): 251–76; see especially 268. See also Rawls, "Justice as Fairness: Political Not Metaphysical," *Philosophy and Public Affairs,* vol. 14 (1985): 251–76; and Rawls, "The Domain of the Political and Over-

lapping Consensus," *New York University Law Review,* vol. 64, no. 2 (May 1989): 233–55.

42. 310 U.S. 296 (1940), 310.

43. See Ronald Dworkin, "Foundations of Liberal Equality," in *The Tanner Lectures on Human Values,* vol. 11, ed. Grethe B. Peterson (Salt Lake City: University of Utah Press, 1990), 1–119.

44. See George W. Dent, Jr., "Religious Children, Secular Schools," *Southern California Law Review,* vol. 61, no. 4 (May 1988): 863–941. Dent analyzes various cases in which we would say that the religious interests of parents are in conflict with the educational needs of children.

45. The movie *Witness* evenhandedly describes the appeal of Amish community solidarity and the appeal of modern individual liberties incompatible with it. See also Justice Douglas's minority opinion in *Yoder* chiding the Burger opinion for taking an overly romantic view of Amish-style religious community.

46. Sandel, "Freedom of Conscience or Freedom of Choice?", 90.

15

IN DEFENSE OF *YODER:* PARENTAL AUTHORITY AND THE PUBLIC SCHOOLS

SHELLEY BURTT

There is much to disagree with in the Supreme Court decision, *Wisconsin v. Yoder* (406 U.S. 205 [1972]). The question the Court confronted was whether to allow Amish parents to end their children's schooling at age fourteen, rather than age sixteen as required by Wisconsin law. In ruling against the state, the Supreme Court first stressed the distinctiveness of the Amish religion and the social respectability of the religion's members. The unfortunate impression given is that the strength of parents' free exercise rights in relation to the education of their children will depend on the insularity of the religion, its longevity, and the law-abidingness of its confessors rather than on the fact of religious belief itself.

The exclusive focus on the free exercise rights of parents is another regrettable feature of the *Yoder* decision. Of course, the Court has always been reluctant to grant children a religious identity independent of their families'. Yet parents' and children's interests are not always identical, even in the spiritual realm. For this reason, it seems important, as Douglas's dissent points out, to hear from the children themselves. I will say more about how best to accommodate children's interests at the conclusion of this chapter. My point here is that by grounding its decision entirely on the free exercise rights of parents, the Court too quickly foreclosed the claims of children to the state's independent attention.

Despite these and other difficulties with its precise reasoning, *Yoder* deserves continued attention. As a ruling on religious liberty, it appears to affirm the rather narrow right of a long-standing, law-abiding sect at the margins of contemporary culture to perpetuate itself in part by keeping its children out of public high school. But consider it as a statement regarding the appropriate scope of parental authority: once certain minimum standards of educational achievement are met, parents may resist a public education that they deem destructive to their children's religious life or sensibilities. In other words, the public, civic education of children takes second place to their religious education. The Court's decision attempts to limit the scope of this conclusion by stressing the unique nature of the Amish religion.[1] Here I make the case for applying *Yoder*'s implicit dicta more widely, defending a conception of familial authority which gives parents wide latitude to shape the educational experience of their children. In this account, I defend state accommodation of parents' educational choices not on free exercise grounds but in terms of parents' and state's shared responsibility to meet children's developmental needs.

This chapter begins by questioning the stark contrast drawn in much of the recent legal and philosophical literature between critical rationality and moral autonomy on the one side and virtually any sort of religious education on the other. I argue in the next section that any account of the authority of the democratic state over the education of young children must make allowance for the many religiously grounded ways in which children might learn to choose well in civic and moral matters.

Some critics of *Yoder* charge the Amish (and others who cite religious objections to the public school curriculum) with inappropriately subordinating their children's educational interests to other issues: their own salvation or the long-term survival of their religious communities, for example. By questioning the motives of religious parents in this way, commentators can frame the parent-public school conflict in easily resolvable terms: indulging religious fanatics out to brainwash their innocent children or supporting levelheaded public servants devoted to serving the interests of the next generation. In debating the merits of *Yoder,* however, it seems both more accurate and more interesting to accept the self-characterization offered by the Yoders and others like them: concerned parents determined to provide their children with the education they believe best serves their children's long-term interests.[2] If we concede that Christian fundamentalists possess the same love for their children that we assume animates mainstream Protestants or militant atheists, the question at issue in parent–public school conflict can be reframed as follows: when parents and state (and perhaps child) disagree on what constitutes the child's educational interests, whose judgment should prevail and why? I answer this question by defending a modified "principle of parental deference" which supports broad but not unlimited parental authority over children's educational experience. I conclude by examining one important exception to this principle, specifying those circumstances in which both parents and the state must respect children's independent claims to shape the content of their education.

It is useful to note at this point that my argument proceeds with little reference to questions of constitutional law. The idea advanced in this chapter (that authority over children ought to be distributed according to the ability and willingness of the relevant parties to meet children's needs) is unfamiliar to most constitutional scholars and absent from current constitutional jurisprudence.[3] And while parents' fundamental right to the care and control of their children is often asserted in judicial decisions, this right rarely survives the presentation of competing interests.[4] We might say of this situation that courts currently misinterpret the constitution, allowing greater state inroads on parental authority than is strictly compatible with the document's guarantees of personal liberty. On the other hand, it may be that in the area of family rights and responsibilities, our constitution provides protection against only the grossest abuses of state (and parental) power. In this case, enforcing the vision of children's and parents' rights that I articulate here would be up to our legislatures, not the Supreme Court.

Disputing *Yoder:* The Case against Accommodation

Many commentaries on *Yoder,* including Arneson's and Shapiro's in this volume, fault the decision for its acceptance of parental choices that appear to violate the basic principles of a liberal democratic order. In this view, polities like the United States owe the children within their borders an education in "the habits and skills of critical reflection."[5] The Court in *Yoder* was thus mistaken to grant Amish parents the right to deprive children of their last years of compulsory education. Adults' right to religious liberty does not include the right to raise children lacking the mental resources to "participate competently in democratic decision-making" or "engage in critical reflection about one's values."[6]

There are a number of difficulties with a critique of *Yoder* along these lines. The first problem concerns the incremental value of two additional years of high school education. I can agree that children deserve an education in autonomy and democratic deliberation and still question whether that end will be substantially advanced by the schooling received in grades nine and ten. Either the process of developing "habits and skills of critical reflection" is sufficiently demanding that a full high school or even college education is necessary or the standard is not to be set so high, in which case it is difficult to see what has not been achieved by age fourteen that will be at sixteen.

A second difficulty with the argument is its misplaced confidence that public high schools in the United States can be reliably expected to offer a curriculum uniquely well suited to developing critical, morally autonomous democratic thinkers.[7] Arneson and Shapiro admit that, "No doubt democratic institutions and educational practices could benefit from improvement," but go on to conclude, "the correct inference from the observation that there is a gap between the obligatory norms we profess and the degree to which we fulfill these norms is that we should narrow the gap by doing more to fulfill the norms."[8] True enough, but why in the meantime should Amish parents be made to send their children to public institutions in the service of ends (education in autonomy and democratic citizenship) which it is conceded the institutions are ill prepared to achieve?

The primary problem with this line of criticism, however, is that religious parents in general and the Amish in particular are portrayed as irredeemably hostile to the development of their children's critical rationality. Arneson and Shapiro, for example, quote a scholar of Amish culture to support their claim that "the Amish acculturation program is expressly designed to limit critical thinking, to get children to accept things on faith without submitting them to reasoned reflection."[9] This is a serious charge because the ability to reflect deliberately on one's personal and civic commitments does seem central to the achievement of both personal autonomy and democratic citizenship. What can be said in the Amish's defense?

I do not want to pursue here any involved sociological inquiry into various religious traditions and their impact on children's cognitive abilities. I cannot make the case here either for or against the value of an Amish education in this regard. Rather what strikes me as odd or at least debatable is the assumption embedded not only in Arneson and Shapiro's work but in most recent philosophical considerations of critical rationality that to reason from the basis of God's word as reflected in Scripture is somehow to abandon the exercise of critical rationality. The long and distinguished traditions of religious scholarship which reflect critically on the requirements of one's (perhaps unquestioned) fundamental commitments are here consigned to political oblivion. To make this point another way: the Amish and other religious parents seeking exemptions from the public school curriculum may not be opposed to the development of "habit and skills of critical thinking" per se—just to the texts and methods used to teach it in the public schools.

Current political theory puts a tremendous premium on developing the ability to "distance [oneself] from prevailing desires and practices" or to engage in "reconsideration of [one's] ends and commitments" as markers of personal autonomy and critical rationality.[10] Because religious education of youth typically does not encourage such radical skepticism, it is often characterized as hostile to critical reasoning more generally. Arneson and Shapiro's assertion in this regard is typical: "In general, the practical alternative to subjecting one's fundamental aims to critical scrutiny is to accept uncritically whatever aims socialization during one's childhood has instilled."[11] Passages such as this one ask us to think of early childhood religious education as one more obstacle to achieving an autonomous moral identity. But this is to describe the nature of religious belief and the import of the sacrament of baptism (in Christian families) or the ritual of circumcision (in Jewish ones) in terms completely alien to those who profess a religious faith.[12] To religious believers, one teaches children about God so that they can reason correctly. To disrupt this process too early is not to facilitate rational deliberation, but to deprive a child of the conceptual tools necessary to make sense of the world.

The academy's tendency to belittle the educational goals of deeply religious parents can be found as well in the judiciary's consideration of cases brought by parents troubled with religious objections to parts of the public school curriculum.[13] Faced with a Minnesotan sect objecting to the use of any audiovisual learning aids in the classroom, one judge contrasted the interests that he was being asked to balance in this way: on one side was "the state's interest in providing its youth with a proper and enabling education"; on the other was the "asserted . . . right of the parents to inculcate and mold their children's religious beliefs to conform to their own."[14] A similar analysis informs Judge Kennedy's concurring opinion in *Mozert v. Hawkins County Board of Education* (litigating a textbook dispute). Here she describes the state as having a compelling interest in "preparing public school students for citizenship and self-government . . . [by] teaching students about complex and controversial social and moral issues." It is a goal that contrasts favorably to the parents' interest in preventing "their children . . . being exposed to controversial ideas in the classroom, and to making critical judgments . . . about anything for which they believe the Bible states a rule or position."[15] In both these examples, religious parents' misgivings about the public school curriculum are characterized in such a way that their educational choices are portrayed as inimical to the values the public schools are trying to develop. Having dismissed the parents' educational goals in this unsympathetic, if not actually contemptuous, manner, courts can refuse to accommodate their objections with a clear conscience. Neither the constitution nor good public policy requires compromise with such benighted educational ideals.[16]

The problem with this judicial strategy is that it defines the substance of the debate between religious parents and public schools in a way that grossly distorts the nature of parental concerns. Those who object to accommodation argue that the question at issue is what sort of education American children will receive: one that encourages autonomy and civic competence or one that does not. Nowhere is the debate framed, more realistically, as a choice between an education for personal autonomy and civic responsibility grounded in religious faith against one grounded in secular certainties. The previous pages have suggested some of the difficulties raised by construing conflicts between public schools and religious parents as primarily about how far the First Amendment allows parents to thwart the civically responsible education the state desires for its citizens. A more promising approach to such cases as *Yoder, Davis,* and *Mozert* would treat them as disputes over who possesses the authority to decide upon the shape and nature of a child's educational experience: parents or public schools. Resolving this question about authority over a child's education requires first an account of how we as a polity should distribute authority over children in general.

Authority over Children: Current Approaches

When asked to consider the limits of state or parental authority over children, courts and philosophers usually proceed in one of two ways, both of which I find unsatisfactory. The first approach relies on a case by case balancing act in which the relevant interests at stake are identified and then weighed: a parent's right to religious freedom versus the state's interest in the safety and health of minors (*Prince v. Massachusetts* 321 U.S. 158 [1944]); a child's liberty interest versus a parent's right to control his whereabouts (*Parham v. J.R.* 442 U.S. 584 [1979]); the state's interest in civic education versus a parent's interest in moral instruction (*Pierce v. Society of Sisters* 268 U.S. 510 [1925]).

One of the greatest drawbacks of this approach is that it displays little consistency across time or across issues. In fact, American jurisprudence as practiced today gives us no principled account of the scope of parental authority or the acceptable reach of state intervention in the family. Setting the scales afresh with each case, courts have produced a patchwork of rulings that fails to reflect any consistent vision—liberal, democratic or otherwise—of the appropriate scope of parental rights and responsibilities.[17]

The most frequently proposed alternative to such ad hoc jurisprudence calls for the judicial thumb to be pressed firmly down on the parents' side of the scales, with public officials given the authority to overrule parental decisions only in a narrowly defined range of cases. This theory holds that public officials must point either to a clear and compelling public interest or to a complete breakdown in parent-child relations in order to justify state intervention in adults' parenting choices.[18] This presumption of parental autonomy has the advantage of articulating a settled principle one might apply somewhat consistently across a range of disputed cases. The problem is that, when applied, it demarcates a line between public concerns and private matters which poorly serves the interests of both parents and children. The reason for this troubling disjunction can be seen by comparing a case like *Mozert v. Hawkins,* discussed above, with one in which a judge or social worker must decide what to do with a child at risk of ongoing abuse or neglect.

In the first case, any presumption of parental autonomy is easily outweighed by the ready availability of a compelling public interest. The undeniable public good of educating a competent citizenry offers sufficient justification for substantial impositions on parental prerogative—or so the argument might go.[19] By contrast, in cases concerning the emotional and physical welfare of individual children, a presumption in favor of parental autonomy severely curtails state interference in the parent-child relationship. While it is not impossible under a presumption of parental autonomy to take the steps necessary to remove children from abusive situations before they get very badly hurt, the principle as articulated by its defenders does not always provide an easy rationale for such measures. Because no substantial risks to broad public interests such as public health or civic competence present themselves, the state must await proof of a complete breakdown in family relations in order to justify any constraint on parental autonomy. But since the proof of irremediable family breakdown is usually the actual injury of the child, the theory requires one to await the very maltreatment one would wish to prevent before intervening.[20] As a method for resolving conflicts of authority in family life, then, a presumption of parental autonomy has the ironic effect of justifying greater interference with children's educational, moral, civic, and religious education than with parental behavior that places children at risk for physical maltreatment.

There have been a number of efforts in recent years to correct for the shortcomings in the "parental autonomy" approach without resorting again to a mere balancing of interests. Some theorists have urged the recognition and protection of children's autonomy interests, arguing that the state ought to step in to protect what one author calls "the child's right to an open future."[21] Others have sought to reduce the scope of parental prerogative by appealing to more demanding standards of democratic process and civic competence than the one used now by courts and liberal theorists.[22] Both these alternatives avoid the inconsistency plaguing the balancing of interests approach and extend greater protection to children than that provided by a presumption of parental autonomy. But they do so by disregarding what I take to be the still valid parental prerogative to shape the moral and religious environment of a maturing child. The following section develops an account of the proper distribution of authority over children that encourages a greater accommodation of the distinctive educational goals of highly religious parents without sacrificing the community's ability to protect children from a wide variety of parental maltreatment.

From Adult Liberties to Children's Needs

How we distribute authority over children is in part a function of our beliefs regarding the proper use of that authority. If Americans believed, with Rousseau, that a free polity must above all ensure that each generation of citizens was committed body and soul to a democratic regime, then our legislatures would seek to distribute authority over children in such a way as to ensure that nothing compromised the established program of citizen education. Perhaps we would not even rule compulsory public education out of order. But both our political and legal traditions eschew this sort of avid republicanism. Liberal democracies such as the United States typically temper the principle of majority rule with expansive respect for citizens' individuated pursuits of the good life. Regimes of this sort gain their authority over individuals not only by establishing and upholding a democratic political process, but also by affording protection (usually through the medium of constitutionally protected rights) to the values, desires, and life plans of individuals over against majoritarian legislation.

But how do we translate these commitments into a principle of action when it comes to children? Should we allow Amish parents to deprive their children of secondary schooling because having children grow up Amish is part of the parents' desired life plan? Free exercise claims aside, is this a liberal solution to the problem? Should we allow other religious parents to pick and choose within the public school curriculum so as to protect their children from coursework offensive to their conception of the good life? Is this an acceptably democratic response?

It seems to me a mistake to imagine that liberal democratic values call for respecting parental choices simply on the basis of a supposed sovereignty of parental will. Granting parents an extensive, if not unlimited, right to do what they want with their children *seems* liberal because it allows adults wide latitude to pursue their own life plans, including the often intensely enjoyable and rewarding challenge of parenthood, with minimal intervention from the state. But this liberal look is purchased at significant cost. By attaching such importance to parental autonomy—whatever the end to which it is put—this approach ends up privileging the rights, desires, and life plans of one class of individuals in our society (parents) over others (their children) without offering sufficient justification for this favoritism.

Those who justify such an expansive conception of parental authority often think of themselves as usefully expanding the realm of individual liberty. In fact, the rights of parents thus conceived are grounded in the decidedly illiberal exclusion of a large and especially vulnerable segment of the population from full membership in the civic community for no other reason than that their parents claim the pleasure of controlling them as part of their personal experience of freedom.[23] While it is possible to justify a second-class citizenship for persons under a given age, this is not an acceptable way to do it.

A better defense of parental claims to authority over children would begin not with adult liberties but children's needs. We would still expect the polity to respect a wide range of parental choices regarding children's care, education, and discipline. But the reason for parental autonomy in these matters would be to allow the satisfactory discharge of parental responsibilities, not the unmonitored satisfaction of adult preferences.

At the beginning of this section, I stated that the proper distribution of authority over children depends in part on how the end of that authority is conceived. My suggestion here is that authority over children in liberal democracies ought to be exercised not to satisfy parents' conception of the good life, but to ensure satisfaction of children's needs. Adults' authority over children will thus depend on their ability and willingness to meet children's developmental needs, broadly conceived.

To make sense of this proposed principle, we need first of all an acceptable account of children's developmental needs, those goods children must receive in order to grow, at a minimum, into socially competent, civically responsible, independent adults. Two points are worth making about whatever list one might draw up. First, one would need to give attention not only to children's primary emotional, physical, and cognitive needs, but to the moral, spiritual, and cultural side of their growth as well. Second, any list of needs would have to be treated both as provisional and as open to public deliberation. We could expect general agreement (even across cultures) on certain core needs of children—food, shelter, and in the late twentieth century, literacy. But the identification of other items as children's needs would depend in part on contestable accounts of what makes for a competent, mature, and flourishing adult. Inevitably, then, any polity's list of those goods that children need to develop would properly be open to debate and revision—not just in journals of child pyschology but in public, deliberative forums. My point: placing needs at the center of an account of how to distribute authority does not end public debate about parent-state relations, but shifts that debate's focus from adult rights over children to adult responsibilities for them.

Of course, a list of children's needs, however arrived at and whatever its content, does not in itself explain who gets to do what to a society's youngest citizens. A polity in the process of rethinking the proper distribution of authority over children must also develop an understanding of the various social and psychological factors that influence adults' ability effectively to provide for a child's needs. These factors include, but are not limited to, the safety of the surrounding environment (including the presence of political stability and the absence of environmental hazards), the material and financial resources at the parent's disposal (whether provided by participation in the labor market or by public assistance), the parent's physical and mental health, his or her conception of the rights and responsibilities of parenthood and of the nature of childhood, and his or her ability to respond constructively to the complex logistical and emotional demands of integrating work and family life in modern society. Certainly, the ability of an adult to meet a child's needs is not determined by any single element such as class background, income level, race, or nationality. On the other hand, the mere physical ability to produce a child does not make one a good parent. Rather, the extent to which an infant can hope to have its myriad developmental needs consistently met over the period of its growth and maturity depends on the complex interplay of numerous factors, like those just listed, which shape the success of the parenting process regardless of class or culture.

The fact that our ability to transform love of a young child into effective parenting depends on many, often difficult to control variables reveals as well the contingent nature of the association we usually draw between biological ties and parental authority. Rather than grant adults authority over children on the basis of biological accident, the approach I propose would ground parental authority in the ability and willingness to meet children's developmental needs. This is not some prescription for mass redistribution of babies at birth. Recognizing the diversity of factors that contributes to one's ability to parent well underscores the shared responsibility of parent and community to create the circumstances in which children's biological parents (or other appointed guardian) can succeed at this extraordinarily demanding task.

Like Arneson and Shapiro, this account envisions parents fundamentally as trustees of their children's interests, with a responsibility (shared by the community at large) to provide an environment in which children can grow into socially competent, civically responsible, independent adults. While willing biological parents are in almost all cases the preferred guardians for any child, what these adults can do to and for a child will be limited by the scope of this responsibility. In particular, parental authority must be exercised with reference to a child's specific short-term or long-term interests and not by reference to a customary right of parents to the "care and control" of their children.[24]

While Arneson, Shapiro, and I agree up to this point, our accounts diverge on the question of what attention to a child's interests requires on the part of parent and polity. Obvious failure to provide for a child's most basic developmental needs—by gross physical abuse, deliberate neglect or the withholding of lifesaving medical treatment—would trigger state intervention and rightly so. But acute physical distress is an easy case under almost any philosophy of family law. The proper course of action becomes harder to discern when we confront the problem at the root of religious parents' conflicts with the public schools. When parents and state differ as to the educational interests of children enrolled in public schools, whose judgment ought to prevail and why?

The Case for Parental Deference

Arneson and Shapiro's version of trusteeship argues for the authority of public schools in this conflict: "Parents must cooperate with other legitimate authorities in society to develop in their children critical reasoning skills that will enable their children to stand back from the values they have been taught and to subject these values to informed critical scrutiny." The reason for this obligation lies in a democratic society's " 'compelling' interest in bringing it about that each member of society is raised with the capacities needed to fulfill the responsibilities of democratic citizenship."[25] The claims of democracy, in this account, require parents to subordinate their judgment regarding their child's educational needs to their local board of education's. But this restriction of parental authority builds on too narrow an account of children's interests, one which excludes from consideration not only the needs of children as moral and spiritual beings, but their interests as members of distinct cultural communities. When we enlarge our understanding of children's developmental needs to include these aspects of their characters, then a division of authority made with reference to children's needs supports what I call a modified principle of parental deference.

I ground this argument for parental deference in a consideration of the reasons that we subject children to parental authority in the first place. Helpless, vulnerable, and without independent access to material resources, children require the nurturing aid of other human beings to reach maturity. But their needs encompass more than physical well-being. Children need an upbringing that enables them not only to discharge their civic and social obligations but to pursue and live a good life as they come to understand it. One reason then that public schools ought to make room for religious parents is that the effort to provide a consistent moral and religious environment for a child represents an important way of building the psychological and cognitive resources which the child will need to choose and live a good life as an adult. This conclusion obviously challenges the views of many liberal theorists that schools must use their authority to counter parental indoctrination, by providing "children with the sense of the very different lives that could be theirs."[26] But to give children the resources for living a good life requires more than simply exposing them to many alternatives.

Our high-tech, consumer-oriented society provides plenty of opportunity for exposure to competing lifestyles, especially for those who are attempting to construct lives that depart significantly from the mainstream. Apostolic Lutherans can forbid their children to watch television, but they cannot shutter the windows of the local toy store with its tempting display of electronic games. Christian fundamentalists can send their children to schools that forbid dates and dancing but they cannot keep them from hearing about the high school prom from the girl next door. We can assume, given the high rates of defection from the Amish community, that even their "unworldly" teenagers become aware, very powerfully, of the life available outside their closed community. When it comes to providing the next generation of American citizens with a sense of the different ways in which one can be a good human being, it seems to me that the message of the dominant secular culture is not in danger of being drowned out by the strictures of marginal sectarians. (Even Waco's Branch Davidians watched television.) Precisely because of the robust pluralism of our culture, then, we would do better to encourage parental efforts to create a moral environment filled with consistent, not conflicting, messages. If we are to take seriously the goal of giving children the material and psychological resources not only to reflect upon but to live and enjoy an individualized conception of the good life, public authorities should generally seek to accommodate, not undermine, parental efforts in this area.

Two examples illustrate my point. Consider first the decision, taken in 1992 by New York City's board of education, to make condoms available in the city's high schools with no provision for a parental "opt-out." In defending this plan, advocates of universal access conjured up a particular image of the objecting parent: a mother unable to discuss sexual matters with her children, rigid in her religious views, and willing to risk her children's lives to AIDS rather than admit that they might reject her church's moral imperatives. Her religious prejudice should not prevent her children from getting free condoms from the guidance counselor. However, one might also imagine a different parent profile: a practicing Roman Catholic who believed and had taught her children that the use of birth control was sinful, who had spoken about sexual matters with her children, urging them to postpone sexual activity until they were older, and who exercised what she hoped was sufficient supervision over her children's social life to discourage casual sexual encounters. I would describe this parent as trying very hard to create, against a great deal of social pressure to the contrary, an environment in which sexual abstinence for adolescents was a morally valued and realistic choice. Although the New York City school board may have a different sense of the realities of adolescent life and the imperatives of AIDS prevention, it would not have the authority, in my account, to substitute its judgment of moral priorities (in which "safe sex" is more sensibly encouraged than abstinence) for the parent's.[27]

A similar argument can be made with respect to schools' practice of corporal punishment. The Supreme Court currently holds that public school officials have the authority to impose whatever disciplinary measures they believe appropriate (and the state legislature allows) without consulting a child's parents.[28] In this model of shared authority over children, parents' at-home commitment to nonviolent methods of discipline has no claim to the respect of school officials. Any student can be paddled, whether parents object to this form of correction or not. The principle of parental deference offers a different model of shared authority which discourages this sort of deliberate undermining of parental choices. In this model, school officials would not be able to substitute their view that children learn and behave better when motivated by fear and physical pain for parents' judgment that "talking it out" is more appropriate in the disciplining of children. Note too that the idea, often suggested in the case of religious parents, that parents can simply counterbalance at home what is taught at school seems especially foolish in this context. How does nonviolent discipline at home "make up" for being paddled at school? The grant of authority to the school in this circumstance completely undermines, rather than usefully supplements, parental choices.

I do not assert here that parents' educational choices be given deference because parents' views somehow weigh more than public officials'. My aim is to avoid the balancing act that plagues judicial reasoning in this area and to elaborate instead those circumstances in which parents rather than the state get to make tough judgment calls about what children need. This broad but not unlimited principle of parental deference affirms the liberal idea that the good life can be defined, not infinitely, but in many different ways, compatible with a wide cultural variety in parenting styles. It accepts the democratic claim that children must be raised not only to embrace their own individual ends but also to discharge their civic and social responsibilities. Parents whose education and disciplinary choices deliberately undermine constitutional principles or actively prevent the development of a moral or civic consciousness would not have a claim to have such choices respected by the state. But in most cases, once certain minimum standards of educational achievement are met, parents should possess the authority to refuse a public education that they deem destructive to their children's religious life or sensibilities. This principle, I argue, allows the state to protect its legitimate interests in democratic citizenship and autonomy while discouraging government officials from simply substituting their view of what makes a good child or good parent for the family in question's approach. (I assume here that Amish education, whatever its weaknesses, does not prevent the formation of either a moral or civic consciousness. The civic consciousness it promotes, of course, is not one likely to be embraced by strong participatory democrats.)

Of course, if all we sought for our children was civic competence we might be content to assign primary authority for educational judgment calls to large bureaucratic institutions run by public authorities. But children need a moral and sentimental education as well; we owe them an upbringing that provides the material and psychological resources that allow for a full and flourishing human life. Most cultures assign the responsibility for providing this sort of upbringing to small social units distinguished by intense emotional attachments: families. Parents cannot advance this end unaided; but neither should their chosen route to their children's well-being endure constant second-guessing from public authorities.

I suspect that some of the opposition to accommodating the religious objections of sectarian parents in the public schools has its roots in a confused conception of fairness. It is true that from the point of view of each newborn child, her parents' choices as to religious beliefs, cultural community, valued activities, and moral ideals are inescapably arbitrary. But justice in parent-child relations does not require that we assign children carbon copy parents who will all instill the same (politically correct) values. Nor should we attempt to approximate this goal by looking to the public schools to undermine or counterbalance certain parental views of the good life while reinforcing those parental moralities which mirror the dominant culture's.

What then can the state demand of those with primary authority for children? My answer is that the state can and ought to demand of parents that they fulfill in some reasonable way children's developmental needs. As long as parental choices can plausibly be seen as advancing this end, they ought not to be overruled or undermined by public officials or institutions. They remain legitimate, if not ideal, exercises of parental authority.

Making Room for Religious Parents

With this account in place, let us reconsider the Amish parents' request (litigated in *Wisconsin v. Yoder*) to remove their children from school two years earlier than required by law. How would the account of parental rights and responsibilities offered here frame and resolve the conflict? First of all, the problem would not be seen as one of balancing interests: the parents' (or child's) interest in free exercise of religion versus the state's interest in democratic citizens. Nor would one wave the flag of civic education as sufficient reason to set aside parental worries about the values taught in the public schools. Rather the question would be this: are the Yoders able to make a case that removing their children from school is a responsible exercise of paternalistic authority? That is, can they show how their action serves the end of enhancing the material and/or psychological resources available to their children for living a satisfying or good life?

If the court were to conduct this exercise in the Amish case, they would almost certainly find that the Amish were able to defend their choice to end their children's schooling at the junior high school level as enhancing the children's opportunity to experience a particular form of good life—the life of an individual committed to an unworldly religious practice. At the same time, the education they do provide is sufficient to allow children, once legally emancipated, to pursue other ways of life should they so choose. In my account, parents have the authority to structure their children's education so as to encourage a life-choice that they deem praiseworthy, as long as they also meet their children's basic developmental needs. Since the Amish fulfill this criterion, they may legitimately act on their judgment that their children's spiritual and educational needs are best met by ending formal schooling at age fourteen.

A similar rationale leads to greater support for those parents seeking to forge some sort of acceptable accommodation between the demands of religious belief and the expectations of a public school education. Children for whom exceptions are being made must be able to demonstrate an adequate level of educational achievement (for example, by passing the state examinations set for homeschoolers). But if these standards are met, public officials ought to excuse students from those aspects of a public school education that their parents consider deeply corrupting or blatantly sinful.[29]

The Limits of Accommodation

As a guide to the distribution of authority over children, the principle of parental deference is not unlimited. In particular, our polity must consider the independent claims of children, of whatever age, to pursue their own conception of the good life—even, or especially, when such conceptions differ from their parents'. These claims represent an important limit to the principle of parental deference for which I have argued.

Consider again the case of the Wisconsin Amish. The rights at issue were those of the parents only and the Supreme Court ultimately ruled that the constitutional guarantee of free exercise of religion allowed the parents to end their children's formal schooling two years earlier than required by law. This essay has defended not the Court's reasoning in this decision, but the outcome itself as vindicating a sincere parental effort to provide children with the resources necessary to choose and live a good life. But what if the Yoders' children wanted to continue in school? What if their sense of the resources needed to live a good life—the good life to which they, at age fourteen, aspired—included those to be obtained at a public high school?

Current jurisprudence treats children in these situations as mere ciphers in the independent conflict between parental desires and state law.[30] Indeed, both the parental autonomy model of parental authority and the balancing of interests approach encourage this privileging of the adult will—the former because parental desires are specifically favored in conflicts with the state and the latter because children's interests are traditionally subsumed under those of the parents. Placing children's developmental needs at the center of questions of parental authority changes this dynamic.

Switching the focus from adult liberties to children's needs would, in particular, encourage courts and policy makers to give children an opportunity to challenge their parents' conceptions of their interests and needs when conflicts over parental choice arise. Young adults willing and able to frame their own conceptions of the good life independently of their parents deserve a voice in decisions regarding their own destiny. Thus, in *Yoder,* the Court should have treated children as parties to the decision to leave school, not by imposing its own paternalistic judgment of what would be best for them but by according their conceptions of the good life the same respect given to their parents'. Thus, if children shared their parents' view of the corrupting nature of the high school curriculum, the Court should have considered the case as one involving the free exercise rights of parents *and* children. But if the children had been able to make a case for attending high school that plausibly challenged their parents' views of what was best for them, the Court should have vindicated their right to do so. (Of course, since Wisconsin law required schooling only through age sixteen, parents would still have the legal right to remove the children at that age.)[31]

One objection to this argument is that we need the state to intervene in family relations to protect the interests of children too young or too cowed to speak up for themselves. This is certainly the case if children's developmental needs are not being met. In the Amish case, however, we have a legitimate difference of opinion about the nature of a child's developmental needs. If one cannot be well prepared for both a worldly life and for Amish devotion, which sort of education is better for children being raised by Amish parents? The account of parental authority offered here suggests that if parents are not absolutely disenabling a child's ultimate choices (which, as the defection rate from the community shows, the Amish are not), the state should not impose its opinion of the better way of life over the parents'. The case is different when the child herself has developed sufficient confidence in her capacities of critical reflection to differ with her parents (or state officials) regarding their decisions concerning her education.

Does this argument mean that children will be able to pursue legal remedies whenever they object to the plans parents lay for them? What happens to the gifted athlete whose parents are not willing to make the sacrifices necessary for her to excel in her chosen sport? The difference between this example and *Yoder* is obvious: athletic training is purely discretionary, neither mandated nor discouraged by public authorities; education through age sixteen is a state law from which the Yoders sought a special exemption. If the Yoder children did not in fact wish to be exempted and had already reached a level of maturity at which they could frame their differences with their parents coherently, the state ought not to side with the parents against the children.

This account of a limited "children's prerogative" modifying the principle of parental deference does not apply with similar force to curricular decisions made at the local board of education level. Consider a dispute about a biology course. Children could oppose their parents' efforts to exclude them from the course if biology was part of a state-mandated education requirement. But they would not have similar standing if their parents simply requested an alternative biology textbook. Again, the frame of reference is the parental effort to meet children's developmental needs by providing a consistent moral message that will enhance the child's opportunity both to reflect upon and to live a good life. Completely to close down a legislatively required option over the objections of the child is not acceptable. To select how particular information will be presented is an acceptable exercise of parental authority.

The previous paragraphs have emphasized an important constraint on the principle of parental deference: children's own maturing conceptions of their developmental needs. It is important to note that this principle is limited as well by considerations of children's well-being, civic responsibilities, and the social context of the community in which it is applied. Thus, my proposal does not give parents the right to fashion an education that severely compromises children's emotional, material, or cognitive needs or that fails to provide them with the skills and dispositions necessary for democratic citizenship.[32] Nor will the principle apply with the same force to communities that are less culturally and politically open than the United States. My argument assumes that, despite the best (or worst) intentions of American parents, they will not be able to shield their children completely from the country's largely secular, highly commercialized mass culture. If the evidence were to suggest the contrary—that parents have succeeded in completely isolating their children from mainstream culture—the state's responsibility to provide an alternative to the parental educational message would be correspondingly stronger. On the other hand, when parents show themselves concerned to foster a distinctive moral, religious, or cultural environment so as to prepare their children to live a full, meaningful, independent life within a larger political community, that effort ought to be accommodated, particularly by the public schools. This accommodation should be seen as neither illiberal nor undemocratic, but rather as an appropriate instantiation of the principles of parental authority.

NOTES

1. Lower courts have eagerly followed this lead. The criterion for granting First Amendment protection in public school cases becomes parents' desire to prepare children for "an existence in an isolated and independent community" (*Davis v. Page* 385 F. Supp. 395 [1974], 400).

2. Evidence for this self-conception can be found in a number of

academic studies of Christian academies including Paul F. Parsons, *Inside America's Christian Schools* (Macon, Ga.: Mercer University Press, 1987); Susan D. Rose, *Keeping Them out of the Hands of Satan: Evangelical Schooling in America* (New York: Routledge, 1988); and Melinda Bollar Wagner, *God's Schools: Choice and Compromise in American Society* (New Brunswick, N.J.: Rutgers University Press, 1990). Also useful is Stephen Bates's account of the *Mozert v. Hawkins* case, *Battleground: One Mother's Crusade, the Religious Right, and the Struggle for Control of Our Classrooms* (New York: Poseidon Press, 1993).

Richard J. Arneson and Ian Shapiro argue in the previous chapter, "Democratic Authority and Religious Freedom: A Critique of *Wisconsin v. Yoder*" that "the parents in *Yoder* did not invoke a fiduciary obligation to their children in support of their actions. Instead they appealed to a mixture of the right of the Amish community to reproduce itself and the parents' own free exercise rights" (384–85). But this is strictly true only of the justices' characterization of the parents' concerns. John A. Hostetler, *Amish Society,* 3d ed. (Baltimore: The Johns Hopkins University Press, 1980), chapter 8, suggests the presence of less selfish motives.

3. Without making a complete review of the literature, one might usefully consult Anne C. Dailey, "Constitutional Privacy and the Just Family," *Tulane Law Review* 67 (1993): 955–1031; Laurence Houlgate, *Family and State: The Philosophy of Family Law* (Totowa, N.J.: Rowman and Littlefield, 1988); "Developments in the Law—The Constitution and the Family," *Harvard Law Review* 93 (1980): 1157–383.

4. Samuel M. Davis and Mortimer D. Schwartz, *Children's Rights and the Law* (Lexington: Lexington Books, 1987).

5. Arneson and Shapiro, "Democratic Authority," 388.

6. Ibid., 376, 399.

7. For attacks on the performance of our public high schools, varying only in their degree of severity, see among others, Theodore Sizer, *Horace's Compromise: The Dilemma of the American High School* (Boston: Houghton Mifflin, 1984); Gerald Grant, *The World We Created at Hamilton High* (Cambridge: Harvard University Press, 1988); Samuel Freedman, *Small Victories: The Real World of a Teacher, Her Students, and Their High School* (New York: Harper and Row, 1990); Jonathan Kozol, *Savage Inequalities: Children in America's Schools* (New York: Crown Publishers, 1991).

8. Arneson and Shapiro, "Democratic Authority," 378.

9. Ibid., 393–94.

10. Cass Sunstein, "Beyond the Republican Revival," *Yale Law Jour-*

nal 97 (1988): 1549; Frank Michelman, "Law's Republic," *Yale Law Journal* 97 (1988): 1528.

11. Arneson and Shapiro, "Democratic Authority," 400.

12. This point is eloquently made in Stephen Carter, *The Culture of Disbelief: How American Law and Politics Trivialize Religious Devotion* (New York: Basic Books, 1993). See also Michael Sandel, "Freedom of Conscience or Freedom of Choice?" in *Articles of Faith, Articles of Peace: The Religious Liberty Clauses and the American Public Philosophy,* ed. James Davison Hunter and Os Guinness (Washington, D.C.: Brookings Institution, 1990).

13. Notable cases include *Davis v. Page* 385 F. Supp. 395 (1974) (dismissing religious objection to use of audio-visual equipment in classrooms); *Moody v. Cronin* 484 F. Supp. 270 (C.D. Ill. 1979) (allowing religious objection to "immodest apparel" in physical education classes); *Grove v. Mead School District No. 354* 753 F.2d 1528 (9th Cir. 1985) (dismissing religious objection to use of the book *The Learning Tree* in English curriculum); *Mozert v. Hawkins County Board of Education* 827 F.2d 1058 (6th Cir. 1987) (dismissing religious objection to basal reading series); *Smith v. Board of School Commissioners* 827 F.2d 684 (11th Cir. 1987) (dismissing religious objection to Mobile, Alabama public school curriculum as teaching "secular humanism"). The Supreme Court has also ruled on the efforts of religious parents to shape the public school curriculum to their liking; see especially *Edwards v. Aguillard* 107 S. Ct. 2573 (1987) (invalidating Louisiana statute mandating teaching of creationism as a "balance" to evolutionary theory).

14. *Davis v. Page* 385 F. Supp. 395 (1974), 399, 398.

15. 827 F.2d 1058 (1987), 1071.

16. *Moody v. Cronin* 484 F. Supp. 270 (1979) is the exception that proves the rule. Here the court ruled in favor of parents who sought to have their children wear more modest clothes during gym class. Where the curriculum itself was not at stake, the court required public authorities to defer to religious sensibility.

17. For an extended critique along these same lines, see Davis and Schwartz, *Children's Rights and the Law,* chapter 4, esp. 73.

18. An influential articulation of this view is Joseph Goldstein et al., *Before the Best Interests of the Child* (New York: Free Press, 1979). The same principle is differently defended in, among others, Barbara Lerner, "Children's Rights in the United States," in *Children: Needs and Rights,* ed. Vincent Greaney (New York: Irvington Publishers, 1985); Ferdinand Schoeman, "Rights of Children, Rights of Parents, and the Moral Basis of the Family," *Ethics* 91 (1980): 6–19; William Galston,

"Civic Education in the Liberal State," in *Liberalism and the Moral Life*, ed. Nancy Rosenblum (Cambridge: Harvard University Press, 1989).

19. See, for example, *Davis v. Page* 385 F. Supp. 395, 398–99 and *Mozert v. Hawkins County Board of Education* 827 F.2d. 1058, 1071.

20. This difficulty is poignantly documented in Robert Dingwall et al., *The Protection of Children: State Intervention and Family Life* (Oxford: Basil Blackwell, 1983) and Vincent Fontana, *Save the Family, Save the Child: What We Can Do to Help Children at Risk* (New York: Dutton, 1991). See also Robert E. Shepherd, Jr., "The Abused Child and the Law," in *The Rights of Children: Emergent Concepts in Law and Society*, ed. Albert E. Wilkerson (Philadelphia: Temple University Press, 1973); Amy Sinden, "In Search of Affirmative Duties toward Children under a Post-*DeShaney* Constitution," *University of Pennsylvania Law Review* 139 (1990): 227–70; Margo Sarasohn, "Does the Constitution Require a State to Protect a Child Who the State Knows Is Being Abused?" *Whittier Law Review* 11 (1990): 811–44.

21. Joel Feinberg, "The Child's Right to an Open Future," in *Whose Child? Children's Rights, Parental Authority, and State Power,* ed. William Aiken and Hugh LaFollette (Totowa, N.J.: Littlefield, Adams, 1980). See also Bruce Ackerman, *Social Justice in the Liberal State* (New Haven: Yale University Press, 1980), chapter 5; Robert Burt, "Developing Constitutional Rights of, in, and for Children," in *Pursuing Justice for the Child,* ed. Margaret Rosenheim (1976); D. A. J. Richards, "The Individual, the Family, and the Constitution," *New York University Law Review* 55 (1980): 1–62.

22. Amy Gutmann, "Undemocratic Education," in *Liberalism and the Moral Life,* ed. Nancy Rosenblum, (Cambridge: Harvard University Press, 1989); Arneson and Shapiro, "Democratic Authority."

23. This theme is given more extended treatment in Martha Minow, "Interpreting Rights: An Essay for Robert Cover," *Yale Law Journal* 96: 1860–915.

24. Laura Purdy, *In Their Best Interest? The Case against Equal Rights for Children* (Ithaca: Cornell University Press, 1992) usefully emphasizes the "considerably higher standard of parenting" established by such a requirement (164).

25. Arneson and Shapiro, "Democratic Authority," 403.

26. Bruce Ackerman, *Social Justice in the Liberal State,* 139.

27. In *Matter of Alonzo v. Fernandez* (December 1993), the New York Supreme Court offered similar arguments to the ones made here in ruling that New York's condom availability program "violates the petitioners' constitutional due process rights to direct the upbringing of their children," 10.

28. *Baker v. Owen* 423 U.S. 907 (1975); *Ingraham v. Wright* 430 U.S. 651 (1977).

29. Again, this conclusion does not reach the constitutionality of such accommodation. On this question, see among others, Nomi Stolzenberg, " 'He Drew a Circle that Shut Me Out': Assimilation, Indoctrination and the Paradox of a Religious Education," *Harvard Law Review* 106 (1993): 581–667; Mary-Michelle Upson Hirschoff, "Parents and the Public School Curriculum: Is There a Right to Have One's Child Excused from Objectionable Instruction?" *Southern California Law Review* 50 (1977): 871–959; and George W. Dent, Jr., "Religious Children, Secular Schools," *Southern California Law Review* 61 (1988): 863–941.

30. See, for example, the ruling in *Davis v. Page* 385 F. Supp. 395 (1974). Plaintiffs originally claimed that compulsory presence in class while audio-visual material was being used violated the free exercise rights of the Davis *children.* But despite testimony of the distress experienced by the children themselves at being required to remain in the classroom, Judge Bownes framed the case as concerning parental rights only, arguing, "It would be naive of the court not to recognize that the children's asserted freedom of exercise of religion is, in essence, that of their parents" (398).

31. Cf. Hostetler, *Amish Society,* 304–7, on current practice.

32. I assume here that being raised in a fundamentalist or evangelical tradition does not automatically compromise one's education as severely as this. For a fuller defense of this view, see Shelley Burtt, "Religious Parents, Secular Schools: A Liberal Defense of an Illiberal Education," *Review of Politics* 56 (1994): 51–70.

16

SPHERES OF POLITICAL ORDER

LAINIE FRIEDMAN ROSS AND DAVID SCHMIDTZ

Introduction

This chapter examines the relation between polis and family as interacting spheres of political order. It will offer a relativistic reinterpretation of the Rawlsian concept of basic structure. A political order, as we use the term, is a kind of social organization. It may be a very loose organization, but a political order is, in any event, an order that governs itself as a distinct social organization. Democracy comes out as an example of political order, a social organization that governs itself by a democratic decisionmaking mechanism. Anarchism is the thesis that a well-functioning social order could exist without political order, without any overarching decisionmaking mechanism. It seems that our way of defining political order is roughly in keeping with ordinary usage, insofar as the term has an ordinary usage.

A few opening remarks about political order so understood: First, political orders are not mutually exclusive. In any society, there is more than one decisionmaker, and more than one level of organization with respect to which decisions are made. A state jurisdiction can be wholly contained within a federal jurisdiction and still be a distinct political entity, or a state board of education and a municipal government can interpenetrate. Their jurisdictions overlap, but neither encompasses the other.

Second, order does not imply design. We observe order in biological or economic realms too, but that does not count as evidence for the existence of a designer. The same is true of political order. As it happens, the political order we call the United States is partly a product of deliberate design, but it is also partly a product of bottom-up cultural and economic evolution combined with piecemeal top-down political and legislative changes that are not even intended to be steps in the implementation of an overall design. A governor can influence the direction in which a political order moves, in the same way a coach can influence the outcome of a sporting event, but that direction is also a function of decisions made within smaller orders encompassed by the larger one. Many decisions that effectively chart our course as a society are largely decentralized. They lie in the hands of corporations, churches, community or professional associations, clubs, and of course, families. Decisions made within families are among the most important decisions made in a liberal society.[1]

Third, we agree with William Galston that a government cannot be, nor would we want it to be, completely neutral with respect to competing conceptions of the good. Galston thinks there is such a thing as liberal bias, and that victims of liberal bias will want to remove themselves from the larger polis and form enclaves within which there is more homogeneity.[2] Surely Galston is right. We want only to add that people removing themselves from the larger polis is not an isolated phenomenon, like the Amish wanting to remove their teenage children from public schools. On the contrary, withdrawal is a matter of degree, and as such, ubiquitous. People withdraw from the larger polis every day, into couples, into families, into clubs, and so on. Secession, or something like it, happens all the time. Everyone withdraws to smaller spheres of social order, and re-enters the larger polis on a drop-in, part-time basis.

Finally, a larger point about principles of justice in a hierarchial political order: As we move toward broader, more encompassing realms of decisionmaking authority, we move toward what Rawls calls basic structure. Now, Rawls claims that his two principles of justice as fairness apply to basic structure. He also claims they apply *only* to basic structure. The second claim seems more arresting. If a principle really is a principle of justice, why would it not apply to every social structure, and indeed to everything we do? What is this property of being "basic" such that only basic structure has to answer to Rawls's two principles of justice? We address this question not only to Rawls scholars, but also to anyone who wonders whether (and if so, why) the requirements of justice vary from one level of political order to another.

In Rawls, we never get a firm sense of what counts as basic structure. Or if Rawls gives us examples of basic structure, we never get a sense of why it is those structures to which principles of justice are uniquely applicable. We thought it might be useful to think of basic structure as a relative concept. In other words, the more encompassing the jurisdiction, the more basic the structure. Thus, a state government is basic relative to municipal governments within its jurisdiction, but not basic relative to the federal government in which it is embedded. That gives us a nonarbitrary and contextually sensitive way of separating basic structure from nonbasic structure. We do not suppose that this is quite what Rawls means when he speaks of basic structure. On the contrary, however unclear Rawls's use of the term may be, it is clear that when he speaks of basic structure he has several quite different things in mind.[3] Our way of defining basic structure is a one-dimensional version of the multidimensional idea that Rawls seems to have in mind, but it will be useful to focus on this single dimension in what follows.

One of the benefits of focusing on the jurisdictional aspect of basic structure is that we immediately get a glimpse into why principles of justice might apply only to basic structure. If, for argument's sake, we assume Rawls's difference principle is genuinely a principle of justice, then our proposal is this: for any social order, there is a presumption that arrangements within it should satisfy the difference principle. Can the presumption be rebutted? Yes it can.

Suppose we look at institution *X* and see that *X* is embedded in a larger jurisdiction, a relatively more basic structure. Now suppose *X* tries to make its worst off members as well off as possible. The question is, would that make the *larger structure's* worst off members as well off as possible? If the answer is no, then from the larger structure's perspective, the difference principle at very least does not require *X* to make *X*'s worst off members as well off as possible. The presumption of the difference principle's applicability to *X* is therefore rebutted by the lights of the difference principle itself. That is our theory about why a goal-directed principle such as the difference principle might apply to an institution without directly applying to substructures within that institution's jurisdiction.

We have recently begun to consider what the theory implies about the legitimate use of force in a hierarchical political order. A family is in principle assessable by the same principles that apply to larger jurisdictions. But the idea that families ought to be forced to satisfy the difference principle is a thesis not about families per se but rather about the more basic structure that would do the coercing. Suppose a state government helps its worst off members by forcing families to pursue some other goal instead. In that case, the difference principle itself says families should not be forced to comply with the difference principle. Or suppose a state government helps its worst off members by imposing constraints on families instead of goals. Or by not imposing much of anything, by leaving families mostly alone. In those cases too, the difference principle, by its own lights, rules out forcing families to comply with it.

In general, one way in which basic structure works to greatest advantage is by nurturing smaller orders within its jurisdiction. The smaller and more intimate the social structure, the greater the potential for sharing and jointly pursuing a "thicker" conception of the good. There is a lot to be said for leaving these smaller orders alone to pursue their own visions of the good, but there also are rationales for imposing constraints on such smaller structures as families. The decentralization of political order that gives groups a measure of decisionmaking autonomy can fail people left vulnerable by the "group right," so to speak, of that thicker social structure. In effect, when the larger polis acts to strengthen boundaries around a group, it effectively weakens boundaries around individuals within the group. The boundaries around the group make the group less answerable for how it treats its own members. The basic structure, though, is supposed to increase opportunities for voluntary and mutually advantageous cooperation rather than increase opportunities for exploitation.[4] So, some constraints, such as laws against child abuse, are meant to minimize exploitation within families. Other constraints are meant to offset emerging disparities between smaller structures. Families, like corporations, churches, clubs, professional associations, and government itself, are hotbeds of unequal opportunity. That is not a problem for the family per se, but it is a problem for the larger jurisdiction within which such disparities are emerging as parts of its internal structure. If more encompassing structures do not offset these inequalities, it may become increasingly difficult over time to view the more encompassing structure as satisfying the difference principle.[5] The following sections take a closer look at Rawls's two principles and how they apply to particular institutions within a hierarchical political order.

I. The Evolution of Rawls's Two Principles

John Rawls begins *A Theory of Justice* with the assertion that "Justice is the first virtue of social institutions."[6] Rawls argues that *all* the social institutions "taken together as one scheme" are the primary subject of justice.[7] Despite some modifications to the principles of justice themselves, Rawls continues to hold this position in *Political Liberalism:* "all the major social institutions fit together into one system" whose first principles "provide reasonable guidelines for the classical and familiar questions of social justice in connection with this complex of institutions."[8] Rawls includes on a sample list of the major social institutions: "the legal protection of freedom of thought and liberty of conscience, competitive markets, private property in the means of production and the monogamous family."[9]

Having mentioned the family, Rawls in effect sets it aside in both works as something to be dealt with by a broader inquiry.[10] This paper considers what it would mean to apply the principles of justice to the institution of the family. First, we consider how these principles have been modified in Rawls's most recent writings.

In *Political Liberalism,* the first principle still has lexical priority, but it no longer guarantees "the most extensive basic liberty."[11] Rather, more modestly, it enshrines "a fully adequate scheme of equal basic liberties which is compatible with a similar scheme of liberties for all"[12] such that "altogether the possession of these basic liberties specifies the common and guaranteed status of equal citizens in a well-ordered democratic society."[13]

Although the second principle is unchanged in *Political Liberalism,* Rawls now speaks of elements of the second principle which are "constitutionally essential" and elements which are "questions of basic justice." "Constitutional essentials" are less demanding. They have a more urgent claim, and it is easier to reach agreement about them as well as to determine whether they are realized. Rawls will be satisfied if the complex of background institutions satisfies the constitutionally essential aspects of the second principle:

> [W]hile some principle of opportunity is surely an essential, for example, a principle requiring at least freedom of movement and free choice of occupation, fair equality of opportunity (as I have specified it) goes beyond that and is not such an essential. Similarly, though a social minimum providing for the basic needs of all citizens is also an essential, what I have called the "difference principle" is more demanding and is not.[14]

In *Political Liberalism,* Rawls also says that the principles of justice as fairness do not apply to the individual institutions within the complex of social institutions:

> In many if not most cases these principles give unreasonable directives. To illustrate: for churches and universities, different principles are plainly more suitable. Their members usually affirm certain shared aims and purposes as essential guidelines to the most appropriate form of organization. The most we can say is this: Because churches and universities are associations within the basic structure; they must adjust to the requirements that this structure imposes in order to establish background justice.[15]

The principles of justice do not hold as a guide for any particular institution, but only for the complex of institutions. Principles that guide an individual institution would take into account the particulars of that institution; e.g., its particular aims and membership. Rawls does not elaborate on what these principles might be.

II. Application of Rawls's First Principle to the Family

How then would these principles impact on the family? Do they even apply to the family or to the family structure? We believe that these questions are in keeping with Rawls's move in *Political Liberalism* from a comprehensive moral theory to a more narrowly defined political theory of justice because of the political roles of the family. It is within the family that the values of a particular culture as well as the values of the larger political community are socially reproduced. Power relationships defined in the family are replicated in other spheres. And the family is not isolated from the political process, but is part of the complex of background institutions to which the principles of justice apply.

In *A Theory of Justice,* Rawls assumed that the family structure would include a monogamous heterosexual couple with children. Against this, Will Kymlicka argues that a discussion about justice within a family cannot assume any particular set of relationships. The assumption that the family is or ought to include a monogamous heterosexual couple assumes too much of what a theory of family justice needs to determine.[16] Francis Schrag even questions whether one can assume that the family is the institution in which child rearing ought to take place.[17] Although Rawls does not address these issues in *Political Liberalism,* his move away from a comprehensive moral theory allows for a wide range of conceptions of the good which may embrace various alternative family structures.

What, then, does Rawls's first principle imply for the family structure and the interrelationships within the family? Presumably, "an adequate scheme of basic liberties" would include the liberty to form personal relationships according to one's own private conception of the good. Also needed are liberties to protect autonomous consenting individuals from government intrusions into their decisions regarding when and with whom they could marry, whether they could have children, and how many.

Consider, for example, if background institutions were just, and family relationships were all purely voluntary. Over time, of course, certain classes of voluntary relationships, although individually just, could create significant cumulative inequalities which might need to be reduced or redressed. But at least when the relationships are voluntarily contracted, one is more willing to accept the consequences, whatever they may be. However, whether particular intimate associations between free and equal moral individuals are consistent with justice in the family must be approached from the perspective of not only the consenting adults but also from the perspectives of the potential offspring to be born into and/or raised by these groupings. That is, an adequate scheme of basic liberties would allow free and equal moral persons not only to form relationships but also to procreate and rear children as an extension of their freedom. It is important, then, to consider these family structures from the perspective of the children who do not choose their parents nor their siblings, but whose life prospects are significantly shaped and influenced by them.

A child has an interest in having parents who want her and who are willing to take her interests seriously. While she does not have a preference for her biological parents per se, as long as they are willing to fulfill her present-day welfare needs and her long-term interests in becoming an autonomous adult, she has no reason to desire other parents. But the child also has no reason to want to exclude other caretakers of her parents' choosing who are willing to take her interests seriously. Thus, the child has no reason to thwart her parent's interest in choosing alternative intimate associations (e.g., extended families, open marriages, or homosexual parenting) provided that all the involved adults are able and willing to take her interests seriously such that she acquires and becomes capable of using her own adequate scheme of basic liberties.

The first principle of justice, then, can accommodate a far wider range of family structures than are presently permitted in our society. If there is more than one kind of family structure that satisfies these requirements in a more or less reliable way, then more than one kind of family is compatible with basic justice. There is no need to proscribe any form of family structure provided that each person, regardless of the family into which he is born, has the basic rights and liberties that are prerequisites for formulating, implementing, and fulfilling his own conception of the good life.

III. Second Principle: Fair Opportunity

In *A Theory of Justice,* Rawls states that the family is an obstacle to fair equality of opportunity.[18] Rawls argues that the institution of the family is in tension with equal opportunity because different families have different beliefs, priorities, values, and wealth, and will choose to distribute them in different ways such that children with the same potential may not have equal opportunities. Although fair equality of opportunity would prevail in an ideally just society as Rawls envisions it, he nevertheless accepts the inequalities in opportunities created by the family because he believes that when all the other background institutions are founded on the principles of justice, the benefits of the family will outweigh the losses caused by the inequalities they produce:

> within the context of the theory of justice as a whole, there is much less urgency to [abolish the family] . . . And when the principles of fraternity and redress are allowed their appropriate weight, the natural distribution of assets and the contingencies of social circumstances can more easily be accepted.[19]

In agreement with Rawls's assertion that the family is in tension with *equality of opportunity,* William Galston says "the family is a prime—perhaps *the* prime—source of inequalities that affect the development of natural talents and the ability to compete."[20] Parental discretion influences the opportunities and resources available to their children. To impose the constraint of equality of opportunity on families would require "at a minimum, very substantial invasions of the family autonomy cherished as a basic freedom in a liberal society."[21] This would not be in keeping with the lexical priority of basic liberties. This is not to say that the government cannot set certain minimum standards (e.g., that the adults do not seriously abuse or neglect their children), but only that parents should have wide discretion in giving their children advantages and opportunities that are not necessarily available to all.

In *Political Liberalism,* Rawls defuses the tension between fair equality of opportunity and the family by de-emphasizing the parental role in assuring fair *equality* of opportunity and instead focusing on securing a minimum set of opportunity "essentials" for all children. All that is required of parents is to fulfill their children's basic needs and interests and give their children the basic liberties essential for the adequate development and full exercise of moral personality. Other advantages and opportunities offered to one's children which yield inequalities are permitted. Most parents will offer their children opportunities and goods that go beyond these basic requirements, and they will do so to different degrees and by emphasizing different skills. A child does not have a claim against his family to be exposed to the widest range of possible ways of life, nor does he have a claim against his competitors to compensate for his handicaps. All that he can demand are the constitutional essentials of fair opportunity: i.e., freedom of movement, free choice of occupation, and the right not to be discriminated against on the basis of irrelevant traits.

The other thing to add on behalf of the family is that it is a primary source of unequal opportunities in part because it is a primary source of opportunities, period. When parents offer their children cultural experiences, material goods, athletic training, or private academic tutoring, they are defining the range of possibilities to which their children can aspire. An individual's dream is nourished or neglected according to the family's thicker conception of the good. This is not to say that other institutions do not play a significant role in offering or expanding an individual's opportunities, but the family is both the first and primary source of opportunities.

The roles that institutions other than the family play in shaping an individual's opportunity help explain why Rawls does not need to hold the family to a strict fair equality of opportunity standard. Children are members of various overlapping but distinct institutions: e.g., a particular family, school, church, race, gender, community, club, group of friends, workplace, and country. So even if parents attempt to restrict their children's opportunities to culturally specific roles, their children cannot help but be exposed to other roles, experiences, and opportunities which reflect different values and beliefs. Even if parents have wide discretion in how they raise their children, their children's membership in other spheres means that their parents cannot fully shelter them from noticing if not considering alternate lifestyles. Galston elaborates:

> from an early age, every child will see that he or she is answerable to institutions other than the family—institutions whose substantive requirements may well cut across the grain of parental wishes and beliefs. Some measure of reflection, or at least critical distance, is likely to result.[22]

That is, differences in opportunities created by family membership is somewhat attenuated by the other background institutions. So it may be in keeping with the principle of fair opportunity for the basic structure to constrain the family in certain respects, but the basic structure does not and should not expect the family to govern itself by the principle of equality of opportunity.

None of this is to deny that the typical modern family is often a source of significant gender discrimination, preventing fair opportunity at a basic level.[23] But whether the state ought to externally impose egalitarian goals on the family is a separate issue. We think not, because less intrusive means of promoting fair opportunity are available. For example, high-quality affordable day-care would permit all parents, including single mothers of young children, the opportunity to seek outside employment. The state need not be neutral between different conceptions of the good particularly when some conceptions have entrenched gendered hierarchies, but the state should not actively intrude upon and destroy families except when they are incompatible with minimum standards (e.g., if the families perpetuates chronic abuse or neglect of any subgroup of their members). Rather, through educational, financial, and political means, the state can support its citizens' ability to determine for themselves whether the values of their subculture are acceptable. To make this decision meaningful, the state must not only foster critical reflection in order that individuals question and demand reform of the prevailing discriminatory hierarchies within their subcommunities, but also it must offer these individuals a viable alternative if their communities do not respond.

IV. The Second Principle of Justice: Difference Principle

Whereas Rawls was acutely aware of the tension between the family and the principle of fair equality of opportunity, Rawls saw the family as a prime example of a setting in which the members act in ways that, from any perspective, accord with the difference principle:

> Members of a family commonly do not wish to gain unless they can do so in ways that further the interests of the rest. Now wanting to act on the difference principle has precisely this consequence.[24]

The problem with this understanding of the family is that it assumes a harmony of interests among family members, and such harmony cannot be assumed. Families must sometimes choose between options in which one or another of its members will be disadvantaged. Consider Thomas Nagel's example in which he must choose whether to live with his two children in an expensive city or in a semi-rural suburb.[25] The first child is normal, the second is handicapped. The advantage of the city is that the second child can receive optimal rehabilitation which will make his life better, but still miserable. Nagel stipulates that the rest of the family will suffer greatly as the neighborhood will be unpleasant and dangerous. If they move to the suburbs, the handicapped child will not receive such extensive rehabilitation and he will suffer a minute worsening of his medical condition, but the rest of the family will flourish. Nagel notes that a strict application of the difference principle would require him to move his family to the city, even though the move has overall negative utility. He adds that the conclusion holds whether they are a family of three or thirty-three—the handicapped child's urgent needs must be given priority.[26] The difference principle seemingly does not even allow for the possibility that the handicapped child himself might not want his whole family to compromise their futures for his sake.

A related question is whether it is appropriate for Nagel to apply the difference principle to his decision to relocate his family. Constraining the family to make its relocation decision in accordance with the difference principle might not make the family as a whole better off. It might not even make the handicapped child better off. The handicapped child, more than anyone else, might benefit from a healthy, loving, intact family environment, an environment in which other family members have no reason to think of the handicapped child's interests as constantly threatening to trump (and not merely outweigh) their own. This is not to deny that there can be serious conflict between the needs of various family members. Rather, the point is that families can, after all, be harmonious and can afford individuals the opportunity to jointly pursue a thicker conception of the good. By its own standards, then, the difference principle, applied at the level of a society's most encompassing decisionmaking mechanisms, may require that principles of decisionmaking other than the difference principle be employed at particular sublevels. That may be how society's basic structure makes the worst off as well off as possible.

Alternatively, the point may be that Rawls's principles of justice are about results. The most liberal and quite possibly most effective way of moving society in the direction of these results involves not forcing or even encouraging mid-level institutions to *aim* at these results, but rather constraining the latitude that mid-level institutions have in selecting methods of pursuing whatever it is that they are going to pursue.[27]

Conclusion

As applied to more encompassing spheres of political order, Rawls's principles of justice can serve as a check on the autonomy of mid-level institutions such as the family, just as families check and balance the basic structure itself. When we reflect upon the characteristics that would make the family a just institution, we consider its influence on all members within a particular family as well as its influence on members of different families. In this chapter, we have tried to show that such an analysis requires an examination of the family from the perspectives of all its members as well as an assessment of the other social institutions with which the family shares its authority to distribute goods and opportunities.[28]

NOTES

1. Of course, it does not do so by design. The evolution of the family as a sphere of political order was strictly from the bottom up.

2. William Galston, *Liberal Purposes: Goods, Virtues, and Diversity in the Liberal State* (New York: Cambridge University Press, 1991), 147.

3. At times, Rawls uses the term "basic structure" to refer to "natural" institutions; i.e., those that evolve in contrast to those that are deliberately put in place. The family may be basic in this sense, but this is not the sense upon which we focus our attention.

4. Consider Will Kymlicka's proposal that group rights be identified for aboriginal peoples. See *Liberalism, Community, and Culture* (New York: Oxford University Press, 1989). How much might that proposal cost members of aboriginal groups (women and children, for example) who are left vulnerable by the basic structure's recognition of that group's right to self-determination? (Some of the opposition to Quebec's secession comes from within Quebec, from minorities who are afraid of how they will be treated if the Quebec government is given a free hand.) Group rights protect people against the tyranny of the majority only by opening the door to possible tyranny within the smaller spheres. Of course, we acknowledge that one advantage of having smaller spheres is that victims tend to be in a better position to exit the spheres in which they are victims. To some extent, they will be in a better position to vote with their feet, unless basic structures limit freedom of exit from the smaller spheres.

5. The moral is not that more basic structure has to show that it cares: the justice of the basic structure lies in its results, not in the intentions of its administrators. Whether intervention is better than benign neglect by the light of the difference principle is an empirical issue.

6. John Rawls, *A Theory of Justice* (Cambridge: Harvard University Press, 1971), 3. Hereinafter cited as *A Theory of Justice.*

7. Ibid., 7.

8. John Rawls, *Political Liberalism* (New York: Columbia University Press, 1993), 258. Hereinafter cited as *Political Liberalism.*

9. *A Theory of Justice,* 7. Rawls, however, drops the family from his enumeration in "The Basic Structure as Subject," *American Philosophical Quarterly,* 14, no. 2 (April 1977): 159. When this article is rewritten and incorporated into *Political Liberalism,* the family is reinstated (258).

10. In part, this omission in *A Theory of Justice* is not surprising given that all the members of the original position are presumed heads of heterosexual monogamous nuclear families (7). In *Political Liberalism,* Rawls is able to do away with this assumption by revising the "just savings principle" (274). Although Rawls distinctly expresses his belief that the family can be accommodated by his theory (ibid., xxix), he resists the challenge. Rawls does not discuss how his theory can apply or be applied to the institution of the family.

11. *A Theory of Justice,* 60.

12. *Political Liberalism,* 291.

13. *Political Liberalism,* 335.

14. *Political Liberalism,* 228–29.

15. *Political Liberalism,* 261.

16. Will Kymlicka, "Rethinking the Family," *Philosophy and Public Affairs* 20 (1991): 77–97.

17. Francis Schrag, "Justice and the Family," *Inquiry* 19 (1976): 193–208, esp. 195–97.

18. *A Theory of Justice,* esp. 298–303.

19. *A Theory of Justice,* 511–12.

20. Galston, *Liberal Purposes,* 195.

21. Ibid.

22. Ibid., 255.

23. Susan Moller Okin argues that the greatest threat to equality of opportunity is *within* and not *between* families. Okin argues that the division of labor along gender lines leads is unfair to children of both sexes because it perpetuates sex-role stereotypes which inhibit the growth of their *human* potential. Her analysis is acute. But the question still remains what role the state should play in promoting greater equality of opportunity. See Susan Moller Okin, *Justice, Gender, and the Family* (New York: Basic Books, 1989).

24. *A Theory of Justice,* 105.

25. Thomas Nagel, "Equality," in *Mortal Questions* (Cambridge: Cambridge University Press, 1979), 123–25.

26. Ibid., 125.

27. Making a similar claim about democracy, Ian Shapiro says that rather than try to design institutional blueprints, we do better to work against particular impediments (chapter 3 of *Democratic Justice,* unpublished).

28. We would like to thank Russell Hardin and Stephen Gardbaum who were the commentators at our presentation before the American Society for Political and Legal Philosophy, September 4, 1993. We would also like to thank the audience for a lively discussion. Finally, special thanks to John Exdell, John Ross, and Elizabeth Willott for their contributions.

17

VIOLENCE AGAINST WOMEN: CHALLENGES TO THE LIBERAL STATE AND RELATIONAL FEMINISM

JENNIFER NEDELSKY

I. Introduction

One of the uncontested objectives of political order in a liberal regime is the protection of its citizens from violence. Yet the liberal state has failed in this basic task with respect to women and children.[1] If we take this failure seriously, we must rethink the scope of the liberal state and the conception of rights optimal for making good on liberalism's most basic aspirations. This rethinking flows from my central claim that violence against women[2] cannot be prevented until the relations between men and women are transformed—which means that transforma-

I had the good fortune to be thinking about revisions for this chapter while visiting the University of Chicago Law School. I would particularly like to thank the following for giving me the benefit of their responses: Carolyn M. Burns, Richard Epstein, Elana Kagan, Larry Lessig, Tracey Meares, Martha Nussbaum, and Stephen Shulhoffer. I also received particularly excellent questions and comments from Owen Fiss and his Feminist Theory class at Yale Law School. And I would like to thank the participants in the discussion at the NOMOS meeting where the first draft of this essay was presented.

tion of these social and intimate relations must be an objective of the liberal state. A conception of rights that routinely directs our attention to structures of relationships is better suited to facilitate that transformation than one, like the traditional liberal conception, aimed at the protection of boundaries.[3] Yet there is no issue that more powerfully evokes the need for legally protected boundaries than violence. Thus violence against women poses a challenge to reconceiving rights as relationship as well as to liberalism.[4] My purpose is to take up this challenge to the relational approach in the context of the liberal state's failure on its own terms.

I begin by outlining the genesis of this chapter: my effort to meet the most compelling challenges I think my work on relational feminism has encountered. I then turn to a lengthy section on background sources which illuminate my core claim that a relational approach is the optimal way of understanding issues of violence. The heart of my argument takes as its starting point Judith Shklar's fascinating defense of liberalism as the "only system devoted to the project of lessening [cruelty]."[5] Shklar's powerful evocation of the horrors of the fear of cruelty serves as an indictment of societies in which women live in fear. Focusing on rape, I explore the limitations of boundary language to capture the horror of rape, then argue that the cycle of fear and domination can only be broken by transforming relations between men and women. But that means that to achieve its minimum goal, security from fear and violence, the liberal state must take on this project of transformation in ways that transcend the limits of the state that Shklar advocates. And Shklar is not alone. Most accounts of liberalism (not merely libertarian ones) would see taking on the kind of transformation I have in mind as dangerously enlarging the appropriate scope of the state with vague, open-ended and inevitably contested objectives, thus inviting both intrusion and expanded state power to which no clear limits could be drawn. I use an analogy to Robert Cover's analysis of how violence was integral to racial subordination in the American South to show why rethinking the scope and role of the state is essential to dismantling hierarchies that are embedded in the culture and sustained by "private" violence.[6] I then briefly address some concerns about why a relational approach to rights might not "work," before turning to my conclusion.

II. Genesis

This chapter reflects my attempt to deal with a worry that I have kept pushing aside while working on my project of reconceptualizing various concepts basic to liberalism, such as autonomy and rights.[7] The core of my concern is whether there is something myopically utopian about my effort to use relational feminism[8] to develop new conceptions of rights, law, autonomy, and constitutionalism. These conceptions are inspired in part by aspirations toward radically different forms of relations among people in which violence and domination do not disappear, but play a far less central role in the structure of society.

Now I take these aspirations to be grounded in an understanding of human beings that is realistic. Indeed, part of my purpose here is to make clear that the feminist conception of human selfhood as constituted by relationship has nothing warm, mushy, or romantic about it. Feminists above all know that the web of relationships in which we exist is not necessarily benign.[9] Nevertheless, I know that I am consistently drawn to the side of feminism that explores the exciting possibilities of transformation rather than the grim realities of people's lives. So I thought it appropriate that I finally confront these realities as a kind of test of my approach. If my reconceptualizations are actually to be useful, something other than a sort of inspirational literature, then they must be able to cope with what is most horrible as well as what is most beautiful and promising about human existence.[10]

More specifically, I want to try to answer a set of "critics' questions"—some from actual external critics and some from my own voices of unease. The questions that began this project arose primarily in response to my arguments that we should abandon "boundary" as the dominant metaphor in law and to my argument that we should reconceptualize rights in terms of the relationships (of power, trust, responsibility) that rights in fact structure.[11] The questions fall into three groups:

1. Given the violence to which women are subject, don't we need more, stronger boundaries? Isn't the appropriate strategic focus to claim the protection of boundaries, of bodily integrity in particular, that men claim? This question comes most powerfully from students who work in areas of violence against women, such as sexual harassment and sexual assault. The underlying issue is whether my approach can protect us from the truly dark and dangerous forces that manifest themselves in the daily lives of millions of women.

2. Will not the magnitude of responsibility implicit in my approach be overwhelming, personally, psychologically, and socially? Will it not end up erasing the divisions of rights, boundaries, and limits that have made freedom and security possible? Doesn't it invite vast intrusion at a collective level?[12]

3. The third issue is one of the central problems toward which this exploration is ultimately directed, and it emerges in the course of my discussion as something still to be resolved: Can the relational approach to rights "work"? Isn't there some degree of mystification, stability, and (apparent) determinacy of rights that is essential to their capacity to provide the protections they do succeed in providing? In other words, can conceptions of rights that routinely turn our minds to an open-ended inquiry into optimal relationships ever provide the appearance of stable, formal content? Will not, at the least, the crucial rhetorical power of rights be destroyed? This question became particularly pressing to me when I heard a version of it from a woman in South Africa[13] where the question of how to promote a culture of rights is an extremely pressing one, and the dangers of fooling around with risky alternatives especially obvious.

I think these problems are serious. And if they cannot be resolved in some serious way, then I would have to abandon my project. Nevertheless, I think they must be posed in the context of another question: from what have the traditional forms (both conceptions and institutions) of liberal rights *not* been able to protect us? I have in mind in particular the pervasive and systemic violence against women and the abuse of children, which we now know to be extraordinarily common. Of course, the problem is not that the rights to bodily integrity and security are not recognized by the liberal state. On the contrary, the problem is that despite the primacy accorded these rights in principle, they are not in practice protected for women. The challenge then is to understand how prevailing conceptions of rights and the scope of the liberal state have participated in this failure, and how an alternative might help.

The violence against women and children is so widespread that it cannot properly be understood simply as a matter of individual pathology or criminality or wickedness. It is a characteristic of our society and, at least in the case of violence against women, we have a general idea of how it serves to keep a structure of power in place.[14] I will suggest that these evils are best dealt with through the sorts of relational reconceptions I propose. Most importantly, I claim that the very features of my approach that generate the "critics questions" are those that make it well suited for tackling these dramatic failures of our current regime of rights.

III. Relational Reflections on Violence

I want to begin with the sources I used to help me think about this daunting topic. I will start with those I refer to least in the main body of the chapter, for they in particular form a kind of background context for my approach, a way of seeing the relational nature of the violence I address. Susan Griffin's *A Chorus of Stones* is subtitled "The Private Life of War."[15] It is a complex interweaving of stories and reflections ranging from the secrets of her own family and the silences and disconnection they bred, to Werner von Braun's development of rockets, to Heinrich Himmler's preoccupation with secrets and the sadistic childrearing practices advocated by a leading child psychologist in the Germany of Himmler's youth. Griffin tells terrifying stories of Hiroshima and the suppression of a report on the safety of nuclear power plants, and of the very ordinary lives of those who work in a nuclear weapons plant and the everyday events that led a particular woman to participate in the suppression of the report. She gives us a sense of the anguish of a brutal murderer and of a survivor of the Holocaust. We see patterns of links between individuals' psyches, their families, and their history, writ large and small. Griffin manages to convey a vision of the connections between the large scale horrors of war and the private, often secret pain of all of us who live in this culture of domination and destruction. This vision is both compelling and illusive.

Griffin does not try to offer neat theoretical synopses of these interconnections which could serve as a framework for my discussion. Her vision serves to remind me of the scope and variety of the violence in our culture, the complexity of its sources, and the means by which it is sustained and perpetuated. Two points matter particularly for my argument here. The first is that although I focus here on conceptions of rights, I am, of course, under no illusion that liberal rights are the essential source of the problem or that simply a better conception of rights will solve it. The second point is that the particular evils I have in mind here are part of a larger pattern. Part of that pattern can crudely be described as patriarchy, in which domination, not just of women by men, is a central dynamic. Now, of course, patriarchy precedes liberal rights and exists in non-liberal regimes. Nevertheless, part of the project (which I have begun in "Law, Boundaries, and the Bounded Self" and "Reconceiving Autonomy") is to see how a particular vision of rights fits with a particular conception of the self, which is in turn connected to a long tradition of patriarchy.

It is important to see that we need not make exaggerated claims about the importance of rights in order to draw connections between the forms of conventional liberal rights and the violence they fail to prevent and the larger culture of which both the rights and the violence are an integral part. And this attention to interconnection need not deny that liberal rights regimes have succeeded in protecting many of their people from important forms of violence, brutality, and fear. Indeed, a basic question driving my inquiry is whether efforts to improve on the conventional conception of rights to address their failures will succeed only in destroying their proven efficacy to protect us from substantial horrors.

Part of the purpose of keeping in mind the broader picture of the culture in which this violence is embedded is to guide the reconceptualization of rights by the broader aspirations for change (while remembering that rights *alone* cannot be the engine for such change). I will argue later that rape in particular cannot be stopped without transforming the relations between men and women, indeed without transforming our very conceptions of ourselves as gendered beings. And these transformations, even in the short run, will affect not only the traditional privileges of men, but their rights. Here, I want turn to another source that I treat as a background guide.

The violence men perpetrate against women (and, I think, against children as well) must be understood in the context of the destructive gender roles that are so central to our psyches. More generally, the violence and pain that are so much a part of our ostensibly safe, civilized North American world must be understood in terms of collective, systemic psychological patterns which take a unique form for each individual yet are comprehensible only in these broader terms.[16] The healing required needs to take place on both the individual and the societal level. If the basic mechanisms of protection, rights, are to be reconceptualized in order to lessen the violence, to be part of a restructuring of the relations of power between men and women, it should be with the guidance of the most thoughtful approaches we have to the destructive patterns built into gender.

The single most illuminating author I have encountered on these subjects is Marion Woodman, a Jungian analyst who has written widely on the nature of the masculine and the feminine in both men and women.[17] I want to describe three ways in which her approach informs mine.[18] First, the attention to patterns of relationship that is required by my notion of "rights as relationship" can be seen as part of a resurgence of a kind of thinking, that is in turn connected to a reconceptualization of the self.[19] This resurgence of what Woodman would call "the feminine" is itself part of the transformation she describes and advocates—so that the very nature of the process (as well as my claims for its outcome) matters.

Second, Woodman's perspective provides a context for reflecting on violence against women which avoids presenting women as helpless victims and men as the agents of evil. Her focus is on the dynamics *between* men and women (and between the masculine and feminine in each) that generate the violence and destruction.[20] Even in the case of rape, our concern must be with restructuring relations, not simply "stopping men"—not because it sounds less condemnatory and threatening, but because men *cannot* be stopped unless relations change.

Third, Woodman helps us see that a simple shift in power between men and women, taking the form of giving women an equal share of the kind of power men hold, will never solve the problem of violence and destruction endemic to North American society. The violence is too much a part of the nature of that power. Woodman tells us that "What this century has brought to light by acting it out in the most public and explicit ways is the psychological condition of the raped woman. Indeed, the raped woman has in some sense replaced the crucified Christ as the most powerful and meaningful of icons."[21] Robert Johnson, another Jungian, adds to this perspective in his exceptionally illuminating insights into the way the thrill of violence replaces something missing at the core of Western culture.[22] A far broader transformation than an equalizing of conventional power (or a more equal enforcement of conventional rights) is required to achieve the minimum aspirations of a liberal society: its members must be able to live free of fear, at least sufficiently so for the purposes of liberty.

Nel Noddings, a leading relational feminist theorist, offers an approach to the problem of evil that I see as another perspective on the importance of a relational approach. Her book, *Women and Evil,* is an attempt to describe a "morality of evil," a "carefully thought out plan by which to manage the evil in ourselves, in others, and in whatever deities we posit."[23] Although her book is not written from a Jungian perspective, she borrows this notion of a morality of evil and draws heavily on a version of the Jungian concepts of "shadow" and projection.[24] Her starting presumption is that there is evil in all of us, and that one of the basic problems in the dominant approaches to evil is that it treats evil as "out there," something other than ourselves. This dangerous mistake is usually part of a projection of our own evil (individual and cultural) onto others. And it is now widely recognized that women, from Pandora to the seductive Eve, have been an important target of such projection. When we consider the special problems of violence against women, it is helpful to remember that when women carry the projection of evil, they will also bear the brunt of evil actions—and that evil will appear justifiable.

Noddings develops a phenomenology of evil from the standpoint of women's experience. She says that "three great categories of evil" emerge: "pain, separation, and helplessness."[25] For my purposes, her identification of separation as a condition as well as a category of evil is particularly important. In the evil of separation, often the issue is compassion and what stands in the way of this ordinary and essential human response. Seeing each other and ourselves as symbols is, of course, part of what sustains our capacity to inflict suffering.[26] It is the move to abstraction, the transformation of a suffering person into a symbol that fosters the separation, the turning away, the infliction of suffering.

I want to suggest that the conception of rights as relationship mitigates the dangerous capacity to treat people as symbols or as removed "others," while the conventional language of rights as boundaries fosters our inclination to project evil onto others, imagining that secure fences and sanctions can keep evil away.

I think it is fairly obvious that part of what permits people to engage in unimaginable cruelty is that they see the objects of their violence as something radically other than themselves, something other than human, or at least so inferior as to be not fully human. It is this otherness that allows me to comprehend the stories of the violence individual whites inflict on individual blacks in South Africa or the United States, not just during slavery or the heyday of the Ku Klux Klan, but on the streets and in the prison cells today. (The violence a brutalized population inflicts on itself must have some different explanation, although I think it may be connected to the dehumanization inherent in their treatment by the dominant population.)[27]

Of course, what makes this experience of otherness possible is extremely complex. The prevailing conception of rights is surely just one tiny piece of the puzzle.[28] The very purpose of the abstraction of rights is to render them applicable to all people regardless of their multiplicity of particular differences. Yet the form this abstraction has taken, and the modes of thinking associated with it, may foster the capacity for distancing ourselves from others that encourages cruelty. I think this is particularly true of what Noddings calls "cultural evil,"[29] such as poverty, racism, and war. For example, our conception of rights insulates us from the pain of the poverty around us, and permits us to let this cruelty continue. As we pass a homeless woman on the street (whether we give her money or not), we can feel secure in the knowledge that we have not done anything wrong, have not violated her rights, while remaining comfortably unconscious that our sense of our property rights in our homes permits us to exclude her. Despite our unease, our sense of rights permits us to avoid thinking about the connection between her plight and the system of property rights, which is a source of privilege for us[30] and misery for her.[31] But if, as I argue in "Reconceiving Rights as Relationship,"

> we come to focus on the relationships that our rights structure, we will see the connection between our power to exclude and the homeless person's plight. We might still decide to maintain that right of exclusion, but the decision would be made in full consciousness of the pattern of relationships it helps to shape. And I think we are likely to experience our responsibilities differently as we recognize that our 'private rights' always have social consequences.[32]

From Noddings's perspective, I think even this phrase "social consequences" sounds rather abstract. What matters is a relational habit of thinking, not just in rights discourse, of course, but in the range of ways she outlines in her idea of "pedagogy for the oppressor" and in Chapter 9, "Educating for a Morality of Evil." What matters, not only at the level of policy making and formal adjudication, but in our individual encounters with specific human beings, is that our conception of rights turns us toward the relationships of which we are a part, rather than permitting us to be blind to them.

The distancing of rights language is not the same as seeing others as less than human. But I think there is a family of capacities for not seeing the human reality of suffering before us, a group of mechanisms for cutting off compassion and responsiveness that are related. The capacity to see another person only as a category operates at an individual level to foster moral evil. It is not the same as seeing someone as subhuman, but it shares a dehumanizing quality, and it shares the features of abstraction and distancing of conventional rights language. Habits of relational thinking seem an antidote to this cluster of human tendencies.

This antidote may be least effective in combatting a radical sense of otherness, for just as the "others" would not be seen as rights bearers in a system of universal rights, they could be seen as outside of the network of relationships to which attention is due. But despite this possibility, I think a relational approach to rights, in the context of a broader respect for relational thinking, discourages the distancing of abstraction and thus encourages the attention to the particular human realities before us. This attention seems to me likely to erode the capacity to use categories such as race and gender to blind us to the full humanness of our fellow beings. It may indeed be the *combination* of a culture of rights with its claims of universal moral equality and the transformations of thinking of rights as relationship that holds out the best possibility of undermining the age-old propensity to see some as "others" not deserving of fully human treatment. (Of course this implicit claim of compatibility begs the question of whether my conception of rights will destroy their function.)

Now let me turn more briefly to the no less important issue of "projection." I am persuaded by Noddings (and the Jungian approach she draws on) that one of the chief problems with the way Western culture has traditionally treated evil is to project it onto others. I see the dominant metaphor of rights as boundaries as linked to this pattern of projection. "The boundaries so central to American law are the boundaries that feel desperately necessary to the separative self to keep the threatening others at bay—a task whose impossibility only fuels the desperation." The separative self, trying to escape from the frightening reality of interconnection, "is on an endless and doomed search for security, a security that seems possible only in power and domination. Thus the sought-after walls of protection (like property) are those that entail domination."[33] The very nature of the security sought entails the projection outward of all that is threatening, at the same time that domination ensures that real threats will appear. Thus, the conceptual structure of the rights to which we turn to protect us from evil carries with it this basic problem of projecting evil outward.

Noddings argues that we should ask "what is wrong with the vast majority of us? The answer . . . is that we do not understand or accept our own disposition toward evil and that we lack a morality of evil. . . . [T]here is a continuum of susceptibility to the evil within, but no one is immune. Evil is neither entirely out-there nor entirely in-here; it is an interactive phenomenon that requires acceptance, understanding and steady control rather than great attempts to overcome it once and for all."[34] When we move away from the dominant metaphor of rights as boundaries toward a conception of rights as relationship, we will be better equipped to use rights to understand that interactive phenomenon and to exert the steady control that has always been claimed as a virtue of liberalism.

Finally, it is important to see the compatibility between my focus on the dangers of projection and my earlier invocation of patriarchy as a source of violence. I do see a pattern of relations and thinking that one can describe with the shorthand of "patriarchy" as intricately connected both to the evils I am concerned with and to the limitations of the traditional modes of dealing with violence. But that does not mean that I make the mistake of projecting all evil onto men or even onto the abstraction "patriarchy." As I noted earlier, the inquiry into gender must be an inquiry into the dynamic of interaction between men and women. It is only to the extent that the concept of patriarchy helps us to understand these patterns of relations and modes of thought that it is useful. Finally, I hope that my discussion of Noddings makes clear that while I think it is possible to have a culture where domination is less central and pervasive, I do not succumb to fantasies that evil can be eradicated. I subscribe to Noddings's advocacy of understanding and control and suggest that my conception of rights will foster both.

IV. "Liberalism of Fear" and Its Failures

In the early stages of thinking about this essay, I read George Kateb's obituary for Judith Shklar. He referred to her defense of constitutionalism as "the system that tends to lessen cruelty because it is the only system devoted to the project of lessening it."[35] This was just the sort of claim on liberalism's[36] behalf that I thought I should take on in order to explore my concerns about violence and relational feminism, and my belief that ultimately it will do a better job than conventional liberalism. Cruelty is not all there is to violence, but it is a good starting place. And indeed I found Shklar's *Ordinary Vices* and her essay "The Liberalism of Fear"[37] extremely helpful, but not quite in the oppositional sense I had anticipated. I agree with Shklar's view that we should "put cruelty first," both in our ordering of vices and as a primary political concern. I even find this a form of universalism that I accept:

> The liberalism of fear in fact does not rest on a theory of moral pluralism. It does not, to be sure, offer a *summum bonum* toward which all political agents should strive, but it certainly does begin with a *summum malum,* which all of us know and would avoid if only we could. The evil is cruelty and the fear it inspires, and the very fear of fear itself. To that extent the liberalism of fear makes a universal and especially a cosmopolitan claim, as it historically has always done.[38]

While it will become clear that I do not agree with Shklar's conclusions about the role of the state (conclusions which are a basic purpose of her argument), I want to begin with her extraordinary evocation of the horror of fear and cruelty and the urgency of making security against them a true priority. I can think of no better introduction to my indictment of the liberal state's failures with regard to women and children.

While "putting cruelty first" is Shklar's recurring theme, her real preoccupation seems to be with fear, and the way the two are linked. Let me provide a sampling of her claims: "In Montesquieu's eyes, fear is so terrible, so physiologically and psychologically damaging, that it cannot be redeemed by consequences."[39]

> When one puts [cruelty] first one responds, as Montaigne did, to the acknowledgment that one fears nothing more than fear. The fear of fear does not require any further justification, because it is irreducible. It can be both the beginning and the end of politi-

> cal institutions such as rights. The first right is to be protected against this fear of cruelty. People have rights as a shield against this greatest of public vices. This is the evil, the threat to be avoided at all costs. Justice itself is only a web of legal arrangements required to keep cruelty in check.[40]

It is really fear that is the bedrock: "It is an undifferentiated evil in which all lesser vices and faults have their origin. . . . Cruelty comes first, then lying and treachery. All, every single one, are the children of fear. . . . One can be afraid of fear, because fear is the ultimately evil moral condition."[41]

Of course, Shklar makes no exaggerated claims that liberal societies have eradicated fear or cruelty, only that they can and will always do better than anyone else. But even with this qualification, Shklar's articulation of the evil of fear cries out for the response that in North America women's lives, *all* women's lives, are defined by fear as are those of many, many children. On Shklar's own terms liberal North American society[42] fails dramatically.[43]

What I have in mind is the incidence and impact of violence against women and children, particularly rape and child abuse. In the case of rape, it is not just the shattering consequences for the staggering numbers of women raped each year, but the fear of rape that pervades and controls the lives of all women, even those whose privilege otherwise provides them with great security. I will focus here on these violent forms of terror, but the picture ought to be completed by the evils of poverty—pain, separation, helplessness, and fear—which our society inflicts disproportionately on women and children.

Rape and child abuse are traumas. But we must now face the contradictory, and thus unassimilable, fact that these traumas are routine:

> In 1980, when post-traumatic stress disorder was first included in the diagnostic manual, the American Psychiatric Association described traumatic events as "outside the range of usual human experience." Sadly, this definition has proved to be inaccurate. Rape, battery, and other forms of sexual and domestic violence are so common a part of women's lives that they can hardly be described as outside the range of ordinary experience. . . . Traumatic events are extraordinary, not because they occur

> rarely, but rather because they overwhelm the ordinary human adaptations to life.[44]

And Judith Herman also gives us a political context for making sense of what seems unimaginable:

> Only after 1980, when the efforts of combat veterans had legitimated the concept of post-traumatic stress disorder, did it become clear that the psychological syndrome seen in survivors of rape, domestic battery, and incest was essentially the same as the syndrome seen in the survivors of war. The implications of this insight are as horrifying in the present as they were a century ago: the subordinate condition of women is maintained and enforced by the hidden violence of men. There is a war between the sexes. Rape victims, battered women, and sexually abused children are its casualties.[45]

The impact of trauma corresponds closely to both Shklar's and Noddings's discussions of basic evil. Trauma shatters the victims sense of safety and security in the world. Not only is the trauma itself characterized by extreme terror and utter helplessness, but the experience lives on. "Being psychologically overwhelmed, the sensation of being 'reduced to nothing' . . . is such a hideous feeling that the victim seeks never to experience the sensation again." Fear of further fear, "fear of fear itself," can not only immobilize victims at the time of the trauma, but may come to dominate their lives.[46] "The very 'threat of annihilation' that defined the traumatic moment may pursue the survivor long after the danger has passed. No wonder that Freud found, in the traumatic neurosis, signs of a 'daemonic force at work.' The terror, rage, and hatred of the traumatic moment live on in the dialectic of trauma."[47]

Those exposed to the primal evil of trauma have surely not been provided with the basic security from fear and cruelty that should be the first principle of Shklar's liberal regime. But can we say that the prevalence of this trauma is such that it is a fundamental failure? Is it something other than the inability of any regime to ensure that all its members are law-abiding?

Clearly Judith Herman, quoted above, sees the fear and violence as systemic.[48] So do Susan Brownmiller and Catherine

MacKinnon, indeed every feminist I know of who has studied the subject. There is, of course, disagreement over the numbers. Getting accurate statistics is difficult since almost everyone agrees that most rapes are not reported and child abuse and domestic battering are even harder to document. Suppose the most conservative estimate of rape is correct: one in ten women are raped. Given the devastation of the trauma, are we not dealing with a problem that is a fundamental challenge to the claims of the regime? And when we add to rape domestic battering and child abuse do we not have a problem that must be treated as systemic?

A recent debate in Canada over the incidence of violence against women is revealing of both the systemic nature of the violence and the problems with "proving" it. A study was recently completed of in-depth interviews with women from the metropolitan Toronto area. The findings were that 98% had experienced some form of sexual violation.[49]

Violence against Women

Highlights of the Findings of the Women's Safety Project

ABUSE OF GIRLS (16 AND UNDER)

54% had experienced some unwanted or intrusive sexual experience
24% of the cases were forced or attempted forced sexual intercourse
17% reported at least experience of incest
34% had been sexually abused by a non-relative
96% of perpetrators of child sexual abuse were men

SEXUAL ABUSE OF WOMEN (16 AND OLDER)

51% have been victims of rape or attempted rape
40% reported at least one experience of rape
31% reported at least one experience of attempted rape
81% of rapes or attempted rapes were perpetrated by men who were known to the women

PHYSICAL ASSAULT IN INTIMATE RELATIONSHIPS

27% experienced physical assault in an intimate relationship
25% of cases involved partners threatening to kill them

50% reporting physical assault also experienced sexual assault in the same relationship
36% feared being killed by their male intimate.

Immediately a flurry of denunciations appeared in the press. In addition to challenging the methods used,[50] the critics complained about an unreasonably broad definition of sexual abuse, ranging from obscene phone calls to sexual assault. While I think that it is important to distinguish between forms of abuse (as of course the report did), I think its shocking cumulative statistic is important.

Two years ago an envelope on the door to my Women's Studies office was defaced with anti-feminist obscenities. I was surprised to find how upset I was. In fact, I was scared. I came to realize in a new way that such obscenities, like jokes about violence against women, and the strong norms against interrupting a class or social occasion to object to any of the routine forms of trivializing violence against women, are all part of a pervasive pattern of reminders to women that we are always at risk of violence and that the violence is tolerated, condoned, and not taken seriously. It does not take a direct threat to keep the fear alive. My sense of vulnerability as a woman and as a publicly identified feminist, and my urge for male protection reminded me of the social control fear achieves, in a way far more compelling than my long-standing theoretical views on the subject.

The wide range of sexual violations women are subject to are of a piece. They serve to remind us of our subordinate status and that this status is maintained by violence and fear. We can constrain our freedom in ways that reduce the likelihood of assault, but it is not possible to be safe. It is not possible to be free of fear.[51] The practical questions are about the degrees of constraint and the modes of defence for coping with the unavoidable reality of fear.

Let us say that you are persuaded that women live in fear and even that that fear is an essential part of what keeps women in a subordinate position. There is still the question of whether this is the sort of fear Shklar had in mind, and whether its impact and pervasiveness amounts to the indictment I claim.

ances of impropriety or as transitory hysteria. Against hys-
cal politics it is necessary to offer protection, make amends,
rd compensation, but not to remake the political structure."
responding to the demands to dismantle Apartheid, the
urt in effect rewrote the Constitution.[59]

The fear and violence to which women are subjected must be
rcome if the aspirations of the liberalism of fear are to
ored—even if in doing so we must challenge the very pur-
e of articulating those aspirations, the maintenance of the
ndaries to the liberal state.

To reflect further on the inadequacy of boundary language
d the advantages of "rights as relationship" in dealing with
lence against women let me return to one of the "critics'
estions": isn't rape quintessentially about boundary violation
d don't women desperately need better protection for the
undaries of their persons? Isn't this of all places where we
ed to claim the same kind of boundary protection men get?

Let me begin with the question whether the metaphor of
undary violation captures the essence of the horror of rape.
t us start with Judith Herman's description of trauma:

> Traumatic events violate the autonomy of the person at the level of basic bodily integrity. The body is invaded, injured, defiled. Control over bodily functions is often lost; in the folklore of combat and rape, this loss of control is often recounted as the most humiliating aspect of the trauma. Furthermore, at the moment of trauma, almost by definition, the individual's point of view counts for nothing. In rape, for example, the purpose of the attack is precisely to demonstrate contempt for the victim's autonomy and dignity.[60]

oreover, "Helplessness constitutes the essential insult of
uma."[61] (Remember Noddings lists helplessness as one of the
sic forms and conditions of evil.) In rape, as in all trauma, the
tim's sense of self is shattered.[62]

In a culture where boundary is a basic metaphor for the
egrity of the self, it is not surprising to describe rape as a
lation of boundaries.[63] The self, after all, has been deliber-
ely violated. However much the physical invasion, the violent
im of contact whose nature is intimate, is part of the horror,

When Shklar describes cruelty and fear as the *summum malum* of liberalism, she goes on to ask "what is meant by cruelty here?": "It is the deliberate infliction of physical, and secondarily emotional, pain upon a weaker person or group by stronger ones in order to achieve some end, tangible or intangible, of the latter." I think there is no question that rape qualifies. And the fact that it is perpetrated regularly (a rape is reported every six minutes in the United States) by members of the group that holds most positions of public power against a relatively powerless group makes it compelling evidence of something seriously wrong.

But the question is still whether this failure goes to the heart of the object of Shklar's liberalism. (I will turn later to the question of whether the failure is of the sort that a more thorough application of liberal principles can cure.) She goes on to say that "public cruelty is not an occasional personal inclination. It is made possible by differences in public power." Bracketing for a moment the issue of publicness, this description still fits rape. But now the issue of publicness becomes central: "[Public cruelty] is almost always built into the system of coercion upon which all governments have to rely to fulfill their essential functions." This is not the minimum fear and coercion inherent in any system of law. "The fear [that liberalism of fear] wants to prevent is that which is created by arbitrary, unexpected, unnecessary, and unlicensed acts of force and by habitual and pervasive acts of cruelty and torture performed by military, paramilitary, and police agents in any regime. . . . Systematic fear is the condition that makes freedom impossible and it is aroused by the expectation of institutionalized cruelty as by nothing else."[52]

We now have a manifest divergence from the practice of rape. Although public officials do use their power to rape, the systematic fear that pervades the lives of North American women is fear of rape by private citizens, not public officials.[53] But it is this very divergence that points to a limitation in Shklar's vision (a limitation I take to be characteristic of many defenders of traditional liberalism) of what it would take to implement the basic principle of protecting people from fear and cruelty. Exploring this limitation will also take us a step toward the broad question of whether the sorts of issues with which I am concerned are beyond the proper scope of law. To address this issue of public versus private violence, I want to draw an analogy to a brilliant argument by Robert Cover about the expansion of the judicial role that was entailed in overturning the Apartheid of the American South.

Cover argues that blacks were not able to use competitive democratic politics to protect themselves, as other minorities had done, "because of white terror and the failure of the will to control it"

> Whether in a one, two or three-party system, the probable losers, who perceived an alliance with Blacks as the road to victory and power, confronted a powerful temptation to cheat on the White bargain. Precisely because that tension was present, racist domination required that the politics of the region be violent and extreme. In a more civilized context the bargain would not have been kept, as it has not been since 1965. Thus terror has always been part of Southern regional politics.[54]

What matters for the analogy with women is not the particulars of the structure of politics, but the ways in which terror, largely privately perpetrated, was an essential part of a social and political system in which one group was kept subordinate.[55] The "close fit between private terror, public discrimination, and political exclusion" distinguishes the treatment of blacks from other minorities. But it has a powerful resonance with the complex mechanisms by which women (a majority, who have had the vote for some time) are kept in their place. Again, it is not the specifics that matter, but the broader issue of the "resonance of society and politics" that "accounted in part for the peculiar intransigence of the state action problem." Cover charts the process by which the Supreme Court came to see that it could not dismantle Apartheid while respecting the traditional boundaries of judicial intervention, defined by state action. In 1935, the Court was still refusing "to pierce the state-action barrier that was the formal embodiment of a distinction between state and society—a distinction that was meaningless when custom and terror could be expected to enforce what the state could not."[56]

If we are to stop the violence against women we will have to

think differently about the task of law and lence-based subordination of women is so c the fabric of our society, that the conventic the liberal state is to protect us from cannot violence of the South, it is neither simply violence nor state-perpetrated.

Let me offer you one more analogy fro mind when thinking about Shklar's descri censed acts of force" and official acts of "cru which the liberalism of fear is aimed. In 19 asked whether the South was fascist. He ans

> 'The South entirely lacks the centralized orga state. . . . The Democratic party is the very party in a modern fascist sense. It has no ideology, no tight regional or state organizati ized and efficient bureaucracy.'
>
> This, then, is the paradox suggested to m observations. Southern Apartheid was in large fragmented, weak administration, of local a itics.[57]

An intricate system of oppression, sustain tioned by officials (although often not tech did not require either conscious ideology or The same is true for the complexities of wom and the role of terror in sustaining it. And a Apartheid, it cannot be overcome without cr boundaries—and risking genuine values. South, the question was whether "the real po ent in local autonomy [could] survive the tional norms in the interest of destroying A case of women, one of the obvious values a tional privacy of the home and of sexual rel value of privacy that provides both the oppo and the justification for noninterference, just omy of the South did.

The problem cannot be solved in terms c boundaries of state and society. The violen like the Apartheid of the South cannot be

I think the language of boundary crossing misdirects our attention. (It is worth remembering that rape laws used to require penetration for the assault to count as rape. But in the lobbying for reform it was widely argued that this was a standard from a male perspective that did not correspond to the women's experience of the horror.)

What Herman emphasizes is the radical disconnection of trauma and the need for reconnection for recovery. Traumatic events "shatter the construction of the self that is formed and sustained in relation to others." They "destroy the belief that one can *be oneself* in relation to others."[64] "The restoration of a positive view of the self [after rape] includes . . . a renewed sense of autonomy within connection." Part of the horror of rape in our society is that the reconnection is often so difficult. In most instances of rape, the offender is known to the victim. "To escape the rapist, the victim may have to withdraw from some part of her social world" and her "feelings of fear, distrust, and isolation may be compounded by the incomprehension or frank hostility of those to whom she turns for help."[65] Part of the reconnection is "the restitution of a sense of a meaningful world." But for this it is essential that the victim be able to share her story with others. This is often particularly hard for victims of rape—and not just in the notorious situations of trials.

> Returning veterans may be frustrated by their families' naive and unrealistic views of combat, but at least they enjoy the recognition that they have been to war. Rape victims, by and large, do not. Many acts that women experience as terrorizing violations may not be regarded as such, even by those closest to them. Survivors are thus placed in the situation where they must choose between expressing their own point of view and remaining in connection with others.[66]

But both the expression and the connection are essential to their recovery.

If this understanding of rape as a shattering of self-in-connection reinforces my objection to boundary language, what should we do instead of relying on boundaries? There are several different, interconnected, levels to this question. I want to start with brief reflections on what it would take to stop rape, mention the kind of language we should aim for to replace boundary, and indicate the sort of shifts in the law that will take us in the right direction. In the process, we will get some sense of the contributions of a shift to thinking of rights as relationship. And we will see why adequate protection for women cannot be achieved simply by enforcing for them the same rights as men—as if such enforcement would have no serious consequences for the rights and privileges of men.

Let me begin with our original issue of fear.[67] To achieve freedom from fear for all, we would have to end men's domination of women.[68] And to end the domination, we must eliminate the fear that keeps it in place. This apparent circularity means that we must work on both at the same time. Beginning to lessen the fear *will* shift the relations of power; and no mechanism for trying to lessen the fear that does not shift the power will work.[69]

In terms of stopping rape in particular, I think we need to end not only the domination of women by men, but the primacy of domination in general, the role of violence in our culture, and its association with masculinity. Catherine MacKinnon makes compelling arguments that dominance itself is eroticized in our culture. Thus, we are not only talking about achieving equality between men and women, but transforming our experience of sexuality, our understanding of what it means to be a man or a woman in our society. Now I am not, of course, saying that law or a reconception of rights can achieve all this. But we must not back off too quickly, assuming that the project must be beyond the scope of law and intrinsically dangerous for any state to embark on. As I have tried to argue, we cannot abandon the project, despite its daunting scope, without abandoning the basic aspirations of liberalism—even if our understanding of the scope of the liberal state requires serious modification.

Since what is required ultimately is a transformation of the relations between men and women, we need language that directs our attention to these relations, and laws that shift them. Few of the basic protections adult women need can be captured adequately by simple prohibitions. Most of the words and touching that can be threatening, frightening, demeaning, and assaultive in one context can be welcome in another. That is the inherent problem in rape as well as sexual harassment. I think a better language than simple prohibition or respect for boundaries is that men have an obligation to make a respectful effort to determine whether and what kind of touch (or contact) is desired, and to maintain a continued alertness to this desire rather than treat the relation as an on/off one in which once permission (which actually implies tolerance rather than desire) is acquired, no further attention to desire is necessary.[70]

Now lest anyone think such an approach is hopelessly inappropriate to law, let me briefly discuss Canada's new rape law.

The preamble states that "the Parliament of Canada is gravely concerned about the incidence of sexual violence and abuse in Canadian society, in particular, the prevalence of sexual assault against women and children." Parliament "recognizes the unique character of the offence of sexual assault and how sexual assault and, more particularly, the fear of sexual assault affects the lives of the people of Canada."[71] Finally, the preamble declares Parliament's wish "to encourage the reporting of incidents of sexual violence or abuse and to provide for the prosecution of offenders within a framework of laws that are consistent with the principles of fundamental justice and that are fair to complainants as well as to accused persons." This preamble is in part an attempt to anticipate constitutional challenges to the Act as a violation of the rights of the accused. But it is also broadly important in its assertion that standards of fairness must be applied to the complainant as well the accused, and that a good law must be one that encourages reporting. (Compare Herman's indictment of American law: "The legal system is designed to protect men from the superior power of the state [as Shklar says it should be] but not to protect women or children from the superior power of men. It therefore provides strong guarantees for the rights of the accused but essentially no guarantees for the rights of the victim.)[72]

In terms of the substantive content of the Act, the redefinition of the meaning of consent has great potential for changing long standing patterns of power and (ir)responsibility. Women routinely have found themselves in the position of willingly engaging in socializing and even sexual contact, and then been told that if the man then forces her to have intercourse that either "she asked for it" or that it is plausible that he believed she consented. The new Act addresses this problem directly: no consent is obtained where "the complainant, having consented to engage in sexual activity, expresses, by words or conduct, a lack of agreement to continue to engage in the activity." Of course, even this leaves open the question of the man's responsibility to pay attention to what the woman is communicating. The central role of intent, of *mens rea* in the criminal law, has long been used to insist that the only option in the law of sexual assault is a subjective standard of intent. The argument goes that the man's perspective, his understanding (or lack of it) of the situation has to be privileged over the woman's experience of violent harm, because the requirement of subjective intent has been at the heart of the common law tradition of criminal law. To hold someone criminally accountable for an act he did not "intend" would violate his basic rights.

The problem long recognized by feminists is that, as I noted above, this approach must give priority to the man's perspective over the woman's. (Remember Herman's statement that "at the moment of trauma, almost by definition, the individual's point of view counts for nothing."[73] It is no wonder that many women experience a rape trial as a second rape.) The problem is particularly acute since in sexual assault men and women often experience the encounter completely differently, even if they agree on a "factual" description of what took place. The law is then faced with an exceptionally difficult situation. Even if everyone is telling the truth, judges will routinely be faced with wildly different accounts of what happened. The way consent is defined will inevitably shape whose story the law validates, and thus whom the law protects. There does not seem to be a "neutral" solution to the problem. Clinging to the common law tradition of intent is obviously one-sided in its impact, and one-sided with respect to one of the most horrific forms of violence against women. When one adds to that the recognition that the prevalence of violence against women is one of the chief means of maintaining their subordination in society, of preventing the possibility of genuine equality, acquiescence in the consequences of the traditional meaning of *mens rea* seems unconscionable.

The alternative has always seemed to me to hold men to a standard of reasonable care in determining whether a woman has consented to intercourse. This could work toward equalizing power relations between men and women, instead of entrenching the patterns of inequality (sustained by violence) as the privileging of the man's perspective does. The new Canadian law is a step in this direction, but it is a less forthright step than that included in the original Bill C–49.

The original wording was as follows: "It is not a defence . . . that the accused believed that the complainant consented to the activity that forms the subject-matter of the charge, where (a) the accused's belief arose from the accused's (i) self-induced intoxication, or (ii) reckless or wilful blindness; or (b) *the accused did not take all reasonable steps, in the circumstances known to the accused at the time, to ascertain that the complainant was consenting.*" In the Act as adopted, the word "all" was deleted from the phrase "all reasonable steps." It will presumably depend on judicial interpretation whether the deletion of the term "all" merely removes the possibility of imposing an unreasonably high standard (say, of all conceivable steps), or virtually reinstates a subjective standard in terms of "what seemed reasonable to him at the time" or something in between. It at least holds out the possibility that the law will impose a new kind of responsibility on men to make some effort to find out if a woman consents to sex. Unexamined stereotypes of "no means yes" would presumably no longer provide a defence, even if the accused had managed to so insulate himself from public education on the subject that he actually believed it, in general and in a particular case. With sympathetic interpretation, the net effect would be to significantly change the degree of impunity with which men inflict violence against women—which in turn would shift the overall relations of power between men and women.

Once we are confronted by the inevitability of the legal systems favoring one perspective over another, and thus of protecting one of the parties rather than the other, then an analysis in terms of how the law affects the relations of power gives us a reasoned means for deciding what to do. Assuming a recognition of the systemic subordination of women and a commitment to equality, it is clear that a commitment to the traditional meaning of *mens rea* is a commitment to inequality. The relational analysis leads us here, as always, out of sterile quandaries about neutrality or the intricacies of conventional legal categories. And, of course, to do so is by no means to simply disregard the rights of the accused. It is to recognize the consequences of those rights as they have been traditionally understood, and to see the incompatibility of those consequences with equality.

Finally, it is worth noting an ironic shift in the affect usually invoked when "subjectivity" is associated with feminism. I have repeatedly heard the argument that the law requires objectivity, and thus the subjectivity inherent in many of the feminist reconceptions of reasoning, of fairness, of adjudication is unsuitable for a legal system as we know it. But when we turn to the criminal law, where a subjective standard has long been the norm, suggesting an "objective" standard of reasonableness is equated with the collapse of civil liberties.

However unreasonable this conclusion, it does point to the reality that men's rights are changed. It does not turn out to be possible to protect women simply by enforcing traditional rights for them as well as men. A law like this in the United States would pose an interesting test of the willingness of the Court to interpret the Constitution in ways necessary to end the subordination (backed by violence) of women as they were willing to do in the case of ending Apartheid in the South.[74]

I must come to a close without fully addressing the problem of child abuse. We are just now coming to recognize its prevalence and its long-term consequences (although the history of our not-knowing is itself fascinating).[75] I see it (as does Judith Herman) as related to the overall pattern of sexual domination and the eroticization of dominance that MacKinnon describes. Thus preventing child abuse involves the same sort of scope of change. I think the issue of the protection of children also makes clear the problematic nature of relying on traditional conceptions of rights. Some have argued that what we need is more rights for children, and better enforcement of those they already have. But I think it is clear that the oppositional nature of conventional rights cannot (at least in many cases) be the best path for reconstructing the damaged relations that bring about and result from child abuse. And, of course, my point is that we cannot say that healing these relationships is beyond the scope of the law, because the healing is necessary for the basic security promised by the liberal state.

Finally, the issue of child abuse points to our society's astonishing indifference to the well-being of children. When we add the pain of poverty to the shocking incidence of child abuse, we have to recognize that we permit fear, cruelty, and violence to dominate the lives of a huge percentage of our children. This toleration of evil is a puzzle to me, for children are hardly "others" in conventional ways. I think the inexplicable turns out to be accounted for, at least in part, by the unimaginable. It is inexplicable how we (here meaning those with relative power and privilege) can fail to act, to find ways of acting effectively to mitigate the pain, poverty, and abuse of children. Yet to face it, to let in the full scope of the horror, threatens to take over our lives. The degree of change entailed seems unimaginable. So we manage not to see the pain, although we know it to be there. How could we continue as we do if we did not protect ourselves by wilful blindness, by a kind of radical dissociation from the pain around us?

This now brings me back to a question I raised at the outset. If our notion of rights as boundaries helps provide this blindness and dissociation, will not abandoning this metaphor and embracing a conception of rights as relationship overwhelm us with responsibility? As I have acknowledged elsewhere, it will increase our responsibility, but I think it need not be as overwhelming as it appears. I think part of the problem is that in our attachment to the secure limits of rights, including the security of limited responsibility, we have had little training in compassion. We know little about how to face the reality of suffering, how to hold it in our minds and not turn away from it, without having it overwhelm us,[76] and how to make reasonable decisions about our responsibility in light of this knowledge.

I think habits of relational thinking, in the realm of rights as in others, would foster this ability. Seeing ourselves in relation to others would not generate inflated and overwhelming ideas about the scope of our responsibility to cure all evils. It could be the basis for a more reasonable judgment about the limits of our power as individuals as well as the desirable scope of power we exercise collectively.

To say this is to acknowledge that the problems of defining that scope remain. I have argued that we must think differently about how to define the scope of the state. I have not tried here (though I have provided hints elsewhere) to say how we should do it. Indeed, my whole project of reconceptualizing some of the terms of liberalism is meant to encourage a shift in focus or perspective. I think we are best off not rejecting the concept of rights, but redefining it. I think the shift in focus can make a big difference, with implications that some defenders of traditional liberalism would strenuously resist. But my aspirations are modest. There need be no radical disjuncture between the ongoing invocation of conventional rights and the urging of a different focus. The new Canadian rape law, for example, emerged out of the ordinary processes of law-making with feminists arguing within the context of liberal rights. Yet I think such legislation is best understood and argued for in relational terms. It is this relational approach that will facilitate the vast scope of change in the relations between men and women that is necessary for women to have genuine freedom from fear.

V. Can the Relational Approach "Work" for Rights?

Let me turn finally to sketch some of my reflections about whether the relational approach can "work."[77] I think the core of the concern about rights as relationship "not working" has to do with the importance of the mythology of rights. We think that rights can only succeed in protecting us if there is something indisputable, or at least peremptory, about claims made in their name. That is, I think, part of the urge to insist on universal rights. If rights are not universal, then there is always room for dispute, for debate over whether they apply in a given situation. And when we claim a right, we do not want to invite debate. We want the claim treated as authoritative, with unassailable moral authority behind it.

There are some good reasons for this. We don't always want to debate everything. Indeed, we want some things to be particularly resistant to debate because we want them to be the most stable dimensions of our society. Rights claims are supposed to provide this resistance on behalf of basic values. But the reality, of course, is that rights claims are disputed. That is what courts do: they arbitrate disputes over rights. When one claim of right conflicts with another, as is the usual case in private law disputes and often the case even in constitutional adjudication, courts must open up the meaning of the rights in question. They must regularly make minor adjustments in the prevailing interpretation, shifting the meaning of the rights slightly. Of course, sometimes there are important moments when the shifts constellate into a major change (e.g., *Brown v. Board of Education, West Coast Hotel*). In any case, the meaning of rights is not in fact static, and claims of rights for legal (as opposed to political) purposes do entail debate, dispute, and change.

My claim on behalf of "rights as relationship" (and moving away from the boundary metaphor) is that the debate will be more productive and the change will occur in more positive directions. Within the framework of courts, my claim is that shifting to the "rights as relationship" approach will not radically alter the kind of inquiries judges engage in anyway. It will make those inquiries more self-conscious and it will help them ask questions that get to what is really at stake, the values people care about most, and help them to think about what definitions of rights will foster those values. In principle, nothing here ought to be radically disruptive of the judicial process.[78] I think what is perceived to be disruptive is not the relational content of the questions I advocate,[79] but the issue of self-consciousness itself. It is this that is connected to the broader concern about rights losing their rhetorical efficacy in the public realm generally.

What I think makes people nervous about "rights as relationship" is that they seem to proclaim what needs to be hidden, to destroy the mythic quality of rights that is essential for their political role, for their rhetorical power, and even for their role in constraining judges, in defining what counts as legal, as judicial. In the case of judges, it doesn't matter that they do in fact engage in the sorts of open-ended inquiries, the inevitable value judgments, and the estimate of consequences that my approach entails. What matters is that all these inquiries, and their behavior more generally, are constrained by their understanding of their role as judges in interpreting "the Law." That role is closely tied to their sense of rights as something not of their creation, if not natural or inherent in human nature, at least the product of something far beyond them and their particular decision: "the Framers," or custom, or the great common law tradition. Indeed, rights do have a quality like that. They take their power from a cumulative process of definition, and are not (properly) simply subject to wholesale revision because a given judge or even court of several judges thinks it would be a good idea. The meaning of rights is tied to long-standing judgments about what will foster the most basic of human needs and values—security, freedom, autonomy, dignity—as these have been interpreted in the tradition. Even moments of major change invoke the tradition. The form of the argument is that the change is necessary to be true to or give effect to the deepest values of the tradition.

My claim is that rights as relationship can still do all this, and do it better. There is no reason why a tradition of relational analysis could not be developed that carries the same weight of respect that is currently accorded to precedent and the traditional mode of legal analysis. There could be the same reluctance to overturn a long established line of reasoning—even though the nature of that reasoning would be somewhat different from that common in courts today. The basic values at stake would be clearly articulated, as would the grounds for believing that the prevailing interpretation best fostered the relationships necessary for those values. There is no reason why cumulative judicial inquiries into the relationships necessary for such a value as autonomy and the contours of legal rights that would foster those relationships could not form a body of authoritative case law, offering the same sort of guidance that current case law does. Just as now, new interpretations constantly would be suggested and some would prevail and others would not—but all in the context of arguments about the tradition.

Two questions about this dimension of the viability of rights as relationship remain. The first is the issue of self-consciousness noted above. But I will begin with the second question, the matter of transition: how do we get fundamental change within a system whose foundation is reverence for tradition? Particularly when what is required is both a change in the mode of reasoning *and* a recognition that parts of that tradition, and worse, woven throughout it, are things at odds with its basic values, or at least at odds with their equal application to all. Part of what then becomes necessary is a redefinition of the basic values so that their patriarchal interpretations can be replaced. Recognizing that patriarchy infuses our entire legal system is akin to recognizing that "the apparently neutral structural characteristics of the Constitution had never been neutral concerning race."[80] It is possible to start to dismantle patriarchy as it was to dismantle Apartheid while invoking as justification the same values that were basic to the system that enforced these two forms of domination. The values require reinterpretation, but it matters that the basic concepts of equality, liberty, and autonomy can still be invoked—even if the new meaning of, say, autonomy, is almost the opposite of such characteristics as independence that were traditionally associated with it.

I do not mean to minimize the difficulties of advocating the wholesale (even if gradual) transformation of a tradition, while claiming a constancy of respect for tradition itself. (I believe that respect for tradition is an essential part of what we mean by law.) I think the challenge of relational feminism may be even greater than that of dismantling the Apartheid of the American South—as the judges of the Supreme Court conceived it.[81] Not only does the state/society barrier have to be reconfigured and the "structural underpinnings" of domination overturned, but the mode of reasoning about how to do this needs to change. (And, of course, feminists are increasingly seeing the complex interconnections between the structural underpinnings of racism and sexism.) Here I will do no more than point out that we do have a precedent for this (still ongoing) process of invoking underlying values as a ground for major changes in the understanding of those values and the system by which they can fostered. Although there are important differences, I think the precedent of race, as Cover describes it, is analogous to the ways in which I deliberately advocate something other than simply "extending" traditional liberal rights to a hitherto excluded, or incompletely protected, group. My point has been that even if we invoke classic liberal values as justification, we cannot achieve those values simply by "extending" conventional liberal rights. The nature of the rights themselves will have to change. Of course, the precedent of race reveals the difficulties as well as the possibility of transformation.[82]

The core of the self-consciousness issue seems to be the fear that if judges (we will consider the public later) were conscious of the choices, evaluations, and even speculations entailed in their decisions, they would experience those decisions as unconstrained. To use language familiar in other contexts, once judges see that case law, abstract conceptions of rights, and the text of the Constitution do not *determine* outcomes, they will become dangerous, free-wheeling policy-makers constrained neither by a tradition nor by accountability to an electorate. But since the actual and the desirable impact of a tradition of discourse works in ways other than by *determining* outcomes, there is no intrinsic reason for this fear. (There *is* reason, as I noted in "Reconceiving Rights as Relationship," to worry about the transition. In particular, if we distrust most of the current judges as defenders of the current regime of multiple domination, we might think they would do even more damage if they interpreted "rights as relationship" as a licence freeing them from some of their traditional constraints.)

There is another dimension of the fear about whether rights as relationship could work that is related to the issue of self-consciousness: the misunderstanding that every time a right is invoked a full-scale inquiry into all the relations at stake would have to take place. But of course there would be shorthand for the inquiries that have become part of the tradition. Everything would not always have to be done over "from scratch." The possibility of shorthand, in turn, raises the issues of reification and the use of rights claims to close down rather than direct fruitful inquiry. I think some degree of these problems is inevitable. But I do not think that this means there is no difference between the sorts of shorthand that would emerge around, say, autonomy in relation and the conventional rights claims of property.

The habits of relational thinking are what matter and if

rights are widely conceived in relational terms, if debates over what should be treated as a right and how rights ought to be interpreted and enforced, take place in relational terms, then the availability of shorthand claims will not undermine the purpose of reconceiving rights as relationship. And thinking of rights as relationship will not undermine the possibility of the shorthand rights claims that are so important rhetorically.

Now for a final point that brings me back to a question I raised earlier. Part of what has been important for the rhetorical power of rights are their claims to universality. Is this dimension of traditional rights compatible with rights as relationship, so that the combination of the two is possible? (I suggested earlier that it might be the combination of the claims of universal moral equality with rights as relationship that had the best hope of overcoming the cruelty to "Others.") I think there are some very basic claims that are universal. Shklar's goal of minimizing cruelty is one. But I do not think that there are simple, universal definitions of cruelty. For example, practices of inducing great pain for the purpose of inviting a sacred vision probably do not count, while female genital mutilation probably does, even though it is not in any simple way done to further the interests of the parents who order it done to their daughters.[83] (It is a kind of cultural cruelty that requires individual, conscious decision to participate in it.) I think the inquiry into the practical meaning basic values should have for the purposes of rights definitions is best pursued in relational terms.[84]

In short, I think we can and should start with a universal claim of equal moral worth,[85] and of some few goals like avoiding cruelty, then use the conception of rights as relationship for the purposes of deciding what that actually entails in any given situation.

VI. Conclusion

Judith Shklar's liberalism of fear provides a powerful indictment of the liberal state she seeks to defend. She offers some of the most effective language I have seen to describe the horror of the failure to protect women and children from pervasive fear. One of Shklar's central purposes was to limit the power of the state, because the state is the most dreaded source of fear and cruelty: "systematic fear is the condition that makes freedom impossible, and it is aroused by the expectation of institutionalized cruelty as by nothing else."[86] My approach to systemic fear cuts against this purpose in the sense that it asks us to expand our conception of the appropriate tasks of the liberal state to include the transformation of the relation between men and women. In reflecting on the unease generated by this task and a relational conception of rights to facilitate it, it is important to remember that I began my argument not with contested claims about equality and dignity, but with the uncontested, minimal objective of the liberal state to protect its members from violence. If I have persuaded you of the liberal state's failure on *these* terms, and the need to go beyond an approach of trying to "stop men" from committing violence, then I hope the relational approach emerges as plausible. It is not obvious that the state would wield more power, control more dimensions of people's lives if we were to focus our attention on the way the law and the state's delegated power (economic as well as familial) *currently* structures relationships not only to the terrible detriment of women, but in ways inconsistent with liberalism's basic goal. It *is* clear that we would need to think in new and challenging ways—but these challenges are what we need to take on the violence that is so deeply rooted in society. The unnerving scope of the task and of collective responsibility, the renegotiation of public/private relations, the self-consciousness, all of these disturbing dimensions to the relational approach are what makes it suitable for addressing the dramatic failure of the liberal state to protect two-thirds of its members from systematic fear. The relational approach does not offer pat answers, but a framework to analyze the problem in ways that can facilitate the necessary change so urgently required.

NOTES

1. For the purposes of this chapter, I believe it makes sense to focus on this particular failure. But while I was teaching in Chicago, it

was brought home to me forcefully that this is not the only such failure. In the United States, the state has failed perhaps even more dramatically to protect young black men from violence, and it might be said that there is a background of violence that pervades the lives of Native peoples in North America. The class of those for whom the liberal state has succeeded in providing routine security from violence (which of course does not mean perfect security) begins to look suspiciously small. Further, it seems that the fever of prison building in the United States is fueled by the perception that even that class is increasingly subject to the fear of violence that has pervaded the lives of so many others. Of course this kind of failure does command political attention.

2. This essay focuses on the issue of violence against women, only briefly returning to children at the end. Although I think the violence against women and children are closely linked, both issues were too much to take on in one discussion.

3. See note 6 for the articles in which I have elaborated this claim.

4. See, for example, my "Reconceiving Rights as Relationship," *Review of Constitutional Studies/Revue d'études Constitutionel* 1 (1993): 1–26; and Martha Minow, *Making All the Difference: Inclusion, Exclusion, and American Law* (Ithaca: Cornell University Press, 1990).

5. This is George Kateb's description of Shklar's argument in *Newsletter, Conference for the Study of Political Thought,* vol. 22, November 1992.

6. This issue of "private violence" also characterizes wife assault, which is an even more widespread source of violence against women. In 1986, the Surgeon General reported that domestic violence was the primary cause of physical injury to women, exceeding car accidents, rapes, and muggings combined. *Report on the Surgeon General's Workshop of Violence and Public Health,* United States Department of Health and Human Services and Department of Justice, Public Health Service (1986).

It has also been reported that homicide, almost always by an abusive partner, is the leading cause of death for black women under forty. E. Stark, "Framing and Reframing Battered Women" in *Domestic Violence: The Changing Criminal Justice Response,* ed. E. S. Buzawa and C. G. Buzawa (Westport, Conn.: Greenwood Publishing Group, 1992), 271 at 273. This statistic is based on medical records at the Yale-New Haven Hospital between 1978 and 1983. I am grateful to Christina Kobi for providing me with this information from her unpublished paper, "The Criminal Justice Response to Domestic Violence: A Feminist Perspective."

7. See Jennifer Nedelsky, "Reconceiving Autonomy," *Yale Journal of Law and Feminism* 1 (1989): 7–36; "Law, Boundaries, and the Bounded Self," *Representations* 30 (Spring 1990): 131–58; "Reconceiving Rights as Relationship"; "Feminist Theory and Practical Alternatives," 87 *Northwestern Law Review* (1993): 1286–301; "Potential Life as Property? A Feminist Perspective on Choosing Legal Categories," *Canadian Journal of Law and Jurisprudence* 6 (1993): 343–65; "Constitutional Dialogue," co-authored with Craig Scott, in *Social Justice and the Constitution,* ed. Joel Bakan and David Schneiderman (Ottawa: Carleton University Press, 1992), 59–84; *Private Property and the Limits of American Constitutionalism: The Madisonian Framework and Its Legacy* (Chicago: University of Chicago Press, 1990), chapter 6.

8. Among my fellow relational feminists are Carol Gilligan, Martha Minow, Joan Tronto, Carrie Menkle-Meadow, Nel Noddings, Sara Ruddick, Catherine Keller, Hester Lessard, and Virginia Held. There is of course disagreement among those using some version of this framework. Sometimes people I think of as relational feminists are called maternal feminists or cultural feminists. I do not particularly like these terms, nor often, the description accompanying them.

9. Feminists have an advantage in avoiding one of the pitfalls of challenges to liberal individualism: women's experience of relationships as oppressive as well as essential has the virtue of making us less likely to be romantic about the virtues of community as such. See Nedelsky, "Reconceiving Autonomy," 9–10.

10. With some self-consciousness, I originally used the grandiose title of "Relational Feminism Confronts the Problem of Evil." I think the essay still shows some of this broad aspiration to see if my relational approach can deal with the darkest parts of human interaction. I changed the title because the term "evil" is so complex, even contentious. What I actually address here is just one dimension of violence, but my driving concern remains the broader problem.

11. See Nedelsky, "Law, Boundaries, and the Bounded Self" and "Reconceiving Rights as Relationship." I will not try to summarize those arguments here, although I refer to them in more detail in section IV.

12. There is a related question which I will not address in this context: will not the relational approach I am advocating entail or invite an intrusiveness, an incapacity to maintain a distance necessary for human thriving that rights have traditionally provided? I hear this question to be implicit in Patricia Williams's defense of rights.

13. Kate O'Regan, who now sits on the new Constitutional Court of South Africa.

14. There is, however, an important nuance and puzzle here. What most women fear, what controls their daily activities, is fear of stranger rape. And what they think will protect them is "having a man." The irony, of course, is that the vast majority of rapes are by men their victims know. The protection they seek is often the real source of the danger. Thus the pervasive fear is in some ways misguided. If the fear were more realistic, it would probably not function in the same way to foster women's dependence on men. The basic terror of vulnerability to rape would, however, still reinforce the power relations.

15. Susan Griffin, *A Chorus of Stones: The Private Life of War* (New York: Doubleday, 1992).

16. See the description of the dark underside of farm life in Jane Smiley, *A Thousand Acres: A Novel* (New York: Knopf, 1991).

17. See particularly Marion Woodman, *The Pregnant Virgin: A Process of Psychological Exploration* (Toronto: Inner City Books, 1985) and *The Ravaged Bridegroom: Masculinity in Women* (Toronto: Inner City Books, 1990).

I have a continuing unease with the use of the terms "masculine" and "feminine" even in Woodman's fully feminist, consistently enlightening reflections. For my brief purposes here, however, I think it is enough to say that "the feminine" does not refer to gender, and that I always find that Woodman's insights are compelling even if I wish for slightly different language.

18. While I have found her approach extremely helpful, I do not think a reader need accept Jungian psychology to accept my argument.

19. I spell out some of these links (though without reference to Woodman) in Nedelsky, "Law, Boundaries, and the Bounded Self."

20. See also Dorothy Dinnerstein, *The Mermaid and the Minotaur* (New York: Harper Colophon Books, 1977), who for all the problems of her universalizing language, has important insights on the mutuality of destructive gender roles.

21. Marion Woodman, *Addiction to Perfection* (Toronto: Inner City Books, 1982), chapter 7, "Rape and the Demon Lover," 132. The passage quoted continues, "D. M. Thomas's novel *The White Hotel* (1981) makes vividly clear the contemporary fate of the feminine."

22. Robert Johnson, *Ecstasy: Understanding the Psychology of Joy,* see especially 18–20. Johnson also sees links to the destructive quality of our gendered roles.

There are also important links here to Catherine MacKinnon's persuasive arguments about the eroticization of dominance and violence. See *Feminism Unmodified: Discourses on Life and Law* (Cambridge: Harvard University Press, 1987).

23. Nel Noddings, *Women and Evil* (Berkeley: University of California Press, 1989), 1.

24. "When I use the word *shadow,* I will refer not to an element in the realm of archetypes, but rather to a set of desires, inclination, and behaviours that are observable in human experience . . . those of which the individual is unaware are part of his or her shadow. Similarly, a group, institution, nation, or culture may have a shadow. Sometimes the traits belonging to the shadow are vehemently denied, even despised, and then we may predict projection" (75).

25. *Women and Evil,* 120.

26. Ibid., 211.

27. This is just one of the many ways in which I do not purport to address all the different forms violence takes.

28. The idea of universal, equal rights only applies to other full humans. The concept itself thus is little, if any, impediment to mistreating those we do not think of as human or as so inferior that they are not entitled to equal rights.

29. "We have also found it useful to distinguish among natural, cultural, and moral forms of evil. The pain of illness and death are natural evils; poverty, racism, war, and sexism are cultural evils; the deliberate infliction of physical or psychic pain—unless we can show convincingly that it is necessary for a desirable state in the one undergoing pain—is moral evil." Noddings, *Women and Evil,* 120–21.

30. I assume the readers of this essay are neither homeless nor impoverished (beyond the temporary constraints of studenthood). I would be glad if the assumption proved incorrect.

31. See "Reconceiving Rights as Relationship," 17, where I discuss this example.

32. Ibid.

33. "Law, Boundaries, and the Bounded Self," 183, 180.

34. *Women and Evil,* 210.

35. *Newsletter, Conference for the Study of Political Thought,* vol. 22, November 1992, 2.

36. Actually, she talks more about liberalism than constitutionalism, and it is more the traditions of liberalism than constitutionalism that I want to take on here. Someone once said that my objective was to have constitutionalism without liberalism. In fact, I want to revise some of the basic terms of liberalism and to transform our understanding of constitutionalism in corresponding ways. The idea of boundaries (to the legitimate authority of the state) is as essential to the American conception of constitutionalism as it is to the dominant conception of rights (as the content of the boundaries).

37. Judith Shklar, "Liberalism of Fear," in *Liberalism and the Moral Life,* ed. Nancy Rosenblum (Cambridge: Harvard University Press, 1989), 21–38; Shklar, *Ordinary Vices* (Cambridge: Harvard University Press, 1984).

38. "Liberalism of Fear," 29.

39. *Ordinary Vices,* 235.

40. Ibid., 237.

41. Ibid., 241–42.

42. The United States is clearly her paradigm liberal society.

43. Which is not, of course, to say that there are not forms of violence and terror to which women are subjected elsewhere, and from which women in North America are relatively well protected. To say that there are worse horrors elsewhere, however, is not to deny the claim that North American liberal society fails to provide some of its weakest and most powerless members with the security from fear that Shklar treats as fundamental.

44. Judith Lewis Herman, *Trauma and Recovery* (New York: Basic Books, 1992), 33.

45. Ibid., 32.

46. Lenore Terr, *Too Scared to Cry: Psychic Trauma in Childhood* (New York: Basic Books, 1990), 37.

47. Herman, *Trauma and Recovery,* 50.

48. She also sees it as part of a broader pattern of violence that affects men as well: "Combat and rape, the public and private forms of organized social violence, are primarily experiences of adolescence and early adult life. The period of greatest psychological vulnerability is also in reality the period of greatest traumatic exposure, for both young men and women. Rape and combat might thus be considered complementary social rites of initiation into the coercive violence at the foundation of adult society. They are the paradigmatic forms of trauma for women and men respectively." (There are strong echoes here of Susan Griffin.) But the fact that men in our culture are subjected to the horrors of war, long sanctioned as inevitable, and that there are links between these different, routine forms of violence, does not mean that the absence of basic security for women and children does not pose a special challenge to the claims of liberalism.

49. Report by the Canadian Panel on Violence Against Women, as reported in *The Toronto Star,* Friday, July 30, 1993, A23.

50. I cannot vouch for the methods used. But it would be interesting to note whether in-depth interviews consistently illicit higher numbers of victims than do questionnaires or telephone surveys. It seems likely to me that something other than interviewer bias (as implied

about the Toronto study) would account for the higher numbers. It makes sense to me that women would be more willing to reveal such painful experiences in a context where some personal rapport had been established.

I should also note a year prior to the report, four national feminist organizations withdrew support for the Canadian Panel on Violence Against Women because it did not sufficiently represent disabled, ethnic, and immigrant women. One of the objections from feminists is that none of the information is new. The money, ten million dollars, would have been better spent on mitigating (e.g., battered women's shelters) or solving the problem. See *The Toronto Star,* Friday, July 30, 1993, A23.

51. Of course, the degree of fear women suffer varies enormously, not only among women, but across the different parts of a woman's daily life. Living in the relatively safe city of Toronto, I experience far less daily intrusion into my life plans than I did while living in Hyde Park in Chicago. Like most women, I make accommodations to the fear that feel so routine that I generally am scarcely conscious of the fear that lies behind the accommodations. For example, I consider my office in a large university building to be inaccessible to me late at night, whereas my male partner will comfortably go there at 4:00 A.M. What brought home to me most clearly the way some level of fear pervades my life was a story of the Michigan Women's Folk Festival, which has a large acreage on which no men are allowed. Although I found it troubling that male infants were part of the exclusion, I realized that for the first time I could imagine what it would be like to spend whole days and nights with no fear at all of male assault. I found the idea of being able to walk alone through woods without anxiety exhilarating—and as a result became more conscious of how such freedom from fear ordinarily feels impossible to me.

52. "Liberalism of Fear," 29.

53. Subtle revisions of this statement might be necessary when we have a full account of the frequency of the sexual abuse perpetrated on children by those in power over them in orphanages, residential schools, and reform schools. We might also need to revise it in light of the complexities of the abuse of power by employers and teachers who sexually harass and rape women subject to their power. Although the common experience of fear is of "stranger rape," it may be that for a very large number of women the original source of the terror is abuse of state-sanctioned power. This description might apply as well to women sexually abused by a step-parent.

It seems likely, however, that recent changes in law and norms have made more headway against these abuses of power than against "private" rape.

54. Robert Cover, "The Origins of Judicial Activism in the Protection of Minorities," *Yale Law Journal* 91 (1982): 1287–316. Quotation cited is at 1303–4.

55. It is probably always the case that violence and fear are necessary to keep a group subordinated. Women were once thought of as an exception, but we can now see that they are not.

56. Ibid., 1307. Cover is referring to a case that upheld the white primary when it was the product of a party convention decision.

57. Ibid., 1308–9.

58. Ibid., 1309.

59. Ibid., 1316. I have not tried to present Cover's central and fascinating argument about the importance for this process of the famous Footnote Four in *United States v. Carolene Products* 304 U.S. 144 (1938), 152 n.4.

60. Herman, *Trauma and Recovery,* 53.

61. Ibid., 41.

62. Ibid., 61, 51.

63. See "Law, Boundaries and the Bounded Self," for a discussion of the disturbing implications of the boundary metaphor, including Andrea Dworkin's vision of intercourse as inherently a violation.

64. Ibid., 51, 53.

65. Ibid., 62.

66. Ibid., 67.

67. Herman's compelling comment reveals the serious constraint on women's freedom that fear and violence entail: "Most women do not in fact recognize the degree of male hostility toward them, preferring to view the relations of the sexes as more benign than they are in fact. Similarly, women like to believe that they have greater freedom and higher status than they do in reality. A woman is especially vulnerable to rape when acting as though she were free—that is, when she is not observing conventional restrictions on dress, physical mobility, and social initiative. Women who act as though they were free are often described as 'loose,' meaning not only 'unbound' but also sexually provocative" (69).

68. It is important to remember that I have not begun to catalog the full range of fears, from economic dependency to a deep sense of inadequacy, that characterize so many women's lives. Indeed, as I read the descriptions of the consequences of trauma, I thought they sounded on a continuum with what most women seem to experience. Now this might turn out to be because such a huge percentage of

women have suffered some kind of trauma, whether of child abuse or adult sexual violation. But I think it is more likely that there is something abusive about the role of women (extraordinarily diverse as the forms of the role are) in our society that itself generates a kind of pathology. I also have not discussed the special fear and pain of poverty that afflicts women disproportionately.

69. There are close parallels here with the issue of wife assault.

70. This is not to say that the communication must be in words. There are many such nuances that I will not fully explore here.

71. In my reading of the preamble, I do not wish to sound overly naive. I am sure many preambles express lofty sentiments that are either routinely ignored in interpretation or actually contradicted by the language of the statute. Nevertheless, in this context, I think these positive interpretations are potentially important in the statute's capacity to shift the relations of power around one of the most important uses of violence to express and maintain male dominance.

72. Herman, *Trauma and Recovery,* 72.

73. Ibid., 53.

74. Of course, the structure of the Canadian Charter of Rights and Freedoms provides greater latitude than the prevailing interpretations of the U.S. Constitution with respect to realignments of civil rights. In Canada, if the new responsibilities assigned to men (through the reasonableness clause) are deemed to be a violation of constitutionally protected rights of due process, then the judges still have open to them the argument that the violation is justified in a free and democratic society (Section 1, Charter of Rights and Freedoms). The legitimate and compelling objectives stated in the preamble, as well as the commitment to equality between men and women, can be used to justify the law (upon showing that the law is a reasonable means to such objectives).

75. See Herman, *Trauma and Recovery,* chapter 1, "A Forgotten History," on the discovery and subsequent repudiation of childhood sexual abuse as the cause of hysteria. Also, I am told that the Kinsey report in the 1950s provided estimates of the frequency of incest and abuse that are close to the "revelations" of recent years.

76. See Joanna Macy, "Taking Heart: Exercises for Social Activists," in *The Path of Compassion: Writing on Socially Engaged Buddhism,* ed. Fred Eppsteiner (N.p.: Parallax Press and the Buddhist Peace Fellowship, 1988).

77. Of course, I have not repeated the details of what this relational approach is. That is to be found in Nedelsky, "Reconceiving Rights as Relationship."

78. However, I think over time it might lead to a reconception of such basic terms of adjudication as impartiality. At least, my theoretical inquiries lead in that direction. The long-run changes might be very significant. But that is compatible with my claim that no radical disruption need be entailed. I will address the question of whether the long-run changes might amount to the sort of disruption that my critics fear.

79. This is not true for those who believe that the content of rights can be deduced from human nature—and a human nature which is given and static and thus does not require any inquiry into actual patterns of relationship. For them, the inquiry into relationship is an unacceptable departure into "consequentialism," abandoning the only defensible foundation for rights, and putting those rights at risk. I think they see the risk as being willing to sacrifice "real" rights for some preferred, consequential outcome.

80. Cover, "The Origins of Judicial Activism in the Protection of Minorities," 1308.

81. This is not to say that eradicating sexism is harder than eradicating racism. I would not make such a claim, not least because in North American culture the two are so deeply intertwined.

82. Not only has racial oppression not been overcome in the United States, but the reconfiguration of state/society bounds has never been integrated into a coherent model of the scope and role of constitutional law. The incoherent state-action doctrine stands as testimony to this incomplete integration. So one might say that the jury is still out on the possibility claim.

83. Compare Shklar's definition in "Liberalism of Fear," 29.

84. Indeed, debates such as those current over whether emphasis on difference is the best way to achieve genuine equality, may best be pursued in relational terms, which also focuses attention on context. It may that at the end of the twentieth century in North America an emphasis on difference is essential, but that in South Africa it is not appropriate, or not in the same way. A relational focus consistently helps resolve apparent quandaries of inconsistency.

85. I will have to postpone the interesting question of how to ground this if we cannot have recourse to the soul.

86. Shklar, "Liberalism of Fear," 29.

18

STRUCTURES OF POLITICAL ORDER: THE RELATIONAL FEMINIST ALTERNATIVE

ROBERT E. GOODIN

I. Political Order and the Problem of Evil

Evil has many faces, many sources.[1] Not all of them are interpersonally hurtful. Sometimes the wicked harm only themselves. Neither are all forms of evil publicly actionable. Sometimes the only remotely plausible preventives or remedies are necessarily private ones. That said, it would be widely (if not, perhaps, universally) agreed that, first and foremost, political arrangements should strive to forestall evil where they can and to rectify its effects as they are able.

A variety of arguments converge on setting that as the first priority of political order. Some of the most compelling have to do with the "fear of fear." Living under constant threat of suffering gross evil engenders a sort of fear that we find utterly crippling in all our ordinary, everyday actions. If we are to live our ordinary lives at all, government must protect us from such crippling fear of extraordinary interventions. Protection from that sort of fear would rank as the primary primary good, in

I am grateful to Moira Gatens, Jenny Mansbridge, Jenny Nedelsky, and Carole Pateman for helping to clarify these issues for me.

much the same way and for much the same reason as "self-respect" is said to do in Rawls's *Theory of Justice.*[2]

Other arguments converging on the same conclusion about the political preeminence of preventing evil have to do with the problems of knowledge facing public officials. The causes of happiness are many and varied, the causes of misery few and common to all. Public officials are able to act with more confidence in rooting out evils, on which almost everyone agrees, than in promoting The Good, which almost everyone understands differently.[3]

Whichever path we take to that conclusion, it certainly is a common proposition that the problem of evil is *the* problem to which political order is a solution. That is widely agreed among liberal political theorists and many others besides. Indeed, it is almost the defining tenet of a liberal political theory that the state ought strive to prevent evils, or at least a certain well-defined subset of evils, rather than to promote The Good; and circumscribing the state's response to the problem of evil, creating a state strong enough to control evil without its being so strong as to submerge the moral personality of its citizens, is liberal political theory's preeminent task.

Within other, more optimistic traditions—anarchist, utopian, socialist, feminist—the problem of evil looms less large and politics performs various other important tasks. Outside the liberal canon order is taken as more natural and evil as more aberrant. Even there, however, the problem of evil remains a (if not the) central problem that political order is required to solve. That is in part because, on those other more optimistic accounts, there will be fewer problems to be solved, politically or otherwise. It is also in large part because those other gentler forms of social arrangement are more susceptible to being undermined by evil influences, however rare.

In short, wherever you start you come quickly to the same conclusion: the problem of evil occupies center-stage, politically. Politics is a matter of "imposing order." That is almost the whole story according to liberalism; it is at least a large part of the story according to most other traditions. And on all accounts, institutional order is designed first and foremost to control the knaves, many or few, among us.[4]

II. Structures of Political Order

Political structures for pursuing that purpose are themselves many and varied. At root, however, there seem to be only three fundamentally different ways of structuring political order.

One classic style of political order is *authoritarian*. This is the Hobbesian approach, adopted and adapted by many others besides. Its core components are a strong central authority, which issues rules and edicts directly to subjects who in turn have minimal discretion in interpreting their content and virtually none in applying them. This is the world of crude legal positivism, Austin's sovereign handing down laws understood as orders backed by threats.[5]

A second style of political order is broadly *hierarchical*. What all these many subspecies of hierarchical rule have in common are notions of superiors and subordinates, with the former empowered by the rules of the system to issue orders (of certain kinds, within certain limits) to the latter—and to empower them (within limits) to issue orders in turn. In the final analysis, the force of the orders comes down, once again, to the threat of force. From within, however, it is the authority of the rules empowering hierarchs to issue the orders, rather than the force with which they can back them up, that is the felt force behind the order.[6]

That is how, subjectively, life in a hierarchy feels different from life in an autocracy. Structurally, the more crucial difference lies in the fact that hierarchical forms of political order devolve authority from the central authority (who still is the ultimate source of all authority) to other lower-level authorities in the political order. Structurally, hierarchy is essentially a matter of *subcontracting* political order.

The clearest case of hierarchical political order, understood in this way, is feudalism. The lord of the manor enjoys his authority by the grace of the monarch, to be sure; but within his realm he is (perhaps within certain limits, perhaps not) the absolute ruler of all those who are tied to him. Likewise, the master is empowered by the crown and its successors to rule (with more limits) over his servants and employers to rule (with still more limits) over their employees.

This model is not without its contemporary advocates. Corporatists, syndicalists, and guild socialists all appeal to essentially this same model.[7] Nor is the model without practical contemporary relevance. The family was traditionally organized on just such a basis, with the law of marriage historically empowering the husband to be (within increasing limits) absolute ruler of his wife and household; and much contemporary feminist writing is devoted to demonstrating the myriad ways in which that basic model still prevails even after formal legal shells have been notionally changed.[8]

Most interesting for present purposes is the limiting case of hierarchical models of political order. That, I submit, is what a regime of rights amounts to. Ascribing to individuals rights, understood as legally protected spheres within which the right-holder's choices will be respected, is tantamount to empowering the right-holder as absolute sovereign within that (admittedly, tightly circumscribed) sphere.[9] It is a model of Everyman his own King—and, ideally, every woman too.

The right-holder's authority is subcontracted authority, to be sure. It is derived from the higher authority of the legal system ascribing those rights in the first place. But being subcontracted in that way is precisely what makes it, structurally, an instance (albeit the limiting one) of hierarchical models of political order. Insofar as we are acting within our rights we are absolute rulers, and others must simply bow to our sovereign determinations.

The defining feature of the third mode of political order, the *decentralist* mode, is its opposition to hierarchy in any form. The ideal there is, somehow, to establish order by everyone controlling everyone. There are no central authorities, no superiors and subordinates, no spheres within which anyone can rule supreme.

Such models have long formed the backbone of radical programs of one sort and another. Anarchists have always insisted upon the possibilities of achieving order without any central authority structures.[10] More recently, decentralization conceived in roughly this way has formed the core of a great many practical (as well as a great many impractical) proposals eminating from New Social Movements in general and Green parties in particular.[11]

Within more narrowly academic discussions, a classic example of such a model would be the market, sufficiently idealized to ensure that no one has any power to dictate (or even to shape significantly) the outcome of market transactions.[12] Democratic pluralism, in its various forms, is another example of this sort of decentralized-control model. The aspiration for everyone to control everyone without the intervention of any (independent) central authority is one which is shared by democratic theorists ranging from populists to advocates of deliberative democracy and communicative ethics to advocates of checks and balances and countervailing power.[13]

There is another variation on essentially decentralist themes. Remembering that the problem to which political order is a solution is the problem of evil, another way of solving the problem would be to make people less evil in the first place. Instead of trying to construct mechanisms to control people's evil impulses, we might strive to remake people so they are less in need of being controlled at all. There are many ways of attempting to achieve that outcome, some more authoritarian, some less so. Once people's characters have been reformed in this way, however, they are in effect controlling themselves, checking their own evil impulses before they issue in action. For this reason, this strategy is properly classed as a decentralized one, although of course the mechanisms by which the character reform was achieved in the first place may have been of a very different sort.

This strategy represents an important, albeit often idealistic, alternative. It was the aspiration of certain sorts of state socialist systems to create the New Socialist Man (and, typically, woman in his image).[14] It is one of the central arguments in favor of participatory democracy, for its potential in furthering people's self-development and the growth of their moral capacities.[15] And it is into this broad mode that "relational feminism" fits.[16] All those represent attempts not so much to *solve* the problem of evil by manipulating the political order in such a way as to contain evil, but to make evil *disappear* altogether—by, in the case of relational feminism, ensuring the right relations among people.

The contrast between these three ideal types is perhaps too strong. Perhaps none can exist in pure form. Just as the second sort of strategy requires a certain element of the first, perhaps so too does the third.[17] Hierarchies, as I have already observed, require central authority to ground the authority of subcontractors. So too do most decentralized mechanisms likewise require or presuppose centralized authority structures of some sort or another. Markets presuppose the structure of property law, contracts and torts; democracy presupposes electoral law, fairly enforced; relational feminism, in so far as it is to be undergirded by and reinforced through socio-legal instruments, presupposes a formal legal code. Any given political order will, therefore, probably always be a blend of these several styles. Even so, it genuinely matters how much of each ingredient you blend in. The contrast among these styles of structuring political order is nonetheless useful for its being something less than absolute.

III. Feminist Critiques of the Liberal Political Order

Contemporary feminist critiques of the received wisdom about the problem of political order focus largely upon the problem of too much (artificially imposed) order—and, of course, upon whose interests are served by that order.[18] While sympathizing with the liberal animus against the oversupply of central state power in authoritarian regimes, feminists are equally anxious to avoid a parallel oversupply of publicly licensed private power being exercised by the state's subcontractors. The problem is power and authority, domination and oppression, whether public or (notionally) private.[19]

The classic liberal solution to the problem of tyranny was to create a "sphere of rights, freedom and autonomy [that] was private . . . [and] to keep the public realm distant, separate, at bay."[20] This system of rights and the public/private split it serves to create, so cherished by liberals, has traditionally had the effect of lending the liberal state's authority to authoritarian rule within the household.[21] Carving out a protected private sphere traditionally protected the husband and father from the state, while within that sphere leaving the wife and children utterly at his mercy.[22]

Of course the details of that traditional settlement can be, and have been, adjusted at the margins. Any grant of authority to subcontractors is always circumscribed to some extent or another. If subcontractors are misbehaving, then their authority can always be circumscribed still further. In the limiting case, the same sort of rights that liberals traditionally granted husbands against the state could be granted to wives and children against brutal husbands and parents.[23]

Some feminist critics of the liberal order would insist that none of this addresses the real problem, however. "Our project," they say, "should not be to try to shore up women's boundaries . . . nor should it be, at least in the long run, to find ways to draw circles of protection around women that are the same as men's."[24] For such feminists, the problem with the liberal solution lies in its structure, not in its details. The problem lies in the use of liberal rights to carve out separate private spheres at all, not in how those private spheres are delimited.

Giving women or children a private sphere within which they, by right, are sovereign simply reinforces separateness rather than encouraging us to think about what sorts of relationships we have and what sorts we want.[25] Liberal rights claims are egoistic in tone and preemptory in form. Relational feminists would join communitarians more generally in saying that in both those respects rights are powerfully subversive of the sort of cooperative thinking required to undergird any proper form of community morality.[26]

Furthermore, any grant of power to some people to act as (more or less) free agents within a sphere defined by liberal rights brings with it the hierarchical subcontracting of authority. Within that hierarchy, in turn, necessarily comes the subordination of those who must yield to the will of others. By their very nature, subordinates are (to some extent or another) dominated by superiors in the authority structure created by liberal rights, as surely as by autocratic rules.

The feminist program, in all its varieties, essentially aims to end domination in all its forms. Its aspiration is to ensure equality, which can be undercut as powerfully by private exercises of power that are at most only implicitly sanctioned by state authority. (The example of Southern lynchings keeping blacks in their place is indeed a powerful case in point.)[27] Feminists typically shy away from seeking the solution in more intervention from central state authorities, however—and understandably so, given their animus against hierarchical authority, with its inevitable corollary of domination and subordination.[28]

IV. Feminist Alternatives: Politics as Personal Relations

There are all those forces pushing feminists away from reliance upon the traditional instruments of the liberal state to protect women and children against many of life's greatest evils. That, however, is only part—and perhaps the lesser part—of the story. Feminists also feel a powerful attraction to alternative, non-state remedies to the forms of domination and subordination that they hope to eradicate.

For many of them, the preferred solution is to be found in what is said to be a peculiarly female "ethic of care," arising principally out of the experience of mothering.[29] That seems to be an essential part, anyway, of what is meant by "relational feminism." The emphasis there is upon getting personal relations right. Caring affection of the sort found within a good friendship is offered as a general model for political life.[30]

This is almost the flip side of the old slogan, "the personal is political." Within this style of relational feminism, the political is personal. Or, more precisely, the personal is the best model for and best ground on which to build the good polis. And since the personal is peculiar to individuals and groups, the emphasis within this strand of feminism (as within many others) is upon respect for "difference," upon particularity rather than universalistic abstractions.[31]

Working within this broad framework, relational feminism reconstructs all manner of received socio-legal instruments—notions of "rights" conspicuously among them—to its own peculiar ends. Of course, rights have always been regarded as being inherently relational: by their very nature, rights connect holders of the rights with those who bear the correlative duties.[32] While that would remain true for relational feminists' rights, as well, that is not the most important sense in which they see their preferred model of rights as being relational.[33]

The goal of rights, on the relational feminist model, would be to cultivate the right relationships at a personal level. A decent political order would follow from that. Rights, on this view, are not so much devices to protect people from one another as devices for binding people together. Rights do not carve out a private sphere within which anyone is sovereign. Rather, they carve out a shared sphere within which we who are bound together by them must act somehow in concert.[34]

On this relational feminist model, invoking rights amounts less to lodging a preemptory claim than to initiating a conversation.[35] Rights conceived in this way would call for negotiation rather than litigation, for mediation rather than adjudication.[36] On this view, disputes betoken the breakdown of ordinary social relations, and the proper goal (or, anyway, highest aspiration) for systems of dispute resolution should be to restore decent social relations among parties to that dispute.[37]

The aim would be not just to find some modus vivendi, not just some common ground upon which all parties can stand, nor even come to that to find some fair compromise to end the controversy. Ideally the aim would instead be genuinely to dissolve the dispute—to find, through this conversation, some way of recasting relationships so that a new consensus genuinely emerges to replace what were previously points of contention.

V. An Assessment: Feminism versus Liberalism

Relational feminists are dead set against models of order achieved by fence building and boundary maintenance. They are appalled by the stark individualism, the neglect of community ties and social relations built into such models. Insofar as those models are given social meaning through regimes of liberal rights, relational feminists are further appalled by the hierarchical authority structures thereby created, and the possibilities (yea, inevitabilities) of domination built into such models. Their preferred alternative might be characterized as decentralized systems of order achieved by subsuming people into relationships—"we"ness, to borrow Buber's term employed by self-styled "new communitarians" to similar effect.[38]

The trouble with subsuming individuals into relationships of "we"ness, however, is precisely that we then risk losing track of the "separateness of people." Within a full Buberian relationship of "we"ness, we are a single entity, a single personality. Then any can speak for all. That, in turn, makes it easy for everyone to impose upon (to exploit, if not strictly dominate) any or indeed every other. Sacrifice of the few for the many, or of the many for some higher group-defining cause—precisely the sort of thing liberal rights were designed to protect against in the first place[39]—is then very much on the cards. Indeed, so too is the sacrifice of the many for the few, for in relationships of "we"ness each one can make in principle limitless claims against all others in the name of the collective "we."

Of course, relational feminists may have something less than the full Buberian program in mind here. They may, for example, mean no more than that we develop our own separate identities in the context of social (primarily family) relationships.[40] They may just be saying that to understand, and hence to alter, socially undesirable differences between men and women we need to understand and to alter socially undesirable differences in the way these family relationships impact upon boys and girls in early childhood socialization.

If that is all the relational feminist emphasis upon relationships amounts to, then it is unexceptionable but also unexceptional. Ameliorating social ills through improved childhood socialization is an old and familiar strategy. Furthermore, it is one with which liberalism has long ago made its peace. Much though it may prefer to focus upon fully-formed, autonomous agents, liberalism needs some account of the genesis of such agents. Insofar as relational feminism merely offers a better account of preference formation and character development than liberalism's own, the two models might be seen as complements to one another rather than as alternatives to one another.

Typically, however, the two are presented as stark alternatives. Relational feminism rejects the stark individualism of liberalism, and not just because of its inadequate account of the shaping of individuals' personalities. Rather, it seems, relational feminists are typically advocating an "ethic of care" that involves subsuming self into relationships in a stronger Buberian sense. Insofar as that is the aim, then relational feminists are as much at risk of losing track of the separateness of people as are Buberians.[41]

Relational feminists thus hope to ground moral and political responsibilities on concrete, existing relationships. But where do those relationships come from, and how far do they stretch?[42] Some relationships clearly exist independently of choice and were in no sense voluntarily assumed. Family relations, especially relations between children and their parents, are the paradigm case of that, as I have remarked elsewhere.[43] But wherever such relations came from, it is at least clear in that case that there is a relationship in existence once the children are on the doorstep.

Within relational feminism, it is unclear what criteria are to be employed for saying whether a relationship does or does not exist. Does an analogous relationship arise when a bag lady appears on your doorstep, for example? It is undeniably true that her well-being is affected (maybe weakly, maybe powerfully) by your actions and choices with respect to her. That is enough on my reckoning to impose some responsibility (weak or strong) upon us for helping her. But that, on my reckoning, is because our acts and omissions will help or harm her, not because we have any "relationship" in any other sense with her. My point would be precisely opposite to that of the relational feminists. I would say that we bear that responsibility regardless of whether or not we have any special relationship, whereas they would insist that we have such responsibility precisely because we have some sort of a relationship with her.

Maybe the relational feminist point could be rephrased to assert not that we *do* have a relationship to her but rather that, because of that power of ours to help or harm her, we *should*.[44] Once we have started rendering assistance, and she has started relying on it, then a relationship clearly will have come into existence; law and morals converge on the conclusion that we then have a strong duty to continue that assistance. Maybe what relational feminists are suggesting is merely that we should cultivate ongoing relationships of interdependence of that sort. But if that is the argument, then the reason for cultivating the relationship is not the existence of a preexisting relationship. Rather, the reason must have to do with the excellence of a life built around relationships, or some such.

There are occasional passages in the writings of relational feminists to suggest that we ought strive to form just such positive relationships with anyone and everyone. More often, though, the appeal is not to universality but rather to particularity. It is our relations with particular others that we ought cherish in these ways. Then, however, that particularized ethic of care threatens to make us literally careless of others outside our particular circle of relations.[45] "Care as a political ideal," Joan Tronto acknowledges, "could [then] quickly become a way to argue that everyone should cultivate one's own garden, and let others take care of themselves, too."[46]

Relational feminists such as Tronto clearly hope to avoid that conclusion. But if they succeed in stretching their notion of relationships far enough that it can in principle embrace large groups, further questions arise. How are those larger groups of "related others" supposed to come to some collective determinations? Given relational feminists' emphasis upon the particularity and situatedness of each party to the relation, and the particular needs and interests arising from that, it would be fatuous for them to postulate some facile consensus to get around the problem. Inevitably, some perspectives will prevail over others, certainly on any given occasion and perhaps systematically across all occasions. Thus we see reemerging *within* relationships risks akin to familiar problems of majority tyranny.

VI. Rights and Right Relations

Why, exactly, should we suppose that relational feminism and liberal rights are necessarily at odds? What exactly is it about structures of order built around liberal notions of rights that is thought to make them inherently hostile to right relations, and what is it about structures of order built around notions of right relations that is thought to make them inherently hostile to liberal-style rights?

The central intuition underlying the analysis at that point seems to be just this: standing on your rights is inimical to close personal relationships. As arbitrators keen to avoid premature hardening of positions often say, standing on your rights gets in the way of sitting down at the table. Close personal relationships, at their best, are "characterized by intimacy, genuine care, love, and emotional involvement." All that is antithetical to the sort of arms-length "respect" that one shows for the other's rights, to say nothing of the sort of "demanding one's due" that is involved in asserting rights claims.[47] Liberal rights are essentially fence-building, boundary-enforcing exercises, and fencing others out is no way to foster a relationship with them.[48]

This is a familiar proposition, in law and in ethics alike. Traditionally courts refused to entertain litigation of any form between husband and wife.[49] At least one of the central rationales for that policy had to do with the way in which "domestic harmony" would be disturbed if husbands and wives were living their lives in the shadow of the courts. In the words of one nineteenth-century case, "The flames which litigation would kindle on the domestic hearth would consume in an instant the conjugal bond."[50] Even as late as the mid-1970s, dissenting members of the U.S. Supreme Court could still mount a spirited challenge to due-process rights for pupils suspended from school on analogous grounds that legalistic remedies would upset the delicate and complex ongoing relationships between teachers and pupils.[51]

Of course all that reflects an attitude toward the sanctity of private spheres that has now been superseded in the courts.[52] And rightly so, feminists would be the first to agree.[53] They are properly keen for ordinary legal remedies to be readily available to battered wives and abused children. They are rightly suspicious of "just so" stories about "domestic harmony" that serve only to shelter abusive behavior in distinctly nonharmonious settings.

Anxious though feminists might be for such legal remedies to be available to battered wives and abused children when ordinary affection has broken down, relational feminists in particular retain strong elements of this old animus against liberal rights as being destructive of ongoing relationships when they are going well. Much though we may need standard liberal rights when things are going badly, they would say, recourse to such remedies is also much to be avoided when things are going well. Liberal-style boundary-protecting rights might be an unfortunate necessity, to which we appeal when relationships have already been destroyed. But by the same token they are destructive of relationships and therefore ought not be invoked prematurely to settle matters that might still admit of other modes of resolution.

The sorts of rights that relational feminists would most like to use most of the time are the other sorts of rights, ones designed to create good relationships and to bind us into cooperative communities with one another. That more positive side of the relational feminists' program amounts, in effect, to equating rights of their preferred sort with right relationships.

That move seems to me to involve a simple fallacy, already familiar in only a slightly different form. It is something of a saw in recent moral philosophy that there is a difference between rights and right conduct.[54] If people have rights, then the right conduct toward them follows (in part) from that fact. But even then, there may be more to right conduct toward them than merely respecting their rights: it might be *wrong* to let them starve, even if they have no right against you to food. Just as there is more to right conduct than just respecting rights, even where there are rights, it is all the more true that there can be notions of right conduct where there are no rights.

The connection within relational feminism between rights and right relations is, I think, similarly deceptive. The best way to build the right sort of relationships might be to forget about our rights altogether; and, conversely, the best way to construct our lists of rights might be to forget about relationships. It is not at all clear that notions of rights, of whatever sort, will ever facilitate relationship-tending on a day to day basis. As Waldron rightly says, rights do not specify how you live your life. They are merely fallback positions, telling you how to govern the unraveling of relations when ordinary affection fails.[55]

It is important for relational feminists and liberals alike to realize that this is precisely how we use liberal rights in our everyday affairs, of both a personal and an impersonal sort. Just as no one within a thriving family would dream of "standing on their rights," so too does no one even within an ongoing business relationship.

Business, of course, typically proceeds through contracts, and those standardly specify what will happen push come to shove.[56] It is an important fact, however, that even in the business world push rarely comes to shove—not just in the sense that things rarely come to actual litigation, but also in the more important sense that accommodations to shifting circumstances are most typically made without reference to the terms of the existing contract at all. Macaulay's classic paper on "Noncontractual Relations in Business" quotes one businessman as explaining,

> If something comes up, you get the other man on the telephone and deal with the problem. You don't read legalistic contract clauses at each other if you ever want to do business again. One doesn't run to lawyers if he wants to stay in business because one must behave decently.

Another says, more succinctly, "You can settle any dispute if you keep the lawyers and accountants out of it. They just do not understand the give and take needed in business."[57]

Upon reflection, there is nothing surprising in that. It simply would not be a particularly effective business firm in which all partners, all customers, all employees were always governing every act every day according to contractual entitlements and how best to defend themselves should the matter end in court. Whatever the formal authority structure within an organization, subordinates almost always enjoy substantially more latitude than the formal organization chart suggests.[58] Whatever the formal rights flowing from their ownership of a firm, shareholders and Boards of Directors inevitably cede almost all effective control to managers technically employed merely to carry out their orders.[59]

That is not to deny that Boards of Directors have rights over managers, and managers over subordinates. Nor is it to deny they can and will stand on them, in extremis. The point is merely that those rights are very much in the background rather than in the foreground in the course of everyday affairs, even in the most impersonal business-like corners of liberal society.

VII. Toward a Reconciliation of Liberalism and Relational Feminism

The upshot would seem to be just this: even relational feminists would (for certain purposes) want rights of the standard liberal sort, and even liberals would (for the most part) lead their ordinary lives in relationships of trust and reciprocity rather than always standing on their rights. In short, more sophisticated forms of liberalism and relational feminism may tend in the end to converge.

The crucial move toward convergence on the side of relational feminism comes with the recognition that relationships encode power as well as affection.[60] The program of these more sophisticated relational feminists consists, in part, in recognizing existing relationships for what they are. But often what they are are relationships of domination and subordination, exclusion, and inclusion.

That recognition leads to the other, more important part of the sophisticated relational feminist program—of recasting power relations in such a way as to empower those who are excluded or subordinated under existing social arrangements. In this reconstructivist "social-relations model for law," a crucial element in recasting power relations works through notions of rights. The aim is "remaking rights so that they do not recreate the differences etched . . . into the structures and crevices of inherited institutions."[61] In effect, that amounts to giving subordinated groups resources for negotiating their way in the world on an improved footing.[62]

The crucial move toward convergence on the liberal side comes with the recognition that formal structures of rights and duties merely set the parameters for bargaining.[63] The lived reality of a liberal world is the experience not merely of formal authority structures and entitlements but of the negotiated order that results from accommodation and exchanges arising from that initial distribution of power and resources. In an ongoing relationship, reliance and trust inevitably emerge as the most profitable strategy, even among arch-liberal agents.[64]

A sophisticated relational feminist, therefore, would be sensitive to power relations and reallocate rights in such a way as to get the power balance more nearly right.[65] She would do so not in the expectation that people would live their lives according to the strict letter of the law thus laid down, but rather in the expectation that relationships would grow and develop in the interstices of the formal structures thus created.

By the same token, a sophisticated liberal would expect formal allocations of rights and duties and authority to be opening gambits in a bargaining game. Assuming society is sufficiently small and stable for people to know one another and their reputations, repeat-players would cultivate relationships of trust and reciprocity among those with whom they will have continuing involvement.

The upshot, therefore, is that the two worlds of liberalism and relational feminism do not really look so very different after all. The differences are largely ones of emphasis, of whether we should focus primarily on formal allocations of power and authority or primarily on the ongoing relationships that grow up in their shadow. The latter may well be the more apt characterization of social life in general. But the former is the more appropriate model of political order, characterized at the outset as primarily a response to the problem of evil.

NOTES

1. See, e.g.: Judith N. Shklar, *Ordinary Vices* (Cambridge: Harvard University Press, 1984); Ronald D. Milo, *Immorality* (Princeton: Princeton University Press, 1984); and S. I. Benn, "Wickedness," *Ethics* 95 (1985): 795–810.

2. Judith N. Shklar, "The Liberalism of Fear," in *Liberalism and the Moral Life,* ed. Nancy Rosenblum (Cambridge: Harvard University Press, 1989), 21–38; John Rawls, *A Theory of Justice* (Cambridge: Harvard University Press, 1971), sec. 67.

3. Barrington Moore, Jr., *Reflections on the Causes of Human Misery* (Boston: Beacon Press, 1970).

4. David Hume, "Of the Independency of Parliament," *Essays: Literary, Moral, and Political* (London: A. Millar, 1760), part 1, chap. 6.

5. John Austin, *Province of Jurisprudence,* as explicated by H. L. A. Hart, *The Concept of Law* (Oxford: Clarendon Press, 1961), chaps. 2–4.

6. If the first model is essentially Austin's, the second is essentially H. L. A. Hart's alternative of power-conferring rules: see his *Concept of Law,* esp. chaps. 5–6.

7. Bob Jessop, "Corporatism and Syndicalism," in *A Companion to Contemporary Political Philosophy,* ed. Robert E. Goodin and Philip Pettit (Oxford: Blackwell, 1993), 404–10.

8. Carole Pateman, *The Sexual Contract* (Oxford: Polity Press, 1988), esp. chaps. 5 and 6; Susan Moller Okin, *Justice, Gender, and the Family* (New York: Basic Books, 1989).

9. H. L. A. Hart, "Definition and Theory in Jurisprudence," *Essays in Jurisprudence and Philosophy* (Oxford: Clarendon Press, 1983), 21–49 at 35 and "Are There Any Natural Rights?" *Philosophical Review* 64 (1955): 175–91.

10. Richard Sylvan, "Anarchism," in *A Companion to Contemporary Political Philosophy,* ed. Robert E. Goodin and Philip Pettit (Oxford: Blackwell, 1993), 215–43.

11. Kirkpatrick Sale, "Bioregionalism—A New Way to Treat the Land," *Ecologist* 14, no. 4 (1984): 167–73; Claus Offe, "New Social Movements: Challenging the Boundaries of Institutional Politics," *Social Research* 52 (1985): 817–68; Robert E. Goodin, *Green Political Theory* (Oxford: Polity Press, 1993), chap. 4.

12. The contrast is nicely drawn by Oliver E. Williamson, "Markets and Hierarchies: Some Elementary Considerations," *American Economic Review (Papers and Proceedings)* 63 (1973): 316–25.

13. Robert A. Dahl, *A Preface to Democratic Theory* (Chicago: University of Chicago Press, 1956); Jürgen Habermas, *Legitimation Crisis,* trans. Thomas McCarthy (London: Heinemann, 1976). See, more generally, Robert A. Dahl and Charles E. Lindblom, *Politics, Economics, and Welfare* (New York: Harper and Row, 1953).

14. Peter Clecak, "Moral and Material Incentives," *Socialist Register* (1969): 101–35.

15. C. B. Macpherson, *Democratic Theory* (Oxford: Clarendon Press, 1973), chaps. 1–3 and *The Life and Times of Liberal Democracy* (Oxford: Clarendon Press, 1977), chap. 3.

16. See Section IV of this chapter for further elaboration and references.

17. So, I shall argue below, do both of the other modes in effect

enshrine something of the third model, in the form of bargaining among those in relations of notional authority.

18. See, e.g.: Catharine A. MacKinnon, *Toward a Feminist Theory of the State* (Cambridge: Harvard University Press, 1989); Martha Minow, *Making All the Difference: Inclusion, Exclusion, and American Law* (Ithaca: Cornell University Press, 1990); and, for an overview, Jane J. Mansbridge and Susan Moller Okin, "Feminism," in *A Companion to Contemporary Political Philosophy,* ed. Robert E. Goodin and Philip Pettit (Oxford: Blackwell, 1993), 269–90.

19. Some feminist writers (MacKinnon, especially) would of course say that an important part of the remedy involves the imposition of different sorts of power and order, regulating even more tightly what sorts of activities we can engage in, what sorts of images we may view, and so on.

20. Jennifer Nedelsky, "Reconceiving Autonomy: Sources, Thoughts, and Possibilities," *Yale Journal of Law and Feminism* 1 (1989): 7–36 at 17.

21. Just as, in the *Lochner* era, enforcement of liberal rights of contract had the effect of protecting employers from the power of the state while lending state authority to their authoritarian rule over their employees (Minow, *Making All the Difference,* 277–83).

22. Note, for example, the way in which courts process child abuse cases and the way in which public policy-makers, when finally forced to face the fact of child abuse, insistently recast it in ways least intrusive into the existing structures of family relations. On the former, see Robert Dingwall, John Eekelaar, and Topsy Murray, *The Protection of Children: State Intervention and Family Life* (Oxford: Blackwell, 1983). On the latter, see Barbara J. Nelson, *Making an Issue of Child Abuse* (Chicago: University of Chicago Press, 1984), esp. chap. 7.

For more general feminist critiques of the public/private dichotomy, see: Jean Elshtain, *Public Man, Private Woman* (Princeton: Princeton University Press, 1981); Mary G. Deitz, "Citizenship with a Feminist Face: The Problem with Maternal Thinking," *Political Theory* 13 (1985): 19–37; Okin, *Justice, Gender and the Family,* chap. 6; and Carole Pateman, "Feminist Critiques of the Public/Private Dichotomy," *The Disorder of Women* (Oxford: Polity Press, 1989), 118–40.

23. Dingwell, Eekelaar, and Murray, *The Protection of Children,* chap. 11; "United Nations Declaration of the Rights of the Child (1959)," reprinted in *Having Children,* ed. Onora O'Neill and William Ruddick (New York: Oxford University Press, 1979), 112–14.

24. Jennifer Nedelsky, "Law, Boundaries, and the Bounded Self," *Representations* 30 (1990): 162–89 at 170.

25. Nedelsky, "Law, Boundaries, and the Bounded Self" and "Reconceiving Autonomy." Cf. Minow, *Making All the Difference,* chaps. 8 and 9.

26. Mary Ann Glendon, *Rights Talk* (New York: Free Press, 1991). For the more general "new communitarian" case against rights, see "The Responsive Communitarian Platform: Rights *and* Responsibilities," *The Responsive Community* 2 (1991/2): 4–20, and Amitai Etzioni, *The Spirit of Community* (New York: Crown Books, 1993).

27. Gunnar Myrdal, *An American Dilemma* (New York: Harper and Row, 1944), chaps. 25–27. Cf. James M. Inverarity, "Populism and Lynching in Louisiana, 1889–1896," and Whitney Pope and Charles Ragin, "Mechanical Solidarity, Justice, and Lynching in Louisiana," *American Sociological Review* 41 (1976): 262–80 and 42 (1977): 363–69 respectively.

28. In some cases, though, the liberal state and the rights it confers can be a powerful force for liberation. That certainly was true in the case of civil rights in the American South, for example. What makes the case of gender so very different from that of race, here?

29. Carol Gilligan, *In a Different Voice* (Cambridge: Harvard University Press, 1982); Virginia Held, "Mothering versus Contract," in *Beyond Self-Interest,* ed. Jane J. Mansbridge (Chicago: University of Chicago Press, 1990), 287–304; Sara Ruddick, "Maternal Thinking," *Feminist Studies* 6 (1980): 342–67 and *Maternal Thinking* (New York: Ballantine Books, 1989); Kathleen B. Jones, *Compassionate Authority* (London: Routledge, 1993), esp. chap. 4; Cass R. Sunstein, ed., *Feminism and Political Theory* (Chicago: University of Chicago Press, 1990); Mansbridge and Okin, "Feminism." Other feminists would, of course, reject the sort of "essentialism" that ascribes to women any such natural caring or nurturing tendencies.

30. On friendship, see Lawrence A. Blum, *Friendship, Altruism, and Morality* (London: Routledge and Kegan Paul, 1980) and Neera Kapur Badhwar, "The Circumstances of Justice: Pluralism, Community, and Friendship," *Journal of Political Philosophy* 1 (1993): 250–76. On caring, see especially: Nel Noddings, *Caring* (Berkeley: University of California Press, 1984); Joan C. Tronto, "Beyond Gender Difference to a Theory of Care," *Signs* 12 (1987); 644–63 and *Moral Boundaries: A Political Argument for an Ethic of Care* (London: Routledge, 1993); and Jeffrey Blustein, *Care and Commitment: Taking the Personal Point of View* (New York: Oxford University Press, 1991).

31. Iris Young, *Justice and the Politics of Difference* (Princeton: Princeton University Press, 1990); Minow, *Making All the Difference.*

32. Wesley N. Hohfeld, *Fundamental Legal Conceptions as Applied in*

Judicial Reasoning (New Haven: Yale University Press, 1923). Hart, "Definition and Theory in Jurisprudence" and "Are There Any Natural Rights?"

33. Minow, *Making All the Difference,* 277–78; Nedelsky, "Law, Boundaries, and the Bounded Self," 171, concedes that "the function of boundaries *is* to structure relationships," but she goes on to argue that "the boundary metaphor consistently inhibits our capacity to focus on the relationships it is in fact structuring."

34. This formulation is meant to pick up the "anti-boundary, anti-separateness" strand in Nedelsky ("Law, Boundaries, and the Bounded Self" and "Reconceiving Autonomy") and Minow (*Making All the Difference,* chaps. 8 and 9).

35. "By invoking rights, an individual or group claims the attention of the larger community and its authorities. At the same time, this claim acknowledges the claimant's membership in the larger group, participation in its traditions, and observation of its forms. . . . Although the language of rights, on its surface, says little of community or convention, those who exercise rights signal and strengthen their relation to a community" (Minow, *Making All the Difference,* 293–94, see similarly 296–97).

36. "The powerful vision of rights-as-limits no longer seems to me the best way of thinking about or trying to institutionalize the notions that in any society there will be competing values. . . . A society should . . . acknowledge the inherent tension between the collective and the individual and find means of mediating as well as sustaining the tension. I say 'sustaining' because the values of neither the individual nor the collective should be collapsed into one another" (Nedelsky, "Reconceiving Autonomy," 35).

37. See especially Lon L. Fuller, "Mediation—Its Forms and Functions" and "The Forms and Limits of Adjudication," in *The Principles of Social Order,* ed. Kenneth I. Winston (Durham: Duke University Press, 1981), 125–57 and 86–124 respectively. This Alternative Dispute Resolution program, advocated by Derek Bok and others, is fairly summarized and roundly challenged by Owen M. Fiss, "Against Settlement," *Yale Law Journal* 93 (1984): 1073–91.

38. Amitai Etzioni, *The Moral Dimension* (New York: Free Press, 1988). See also Mansbridge, ed., *Beyond Self-Interest.*

39. H. L. A. Hart, "Between Utility and Rights," *Essays in Jurisprudence and Philosophy* (Oxford: Clarendon Press, 1983), 198–222.

40. Often "communitarians" seem to be saying no more than that; see, e.g., Michael Sandel, *Liberalism and the Limits of Justice* (Cambridge: Cambridge University Press, 1982).

41. While relational feminists might be enamored of the "ethic of care," there are of course other strands of feminism that would be keenly sensitive to the costs to women of being relied upon to provide disproportionate shares of such caregiving. See, e.g., Diane Gibson and Judith Allen, "Parasitism and Phallocentrism in Social Provision for the Elderly," *Policy Sciences* 26 (1993): 79–98.

42. Tronto raises these issues in her early paper ("Beyond Gender Difference to a Theory of Care," 659–61) but does not get very far toward resolving them in the book that grew out of that work (*Moral Boundaries,* 142–43, 170–73).

43. Robert E. Goodin, *Protecting the Vulnerable* (Chicago: University of Chicago Press, 1985).

44. On such themes, see the title essay in Harry Frankfurt, *The Importance of What We Care About* (Cambridge: Cambridge University Press, 1998).

45. This might be rationalized, in terms of "respect for difference," in terms of not being imperialistic about unknown others' values. But ignorance is always a weak excuse, carrying with it a duty to find out.

46. Tronto, *Moral Boundaries,* 171. She continues, lamely, "The only solution that I see . . . is to insist that care needs to be connected to a theory of justice and to be relentlessly democratic in its disposition," suggesting that "what would make care democratic is . . . its focus on needs, and on the balance between care-givers and care-receivers." That might make the theory democratic, and instill a concern for justice, but I cannot see how that would do anything (except via the sort of extrapolation and abstraction that relational feminists eschew) to instill a concern for justice or democracy that would go beyond those particular individuals thus linked by caring relations.

47. John Hardwig, "Should Women Think in Terms of Rights?" in *Feminism and Political Theory,* ed. Cass R. Sunstein (Chicago: University of Chicago Press, 1990), 53–67 at 54–55.

48. To borrow the terminology of Nedelsky, "Law, Boundaries, and the Bounded Self."

49. The principle was taken to absurd extremes: if a man negligently driving a car hits a woman pedestrian, causing her serious injuries, she ordinarily could sue for damages; but not, traditionally, if the driver in question were her husband. See "Note: Litigation between Husband and Wife," *Harvard Law Review* 79 (1966): 1650–65 at 1650–51.

50. *Ritter v. Ritter,* 31 Pa. 396, 398 (1858), quoted ibid., 1650–51.

51. Justice Lewis Powell, dissenting, in *Goss v. Lopez,* 419 US 565 (1975), at 593–94.

52. "Developments in the Law—Legal Responses to Domestic Violence," *Harvard Law Review* 106 (1993): 1499–620.

53. Minow, *Making All the Difference,* 289–95.

54. And not-so-recent moral philosophy, come to that: see George Cornewall Lewis, *Remarks on the Use and Abuse of Some Political Terms* (London: Fellowes, 1832), 7–32, distinguishing between the very different uses of "right" as an adjective and as a noun. See similarly Jeremy Waldron, "A Right to Do Wrong," *Ethics* 92 (1981): 21–39.

55. Jeremy Waldron, "When Justice Replaces Affection: The Need for Rights," *Harvard Journal of Law and Public Policy* 11 (1988): 625–47; Onora O'Neill, "The Prerogatives of the Premature," *Times Literary Supplement,* March 26, 1982, 332.

56. Surprisingly often, however, there are no contracts at all or no default clauses written into them; see Stewart Macaulay, "Noncontractual Relations in Business: A Preliminary Study," *American Sociological Review* 28 (1963): 55–67.

57. Macaulay, "Noncontractual Relations in Business," 61.

58. Herbert A. Simon, *Administrative Behavior,* 2d ed. (New York: Free Press, 1957), esp. chap. 7; Peter M. Balu, *The Dynamics of Bureaucracy,* rev. ed. (Chicago: University of Chicago Press, 1963), chaps. 7–9; Richard Cyert and James G. March, *A Behavioral Theory of the Firm* (Englewood Cliffs: Prentice-Hall, 1963); David M. Kreps, "Corporate Culture and Economic Theory," in *Perspectives on Positive Political Economy,* ed. James E. Alt and Kenneth A. Shepsle (Cambridge: Cambridge University Press, 1990), 90–143.

59. Adolf A. Berle, Jr., and Gardiner C. Means, *The Modern Corporation and Private Property* (New York: Macmillan, 1932); Oliver E. Williamson, "Corporate Governance," *Yale Law Journal* 93 (1984): 1197–230.

60. For a particularly clear statement of this proposition, see Catharine A. MacKinnon, "Difference and Dominance: On Sex Discrimination," in *The Moral Foundations of Civil Rights,* ed. Robert K. Fullinwider and Claudia Mills (Totowa: Rowman and Littlefield, 1986), 144–58.

61. Minow, *Making All the Difference,* 228.

62. In ways akin to the "protective state" of liberalism: see Macpherson, *Life and Times of Liberal Democracy,* chap. 2.

63. Thomas C. Schelling, "An Essay on Bargaining," *The Strategy of Conflict* (Cambridge: Harvard University Press, 1960), 21–52.

64. On the theory, see: Russell Hardin, "Exchange Theory on Strategic Bases," *Social Science Information* 21 (1982): 251–72 and *Collective Action* (Baltimore: Johns Hopkins University Press, 1982); Robert Axelrod, *The Evolution of Cooperation* (New York: Basic Books, 1984); Mi-

chael Taylor, *The Possibility of Cooperation* (Cambridge: Cambridge University Press, 1987); and Partha Dasgupta, "Trust as a Commodity," in *Trust,* ed. Diego Gambetta (Oxford: Blackwell, 1988), 49–72. For practical examples, see Elinor Ostrom, *Governing the Commons* (Cambridge: Cambridge University Press, 1990) and Robert C. Ellickson, *Order without Law: How Neighbors Settle Disputes* (Cambridge: Harvard University Press, 1991).

65. That arguably is what is going on in Nedelsky's prize example of Canadian rape law, resetting the standard of proof in rape cases in such a way as to advantage victims as against perpetrators.

Index

accountability, 181; of political leaders, 179
Ackerman, Bruce, 121-22, 123, 138, 148, 150, 152, 162
agenda, deliberative, 279-80, 281, 283; contestibility of, 261-66; setting of, 267-68
agriculture, 42, 77; policy for, as revealing differences between European and United States consensus and institutions, 105-6
Amish, 11, 366-68, 374, 378, 382, 385-88, 390-92, 395, 400-402, 405, 412, 415-16, 421, 428-31; acculturation processes of, 369-70, 393-94; and compulsory education, 370-71, 372; educational practices, 405-6; free exercise of religion by, 379-80; socialization processes, 375-76;
Aristotle, 176; *Nicomachean Ethics*, 322; *Politics*, 24-25; theory of politics and anatomy of city, 24-25
Arneson, Richard J., 11-12, 415, 416-17, 424
Arrow, Kenneth, 218; Impossibility Theorem, 90
associations, differences among, 262-66
authority, 400, 510, 503, 504; over children, 414, 418-19, 420-21, 423, 427; political, 14; subcontracting, 504. *See also* parents
autonomy, 359, 391, 393-97, 398-402, 404, 413, 415-16, 418, 428, 456, 484-85, 503; individual, 388-90. *See also* parents

beliefs, 3; contrasted with preferences, 87-88; role of, in electoral response, 96-97
Berlin, Isaiah, 347, 348, 357, 360
borders, 310, 312-13, 317, 334, 337
Bosnia, 294-95, 300, 303, 310, 319
boundaries, 477; language of, 474-75; metaphor of, 483
Bruges, 59 (picture), 63
Burnham, Walter Dean, 3-5, 116, 118-21, 123, 127, 138, 162, 167
Burtt, Shelley, 12

Canada, 469; rape law in, 477-78, 482
causality, 118, 142; causal models, 126
change, 113, 140, 163-64; and order, 120
chaos, 94; dimension of voting process, 90-91; in former Soviet Union and Eastern Europe, 92; in Japan, 101; possibility of, 106; voting theorems, 92; within collective choice mechanisms, 89
chaotic systems, defined, 89
Chicago, 61, 62 (picture), 63
child rearing, 374, 444

children, 11, 366, 380-81, 397, 401, 403-4, 406, 416, 424, 446; abuse of, 457, 467-69, 480-81; basic interests of, 11, 12, 447; best interests of, 387; educational interests of, 413; independent claims of, 430; influences on, 447-48; interests, 385, 412, 425; and justice, 445; life options of, 392-93; long-term interests of, 414; needs of, as basis of claims to authority, 422-24; prerogative, 432; rearing of, 374, 444; rights of, 389-90
Christian fundamentalists, 414, 426
Christiano, Thomas, 8
citizenship, 298, 311-12, 367, 375, 394-95, 403, 405-6, 415-16, 425, 428, 433; education for, 386; responsibilities of, 376-77
city, hatred of, and nationalism, 294; as site of problem of political order, 19-28, 29, 30, 31; and spatial order, 59-65
civil institutions, 11, 366, 368, 372-74; undemocratic, 405
civil society, 12, 292, 306, 348, 353-54, 356-57, 365, 372-74, 404-5; features of, 350-51; liberal, 10, 351, 355
cleavage politics, 8, 208, 240; characteristics, 213-14; and majority rule, 220; multiple-issue, 227-29; single-issue, 221; two-issue, 222-24
cleavages, social, 373-74, 404
collective action, 261; problems, 263, 277-78, 337
collective choice, 207, 226, 229-31; criteria for, 216-17; contrasted with individual choice, 87-88; minority impact on, 235, 236; theory, 88
collective decision making, 252, 267, 279, 282
collective good, 253; information as, 271-72; understanding as, 273-74
commission, regulation by, 129
common good, 189, 251; and special interests, 264-65
communism, 66, 289, 306, 314
communitarians, 11, 253, 292, 375, 406, 507; critique of liberal order, 504; critique of liberalism, 366
compulsory education, 367, 370-71, 375-76, 379, 387-88; and free exercise, 385-86
conceptions of the good, 394, 441
Condorcet, 96; Condorcet winner, 216-19, 226, 229-30, 232
conflict, as threat to political order, 29; management of, 28; over religious truth, 29-31
Congress (United States), 113, 118, 120, 125-26, 127-29, 130-33, 149-51, 157-58, 160-61, 168-69, 220, 241; cleavages in, 97; and economic policy, 104
consensus, 180; and equilibrium, 91; overlapping, 2; political, 3; social, 105-6
consociationalism, 105, 178, 191, 195, 317
constitutional arrangements, 175, 176, 185; ability of, to overcome unfavorable conditions for democracy, 189-90; adaptation to special circumstances, 195-96; choice of, 178; criteria for judging, 179-81; range of, 183-85, 188-89
constitutionalism, 456, 466; as response to threat of disorder, 20
constitutions, 147; and bills of rights, 183; democratic, 6; distinguished from institutions and conditions of polyarchy, 177; United States, 4, 113, 121, 175, 316, 366, 386, 414, 474, 480, 486; written vs. unwritten, 183
critical rationality, 367, 376, 388, 393-94, 396, 402-4, 406, 413, 415-16, 425, 432; and religious faith, 416-18; state fostering of, 448-49
cultural diversity, 11, 334, 352, 354; lack of, 178, 300
cultural inclusion, 315; processes of, 318; strategies of, 319

delegation, 5, 133, 160-62, 164
deliberation, 8, 251, 257, 261, 269, 396, 404, 415; among equals, 252; critical, 401; deliberative democracy, 502
democracy, 5, 6, 254, 314, 357, 367, 372-74, 395, 404-5, 438; ambiguity in, 284; and deliberation, 251, 502; and nationalist aspirations, 290; and political institutions, 176-77; tension with stability, 8
democratic decision making, 253, 376; components of, 255; and secondary associations, 280
democratic institutions, 315, 356; conditions for, 178-79; maintenance of, 185; stability, 91, 179
democratic society, 252, 394, 396-97, 403, 443
democratic theory, 365, 367, 372-74, 404, 405, 502
denationalization, 308-9, 313-14, 335
difference, 289, 300-301, 307-8, 321, 505; ethnic, 288; political and moral significance, 334; and political order, 295
disorder, 2; as compatible with reasonable ordering of collective choice, 90; sources, 27, 29; as result of economic dislocations, 106
dissatisfaction, 230-31; formally defined, 229
distributive politics, 8, 208-9, 240; characteristics, 214
domination, 459, 464-65, 476, 480, 504-6; structural underpinnings, 485

economic regulation. *See* regulation
education, 11, 178, 317, 366, 375, 382, 385, 387, 391-92, 394, 397-98, 401, 404, 414-15, 418; and citizenship, 377-79; for rational autonomy, 388, 393-94; religious, 416-17; right to, 390, 405; system of, 374
elections, 376; and congressional behavior, 128-30, 159-60, 169. *See also* proportional representation; pluralities
electoral systems, 3, 97-101; and democratic stability, 192; interaction with other constitutional arrangements, 184
equal protection, 121-22, 298
equality, 8, 251, 253, 262, 373, 476, 478-79, 480, 485; in deliberation, 258-62, 271, 275-76; democratic, 252, 267, 279, 283-84; institutions of, 252-53; numerical, 258, 279; of opportunity, 446-49; and political instability, 9; qualitative, 258, 260, 261, 263, 266, 267, 279-80, 282; of resources, 255, 257, 260-61; of welfare, difficulties with, 254
equilibrium, 101, 106, 124-25, 132, 136, 140; and institutional structures, 92; maintenance of, 92; as order, 3
Esperanto, 69-70
ethic of care, 505, 508-9
ethnic nationalism, 9, 289, 301-2, 304, 314, 334-36, 341; defined, 290-91; distinguished from state-centered nationalism, 336; European, 305; as human construct, 308; as mobilizing force, 306; and political order, 296, 306-7, 312, 315, 316, 321-22, 335; as political phenomenon, 291-92; psychological economy of, 294; and respect for human rights, 317-19, 322; self-definitions of, 292; as threat to common human identity, 293-94
Europe, 314, 317, 320, 339, 355-56; nationalism in, 290, 294, 304, 307, 310, 318
evil, 462, 464, 465, 468, 474, 481, 498, 502
expression, value of, 259-60

family, 113, 365, 404, 428, 442, 501; authority, 451; autonomy of, 13; and fair equality of opportunity, 446-49; interests of members, 449-

family *(Continued)*
50; as just institution, 450-51; and political process, 444; rights and responsibilities of, 414; and Rawls's difference principle, 449-50; as sphere of political order, 12, 438
Fan condition and existence of chaos in voting process, 91
fear, 473, 474, 476-77, 498-99, social control achieved by, 470; as *summum malum* of liberalism, 471
federalism, 183, 195-96, 317; and judicial review, 184; and parliamentary vs. presidential systems, 186
feminism, 11, 480, 501, 503; critique of liberalism, 366, 504; and hierarchical authority, 505
Ferejohn, John, 135-36, 138, 141
fiduciary obligations (of parents), 367, 380, 383-84
Fiorina, Morris P., 3-5, 126-28, 132-33, 136, 138, 168-70
first past the post. *See* plurality systems
forestry, 42-47, 65
formal political theory, 161, 208. *See also* rational choice theory
Foucault, Michel, 51-70
free exercise, 372, 379-80, 386, 390, 412, 429-31; and children's interests, 382-85; and compulsory education, 385-86
freedom, 457, 471, 503; of association, 385; of expression, 395-98, 403. *See also* liberty
fundamental, contrasted with *superstruction,* 31

Galston, William, 12, 394-96, 439, 446
game theory, 88, 126, 135-36. *See also* rational choice theory
gender, 464-65; as basis of discrimination, 448; politics of, 294; transformation of gender relations, 454-55, 461; roles, 460
Goodin, Robert E., 13-14
government, competence, 180-81; comprehensibility, 181; legitimacy, 181; transparency, 181
Gray, John, 10-11
Griffin, Susan, 458-59
Guinier, Lani, 7, 207, 210

heart, in voting models, defined, 95
Herman, Judith, 468, 474-75, 477, 480
hierarchy, 365, 373, 455, 503, 506; as type of political order, 500
high modernism, 3; and authoritarianism, 71; defined, 67-68; distinctive features, 69-71; as ideology, 66, 71; and intelligentsia, 73; rejection of history and tradition, 67; and rural development, 78-79; spread of, 68
historical institutionalism, 114, 119, 162; and positive theory of institutions, 164. *See also* intercurrence
history, institutional character, 113, 114; juxtaposed with rational choice analysis, 136-37; and theory, 126, 129
Hobbes, Thomas, 28; *Elements of Law,* 28, 30, 31; *Leviathan,* 20, 22
human identity, 293, 315, 319; and nationalism, 288
human rights, 9, 295, 297-99, 300, 312-14, 315-16, 320, 335, 338, 341; and ethnic nationalism, 317-19, 322
humanity, 341; claims of, 315, 335; moral claims of, 296, 335; as moral community, 297, 313

identities, 300, 309, 312; ethnic, 289; of nations, 302; as political constructions, 315; and public resources, 314
ideological politics, 8, 208, 240; characteristics, 214; defined, 229; and ideological cohesion, 234-35; and means of distributions, 234; on single preference distribution, 230-32; and size of minority, 234

Ignatieff, Michael, 289, 293-96, 303, 307, 309-11, 318
individual choice, 3; contrasted with collective choice, 87-88
individual, freehold tenure, 51, 52, 53; as ordering principle, 53
individualism, 506, 507
individuals, boundaries around, 441
inequality, 315, 342, 442, 445, 479-80; among nations, 10
information, 269, 274; as collective good, 271; inequalities, 272
institutions, 141, 147, 150, 162; of civil society, 348; democratic, 176-77, 251, 283, 315, 356, 374, 376, 378, 395; design, 316-18; of discussion and deliberation, 257, 279; historical character, 113, 114; and nationalism, 288; ordering propensities, 2, 112, 117, 137-38; political, 97, 124, 138; of political equality, 252-53, 255; politics of, 113, 114, 125, 127, 134, 140, 164; primacy of, 5; public, 365; and their environments, 141; social, 451; and strategies of ethnic accommodation, 9; structures of, 92, 130; and time, 111, 140-42; transparency of, 8
intercurrence, 4-5, 114, 131, 138-42, 147, 149, 154, 157, 163-64, 168-69; defined, 112-13; dependence on identifying patterns through time, 167; formal models and, 161-62; as foundation for historical institutionalism, 137-38; and institutional view of history, 117
interest groups, 101, 258, 262-66, 272, 273
interests, 251, 253-54, 260-61, 267, 269, 274, 277, 279-80, 283, 399, 401; balancing of, 418-19, 420; basic interests of children, 383, 387; best interests of children, 387; comprehension and advancement of, 255-57; integration of, 180; of family members, 449-50
Interstate Commerce Act, 130, 132-33, 156-58, 160, 168
Interstate Commerce Commission, 127, 168-69
issue preferences, and two-issue cleavage politics, 223

judicial review, 183-84, and stability, 193-95
judiciary, and other institutions, 122

Kiss, Elizabeth, 9, 334-36, 341
knowledge, local, 53, 60, 61; of politics and interests, 257-58; relation between kinds of, 77-78; scientific, 69. *See also metis*

land tenure, 3, 42, 47-54
law, proper scope of, 472; task of, 473
legislative delegation, 5
legitimacy, 252, 345; claims to, 190
levels of analysis, 148, 150
liberal democracy, 11, 315-16, 421; order of, 415; reconciliation with nationalist sentiment, 10; regimes of, 11
liberal rights, 14, 455, 482, 485-86, 506-7; as boundaries, 410; inability to protect women and children, 457-59; scope of, 476
liberal state, 13, 455, 457-58, 473, 505; boundaries, 474; failure to protect women and children, 454-455, 466; Sieyes's theory of, 20; tasks of, 488
liberalism, 10, 19-21, 292, 314, 349-50, 358-59, 394, 405, 456, 465-66, 474, 476, 482, 507; agonistic, 347-48, 357, 358, 360; bias of, 439; critiques of, 366; libertarian accounts of, 13; of fear, 487-88; and nationalism, 319; project of, 345-47, 357, 360; theory, 20, 337, 345, 352, 360. *See also* liberal democracy; liberal rights; liberal state
liberty, 346, 359, 414, 443-46, 422, 485; guardianship of, 27; religious,

liberty *(Continued)*
395, 413, 415; state power as precondition of, 21

Machiavelli, Niccolò, on Christianity and political order, 29-30; *Discourses,* 26; *Discourses on Livy,* 21, 22, 24; *Discursus florentinarum rerum,* 25; *Florentine Histories,* 23; *The Prince,* 23, 26; use of Aristotle's definition of parts of the city, 25
MacKinnon, Catherine, 468-69, 476, 480
majority rule, 7, 8, 92, 103, 213, 235, 240, 377; chaotic, 219; and cleavage politics, 220; collusive, 239; and discrimination against minorities, 241; as formal decision rule, 209; in ideological politics, 230; and minorities, 207-8, 214, 221, 229, 241, 242; multiple alternatives in, 216; and multiple issue dimensions, 219; and political process, 219-20; properties, 214-20; shifting majorities in, 217
market, 86-87, 178, 267, 357, 502, 503; capitalism, 351; and equality, 282; equilibrium in, 93; institutions, 10; political intervention in, 101-3
marketplace of ideas, 272, 276-79; bias in, 270-71; critique of, 275; in literal sense, 268-70; as metaphor, 268
median voter theorem, 218-19, 234-35
membership, 311-12, 334-35, 337; group, 331
metis, 3, 74; contrasted with simplification, 76; defined, 75; situations where relevant, 75-76; social engineering's failure to incorporate, 75
Mill, John Stuart, 310, 315, 346, 360, 394
Miller, Nicholas R., 6, 7-8
minorities, 315, 339, 374; coalitions of, 224-28; dissatisfaction of, 235, 236; ethnic, 312; ideologically distinct, 232-33; and ideological politics, 230, 234; impact of, 237-38; interests of, 8, 224, 236, 240; preferences of, 242; rights of, 179, 209, 317, 318. *See also* majority rule
mixed government, 21; Aristotle's preference for, 24, 26; contrasted with democracy, 25-27; as disciplining and institutionalizing disorder, 27; Hobbes's and Bodin's critique of, 28-29; Machiavelli's defense of, 23-24, 26
moral community, 296; humanity as, 297, 313, 322, 334

Nash equilibrium, 94
nationalism, 5, 6, 9, 288, 315, 334-36, 339-40; humanity's claims and, 335; and liberalism, 319; historical links with democracy, 290, 294; as modern phenomenon, 302; in opposition to imperialism, 304-6; and political order, 9, 309-10; as rational response, 307; reconciliation with humanity's claims, 319; and territorial order, 313; and world inequality, 340. *See also* ethnic nationalism
nations, construction of, differences, 295-96; identities of, 304; sovereignty of, 311, 338
nation-states, 295, 338, 342, 356; homogeneous, 311
Nedelsky, Jennifer, 13
needs, children's, 425, 428; as basis of authority, 430-33
neutrality, 179, 352, 360, 439, 448, 480, 485
Noddings, Nel, 461-63, 465, 474
nondemocratic regimes, 175, 178, 180
norms, 111, 112

Olson, Mancur, *The Rise and Decline of Nations,* 102-3; United States experience as contrary to interest group thesis of, 104

order, and change, 120; and institutions, 111-14; relation to time, 114. *See also* political order
Orren, Karen, 3-5, 147, 149-50, 156, 158-61, 163-64
overlapping consensus of Christian religion, 31-32

parental authority, 413, 419, 422, 429
parental autonomy, 366, 367, 414, 419-20, 433
parental deference, argument for, 424-25, 427, 428; limits to, 430-32; principle of, 414
parental discretion, 446
parental obligations, 380-82
parental rights, 380, 387; and responsibilities, 422, 429
parenting, 423-24
parents, 377, 380-81, 382, 392-93, 401-3, 405, 416, 423-24; authority of, 413, 419, 422, 429; autonomy of, 12, 366, 367, 414, 419-20, 433; conflict with public schools, 413-14, 418, 424; deference to, 414, 424-25, 427, 428, 430-32; discretion of, 446; fiduciary obligations of, 386-87; interests of, 412; obligations of, 380-82; relations with state, 422; religious interests of, 404; responsibilities of, 422, 429; rights of, 380, 387, 414; as trustees of children's interests, 424
parent-state relations, 422
Pareto criterion, 90
Pareto equilibrium, 86
Pareto optimality, 87, 101
Pareto set, 90, 92
Paris, 63, 64 (picture)
parliamentary government, and presidential systems, 184, 187; choice of, 185; and proportional representation, 186-87; stability of, 189, 191, 193
parties, 113, 216, 258, 272, 276; competition among, 128; minority, 7; multiparty systems, 95, 99-100; system of, 119, 149; two-party system, 133
Pasquino, Pasquale, 2
paternalism, 365
patriarchy, 113, 459, 465; and values, 485
patronyms, 3, 58
periodization, 3, 113, 114, 115, 117-22, 124; analytic moves in, 115-16; purpose of, 116; schemes of, 124, 127
pluralism, 11, 140, 148, 178, 251, 339, 347, 351, 354, 356-57, 360, 372-74, 426, 502; distinguished from post-liberalism, 353; ethical, 11; legal, 352, 355-56; political orders of, 353; theory of, 356; of values, 352
pluralities, vs. proportional representation elections; and representation, 182
plurality systems, 184, 192; choice of, 185
plurality winner, 216-17, 231
political change, 5, 112; relation to political order, 4
political culture, 141, 178, 356; and democratic stability, 190-91
political development, 112, 113; American, 116
political order, 295, 308, 341, 503; anti-liberal view of, 354-55; borders and, 317; as consequence of spatial order in cities, 59-65; as result of standardization, 46; city as site of problem, 19-28, 29, 30, 31; conflict as threat to, 29; democracy as challenge to, 5; democratic, 8, 372, 405; design and evolution, 439; and difference, 295; as distinct social organization, 438-40; and ethnic nationalism, 292, 296, 306-7, 312, 315-16, 321-22, 335; equilibrium as, 3; as forestalling evil, 498-99; global, 288; hierarchical, 439, 441, 442; human rights and, 299; individual, freehold land tenure as source of,

political order *(Continued)* 53,54; hierarchical, 500; and institutions of equality, 252; in liberal regime, 454; modernity as, 3; multiple, 438-39; and nationalism, 5, 309-10; overlapping consensus of Christianity as source of, 31-32; pluralist view of, 353-56; political change and, 4; of polyarchy, 176; as protecting citizens from violence, 454; questions about, 1-2; simplification as, 3; as solution to the problem of evil, 14; spheres of, 438, 450-51; subcontracting, 500-501; threat from disagreement over nature of threat, 32; as transmitting ways of life, 357-58; ways of structuring, 500. *See also* disorder; order; political change
political philosophy, 347. *See also* political theory
political system, 115; contrasted with intercurrence thesis, 112; ingredients of, 210
political theory, 2, 289, 292, 310, 334, 355, 416; as texts on means of avoiding disorder, 19; liberal, 11, 499; contextual dimension of, 22. *See also* political philosophy
politics, 115; as imposing order, 499; temporal dimension of, 112
polyarchy, 176-77, 178, 185
positive theory of institutions, 133-35, 138, 157, 160-62, 164; as equilibrium theory, 124; and historical institutionalism, 164; time in, 125-26. *See also* rational choice theory
post-liberalism, 345, 347-48, 351, 352, 360; distinguished from pluralism, 353
poverty, 467, 481
power, 461, 464, 471, 476, 502, 505
power relations, 479; affected by law, 479; in relational feminism, 513; and political order, 54
preferences, 3, 217, 225, 390-91, 422; characteristics of citizens', 211-12; of children, 384; contrasted with beliefs, 87-88; crosscutting, 227, 228; interchangeability, 239, 240
presidential government, 184-85; instability, 192-93; and plurality elections, 187; and proportional representation elections, 187-88; stability, 189, 191
proportional representation, 3, 7, 99-100, 105-6, 180, 184-85, 192, 317, 336; and representation, 182; stability, 193; vs. plurality elections, 177
public education, 413-14, 415-18, 421, 428, 429
public goods, 86-87, 94, 101, 103-5, 317, 337; and political mechanisms, 103
public interest, 419-20

race, 340, 455, 464, 485-86
Rae-Taylor-Straffin Theorem, 215-16, 224
rape, 13, 294, 460-61, 467-71, 474-76, 477; perceptions of, by men and women, 478-79
rational behavior, 93, 94
rational calculation, information for, 93
rational choice theory, 3, 4, 7, 126-35; four interconnected facets of, 87-88; juxtaposed with history, 136-37. *See also* positive theory of institutions
rational social deliberation, 275
rationality, 86, 125, 136, 138
Rawls, John, 12-13, 230, 251, 346-47, 352, 358, 360, 394-96; concept of basic structure, 438, 439-42, 450; difference principle, 441, 449-50; first principle of justice, 444-49; justice as fairness, 439-40; principles of justice applied to families, 442-50; principles of justice and political order, 450-51; *A Theory of Justice,* 292, 442, 444, 446, 499; *Political Liberalism,* 442-43, 444, 447

Raz, Joseph, 347-48, 357, 359, 360
realignment, 5, 116, 121, 139, 167-68; 1994 election as, 147, 153; of 1896, 118; theory of, 148
redistribution, 340-41
regulation, 113, 126-27, 132, 157-59, 170
relational feminism, 13, 14, 455, 456, 461, 466, 480, 482, 485, 488, 502-3; convergence with liberalism, 513-14; critique of liberal order, 504; and ethic of care, 505; at odds with liberal rights, 509-10; problems with, 507-9; and rights, 505-6; as way of thinking, 464, 481, 486-87
representation, 175, 179-80, 182, 291, 305, 317, 338
republicanism, 21-28
resources, 274; and deliberation, 270; equality of, 277; inequality, 271, 298
responsibility, 457; to children, 413; and relationship, 508
rights, 2, 113, 179, 298, 354-55, 454, 456, 465, 480, 484, 503-4; as boundaries, 13, 455-56, 464-65, 457, 481; conventional language of, 462-64; disputes over, 483; as fall-back positions, 511-13; of groups, 385; kinds of, 183; of majority, 179; as parameters, 513-14; as protected choices, 14; protection of, 194-95; public power as threat to, 19; reconceptualization of, 459-60; regime of, 501; and relational feminism, 505-6; as relationship, 13, 455-58, 460, 464-65, 476, 481, 483, 486; and right conduct, 511-12; traditional conceptions of, 480
Ross, Lainie Friedman, 12-13
rules, 111, 112, 117, 140-41, 500; institutional, 139; and norms, 139; rule-bound settings, 126

satisfaction, 224-25, 227, 229
Satz, Debra, 9-10
Schmidtz, David, 12-13
Schofield, Norman, 3
Scott, James, 2-3
secondary associations, 276, 280; circularity problem and, 280-83; subsidy of, 279-80; voucher scheme for, 276-79
self, 459; construction of, in relation to others, 475; encumbered, 406; sense of, 474
self-interest, 251, 273
Shapiro, Ian, 11-12, 415-17, 424
Sherman Anti-Trust Act, 118-20
shift-the-responsibility model of delegation, 128, 156-59, 168-69
Shklar, Judith, 14, 455, 465-68, 470-71, 473, 487-88
simplification, as order, 3; of land tenure, 51; as providing official view of reality, 55; state, character, 56-57; utilitarian logic of, 44
Sklar, Martin, 114, 118
social choice theory, 208-9; as representation of political system, 210-14. *See also* rational choice theory
social engineering, 65, 66
social groups, integration of, 25-26; resources of, 266
socialism, 66, 289, 373; and high modernism, 72-73
sovereignty, 2, 28-29, 339; national, 311; world, 338
special interests, and the common good, 264-65
stability, 164; and constitutional arrangements, 6; and electoral systems, 192; of democratic institutions, 179; as depending on institutions, 111; dimension of voting process, 90; of presidential vs. parliamentary systems, 189; tension with democracy, 8; threatened by equality, 9
standardization, 45-46, 52-53, 57-60
state, 2, 10, 42, 346, 372, 448; appropriate scope of, 13; boundaries, 473; and children, 11, 12, 387, 389-90, 413; and critical reflection, 448-

state *(Continued)*
49; democratic, 405; distinguished from society, 472, 485; form of organization, 356; insistence on standardized documents, 54; interests of, 47; intervention in families, 419-21; multi-ethnic, 290; necessity of, for protecting liberty, 21; power of, 22, 66, 488; role of, 466; and standardization, 43-47, 49, 71; state-centered nationalism, 9, 336-38; task of, 473
subordination, 473, 505
superstruction, contrasted with fundamental, 31
Supreme Court (United States), 118, 121, 131-32, 151, 152, 194-95, 366-68, 375, 386, 392-93, 397-98, 404, 412-15, 427, 430; conflict with party system, 119; decision making by, 123; and racism, 472
system of 1896, 118-20, 149, 150-52, 168

territorial claims, 295, 310
threats to order, changing conceptualizations of, 19
time, as dimension of politics, 112; and institutions, 140-42; political action in, 143; in positive theory of institutions, 125; relation to order, 114; systems in, 149
titular nationalities, 305-6
tolerance, 289, 320, 353, 395, 404

unanimity rule, 282
understanding, as collective good, 273-74
unintended consequences, 131, 142
United Kingdom, economic decline in, 102-3; Labour Party, 95; and centrist government policies, 100, 220; Parliament, 98; uncertainty created by electoral system in, 99
United Nations, 318, 338
United States, 139, 309, 340, 355, 421, 433; electoral preferences of population, 98; immigrant politics, 291; public goods in, 103-5; relations between Congress and president, 98; specificity of system, 196. *See also* Congress; Supreme Court
universalism, 10, 300, 347, 357, 321, 360
urban planning, 3, 42
utopianism, 69, 70, 298; and state power, 67

values, 12, 347-48, 358, 390-91, 399, 403-4, 406, 417, 429, 444, 448, 483-84, 486; critical reflection on, 400; incommensurable and conflicting, 10; pluralism, 10, 348, 351, 358, 360
violence, 462, 465, 466, 488; against children, 467; against women, 457, 460-62, 467, 470, 472-74, 478, 480; in culture, 459, 476; in North American society, 461; relational nature of, 458
voting, 90, 255; cycles, 90, 218; obligation of, 378-79; paradox of, 218

Westminster model, 196
Wisconsin v. Yoder, 11, 12, 365-68, 369, 371-72, 374-75, 379-80, 382-85, 388, 389, 393-94, 404, 406, 412, 413-15, 429, 431-32
women, 474; protection of, 476. *See also* violence
Woodman, Marion, 460-61